DESIGN THINKING

DESIGN THINKING

A Hands-on Approach

Chandramouli Subramanian

Ph.D. (Management); PfMP; PMP; PMI-ACP

Associate Director, Cognizant Technology Solutions,
Chennai, Tamil Nadu

Thiyagarajan Paramasivan

Post-Doctorate Fellowship (Department of Atomic Energy);
Ph.D. (Computer Science and Engineering)

Assistant Professor, Department of Computer Science,
Central University of Tamil Nadu, Thiruvarur, Tamil Nadu

Sankaran Venkataramani

Ph.D. (Management);
Post-Graduate Diploma (Human Resource and Personnel Management);
B.E. (Industrial and Production Engineering)

Partner, KPMG India, Chennai, Tamil Nadu

Universities Press

DESIGN THINKING: A HANDS-ON APPROACH

UNIVERSITIES PRESS (INDIA) PRIVATE LIMITED

Registered Office
3-6-747/1/A & 3-6-754/1, Himayatnagar, Hyderabad 500 029, Telangana, India
info@universitiespress.com; www.universitiespress.com

Distributed by
Orient Blackswan Private Limited

Registered Office
3-6-752 Himayatnagar, Hyderabad 500 029, Telangana, India

Other Offices
Bengaluru / Chennai / Guwahati / Hyderabad / Kolkata
Mumbai / New Delhi / Noida / Patna

First published 2025

Cover and book design

ISBN: 978-81-974249-2-2

502160

Typeset in Times Ten LT Std 10 *by*
SRS Technologies, Puducherry

Printed in India by
B.B. Press, Tronica City, Ghaziabad 201 102

Published by
Universities Press (India) Private Limited
3-6-747/1/A & 3-6-754/1, Himayatnagar, Hyderabad 500 029, Telangana, India

About the Authors

Chandramouli Subramanian is Associate Director in Cognizant Technology Solutions, Chennai. He is an alumnus of IIM-K and a Certified Global Business Leader from Harvard Business School. He is a prolific writer of business management articles dealing with technology management, delivery management, competitiveness, IT, organizational culture, and leadership. He is a certified Green Belt in six-sigma methodology and a certified master practitioner of neuro-linguistic programming (NLP). He has presented papers on project management in various international forums and has more than 30 publications in national and international journals and conferences.

He implements design thinking principles across all his projects. He was an active member in the Project Management Institute's Organization Project Management Maturity Model (OPM3) and Project Management Competency Development Framework (PMCDF) assignments. He has been invited to speak at various technology and management conferences and has addressed more than 15,000 software professionals worldwide on a variety of themes associated with blockchain, artificial intelligence, machine learning, big data analytics, delivery management, competitiveness, and leadership.

Thiyagarajan Paramasivan is Assistant Professor in the Department of Computer Science, Central University of Tamil Nadu (CUTN), Thiruvarur. He worked as Dean (Research), Associate Professor and Head in the Department of Computer Science (Cyber Security) at the Rajiv Gandhi National Institute of Youth Development in Sriperumbudur.

He completed his integrated masters from the College of Engineering (CEG), Guindy, and his Ph.D. in Computer Science and Engineering from Pondicherry University. He was awarded a Post-Doctorate Fellowship from the Department of Atomic Energy at the Indira Gandhi Centre for Atomic Research (IGCAR) in Kalpakkam.

He was the founder head of the Department of Computer Science, Central University of Tamil Nadu (2016–2020). He was the Nodal Officer of the Campus Connect Wi-Fi project and was selected by the University Grants Commission (UGC) as an expert in Information Communication Technology for the Malaviya Mission Teachers Training Programme.

He has developed a MOOC course on Internet of Things (IoT) and published one patent. He has authored two books and has received the Young Scientist Award from Tamil Nadu State Council for Science and Technology. His research interest includes threshold cryptography, information security, network security, steganography, big data analytics, security aspects in smart cities, machine learning and blockchain technology. He has published more than 50 papers and has delivered 100+ invited technical talks across educational institutions such as IIT Madras, NIT Trichy, NIT Puducherry, Pondicherry University and CUTN.

Sankaran Venkataramani is a Partner with KPMG India in Chennai. He is a passionate management professional and researcher with more than 28 years of rich experience in the fields of strategic operating model advisory, transformational process consulting and leadership competency development, and coaching programs. His experience spans multiple industry domains such as Information Technology, Manufacturing, Engineering, Services, and Education.

He is fluent in global benchmarking models such as Capability Maturity Model Integration, Scaled Agile Framework for Enterprise, SCRUM Agile, People CMM, ISO 9001 and 20k, European Foundation for Quality Management, Lean 6σ, and Design Thinking. He has leveraged the principles and premise of Design Thinking along with the SAFe Agile Framework to build organizational capabilities in applying the Design Thinking philosophy around solution design and development. He has also conducted various management workshops. A part of Industry bodies such as NASSCOM, CII Connect, and Chennai SPIN, he has presented and been part of panel discussions in various Industry forums.

Preface

Design thinking is a creative problem-solving process that places the user at its core, ensuring their needs and experiences are valued and considered. It involves understanding the user, looking at the problem from multiple perspectives, creating different ideas, and exploring opportunities. This user-centric approach can help create better products, services, processes, and experiences that meet people's needs more meaningfully. It is, thus, a way of thinking or approaching a problem or challenge focused on understanding users and finding creative solutions that are centered on them. In addition, design thinking takes an iterative approach by testing ideas quickly and making changes based on feedback. In other words, it is all about putting people first!

This book aims to provide a comprehensive and practical introduction to design thinking, its methods, tools, and applications. It covers the theoretical foundations, the core phases, and the fundamental principles of design thinking. It also showcases how design thinking can be applied to different contexts, such as engineering, business, education, healthcare, and social innovation. The book includes numerous case studies and examples of design thinking in action, as well as exercises and activities to help readers practice and master design thinking skills.

The book is organized into 13 chapters, each focusing on a specific topic related to design thinking:

Chapter 1—Introduction to Design Thinking: This chapter lays the groundwork by defining design thinking, exploring its history and benefits, and outlining the core stages of the process.

Chapter 2—The Empathize Stage: Understanding the user is paramount. This chapter delves into techniques for building empathy and gathering insights.

Chapter 3—The Define Stage: Transforming empathy into actionable insights, this chapter covers problem definition, need identification, and framing of the design challenge.

Chapter 4—The Ideation Stage: Unleash creativity! This chapter explores various techniques for generating innovative ideas and solutions.

Chapter 5—The Prototype Stage: Bring ideas to life! This chapter focuses on creating tangible representations of ideas for testing and refinement.

Chapter 6—Testing and Implementation: This final phase involves testing prototypes, gathering feedback, and successfully launching the solution.

Chapter 7—Sustainable Design Approaches: This chapter explores how design thinking can contribute to a more sustainable future through eco-friendly solutions.

Chapter 8—Analyzing User Experience: Here, we understand the importance of user experience and learn how to analyze user behavior and needs.

Chapter 9—Integrating Design Thinking with Other Disciplines: In this chapter, we discover how design thinking can be applied in various fields, such as business, technology, and healthcare.

Chapter 10—Measuring the Impact of Design Thinking: Here, we learn how to evaluate the effectiveness of design thinking initiatives and measure their impact.

Chapter 11—Ethical Considerations in Design Thinking: This chapter emphasizes the importance of ethical practices in design and addresses issues like privacy and inclusivity.

Chapter 12—Design Thinking Case Studies: Learn from real-world examples of successful design thinking projects across different industries.

Chapter 13—Capstone Projects: Put your knowledge into practice with various project ideas that allow you to apply design thinking principles to real-world challenges.

At the end of each chapter, you will find objective questions that test your understanding of the main concepts and ideas. You will also find short answer and essay questions that will challenge you to apply your knowledge and skills to specific scenarios and cases. The explanations and solutions to these questions are provided in the app/website that accompanies the book.

This book is written in simple language, with clear explanations and examples. It is suitable for anyone who wants to learn about design thinking, from beginners to practitioners. Whether you are a student, a teacher, a manager, an entrepreneur, or a social innovator, this book will help you develop your creative confidence and competence and enable you to create positive change in the world.

Chandramouli Subramanian
Thiyagarajan Paramasivan
Sankaran Venkataramani

Acknowledgements

The journey through traditional Project Management, Agile Project Management, and Program and Portfolio Management, along with the use of artificial intelligence, machine learning, blockchain technologies, and big data analytics, has been very rewarding, as it has given me the opportunity to work for some of the best organizations in the world and learn from some of the best minds. Along the way, several individuals have been instrumental in providing me with the guidance, opportunities and insights needed to excel in this field: Mr Alexis Samuel, Senior Vice-President, Cognizant Technology Solutions; Mr Sriram Vaithamanithi, Senior Vice-President, Cognizant Technology Solutions; Mr Hariharan Mathrubutham, Former Vice-President, Cognizant Technology Solutions; Mr Krishna Prasad Yerramilli, Vice-President, Cognizant Technology Solutions; Mr Dharmendraraj Govindarajan Nagarajan, Associate Vice-President, Cognizant Technology Solutions; Ms Anand Prabha, Vice-President, Cognizant Technology Solutions; and Mr Balasubramanian Narayanan, Senior Director, Cognizant Technology Solutions. I would like to thank them for their inspiration and help in creating this book. They have contributed immensely towards improving my skills.

This book is the result of all the learning I have gained from many highly reputed professionals in the industry. I was fortunate to work with them and in the process, acquire knowledge that helped me in molding my professional career. I am obliged to Mr V Chandrasekar, Former CIO, Standard Chartered Bank, for demonstrating how the lives, thoughts, and feelings of others in professional life are to be valued. He is a wonderful and cheerful man who inspired me and gave me a lot of encouragement when he launched my first book.

My parents, Mr Subramanian and Mrs Lalitha, have always been enthusiastic about this project. Their unconditional love and affection provided much-needed moral support. My son, Shri Krishna, and daughter, Shri Siva Ranjani, constantly added impetus to my motivation to work hard.

This book would not have been possible without the constant inspiration of my wife, Ramya. She was unfailingly supportive and encouraging during the long months that I spent glued to my laptop while writing this book. Last but not the least, I beg forgiveness of all those who have been with me over the years and whose names I have failed to mention here.

Chandramouli Subramanian

There are countless people I would like to thank for their help throughout my life, without whom I would not be who I am or doing what I do. For the sake of brevity, I would like to thank and acknowledge the people who supported me throughout the process of writing this book. My deepest gratitude to Central University of Tamil Nadu (CUTN) for its invaluable support throughout the development of this book.

Thank you, Mom (Mrs P. Kamala), Dad (Mr V. S. Paramasivan), my wife (Mrs T. Revathi), and my children (T. Thamaraichelvi and T. Sivagurunathan), for their unconditional love and gracious support without which my contribution towards this book would not have happened.

Of course, I am very grateful to my co-author, Dr Chandramouli Subramanian, for inviting me to join him in this inspiring and fun-filled project. Your support, motivation and guidance in the entire process of writing this book has been indispensable. Thank you for your patience and the wonderful collaboration.

It has been a privilege to collaborate with Dr Sankaran Venkataramani. Your fresh perspectives kept this project moving forward with energy and enthusiasm.

I would like to express my deepest gratitude to the Almighty for providing me with the strength and perseverance to contribute to this well-crafted book.

Thiyagarajan Paramasivan

Gracias to many people who have helped and supported me in my life. To maintain brevity, I would like to express my gratitude and acknowledge the people who extended their untiring support and encouragement during the process of co-authoring this book.

Let me start by thanking my mother, Mrs V. Meenakshi; father, Mr N. Venkataramani; and brother, Mr V. Krishnamurthy, for their flowing guidance and knowledge. I would like to extend my gratitude to my wife, Mrs Shubha S., and my daughters, Ms Srinidhi S. and Ms Sripradha S., for their constant affection, love, and continued support.

Co-authoring this book is such an honour for me and this would not have been possible without Dr Chandramouli's motivation and tutelage. His constant support, guidance, and dedication is highly inspirational. Thank you for extending this wonderful opportunity to me.

Thanks to Dr Thiyagarajan Paramasivan for making me a part of this endeavour and for sharing his deep knowledge and thoughts.

Thank you, the Almighty, for the blessings bestowed on me to be part of this insightful book.

Sankaran Venkataramani

We are grateful to Universities Press, who came forward to publish this book. Thomas Mathew Rajesh, Kallol Das and Madhavi Sethupathi were always kind and understanding. Madhavi reviewed this book with abundant patience and helped us say what we had wanted to, enhancing each page of this book with care.

Chandramouli Subramanian
Thiyagarajan Paramasivan
Sankaran Venkataramani

Table of Contents

To
My parents, Subramanian and Lalitha
My wife, Ramya
My son, Shri Krishna
My daughter, Shri Siva Ranjani
And my colleagues and friends
Chandramouli Subramanian

To
My parents, V S Paramasivan and P Kamala
My wife, Revathi T
My daughter, Thamaraichelvi T
My son, Sivagurunathan T
And my colleagues and friends
Thiyagarajan Paramasivan

To
My parents, V Meenakshi and N Venkataramani,
and my brother, V Krishnamurthy
My wife, Shubha S
My daughters, Srinidhi S and Sripradha S
And my colleagues and friends
Sankaran Venkataramani

CHAPTER 1

Introduction to Design Thinking

Learning Objectives

At the end of this chapter, you will be able to:

- Describe sustainable business models and how design thinking contributes to their development
- Define design thinking and give an explanation of its unique way of working
- Provide insights into the 'sweet spots' of design thinking where it can be most effectively applied
- Explore the four critical questions that design thinking addresses
- Explain the need for design thinking in modern problem-solving and innovation
- Provide a historical perspective on the evolution of design thinking and its impact over time
- Give an overview of the 10 essential tools of design thinking and how they facilitate the process
- Provide a step-by-step breakdown of the five stages of design thinking
- Offer guidance on planning and executing a design thinking project from start to finish
- Enumerate the benefits of using design thinking in various contexts
- List the criteria for when to employ design thinking and when it might not be the best approach
- Compare design thinking with alternative methodologies
- Distinguish between design thinking and traditional problem-solving techniques

1.1 If You Want to Think Out-of-the-Box, First Get Rid of the Box

Consider the photographs shown in Fig. 1.1. They depict innovative problem-solving ideas and creativity in everyday scenarios. The first picture shows a bicycle seat that has been replaced with a chair cushion, in an effort to enhance riding comfort. The second image shown a shoe sole attached to a water faucet to regulate water pressure or minimize splashing. In the third image, a shoe bottom has been used as a receptacle for a phone charger, possibly to prevent it from dropping or becoming entangled. The fourth image depicts the utilization of the outer layer of a plastic water tank as an improvised roof for a public toilet, presumably to offer privacy and shield from weather conditions.

Figure 1.1 Simple and effective ideas for solving common problems

In the fifth image, a primary water container has been converted into a functional shower by puncturing holes at the base, providing a practical means of personal hygiene. The sixth image showcases the innovative use of a water tank's outer cover as a protective barrier for motorcycles, potentially safeguarding them from dust or rain. These photographs exemplify how individuals perceive things from varying perspectives and discover inventive solutions to their difficulties.

Design Visualization Question 1.1

Have you encountered any similar cases of innovation in everyday life?

Please identify and describe five such examples of ingenious solutions that address a specific challenge or need.

Creating something new or improving something that already exists is the process of **innovation** (Fig. 1.2). It could be a brand-new concept, product, procedure, item, or service. Finding more effective and efficient methods to do things is another definition of innovation. Everyday problems are solved through innovation, which makes life simpler, more effective, and more pleasurable.
Innovation can solve current problems, create new opportunities, and improve efficiency and effectiveness (Fig. 1.3):

- Thanks to technological advancements, vehicles can now drive at higher speeds and more safely than with previous versions.
- Healthcare innovation is crucial for increasing human progress and encouraging well-being and is a source of optimism. Imagine living longer, healthier lives! That is the promise of healthcare innovation.
- New market innovation can generate new markets or occupations that were earlier not feasible or accessible, stimulating economic growth and employment opportunities for people across the globe. For instance, it has enabled the emergence of e-commerce, digital media, renewable energy, and biotechnology.

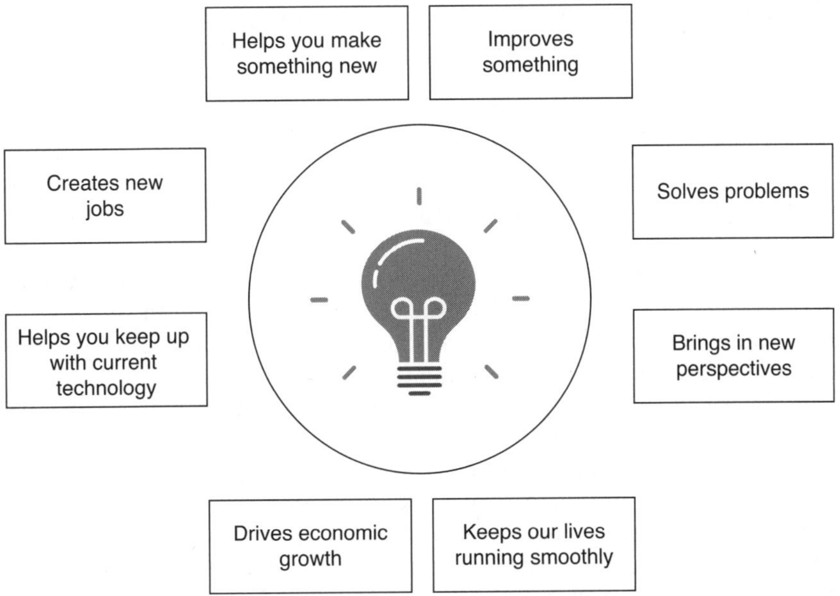

Figure 1.2 What and why of innovation

	Technological innovation has led to the development of vehicles that can travel faster and which are safer, reducing the risk of accidents and saving time and fuel.
	Healthcare innovation can create new vaccines, diagnostic tools, surgical techniques, and telemedicine platforms to prevent, detect, and treat diseases.
	New market innovation has enabled the emergence of e-commerce, digital media, renewable energy, and biotechnology sectors that can offer new products, services, and jobs.
	Internet technology facilitates team collaboration and coordination to accomplish tasks faster and better. We have more choices and possibilities, fostering innovation and skill development.
	Innovation thinking can enable us to address some of the most pressing challenges we face today, such as climate change and global poverty. By applying our creativity and knowledge to these problems, we can develop novel and practical solutions.

Figure 1.3 Different kinds of innovation

- Internet technology advancement is a significant enabler of internet innovation, allowing us to create, learn, and experiment with new things. We can access information online, consult experts remotely, and watch instructional videos. Technology also facilitates team collaboration and coordination to accomplish tasks faster and better.
- Employing creative thinking can lead to unique encounters that enrich our lives and expand our viewpoints. Innovative thinking can also enable us to address pressing issues that we currently face, such as climate change or global poverty.

Collaborative thinking elevates the potential for individuals to generate more innovative and effective solutions compared to those working in isolation by leveraging the collective intellect of diverse groups of people. **Collective wisdom** is the synthesis of varied perspectives, experiences, and understanding stored in a shared repository. This intellect can produce innovations that exceed the limitations imposed by conventional reasoning.

1.2 Sustainable Business Models

Product innovation allows us access to opportunities for growth, both professional (such as by starting a business) and personal (such as hobbies). There are no limits when it comes to what you can create – anything from an app for smartphones to something made out of local material. Product innovation can lead to many benefits such as jobs, which help the economy by providing people with the employment and money they need to buy the goods and services. Innovation is also required to stay up-to-date with quickly changing technology to uphold a high quality of life.

Albert Einstein once said, "A problem cannot be solved with the same mentality that generated it." Thought process quality is directly proportional to outcome quality. Consequently, every organization and institution must employ differential thinking.

In today's marketplace, customers expect more from their service providers. They also anticipate a long-term constructive partnership founded upon trust, cooperation, and reciprocal advantage. A holistic and integrated approach to success is gaining traction in the industry, instead of emphasizing isolated accomplishments. Consequently, to deliver value and ensure customer satisfaction, service providers must synchronize their objectives and strategies with their clients and collaborate across all enterprise functions and divisions. A strategic business model that integrates environmental and social considerations into its fundamental operations is one method for sustainable business development.

The **circular model** (Fig. 1.4) is an approach to designing and managing products and processes to minimize the environmental impact of production and consumption. It involves creating products and processes that can be easily recycled, reused, repaired, or regenerated instead of discarded or burnt up. A circular product could be made of biodegradable or recyclable materials, designed for easy disassembly and repair, and offered with a service or leasing model that ensures its return to practice after quick repair and reuse. Some examples of circular products in day-to-day life are given in Fig. 1.5.

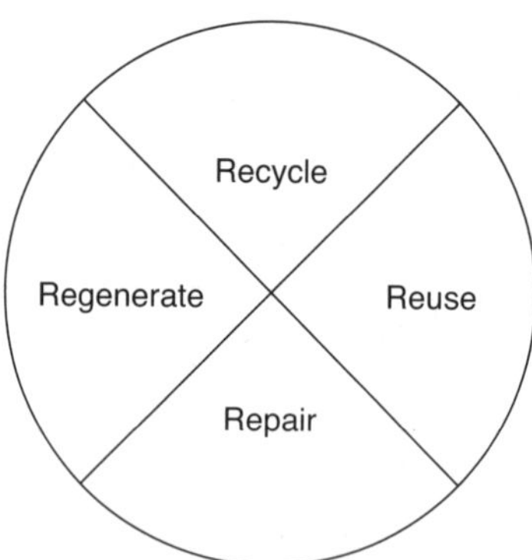

Figure 1.4 Circular model of sustainable business

Design Visualization Question 1.2

Give three examples of circular products that are commonly used in everyday life and which contribute to the principles of reuse, recycle, and regenerate.

	Coffee pods made of compostable materials can be returned to the manufacturer for composting and reuse.
	Mobile phones that are designed to be modular and easy to upgrade, repair, or recycle and that come with a subscription service that includes regular maintenance and replacement of parts.
	Clothing made of organic or recycled fibers and dyed with natural or low-impact dyes can be rented, swapped, or donated to extend its lifespan and reduce waste.
	Furniture made of durable and renewable materials such as wood or bamboo can be disassembled and reassembled into different shapes or functions or refurbished and resold.
	Food packaging made of edible or biodegradable materials such as seaweed or corn starch can be composted or consumed along with the food.
	Toys made of safe and recyclable materials such as plastic or metal can be customized, repaired, or exchanged with other users or returned to the manufacturer for recycling or donation.
	Books printed on recycled paper or digital formats can be borrowed, lent, or donated to libraries or schools or accessed online through subscription services or platforms.
	Cosmetics made of natural or organic ingredients and packaged in reusable or refillable containers can be purchased in bulk or through subscription services or be returned to the manufacturer for recycling or refilling.

Figure 1.5 Examples of circular products in day-to-day life

The **triple bottom line (TBL) model** (Fig. 1.6) is a framework for assessing and reporting the performance of a corporation based on three dimensions: financial, social, and environmental.

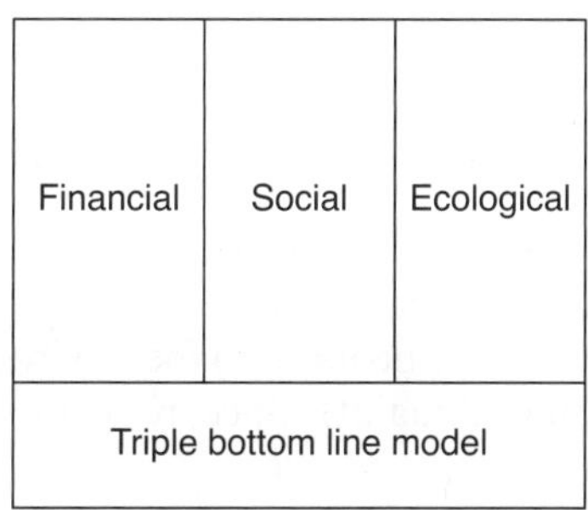

Figure 1.6 TBL model of sustainable business

Financially, it covers earnings, expenses and costs – ensuring the company can make money for investors. Socially, it is about being responsible – treating workers well, helping communities, and making customers happy. Environmentally, it means being accountable and reducing bad impacts – managing waste properly, protecting nature, and cutting emissions. The financial part allows the company to exist. The social part enables it to be accepted. The environmental part makes sure it does not do harm. Together, these three parts make up the whole model. Some examples of TBL models are given in Table 1.1.

Table 1.1 Examples of TBL models

S.No	Organization	Financial Dimension	Social Dimension	Environmental Dimension
1	Apple Inc.	Revenue growth and profitability	Investment in improving labor conditions	Aims to become carbon neutral by 2030
2	Patagonia	Stable financial returns	Environmental activism and community engagement	Sustainable business practices
3	Microsoft	Consistent revenue increase	Corporate social responsibility initiatives	Use of AI for environmental preservation

Design Visualization Question 1.3

Write an essay on Amul, the largest dairy cooperative in India, about their triple bottom line (TPL) model implementation.

Servitization is a business model (Fig. 1.7) that transforms a company's value proposition, from selling products to delivering services or solutions that address customers' specific needs and expectations.

Selling products
to
Delivering services

Figure 1.7 Servitization model of sustainable business

By adopting this model, a company can establish long-term customer relationships, enhance satisfaction and loyalty, and generate recurring and stable revenue streams and higher profit margins. Moreover, servitization can also contribute to the environmental sustainability of products by ensuring their optimal utilization and maintenance, reducing waste and resource consumption (Table 1.2).

Table 1.2 Examples of companies that use the servitization model

S.No	Company	Sector	Product	Services
1	Tata Motors	Automotive	Vehicles	Fleet management, maintenance, insurance, financing
2	Godrej Appliances	Consumer durables	Refrigerators, air conditioners	Cooling as a service (CaaS), pay-per-use, remote monitoring
3	Mahindra & Mahindra	Agriculture	Tractors, farm equipment	Farming as a service (FaaS), crop advisory, soil testing
4	Larsen & Toubro	Engineering	Machinery, equipment	Asset management, performance optimization, life cycle support

Design Visualization Question 1.4

Based on the number of employees, identify the top three IT organizations in India. Then, investigate how these organizations implement servitization in their business models and processes.

The process of generating ideas is not driven by the monetary value of the content but by the type of problems that the ideas can address in a lasting way. The key to successful ideation (Fig. 1.8) is to have a deep understanding of the problems or challenges and to break them down into manageable components that can lead to practical and straightforward solutions that can remove the barriers or pains caused by those challenges.

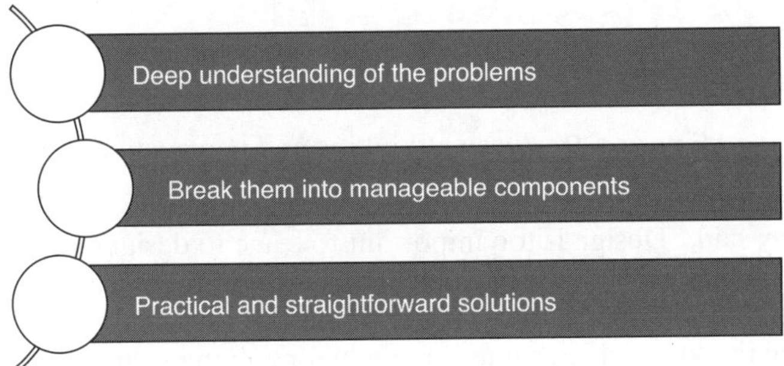

Figure 1.8 Key to successful ideation

No idea can be considered innovative unless it is implemented. Ideation without implementation is only a false start. Putting ideation in action is essential to fully assess its outcome. Design thinking helps to put ideation in action by defining a life cycle model for the implementation of the innovation.

1.3 Definition of Design Thinking

Once, there lived a girl called Tara who loved drawing pictures. Her talent impelled her to create something exceptional. So, Tara decided to use design thinking! First, she pondered what her project should be – how could her artwork help others? Then, she thought about the tools or materials she needed to achieve this goal. To gather ideas, Tara spoke to friends and family, and researched online. Next, using insights from these conversations, she designed prototypes or small models showing how her finished project would look. Tara kept modifying this until she found a satisfactory design. Then, Tara created a beautiful mural that made everyone smile! This is how design thinking works – by combining creativity and problem-solving in one great idea!

Design thinking helps inventors develop new solutions to problems. It looks at issues from multiple viewpoints to understand users' needs. Inventors then generate different ideas and explore opportunities for innovation. This creative problem-solving process leads to improved products, services, experiences, and processes that cater to people's needs more meaningfully.

Design thinking puts users first and involves an approach focused on understanding them and finding creative user-centric solutions. It also uses an iterative method. Ideas are quickly tested and changes are made based on feedback (Fig. 1.9).

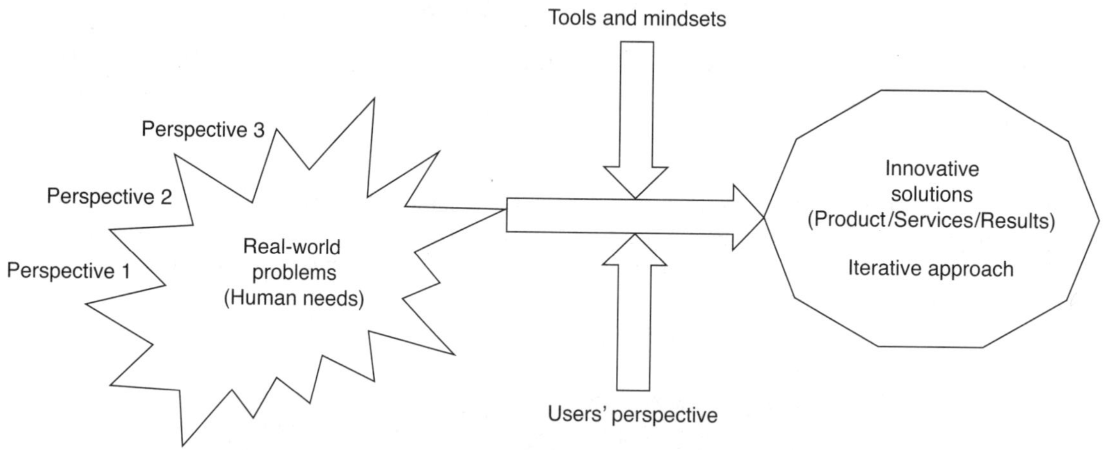

Figure 1.9 Design thinking and perspectives

Design thinking thus involves grasping challenges, finding solutions, and checking if they work well. Raymond Loewy said, "Design is too important to leave to designers alone." So, experts from various fields must collaborate effectively to create solutions/products. The mindset and practical methods of design thinking aid problem solving in numerous ways.

It includes critical thinking, which comes in handy for gaining valuable insights into a problem. Adopting a different perspective and breaking free from our comfort zones is crucial. This shift in positioning allows for a new world to unfold, presenting a variety of choices.

According to Tim Brown, design thinking is not an art, science, or religion but the capacity for integrative thinking (Fig. 1.10). Brown emphasizes that design thinking involves a human-centered approach to innovation that integrates people's needs, technology's possibilities, and business success requirements, drawing on the designer's toolkit. Thus, design thinking advocates a hands-on, learning-by-doing approach. It shifts the focus from a business-centric engineering solution to a customer-centric solution.

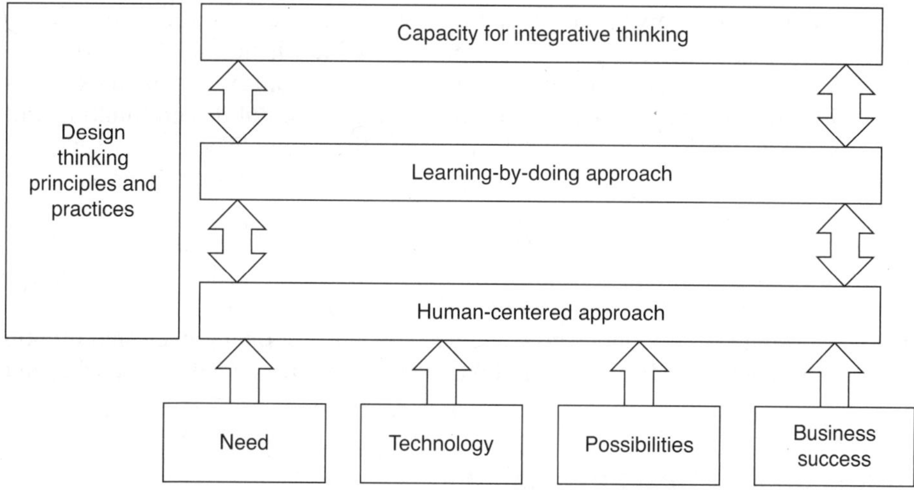

Figure 1.10 Tim Brown's definition of design thinking

1.4 Way of Working (WoW) of Design Thinking

People from many fields need to work together to find solutions. Design thinking lets us understand users, identify issues, brainstorm ideas, prototype, and test solutions in a feedback loop. We must understand our company's culture, values, and goals. Then we align these with design thinking principles and practices (Fig. 1.11).

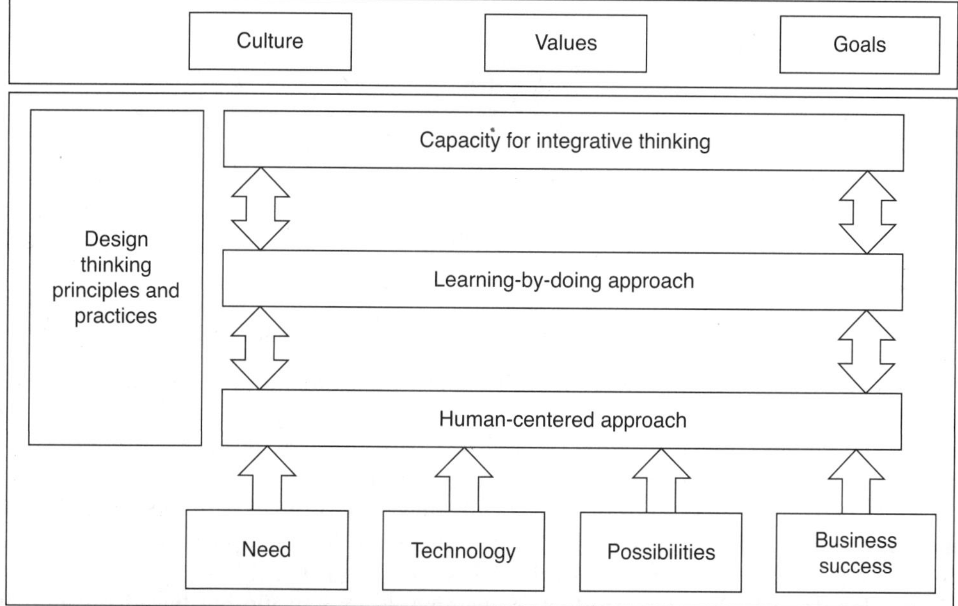

Figure 1.11 Design thinking as a way of working

Focused enablement sessions must be provided to employees to ensure they have a common and consistent understanding of the design thinking principles and further deliberate on the adoption and ways of making these concepts work within the company's context. Enablement sessions need to be curated with sufficient depth to drive knowledge acquisition of design thinking and practice the tenets in real-world implementation to demonstrate the results. These sessions should not be superficial or generic but instead tailored to the specific needs and goals of the employees and their projects.

Employees must be given many chances to practice their design thinking skills. They should work on realistic cases and obtain feedback from experts. This way, they will understand design thinking and learn how to use it to create value and solve problems.

The way of working (WoW) guides how people think and act on a job. Design thinking shapes WoW's principles and practices. It stresses understanding others, trying new approaches, and making adjustments.

1.5 Sweet Spot of Design Thinking

Design thinking involves understanding the customers' needs, desires, and preferences, as well as the organization's capabilities, constraints, and opportunities. One way to apply design thinking is to use a framework of three dimensions: desirability, feasibility, and viability. These dimensions help evaluate a solution or value or product's potential value and impact from different perspectives (Fig. 1.12).

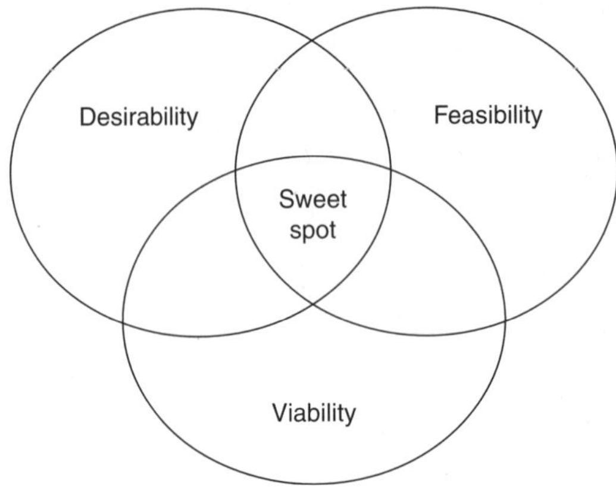

Figure 1.12 Sweet spot: desirability, feasibility, and viability

Desirability is about how well a product meets people's needs, wants, and expectations. It asks: Do customers want it? To understand this, you can map customer feelings, track their journey, interview people, send out surveys, make prototypes, and test with users. A desirable product solves real problems, fills unstated needs, or creates positive experiences.

Feasibility refers to whether you can realistically make the product with the available resources, skills, and know how. It asks: Can we build it? Brainstorming, coming up with ideas, experimenting, validating assumptions, and iterations help check if something is feasible.

Viability denotes whether the product is sustainable and profitable based on demand and competition. It asks: Will it work? To assess this, you create business models, define value propositions, research the market, analyze rivals, and forecast financials.

Finding a solution that satisfies the customer's needs, business goals, and competitors' offerings is design thinking's sweet spot. A viable product delivers value to customers and the company, stands out from alternatives, and enables long-term growth and success.

Design thinking is not a linear process, but a dynamic, iterative one, requiring collaboration, experimentation, and multi-disciplinary learning. This approach is different from other methods that focus on appearance, function, or efficiency. Design thinkers use three factors: experimenting, learning by doing, and collaboration (Fig. 1.13).

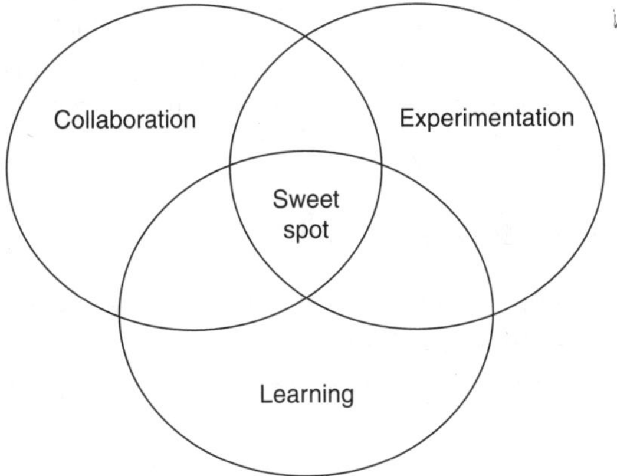

Figure 1.13 Sweet spot: collaboration, experimentation and learning

Often, project staff are organized using a cooperation approach, where they work jointly but do not perform every process step. Each person has a set role or task contributing to the total project outcome. In the design thinking approach, staff collaboratively make decisions by being hands-on throughout. Here, each member offers diverse skills and viewpoints, actively participating in all project stages.

A collaborative approach requires three key elements: talent, methods, and workspace (Fig. 1.14). Talent involves the project members, their skills, mindsets, and attitudes. Methods encompass techniques like brainstorming, prototyping, testing, and feedback. The workspace refers to the physical and social environment, including resources, equipment, time, and support.

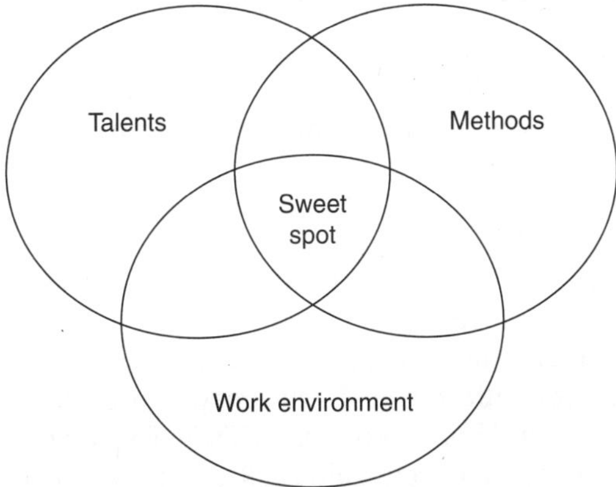

Figure 1.14 Sweet spot: Talents, methods and work environment

For instance, imagine a hospital enlisting designers to enhance patient experiences in the emergency room. The team includes diverse professionals, such as graphic designers, service designers, psychologists, and nurses. They possess talents in empathizing, experimenting, and iterating. Utilizing various methods, they conduct interviews and observations to identify user needs, pain points, and expectations. They synthesize findings into personas, journey maps, and insights. Through brainstorming and sketching, they generate potential solutions, like improving signage, layout, and communication. They create low-fidelity prototypes, testing them with users and collecting feedback and data. Refining their prototypes based on this feedback, they continue testing until achieving satisfactory outcomes. This team also has a conducive workspace, with dedicated areas for displaying research, ideas, and prototypes, along with necessary tools and materials. They are given ample time and budget, as well as support and trust from hospital management and staff open to change and innovation.

1.6 Four Questions of Design Thinking

Design thinking encourages people to think outside the box to solve problems. Four key questions are part of the design thinking process (Fig. 1.15).

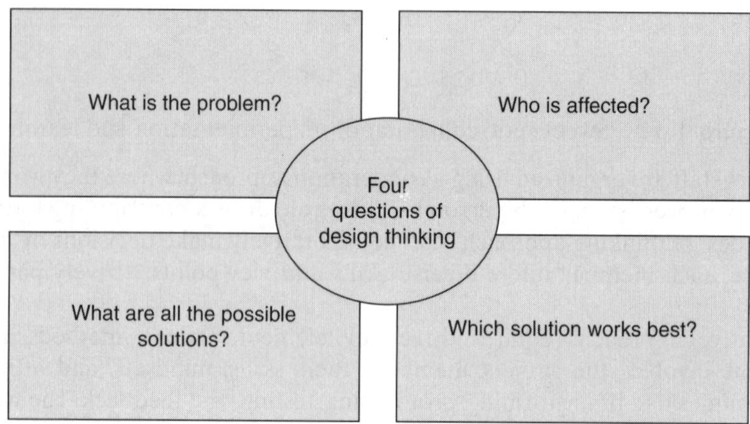

Figure 1.15 Four key questions of design thinking

- **What is the problem?** Design thinking starts by understanding what needs solving. First, identify the real problem and why it exists. Then, you can find the best solution.
- **Who is affected?** Knowing who benefits from your solution is key. It leads to smarter choices, better designs, and improved results for all.
- **What are all the possible solutions?** Brainstorming represents a vital design thinking component. The goal should be to generate numerous potential solutions, initially disregarding their perceived outlandishness or impossibility. This openness nurtures creativity when selecting the optimal solution later.
- **Which solution works best?** After evaluating all the potential solutions, one must assess them against criteria such as cost effectiveness, efficiency, and user experience to determine the optimal choice for the specific situation or goal. This final step ensures selection of a practical, aesthetic solution that most effectively guides all the parties involved towards their desired outcomes!

Design Visualization Question 1.5

Apply the four questions of design thinking for designing a better user interface for an online shopping website. The challenge is to make the website more user-friendly, engaging and accessible.

1.7 Need for Design Thinking

Design thinking helps people solve problems in creative ways. It helps us think outside the box and develop new solutions (Fig. 1.16).

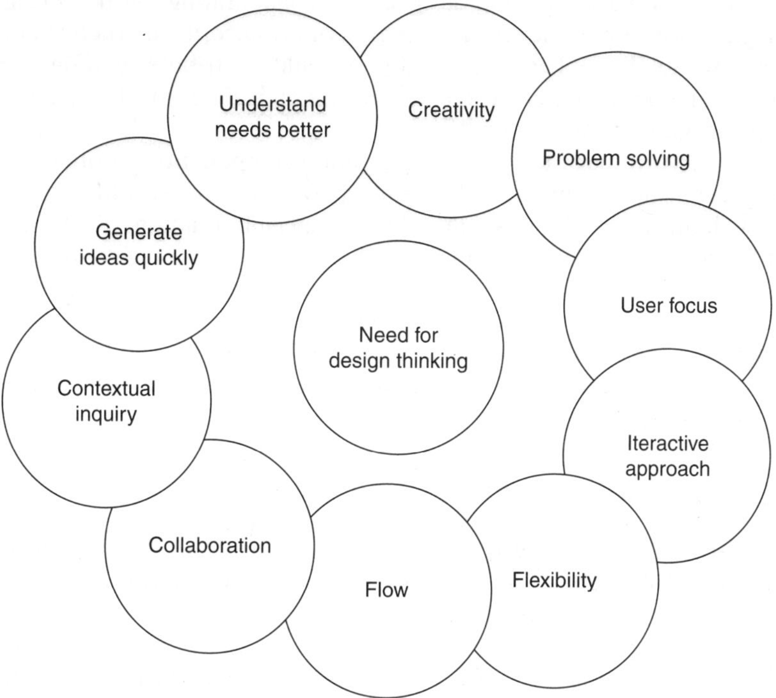

Figure 1.16 Need for design thinking

- **Creativity:** Design thinking promotes creativity to develop solutions for issues. For instance, Apple used design thinking to create the iPod. It enabled us to carry thousands of songs on a small device.
- **Problem-solving:** Design thinking helps us understand issues from different angles and find practical solutions. Firms like Google have used it to create products like Gmail and Maps that address user needs creatively.
- **User Focus:** Design thinking focuses on understanding users' needs and desires, so products are customized for them. For instance, websites or apps may need large buttons for easy navigation by tech novices. They should also be simple and intuitive so as not to confuse users. Considerations like these help create enjoyable user experiences.
- **Iterative Approach:** Design thinking involves an iterative approach where designs are constantly tested and refined until optimal results are achieved. For example, when creating a new mobile game, developers would need to playtest it multiple times before sending it out to

the public. This means they would have to try out the game and see how it works to ensure it runs smoothly and all the features work correctly.

- **Flexibility:** Although design thinking relies on known techniques, its main objective is user centricity. This means designers can adapt as needed, provided they prioritize users' best interests. For example, if customer input suggests making specific revisions during development, this could swiftly happen without major changes to the original product concept.
- **Flow:** Design thinking helps our brain process information step by step, enabling us to find solutions quickly while staying focused. For example, when setting up an art exhibit, designers follow each preparation step, ensuring smooth operation once the show begins. Even tiny mistakes can ruin the event's flow.
- **Collaboration:** Design thinking emphasizes teamwork between various professionals, including developers, marketers, and designers, all collaborating towards the shared objective of enhancing the user experience for customers. For instance, if a marketing department wants to launch a new mobile application, developers could contribute by programming the app's functionality, while designers could create visually appealing interfaces, ensuring customers find the app engaging and user friendly.
- **Contextual Inquiry:** Rather than analysing separate components in isolation, design thinking encourages the holistic examination of a challenge within its real-world setting. This contextual inquiry allows innovative solutions tailored to the specific situation.
- **Generates Ideas Quickly:** Design thinking helps people find creative solutions to problems. It involves research, brainstorming, and testing ideas. Using design thinking, you can quickly develop creative ideas that work well when put into practice.
- **Better Understand the Needs of Different Groups of People:** Design thinking helps build trust between customers and brands. It leads to higher satisfaction overall. It makes sure what we make is helpful and enjoyable.

1.8 History and Evolution of Design Thinking

Design thinking was created in the 1960s by designers such as Charles Eames, Robert Propst, and Richard Buckminster Fuller. They thought design thinking could solve complex issues in many areas, such as engineering, architecture, education, and urban planning.

Design thinking uses ideas from science to create better solutions for people. It starts by understanding how people think, feel, and act in different situations. Design thinkers learn from experts like psychologists, anthropologists, and sociologists. Psychology helps understand how humans think, make choices, and solve problems. Anthropology studies cultures and societies. Sociology examines social behaviors. These subjects help designers grasp perspectives of different groups.

Designers also observe how people interact with each other to create better designs that reflect their behaviors. By understanding social dynamics such as communication styles, customs, shared values, and beliefs, designers can make their products more user-friendly for everyone, regardless of background or culture.

The speed of transformation has multiplied drastically over the past couple of decades. With a paradigm shift in emerging technologies and newer ways of leveraging artificial intelligence, robotic process automation will continue contributing towards human-influenced creativity. It will enable more unique ways to become agile and adaptable.

Twentieth-century approaches and mindsets, such as revenue-driven management based on traditional hierarchical directives, have worked to achieve wealth and prosperity sporadically, leaving many others behind. In today's context, companies need to strive in the era of ESG, focusing on Environmental, Social, and Governance, taking responsibility for the community at large. Business houses need to conduct their business by combating the PESTLE (Political, Economic, Social, Technological, Legal, and Environmental) factors.

Hasso Plattner, founder of the software company SAP, noticed that David Kelley's design school was connected to Stanford University in Palo Alto. Kelley used a method/process that he called design thinking to enable students to collaboratively work on problems that were not easily analyzed. At Stanford, Kelley invited students from multiple disciplines to what he called the d.school. He wanted to teach his students to become innovators rather than administrators in their respective domains and even across multiple disciplines.

The subsequent meeting between Plattner and Kelley accelerated the rise of design thinking. Plattner funded the d.school at Stanford, which spread worldwide, from Potsdam, Germany; to Cape Town, South Africa; Kuala Lumpur, Malaysia; and to Beijing in China. Other schools from various backgrounds have also introduced a design thinking approach.

SAP embraced design thinking, as did PepsiCo, Daimler, IBM, and even traditional consultancies such as McKinsey and Accenture.

1.9 Ten Tools of Design Thinking

Design thinking is a creative problem-solving process used by many people to come up with innovative solutions. It aims to generate valuable and meaningful ideas for people. To do this, it uses 10 different tools and strategies to produce the best possible results (Fig. 1.17).

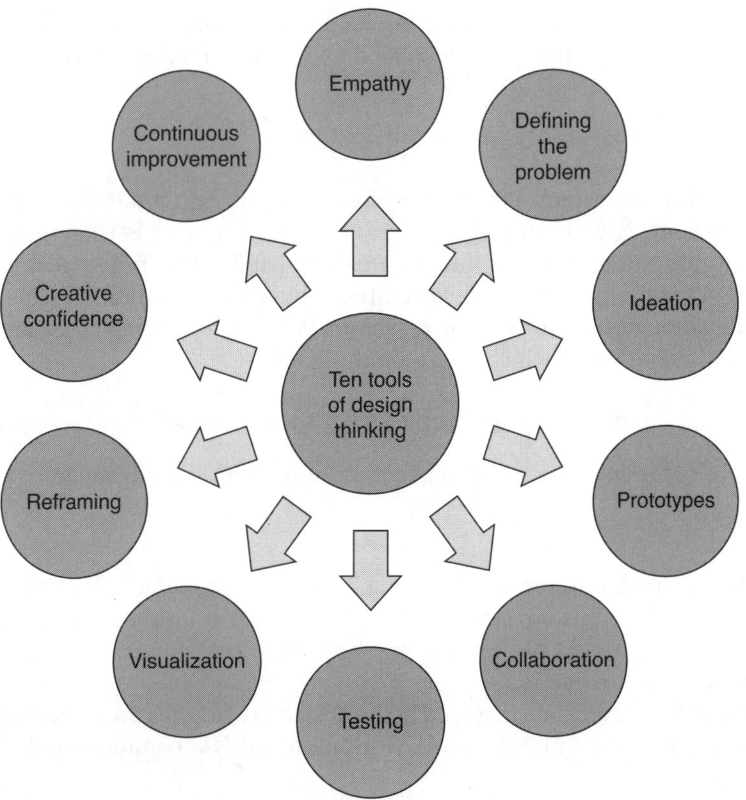

Figure 1.17 Ten tools of design thinking

Empathy helps us grasp what others want from a product or service. We use this tool to imagine ourselves in someone else's shoes before finding solutions. For instance, designers wish to create an app for managing blood sugar levels in diabetes patients. They interview and observe potential users to find their challenges and goals. They learn about users' daily routines. They use this user information to create user profiles, empathy maps, and journey maps to guide their work.

Design Visualization Question 1.6

A school wants to redesign its curriculum and pedagogy to foster more creativity and innovation among students.

List three pointers on how empathy can be used in the above example.

The second tool is **defining the problem**. This involves identifying the root cause of an issue so we can create effective solutions. Here, you need to ask questions and gather information about the problem areas. You start by understanding what people are trying to do and look for clues as to why it is not working. For example, your parents have trouble getting dinner on the table each night. You can ask them why they do not have time for dinner. What holds them up during the day? Do they have enough ingredients or equipment? This can help you understand the problem and then come up with solutions.

Design Visualization Question 1.7

A hospital wants to improve the patient experience and satisfaction in their facility. They use design thinking to define the problem by collecting data and feedback from patients, staff, and visitors.

List 2–3 problems that are possibly faced by the patients.

The third tool is **ideation**, which encourages creativity through brainstorming sessions where everyone contributes ideas without judgment or criticism. The goal is to generate many options. Then, the most feasible and successful solutions are shortlisted before implementation. For instance, imagine your class wants to make the college eco-friendly. During ideation, classmates could suggest bringing reusable water bottles instead of plastic ones and or planting trees around the college grounds. They could then discuss which idea would work best.

Design Visualization Question 1.8

A school wants to redesign its library to make it more inviting and engaging for students.

List 2–3 ideas for the above.

Prototype designs are created to test an idea quickly, cheaply, and effectively before a lot of time or money is invested in it. With this, we can see how practical our solution is by objectively evaluating it against users' needs identified during the empathy stage and any other potential issues raised further down the development cycle.

Collaboration ensures everyone involved in the design process has the opportunity to contribute their skill set, experience and opinions while working towards a common goal. For example, if a group wants to create a new kind of bike, they would need help from many different people. The designer might come up with the look and shape, while an engineer might figure out how it should be built. A mechanic could test the bike while someone else might work on finding materials for it. By working together, everyone can use their skills to create something unique!

Testing allows designers to receive honest feedback from the target audience regarding design concepts/prototypes and identify areas where improvements could be made before the product launch. For example, a designer might perform user testing on a new mobile app for ordering food online. Let us say you want to order food online. The company would ask you to go through the steps. You would then give feedback on your experience. This helps the company find out which parts need improvement.

Visualization uses drawings, diagrams and sketches to help communicate concepts quickly and efficiently, showing how various elements fit together, forming a cohesive whole. This technique allows the entire team to gain a comprehensive view of the project's progress/status and make necessary adjustments easily in the early stages itself. For example, a map is filled with different shapes like squares, circles, rectangles, and triangles. Each shape on the map has its purpose or meaning. For example, the squares may be cities or towns, while the circles may represent oceans or other bodies of water. The rectangles are roads that connect these places, while the triangles represent mountains or other landmarks. All these shapes combine to create one big picture that tells us where we are going and how to get there. Visualization can also be used when creating stories or explaining complex concepts.

Reframing forces designers to think differently about the same problem, providing fresh perspectives and enabling them to come up with innovative solutions that may have been overlooked otherwise. In addition, reframing questions provides greater clarity surrounding issues tackled as part of the design process, increasing the likelihood of success when finally launched! For example, if you want school lunches to be healthier, reframing could mean looking at what other countries do. Or looking at popular home-cooked recipes people love. When you reframe things, you can find creative solutions others may not think of.

Creative confidence boosts the designers' confidence, encouraging them to take risks and try new things even when there is uncertainty. Ultimately, fostering an environment of risk-taking experimentation leads to more unique products being developed. Creative confidence is the belief in your creative abilities and knowledge that you have the power to use to make great things. For example, you want to draw a picture of your favorite animal. If you have only ever drawn cats before, having creative confidence means being brave enough to try drawing something completely different, like a giraffe or an elephant, for the first time – even if it feels uncertain. The result may be better than imagined

Continuous improvement encourages the team to constantly review the processes and methods used during the development cycle, making adjustments as needed to stay competitive over rivals providing similar services and goods.

All these tools, taken together, form a robust framework used successfully countless times worldwide, and which help to generate truly great designs.

1.10 Five Stages of the Design Thinking Process

Design thinking is a creative process used to solve problems. It consists of five stages (Fig. 1.18): empathize, define the problem, ideate, create a prototype, and test.

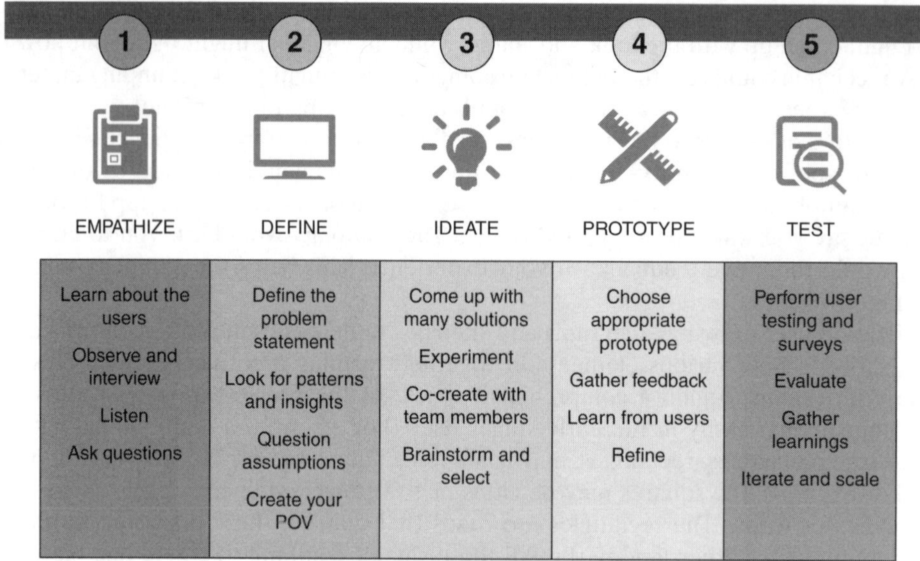

Figure 1.18 Five stages of the design thinking process

1.10.1 Empathize

In design thinking, empathy means seeing things the user's way. You put yourself in their shoes, move past assumptions and biases, and try to view the world as they do. This helps make products perfect for the users' specific needs.

Let us think about creating a new car seat for children. You can watch parents shopping for car seats. Ask them questions like:

1. What features did they look for when choosing a seat?
2. What made them pick one seat over another?
3. What would make using the seat with their child easier?

By asking questions and watching shoppers, you can learn about what is important when choosing a car seat.

Why is the Empathize Step Important?

This step is essential for several reasons. Designers must try to understand the needs of people who will use their products. When designers truly know their users, they can solve real problems. The empathize step also prevents designers from making incorrect guesses about users. Designers sometimes think everyone uses technology the same way they do. But people have different skills. By learning about users, designers avoid these faulty assumptions. This allows them to create products suitable for everyone.

How Can the Empathize Step Be Performed?

Here are some methods that designers can use to empathize with their users:

- **Conduct Interviews:** Do you want to know what the user needs? Ask questions! Speak to users and ask them about their wants and experiences. Open-ended questions let you empathize and understand them. By listening carefully to what the user says, designers can better understand their perspective.

- **Observe Users:** Another way to empathize with users is to observe them in their natural environment. Designers can look at how people use products and get the work done. As designers watch, they can see where people struggle. Then designers can make those tasks easier.
- **Use Empathy Maps:** An empathy map helps designers understand users. It has four parts: thinking, feeling, saying, and doing. Designers fill out each part. This gives them a better idea of what users think, feel, say, and do. Then designers can improve the users' experience of the product.
- **Conduct Surveys:** Surveys can be used to gather quantitative user data. Surveys help us collect facts about users.
- **Research:** This involves researching any existing literature surrounding the topic area, such as case studies or market reports, which provide relevant data points so designers can make informed decisions regarding potential solutions later on in the process.

In conclusion, gaining insights from observing, speaking directly with users, and researching existing literature helps designers increase empathy for their target audience.

1.10.2 Define

The user problem you want to solve needs to be defined in the second stage of the design thinking process. Collect all your findings from the empathize phase and begin piecing them together. What recurring themes and patterns did you notice? What user needs and challenges arose repeatedly? You can write a problem statement after you have put together your discoveries. A problem statement explains the issue or challenge you want to solve. It is also called a point of view (POV) statement. Like everything else in the design thinking process, the problem statement keeps the user in mind. Instead of framing your problem statement as a business goal, frame it from the user's perspective.

You can use the following techniques to help you define the problem and guide your process:

- **Data analysis** is the process of identifying and defining the user's problem based on the data gathered during the empathy stage.
- **Analyse the user journey:** A user journey visually represents the user's journey through the solution. The user journey considers a user's actions, feelings, pain points, and moments of delight.
- **How might we go about it?** Try rephrasing questions to start with "how might we..." The phrase "how might we" followed by a specific pain point can encourage team members to think about the problem space more deeply.

1.10.3 Ideate

This is the most creative stage in which potential solutions are generated and explored. This phase helps designers generate creative ideas, explore them collaboratively, and produce innovative solutions. During this exploration process, it is important to encourage discussion among team members about different aspects of each idea so that great ones are not overlooked just because they seem too startling at first glance (or vice versa).

The ideate stage can be broken down into three steps:

1. **Brainstorming:** Brainstorming means thinking of lots of ideas about a problem. Do not judge any idea as good or bad in this step. For example, if you wanted ideas to reduce traffic jams in cities, you might think of carpooling programs or self-driving cars. This step lets you and your team explore freely. This encourages creativity to find new solutions.

2. **Visualizing:** Once all the initial possibilities have been explored through brainstorming, it is time to visualize what these ideas might look like if implemented; this step allows for more concrete understanding by visualizing how each potential solution would work in practice by means a simple diagram such as flow charts or storyboards. A key component here is using visuals rather than words alone so that everyone involved (especially those who are less familiar with technical details) can understand what is being proposed without having extensive knowledge about it beforehand.For example, visualizing how driverless cars could operate might involve creating diagrams that show how they would interact with other drivers on roads, pedestrians, etc.
3. **Refining:** After generating multiple potential solutions through visualization, we need to refine them so only viable options remain before moving on to prototyping. This requires critical analysis of each idea/diagram while taking into account factors such as cost/benefit ratio, practicality and feasibility. This step will help make sure any solution chosen has gone through a rigorous vetting process and meets specific criteria set out earlier. In addition, it makes room for changes/additions based on feedback. For instance, after refining the driverless car concept, one may decide to add features like sensors that detect nearby objects and adjust speed, thereby increasing the safety factor significantly.

1.10.4 Prototype

This stage starts after finding a potential solution. Here, teams build an early design version and test it with users. They get feedback before investing more time and resources. Prototyping allows teams to quickly change their designs without committing too much time or money. It also helps them identify areas where they need more research or development before launching the product.

The first step is building the prototype physically or digitally, creating the core parts of the design solution. You can then see how all the parts fit together and interact. Once you have built your prototype, you can test it by inviting users to provide feedback on its usability, appearance, functionality, etc. This helps teams identify areas for improvement before beginning work on the production version.

Let us look at some examples from everyday life:

- **A new car model**: Car manufacturers often use prototypes when designing new cars in order to get feedback from prospective buyers. These prototypes can also be made available for interaction by customers during events such as auto shows. The valuable customer insights become part of the finalized model, thereby adding tangible value to the company and customer.
- **A mobile app**: Before releasing any new mobile application, most companies opt to go through a rigorous prototyping process, ensuring that all aspects of the user experience are covered comprehensively.

1.10.5 Test

In this phase, designers get opinions from users to improve the design. They also perform usability tests.

Usability testing involves observing real users as they interact with a product or service for a predetermined period while recording any comments or suggestions they make. During this stage, designers will pay attention to how easy it was for users to complete tasks and where they experienced difficulties when using different features. In addition, focus groups may be conducted during this stage so that designers can get direct feedback regarding their products/services.

A/B tests involves launching two versions of a product simultaneously (with slight variations), so you can compare which one performs better over time among your customer base.

Once data has been gathered from these tests, it will need to be analyzed thoroughly so that any areas where improvement may be needed are identified quickly and accurately. After making sure all changes have been made according to specifications and user requirements, designers may want to conduct one final test known as 'beta' before releasing the product in the market. Beta tests generally involve higher scale efforts than in the previous stages.

1.11 Ten Stages of the Design Thinking Process

Design thinking has various approaches. One view describes five stages, as mentioned earlier. Another perspective outlines 10 steps, going into more detail (Fig. 1.19): empathize, define, ideate, prototype, choose, implement, learn, reflect, iterate, and engage.

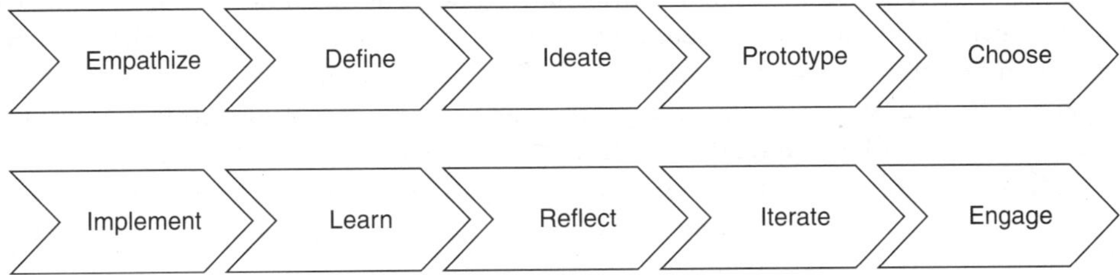

Figure 1.19 Ten stages of design thinking

1. **Empathize:** This means understanding the people you are designing for. You observe how they interact with their surroundings. You gather information on what they need and want. This helps designers understand their users.
2. **Define:** Here you need to define the problem. You lay out the important objectives for designing a product or service. You identify potential limits, such as budget or timeline.
3. **Ideate:** With an understanding of user problems, designers can brainstorm ideas. They can use different methods to solve those problems.
4. **Prototype:** Instead of creating a detailed solution right away, designers build prototypes, which replicate what would eventually become the end product. This is faster than if they had already built the final product from scratch.
5. **Choose:** After exploring different prototypes, designers will develop a final idea that should cover all the objectives during the definition stage while also adhering to any previously identified constraints.
6. **Implement:** Designers will take their chosen concept through further development steps, including coding and testing, until it eventually becomes ready for release into production environments where real users will use it.
7. **Learn:** Here, we can observe how people interact with the product and evaluate if our initial assumptions were correct or whether there are any areas where improvements could be made by introducing new features or tweaking existing ones.
8. **Reflect:** After getting feedback from live usage, it is vital that we take some time away from our project (before moving on to another) so we can step back and think through everything we learned throughout this process.
9. **Iterate:** Armed with newfound knowledge from our reflection session, it is now possible (and encouraged) to make changes/improvements based on what was observed.
10. **Engage:** Last but not the least, get the users involved! Ask people using your product/service what features/functions would help improve their overall experience.

1.12 Benefits of Design Thinking

In India, there was a small tea company called Chai Wala, owned by Babloo. In summer, he struggled to sell tea. One day, Babloo visited Chintu, an expert in design thinking. Chintu explained that design thinking helps us understand customer needs and provide solutions. Babloo wanted Chintu to help him sell more tea in summer.

Chintu observed people walking with umbrellas due to the heat. He proposed an idea: "Chai with an Umbrella." Initially, Babloo did not understand this idea. But Chintu clarified that offering umbrellas to tea buyers would let them enjoy tea while avoiding the sun. Though sceptical, Babloo implemented it. Surprisingly, it became popular! People loved shielding themselves from the sun while sipping tea.

Babloo's sales improved tremendously. He credited Chintu and design thinking with resolving his problem. Known as "Umbrella Chai Wala," Babloo's successful business grew.

Thus, at the heart of design thinking is a profound respect for the end user. Design thinking also encourages teamwork and novel ideas. Teams with varied expertise collaborate, sparking innovation across fields. Another plus is rapid experimentation. Traditionally, companies spend months or years on new products. With design thinking, designers quickly make prototypes to test ideas. Frequent iterations allow faster feedback and adjustments, leading to more successful offerings.

Design thinking is a helpful approach. It lets companies adjust to changes quickly and meet customers' needs. Design thinking supports constantly improving products. It makes companies flexible, letting them stay ahead of competitors.

Design thinking also results in responsible solutions. By focusing on empathy and user needs, designers create effective products. They consider the broader effects of solutions on society and the environment.

In summary, the benefits of design thinking include user focus, teamwork, creativity, fast experiments, flexibility, ethics, and sustainability.

1.13 Misconceptions about Design Thinking

Several common misconceptions about design thinking can hinder its effectiveness in practice. We will discuss some of these misconceptions (Fig. 1.20) and how they can be addressed.

Misconception 1: Design thinking is just for designers.
Design thinking is not just for designers. It is for everyone. Design thinking helps solve problems. It focuses on the user's needs. Anyone can use design thinking. Say, you want to improve customer service at a restaurant. First, understand what frustrates customers. What makes their experience bad? Next, explore ideas to make it better. How can customers have a great experience? Then, test your ideas. Do customers find them helpful? This approach works for any problem.

Misconception 2: Design thinking is only for big, complex problems.
You can apply design thinking to minor, tangible problems that are easy to test and improve quickly. This approach lets you try new solutions, learn from them, and find effective answers faster. For example, let us say your kitchen sink gets clogged. Instead of buying drain cleaners or tools, design thinking means understanding what caused the clog first. Did too much food go down the drain? Could a filter help? This approach looks for tailored solutions before using traditional methods. The same ideas work for bigger problems.

Misconception 3: Design thinking is a linear process.
Design thinking encourages back-and-forth exploration. This helps teams find successful solutions faster than traditional methods. With other methods, teams do lots of research upfront, then develop

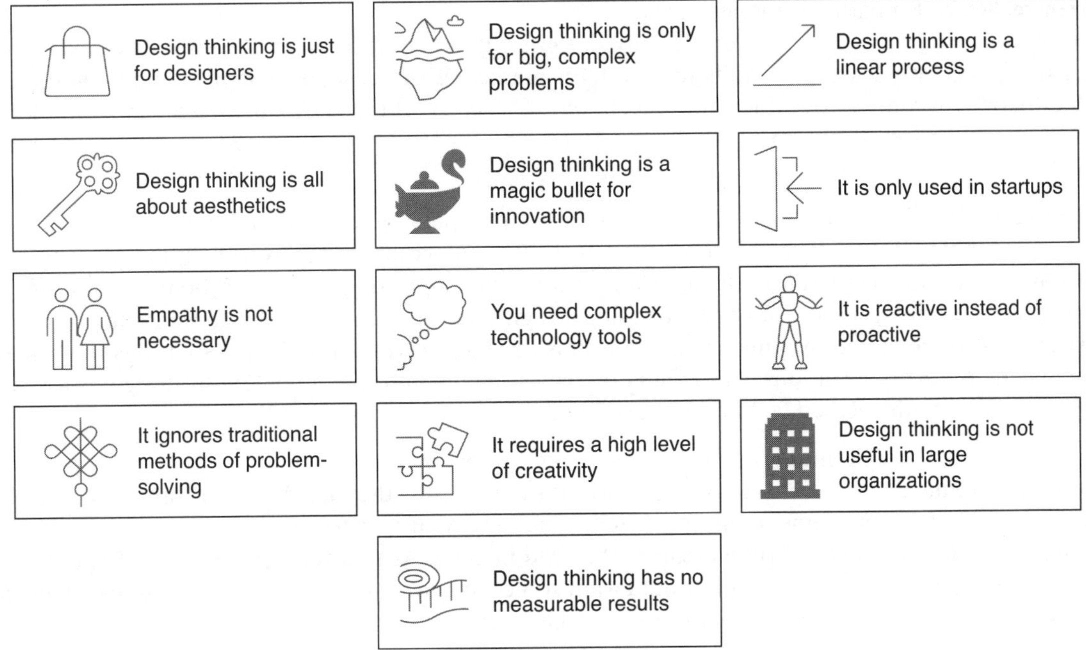

Figure 1.20 Some misconceptions about design thinking

without testing. But design thinking lets stakeholders collaborate at every stage. Teams use customer feedback to shape their designs, not just assumptions from early research.

Misconception 4: Design thinking is all about aesthetics.
Many people wrongly think design thinking is only about how things look visually. While visuals are essential, design thinking is about solving problems to help users. For example, when designing a website, how it looks is one part. Another big part is the user experience (UX). This means how easy it is to use the website and find what you need quickly. Attractiveness is less crucial than ensuring visitors achieve their goals quickly.

Misconception 5: Design thinking is a magic bullet for innovation.
Design thinking is not a quick fix for innovation. It does not ensure that new solutions will be successful or innovative. Design thinking involves understanding user needs and creating solutions based on those insights. However, design thinking alone does not guarantee success. Good ideas still need careful planning and testing. Even if a team develops innovative designs, they may fail due to poor implementation or lack of testing. Innovations require generating creative ideas and executing them well through proper planning and testing.

Misconception 6: Design thinking is only used in startups.
Any organization, big or small, can use design thinking. For instance, Kaiser Permanente and Stanford Children's Health have adopted design thinking. They used it to understand patients better. Another company using design thinking is Amazon Web Services (AWS). AWS created a platform called Cloud Workflows that uses machine learning to automate tasks like deploying apps or scaling resources up or down.

Misconception 7: Empathy is not necessary.
Empathy is vital for design thinking. It helps designers make solutions that users want. For example, say there is an app for older adults to take their medicine. The designers need to understand that older people may not know much about technology. They should focus on making an app that older adults can use easily. Empathy is thus key to design success. It ensures user needs are met accurately, leading to satisfied, engaged users of the final product.

Misconception 8: You need complex technology tools to implement design thinking.
While technology tools such as prototyping software may come into play during the later stages of implementation, essential tools like sketchbooks, paper prototypes, or storyboarding are often enough for starting your journey towards using design thinking principles. Design thinking primarily uses the knowledge and insights gained from this process to create innovative solutions that meet user needs. Even organizations with smaller budgets can benefit from implementing design processes without using sophisticated technological resources.

Misconception 9: Design thinking is reactive instead of proactive.
Design thinking is often seen as a way to solve problems after they happen. But this is not true. It can be used before problems occur, too. It helps find new solutions to complex issues. For example, Apple used design thinking when creating the iPod in 2001. At that time, people were happy with CD players. But Apple knew people would want something more portable and easier to use if given a choice. The iPod met people's needs in ways CDs could not.

Misconception 10: Design thinking ignores traditional methods of problem-solving.
Design thinking considers traditional problem-solving methods, but adds a new perspective. It finds new and better solutions. But it still respects established processes. For example, you want to design a new tech product. First, you research popular products in your industry. You use that as a starting point for something new and innovative. This initial step uses traditional research methods like surveys and interviews. Design thinking then focuses on human-centered design. That involves understanding user needs before developing ideas. You may then build prototypes or models based on user insights.

Misconception 11: It requires a high level of creativity.
Design thinking can help people work through problems that range from the mundane to the complex without relying on the most creative solutions. At its heart, design thinking requires more creativity than structured thinking and a willingness to explore all available options to find the best solution. As such, even those with limited knowledge or experience may succeed with this methodology if they are willing to adopt an open mind and use their critical analysis skills. For example, let us say you have been tasked with creating a new product line for your company. Instead of trying to come up with radical new ideas, you could use design thinking principles like defining customer pain points first before coming up with potential solutions. This way you can ensure your product fits customers' needs better than competitors.

Misconception 12: Design thinking is not useful in large organizations.
Large organizations have more complex problems, so they need well-thought-out solutions which only come through taking part in comprehensive yet thorough processes like designing thinking which involves analysis from different perspectives leading up towards discovering effective solutions efficiently.

For example, at IBM, design thinking was implemented through its design thinking methodology, which the company developed to help guide its employees' design process from start to finish. With this system in place, IBM was able to build high-functioning products that were tailored to their customer's needs and wants. Microsoft also utilized design thinking principles when building its Xbox video game console to create an engaging experience for gamers.

Misconception 13: Design thinking has no measurable results.
By applying measures like benchmarking and user feedback, companies can easily measure results produced by implementing design thinking principles within their operations. For example, a company wants new ways to improve how customers use their website. Through design thinking, they can create prototypes of potential solutions. These prototypes can then be tested before putting them on their website. This allows them to track what works well and what does not, so they can make informed decisions when it comes time to roll out any changes across their entire platform. These metrics also serve as a valuable tool for organizations when it comes time for budgeting purposes or investing in future projects.

1.14 When to Use Design Thinking and When Not to

Design thinking works well when there are no clear answers or multiple stakeholders involved who need to be considered while coming up with an effective solution. However, there will be cases where design thinking may not be suitable due mainly because it requires significant time investment while also involving multiple stakeholders. In addition, design thinking may not work as effectively when working on straightforward tasks, such as managerial reports, due to its focus on creativity and innovation rather than linearity and structure

1.15 Alternatives to Design Thinking

Several alternatives to design thinking can be used to solve different problems or issues (Fig. 1.21):

- **Human-centered Design:** This focuses on making products that meet people's needs. It involves getting user feedback at every step. This helps understand what users want from a product or service. For example, a company creates a new product but talks to people who would use it. This ensures the design meets user expectations before launching it.
- **Systems Thinking:** This studies how different parts of a system interact to get the desired results. It looks for patterns between various system components. Examples include using techniques like data mapping or process flow diagrams.

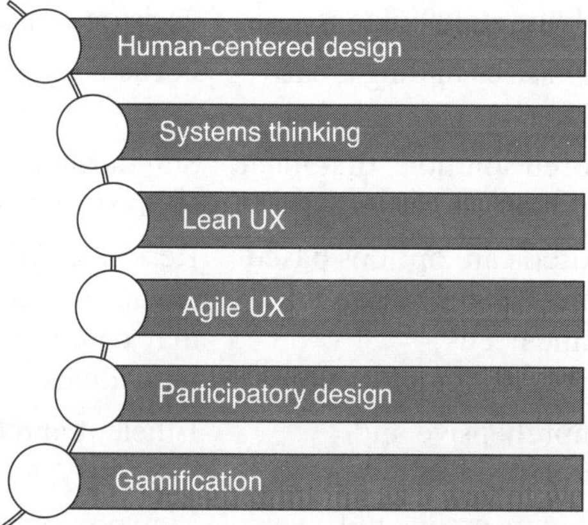

Figure 1.21 Alternatives to design thinking

- **Lean UX:** Lean UX relies heavily on prototyping through rapid iterations as well as user research sessions with small groups rather than large-scale surveys/focus groups. It also embraces Agile principles such as rapid iteration cycles followed by short feedback loops for quick improvements. An example might be implementing an iterative design process where certain features are tested quickly using prototypes before being refined based on customer feedback over time.
- **Agile UX:** Agile UX combines traditional UI/UX design practices with Agile software development principles such as continuous integration and deployment cycles to quickly release incremental updates. An example may involve conducting user testing across multiple sprint cycles throughout each phase of the development process before releasing final product updates into production.
- **Participatory Design:** Participatory design takes advantage of collaborative methods such as workshops and brainstorming sessions that involve stakeholders and end users. An example is hosting weekly meetings where designers get direct input from target audiences about their experiences.
- **Gamification:** This involves utilizing game mechanics like rewards systems and leader boards to drive engagement amongst users. Examples include incorporating achievement badges within mobile applications or adding leader boards that rank top performers.

1.16 How Design Thinking Differs From Traditional Problem-solving Approaches

Table 1.3 compares design thinking with traditional problem-solving approaches.

Table 1.3 Design thinking versus traditional problem-solving

S.No	Characteristics	Design Thinking	Traditional Problem-solving Approaches
1	Approach	Human-centered, empathetic, collaborative	Data-driven, systematic, analytical
2	Focus	User needs, user experience, addressing underlying issues	Efficiency, cost reduction, optimizing resources
3	Ideation	Collaborative process involving stakeholders	Individual or small team analysis and decision-making
4	Creativity	Emphasizes finding creative solutions	Focuses on practical, proven solutions
5	Outcome	Tailored solutions that meet all parties' needs	Standardized solutions that may not address individual needs
6	Example (Healthcare)	Tailored care options based on medical history and specific needs	Resource optimization and technological advancements to improve efficiency, but may compromise quality of care for some individuals
7	Advantages	Comprehensive and personalized solutions	Efficient and time-tested solutions
8	Disadvantages	Time-consuming and potentially costly	May not address underlying issues or individual needs

Two brothers, Rohan and Arjun, liked solving problems but they did it differently. Rohan used traditional methods. He would break problems into smaller parts. Then, he would find a solution. Arjun used design thinking. He would understand people's needs first. After that, he would think of creative ideas. He would then test them to see what worked best.

One day, the brothers had to solve a problem. The village did not have enough water. Rohan analyzed the problem first. He looked at the data. He planned to build a new well in the village center. He thought this was the best solution. Arjun decided to use design thinking. He talked to the villagers. He learned that the villagers had to walk far to get water. They were also worried about the water as it was not clean.

So, Arjun and Rohan worked together. They built a well in the center of the village. They also put in a water filter. This made the water safe to drink. They built pipes to bring water to each house. The villagers did not have to walk far now. The village water problem was solved.

When faced with a problem, many people tend to rely on information or technology to find a solution. Their focus is on improving efficiency and reducing costs, which can be effective in some cases. However, this approach often overlooks the real needs of people and fails to address issues with how things are used in practice. Design thinking first tries to understand the situation. It involves working with different people throughout the process. People explore many angles, not just one. This may lead to a solution that works for everyone.

We can see how traditional and design thinking differ when used for healthcare. A conventional approach might try to reduce wait times by using resources better, like staff or equipment. It might also use technology like patient tracking software. The goal is to serve many patients quickly and efficiently. But there is little focus on giving each patient care based on their specific medical needs (which may take more time). On the other hand, design thinking takes a much more holistic view. Here, we would first identify what exactly patients need before going on to explore potential ways to meet these requirements.

So overall, we can see how design thinking offers greater scope when compared to traditional methods in tackling complex problems like healthcare delivery due to its ability to provide both comprehensive yet personalized solutions.

Summary

- Design thinking is a creative problem-solving process that involves understanding the user, examining the problem from multiple perspectives, and creating creative solutions.
- It takes an iterative approach, testing ideas quickly and making changes based on feedback.
- The four key questions of design thinking are:
  - What is the problem?
  - Who is affected?
  - What are the possible solutions?
  - Which solution works best?
- Design thinking helps solve problems creatively and develop new solutions.
- It was developed in the early 1960s by design professionals like Charles Eames, Robert Propst, and Richard Buckminster Fuller and is rooted in cognitive psychology, anthropology, sociology, and other disciplines related to understanding people's thinking.
- The five stages of the design thinking process are:
  - Empathize: Understanding the needs, wants, and problems of the people you are designing for.
  - Define: Define the problem that needs to be solved.

  - Ideate: Come up with various ideas to solve the problem.
  - Prototype: Create a rough draft or model of the solution.
  - Test: Try out the prototype and see if it works.
- Misconceptions about design thinking include: it is only for designers, or only for big, complex problems; it is a linear process only used in startups; empathy is not necessary; complex technology is needed; it is reactive instead of proactive, ignores traditional methods, and requires a high level of creativity; it is not useful in large organizations and has no measurable results.
- Includes human-centered design (HCD), systems thinking (ST), lean UX (LU), agile UX (AU), participatory design (PD), and gamification (GM).

Solutions to Design Visualization Questions

Q 1.1

Here are five examples of ingenious solutions:

- **Soda Tab Can Opener:** Norwegian inventor Trygve Varmestad, in 1970, noticed that by bending a small tab on the underside of a soda can, it could be used to pry open another can. This clever hack, utilizing a readily available tool, continues to be a handy trick.
- **Braille LEGO Brick:** In 2016, a LEGO enthusiast named Matthew Shifrin noticed the lack of accessibility options for visually impaired children who enjoy building with LEGOs. He developed a system of raised Braille bumps on LEGO bricks, allowing blind and visually impaired children to participate in the creative world of LEGO.
- **LifeStraw Water Filter:** Dirty water is a major health concern in many parts of the world. In 2005, Danish designer Henning Larsen came up with a portable straw containing a built-in filter that removes harmful bacteria and parasites from contaminated water, making it safe to drink.
- **Speed Bump:** Traffic calming measures are crucial for safety, and the speed bump is a prime example of a simple yet effective solution. Invented by Dutch traffic engineer Adrianus Johannes Loudon, these raised sections in the road were first used in the Netherlands in the 1950s and have since become a ubiquitous tool for slowing down traffic.
- **Sharing Economy Platforms:** Platforms like Airbnb and Uber, created by people looking for alternative solutions, have transformed industries like hospitality and transportation.

Q 1.2

Here are three examples of circular products commonly used in everyday life that contribute to the principles of reuse, recycle, and regenerate:

- **Refillable Water Bottles:** They can be filled and refilled countless times, significantly reducing plastic waste. This promotes reuse and reduces the need for constant virgin plastic production.
- **Clothing Made from Recycled Materials:** Many clothing brands are now incorporating recycled materials like polyester made from plastic bottles or cotton scraps from textile production into their clothing lines. This practice helps divert waste from landfills and gives new life to existing materials, promoting both reuse and recycling.
- **Compostable Packaging:** Compostable packaging is made from organic materials like cornstarch or cellulose that can decompose naturally in a compost bin. This eliminates the

need for plastic packaging, which often ends up in landfills or pollutes the environment. Composting these materials regenerates nutrients that can be returned to the soil for future plant growth.

Q 1.3

Established in 1946, Amul (Anand Milk Union Limited) is the largest dairy cooperative in India, boasting a network of over 3.6 million milk producers across the country. What truly sets Amul apart is its commitment to the triple bottom line (TBL) principle, a philosophy that emphasizes environmental, social, and economic sustainability.

- **Environmental Stewardship:** Amul champions sustainable dairy practices. Its village cooperative structure ensures milk collection takes place close to its source, minimizing transportation-related emissions. In addition, Amul promotes energy-efficient processes in its manufacturing facilities and encourages responsible water usage. Furthermore, by focusing on efficient milk collection and processing, Amul minimizes food waste, a significant contributor to environmental degradation.
- **Social Upliftment:** Amul empowers rural milk producers, primarily small and marginal farmers. The cooperative model ensures fair prices for their milk, providing them with a steady income source. Amul also invests in rural infrastructure development, improving milk collection facilities and providing veterinary services. This empowers villages and creates a ripple effect of economic and social upliftment.
- **Economic Sustainability:** Amul's success hinges on its focus on economic viability. By operating as a cooperative, Amul eliminates middlemen, ensuring that a larger share of the profits goes back to the producers. This incentivizes them to invest in better quality cattle and dairy practices. In addition, Amul's focus on innovation and product diversification has led to a robust product portfolio, catering to diverse consumer needs and generating consistent revenue.

Q 1.4

Top 3 IT Companies in India by Employee Count (as of April 2024)

TCS

- **Outcome-based Solutions:** TCS offers solutions focused on delivering business outcomes rather than just building software. This could involve offering 'pay-per-use' models or guarantees on specific metrics like increased efficiency or reduced costs.
- **IoT and Sensor Integration:** TCS leverages its expertise in Internet of Things (IoT) to integrate sensors and data analytics into their services. This allows them to offer 'as-a-service' solutions, like remote equipment monitoring and predictive maintenance.
- **Industry-specific Solutions:** TCS tailors its services to specific industry needs. This might involve developing platforms that integrate with existing industry-specific software or hardware, creating a more comprehensive service offering.

Infosys

- **Managed Services:** Infosys offers comprehensive managed services packages that includes infrastructure management, application management, and security services. This allows clients to focus on their core business while Infosys ensures their IT systems run smoothly.
- **Cloud Enablement:** Infosys helps clients migrate to cloud platforms and develop cloud-based solutions. This can involve managing cloud infrastructure, developing cloud-native applications, and providing ongoing support. This servitization approach helps clients leverage the scalability and flexibility of the cloud.

- **Cognitive Automation:** Infosys incorporates AI and machine learning (ML) into their services to automate repetitive tasks and optimize workflows. This can involve building chatbots for customer service, using AI for network management, or implementing automation tools for software testing.

Wipro

- **Digital Transformation Consulting:** Wipro offers consulting services to help companies develop and implement digital transformation strategies. This might involve identifying areas for automation, recommending new technologies, and developing a roadmap for digital transformation.
- **Digital Experience Platforms (DXPs):** Wipro designs and implements DXPs to create seamless digital experiences for clients' customers. This can involve integrating various digital marketing tools, building customer portals, or developing e-commerce platforms.
- **Product Engineering Services:** Wipro offers product engineering services that go beyond traditional software development. This might involve designing hardware components, managing the entire product lifecycle, and providing ongoing product support. This servitization approach creates a more holistic product development experience for clients.

Q 1.5

Here's how we can leverage the four questions of design thinking to create a user-friendly, engaging, and accessible online shopping website:

1. What is the problem? (Empathize)
    - **User Research:** Conduct surveys, interviews, and usability testing to understand user frustrations with the current website. Analyze data such as heat maps and clickstreams to identify areas of difficulty. Create user personas representing your target audience, outlining their needs and online shopping habits.
2. Who is affected? (Empathize)
    - **Website users:** Consider the spectrum of users, including those with varying levels of technical expertise and accessibility needs.
    - **Business:** An ineffective user interface (UI) can lead to lost sales, decreased customer satisfaction, and higher customer service costs.
3. What are all the possible solutions? (Ideate)
    - **Navigation:** Implement clear and intuitive navigation menus, breadcrumb trails, and advanced search filters to make product discovery easier.
    - **Search:** Improve search functionality by incorporating auto-complete suggestions, synonym recognition, and faceted search options.
    - **Information Architecture:** Organize product categories logically, ensuring a user-friendly hierarchy that simplifies browsing.
    - **Visual Design:** Design a clean and visually appealing interface with high-quality product images, clear product descriptions, and easy-to-read text. Consider color contrast and font choices for accessibility.
    - **Accessibility Features:** Include features like screen reader compatibility, alt text for images, and keyboard navigation for users with disabilities.
    - **Engagement Strategies:** Implement features like personalized product recommendations, customer reviews, and loyalty programs to increase user engagement.
4. Which solution works best? (Prototype and Test)
    - **Prototyping:** Create low-fidelity prototypes (wireframes/mockups) to visualize your design ideas. Focus on functionality and user flow rather than aesthetics.

- **Usability Testing:** Conduct usability testing with your target user personas to evaluate your prototypes. Observe user interactions, identify usability issues, and gather feedback on their overall experience.
- **Iteration and Refinement:** Based on user feedback, iterate on your design, refining the UI to address identified issues. Repeat the testing process until you have a website that is user-friendly, engaging, and accessible.

By following these steps, you can design an online shopping website that prioritizes user needs and offers a superior user experience. This approach will not only improve customer satisfaction and engagement but also lead to increased sales and business growth.

Q 1.6

Here are three ways by which empathy can be used to foster creativity and innovation in a school curriculum redesign:

Understanding Student Needs and Interests

- **Empathize with Students:** Teachers can use empathy to understand students' existing knowledge, interests, and learning styles. This can be achieved through surveys, discussions, or even observing how students interact with current curriculum materials.
- **Tailored Learning Experiences:** By empathizing with students, teachers can design projects and activities that resonate with their interests. This can spark curiosity and a sense of ownership in their learning, encouraging them to think creatively and explore solutions from their unique perspectives.

Building Safe Spaces for Exploration

- **Empathy for Mistakes:** Fostering a classroom environment where mistakes are seen as learning opportunities can be crucial. By showing empathy for students' struggles and uncertainties, teachers can create a safe space where students feel comfortable taking risks, experimenting with ideas, and learning from their failures.

Encouraging Collaboration and Empathy for Others

- **Empathy for Diverse Perspectives:** Empathy is a cornerstone of effective teamwork. By incorporating group projects and collaborative learning exercises, students learn to communicate their ideas, listen to and understand different viewpoints, and build on each other's strengths. This collaborative approach encourages creative problem-solving and innovation.

Q1.7

Based on patient feedback collected during the design thinking process, here are some possible problems faced by patients in the hospital:

- **Inefficient communication and information flow:** Patients might report feeling lost, uninformed, and frustrated due to:
  - Lack of clear communication regarding wait times, procedures, and discharge instructions.
  - Difficulty reaching staff members for assistance or clarification of information.
  - Inconsistent information provided by different staff members.
- **Uncomfortable and impersonal environment:** Patients might express concerns about the physical environment and emotional well-being, including:
  - Long wait times in uncomfortable waiting areas with limited seating or amenities.
  - Lack of privacy in shared rooms or during examinations.
  - Feeling impersonal or like a "number" rather than an individual with unique needs.

Q 1.8

Here are some ideas to make a school library more inviting and engaging for students:

Create Flexible and Engaging Spaces

- **Multi-functional Zones:** Designate areas for different activities. This could include quiet reading nooks with comfortable chairs and beanbags, collaborative study areas with large tables and whiteboards, and even a designated 'maker space' equipped with arts and crafts supplies or technology for creative projects.
- **Interactive Displays:** Incorporate interactive displays showcasing new books, author interviews, or even virtual tours of famous libraries around the world. This digital engagement can spark curiosity and encourage exploration.

Promote Student Choice and Ownership

- **Student-curated Shelves:** Dedicate sections of the library shelves for student recommendations or curated collections based on popular genres, current events, or upcoming school projects. This allows students to see their peers' interests reflected and gives them a sense of ownership in the library space.
- **Student-led Programs:** Empower students by encouraging them to host book clubs, poetry slams, or author talks featuring local writers. This not only promotes student creativity but also fosters a sense of community and belonging within the library.

Embrace Technology and Comfort

- **Comfortable Technology Integration:** Invest in comfortable seating with built-in charging ports for laptops and tablets. This allows students to utilize technology for research, reading ebooks, or simply relaxing with educational apps and games while staying connected.
- **Digital Lending and Interactive Activities:** Offer e-readers or tablets preloaded with ebooks and audiobooks to cater to different learning styles. Consider incorporating educational games, virtual reality experiences, or interactive displays related to specific books or topics. This blend of technology and physical resources caters to a wider range of student interests and learning preferences

Exercises

Part A (Objective Questions)

1. You are a designer working for a company that wants to create a new app for online learning. You want to use design thinking to develop a solution that meets the needs of your target users. Which of the following steps would you do first?
   (a) Brainstorm different ideas for the app features and functions
   (b) Develop a prototype of the app and test it with users
   (c) Observe and interview potential users to understand their pain points and goals
   (d) Implement the final solution and launch the app to the market
2. You are a designer working for a company that provides food delivery services. You have used design thinking to create a new feature that allows users to customize their orders based on their preferences and dietary restrictions. You have developed a prototype of the feature and tested it with some users. You received some positive feedback, but also some suggestions for improvement. What should you do next?

(a) Implement the feature as it is and launch it to the market
(b) Go back to the ideation stage and generate more ideas for the feature
(c) Go back to the clarification stage and redefine the problem statement
(d) Reiterate the feature based on the feedback and test it again with users

3. You are a designer working for a company that produces smart home devices. You have used design thinking to create a new product that allows users to control their home appliances remotely using voice commands. You have implemented the product and launched it to the market. How can you measure the impact of your product on your customers?
(a) By comparing your product with your competitors' products
(b) By tracking your product sales and revenue
(c) By collecting user feedback and satisfaction ratings
(d) By observing how your product improves people's lives

4. You are a design thinking consultant hired by a company that wants to improve its customer service. You decide to use the design thinking process to help them. Which of the following is the first question you should ask?
(a) What are all possible solutions?
(b) What is the problem?
(c) Which solution works best?
(d) Who is affected?

5. You are a design thinking student working on a project to create a new product for people who love gardening. You have brainstormed many ideas and now you want to develop them further. Which of the following is the best way to do that?
(a) Test your ideas with potential users and get feedback
(b) Choose one idea and start making a prototype
(c) Evaluate your ideas based on feasibility and desirability
(d) Ask your instructor for advice

6. You are a design thinking practitioner working for a non-profit organization that aims to reduce food waste. You have implemented a solution that involves collecting surplus food from restaurants and distributing it to low-income communities. How can you measure the impact of your solution?
(a) Compare the amount of food waste before and after your solution
(b) Survey the satisfaction of the restaurants and the communities
(c) Calculate the cost–benefit ratio of your solution
(d) All of the above

7. You are a design thinking consultant hired by a school that wants to have more space for students. What is the first step you would take to help them solve this problem?
(a) Brainstorm ideas for adding another floor to the building or finding a way to store books in less space.
(b) Build a prototype of a new classroom layout and test it with students and teachers.
(c) Research the needs and preferences of the students, teachers, and staff using interviews and observations.
(d) Define the problem statement and the criteria for success.

8. You are a design thinking facilitator leading a workshop for a family that wants to have a fun activity together. How would you help them generate creative solutions for this challenge?
(a) Ask them to list all the possible activities they can think of, without judging or filtering them.
(b) Ask them to choose one activity they like and explain why it is fun for them.
(c) Ask them to draw their ideal activity and share it with the group.
(d) Ask them to test different activities and give feedback on what they liked and disliked.

9. Which stage of the design thinking process involves creating a rough draft or model of the solution?
   (a) Empathize (b) Define (c) Ideate (d) Prototype
10. What is the main aim of the empathize stage of design thinking?
    (a) To gain an empathic understanding of the problem and the users
    (b) To state the users' needs and problems in a human-centered way
    (c) To challenge assumptions and create many ideas to solve the problem
    (d) To try out the solution and see if it works
11. What is the difference between problem-based thinking and solution-based thinking in design thinking?
    (a) Problem-based thinking focuses on obstacles and limitations, while solution-based thinking focuses on outcomes
    (b) Problem-based thinking focuses on outcomes, while solution-based thinking focuses on obstacles and limitations
    (c) Problem-based thinking focuses on human needs, while solution-based thinking focuses on technical feasibility
    (d) Problem-based thinking focuses on technical feasibility, while solution-based thinking focuses on human needs
12. What is the main goal of the empathize phase of design thinking?
    (a) To create numerous ideas in brainstorming sessions
    (b) To understand the needs, desires, and experiences of the people using the product or service
    (c) To start to create solutions using prototypes
    (d) To try your solutions out and get feedback
13. What are some methods that can help you gain empathy towards your users?
    (a) Talking to people, observing them in their environment, or doing surveys or interviews
    (b) Consulting experts, conducting observations, or immersing yourself in your users' physical environment
    (c) Both (a) and (b)
    (d) Neither (a) nor (b)
14. Why is empathy crucial to problem solving and a human-centered design process?
    (a) Because it allows design thinkers to set aside their own assumptions about the world and gain real insight into users and their needs
    (b) Because it allows design thinkers to define the problem statement in a human-centered manner
    (c) Because it allows design thinkers to challenge assumptions and create ideas
    (d) Because it allows design thinkers to prototype and test solutions
15. What is the name of the statement that describes the issue or challenge you intend to address in the design thinking process?
    (a) Problem statement (b) Point of view statement
    (c) User statement (d) Challenge statement
16. Which stage of the design thinking process involves conducting observations to engage and empathize with your users?
    (a) Empathize (b) Define (c) Ideate (d) Prototype
17. How do you frame your problem statement in the design thinking process?
    (a) From your own perspective (b) From the user's perspective
    (c) From the business goal perspective (d) From the solution perspective

18. You are a designer working on a project to improve the user experience of a travel app. You have completed the empathize and define stages of the design thinking process and now you are ready to ideate. What is the main goal of this stage?
    (a) To generate a large number of ideas without judgment or evaluation
    (b) To test your ideas with real users and get feedback
    (c) To narrow down your ideas to the most feasible and desirable ones
    (d) To implement your ideas into a functional prototype
19. You are a designer facilitating an ideation session with your team. You want to encourage discussion among team members about different aspects of each idea so that great ones don't get overlooked because they seem too out there at first glance (or vice versa). What is one method you can use to achieve this?
    (a) Brainstorm (b) Braindump (c) SCAMPER (d) Provocation
20. You are a designer participating in an ideation session with your team. You want to step beyond the obvious solutions and increase the innovation potential of your solution. What is one technique you can use to achieve this?
    (a) Challenge assumptions (b) Mind map
    (c) Sketchstorm (d) Analogies
21. What is the main purpose of prototyping in the design thinking process?
    (a) To build a final version of the design
    (b) To test the design with users and get feedback
    (c) To explore a wide range of possible solutions
    (d) To understand the problem better
22. Which of these skills is not associated with design thinking?
    (a) Empathy (b) Creativity (c) Analysis (d) Memorization
23. You are a designer who has created a prototype of a new app for online learning. You want to test your prototype with real users and get feedback. Which phase of the design thinking process are you in?
    (a) Empathize (b) Define (c) Ideate (d) Test
24. You are a designer who has conducted a usability test of your website with a group of potential users. You have collected data on how they interacted with your website and what problems they encountered. What should you do next with this data?
    (a) Implement your website as it is
    (b) Refine your website based on the data
    (c) Discard your website and start over
    (d) Ignore the data and trust your intuition
25. You are a designer who has developed a solution for reducing food waste in restaurants. You have tested your solution with a few restaurant owners and received positive feedback. How can you determine if your solution is viable before implementation?
    (a) Ask for more feedback from other stakeholders
    (b) Conduct a cost–benefit analysis of your solution
    (c) Compare your solution with existing alternatives
    (d) All of the above
26. What is the name of the design company whose CEO and president wrote the 2008 Harvard Business Review article on design thinking?
    (a) IDEO (b) Canva
    (c) d.school (d) Interaction Design Foundation
27. What type of problems are best suited for design thinking according to the Interaction Design Foundation?

(a) Problems that are well-defined and known
(b) Problems that are ill-defined or unknown
(c) Problems that are simple and easy
(d) Problems that are technical and specific

28. Is design thinking only useful for big, complex problems?
(a) Yes (b) No

29. Can design thinking guarantee innovation?
(a) Yes, it is a magic bullet for innovation.
(b) No, it cannot guarantee innovation.
(c) It depends on the industry.
(d) All of the above.

30. Which of the following examples of gamification involves competition as a key factor?
(a) Adding achievements badges to a mobile application.
(b) Including a progress bar within an online course.
(c) Offering discounts to customers who make frequent purchases.
(d) Providing a reward for completing a survey.

31. What is the purpose of incorporating game mechanics like rewards systems and leader boards in gamification?
(a) To make the app activities more challenging.
(b) To create a sense of community among participants.
(c) To drive engagement among users.
(d) To provide customers with discounts.

32. You are a design consultant hired by a company that wants to improve its customer satisfaction and loyalty. You decide to use one of the alternatives to design thinking to understand the users' needs and expectations better. Which alternative would you choose and why?
(a) Human-centered design (HCD), because it focuses on empathizing with the users and involving them in the design process.
(b) Systems thinking (ST), because it helps you analyze the complex interactions and feedback loops between the users and the company.
(c) Lean UX (LU), because it allows you to test your assumptions and validate your solutions quickly and cheaply with the users.
(d) Agile UX (AU), because it enables you to adapt to changing user requirements and deliver value incrementally and iteratively.

33. You are a design researcher working on a project that aims to reduce food waste in households. You want to use one of the alternatives to design thinking to explore the root causes and consequences of food waste and identify potential opportunities for intervention. Which alternative would you choose and why?
(a) Systems thinking (ST), because it helps you understand the interrelationships and dynamics of the food system and its impact on society and the environment.
(b) Participatory design (PD), because it involves the stakeholders and beneficiaries of the food system in co-designing solutions that meet their needs and preferences.
(c) Gamification (GM), because it applies game elements and mechanics to motivate and engage the users in changing their food consumption behaviors.
(d) Lean UX (LU), because it helps you experiment with different solutions and measure their effectiveness in reducing food waste.

34. You are a design educator teaching a course on design thinking to a group of students from different disciplines. You want to use one of the alternatives to design thinking to introduce

them to the basic principles and practices of design thinking in a fun and interactive way. Which alternative would you choose and why?
(a) Gamification (GM), because it uses game-like scenarios, challenges, rewards, and feedback to stimulate creativity and collaboration among the students.
(b) Agile UX (AU), because it teaches the students how to work in cross-functional teams, deliver working prototypes, and incorporate user feedback in short iterations.
(c) Participatory design (PD), because it encourages the students to engage with real users and stakeholders in co-creating solutions that address their needs and values.
(d) Lean UX (LU), because it trains the students how to formulate hypotheses, design experiments, test assumptions, and learn from failures.

Part B (Short Answer Questions)

1. What are the four key questions which are part of the design thinking process?
2. What are the needs of design thinking?
3. Write a short note on the empathize phase of design thinking.
4. Write a short note on the define phase of design thinking.
5. What is POV in design thinking?
6. Write a note on the ideate phase of the design thinking process.
7. Write a note on the prototype phase of the design thinking process.
8. Write a note on the testing phase of the design thinking process.
9. What are the benefits of the design thinking process?
10. Write any five misconceptions of design thinking.
11. When do we use design thinking?
12. What are the alternatives to design thinking?
13. What is reframing?
14. Why is empathizing important?
15. How will you break the ideate phase of the design thinking process?
16. Write a note on human-centered design.
17. Define system thinking.
18. Define lean UX.
19. Define agile UX.
20. What is participatory design?
21. What is gamification?

Part C (Essay Questions)

1. Explain the four questions of design thinking.
2. Explain the need for design thinking.
3. Write an essay on the 10 tools of design thinking.
4. Write an essay on the five stages of the design thinking process.
5. How can the empathize step be performed?
6. The ideate phase can be broken down into four steps: brainstorming, visualizing, refining, and prototyping. Explain these in detail.
7. What are the benefits of design thinking?
8. Explain the misconception: Design thinking is just for designers.
9. Explain the misconception: Design thinking is only for big, complex problems.
10. Explain the misconception: Design thinking is a linear process

11. Explain the misconception: Design thinking is all about aesthetics.
12. Explain the misconception: Design thinking is a magic bullet for innovation.
13. Explain the misconception: Design thinking is only used in startups.
14. Explain the misconception: Empathy is not necessary for design thinking.
15. Explain the misconception: You need complex technology tools to implement design thinking.
16. Explain the misconception: Design thinking is reactive instead of proactive.
17. Explain the misconception: Design thinking ignores traditional methods of problem-solving.
18. Explain the misconception: Design thinking requires a high level of creativity.
19. Explain the misconception: Design Thinking is not useful in large organizations.
20. Explain the misconception: Design thinking has no measurable results.
21. When do we use design thinking and when should we not use it?
22. How does design thinking differ from traditional problem-solving approaches?

Answer Key

Part A

1. (c) **2.** (d) **3.** (d) **4.** (b) **5.** (a) **6.** (d) **7.** (c) **8.** (a) **9.** (d) **10.** (a)
11. (a) **12.** (b) **13.** (c) **14.** (a) **15.** (a) **16.** (a) **17.** (b) **18.** (a) **19.** (d) **20.** (d)
21. (b) **22.** (d) **23.** (d) **24.** (b) **25.** (d) **26.** (a) **27.** (b) **28.** (b) **29.** (b) **30.** (a)
31. (c) **32.** (a) **33.** (a) **34.** (a)

CHAPTER 2

The Empathize Stage

Learning Objectives

At the end of this chapter, you will be able to:

- Explain the significance of empathy in design thinking and how it forms the foundation for understanding end-user needs and experiences
- Describe the strategies for adopting a user-centered approach in design, ensuring that products and services are tailored to meet real user requirements
- List a variety of user research techniques, including user interviews, focus groups, surveys, observation, shadowing, immersion, empathy maps, user personas, cultural probes, and user diaries, and how each can contribute to a deeper understanding of the user's world
- Explain practical methods for seeing through the eyes of the end-user, which is crucial for creating solutions that resonate on a personal level with the target audience
- Describe the process of developing empathy maps and user personas, which are instrumental in capturing the essence of user demographics, behaviors, and motivations

2.1 Introduction

There was a small village in the hills. For many years, the villagers lived simple but happy lives. They used the natural resources around them for all their needs. But one day, something distressing happened. Their water supply dried up completely. This caused a big problem. The villagers needed water for drinking, farming, and other things. The village elders asked the design thinking team for help to solve this problem.

First, the team talked to the villagers to understand how the lack of water affected them. They interviewed people from different backgrounds. They found that everyone faced difficulties without water. However, different groups of people had different problems based on their age and gender. This showed them that to find a suitable solution, they needed to understand each person's story. The team then moved to the next stage. They brainstormed different solutions based on what they had learned from the villagers. After this, they identified some practical solutions. These solutions were quickly put into action. Soon, every household in the village had access to clean water again!

2.2 Importance of Empathy in Design Thinking

Empathy is the ability to understand and share the feelings of others. It is an essential component of design thinking. When designers put themselves in the end-users' shoes, they can gain a deeper understanding of the problems they face and develop more effective solutions (Fig. 2.1).

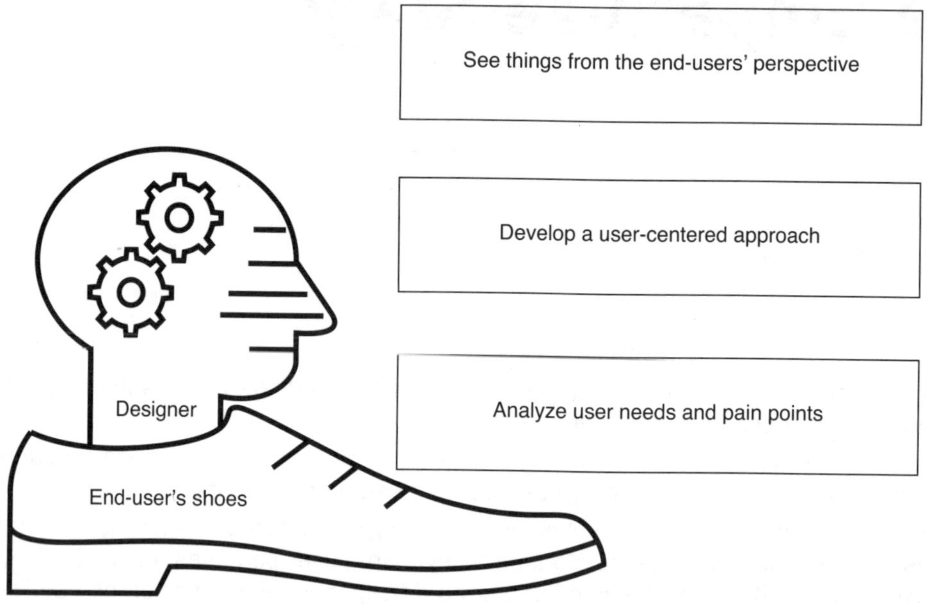

Figure 2.1 The importance of empathy in design thinking

For example, making things easy to use for people with disabilities is a good choice. Another example is avoiding unintended harm in design choices, such as reinforcing harmful stereotypes, by being mindful of how different groups of people could interpret certain elements.

Understanding each other makes it easier to work together. Empathy helps people see things from a different point of view. It enables teams to connect better and work more productively. For example, when two teams work on a new product, empathy helps them listen to each other's ideas.

Let us consider an organization that makes new websites to sell products online. They may design a website they feel is helpful for customers. But if they understand the customers' needs, they can create a much better website. They can observe how customers use other online stores and learn what parts the customers like the most and what problems they have. They can thus make their website easy to use, with helpful features.

2.2.1 See Things From the End-users' Perspective

This means understanding the end-users' motivations, behaviors, and pain points (Table 2.1). By understanding the end-users needs, designers can create solutions tailored to their requirements. This results in more effective and efficient solutions that address the users' problems.

Table 2.1 End-users' needs, pain points, and goals

S.No	Design Project	End-users	Needs and Wants	Pain Points and Frustrations	Goals and Challenges
1	Website for a school	Students	Find information, such as grades, assignments, and schedules; view appealing and engaging content	Difficult to navigate, boring or outdated design, slow or unreliable performance	Access information easily and quickly, enjoy and learn from the website
2	Backpack for hikers	Hikers	Comfortable, durable, and spacious backpack; suitable for different weather conditions and terrains	Heavy, flimsy, or cramped backpack; unsuitable for extreme or varied environments	Carry their essentials and equipment, enjoy and explore nature
3	Game for children	Children	Fun, educational, and creative game; safe and appropriate for their age group	Boring, irrelevant, or complex game; unsafe or inappropriate content or interactions	Engage and learn from the game, express and develop their creativity
4	Coffee machine for office workers	Office workers	Fast, easy, and reliable coffee machine; customizable and compatible with different types of coffee	Slow, complicated, or faulty coffee machine; limited or incompatible with their coffee preferences	Drink coffee conveniently and quickly, satisfy and improve their productivity
5	Toothbrush for elderly people	Elderly people	Gentle, effective, and ergonomic toothbrush; accessible and affordable	Harsh, ineffective, or uncomfortable toothbrush; difficult or costly to obtain or use them	Brush their teeth gently and thoroughly, maintain and improve their oral health and well-being

Design Visualization Question 2.1

As a music app designer for the teenage market, you need to understand the current trends, social aspects, and diversity of this segment. You also need to ensure that your app is easy to use and compatible with various devices and platforms.

To achieve this, you must empathize with the teenage users. What are their motivations and preferences when they listen to music? What are their aesthetic and cultural influences? How do they interact with the music app?

Answer these questions, and define and document their 1) Motivations and Preferences, 2) Pain Points and Frustrations, 3) Goals and Challenges.

Some examples of how designers can create solutions that meet the user's needs are shown in Fig. 2.2.

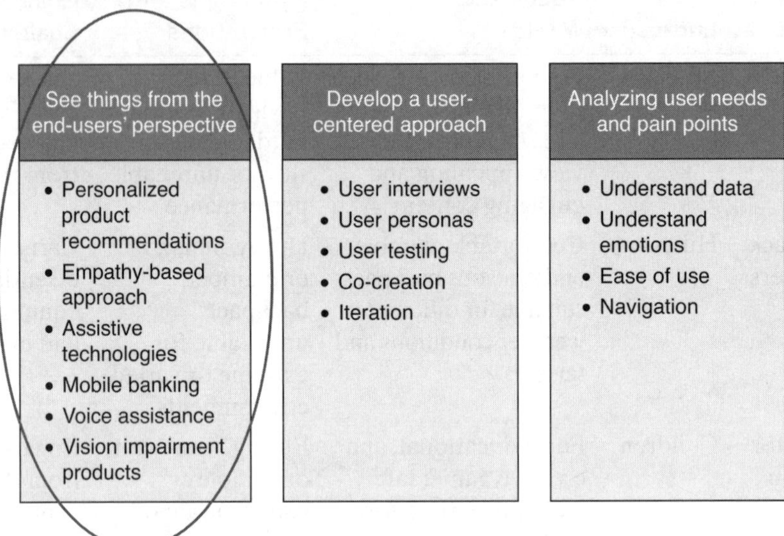

Figure 2.2 See things from the end-users' perspective

2.2.1.1 Personalized Product Recommendations

Personalized product recommendations are a way of using design thinking to create better experiences for end-users. They present the customers with the products they are likely to buy.

Think about shopping online for books. There are thousands to choose from. How do you pick the right one? You could look at reviews. But people have different tastes. Other people's favorite books might not match what you like. That is where recommendations help. Sites like Amazon and Netflix study what you look at, buy, and rate. They find patterns in this data to see what products are more desirable for you. Then they suggest books, movies, and more that match your interests.

Design Visualization Question 2.2

Imagine you are a developer for Netflix and you want to create a system that can recommend movies to your customers based on their preferences. This system will use various factors to determine the best recommendations for each customer.

List the top 5 factors that the recommendations will be based on.

As a customer, personalized product recommendations can satisfy your online shopping experience, as you are more likely to find products that meet your needs. They can also help you discover new products you might not have known otherwise. They can save you time and effort by narrowing down your options and making it easier for you to decide what to buy or watch.

2.2.1.2 Empathy-based Approach

IndiGo has created an empathy-driven approach to its services to meet their passengers' needs. This approach is used by airport workers, customer service personnel, flight crew, and cabin workers. IndiGo tries to make each passenger's experience smooth and pleasant. They help passengers, give useful information, and find solutions. IndiGo 6E Care, IndiGo 6E Tiffin, and IndiGo 6E Voice are examples of their empathy-based approach (Table 2.2).

6E Care is for passengers who need medical help or have special needs. This service gives priority check-in, boarding, baggage help, wheelchair support, oxygen help, and stretcher facilities. 6E Tiffin is for passengers who want to eat home-cooked food on the flight. Passengers can pre-book their tiffin boxes online and collect them at the airport before boarding. 6E Voice is for passengers who want to share opinions or suggestions about their flight experience. Passengers can scan a QR code on their seatback screens or boarding passes to access a survey on their smartphone.

Table 2.2 IndiGo 6E Care, IndiGo 6E Tiffin, and IndiGo 6E Voice

S.No	Design Project	Segment	Description
1	6E Care	Passengers who require medical assistance or have special needs	This service provides priority check-in, boarding, baggage delivery, wheelchair assistance, oxygen support, and stretcher facilities.
2	6E Tiffin	Passengers who want to enjoy their home-cooked food	The passengers can pre-book their tiffin boxes online and collect them at the airport before boarding. The tiffin boxes are designed to fit in the overhead bins and are sealed with tamper-proof stickers.
3	6E Voice	Passengers who want to share their opinions or suggestions about their flight experience	The passengers can scan a QR code on their seatback screens or boarding passes and access a smartphone survey. The survey asks questions about various aspects of the flight, such as cleanliness, comfort, entertainment, food, and service.

Design Visualization Question 2.3

Empathy plays a crucial role in creating a more inclusive society for differently-abled individuals in India.

List any five empathy-based approaches that can help improve the lives of people with disabilities.

2.2.1.3 Assistive Technologies

Assistive technologies are devices that aid individuals with disabilities in performing tasks they may otherwise struggle with. For example, some people have trouble hearing what others are saying, especially in noisy places. Speech-to-text software can convert spoken words into written text on a screen. This way, they can read what is being said and respond accordingly.

Screen readers help people who have vision problems by reading out what is displayed on the screen. They use a computer voice or a braille device. This way, people can understand the information and use the computer.

Assistive technologies are made to meet the needs of users. They are not one-size-fits-all but customized to each person's abilities and preferences. Design thinking helps designers create functional, usable, and desirable assistive technology for users.

Design Visualization Question 2.4

Smart glasses: These are glasses that use augmented reality to provide information or assistance for people who have various disabilities or needs.

List any 3 problems that are solved by smart glasses.

2.2.1.4 Mobile Banking

Mobile banking apps help people carry out transactions from their phones instead of at banks. People can use their phones anywhere, which is easy. Apps are useful for busy people or those who live far away from banks.

Designers make apps easy to use and protect financial and customer details. Some apps use fingerprint or face scans to allow access only to account-holders. Other apps encrypt the data so only the sender and receiver can see it. This prevents hackers from stealing data.

2.2.1.5 Voice Assistants

Voice assistants can process spoken commands and execute tasks accordingly. For example, you can ask Alexa to order pizza or Siri to call your mother. Voice assistants are designed to make your life easier and perform tasks because you do not have to type, tap, or swipe on a screen.

2.2.1.6 Fitness Apps

Design thinking helps solve problems by understanding users' needs. For example, for creating a fitness app, you need learn what users want from it. You can achieve this by talking to them, watching how they use it, and testing your ideas with them. Fitness apps like MyFitnessPal and Nike Training Club use design thinking. MyFitnessPal lets users log food and calories burned, and compare their progress to their goals. It also connects users with others trying to lose weight or be healthy. This way, users get support and encouragement from people facing similar challenges and successes.

Nike Training Club offers workouts. The workouts match your fitness level, goals, and likes. The app also gives coaching tips. It gives audio cues and video demos that guide you through each exercise. Plus, the app rewards you with badges, trophies, and achievements. The rewards celebrate your milestones. They motivate you to keep going.

2.2.1.7 Vision Impairment Products

Products for visually impaired people often have big buttons and text. The items should be easy to use. Simple graphics also help. The products may need braille or voice controls. Designers test products with visually impaired people. This way, they can make sure the product meets their needs.

2.2.2 Develop a User-Centered Approach

Empathy enables designers to adopt a user-centered approach to problem-solving. By putting the users at the center of the design process, designers can create more relevant and meaningful solutions (Fig. 2.3).

Let us explore some examples of how empathy can help designers adopt a user-centered approach to problem-solving:

- **User Interviews:** Designers ask users open-ended questions. They listen carefully to the user's needs, wants, and struggles. For example, designers of a new medical device talk to doctors and patients. They learn what is important, like ease-of-use, accuracy, and patient comfort.

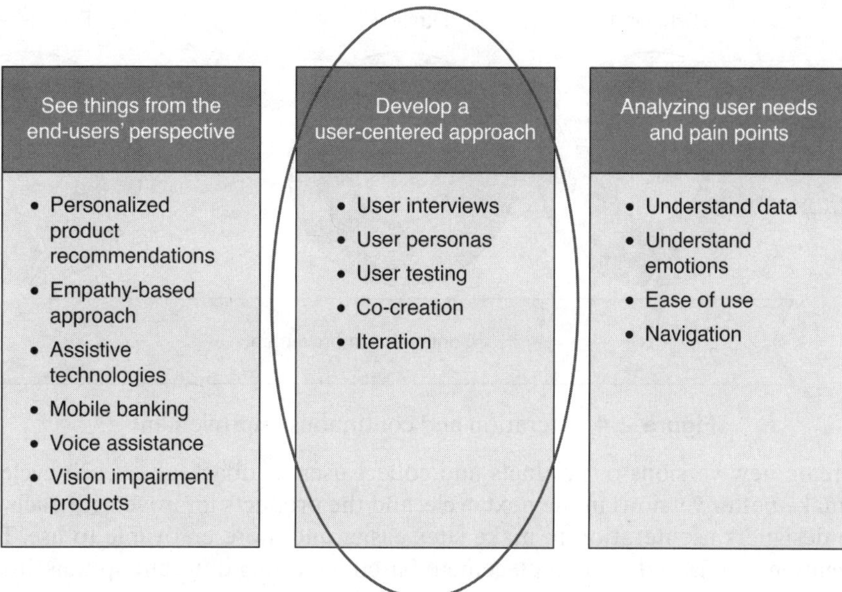

Figure 2.3 Develop a user-centered approach

- **User Personas:** Designers create mock user profiles. These profiles show details such as age, job, and habits for different user groups. Designers can then find solutions that fit each group's needs.
- **User Testing:** Designers watch users try product prototypes or existing products. Observing users' experience shows what works well and what needs improvement. For instance, a website designer may test the site to see if it is user-friendly and accessible.
- **Co-creation:** Designers work with users to make products users want. They ask users what they need. They use ideas from users to build things. This helps designers create products users will like.

For example, a healthcare company created a digital platform with patients and doctors. The platform helps people with long-term health issues. It allows patients to check their health conditions. Patients can also see care plans created just for them. They can talk to their doctors and nurses through the platform.

A museum co-created an exhibition with its visitors. The museum asked visitors to share stories, memories, and experiences about a certain topic. The museum put together all these contributions in the exhibit.

Design Visualization Question 2.5

A school wants to co-create its curriculum. Who are the different types of users they will interact with?

Iteration: Designers go through an important process called design iteration. It helps them improve their work and make it better and more useful. In software development, teams use methods like Agile. These involve getting input from users and making changes based on that. The teams release small portions of the software at a time. They ask users for feedback on each portion. Then they make updates based on that feedback. Iteration means releasing a product in small chunks. Each chunk focuses on one part of the product or a basic version (Fig. 2.4).

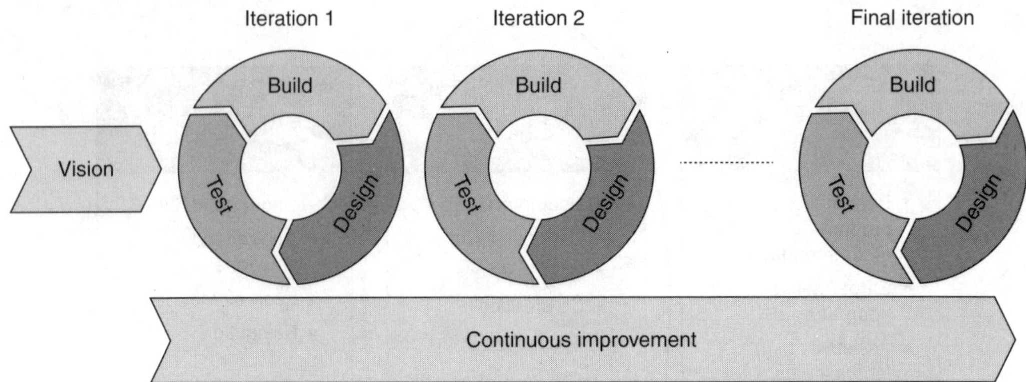

Figure 2.4 Iteration and continuous improvement

Designers create new versions of products and collect user feedback after each cycle. This input helps them make better versions in the next cycle, and the products improve with each iteration.

Website designers use iteration to make sites easier and more enjoyable to use. They change layouts, navigation menus, and content placement based on testing different options. Iteration helps websites stay modern and meet changing user expectations.

2.2.3 Analyzing User Needs and Pain Points

Understanding what problems people face is crucial (Fig. 2.5). The first step involves learning about users' experiences and feelings. By analyzing the issues users struggle with, designers can grasp how to help them. Thus, the empathize stage focuses on understanding users' emotions and needs.

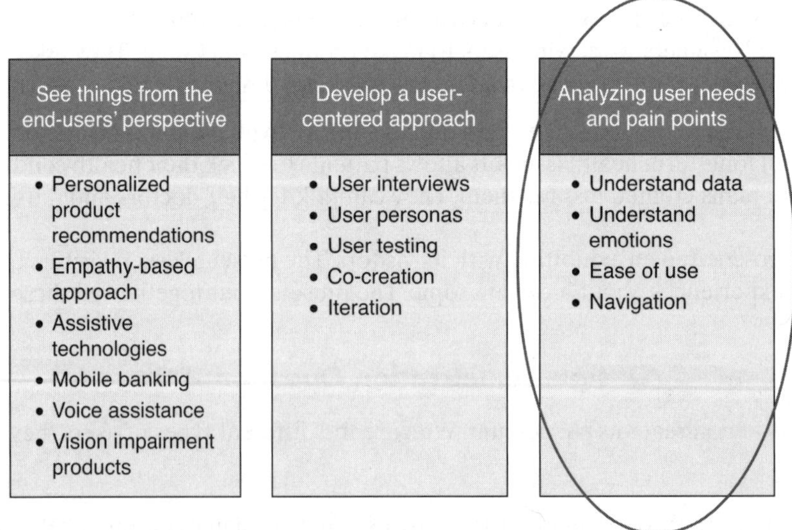

Figure 2.5 Analysing user needs and frustrations

Let us say you want to create an app for parents. They want to view their children's homework and grades. First, you must know what parents need the app to do. You also need to know about issues with other homework apps. Maybe they are too hard to use, or perhaps family members cannot view everything. Understanding these needs and issues can help you create an app that works well.

2.3 Techniques for Conducting User Research and Gathering Insights

When you create something, it is very important to think about the people who will use it. The empathize stage helps designers do exactly that. In this phase, designers try to understand what users need and how they feel when using a product or service. They use tools like interviews, focus groups, surveys, and watching people use the product. This helps designers learn how people use the product and how it affects them (Fig. 2.6).

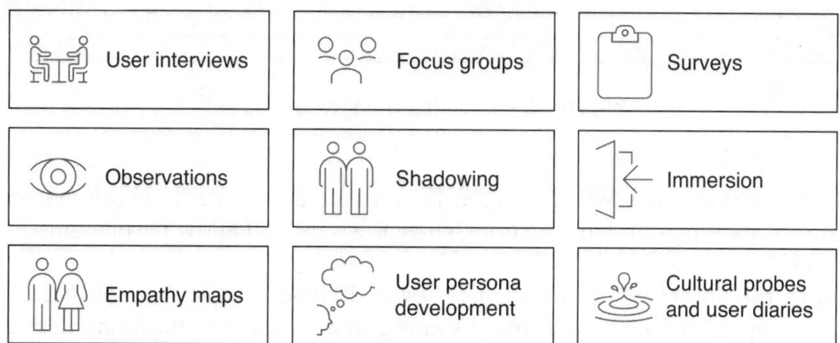

Figure 2.6 Techniques for conducting user research

The first step of user research is to identify who the users are and the problems they face. It ensures that designers understand who will benefit from the product or service. By knowing the users, designers gain insight into how they behave around similar products. For instance, if nurses at a hospital use an app to manage patient records, research helps clarify struggles such as long waiting time or difficulty retrieving information quickly. Insights like these guide designers towards creating effective solutions to address major pain points.

Usability tests with prototypes provide an up-close look at real-world use. Observing natural behaviors, such as gestures on phones, exposes design flaws and successes. This knowledge informs better experiences in the future.

2.3.1 User Interviews

People have different experiences. Designers talk to them to comprehend their views. Interviews shed light on behaviors, reasons, and preferences. Questions are key in extracting useful insights. For instance, if someone stopped utilizing our product, we ask: "Why did you discontinue usage?" Such open-ended queries reveal hidden motivations. Conversations allow exploration of complex subjects. People's perspectives offer invaluable knowledge unattainable elsewhere. Consequently, interviews play a pivotal role in understanding users intimately.

2.3.1.1 The User Interview Process

There are several essential steps (Fig. 2.7) when conducting user interviews as part of the design thinking process. These include:

1. **Defining the objective**: Designers should grasp their research aims, the specific objectives they wish to tackle, and the key questions they need to address with users. This crucial first step ensures a solid foundation for the entire process.
2. **Recruiting the participants:** Next, designers carefully choose and recruit participants who reflect the project's target user group. Various methods, such as social media, emails, and in-person outreach, can help find suitable candidates.

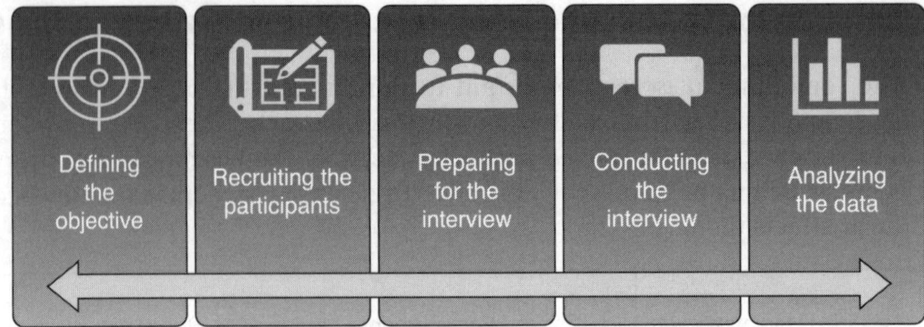

Figure 2.7 User interview process

3. **Preparing for the interview**: With foresight, designers create an interview guide covering essential discussion topics. Open-ended questions, chosen wisely, will allow participants to freely share their perspectives.
4. **Conducting the interview**: During interviews, designers build rapport with participants, encouraging open dialogue: attentive listening and follow-up questions deepen designers' understanding of user needs and viewpoints.
5. **Analysing the data**: After the interviews are concluded, designers meticulously analyze data to uncover emerging patterns and valuable insights. Creating personas or user journeys encapsulating needs, behaviors, and pain points then shapes the design direction.

2.3.1.2 Tips for Conducting Effective User Interviews

Gathering insights during user interviews necessitates posing open-ended queries that prompt participants to openly share their perspectives and encounters. This approach unveils deeper understanding (Fig. 2.8).

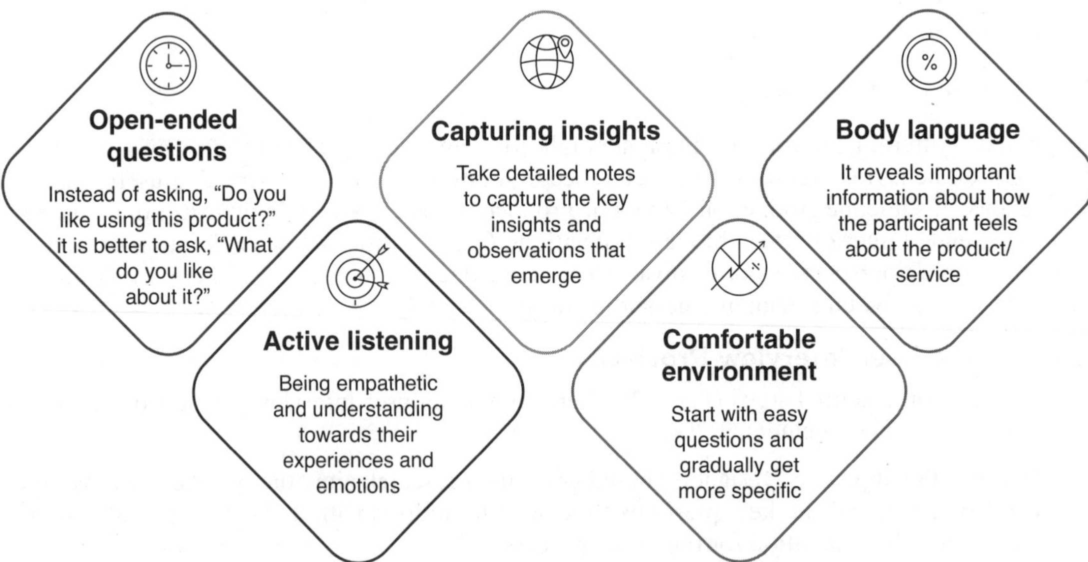

Figure 2.8 Conducting effective user interviews

Experts recommend that researchers concentrate on **actively listening** to participants' statements and demonstrating empathy. Avoid guiding questions that influence responses.

Capturing insights during interviews is important. Interviewers document notable comments and observations. Establishing a comfortable environment for the interviewee is crucial. Begin with simple inquiries and gradually delve deeper as rapport builds.

Design specialists must note body language cues during interviews, as non-verbal communication often reveals attitudes about the product or service. Probing follow-up questions based on initial responses may uncover valuable user needs that generic questioning misses. For instance, asking "What improvements would you suggest?" after "What are your thoughts on our offering?" could yield insightful feedback for enhancement from the user's perspective.

Design Visualization Question 2.6

Can you think of any other tips (3) for conducing effective user interviews?

2.3.1.3 Drawbacks of the Interview Method

The interview technique used in the empathize stage of design thinking has some drawbacks. One main concern is that the results may need to be more accurate because interviews rely on **subjective responses**, which can influence bias, preconceptions, and misunderstandings. Consequently, interview data should be **interpreted cautiously** and used in conjunction with other research sources when making decisions. Another issue with interviews is that they can be **time-consuming and costly** since they require researchers to speak with people who may not be easily accessible or require significant travel time or resources. In addition, conducting interviews **requires training** for both the interviewer and participants. Researchers must be careful to protect participants' **privacy** and obtain informed consent. Finally, **biased questions** may lead to biased answers, so researchers must craft neutral questions to minimize the risk of influencing participants' responses.

Design Visualization Question 2.7

Can you think of any other drawbacks (3) of the interview method?

2.3.2 Focus Groups

Focus groups are a way to gather information from a **small group of people** about a product or service. This is done to gain specific insights from the participants' perspectives (Fig. 2.9).

For example, parents often wonder how their child's progress compares to that of other children. Focus groups allow designers to gather insightful feedback. A few parents meet to discuss a topic. The discussion leader asks questions to guide the conversation. Parents share perspectives on a common challenge, like tracking developmental milestones. New mothers and seasoned parents have diverse experiences. They might discuss struggles like: "How do I know if my baby is on-track?" or "Where can I find simple information on what skills to expect?" Hearing directly from users highlights real needs and pain points.

Focus groups offer valuable user feedback during the design thinking process. However, careful consideration is needed to address potential **drawbacks**:

- **Bias:** Group dynamics may influence participants to align with popular views or present inaccurate information to gain acceptance. This skews data as responses may not reflect true user preferences or behaviors.

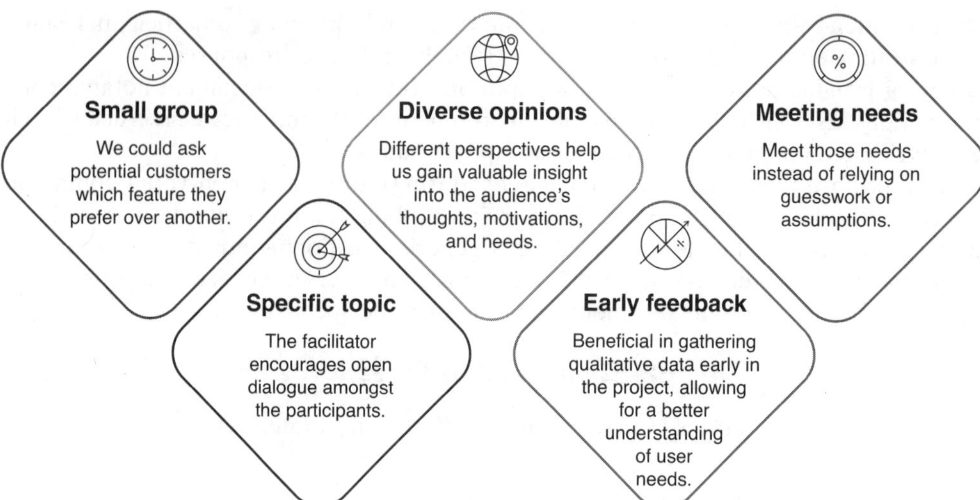

Figure 2.9 Conducting effective focus group discussions

- **Pressure:** Participants may also feel compelled to provide socially acceptable answers rather than honest opinions or feelings, leading to inaccurate data. They could understate issues or overstate satisfaction to avoid criticism or conflict, preventing identification of real pain points or improvement opportunities.
- **Cost:** Facilitating a focus group can be expensive due to hiring facilitators and renting suitable venues. This significant investment may yield uncertain returns if insights or actionable recommendations are lacking. In addition, recruiting and compensating participants can add up to substantial costs depending on group size and duration.
- **Time constraints:** Focus groups face limits on duration and scope, potentially missing crucial perspectives if ideas are not raised promptly or explored thoroughly. In addition, a dominant voice can steer discussions off-track, hindering others from fully sharing their views and insights. This narrows the feedback's diversity and quality.

Design Visualization Question 2.8

Can you think of any other drawbacks (3) of the focus group method?

2.3.3 Surveys

Customer surveys provide important data quickly and easily. Designers ask targeted questions to learn about consumer preferences, such as desired product features.

Design Visualization Question 2.9

Campus Sustainability Survey

Encourage students to survey fellow students, faculty, and staff about sustainable practices on campus. Collect data on recycling habits, energy consumption awareness, and attitudes towards sustainability. Use the survey results to propose actionable steps for enhancing campus sustainability.

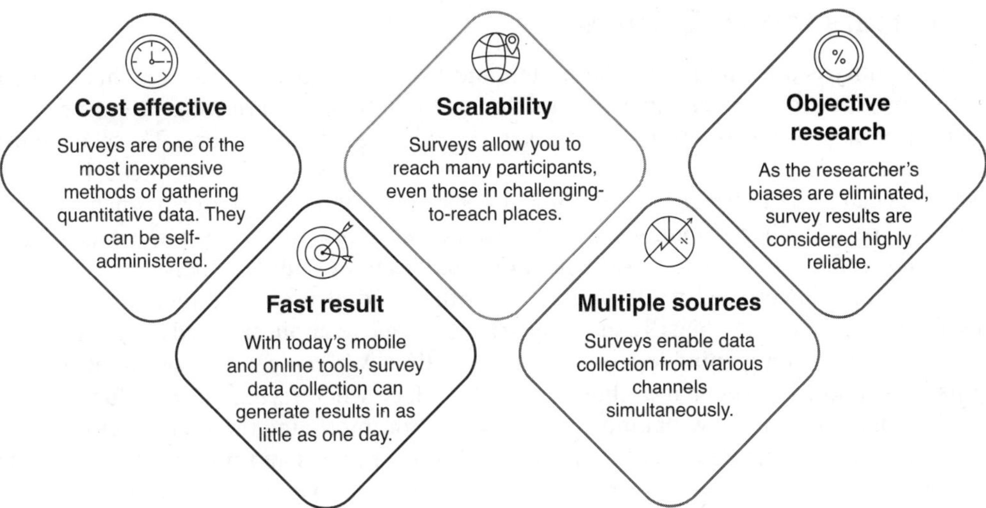

Figure 2.10 Conducting effective survey-based research

Here are the top advantages of survey-based research (Fig. 2.10):

- **Cost-effective:** Surveys are one of the most inexpensive methods of gathering quantitative data. They can be self-administered, avoiding the need for in-person interviews. You can collect a massive amount of information from a large demographic relatively quickly.
- **Fast results:** With today's mobile and online tools, survey data collection can generate results in as little as one day. You no longer need to wait for another company to deliver solutions because these questionnaires provide immediate insights.
- **Scalability:** Surveys allow you to reach many participants, even those in challenging-to-reach places. Online and mobile surveys enable people worldwide to provide feedback on critical ideas, services, or solutions.
- **Data from multiple sources:** Surveys enable data collection from various channels simultaneously. You can place surveys on your website, email them to individuals, or post them on social media profiles.
- **Objective research:** Surveys help maintain objectivity during research. As the researcher's biases are eliminated, survey results are considered highly reliable.

However, using surveys also has some drawbacks. People may only sometimes answer surveys **honestly** and may give answers they think are expected of them. Surveys can also be **biased** if questions are worded to lead participants to give specific responses. This can lead to incorrect conclusions drawn from survey data that do not accurately reflect reality. **Low response rates** and **errors in participant responses** can also result in incomplete or inaccurate data being collected. Surveys focus on factual information and **may not capture how people feel** about something or how their experiences shape their opinions and behavior. Online surveys can collect large amounts of data quickly, but incomplete entries and **multiple responses** from single participants can lead to inaccurate results being reported. Finally, survey respondents may have **difficulty articulating their thoughts** and feelings when answering questions that require long-form written answers, limiting the depth of understanding gained by design thinkers about users' needs and wants.

2.3.4 Observational Studies

Contextual inquiry is a technique for observing and learning from users. Researchers watch how people use products or services in real situations rather than interviewing after the fact. This first-hand approach provides insights into user behaviors and motivations. These insights help designers better understand user needs when developing effective solutions to meet those needs.

Designers can also observe user activity online using social media platforms such as Facebook or X, where people share opinions about products/services they use regularly. (Fig, 2.11). Observational studies allow us to **observe people while they use** our products/services to identify problems they may have faced while interacting with it and also capture their natural reactions towards it without having any biases caused by prior knowledge about the study itself. For example, suppose an app has been gaining less popularity over time. We can conduct observational studies among its users and observe what usability issues they face when trying out new functions within the app. We can then come up with innovative solutions for improving the user experience. Observations can also help designers gain insights into user needs and preferences by identifying **patterns in user behavior**. This information can be beneficial when designing new products or services as it can help refine ideas before investing too much time and money on development costs.

Another benefit of observing people interacting with products is **understanding different contexts** in which these interactions occur, such as at home versus work environments or while someone is standing versus sitting in front of their computer screen. Different contexts often lead to different behaviors, so designers must understand them to create better experiences explicitly tailored around each type of user interaction model instead of trying a one-size-fits-all approach.

Finally, observing designs created by other organizations or individuals can give insight into trends within respective industries giving us the tools needed to evaluate current design processes against market dynamics. This enables **organizations to stay competitive** while continuously improving product quality over time.

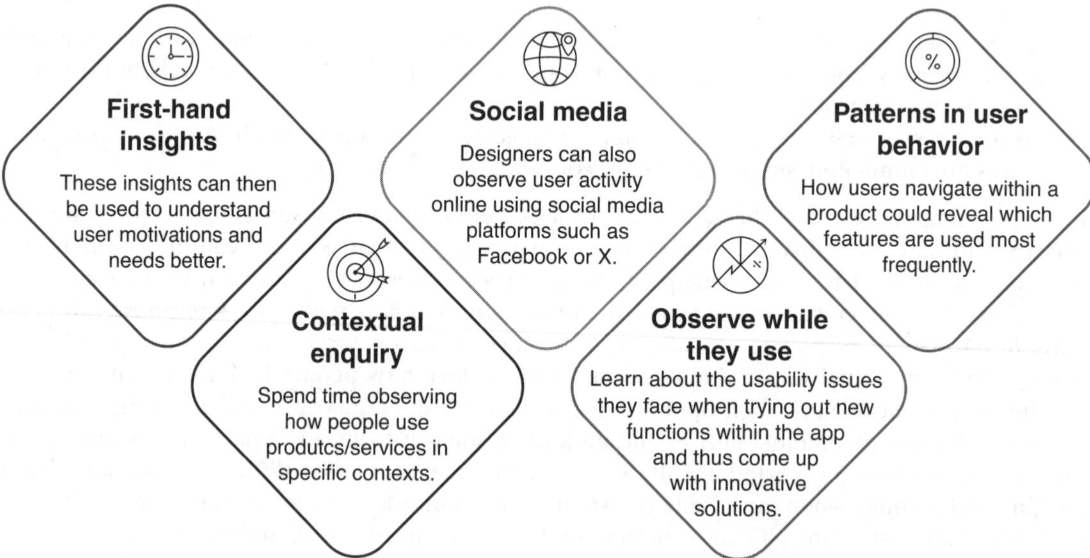

Figure 2.11 Conducting effective observational studies

Design Visualization Question 2.10

In educational settings, exams are pivotal moments that evoke a range of emotions in students.

Conduct an observational study in your college aimed at investigating the prevalence of examination anxiety. Select an equal number of male and female participants. Use the Westside Test Anxiety Scale to assess exam-related anxiety.

Several drawbacks exist when utilizing observational studies during the empathize stage of design thinking. Primarily, conducting such studies can prove **time consuming and challenging**. Observational studies require researchers to physically observe people in their natural environments, which can be difficult due to logistical challenges like scheduling and coordination. In addition, **research bias** poses a potential issue. As observational studies are subjective, there is no guarantee that observations accurately represent reality or remain uninfluenced by researchers' preconceived notions or biases. Furthermore, observational studies **may not always provide sufficient information** about how people feel or why they behave a certain way, as they only capture surface level behaviors without deeper context or insight into users' thoughts or feelings about a subject.

Thus, observational studies alone **may not provide enough data** for successful product design and development decisions since user behavior does not always accurately reflect user intent or feelings on a given topic. Finally, because conducting an observational study takes significant time commitment. It can also be **costly** if performed incorrectly due to inexperience with research techniques or by missing essential elements during observation.

2.3.5 Shadowing

User observation and shadowing provide first-hand insights into how users interact with products or services. During user observation, designers observe users completing tasks and achieving goals with a product or service. They note which elements users utilize, the difficulties they face, and how they resolve problems. Shadowing involves following users as they engage with a product or service to understand what motivates certain behaviors and actions in specific contexts. For example, if someone has trouble setting up a new device because they are unsure where to begin, shadowing them while they try different steps could reveal why certain steps confuse some users. Designers can then address these issues more accurately in later design phases.

Design Visualization Question 2.11

1. Library Usage through Shadowing

Shadow students as they navigate the library.

Observe how they search for books, use digital catalogs, and interact with librarians.

Identify pain points and opportunities for improvement.

2. Transportation

Shadow students using campus transportation (buses, shuttles).

Identify pain points related to schedules, stops, and overcrowding.

Suggest improvements for efficient transportation options.

2.3.6 Immersion

Putting yourself in users' shoes is key to designing user-centered solutions. Immersion is a powerful empathy method that lets designers fully experience the environments and daily lives of users. From living with them to working side-by-side, immersion allows an intimate look into users' experiences, emotions, and behaviors.

Imagine a designer creating an app for healthcare professionals. Working alongside doctors and nurses, observing their routines, and grappling with their challenges would allow the designer to build an intuitive, user-centric app that improves patient care.

While time and resource intensive, immersion empathy gives designers unparalleled access to user perspectives. It requires an open mindset to leave one's comfort zone and directly experience users' environments, which is a valuable learning process. Yet the insights gained fuel tailored, impactful design solutions.

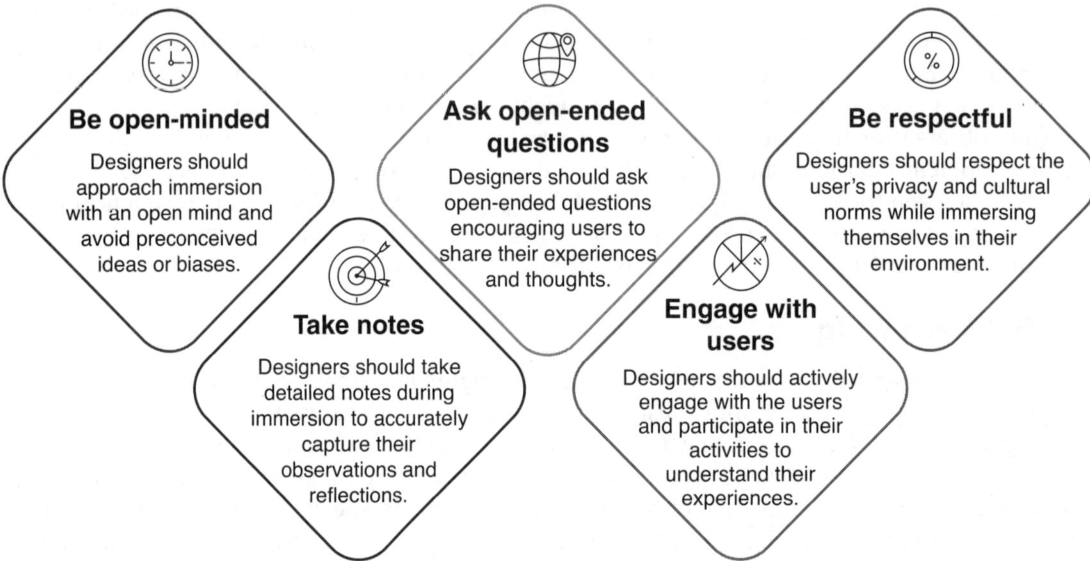

Figure 2.12 Conducting effective immersion study

To understand users thoroughly while immersing in the empathize phase, designers should heed certain tips and tricks (Fig. 2.12). These include:

- **Be open-minded and non-judgmental:** As designers, it is vital to approach immersion without preconceived notions or judgments. Maintain an open mindset and a genuine desire to understand.
- **Take notes:** Throughout the immersion process, take thorough notes, capturing observations and reflections accurately. This documentation will prove invaluable later.
- **Ask open-ended questions:** Ask open-ended questions that invite users to share their experiences and perspectives freely. Engage in active listening.
- **Engage with the users:** Actively engage with users, immersing yourself in their activities and environment. This hands-on approach will deepen your understanding of their realities.
- **Be respectful:** While immersing yourself, remain mindful of users' privacy and cultural norms.

Design Visualization Question 2.12

User-centered Campus Map Redesign

Collaborate with students and faculty to redesign the campus map. Consider user needs, accessibility, and ease of navigation. Use design thinking principles to create a more intuitive and user-friendly map.

While immersion is a powerful tool in the empathize stage of design thinking, it also has some drawbacks. Immersing oneself can demand **significant time and resources**, making it difficult in specific scenarios. Moreover, designers risk **losing objectivity and developing biases** when deeply embedded in the users' environments. While valuable for fostering empathy and insights, immersion necessitates caution. Designers must observe, participate, and reflect thoughtfully. However, they should also acknowledge **immersion's limitations**. By following best practices, designers can comprehensively grasp users' experiences to inform the design process effectively.

2.3.7 The 'I Like, I Wish' Game

The 'I like, I wish' game is an insightful way to gather user feedback during the design thinking process. This simple method involves asking users what aspects they appreciate and what improvements they desire regarding a product, service, or experience under evaluation. It offers a direct path to understanding user needs and aspirations, enabling designers to develop genuinely user-centric solutions.

While the 'I like, I wish' format is straightforward, it can be adapted to different contexts and goals. For instance, using Post-it notes instead of paper or introducing a third 'What if?' column. Defining clear objectives and guiding questions is crucial for productive feedback. In addition, visual aids can enhance user engagement and feedback quality. Fostering an open, judgment-free environment is essential for participants to share ideas and opinions freely. This approach helps identify user pain points and improvement opportunities.

However, implementing the 'I like, I wish' game can present challenges. It may be difficult to elicit honest, meaningful feedback from users unfamiliar with the game or product. Collecting and analyzing large volumes of feedback data can be time-consuming and tedious. Balancing feedback from diverse user groups and stakeholders, especially those with conflicting perspectives, can be challenging. In addition, designers must avoid biases or assumptions that could influence the feedback process.

2.3.8 Empathy Maps

Empathy maps are a tool used in the empathize stage to understand the user's feelings, thoughts, and behaviors when using a product or service (Fig. 2.13).

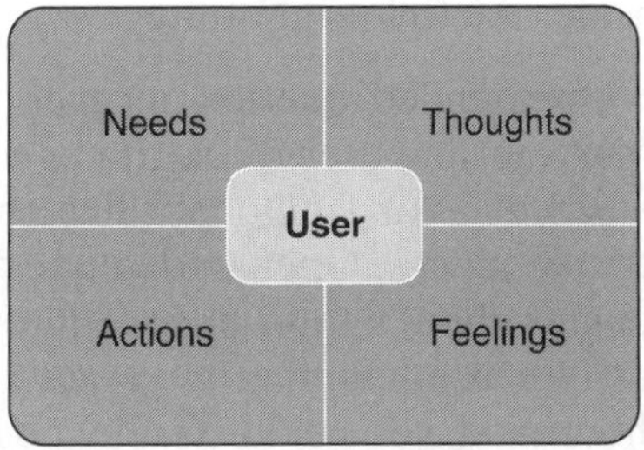

Figure 2.13 Empathy map

It has four key parts:

- **Thoughts:** It includes what someone might think about a situation or person. If discussing work, this covers opinions on the environment or how their boss views them.
- **Feelings:** It involves emotions felt in certain scenarios or with certain people. When describing a tough conversation with a boss, this covers feeling overwhelmed by pressure or undervalued based on expectations.
- **Needs:** This component centers around what an individual may need to make themselves more comfortable or happy in a particular situation or with specific people (such as supportive feedback from colleagues).
- **Actions:** This final component focuses on how an individual might respond to certain situations/people based on their needs/feelings/thoughts expressed previously in the empathy map (taking actionable steps such as researching new job opportunities).

Empathy mapping helps comprehend different perspectives. First, identify the individual's characteristics (age, gender, occupation). Next, brainstorm their words, emotions, thoughts, actions, and environment. Record these aspects on an empathy map, noting frequency and importance.

For instance, imagine designing a healthy food delivery service for parents with children aged 4–10. After identifying the target audience as parents aged 25–45, an empathy map could look like this:

> **Say:** I need quick, easy meal ideas. **Feel:** Frustrated, overwhelmed. **Think:** What ingredients are available? Can I make something healthy? **Do:** Search recipes online, buy precut vegetables. **Hear/See:** Fast food commercials, children requesting unhealthy snacks.

2.3.8.1 Strategies for Creating Empathy Maps

Empathy maps allow deeper insight into users' perspectives by exploring their rational thoughts, emotions, words, and actions. For instance, an empathy map for Jane, a 21-year old living in New York City, might look like this:

Feelings/Emotions: Overwhelmed by current happenings; anxious about informed decision-making; frustrated with unreliable information sources.

Thinking: Desires easy access to relevant news stories; wants accurate reporting from trusted sources; seeks multiple viewpoints before deciding.

Verbal: Shares current event articles with friends on social media; discusses topics by text or video chat.

Actions: Reads articles online multiple times daily from various publications for story updates.

To create user empathy maps, consider the following strategies:

- **Ask open-ended questions:** Open-ended queries uncover insights that may otherwise be hidden. Conduct interviews, surveys, and user focus groups to better understand motivations, attitudes, and behaviors. Instead of asking, "Do you like this product?", ask "What do you like or dislike about using this product?". Open-ended questions help comprehend people's motivations, feelings, and thoughts about a topic or situation.
- **Ask unconstrained questions:** When attempting to create a useful empathy map for those living solitarily in your neighborhood, you could start by posing some unconstrained queries such as "How do you cope when experiencing loneliness?" or "Which activities bring you the most joy?". These kinds of inquiries allow for honest self expression and divulge more than

just plain answers, aiding in better comprehending their lives and experiences. Unrestricted questions also assist in eliciting personal anecdotes from the intended audience, which can unveil unforeseen information about their perceptions or navigation of pertinent life events.

- **Watch users interact with products:** When possible, observe users completing tasks with the product. Note what they say and do to inform your empathy map designs. For example, if designing a website for parents with young children at home, visiting playgrounds or participating in parent activities like playgroups could provide insight into their needs and wants for the website.
- **Examine data from research techniques:** Looking data from interviews, surveys, focus groups, and observations is crucial. Over time, noticeable patterns and trends will emerge. These patterns will help create meaningful categories and themes within your empathy map design.

Design Visualization Question 2.13

Faculty Empathy Map

Students interview a faculty member about their teaching approach and challenges.

1) What do you think about teaching students? What motivates you?
2) What and how do you feel about the work environment?
3) What can be improved in the environment? What is the need?
4) What action can be taken to improve?

Create an empathy map for the faculty member to appreciate their role in student learning.

2.3.9 User Persona Development

A user persona is a representation of the target audience, encompassing their age, gender, interests, goals, and driving forces. These personas originate from interviews or surveys with individuals fitting the target demographic, providing invaluable insights for designing tailored solutions. Crafting a persona involves thorough research into the end-users' demographics, psychographics, and behavior patterns. With this data, designers can create an archetype that embodies the end-users' needs, desires, and pain points.

For instance, a mobile app designer targeting college students might develop a persona named Samantha. Samantha is a 21-year-old psychology major. Her interests revolve around social media, music, and fashion. As a commuter relying on public transportation, Samantha seeks better time management and organizational skills.

Name:	Samantha
Age:	21
Study:	College
Subject:	Psychology
Interests:	Social media, music, and fashion
Travel mode:	Public transport
Needs:	To work on managing time and staying organized

Personas allow designers to comprehend the requirements and challenges faced by typical college students like Samantha. This insight enables the creation of mobile apps tailored to cater to her needs, such as a task manager that aids in organization and time management.

Multiple personas representing diverse user groups can also be developed during persona creation. For instance, a fitness app designer could create personas for gym enthusiasts and outdoor activity lovers. Distinct solutions addressing the specific needs of each group can then be crafted by utilizing these different personas.

2.3.9.1 Steps in Creating User Personas

1. **Collecting Data:** First, gather details about your intended audience. Conduct surveys or interviews with potential users or observe them in their natural environment. This data will help create realistic user profiles representing each segment within your target market. It should include demographic information like age and gender, job details, and psychographics like interests and values.
2. **Analysing Data:** Once the relevant data is collected, analyse it to identify patterns and draw conclusions about your target customer and their needs from your product or service. This analysis will uncover customer insights that inform the creation of detailed user personas.
3. **Creating User Personas:** Finally, use all the insights gathered during research activities and analytical findings to build accurate representations (personas) for each identified segment. Each persona should contain detailed demographic and psychographic information, including values, beliefs, lifestyles, etc. Ensure that these are realistic representations, not stereotypes. Add specific objectives related to what success means for those users when interacting with your product/service offering so that designers can focus on meeting those objectives when creating solutions.

2.3.9.2 User Persona Types

There are two main types of user personas: primary and secondary. The primary persona is the central representation of users that designers use to focus their design process. They represent a typical user who shares similar characteristics like age range, occupation, lifestyle, etc., emphasizing particular behavior patterns that may affect product usage or design decisions. An example would be a 'college student' persona who is tech-savvy but has limited time for personal projects or work tasks due to attending classes or studying for exams; this might affect how they interact with specific products regarding usability and task completion times.

Secondary personas represent more niche or specific groups within the larger target audience; for example, there could be a 'video gaming college student' persona who has more time than the average college student to play games but also requires higher performance from products being used in gaming sessions due to more pressure exerted by high-stakes competitions; this could influence product specs when designing hardware intended for such users (like higher refresh rate screens).

Design Visualization Question 2.14

Persona of a Faculty Member

Collect data about the target audience by conducting surveys or interviews or observing them in action in their environment. It should contain detailed demographic and psychographic information, including values, beliefs, lifestyles.

Add specific objectives related to what success means for this persona.

2.3.10 Journey Map

Journey mapping is a tool used in design thinking to understand the user's experience and identify pain points and opportunities for improvement. It involves visualizing the user's journey, including their emotions, touchpoints, and goals. Journey mapping can help designers create better products and services that meet the users' needs and expectations.

There are different types of journey maps, such as current state, future state, and service blueprints. **Current state maps** focus on the user's experience, while **future state maps** envision a desired future state. **Service blueprints** map out the different touchpoints the user interacts with, providing a holistic view of the user's journey.

To create a journey map, the first step is to define the user persona and the problem to be solved. The next step is to map out the user's journey, including their emotions, pain points, and opportunities. The final step is to use the journey map to identify areas for improvement and inform design decisions.

Journey maps can communicate the user's experience to stakeholders and ensure everyone is aligned on the problem and solution. Journey maps can also inform usability testing and ensure that the testing focuses on critical areas of the user's journey.

Examining a user's journey through a product or service offers valuable insights. It fosters empathy by revealing their motivations and frustrations. This understanding highlights areas needing improvement. As an essential design thinking practice, journey mapping steers design decisions. It exposes pain points and opportunities that may otherwise be overlooked.

2.3.11 Cultural Probes and User Diaries

Cultural probes are utilized to obtain an understanding into how people live their lives through creative activities involving story collection, photographs, surveys, and user artifacts. They offer a qualitative user research approach when face-to-face interactions are impractical or inappropriate. Probes comprise prompts, inquiries, instructions, and artifacts for recording thoughts and feelings. These can range from simple diaries to single-use cameras. Cultural probes are particularly beneficial when conducting remote research or when in-person interactions pose challenges. For instance, Digital Ocean, a cloud computing company, developed a probe sending postcards inquiring about customers' perspectives on cloud computing technology. The results informed product design decisions and service customization for diverse customer types.

User diaries are another valuable tool in the empathize phase, enabling designers to comprehend how people utilize products or services over time by tracking behavior patterns such as frequency of use or location preferences. For example, Airbnb incorporates user diaries into their design process, requesting customers to complete online questionnaires about their experiences using Airbnb services like booking properties and communicating with hosts. These insights facilitate better decision making when designing new features or improving existing ones based on customer feedback.

Design Visualization Question 2.15

Food Habits and Aspirations

Design a cultural probe kit that explores participants' food habits and aspirations.

Include activities such as capturing photos of meals, keeping a food diary, and writing about emotional reactions to specific foods. Why do they like that food? How does it help them?

The goal is to understand how food influences their daily lives.

2.4 Empathetic Dimension to Leadership

Empathy is essential for leadership, particularly in today's complex and rapidly changing world. Empathetic leaders can empathize with their employees, clients, and stakeholders by understanding their viewpoints and worries. As a result, they are better equipped to make informed decisions that benefit everyone involved.

By demonstrating empathy, leaders can build trust and create a positive work environment, even in uncertain times. A leader who appreciates and considers the viewpoints of their team members can promote a feeling of collective ownership and accountability for the organization's achievements. Consequently, this can result in increased levels of involvement, efficiency, and contentment in the workplace.

Oprah Winfrey, a well-known talk show host, actress, and philanthropist, has emphasized the importance of empathy in leadership. According to her, empathy is the key to connecting with people and inspiring and empowering their lives.

Daniel Coleman, a psychologist, and author, also believes that empathy is a crucial trait for effective leadership. He proposes that empathetic leaders use their relationships to enhance their companies in nuanced yet significant ways. For example, an empathetic leader may take the time to understand their employees' challenges and provide them with the necessary resources and support to overcome those challenges. They may also listen to their employees' ideas and suggestions and implement them to improve the organization's overall performance.

The **servant leadership** style is increasingly becoming popular in today's industry due to the need for agile and flexible business and operating models. This leadership style emphasizes putting the needs of employees first, and it involves leaders serving their teams and organizations instead of the other way around. Empathy is the main characteristic of servant leadership.

EY recognized the importance of empathy during the pandemic by appointing its first Chief Wellness Officer. EY integrated empathy into its leadership approach, allowing individual employees to seek resources for well-being while helping managers develop empathetic skills when managing teams.

Leaders who led large transformative engagements have successfully demonstrated the contributions of being empathetic, resulting in beneficial results. The focus of empathetic leaders has always been the selfless approach to achieve immense value for all stakeholders, and such leaders place others first, then the self. By exploring through the lens of empathy, designers can not only see the problem but also internalize the consumers' challenges and pain points to evolve features and traits in the products that can strike the appropriate balance of sustainable solutions.

Summary

- Empathy is crucial in design thinking as it enables designers to understand and empathize with end-users' needs and wants. It allows designers to create tailored solutions based on end-users' motivations, behaviors, and pain points.
- Empathy fosters collaboration and trust among teams working on similar projects.
- Techniques for conducting user research and gathering insights include user interviews, focus groups, surveys, observational studies, shadowing, immersion, and empathy maps.
- The empathy map consists of four main components: thoughts, feelings, needs, and actions.
- User personas represent the real-life user of a product or service.
- Cultural probes gather insights into how people live their lives.
- User diaries track behavior patterns to understand how people use products or services over time.
- Empathetic leaders can empathize with employees, clients, and stakeholders, enabling informed decisions that benefit everyone involved.

Solutions to Design Visualization Questions

Q 2.1

Teenage Music App User Exploration: Understanding Their World

1. **Motivations and Preferences**
   - **Emotional Connection:** Music plays a significant role in a teenager's emotional landscape. It can be a source of comfort, motivation, self-expression, and identity exploration.
   - **Social Currency:** Music is a way for teens to connect with friends and peers. They share playlists, discover new artists together, and bond over shared musical tastes.
   - **Music Discovery:** Teens are constantly seeking fresh sounds and artists. They are influenced by social media trends, recommendations from friends, and music streaming algorithms.
   - **Customization and Curation:** Creating personalized playlists, setting moods, and customizing the listening experience is crucial. (Imagine themed playlists for studying, working out, or chilling).
   - **Offline Listening:** Uninterrupted access to music is essential, even without an internet connection. (Think downloading playlists for commutes or aeroplane rides).
2. **Pain Points and Frustrations**
   - **Limited Data Plans:** Mobile data restrictions can limit streaming and downloading music. (Consider offering offline listening options and data-saving features).
   - **Unwanted Ads:** Excessive or disruptive advertising can interrupt the listening experience. (Focus on non-intrusive ad placements or offer premium ad-free subscriptions).
   - **Unintuitive Interface:** A complex or confusing user interface can frustrate users and prevent them from enjoying the music. (Prioritize a clean, easy-to-navigate design with intuitive features).
   - **Limited Free Features:** Free versions with restricted features can leave users feeling frustrated. (Offer a balance of free and premium features, ensuring the free tier is still valuable).
   - **Irrelevant Recommendations:** Generic or irrelevant music recommendations can be a turn-off. (Develop a system that personalizes recommendations based on listening habits and user preferences).
3. **Goals and Challenges**
   - **Discover New Music:** Teens want to be exposed to new artists and genres, staying ahead of the curve. (Implement features like curated playlists, artist discovery tools, and social music exploration).
   - **Share Music with Friends:** Seamless sharing of music and playlists fosters social connection and strengthens friendships. (Integrate social features for playlist sharing, collaborative playlists, and music recommendations to friends).
   - **Express Themselves:** Music allows teens to express their individuality and explore their evolving identities. (Offer customization options like personalized profiles, mood-based playlists, and artist biographies).
   - **Organize their Music:** Create a system for organizing and easily accessing their favorite songs and playlists. (Implement search features, library filters, and playlist organization tools).
   - **Listen on the Go:** Access to music is essential for various activities, from commutes to workouts. (Ensure seamless integration with different devices and offline listening capabilities).

Q 2.2

Here are the top 5 factors a Netflix recommendation system would likely consider:

- **Watch History:** This is the most crucial factor. It analyzes what a user has watched previously, including movies and TV shows, genres, actors, directors, and even specific completion rates (Did they finish the entire movie?).
- **Ratings and Reviews:** User ratings and reviews provide valuable insights into a user's preferences. The system can analyze shows a user has rated highly and recommend similar movies/shows based on genre, theme, or actors.
- **Viewing Behavior:** Beyond just what they watch, a system can consider how users watch. Do they prefer comedies? Do they tend to binge-watch entire seasons? Do they revisit favorite shows often? This behavioral data can refine recommendations.
- **Demographic Information:** While not the most important factor, some demographic data like age, location, and even language preferences can be helpful. For example, a system might recommend family-friendly movies for users with young children.
- **Trending Content and Popularity:** Understanding what other users with similar tastes are watching can be a good indicator. The system can factor in trending shows, movies recently added to the platform, and overall popularity within specific genres or demographics.

Bonus Factors

- **Implicit Feedback:** Netflix can also analyze a user's browsing behavior, like pausing on a specific trailer or hovering over a particular genre, to understand implicit preferences.
- **Social Connections:** Incorporating data from a user's social network (if enabled) could show what movies/shows their friends are watching, potentially leading to recommendations based on shared interests.

By combining these factors, a recommendation system can create a personalized and engaging experience for each Netflix user, keeping them hooked and discovering new favorites.

Q 2.3

Five Empathy-Based Approaches to Improve the Lives of People with Disabilities in India

Accessibility Audits and User Experience (UX) Design

- Conduct empathy-driven accessibility audits of public spaces, websites, and mobile apps.
- Include people with disabilities in the design process to understand their challenges and preferences.
- Prioritize features like screen readers, closed captions, ramps, Braille signage, and clear visual design for better navigation.

Community Outreach and Awareness Campaigns

- Organize workshops and campaigns to educate the public about different disabilities.
- Promote empathy by encouraging people to experience challenges faced by individuals with disabilities through simulations or role-playing exercises.
- Partner with disability rights organizations to create informative and engaging content.

Inclusive Employment and Skill Development Programs

- Develop targeted training programs to equip people with disabilities with relevant skills for the job market.
- Partner with companies to create a more inclusive hiring process, providing reasonable accommodations and fostering an understanding workplace culture.
- Promote entrepreneurship and self-employment opportunities for people with disabilities.

Accessible Public Transportation and Infrastructure

- Advocate for accessible public transport options with features like ramps, low-floor buses, audio announcements, and designated seating areas.
- Ensure public infrastructure like roads, buildings, and parks are accessible with features like ramps, elevators, and tactile paving for visually impaired individuals.
- Prioritize accessible public restrooms and designated parking spaces for individuals with disabilities.

Empowerment and Access to Assistive Technologies

- Provide financial aid or subsidies for individuals with disabilities to acquire assistive technologies like wheelchairs, prosthetics, screen readers, or communication devices.
- Offer training on using assistive technologies effectively to promote independence and participation in daily activities.
- Support government initiatives for research and development of affordable and innovative assistive technologies geared towards the Indian context.

These empathy-based approaches can foster a more inclusive society where people with disabilities have equal access to opportunities, resources, and can participate fully in all aspects of life.

Q 2.4

Three Problems Solved by Smart Glasses for People with Disabilities

Visual Impairment: Smart glasses with integrated cameras and object recognition software can assist visually impaired individuals by:

- Describing objects and surroundings through voice prompts.
- Reading text aloud from signs, documents, or product labels.
- Providing navigational assistance by highlighting obstacles or guiding users on their route.

Hearing Impairment: Smart glasses can transcribe spoken words into text displayed on the lens, allowing people with hearing impairments to:

- Follow conversations in real-time.
- Understand lectures, presentations, or public announcements.
- Communicate more effectively by converting their speech to text for others to read.

Learning Disabilities: Smart glasses with augmented reality features can be used to:

- Overlay digital information on real-world objects, aiding information retention and comprehension for people with learning disabilities.
- Offer visual prompts and reminders to assist with tasks and daily routines.
- Provide real-time translation for people with dyslexia or language processing difficulties.

Q 2.5

A school creating its curriculum will interact with several user groups, both internal and external. Here's a breakdown of the key user types:

Internal Users

- **Teachers:** The primary curriculum implementers. They need a curriculum that aligns with their expertise, allows for flexibility in teaching styles, and effectively engages students.
- **Curriculum Developers:** These educators or specialists are responsible for creating and revising the curriculum. They need resources, support from leadership, and input from other stakeholders.

- **School Administration:** Principals, vice principals, and other administrators set the overall educational vision and ensure alignment with state and national standards. They need a curriculum that meets these benchmarks and is feasible to implement.
- **Guidance Counselors:** They help students plan their academic pathways and course selection. They need a curriculum with clear learning objectives and pathways for different student needs.
- **Special Education Teachers:** These educators work with students who have disabilities. They require a curriculum that can be adapted to meet individual learning needs and incorporates inclusive practices.

External Users

- **Students:** The ultimate beneficiaries of the curriculum. They need a curriculum that is engaging, challenging, and relevant to their interests and future goals.
- **Parents and Guardians:** They have a vested interest in their child's education and want to understand the curriculum content and learning objectives. They need clear communication and opportunities to provide feedback.
- **Subject Matter Experts:** Professionals or academics in specific fields can provide valuable insights and ensure the curriculum is current and accurate.
- **The Community:** Local businesses, organizations, and community leaders can offer real-world contexts and potential partnerships for learning experiences.
- **Government Agencies:** The school curriculum needs to comply with national and state educational standards set by government agencies.

By understanding the needs and perspectives of all these user groups, the school can create a well-rounded and effective curriculum that caters to all stakeholders and ultimately benefits the students it serves.

Q 2.6

Here are 3 additional tips for conducting effective user interviews:

Active Listening and Encouraging Elaboration

- Do not just listen for keywords or confirmation of your assumptions. Actively listen to the user's responses, body language, and tone.
- Use open-ended follow-up questions to encourage them to elaborate on their experiences, thoughts, and feelings.
- Techniques like paraphrasing and summarizing can show you are paying attention and ensure understanding.

Minimize Bias and Maintain Neutrality

- Be aware of your own biases and preconceived notions. Avoid leading questions or phrasing questions in a way that suggests a preferred answer.
- Maintain a neutral stance throughout the interview, allowing the user to share their honest opinions and experiences without judgment.
- Focus on understanding their perspective rather than trying to convince them of your ideas.

Pilot Testing and Iteration

- Before conducting interviews with a large group, consider piloting your interview script with a few participants. This helps identify any confusing questions, areas that need further exploration, or the overall flow of the interview.
- Based on pilot feedback, refine your interview guide and approach to ensure you are gathering the most valuable information.

Q 2.7

Here are 3 additional drawbacks of the user interview method:

Social Desirability Bias: Interview participants may unconsciously provide answers they think the interviewer wants to hear, or what they perceive as the "correct" answer. They might downplay negative experiences or exaggerate positive ones to appear knowledgeable or agreeable.
Mitigation Strategy
- Frame questions in a way that reduces pressure for a "correct" answer.
- Focus on understanding behaviors and experiences rather than opinions.
- Acknowledge that there are no right or wrong answers and encourage honesty.

Memory Limitations: Recalling past experiences can be challenging. Participants may forget details, misremember events, or unintentionally distort their experiences over time.
Mitigation Strategy
- Use prompts like pictures, objects, or timelines to jog participants' memories.
- Focus on recent experiences to improve recall accuracy.
- Acknowledge the limitations of memory and triangulate findings with other research methods.

Interviewer Bias: The interviewer's own background, experiences, and biases can influence how they ask questions, interpret responses, and analyze data.
Mitigation Strategy
- Be aware of your own biases and actively work to set them aside.
- Conduct interviews with a diverse team to gain multiple perspectives.
- Utilize structured interview techniques to minimize interviewer subjectivity in questioning.

Q 2.8

Here are 3 additional drawbacks of the focus group method:

Group Dynamics and Domination: Focus groups can be susceptible to groupthink, where participants conform to the opinions of the most vocal or assertive members. Shyness or cultural differences might prevent some individuals from expressing their true thoughts and feelings.
Mitigation Strategies
- Employ a skilled moderator who can ensure balanced participation and encourage quiet voices.
- Utilize techniques like anonymous voting or written exercises to allow everyone to contribute anonymously.
- Consider smaller group sizes or individual interviews for more introverted populations.

Lack of Representativeness: The findings might not generalize to the entire target audience if the focus group participants do not accurately represent the demographic diversity you are researching.
Mitigation Strategies
- Recruit a diverse group of participants based on relevant demographic criteria to ensure a well-rounded perspective.
- Conduct multiple focus groups with different sub-segments of your target audience to capture a broader range of experiences.
- Supplement focus groups with other research methods like surveys or online polls to reach a larger sample size.

Cost and Time Considerations: Recruiting, facilitating, and analyzing focus groups can be time-consuming and expensive.

Mitigation Strategies

- Consider alternative research methods like online surveys or usability testing that might be more cost-effective for certain research questions.
- If conducting focus groups, plan efficiently and keep discussions focused to maximize the value of the invested time.

Q 2.9

Sustainable Practices on Campus: A Student-Led Initiative

This project aims to assess current sustainability practices on campus and propose actionable steps for improvement. Your participation is crucial in making our campus more eco-friendly!

The Survey: We will be surveying students, faculty, and staff to gather data on three key areas:

- **Recycling Habits:** We want to understand how familiar you are with our campus recycling program and how often you recycle different materials.
- **Energy Consumption Awareness:** We will explore your awareness of energy-saving practices on campus and your personal habits regarding energy use.
- **Attitudes towards Sustainability:** We will gauge your overall interest in sustainability initiatives and your openness to potential improvements.

The Goal: The data collected will be used to create a proposal outlining actionable steps for enhancing campus sustainability. This proposal will be presented to relevant authorities, aiming to implement solutions that benefit everyone.

How to Participate: Look out for a short survey distributed through [mention preferred distribution channels – email, campus app, flyers]. Your honest responses are valuable in shaping a more sustainable future for our campus.

Here are some ideas for questions in the survey:

- **Recycling Habits**
  - How familiar are you with the types of materials accepted in our campus recycling program? (Very familiar, Somewhat familiar, Not familiar)
  - Do you recycle regularly on campus? (Always, Sometimes, Rarely, Never)
  - What challenges do you face when trying to recycle on campus? (Limited bins, Unclear signage, Other - specify)
- **Energy Consumption Awareness**
  - Are you aware of any energy-saving initiatives on campus (for example, turning off lights in unoccupied rooms)? (Yes, No)
  - Do you personally leave lights or electronics on in unoccupied spaces? (Always, Sometimes, Rarely, Never)
  - How interested are you in learning more about ways to conserve energy on campus? (Very interested, Somewhat interested, Not interested)
- **Attitudes Towards Sustainability**
  - How important do you consider sustainability efforts to be on our campus? (Very important, Somewhat important, Not important)
  - Would you be open to adopting more sustainable practices on campus, even if it requires minor adjustments? (Yes, No, Maybe)
  - Do you have any specific ideas for improving sustainability on campus? (Open-ended question)

Remember:

- The survey is anonymous.
- Your feedback is valued.

Taking Action: Once the survey concludes, the data will be analyzed and a proposal for improvement will be drafted. This proposal will outline specific, measurable, achievable, relevant, and time-bound (SMART) goals for enhancing campus sustainability. The proposal will be presented to relevant authorities, such as student government, campus administration, or the sustainability committee, advocating for the implementation of the suggested solutions.

By working together, students, faculty, and staff can create a more sustainable campus, fostering a more environmentally conscious community.

Q 2.10

Observational Study of Examination Anxiety in College Students

Objective: This observational study aims to investigate the prevalence of examination anxiety among college students and its potential relation to gender.

Methodology

Setting: This study will be conducted at [Your College Name].

Participants: A total of 60 students will be included in the study, with 30 male and 30 female participants selected randomly.

Data Collection

Observation: Researchers will observe students in common study areas (library, study lounges) during exam weeks. Observations will focus on students' behavior related to anxiety, including:

- Fidgeting or nervous movements
- Difficulty concentrating
- Frequent sighing or heavy breathing
- Social withdrawal
- Appearance of physical distress (sweating, rapid heartbeat)

Westside Test Anxiety Scale (*WTAS*): All participants will be invited to complete the validated WTAS anonymously. This self-report questionnaire assesses cognitive, somatic, affective, and behavioral aspects of test anxiety.

Data Analysis

Observations will be documented using a standardized observation form, recording the observed behaviors and their frequency. WTAS scores will be analyzed statistically to determine the prevalence of test anxiety among participants and any potential differences between male and female students.

Ethical Considerations

- Informed consent will be obtained from all participants before the study begins.
- Participation is voluntary and anonymous.
- Students can withdraw from the study at any point.
- All data will be kept confidential.

Expected Outcomes: This study will provide valuable insights into the prevalence of examination anxiety among college students and its potential association with gender. The findings may be used to develop programs and strategies to support students and reduce their exam anxiety.

Limitations

- Observational design cannot establish causation.
- Self-reported data on the WTAS may be subject to social desirability bias.
- The study focuses on a limited sample size and may not generalize to the entire student population.

Future Research: This could explore interventions and support mechanisms to help students manage exam anxiety. In addition, in-depth interviews could provide qualitative data on students' experiences with test anxiety.

Conclusion: Examination anxiety is a prevalent issue among college students. By understanding its prevalence and potential gender differences, we can create a more supportive learning environment for all students.

Q 2.11

Research Methods: Shadowing Students

1. Library Usage

Method: Shadowing

Procedure: Recruit a diverse group of students (different majors, years) who are willing to be shadowed. With informed consent, observe students as they complete typical library tasks:

- Searching for books by topic or title.
- Using the library catalog system (online or physical).
- Accessing online resources (e-journals, databases).
- Interacting with librarians for reference help.

Data Collection: Observe and document student behavior:

- Success rate in finding materials.
- Time spent searching for materials and resources.
- Difficulty level using the library catalog.
- Nature and frequency of interactions with librarians.
- Non-verbal cues of frustration or confusion.

Analysis: Identify common pain points:

- Difficulty navigating the library layout.
- Confusing library catalog interface.
- Lack of awareness of available resources.
- Hesitation to approach librarians for help.

Improvement Opportunities

- Develop library orientation sessions for new students.
- Create online tutorials or video guides for using the library catalog.
- Improve signage and wayfinding within the library.
- Train librarians on proactive outreach strategies.
- Offer workshops on specific research skills and resource utilization.

2. Campus Transportation

Method: Shadowing

Procedure:

- Select routes with high student traffic (dorms to classrooms, main buildings).
- Observe students using different modes of campus transportation (buses, shuttles).
- Track their experience during peak usage times and off-peak hours.

Data Collection: Observe and document student behavior:

- Waiting time for transportation arrival.
- Level of crowding on board vehicles.
- Difficulty boarding or disembarking.

- Route efficiency (directness, stops).
- Student communication regarding schedules or delays.

Analysis: Identify pain points:
- Long wait times for transportation.
- Overcrowding on buses/shuttles, leading to discomfort and safety concerns.
- Inefficient routes with unnecessary stops.
- Lack of clear and up-to-date schedule information.
- Difficulty accessing transportation during peakhours.

Improvement Opportunities
- Increase the frequency of buses/shuttles during peak usage times.
- Explore alternative routes to reduce travel time and congestion.
- Implement a real-time tracking system for bus arrival times.
- Develop a mobile app for students to access transportation schedules and updates.
- Consider alternative transportation options like bike-sharing programs.

By shadowing students in these settings, we gain valuable insights into their real-world experiences. This allows us to identify areas of frustration and inefficiency and develop targeted solutions to improve library usage and campus transportation for a more positive student experience.

Q 2.12

User-Centered Redesign of Campus Map: A Design Thinking Approach

Problem Statement: The current campus map is confusing, difficult to navigate, and does not cater to the needs of diverse users.

Solution: We will redesign the campus map using a user-centered design thinking approach, focusing on user immersion, accessibility, and ease of navigation.

1. Empathize

User Immersion:
- Collaborate with students and faculty from different backgrounds and abilities.
- Conduct shadowing sessions, observing users navigating campus with the existing map.
- Organize focus groups to gather feedback on pain points and desired functionalities.

Information Gathering:
- Analyze existing data on building usage, student traffic patterns, and accessibility needs.
- Review competitor campuses and their map designs for inspiration.

2. Define

User Needs:
Identify key user needs based on the gathered information:
- Easy wayfinding for new and returning students.
- Clear location identification for buildings, departments, and services.
- Accessibility features for users with visual impairments or mobility limitations.
- Real-time information on building hours, closures, and events.

3. Ideate
- Brainstorm creative solutions based on user needs:
- Interactive map format with zoom capabilities and search functions.

- Color-coded sections for different academic areas or building types.
- Integrated points of interest (POI) highlighting key locations (dining halls, restrooms, ATMs).
- Multiple map versions with varying levels of detail (e.g., overall campus, individual buildings).

4. Prototype

- Develop low-fidelity prototypes (paper sketches, digital mockups) of the redesigned map.
- Conduct user testing with the prototypes, allowing participants to interact and provide feedback.

5. Test and Refine

- Analyze user feedback from testing sessions.
- Refine the prototype based on user suggestions, iteratively improving clarity, usability, and accessibility.

6. Implement

- Develop the final high-fidelity map based on user testing results.
- Choose the appropriate format for distribution (printed copies, interactive online map, mobile app integration).

Design Thinking Principles

- **Emphasize User Needs:** Throughout the process, focus on catering to the needs and preferences of students and faculty.
- **Embrace Iteration:** Be prepared to iterate and refine the map design based on user feedback and testing.
- **Promote Collaboration:** Engage students, faculty, and accessibility experts to create a map that benefits everyone.
- **Prioritize Accessibility:** Ensure the map is accessible to users with disabilities, including those with visual impairments or mobility limitations.

Outcomes

- A user-friendly campus map that promotes campus exploration and wayfinding for all users.
- Increased student satisfaction with the campus environment and resources.
- Enhanced accessibility for users with diverse needs.
- An improved sense of community and belonging on campus.

By following these steps and incorporating user immersion techniques, this user-centered approach will result in a redesigned campus map that is not only aesthetically pleasing but also highly functional and inclusive for all members of the college community.

Q 2.13

Faculty Empathy Map

Says

"I love seeing the 'aha' moment when students grasp a concept."
"It's frustrating when students don't participate in class discussions."
"Grading papers can be tedious, but I enjoy providing constructive feedback."
"I wish I had more time for office hours to support struggling students."
"Keeping my courses engaging and relevant can be challenging."

Does

Prepares engaging lectures and presentations.
Uses active learning techniques to promote student participation.
Provides students with clear learning objectives and rubrics.

Offers office hours and responds to student emails promptly.
Attends professional development workshops to improve teaching skills.

Feels
Motivated by seeing students succeed.
Frustrated by a lack of student engagement.
Rewarded by positive student feedback.
Overwhelmed by workload (teaching, research, administrative tasks).
Uncertain about the effectiveness of teaching methods.

Needs
Supportive and collaborative work environment.
Access to resources for developing innovative teaching methods.
Smaller class sizes for more individualized attention.
Efficient technology and administrative support.
Opportunities for collaboration with colleagues and professional development.

Wishes
Students who are actively engaged and come to class prepared.
More time for research and scholarly pursuits.
Recognition and appreciation for teaching efforts.
A better work-life balance to avoid burnout.
A sense of community among faculty members.

By understanding these aspects of a faculty member's experience, students can appreciate the challenges and rewards of teaching. This empathy can foster better communication and collaboration between students and faculty, ultimately leading to a more positive learning environment for everyone.

Q 2.14

Faculty Persona: Dr. Anita Shah

Data Collection: Interviews with faculty members, surveys on teaching styles and priorities.

Demographics
Age: 45
Education: Ph.D. in Literature
Years of experience: 15
Department: English Literature
Marital status: Married, 2 children

Psychographics
Values: Lifelong learning, intellectual curiosity, critical thinking, fostering student growth.
Beliefs: Education is the key to a better future, all students deserve equal opportunities to learn.
Lifestyle: Busy schedule balancing teaching, research, and family life. Enjoys attending academic conferences and staying current in her field.

Objectives of Success
Teaching:
- Students are actively engaged and demonstrate critical thinking skills in class discussions.
- Students achieve a deep understanding of course material as evidenced by high-quality assignments and strong performance on exams.
- Students feel supported and encouraged to pursue their academic goals.

Research:

- Publish high-quality research articles in reputable academic journals.
- Secure grants to support ongoing research projects.
- Contribute to the advancement of knowledge in her field.

Professional Development:

- Stay informed about the latest teaching methods and educational technology.
- Continuously improve teaching skills and course content based on student feedback and best practices.
- Present research findings at conferences and contribute to the academic community.

Challenges:

- Balancing teaching, research, and service workloads.
- Dealing with large class sizes and limited resources.
- Motivating students who are uninterested in the subject matter.
- Keeping teaching methods engaging and relevant in a fast-paced digital world.
- Managing administrative tasks and faculty meetings.

Quotes

"The most rewarding part of my job is seeing students develop a passion for literature and become strong critical thinkers."

"I'm always looking for new ways to engage students and make my courses more interactive."

"It can be frustrating when students don't come to class prepared or don't put in the effort."

"I believe that every student has the potential to succeed, and I'm here to support them on their academic journey."

By understanding Dr. Shah's persona, administrators can develop programs and resources that address her needs and support her success as an educator and researcher. This can include workshops on innovative teaching methods, providing research grants, or streamlining administrative processes to free up faculty time. In addition, students can gain insights into the dedication and challenges that faculty face, fostering a more respectful and productive learning environment.

Q 2.15

Food and Mood: A Cultural Probe Kit

This kit explores your relationship with food! We're curious about how the foods you eat influence your daily life, emotions, and aspirations.

The kit includes:

- **A mini disposable camera (24 exposures):** Capture what you eat throughout the day! Don't worry about being a professional photographer – we want to see the reality of your meals and snacks.
- **Food Diary:** For one week, jot down what you eat and drink each day. Include details like time, location, and how you felt before and after consuming it.
- **Emotion Cards:** A set of cards depicting various emotions (joy, sadness, energy, comfort, etc.). After snapping a photo of a specific meal or snack, circle the emotion(s) that best describe how it makes you feel.

- **Food Story Worksheet:** Choose a food that holds special meaning for you. Write a short story about it – why do you love it? What memories or traditions are associated with it? How does it connect to your aspirations or cultural background?

Instructions:
Capture Your Food Journey: Use the camera to document your meals and snacks throughout the week. Don't forget to capture the environment (at home, restaurant, work) and who you're eating with (if applicable).

Track Your Food Diary: For each day, note down:
- Time of day
- What you ate and drank
- Where you ate it (home, work, etc.)
- How you were feeling before and after consuming it (circle emotions on the Emotion Cards)

Tell Your Food Story: Choose a dish that has a special meaning for you. On the Food Story Worksheet, write about:
- The food itself (name, ingredients)
- Why you love it (taste, memories, cultural significance)
- Memories or traditions associated with this food
- How it connects to your aspirations or cultural background

Why We Care: Understanding your food habits and emotional connections to specific foods helps us gain valuable insights into how food shapes your daily life. This information can be used to:
- Develop more interesting and relevant food options.
- Create a more positive and mindful relationship with food.
- Explore how food choices impact overall well-being and aspirations.

Thank you for participating!

Optional:
- Include a small pouch or reusable bag for participants to keep the kit organized.
- You can add a return envelope for participants to easily mail back their completed kits.

Additional Ideas
- Consider including a blank recipe card for participants to share a favorite recipe or a dish they'd like to learn to cook.
- Depending on your target audience, you could include a short questionnaire about dietary restrictions, cultural influences on food choices, or access to healthy food options.

This cultural probe kit offers a fun and engaging way to gather rich data on people's food habits and emotional connections to food.

Exercises

Part A (Objective Questions)

1. You are a designer working for a company that sells online courses. You want to create a personalized product recommendation system that suggests relevant courses to potential customers based on their interests and preferences. Which of the following steps would help you see things from the end-users' perspective?

(a) Conducting surveys and interviews with existing and potential customers
(b) Analyzing data on customer behavior and feedback
(c) Creating user personas and scenarios
(d) All of the above

2. You are a designer working for a company that develops assistive technologies for people with vision impairments. You want to create a mobile app that helps users navigate their surroundings using voice commands and feedback. Which of the following is an example of innovation in this context?
   (a) Developing a new algorithm that improves the accuracy and speed of voice recognition
   (b) Adopting an existing technology that converts text to speech
   (c) Exploiting a value-added novelty in the social sphere
   (d) Establishing a new management system that allows for agile development
3. What is the main purpose of empathy maps in the empathize phase of the design thinking process?
   (a) To create a shared understanding of user needs and aid in decision making
   (b) To generate a list of features and functions for a product or service
   (c) To test the usability and desirability of a product or service
   (d) To define the scope and goals of a product or service
4. Which quadrant of an empathy map captures what the user is thinking throughout the experience?
   (a) Says (b) Thinks (c) Does (d) Feels
5. You are designing a new app for online shopping. You want to create an empathy map for your target users. Which of these questions would be an open-ended question that you can ask them?
   (a) How often do you shop online?
   (b) What do you like about online shopping?
   (c) Do you prefer online shopping or in-store shopping?
   (d) How much do you spend on online shopping per month?
6. You are conducting a user observation for your empathy map. You visit a user's home and watch them use your app. You notice that they smile when they see a product they like, but they frown when they see the shipping cost. Which quadrant of the empathy map would you put these observations in?
   (a) Says (b) Thinks (c) Does (d) Feels
7. Which of the following is not one of the four main components of an empathy map?
   (a) Thoughts (b) Feelings (c) Needs (d) Goals
8. What is the main purpose of creating user personas in design thinking?
   (a) To represent the different user types that might use your product or service in a similar way
   (b) To test the usability and functionality of your product or service with real users
   (c) To generate ideas and solutions for your product or service based on user feedback
   (d) To evaluate the success and impact of your product or service on user satisfaction
9. Which of the following methods can help you create user personas based on actual data?
   (a) Interviews or surveys with people who fit your target demographic
   (b) Brainstorming sessions with your design team and stakeholders
   (c) Online research and analysis of existing products or services
   (d) Prototyping and testing your product or service with potential users
10. You are a designer working on a new app that helps people learn a foreign language. You have created two personas: Anna, a 25-year-old college student who wants to travel abroad and learn new cultures, and Raj, a 40-year-old business executive who wants to improve his

career prospects by learning a new language. Which persona is more likely to be your primary persona?
(a) Anna (b) Raj (c) Both (d) Neither

11. You are a designer conducting user research for a new website that sells organic products online. You have interviewed several potential users and collected data about their preferences, behaviors, and motivations. How can you use personas to synthesize your research findings and guide your design decisions?
(a) By creating fictional characters based on your assumptions about your users
(b) By creating fictional characters based on actual data collected from multiple individuals
(c) By creating fictional characters based on the preferences of the design team
(d) By creating fictional characters based on the most extreme or atypical users

12. You are a design researcher working on a project to improve the quality of life of elderly people living alone. You want to use cultural probes to gain insight into their daily routines, challenges, and aspirations. Which of the following is not a suitable artifact to include in your cultural probe kit?
(a) A disposable camera with instructions to take pictures of things that make them happy or sad
(b) A diary with prompts to write about their feelings, memories, and hopes
(c) A map with stickers to mark places they visit frequently or avoid
(d) A questionnaire with multiple-choice questions about their health, income, and social support

13. You are a design student learning about the design thinking process. You have been assigned to create a cultural probe kit for a group of teenagers who are interested in music and fashion. You want to make your kit engaging and fun for them. Which of the following is a good way to gamify your cultural probe kit?
(a) Include a reward system that gives points or badges for completing certain tasks or challenges
(b) Include a timer that limits the amount of time they can spend on each activity or artifact
(c) Include a randomizer that assigns different activities or artifacts to different participants
(d) Include a feedback mechanism that gives positive or negative comments on their responses

14. You are a UX designer working on a new mobile app that helps users track their daily expenses. You want to understand how users currently manage their finances and what challenges they face. Which research method would be most suitable for this purpose?
(a) Diary studies (b) Surveys
(c) Usability tests (d) Interviews

15. You are conducting a diary study with 20 participants who use your online learning platform. You ask them to log their activities and experiences every day for two weeks using an online tool. How can you increase the response rate and quality of your diary study?
(a) Send them periodic prompts and reminders to fill in their diary
(b) Offer them incentives and rewards for completing the diary
(c) Provide them with clear instructions and examples of diary entries
(d) All of the above

16. You are a design thinker working on a project to improve the user experience of an online shopping platform. You have conducted user research and gathered insights during the empathize stage. What is the next step you should take in the design thinking process?
(a) Start creating solutions based on your assumptions.
(b) State your users' needs and problems in a human-centered manner.
(c) Test your solutions with real users and collect feedback.
(d) Challenge your assumptions and create ideas for possible solutions.

17. You are a design thinker working on a project to improve the accessibility of public transportation for people with disabilities. You have defined the problem and decided what the project should cover during the define stage. What is the next step you should take in the design thinking process?
    (a) Start creating solutions based on your problem statement.
    (b) Test your solutions with real users and collect feedback.
    (c) Challenge your assumptions and create ideas for possible solutions.
    (d) Conduct user research and gather insights about their needs and experiences.

Part B (Short Answer Questions)

1. Write a note on analyzing user needs and pain points.
2. What are the techniques for conducting user research?
3. What is an empathy map? What are the strategies for creating user empathy maps?
4. What are the types of user personas?
5. What is a cultural probe? Give an example.
6. Define user diaries.
7. What is a user journey? How does it help identify problems?
8. What is a user story?
9. What is a scenario?
10. Give examples of user stories.
11. Define co-creation.
12. List the five steps of the user interview process.
13. How do open-ended questions help in interviews?
14. How does active listening help in user interviews?
15. How do follow-up questions help in user interviews?
16. What are the drawbacks of the interview process?
17. What are the drawbacks of focus group discussions?
18. List any three drawbacks of using surveys in the empathize phase of design thinking.
19. List any three drawbacks of using observational studies.
20. What is immersion?

Part C (Essay Questions)

1. How can empathy help designers adopt a user-centered approach to problem-solving?
2. Explain the importance of analyzing user needs and pain points with examples.
3. What are user interviews? Explain the process in detail.
4. What are focus groups? How are they useful in the empathize phase? What are their drawbacks?
5. What are observations studies? How are they useful in the empathize phase?
6. What are the drawbacks of observational studies?
7. Write an essay on immersion and how it is useful in the empathize phase.
8. Write an essay on empathy maps.
9. Discuss the strategies for creating user empathy maps.
10. Explain the steps in user persona creation in detail.
11. How does user journey analysis help to identify problems?

Answer Key

Part A

1. (d) **2.** (a) **3.** (a) **4.** (b) **5.** (b) **6.** (d) **7.** (d) **8.** (a) **9.** (a) **10.** (a)
11. (b) **12.** (d) **13.** (a) **14.** (a) **15.** (d) **16.** (b) **17.** (c)

CHAPTER 3

The Define Stage

Learning Objectives

At the end of this chapter, you will be able to:

- Explain how to effectively transition from the empathize phase to the define phase in design thinking, ensuring a seamless progression in the innovation process
- Describe techniques for analyzing and synthesizing data, including identifying patterns and themes, linking insights to observations, and building a shared understanding among team members
- List the strategies for defining the core problem with a user-centric focus, ensuring specificity and clarity, and framing the problem in an actionable manner that encourages diverse perspectives and iterative refinement
- Explain the methods used to identify user needs and opportunities, prioritize these needs, and diversify perspectives to uncover innovative solutions
- Describe the process of developing a strong point of view (POV) by formulating, refining, and validating the POV statement to guide the design process
- Explain the art of creating 'how might we' (HMW) questions that are focused on the POV, driving the ideation phase towards user-centered solutions

3.1 Transition from the Empathize Stage to the Define Stage

The define stage creates a framework that allows us to further our exploration of design thinking. It involves turning insights into actionable opportunities. The transition between the empathize and define stages (Fig. 3.1) of design thinking involves unpacking. This is a process in which designers take all the information gathered during the empathize stage, including observations, conversations, and research findings, and break it down into smaller, more manageable pieces.

For instance, imagine a designer who observed that 'People in a community lack access to healthy food options'. In the empathize stage, they collected information from various interviews with people from this community about their experiences with accessing food.

Now during the define stage, they will need to go through each observation or interview individually and 'unpack' them to better understand the problems people are facing when trying to access healthy food options. Table 3.1 indicates the set of activities that can be carried out in the define stage.

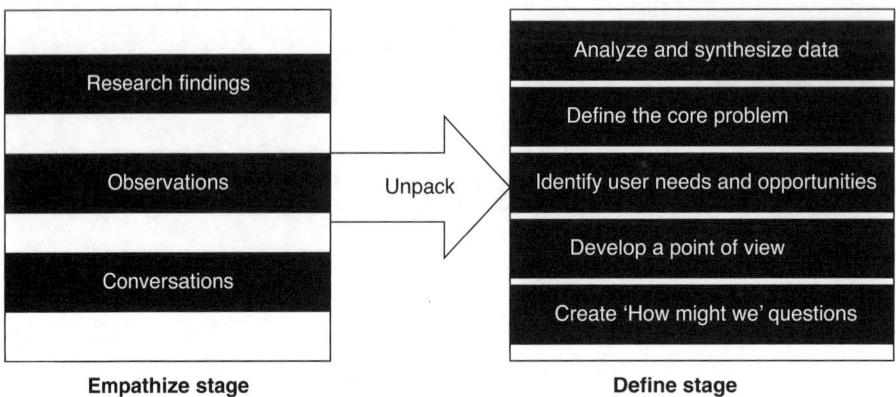

Figure 3.1 Empathize stage to define stage

Table 3.1 Define stage of design thinking activities

Step	Description	Example
Step 1	Analyze and synthesize data	Look for insights and common challenges related to access to healthy food options. What are the barriers people face? Are there specific dietary needs that need to be met?
Step 2	Define the core problem	Community members struggle to access fresh and affordable fruits and vegetables due to limited grocery store options and unreliable transportation.
Step 3	Identify user needs and opportunities	What are their desires and aspirations regarding their food choices? Look for opportunities to address the core problem and user needs creatively. This might involve exploring potential solutions from various angles.
Step 4	Develop a point of view (POV)	We believe that by providing a community-supported agriculture (CSA) program with flexible pick-up points and affordable pricing, we can empower residents to access fresh and healthy produce.
Step 5	Create 'how might we' questions	How might we create a sustainable and affordable food delivery system for residents who lack transportation? or How might we encourage local farmers to participate in a community-supported agriculture program?

Step 1. Analyze and Synthesize Data: Study the interview findings (from the empathize stage) meticulously. Employ analytical methods like affinity diagrams and coding to discern patterns and critical insights. Connect the recognized insights to observations, fostering a collective understanding of the challenge.

Step 2. Define the Core Problem: Grounded in analysis and synthesis, formulate a clear, concise problem statement that encapsulates the core issue's essence. This statement should revolve around the users (community members) and their needs. For example, instead of 'There is a scarcity of healthy food options in the community,' it could be rephrased as 'Community members face difficulties accessing fresh, affordable fruits and vegetables due to limited grocery store availability and unreliable transportation.'

Step 3. Identify User Needs and Opportunities: Having defined the core problem, the next step involves identifying specific needs and aspirations, and prioritizing them accordingly. Recognize potential opportunities from diverse perspectives and connect the needs and opportunities. For example, identify user needs related to healthy food accessibility. What desires and aspirations do they hold regarding their dietary choices? Seek opportunities to creatively address the core problem and user needs.

Step 4. Develop a Point of View (POV): After analyzing the defined issue, user needs, and opportunities, formulate a point of view (POV) statement. This statement should convey the team's perspective on addressing the problem and meeting user needs. It should be specific and actionable. For example, 'We believe providing a flexible community-supported agriculture (CSA) program with convenient pick-up locations and affordable pricing can empower residents to access fresh, healthy produce.'

Step 5. Create 'How Might We' Questions: Craft questions beginning with 'How might we...' to guide the ideation phase. Focus these questions on potential solutions for the POV and user needs. For example, 'How might we establish a sustainable, affordable food delivery system for residents lacking transportation?' or 'How might we encourage local farmers' participation in a community-supported agriculture program?'

After completing these define stage steps, the designer will clearly understand the issue, user needs, and potential opportunities. This paves the way for ideation, where creative solutions can be brainstormed to address the defined problems.

Let us now take a closer look at each of the define stage steps.

Design Visualization Question 3.1

Accessibility Issues: The designer might observe that "Public transportation in the city is not accessible for people with disabilities." Here, the focus would be on understanding the specific challenges faced by users with disabilities when using public transport. This could involve interviewing users, observing their journeys, and identifying pain points related to inaccessible bus stops, lack of ramps on trains, or difficulty navigating crowded platforms.

Collect data for the above issues from physically challenged people and explain the steps given below for these issues. (You can also do it imaginatively).

Step 1. Analyze and synthesize data
Step 2. Define the core problem
Step 3. Identify user needs and opportunities
Step 4. Develop a point of view (POV)
Step 5. Create 'how might we' questions

3.2 Analyze and Synthesize Data (Step 1)

Here, the designer dives deep into the data collected in the empathize stage, primarily focusing on interviews with community members. This step involves analyzing and synthesizing the data to extract valuable insights for defining the core problem. Table 3.2 provides a breakdown of how this step can be approached.

Table 3.2 Analyze and synthesize data

Step	Description	Example
Step 1	Data analysis techniques	**Affinity Diagram:** For example,you might see clusters related to limited grocery stores, transportation issues, affordability concerns, or specific dietary requirements. **Coding:** For example, codes might be assigned for 'limited grocery store options,' 'transportation issues,' 'affordability concerns,' or 'cultural/religious dietary needs.'
Step 2	Identifying patterns and themes	**Identify Key Themes:** Look for dominant and recurring themes related to accessing healthy food options across multiple interviews. These themes may center around: 1) **Accessibility:** Limited grocery stores, transportation barriers, and lack of access to food sources within walking distance. 2) **Affordability:** High cost of fresh produce, food budgets, income limitations. 3) **Dietary Needs:** Lack of culturally appropriate foods, limitations imposed by health conditions, or food allergies. 4) **Awareness and Knowledge:** Food deserts making it challenging to find healthy options, limited understanding of healthy eating and nutritional value.
Step 3	Linking insights (themes) to observations	The identified themes and patterns should be linked back to the initial observations made during the empathize stage. **Observation:** Lack of access to healthy food options in the community. **Linking:** The lack of accessible and affordable healthy food options (observation) is caused by limited transportation (insights) and affordability challenges (insights). Community members desire convenient and affordable access to fresh produce to make healthier choices and improve their well-being (user needs).
Step 4	Building a shared understanding	It is crucial to document the analysis process and findings clearly. Sharing these findings with the design team or stakeholders creates a shared understanding of the problem.

3.2.1 Data Analysis Techniques

Employing meticulous examination, data analysis encompasses an in-depth comprehension of information (obtained from the empathize stage) to facilitate informed decisions or draw logical conclusions. This complex process entails going through substantial quantities of data, identifying recurring patterns, and deriving inferences (Fig. 3.2).

To illustrate, a company may seek to revamp its website with the objective of enhancing user engagement. During the define phase, the organization may leverage data analysis to scrutinize user behavior patterns on the current website. This could encompass evaluating metrics such as page views, bounce rates, and duration of time spent on the site. Through this analysis, the company might detect that users promptly abandon the site due to difficulties encountered while seeking specific information. Grounded in this insight, the problem statement could be formulated as optimizing the website's navigation and information architecture, thereby facilitating users' ability to locate the desired content with ease. Furthermore, this problem statement possesses the desirable qualities

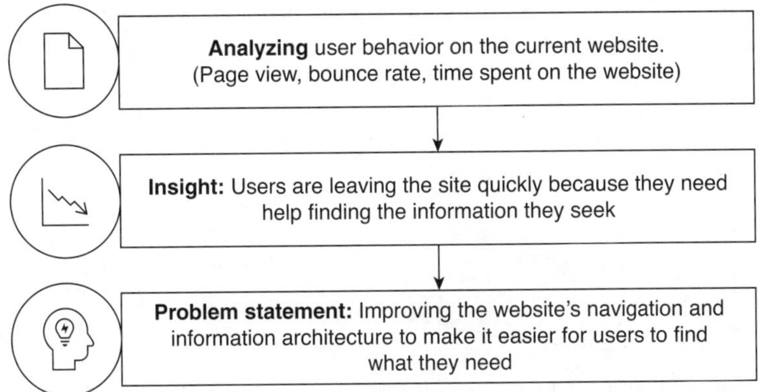

Figure 3.2 Data analysis techniques: Revamping a website to enhance user engagement

of specificity, actionability, and measurability, consequently enabling designers to develop efficient solutions.

Another example could be a healthcare company that wants to improve patient satisfaction. The company may use data analysis to examine patient feedback surveys in the define phase. Through this analysis, the company may discover that patients are dissatisfied with the long wait times in the clinic. Based on this insight, the problem statement could be defined as 'reducing patient wait times in the clinic' (Fig. 3.3).

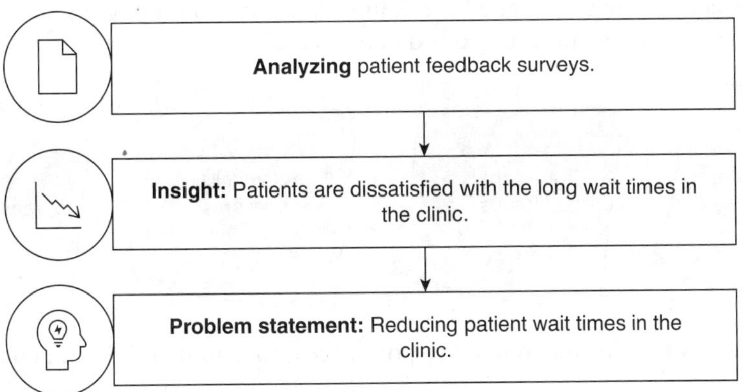

Figure 3.3 Data analysis techniques: Patient wait time reduction

Analysts need to possess robust analytical abilities as well as technical expertise with databases and programming languages like Python or R. This allows them to efficiently process large data sets and derive valuable insights from them. Analysts should also communicate their analyses clearly so that others can fully comprehend what the data revealed.

Affinity Diagramming: This is a design thinking tool used to organize information and structure ideas during problem-solving. It is a visual mapping method that identifies relationships between data or information sets. The process involves grouping data points (like quotes, observations, and critical interview points) based on similarities. Doing so helps uncover recurring themes and patterns within the data.

For example, for the poor access to healthy food problem, you may see clusters related to limited grocery stores, transportation issues, affordability concerns, or specific dietary requirements (Fig. 3.4).

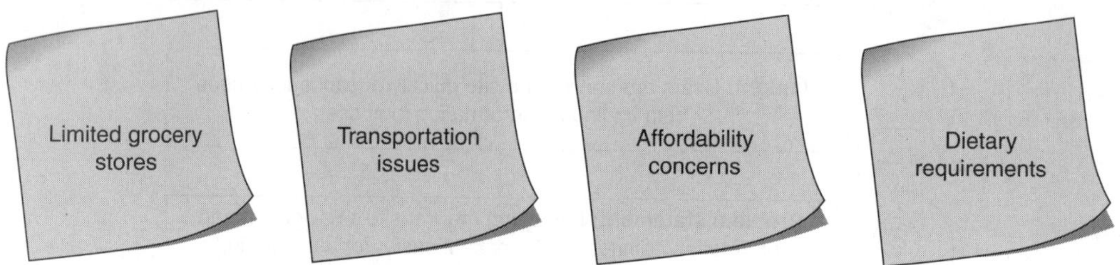

Figure 3.4 Clusters related to poor access to healthy food

These clusters are then presented on an affinity diagram where each can be viewed in relation to other clusters to uncover connections and relationships.

This approach encourages team collaboration by providing multiple perspectives on how best to solve a given problem. It also allows them to work efficiently by breaking down large amounts of complex data into smaller chunks that are easier to manage over time (tackling one cluster at a time).

Coding: This method involves assigning codes (labels) to different data segments based on their content and meaning (Fig. 3.5). This allows for efficient sorting and grouping of similar ideas and identifying major themes.

For example, codes may be assigned for 'limited grocery store options', 'transportation issues', 'affordability concerns', or 'cultural/religious dietary needs'.

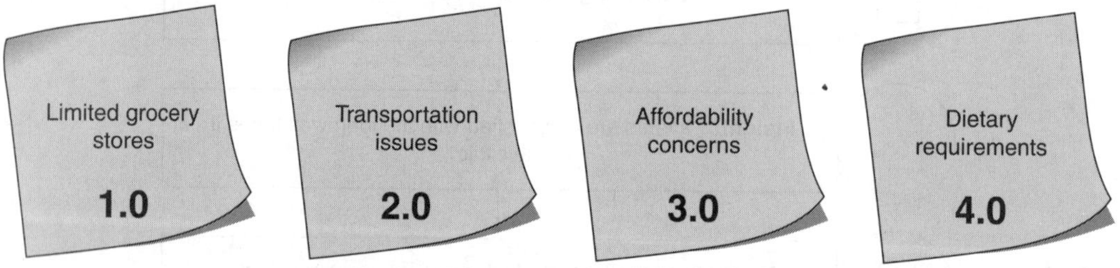

Figure 3.5 Clusters related to poor access to healthy food, with coding

Qualitative Data Analysis Software: These powerful tools can be your ally in data analysis and visualization. They can help you manage large amounts of data, streamline the coding process, and generate reports summarizing key themes. However, remember that your critical thinking and interpretation skills are still crucial. Do not rely solely on software outputs for understanding the data.

3.2.2 Identifying Patterns and Themes

Identifying patterns and recurring themes involves identifying common challenges faced by the community, along with specific needs and preferences. In addition, the analysis should consider unique perspectives or needs of subgroups within the community. This will reveal key themes and highlight the most significant pain points.

Analyzing access to healthy food options across multiple interviews likely reveals recurring themes. These may center around accessibility challenges – limited grocery stores, transportation issues, and lack of sources within walking distance. Affordability can be a major concern, with residents facing high costs of fresh produce and struggling with food budgets due to income limitations (Fig. 3.6). Dietary needs may not be met due to a lack of culturally appropriate options, health conditions, or food allergies.

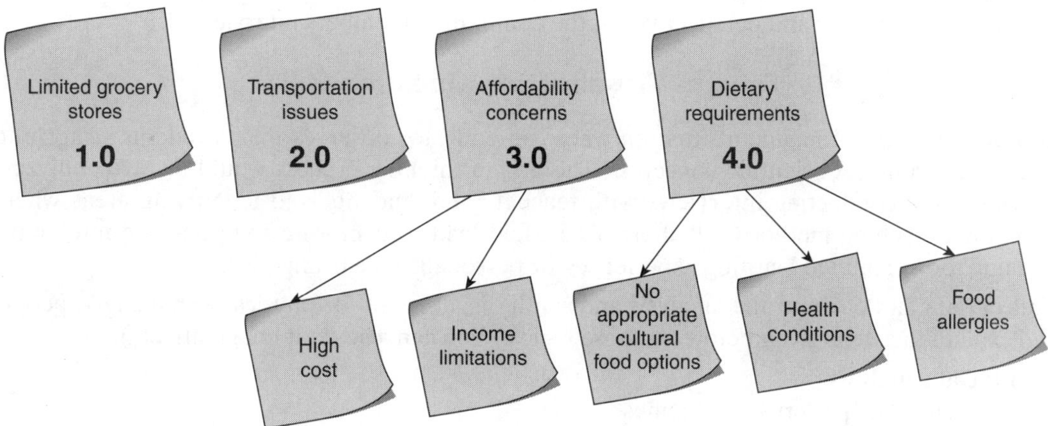

Figure 3.6 Clusters related to poor access to healthy food, with sub-clusters

Prioritization in design thinking involves analyzing the identified themes through a dual lens. First, consider the impact and frequency of each theme to understand which challenges are most widespread and critical for the community. Second, connect these themes to the user experience by examining how they directly affect residents' lives – their ability to access healthy food, make choices, and ultimately impact their health and well-being.

Documentation and collaboration are key during this stage. Visualizations like charts, graphs, or mind maps help solidify understanding of the identified patterns and themes.

3.2.3 Linking Insights to Observations

The themes and patterns identified should be linked back to the initial observations made during the empathize stage. This helps ensure that the analysis aligns with the overall problem and clarifies how user voices are being reflected in the findings.

For instance, transportation and affordability challenges (insights) directly contribute to the observed lack of access to healthy food (observation). Examining specific examples from the interviews can further solidify these connections (Fig. 3.7).

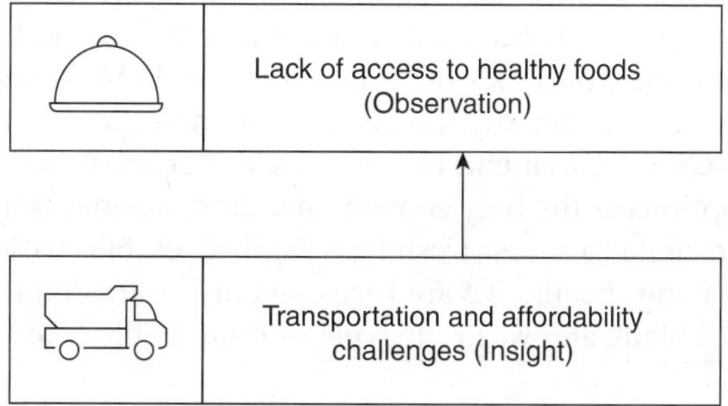

Figure 3.7 Linking insights to observations

3.2.4 Building a Shared Understanding

It is crucial to document the analysis process and findings clearly. This can be done through visual representations like affinity diagrams or reports summarizing key themes. Sharing these findings with the design team or stakeholders creates a shared understanding of the problem and facilitates further discussion in the define phase. By thoroughly analyzing and synthesizing the data, the designer lays the groundwork for defining the core problem and user needs in a way that is grounded in the lived experiences and perspectives of the community members interviewed.

Design Visualization Question 3.2

Educational Gaps: Imagine a situation where an educator observes that "Students struggle to understand complex scientific concepts." The design thinking process would involve analyzing student work, conducting interviews with teachers and students, and identifying areas where traditional teaching methods fall short. This could lead to exploring solutions like interactive learning tools, gamified learning experiences, or personalized learning plans.

Collect data and perform the 'analysis and synthesis' exercise for physically challenged people and explain the steps given below for these issues. (You can also do it imaginatively).

Step 1: Data analysis
Step 2: Identifying patterns and themes
Step 3: Linking insights (themes) to observations
Step 4: Building a shared understanding

3.3 Define the Core Problem (Step 2)

Step 2 of the define stage involves formulating a clear and concise problem statement that accurately reflects the core issue identified through data analysis in Step 1. This step requires careful consideration of several key aspects (Table 3.3).

Table 3.3 Steps in defining the core problem

Step	Description	Example
Step 1	User-centric focus	**Initial statement (not user-centric):** The community lacks access to healthy food options. **User-centric reframing:** Due to limited grocery stores and high food costs, community members struggle to find and afford fresh fruits and vegetables, leading to a scarcity of healthy food options in their daily diet.
Step 2	Specificity and clarity	Due to limited grocery stores and high food costs, community members struggle to access fresh and affordable fruits and vegetables **due to limited grocery store options and unreliable transportation**, leading to a scarcity of healthy food options in their daily diet. **Refined statement:** Due to a lack of grocery stores and limited affordable options at the only convenience store, residents in this community struggle to access fresh fruits and vegetables **within a one-mile radius**. (Being specific, we are focusing only on the limited grocery store problem, and we are leaving out unreliable transportation).

(Continued)

Step	Description	Example
Step 3	Actionable framing	'How might we **increase access to fresh and affordable fruits and vegetables** within a one-mile radius for residents in this community, by exploring alternative food sources and distribution channels?'
Step 4	Considering different perspectives	**Considering other perspectives:** **Local businesses:** Existing grocery stores might be concerned about competition from new food sources. **Local government:** Public health agencies might see this as an opportunity to promote healthy eating initiatives. **Non-profit organizations:** Food banks might be interested in collaborating to ensure access to nutritious food.
Step 5	Iterative refinement	**Refined statement (after considering stakeholders):** 'How might we create a **collaborative and sustainable solution to increase access to fresh, affordable, and culturally appropriate** fruits and vegetables within a one-mile radius for **all residents** in this community, considering the needs of existing businesses, local organizations, and government agencies?'

3.3.1 User-Centric Focus

A well-defined user-centric problem statement is the cornerstone of a successful design thinking process, particularly in the define stage. This statement should shift the focus from simply observing a lack of healthy food options to understanding the user's (community members') needs and challenges in accessing them.

Reviewing User Interviews: Revisit interview transcripts from the empathize stage. Pay close attention to recurring themes, challenges mentioned, quotes, and stories that illustrate difficulties in accessing healthy food.

Identifying User Pain Points: Analyse the user data to pinpoint pain points and frustrations related to availability, affordability, transportation, and cultural preferences. Are there limited options for fresh produce? Is cost a major barrier? Is access to grocery stores limited due to transportation issues?

Reframing the Problem Statement: Move away from simply stating the lack of healthy options. Instead, use user-centric language that emphasizes their experience. Phrases like 'struggle to find', 'difficulty in accessing', or 'cannot afford' effectively communicate the user's perspective.

Refine and Iterate: Continuously refine the statement to ensure user-centered accuracy and eliminate bias or assumptions. Share the draft statement with community members for feedback and iterate based on their input. This iterative process ensures the final statement captures the core user challenge.

For example,
Initial problem statement (not user-centric): The community lacks access to healthy food options

Refined core problem statement: Due to limited grocery store access, unreliable transportation, high food costs and a lack of knowledge about healthy food preparation, community members **struggle to find** and **cannot afford** fresh healthy fruits and vegetables, leading to a scarcity of healthy food choices in their daily diet.

Explanation:

- *Limited grocery store access*: This could mean there are few stores in the community, especially those offering fresh produce. Existing stores might be too far away or not cater to budget-friendly options.
- *Unreliable transportation*: This could be due to a lack of public transportation, limited personal vehicle access, or unreliable taxi services, making it difficult for residents to reach grocery stores.
- *Lack of knowledge about healthy food preparation*: This might prevent residents from making the most of potentially affordable ingredients to cook healthy meals.

By following these steps, you can create a user-centered problem statement that accurately reflects the needs and challenges faced by the community regarding access to healthy food.

Design Visualization Question 3.3

1. **Public Park Usage**
   Initial Problem Statement: The public park is underutilized.

2. **Recycling Program Participation**
   Initial Problem Statement: Residents are not recycling properly.

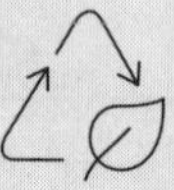

3. **Customer Retention Rates**
   Initial Problem Statement: Our online store is losing customers.

Create user-centered problem statements that accurately reflect the initial problem statements given above.

3.3.2 Specificity and Clarity

Refine the initial user-centric problem statement for clarity and specificity. Here's why this is crucial: The problem statement should avoid generalizations or ambiguous terms. It should accurately represent the core issue and its impact on the users. Having identified the user-centric problem, the designer now plays a critical role in refining it for clarity. This ensures the core problem is well-defined and sets the stage for effective brainstorming in subsequent phases.

Key Considerations

- **Conciseness:** Clearly and concisely articulate the core challenge faced by the community in accessing healthy food.
- **Specific Details:** Utilize specific details gathered from the user-centric analysis. Instead of 'limited access', pinpoint specific limitations like 'residents have limited access to fresh produce within a one-mile radius due to...'
- **Avoiding Assumptions:** The statement must reflect actual user data, not personal biases.
- **Single Issue Focus:** While multiple challenges may exist, define one core problem at a time to create a clear target for solution development.
- **Testing for Clarity:** Share your draft statement with individuals not involved in the research to ensure it is easily understood and accurately reflects the user data.

For example,

1. **Before specificity and clarity:** Due to limited grocery store access, unreliable transportation, high food costs and a lack of knowledge about healthy food preparation, community members

struggle to find and **cannot afford** fresh healthy fruits and vegetables, leading to a scarcity of healthy food choices in their daily diet.

2. **After specificity and clarity:** Due to limited grocery store access, high food costs and a lack of knowledge about healthy food preparation, community members **struggle to find** and **cannot afford** fresh healthy fruits and vegetables **within a one-mile radius,** leading to a scarcity of healthy food choices in their daily diet.

By following these steps and refining the problem statement for specificity and clarity, we can establish a solid foundation for the next stages of design thinking.

Design Visualization Question 3.4

Before Specificity and Clarity: In employee onboarding, due to lack of structure, unclear expectations, and limited opportunities for mentorship, new employees feel overwhelmed and confused, hindering their ability to integrate smoothly and reach full productivity.

Convert the above statement by applying specificity and clarity.

3.3.3 Actionable Framing

Crafting a well-defined problem statement in design thinking should not merely pinpoint the challenge but also serve as a springboard for innovative solutions.
Problem statement from the previous step: Within a one-mile radius, community members face difficulties in accessing fresh, healthy fruits and vegetables due to limited grocery store availability and high food costs, coupled with a lack of knowledge about how to prepare nutritious meals. This leads to a scarcity of wholesome food choices in their daily dietary intake.
To achieve this transformation, here are the steps:

1. **Identifying the desired outcome:** Envision the ideal scenario – how would the community benefit from readily available healthy food options?
2. **Shifting the perspective:** Reframe the problem statement as an opportunity or challenge statement focused on attaining this desired outcome. Rather than stating 'residents lack access to...', phrase it as 'how might we ensure residents have...' This shift fosters viewing the problem as an opportunity for positive change.
   'Residents struggle to find fresh fruits and veggies within a one-mile radius due to limited grocery store access, leading to a scarcity of wholesome food choices in their diet. This poses a challenge in incorporating a nutritious diet. How might we enhance residents' access to fresh produce within their neighbourhoods?'
3. **Action verbs:** Utilize action-oriented verbs like 'enhance', 'improve', or 'create' to accentuate the desired positive transformation.
   'Because residents face difficulties locating fresh fruits and vegetables within a one-mile radius due to limited grocery store access, they struggle to incorporate healthy food choices into their diet. This obstacle restricts their ability to maintain a nutritious lifestyle. How can we enhance residents' access to fresh produce within their neighbourhoods?'
4. **Preserving the user perspective:** The reformulated statement should continue to reflect the user's needs and challenges identified previously, ensuring that the solutions directly address their concerns.
5. **Refining for clarity:** Craft a concise and actionable statement that clearly outlines the opportunity for positive change, avoiding ambiguity and promoting easy comprehension and implementation.

'Limited access to grocery stores within a one-mile radius hinders residents' ability to find fresh fruits and vegetables, restricting their healthy food options. How might we increase residents' access to fresh produce within their neighbourhoods?'

This statement is concise and actionable. It clearly identifies the user group and their challenge (limited access to fresh produce). It also highlights the desired outcome (increased access) and maintains the geographical constraint (one-mile radius). In addition, it focuses on the specific issue of limited grocery store access.

By following these steps, the core problem is transformed into an actionable statement that guides the design team towards solutions.

Design Visualization Question 3.5

Problem Statement: Overflowing trash cans and limited recycling options in apartment buildings contribute to an unsightly and unsanitary environment for residents, negatively impacting their well-being.

Convert the above statement into an actionable framing statement.

3.3.4 Considering Different Perspectives

Crafting an impactful design thinking approach necessitates a robust problem statement. It should encompass user needs and a comprehensive understanding of the broader landscape. This involves acknowledging diverse perspectives from stakeholders who could be influenced by the issue or potential resolutions.

Identifying stakeholders: Initiate the process by brainstorming a list of individuals and groups that might be affected by the problem or its proposed solutions. This could include community residents (considering varied demographics), local businesses (such as grocery stores and farmers markets), local government agencies (public health, transportation), and non-profit organizations (food banks, community gardens).

Stakeholder analysis: Analyze the potential impact of the problem and solutions on each stakeholder group. Consider questions such as: how might this issue affect them, what are their needs/concerns regarding the problem or solutions, and are there potential benefits or drawbacks for each group?

- **Residents**
  - **Problem impact:** Difficulty finding fresh produce, reliance on processed foods, potential health issues.
  - **Needs/Concerns:** Affordability, convenience, product variety, cultural relevance.
  - **Benefits:** Improved health, increased access to healthy options, potential cost savings.
- **Local Businesses**
  - **Problem impact:** Potential loss of customers if new options arise.
  - **Needs/Concerns:** Maintaining profitability, adapting to changing consumer needs.
  - **Benefits:** Increased customer base if solutions involve partnerships or support local businesses.
- **Local Government**
  - **Problem impact:** Public health concerns due to limited access to healthy food.
  - **Needs/Concerns:** Promoting healthy eating initiatives, supporting community well-being.
  - **Benefits:** Improved public health outcomes, potential cost savings on healthcare.

- **Non-profit Organizations**
  - **Problem impact:** Increased demand for their services if residents struggle to access healthy food.
  - **Needs/Concerns:** Ensuring food security within the community, collaborating with other stakeholders.
  - **Benefits:** Collaboration could lead to more efficient solutions, potential funding opportunities.

Integrating stakeholder insights: Based on this analysis, here are some insights to refine the problem statement and solution development:

- **Resident needs:** Consider diverse demographics and cultural preferences when designing solutions. Affordability and convenience remain key factors.
- **Local business concerns:** Explore partnership opportunities or incentives to encourage participation in solutions that benefit residents and businesses alike.
- **Government support:** Public health agencies might offer resources or collaborate on initiatives promoting healthy eating and supporting solutions.
- **Non-profit collaboration:** Food banks and community gardens could be valuable partners in expanding access to fresh produce.

Refined problem statement: Certain residential districts face limited proximity to grocery outlets, posing challenges for inhabitants in accessing fresh produce due to diverse needs and potential concerns of local enterprises. Therefore, the question arises: How can we enhance the availability of affordable and convenient fresh fruits and vegetables within these neighbourhoods, exploring partnerships with local businesses and non-profit organizations to create a sustainable solution?

By comprehensively considering the perspectives of all stakeholders, the design team gains a deeper understanding of the situation, enabling the development of solutions that are more inclusive, sustainable, and beneficial for the entire community. This holistic approach helps mitigate unintended consequences and fosters successful implementation of the proposed initiatives.

Design Visualization Question 3.6

Problem Statement: Lack of wheelchair-accessible features on public buses and train platforms hinders mobility for physically challenged people, restricting their ability to commute independently and participate in community activities.

Consider the perspective of different stakeholders and rewrite the above statement.

3.3.5 Iterative Refinement

Establishing a well-defined issue to address is an ongoing procedure. This guarantees the statement is crystal clear, succinct, and encapsulates the challenge comprehensively. Here's how this refinement unfolds:

- **Reviewing your analysis:** Revisit your initial assessment, verifying the statement incorporates a user-centric emphasis, specific particulars, actionable framing, and stakeholder considerations. 'Numerous residents confront obstacles in accessing grocery stores offering fresh produce within a convenient radius, often exceeding one mile, particularly those with restricted transportation means and limited financial resources. This impediment hampers their capability to sustain a balanced dietary regimen. How might we substantially enhance these residents' access to fresh fruits and vegetables within their locales in an affordable and convenient manner while concurrently exploring collaborative partnerships with local enterprises and non-profit organizations to cultivate a long-term, mutually beneficial solution?'

- **Pinpointing areas for advancement:** Scrutinize for inconsistencies, omitted information, or potential biases that may have inadvertently arisen throughout the process.
  'A substantial segment of the community encounters restricted access to grocery stores offering fresh produce, often exceeding a one-mile radius, particularly those with limited transportation options and financial constraints. This impediment hampers their capability to sustain a balanced dietary regimen. In addition, existing local businesses might harbor apprehensions concerning potential competition from novel solutions. How might we substantially enhance these residents' access to fresh fruits and vegetables within their locales in an affordable and convenient manner while concurrently exploring collaborative partnerships with local enterprises and non-profit organizations, such as food banks and community gardens, to cultivate a long-term, mutually beneficial solution that caters to all stakeholders?'
- **Refine the statement iteratively:** After reviewing the initial statement and gaining new insights, make necessary adjustments by clarifying any unclear wordings, incorporating missing perspectives from stakeholders or users, and ensuring the statement remains focused and actionable.
- **Gather collaborative feedback:** Share your revised problem statement with the design team, relevant stakeholders, and potentially external individuals for feedback. This collaborative approach helps refine the statement further, ensuring it accurately captures the multifaceted nature of the problem.
- **Embrace continuous improvement:** Remain open to further refinements based on the feedback received, as this is an iterative process, allowing you to continuously improve the problem statement throughout the design thinking journey.
  'Many residents, particularly those with limited transportation and low income, face significant challenges in accessing affordable and healthy food choices, as fresh produce is often unavailable within a one-mile radius of their neighborhoods. This limitation restricts their ability to maintain a balanced diet. In addition, existing local businesses may have concerns about potential competition from new solutions. Therefore, we must strive to substantially enhance residents' access to fresh fruits and vegetables within their communities in a way that is both affordable and convenient. To ensure a long-term solution that benefits all stakeholders, we need to foster mutually beneficial partnerships with local businesses (such as offering incentives for stocking fresh produce) and non-profit organizations (such as food banks and community gardens).'

Design Visualization Question 3.7

Safe Playgrounds for Children

Problem Statement: The lack of well-maintained playgrounds and safe play areas in certain neighborhoods restricts children's opportunities for outdoor recreation and physical activity.

Iteratively refine the above problem statement. Ensure the statement incorporates a user-centric focus, specific details, actionable framing, and stakeholder considerations. Look for inconsistencies, missing information, or potential biases that may have been introduced throughout the process.

By iteratively refining the core problem statement, you lay a solid foundation for the ideation stage. This meticulous process ensures your brainstorming session is well-directed, helping you generate creative solutions that address the diverse needs of the community and all the stakeholders involved.

Design Visualization Question 3.8

Workplace Inefficiency: A business analyst might identify that "Employees waste significant time searching for internal documents." Here, the focus would be on understanding how employees find and access information within the company. By analyzing user workflows, interviewing employees, and observing their document search patterns, the designer could identify opportunities for improved document organization, search functionality, or knowledge-sharing platforms.

Collect data and perform the 'analysis and synthesis' exercise for physically challenged people and define the core problem with the help of the steps given below. (You can also do it imaginatively).

Step 1: User-centric focus
Step 2: Specificity and clarity
Step 3: Actionable framing
Step 4: Considering different perspectives
Step 5: Iterative refinement

3.4 Identify User Needs and Opportunities (Step 3)

Step 3 of the define stage focuses on understanding the user's needs and identifying potential opportunities to address the core problem. Table 3.4 provides a breakdown of what this step involves.

Table 3.4 Steps in identifying user needs and opportunities

Step	Description	Example
Step 1	Identifying user needs	**Accessibility:** Closer and more convenient access to healthy food options. **Affordability:** Affordable options for healthy food within budget. **Variety and Choice:** Diverse range of fresh and culturally relevant healthy food options. **Quality and Safety:** Confidence in the quality and safety of available food options. **Convenience:** Convenience of purchasing and preparing healthy food options.
Step 2	Prioritizing needs	**Affordability:** This is prioritized as it likely impacts everyone in the community and directly affects their ability to purchase healthy food. **Accessibility:** This is prioritized as it addresses a significant barrier for many residents. **Variety and Choice:** This is important but might be addressed slightly later due to potential resource limitations. **Quality and Safety:** While crucial, this might be addressed through existing regulations and might not require immediate, specific solutions. **Convenience:** This might be explored in the future but might not be the most immediate priority.

(Continued)

Step	Description	Example
Step 3	Identifying opportunities	Prioritized user needs {Top 2}: Affordability and Accessibility **Potential opportunities** **Partner with existing grocery stores:** Offer subsidies or incentives to encourage them to stock more affordable and diverse healthy food options. **Develop a mobile app:** Create an app that helps residents find the nearest and most affordable sources of healthy food options,including farmers' markets and community gardens. **Advocate for policy changes:** Lobby for local policies that increase access to healthy food options through food banks, nutrition programs, or transportation subsidies.
Step 4	Diversifying perspectives	1. **Seek diverse voices:** **Interview stakeholders beyond the initial group:** This could include community leaders, local businesses (such as farmers, grocers), healthcare professionals, and policymakers, each offering unique perspectives. **Consider demographic factors:** Include individuals of different ages, ethnicities, income levels, and abilities to gain a holistic understanding of the challenges faced by various subgroups within the community. 2. **Question our own biases:** Acknowledge and challenge our preconceived notions about the community and the problem. **Engage in critical thinking:** Analyze the collected data from different angles, looking for potential inconsistencies or overlooked aspects. 3. **Consider unexpected perspectives:** **Think outside the box:** Explore viewpoints of individuals not directly impacted by the problem, such as environmentalists, urban planners, or technology enthusiasts.

3.4.1 Identifying User Needs

Following the empathize stage, a crucial step in design thinking involves analysing user data, particularly interview transcripts, to gather the underlying needs and desires of the community regarding healthy food access.

Here's how to unlock these insights: Revisit interview transcripts, notes, and observations collected during the empathize stage. Analyze the data for recurring themes and patterns related to user needs, desires, and struggles when accessing healthy food. Pay close attention to both explicitly stated needs and those implicitly revealed through user challenges:

- **Accessibility:** Closer and more convenient access to healthy food options.
- **Affordability:** Affordable options for healthy food within budget.
- **Variety and Choice:** Diverse range of fresh and culturally relevant healthy food options.
- **Quality and Safety:** Confidence in the quality and safety of available food options.
- **Convenience:** Convenience of purchasing and preparing healthy food options.

Suppose individuals express sentiments such as 'The sole grocery establishment is situated an inconvenient distance away, and its pricing is exorbitant' or 'I desire access to fresh produce reminiscent of my former abode' or 'Preparing nutritious meals is arduous due to the paucity of available options'.

Through meticulous examination of user data and granular identification of user requirements, a profound comprehension of the underlying quandaries is attained. This comprehensive analysis facilitates the subsequent phase prioritizing the most critical needs to concentrate on during the solution development process.

Design Visualization Question 3.9

Problem Statement 1: *Public Transportation Reliability*: Frequent delays, cancellations, and overcrowded buses and trains create frustration and inconvenience for commuters, hindering their ability to rely on public transportation and impacting their time management.

Problem Statement 2: *Limited Access to Mental Healthcare*: The high cost of therapy and limited availability of mental health professionals create significant barriers for individuals seeking mental health support, impacting their overall well-being.

Identify various needs based on the above problem statements.

3.4.2 Prioritizing Needs

Addressing every requirement with equal importance can hinder progress. Prioritizing crucial needs based on user impact and feasibility within project constraints becomes paramount. This strategic approach allows the design team to concentrate on solutions that significantly elevate the user experience. Having identified various user needs previously, the next logical step involves prioritizing them according to importance and impact. Understanding the end-users' challenges, preferences, and objectives is key to determining the most critical needs. By prioritizing user needs, designers ensure solutions tailored to specific user requirements, resulting in more effective and satisfying outcomes.

For instance, if a designer works on a healthcare app, they may prioritize easy access to medical information for users managing chronic conditions. With this priority in focus, the designer can develop features such as personalized health tracking and reminders, enabling users to effectively manage their health (Fig. 3.8).

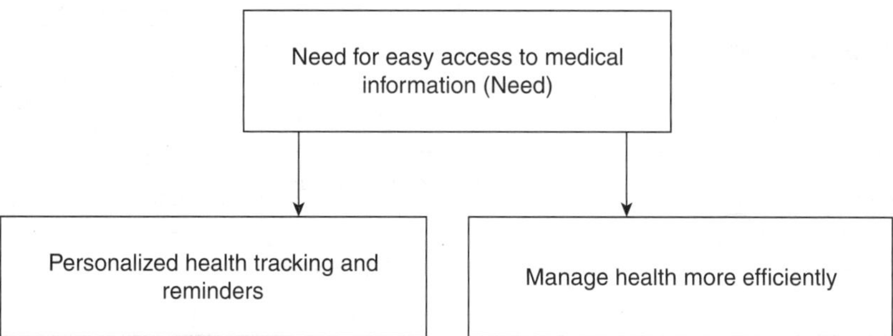

Figure 3.8 Prioritizing needs

Designers should understand user needs and wants to create successful products. They can use surveys and interviews to gather information on desired features, like easy-to-use interfaces or personalized options. With this user data, designers pinpoint the most important requirements for most users. Empathy mapping also helps designers better comprehend user perspectives, wishes, and frustrations.

Addressing real user needs, rather than guessing preferences, enhances product success. This user-centered approach fosters more innovation than trial-and-error development methods. Accounting for user wants creates products better suited to requirements versus conventional options. Ultimately, this method boosts satisfaction since designs consider user input from the start. Prioritizing user needs helps ensure you focus on the needs that matter most to the The needs identified in the previous step can be prioritized as follows:

- **Affordability:** This is prioritized as it likely impacts everyone in the community and directly affects their ability to purchase healthy food.
- **Accessibility:** This is prioritized as it addresses a significant barrier for many residents.
- **Variety and Choice:** This is important but might be addressed slightly later due to potential resource limitations.
- **Quality and Safety:** While crucial, this might be addressed through existing regulations and might not require immediate, specific solutions.
- **Convenience:** This might be explored in the future but might not be the most immediate priority.

3.4.3 Identifying Opportunities

Based on the understanding of user needs and the defined core problem, identify potential opportunities to create solutions. This involves exploring different ways to overcome the challenges and fulfill user needs. Think creatively and consider various approaches. Let us take two needs that are on the top of the list: Affordability and Accessibility (Fig. 3.9).

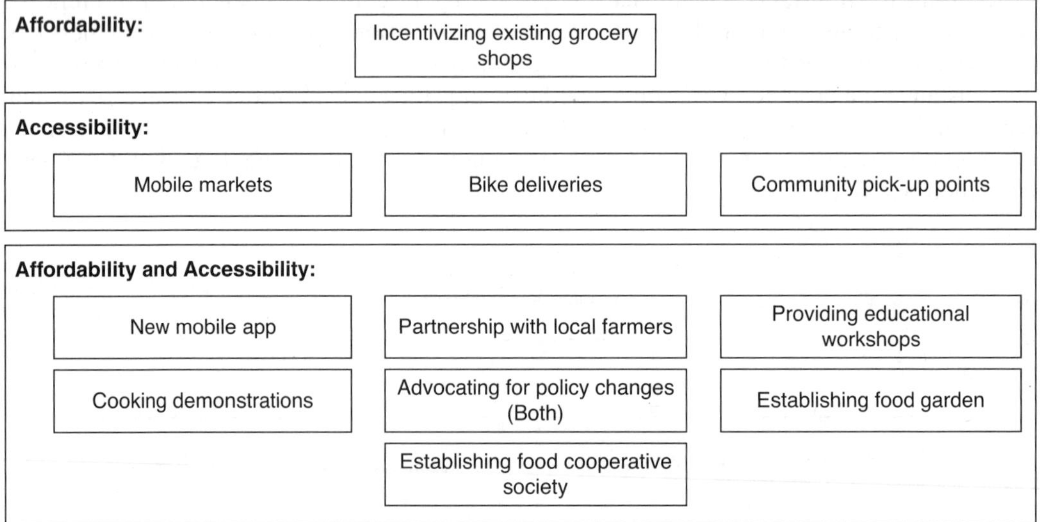

Figure 3.9 Affordability and Accessibility needs

Need 1: Affordability

Incentivizing existing grocery shops: Offering tax breaks or rebates incentivizes stores to stock and promote affordable healthy options.

Need 2: Accessibility (High Priority)

Implementing innovative delivery systems for fresh produce: Explore options such as:

- Mobile markets
- Bike deliveries
- Community pick-up points for pre-ordered produce boxes

Both Affordability and Accessibility

- **Develop a mobile app:** The app can highlight stores with ongoing promotions, discount coupons, and information about food banks or assistance programs (affordability). The app can include features like filtering by accessibility options (delivery available, ramps present), real-time inventory levels, and directions with public transportation options (accessibility).
- **Partnerships with local farmers or grocery stores:** This can potentially address both affordability and accessibility by negotiating lower prices and implementing delivery solutions. This can lead to bulk discounts, negotiated pricing on fruits and vegetables, or participation in CSA programs, making healthy food more affordable (affordability). Work with stores to improve delivery options for residents with limited mobility or transportation issues (accessibility).
- **Providing educational workshops:** Workshops can teach residents how to grow their own food (accessibility) and cook healthy meals on a budget (affordability).
- **Facilitating cooking demonstrations:** Like workshops, demonstrations can address both needs by teaching how to use affordable ingredients (affordability) and potentially offering mobile demonstrations in areas with limited access to stores (accessibility).
- **Establishing a food cooperative society:** Provides both affordability (lower prices) and accessibility (community ownership and potentially more convenient locations).
- **Establishing a food garden:** Offers affordability (low-cost produce) and accessibility (increased availability in the community).

By identifying potential opportunities that align with user needs and the available context, you lay the groundwork for the next step in the design thinking process: developing a point of view (POV) that frames the design challenge and guides the creation of innovative solutions.

Design Visualization Question 3.10

Public Park Safety

Problem Statement: Poor lighting, limited security measures, and a lack of engaging activities in public parks after dark deter residents from using them, hindering opportunities for outdoor recreation and community interaction.

Prioritized Needs

1. **Safety:** This is the highest priority as it directly impacts residents' well-being and discourages park usage.
2. **Accessibility:** Ensuring parks are accessible for people with disabilities is vital but may be secondary.
3. **Engagement:** Creating a more engaging atmosphere might be considered later.

Identify different opportunities based on the above prioritized needs.

3.4.4 Diversifying Perspectives

It is essential to consider diverse perspectives when brainstorming opportunities. Encourage team members to think creatively and explore different viewpoints. This approach fosters innovative solutions that address the needs and opportunities identified. Avoid limiting solutions to traditional approaches. Instead, broaden your understanding by considering various viewpoints. This process ensures inclusive solutions that cater to the entire community's requirements, rather than catering to a narrow segment.

Here's what we can do to diversify perspectives in the scenario of limited access to healthy food:

- **Seek diverse voices**
  - **Interview stakeholders beyond the initial group:** This could include community leaders, local businesses (such as farmers, grocers), healthcare professionals, and policymakers, each offering unique perspectives.
  - **Consider demographic factors:** Include individuals of different ages, ethnicities, income levels, and abilities to gain a holistic understanding of the challenges faced by various subgroups within the community.
- **Utilize creative methods**
  - **Conduct workshops or focus groups:** These activities can gather diverse opinions and spark new ideas for solutions.
  - **Review existing research and data:** Look for reports, studies, or surveys conducted in similar communities or on related topics.
  - **Consider the historical context:** Explore how historical events or policies might have contributed to the current situation.
- **Challenge assumptions**
  - **Question our own biases:** Acknowledge and challenge our preconceived notions about the community and the problem.
  - **Engage in critical thinking:** Analyze the collected data from different angles, looking for potential inconsistencies or overlooked aspects.
- **Consider unexpected perspectives**
  - **Think outside the box:** Explore viewpoints of individuals not directly impacted by the problem, like environmentalists, urban planners, or technology enthusiasts.

3.5 Develop a Point of View (POV) (Step 4)

Step 4 of the define phase involves creating a point of view (POV) statement. This statement encapsulates the design team's perspective on how to address the core problem, opportunities and fulfill user needs. Table 3.5 provides a breakdown of what this step entails.

Table 3.5 Developing a point of view (POV)

Step	Description	Example
Step 1	Formulating the POV statement	To improve the health and well-being of our community, particularly low-income residents and those with limited transportation, we need to design a user-centered network of accessible and affordable fresh produce distribution points, partnering with local businesses and organizations while fostering a sense of community ownership.
Step 2	Refining and validating	A well-defined POV acts as a guiding principle for the design process. It keeps the team focused on the intended outcomes and helps ensure that all brainstorming and ideation efforts are directed towards solutions that address the defined problem and meet user needs.

3.5.1 Formulating the POV Statement

Creating an actionable statement that encapsulates the team's vision and roadmap for tackling the issue is crucial. The POV should articulate assumptions about the user, their requirements, and how the design can cater to them. A well-crafted POV statement guides designers to maintain a user-centric focus, which is essential for developing effective solutions. An ideal POV statement should prioritize human needs, be actionable, and be specific.
Here's how we can proceed:

Combine insights and needs: Connect the core challenge with user needs. Refer to the core problem statement and the identified user needs from previous stages. Consolidate these insights into a concise statement.

'Individuals with limited financial resources and transportation options face significant obstacles in accessing fresh, affordable produce due to a scarcity of nearby grocery stores. This restricts their ability to incorporate healthy dietary choices (problem statement). Consequently, these residents prioritize accessibility (proximity and convenience) and affordability (options within their budget) when seeking nutritious food (user needs 1 and 2).'

Introduce a design solution approach: Briefly outline how the design process aims to address the identified problem and user needs. Emphasize that the solution will be developed with the user at the forefront, considering their specific needs and preferences. A user-friendly solution addressing these obstacles involves establishing easily accessible and cost-effective outlets for distributing fresh produce within local neighbourhoods. This approach will be developed through active collaboration with community members, carefully considering their specific requirements and preferences.

Craft a clear and concise statement: Consolidate the previously formulated statements into a cohesive, straightforward sentence that encapsulates the core issue, user needs, and the proposed solution strategy.

'POV: To foster improved well-being and health among our community, particularly those with limited transportation or low-income circumstances, we must design an accessible and affordable network of fresh produce distribution points centered around user needs. This initiative will involve partnerships with local businesses and organizations while nurturing a sense of community ownership.'

Design Visualization Question 3.11

Public Park Safety

Problem Statement: Poor lighting, limited security measures, and a lack of engaging activities in public parks after dark deter residents from using them, hindering opportunities for outdoor recreation and community interaction.

User Needs
Safety: Residents prioritize feeling safe while using the park.
Accessibility: Ensure parks are accessible for people with disabilities.
Engagement: Create a more inviting atmosphere to encourage park usage.

Create a point of view (POV) based on the above problem statement and user needs.

This POV statement encompasses the following key elements:

- **Human-centered:** Prioritizes enhancing the health and well-being of specific user groups.
- **Actionable:** Identifies the design of a user-centered network as a potential solution.
- **Specific:** Emphasizes accessibility, affordability, local partnerships, and fostering community ownership.

3.5.2 Refining and Validating

Working closely with the team and key people involved, explore the draft problem statement in depth. Gather input and refine it repeatedly to ensure it mirrors the group's goals and aligns with user needs accurately. We refine and validate the draft problem statement from the previous stages. This involves collaboration and feedback to verify that the statement accurately captures the collective understanding of the issue, user needs, and design direction. Share the proposed statement with the entire design team and any crucial stakeholders for the project. Facilitate an open discussion where everyone contributes their viewpoints, asks clarifying questions, and provides constructive feedback on the statement. Does it convey the intended message clearly and concisely? Does it accurately reflect the identified user needs and challenges? Does it provide clear guidance for generating potential solutions in the next phase? Encourage diverse voices and perspectives within the team and from stakeholders.

Incorporate the gathered feedback to revise the problem statement, addressing identified points to ensure clarity, user-centricity, and actionable direction. While integrating feedback, ensure that revisions stay aligned with the project's core message and vision. Depending on the project's complexity and feedback received, you may need to repeat the discussion and refinement process iteratively until you achieve a comprehensive and well-rounded problem statement. Once finalized, consider sharing the problem statement with a representative sample of potential users to gather feedback and ensure it resonates with their experiences and needs. This collaborative and iterative process helps ensure the final problem statement is robust, accurate, and effectively guides the design team towards developing solutions that genuinely address the community's needs. Remember, the problem statement is a living document that can be revisited and refined throughout the design thinking process as new information and insights emerge.

Importance of POV: A concise POV fuels the design journey, steering the team's creativity towards meaningful solutions. It acts as a compass, ensuring all brainstorming efforts align with the core challenge and user needs. The POV distils key insights about the problem, user requirements, and potential opportunities into a clear, focused direction. This guiding principle cements a shared understanding of the design objective. It highlights the user's perspective, embedding a user-centric approach.

3.6 Create 'How Might We' Questions (Step 5)

Step 5 of the define phase involves crafting 'how might we' (HMW) questions. These questions serve as prompts for brainstorming and ideation in the next phase of the design thinking process. These questions are open-ended and help to generate a wide range of ideas and solutions (Table 3.6).

Table 3.6 Creating 'how might we' questions

Step	Description	Example
Step 1	Formulating HMV questions	How might we simplify access to fresh produce for community members with limited transportation options? (Addresses affordability and accessibility for a specific sub-group)
		How might we design a mobile app that combines grocery ordering with nutrition education for residents of all ages? (Integrates technology and addresses knowledge gaps)
		How might we incentivize local restaurants to offer healthier menu options while maintaining affordability? (Focuses on collaboration and addresses pricing concerns)
		How might we encourage local grocery stores to offer discounts on healthy food options?
Step 2	Focusing on the POV	**Original HMW question:** How might we encourage local grocery stores to offer discounts on healthy food options?
		Revised HMW question: (Considering the POV focuses on affordability and accessibility) How might we incentivize local grocery stores to offer affordable, culturally relevant healthy food options in easily accessible locations within the community?

Purpose of HMW questions: HMW questions play a pivotal role in problem-solving. They steer the design team towards brainstorming potential solutions while staying true to the established POV. Moreover, they foster divergent thinking, discouraging immediate convergence on a single solution and encouraging open-ended exploration. The open-ended nature of the questions helps spark creativity and generate innovative ideas that might not be readily apparent. HMW questions maintain a user-centric focus. By aligning with the POV, they ensure the ideation process remains laser-focused on the needs and challenges of the target users.

3.6.1 Formulating HMW Questions

Each HMW question should begin with the phrase 'how might we...' followed by a specific aspect of the core problem or user need. The question should be phrased in a way that prompts creative problem-solving and encourages the generation of diverse ideas.

- **Follow the basic structure**
  - **Begin with HMW:** Each question should start with this phrase, establishing the open-ended and exploratory nature of the question.
  - **Focus on specific aspects:** The second part of the question should address a specific aspect of the core problem or user needs identified in previous steps.
  - **Encourage problem-solving:** The question needs to be phrased in a way that prompts creative thinking, encourages exploration, and invites the generation of diverse solutions.

- **Avoid common pitfalls**
  - **'Yes/No' questions:** Avoid HMW questions that can be answered with a simple yes or no, as they limit the brainstorming process.
  - **Narrow focus:** Avoid questions that are too specific, as they restrict the exploration of broader possibilities.
  - **Solution-oriented questions:** Avoid framing the question with a particular solution in mind, as this hinders creative thinking.
- **Leverage the POV**
  - **Align with the POV:** Ensure each HMW question aligns with the established POV statement. This guarantees that the generated solutions remain focused on the identified needs and direction outlined in the POV.
  - **Use keywords:** Consider incorporating keywords from the POV statement into the HMW questions to maintain coherence and ensure the exploration adheres to the user-centric approach.

Following these steps and considerations, we can structure practical HMW questions as effective launching pads for the ideation phase. Building on the scenario, here are some examples of well-structured HMW questions:

- How might we simplify access to fresh produce for community members with limited transportation options? (Addresses affordability and accessibility for a specific sub-group)
- How might we design a mobile app that combines grocery ordering with nutrition education for residents of all ages? (Integrates technology and addresses knowledge gaps)
- How might we incentivize local restaurants to offer healthier menu options while maintaining affordability? (Focuses on collaboration and addresses pricing concerns)
- How might we partner with local chefs to develop affordable and culturally relevant healthy meal kits for residents to purchase and prepare at home? (Addresses affordability, collaboration, and education)
- How might we gamify healthy eating habits and incentivize residents to participate in community-based cooking classes and nutrition workshops? (Addresses education, technology, and community involvement)

3.6.2 Focusing on the POV

We ensure that all HMW questions generated align directly with the defined POV statement. This maintains the user-centric approach and guarantees that brainstormed solutions remain relevant to the identified core problem and user needs.

- **Original HMW question:** How might we encourage local grocery stores to offer discounts on healthy food options?
- **Revised HMW question:** (Considering the POV focuses on affordability and accessibility) How might we incentivize local grocery stores to offer affordable, culturally relevant healthy food options in easily accessible locations within the community?

By aligning the HMW questions with the POV, we guide the ideation phase towards exploring user-centered solutions, address the core problem effectively, and ultimately benefit the community meaningfully.

Design Visualization Question 3.12

Limited Access to After-School Care
Problem Statement: The scarcity of affordable after-school childcare options forces working parents to choose between work and childcare, creating a significant burden for families and potentially hindering children's academic and social development.

User Needs
- **Affordability:** Families prioritize finding cost-effective after-school childcare.
- **Availability:** Ensure enough after-school programs exist to meet the demand.
- **Quality:** Maintain a high standard of care and educational enrichment for children.
- **Safety and Security:** Guarantee a safe and secure environment for children after school hours.

Define opportunities, create a point of view (POV) and formulate possible HMW questions based on the above problem statement and user needs.

Summary

- The transition from the empathize to the define phase entails understanding needs and gaining insights from the empathize stage.
- The define stage creates a framework for further exploration of design thinking, turning insights into actionable opportunities.
- A well-framed problem statement is crucial in this stage, focusing on end-users and their needs.
- Data analysis is a powerful tool in the define phase, identifying patterns and insights that inform the problem statement.
- Open-ended questions starting with 'how might we' generate a wide range of ideas and solutions.
- Creating a point of view (POV) is essential in the define phase, synthesizing information from the empathize stage to create a clear statement that captures the core problem.
- An affinity diagram is a visual mapping method used to organize information and structure ideas during problem-solving, breaking down complex problems into manageable parts.

Solutions to Design Visualization Questions

Q 3.3

1. **Public Park Usage**
   Initial: The public park is underutilized.
   Refined: Due to a lack of engaging activities and limited accessibility features, residents rarely visit the park, hindering opportunities for community recreation and social interaction.
2. **Recycling Program Participation**
   Initial: Residents are not recycling properly.
   Refined: Confusing recycling guidelines and limited access to bins in certain neighborhoods lead to residents discarding recyclables incorrectly, reducing the program's effectiveness.

3. **Customer Retention Rates**
   Initial: Our online store is losing customers.
   Refined: Frustrated by a complex check-out process and lack of transparency regarding shipping costs, customers abandon their carts before completing purchases, leading to decreased sales and customer retention.

Q 3.4

Before Specificity and Clarity: In employee onboarding, due to a lack of structure, unclear expectations, and limited opportunities for mentorship, new employees feel overwhelmed and confused, hindering their ability to integrate smoothly and reach full productivity.

After Specificity and Clarity: During their first week, new employees at [Company Name] often report feeling overwhelmed due to a lack of structure in the onboarding program. Unclear expectations about their roles and responsibilities, coupled with limited opportunities for mentorship from experienced colleagues, contribute to confusion and hinder their ability to integrate smoothly into the team. This delays their ramp-up time and impacts their ability to reach full productivity within the first [Target Timeframe].

Q 3.5

Problem Statement: Overflowing trash cans and limited recycling options in apartment buildings contribute to an unsightly and unsanitary environment for residents, negatively impacting their well-being.

Refined Problem Statement: Limited trash can capacity and a lack of convenient recycling options in apartment buildings lead to overflowing bins and create an unsanitary environment for residents. How might we create a more efficient and user-friendly waste management system within apartment complexes?

Q 3.6

Public Transportation Accessibility

Problem Statement: Lack of wheelchair-accessible features on public buses and train platforms hinders mobility for physically challenged people, restricting their ability to commute independently and participate in community activities.

Refined Problem Statement: The current public transportation system lacks sufficient wheelchair-accessible features on buses and train platforms, significantly limiting mobility and independence physically challenged people. How might we create a more inclusive transportation system by ensuring all public vehicles and stations are fully accessible for physically challenged people?

Q 3.7

Safe Playgrounds for Children

Problem Statement: The lack of well-maintained playgrounds and safe play areas in certain neighborhoods restricts children's opportunities for outdoor recreation and physical activity.

Refined Problem Statement: Unequal access to safe and well-equipped playgrounds within the community limits opportunities for outdoor play and physical activity for children in certain neighborhoods. How might we create a network of accessible and inclusive playgrounds throughout the city, ensuring all children have spaces for safe and healthy recreation?

Q 3.9

Here are some examples showcasing problem statements and their corresponding identified needs:

1. Public Transportation Reliability

Problem Statement: Frequent delays, cancellations, and overcrowded buses and trains create frustration and inconvenience for commuters, hindering their ability to rely on public transportation and impacting their time management.

Identified Needs:

- **Reliability:** Consistent schedules and on-time arrival/departure of public transportation.
- **Frequency:** Availability of frequent services to reduce wait times and overcrowding.
- **Capacity:** Increased capacity within vehicles to ensure comfortable and safe travel.
- **Accessibility:** Services that cater to people with disabilities, including features like ramps and designated seating.
- **Real-time Information:** Access to real-time information on schedules, delays, and disruptions.

2. Limited Access to Mental Healthcare

Problem Statement: The high cost of therapy and limited availability of mental health professionals create significant barriers for individuals seeking mental health support, impacting their overall well-being.

Identified Needs:

- **Affordability:** Affordable therapy sessions or subsidized programs for low-income individuals.
- **Accessibility:** Increased availability of mental health professionals within the community.
- **Awareness:** Educational campaigns to raise awareness about mental health and reduce stigma.
- **Telehealth Options:** Availability of telehealth services to provide remote access to mental health professionals.
- **Culturally Competent Care:** Access to mental healthcare professionals trained in cultural competency.

Q 3.10

Public Park Safety

Opportunities:

- **Partnerships with local organizations:** Collaborate with police departments and community watch groups to increase park security patrols.
- **Community programming:** Organize events and activities like movie nights, fitness classes, or art workshops to attract diverse user groups.
- **Upgraded facilities:** Improve park infrastructure by including accessible restrooms, playgrounds, walking paths, or dog parks.
- **Public art installations:** Encourage local artists to create interactive installations to add visual interest and spark community engagement.

Q 3.11

Public Park Safety

POV: To revitalize our public parks and promote a sense of community, we need to design a solution that prioritizes safety through improved lighting and security, while fostering engagement with exciting activities and programs. This will be achieved through collaboration with local residents and stakeholders.

Q 3.12

Limited Access to After-School Care

Problem Statement: The scarcity of affordable after-school childcare options forces working parents to choose between work and childcare, creating a significant burden for families and potentially hindering children's academic and social development.

User Needs:

- **Affordability:** Families prioritize finding cost-effective after-school childcare.
- **Availability:** Ensure enough after-school programs exist to meet the demand.
- **Quality:** Maintain a high standard of care and educational enrichment for children.
- **Safety and security:** Guarantee a safe and secure environment for children after school hours.

Opportunities:

- **Partnerships with schools:** Collaborate with schools to utilize existing facilities and resources for after-school programs.
- **Government funding and grants:** Explore opportunities for government funding or grant programs to subsidize after-school care costs.
- **Volunteer recruitment and training:** Develop a program to recruit and train volunteers from the community to assist with after-school care activities.
- **Flexible scheduling options:** Offer various scheduling options to cater to the diverse needs of working families.
- **Educational enrichment activities:** Integrate engaging and educational activities into the after-school programs to support children's development.

POV Statement: To support working families and provide enriching experiences for children, we need to design a network of accessible and affordable after-school care programs. This solution will be developed through collaboration with schools, government agencies, and the community, prioritizing affordability, quality care, and a safe environment.

HMW Questions:

1. HMW design a sliding-scale fee structure for after-school care programs, ensuring affordability for low-income families? (Addresses affordability and accessibility)
2. HMW leverage technology to create a central platform where parents can easily search for, register for, and manage their children's after-school care arrangements? (Addresses accessibility through technology)
3. HMW create a training program for volunteers that equips them with the skills and knowledge to provide effective after-school care and educational enrichment activities? (Addresses quality, affordability through volunteer integration, and educational needs)

Exercises

Part A (Objective Questions)

1. You are a design thinker working on a project to improve the user experience of an online shopping platform. You have conducted user research and gathered insights during the empathize stage. What is the next step you should take in the design thinking process?
   (a) Start creating solutions based on your assumptions.
   (b) State your users' needs and problems in a human-centered manner.

(c) Test your solutions with real users and collect feedback.
(d) Challenge your assumptions and create ideas for possible solutions.

2. You are a design thinker working on a project to improve the accessibility of public transportation for people with disabilities. You have defined the problem and decided what the project should cover during the define stage. What is the next step you should take in the design thinking process?
(a) Start creating solutions based on your problem statement.
(b) Test your solutions with real users and collect feedback.
(c) Challenge your assumptions and create ideas for possible solutions.
(d) Conduct user research and gather insights about their needs and experiences.

Part B (Short Answer Questions)

1. Write a short note on the define phase of the design thinking process.
2. What is a problem statement? What is an actionable and measureable problem statement?
3. What is an affinity diagram?
4. What are the steps in defining a point of view?
5. Give examples of assistive technologies.
6. Why is the define phase crucial in the design thinking process?
7. Define a well-framed problem statement.
8. Write a short note on the importance of 'how might we' questions.
9. A problem looks like this, before specificity and clarity: "Due to limited grocery store access, unreliable transportation, high food costs and a lack of knowledge about healthy food preparation, community members struggle to find and cannot afford fresh healthy fruits and vegetables, leading to a scarcity of healthy food choices in their daily diet." Convert this to include specificity and clarity.

Part C (Essay Questions)

1. What are the different techniques for defining and reframing the problem?
2. How is the affinity diagram used in design thinking?

Answer Key

Part A

1. (b) **2.** (c)

CHAPTER 4

The Ideation Stage

Learning Objectives

At the end of this chapter, you will be able to:

- Explain the essence and significance of the ideation phase in design thinking, including a comprehensive understanding of its purpose and the importance of clearly articulating the problem statement to uncover latent needs
- List a variety of ideation techniques and tools, such as brainstorming, brainwriting, reverse brainstorming, mind mapping, rapid prototyping, role-playing, storytelling, sketching, SCAMPER, and visualization, and how to apply them effectively to foster creativity and innovation
- Describe the concepts of divergence and convergence in the context of idea generation and how to balance these opposing forces to enhance the ideation process
- Explain the methods for evaluating ideas critically and the use of various ideation tools like sticky notes, whiteboards, Post-its, pens and pencils, 3D sketches, and idea management software to organize and refine concepts
- Provide insightful case studies on ideation and the application of systematic inventive thinking (SIT) to generate novel solutions
- Explain the techniques for recognizing and interpreting weak signals in the ideation process and the strategic approach of three-box thinking to manage present challenges while simultaneously creating future opportunities

4.1 Introduction

Once upon a time, a group of designers were asked to design a new car. They wanted it to be eco-friendly and knew what their users would need. So, they gathered pens, paper, sticky notes, and their brains to brainstorm! They used mind maps, sketches, and storytelling to develop ideas like solar-powered engines and car seats made from recycled materials.

First, they organized their thoughts into themes to decide which ideas had the most potential. Then they used clay models and cardboard cutouts for prototyping the features they liked best. After a lot of testing and refining, the team was finally happy with the design for their eco-friendly car! It had an aerodynamic shape, was made from recycled materials, had a solar-powered engine, and included comfortable seating for passengers. All these ideas were born in the ideation stage, when the team brainstormed new ideas. This allowed them to quickly develop many innovative possibilities without wasting time or resources. The extraordinary result met all their users' needs.

4.2 What and Why of the Ideation Stage

Coming up with ideas is a vital part of the design thinking process. This stage encourages creative and innovative thinking to find unique answers to complex issues. Ideation promotes divergent thinking. It enables the generation of many ideas without judgement or criticism. It also enables designers to explore and develop innovative solutions. Ideation helps designers concentrate on user needs and insights from research. It ensures that the solutions address the target audience's needs.

When creating a new product, the design thinking team may use mind maps to brainstorm ideas. They could use SCAMPER (Substitute, Combine, Adapt, Modify, Put to another use, Eliminate, and Reverse) to modify existing products. Or random words to spark novel concepts. They could try reverse brainstorming to generate alternative solutions. The team can develop as many concepts as possible. Even those that seem unrealistic or absurd.

For instance, when ideating a new restaurant concept, the team can suggest unconventional ideas, such as a restaurant in a treehouse or serving food on a conveyor belt.

A team designing a new personal finance app analyses ideas based on feasibility, such as the development resources required, and impact, like helping users save money or track spending (Fig. 4.1). They consider each idea's novelty and alignment with the user's needs. After evaluation, a few ideas may advance, such as using machine learning for personalized budgets or gamified savings challenges. These ideas then undergo refinement and further development during the prototyping and testing phases.

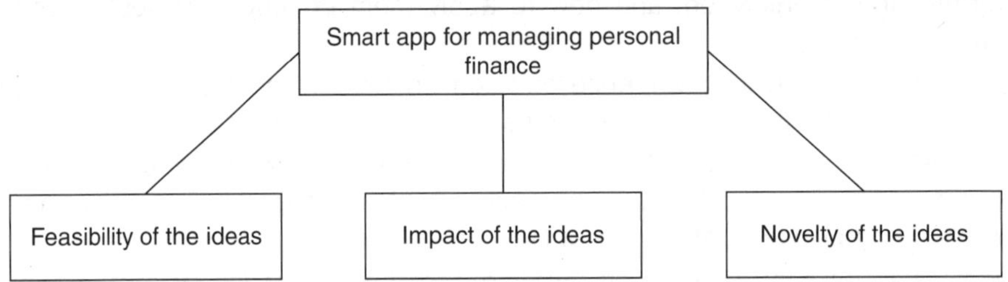

Figure 4.1 Smart app for managing personal finance

Ideation prioritizes user needs, so designers consider the proposed solutions' impact on the end-user experience.

For example, a debt management platform equipped with intuitive tracking tools can grant users a transparent view of their repayment journey, amplifying motivation through tangible visualizations of progress made. This empowers individuals to take control and effectively navigate the path to financial freedom. Leveraging artificial intelligence (AI)-driven analytics, the personalized insights feature offers tailored advice and recommendations meticulously crafted for each user's unique financial circumstances.

4.3 Clear Articulation of the Problem Statement with Focus on Latent Needs

Clear articulation of the problem statement is crucial in the design thinking process. It enables designers to identify and understand the users' needs. Often the problem statement is limited to the evident surface-level problems. However, it is also essential to identify the latent needs of the users. Latent needs are unmet or unarticulated needs that the user may have, need to be made aware of, or need help to express clearly (Fig. 4.2).

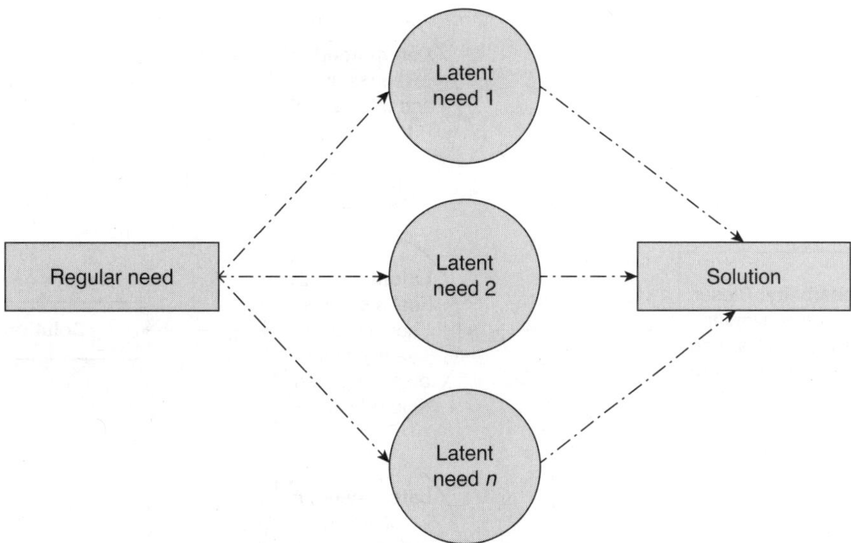

Figure 4.2 Needs and latent needs

Discovering latent needs can prove advantageous during the ideation stage of design thinking, empowering designers to craft groundbreaking solutions catering to unaddressed user needs. This methodology entails deeply understanding users, gleaning insights into their behavior, and observing their interactions with products and services. By delving beneath surface-level problems, designers unearth profound issues influencing the user experience.

Going back to the example of access to healthy food options, here are some **surface-level** needs:

- **Accessibility:** Closer and more convenient access to healthy food options.
- **Affordability:** Affordable options for healthy food within budget.
- **Variety and Choice:** Diverse range of fresh and culturally relevant healthy food options.
- **Quality and Safety:** Confidence in the quality and safety of available food options.
- **Convenience:** Convenience of purchasing and preparing healthy food options.

Let us now identify the **latent needs** for accessibility, a surface-level need (Fig. 4.3):

- **Latent Need 1:** Reduce time and effort spent traveling to acquire fresh produce. This could involve minimizing walking distance, reducing reliance on public transportation schedules, or offering alternative delivery options (such as, bike deliveries, community pick-up points).
- **Latent Need 2:** Feel a sense of security and safety when obtaining fresh produce, especially for residents with mobility limitations. This could involve well-lit locations, accessible entrances and exits, or assistance programs for carrying groceries (such as, volunteer grocery shoppers, designated bagging areas).
- **Latent Need 3:** Maintain independence and dignity when acquiring fresh produce. This could involve offering self-service options with clear signage and assistance readily available upon request, or exploring mobile market formats that cater specifically to senior citizen residences.

Effectively communicating the issue at hand while zeroing in on underlying requirements is vital during the ideation stage of design thinking.

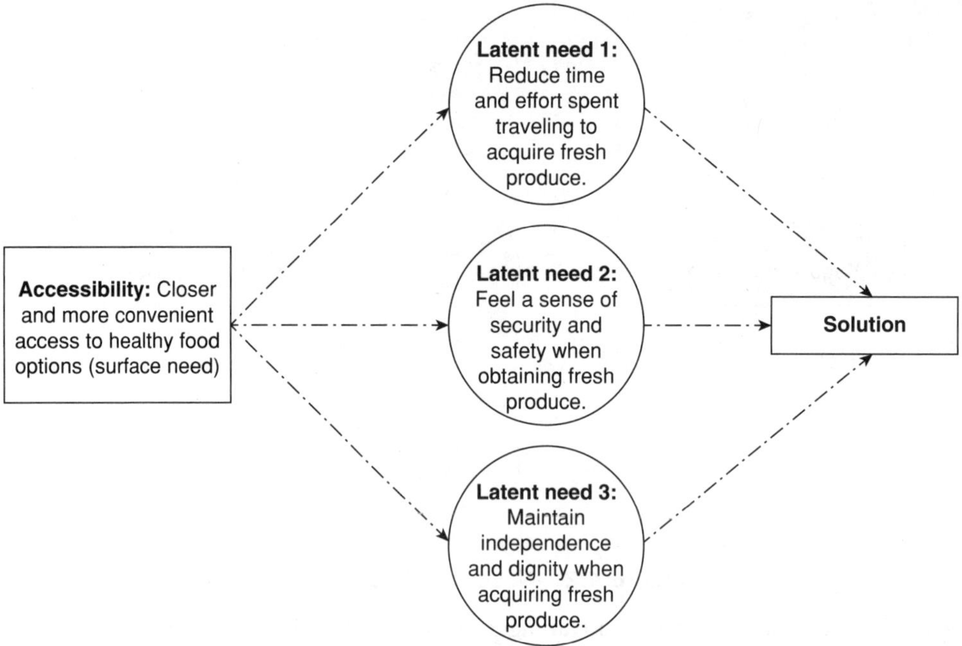

Figure 4.3 Latent needs example

Design Visualization Question 4.1

User Needs

Affordability: Affordable options for healthy food within budget.
Variety and Choice: Diverse range of fresh and culturally relevant healthy food options.
Quality and Safety: Confidence in the quality and safety of available food options.
Convenience: Convenience of purchasing and preparing healthy food options.

Identify at least 3 latent needs for each of the above user needs.

4.4 Techniques for Ideation

The ideation stage of the design thinking process emphasizes creativity and innovation. In this phase, designers explore numerous concepts without limitations. They then refine these ideas to devise an effective solution. To generate and refine ideas in the ideate phase, designers follow a creative approach. This typically involves several steps, beginning with gathering information about the problem they aim to solve. After understanding the issue, designers utilize brainstorming techniques like mind maps and SCAMPER to spark ideas. A crucial aspect of the creative process is avoiding overly critical evaluation during the brainstorming stage. The goal is to generate as many ideas as possible, even if they seem unrealistic.

Once ideas have been generated, the next step involves evaluating and refining them. This entails examining each concept, identifying its strengths and weaknesses, focusing on the most promising ideas, and discarding those that may be less feasible. During the ideate phase, designers can apply several creative principles to think innovatively and generate ideas that can lead to successful solutions.

4.4.1 Warm-up Games

Warm-up games are an essential element of design thinking as they help teams get the right mindset for creative problem-solving. They are designed to relax the team members, free their minds from distractions, and encourage them to think outside the box. They can help teams build trust, overcome communication barriers, and generate ideas in a relaxed and playful environment.
Some of the popular warm-up games are as follows:

- **Two Truths and a Lie:** A popular icebreaker game, in which each participant shares three statements about themselves, two of which are true and one false. Other participants then try to guess which statement is a lie, encouraging creativity, collaboration, and trust among participants.
- **Word Swap:** A game where each participant writes down a word related to the challenge or topic on a sticky note and places it on a wall. Then, each participant randomly picks a word from the wall and tries to generate ideas using that word as a starting point. This game encourages divergent thinking, association, and brainstorming skills.
- **Yes, And:** A game in which participants form a circle and take turns to build on each other's ideas by saying 'Yes', and then adding something new. This game promotes positive reinforcement, collaboration, and improvization skills.
- **Blind Drawing:** A game in which pairs of participants sit back to back, one with a picture and the other with a blank paper and a pen. The person with the picture has to describe it to the other person without naming the object, while the other person tries to draw it based on the description. This game fosters communication, listening, and feedback skills.
- **Word Association:** This straightforward exercise involves participants sequentially stating a term, with the subsequent individual offering a word connected to the preceding one. It nurtures ingenuity and teamwork, cultivating a constructive, affirmative dynamic within the collective.

These introductory activities are invaluable in fostering rapport, stimulating resourcefulness, and promoting collaboration during design thinking workshops. Engaging in such games orients teams toward the optimal mindset for innovative problem resolution, yielding superior outcomes.

4.4.2 Brainstorming

Brainstorming enables a team to ingeniously craft innovative and captivating concepts. This straightforward technique, applicable in person or virtually, swiftly generates a multitude of ideas. During a brainstorming session, team members are actively encouraged to share their thoughts freely, building upon each other's suggestions without judgment or critique. For instance, a marketing team might brainstorm to devise an advertising campaign; they could commence by setting a 10-minute timer and documenting as many ideas as feasible within that timeframe, without pausing to evaluate or deliberate upon them. Subsequent to the expiration of the allotted time, the group can analyze their list of ideas, identifying patterns or areas where they could refine their approach. This process empowers the team to develop creative solutions that may otherwise have remained unexplored.

Similarly, product teams can also use brainstorming to generate new product ideas. The process begins with the same basic steps: setting aside some time for free thinking and then discussing each idea further until patterns emerge from which teams can create more specific solutions. Allowing everyone in the room (or virtual space) to contribute freely during this session gives teams access to multiple perspectives, leading them towards more exciting solutions than working alone on their projects. Overall, brainstorming offers teams an effective way of generating multiple possible solutions quickly while fostering collaboration among their members – all it takes is some dedicated time!

The brainstorming process presents numerous advantages during the ideation stage of design thinking:

- **Boosts Creativity:** Brainstorming encourages innovative thinking by allowing participants to freely express novel ideas without judgement. Together, groups dissect complex problems, combining diverse viewpoints to formulate creative solutions. This open exchange of perspectives fosters more comprehensive outcomes than working alone.
- **Enhances Collaboration:** Brainstorming sessions bring together teams with varied expertise, enabling them to build upon each other's contributions for more robust solutions.
- **Widens Solution Scope:** By generating numerous ideas, brainstorming broadens the range of potential solutions, increasing the likelihood of identifying the most effective approach.
- **Facilitates Iteration:** Multiple ideas emerge during brainstorming, enabling continuous refinement toward optimal outcomes. For instance, when developing a video game, teams can explore various concepts before selecting one. Each idea undergoes evaluation, discussion, and improvement until its best version is reached. This iterative process applies across creative projects, from website design to essay writing, yielding superior results through repeated enhancement. Moreover, iteration encourages deeper contemplation, leading to more thoughtful solutions than settling for initial ideas.
- **Facilitates Prioritization:** Generating numerous concepts is just the start; participants then prioritize them based on feasibility, impact, and problem alignment. This narrows down the options, highlighting promising solutions. Prioritization also clarifies direction and resource allocation among plans.

Fundamentally, ideation stage brainstorming builds consensus among stakeholders, unifying perspectives for productive progress toward solving problems or achieving goals. Collaboration throughout this problem-solving stage enables insight sharing and efficient strategy formulation for tackling emerging issues.

Given below is an example of brainstorming.

Challenge: How might we reduce time and effort spent traveling to acquire fresh produce? (Latent need 1).

Design Thinking Experts

Expert 1: You (Design Thinking Expert)
Expert 2: (Technology and Innovation Specialist)
Expert 3: (Urban Planning and Logistics Specialist)
Expert 4: (Sustainability and Community Engagement Specialist)

Idea 1: Hyperlocal Micro-markets (Expert 3)

- Establish a network of small, walk-in kiosks stocked with fresh produce in strategic locations throughout neighborhoods.
- Partner with local farmers or distributors to ensure freshness and variety.
- Utilize technology for self-service check-out or integrate with a mobile app for pre-ordering and contactless pick-up.

Idea 2: E-grocery Bike Delivery with Incentives (Experts 2 and 4)

- Develop a user-friendly mobile app for ordering fresh produce from local grocery stores or farmers markets.
- Partner with local delivery services utilizing cargo bikes or e-bikes for environmentally friendly and efficient delivery.

- Offer subscription options with discounted delivery fees or loyalty rewards programs to encourage frequent use.

Idea 3: Community-supported Agriculture (CSA) Pick-up Points (Experts 3 and 4)

- Partner with existing CSA programs to expand their reach beyond traditional farm pick-up locations.
- Establish a network of convenient pick-up points throughout the community, like schools, community centers, or even local businesses.
- This promotes a sense of community ownership and reduces travel time for CSA members.

Idea 4: "Fresh Produce on Wheels" Mobile Market (Experts 1 and 3)

- Design a converted van or truck equipped with a refrigerated storage unit and point-of-sale system.
- Create a dynamic schedule that allows the mobile market to visit underserved areas with limited access to fresh produce.
- Utilize a mobile app or community outreach to inform residents of upcoming stops and ensure timely access.

Idea 5: Neighborhood Bartering and Seed Libraries (Expert 4)

- Facilitate a platform through a mobile app or community center for residents to barter homegrown produce, surplus pantry items, or cooking skills for fresh produce from local farmers or gardens.
- Establish seed libraries offering culturally relevant seeds and educational resources on home gardening, promoting self-sufficiency and local food production.

Idea 6: Gamified Walking Routes with Incentives (Experts 2 and 4)

- Develop a mobile app with gamified walking routes that lead users past grocery stores or farmers markets selling fresh produce.
- Integrate features like points, badges, or even small discounts on produce purchases for completing walking challenges.

These ideas explore various approaches to reducing travel time and effort, from hyperlocal micro-markets to alternative delivery models. Each option prioritizes user convenience and caters to different needs and preferences. Remember to consider factors like sustainability, community engagement, and existing infrastructure when evaluating and refining these solutions.

Design Visualization Question 4.2

Latent Need 2: How might we feel a sense of security and safety when obtaining fresh produce, especially for residents with mobility limitations. This could involve well-lit locations, accessible entrances and exits, or assistance programs for carrying groceries (volunteer grocery shoppers, designated bagging areas).

Perform brainstorming with other design thinking experts and identify at least 5 ideas for the above latent need.

4.4.3 Brainwriting

Brainwriting is a valuable tool used in the design thinking process to generate a wide range of ideas. Table 4.1 compares brainstorming and brainwriting techniques.

Table 4.1 Brainstorming versus brainwriting

S.No	Feature	Brainstorming	Brainwriting
1	Participation	Active, discussion-based	Silent, individual writing
2	Anonymity	Ideas typically attributed	Ideas often anonymous
3	Evaluation	Ideas may be judged during session	Ideas not judged until after session
4	Structure	Less structured, relies on conversation flow	Follows a specific structure (round-robin, etc.)
5	Focus	Quantity of ideas	Quality and individual reflection
6	Process	Group-driven, building on each other's ideas	Individual thinking and written expression
7	Suitability	Energizing groups, collaboration, shared ownership	Anonymity, introverts, large volume of diverse ideas
8	Materials	Minimal (whiteboard, flipchart)	Specific materials (worksheets, notecards)
9	Time Management	Easily time-boxed	May require slightly more time
10	Output	List of ideas on whiteboard/flipchart	Collection of written ideas on separate sheets

Brainwriting emphasizes individual thinking and written expression of ideas. Participants silently write down their ideas without interrupting or being influenced by others. Ideas are often anonymous, fostering a more equal playing field and encouraging participation from introverts or those hesitant to speak up in a group setting.

Brainwriting creates a 'judgment-free zone' where ideas are not critiqued or evaluated in the session. This allows for a broader range of unfiltered and creative ideas to emerge. Brainwriting typically follows a specific structure, with techniques like 'round-robin' writing, where participants pass sheets with their ideas to build upon or individual worksheets with prompts. While quality ideas are essential, brainwriting initially prioritizes generating diverse ideas to explore a problem from multiple angles. These ideas are discussed after the writing phase is complete. This allows for individual reflection and prevents groupthink or dominance by certain participants.

Brainwriting utilizes written communication, which allows for clearer expression and organization of ideas compared to a fast-paced verbal discussion. It encourages individual thinking and helps capture a wider range of perspectives and experiences within the group. Combining individual reflection, deferred judgment, and written format can lead to higher-quality ideas than traditional brainstorming. Brainwriting provides a safe space for introverts and quieter participants to contribute meaningfully to the ideation process.

Brainwriting Simulation: Reduce Travel Time for Fresh Produce

Challenge: How might we reduce time and effort spent traveling to acquire fresh produce? (Latent need 1).

Instructions

1. Imagine you are a busy resident who wants to minimize the time and effort spent traveling to acquire fresh produce.

2. Silently write down ideas on separate sheets of paper for 5 minutes, focusing on ways to reduce travel time and effort.
3. Do not judge or discuss your ideas yet.

   (Individual Brainstorming: 5 minutes)
   (Timekeeper's Note: Ring a bell or announce the end of the 5-minute period)

Sharing and Building on Ideas

1. Now, let us share our ideas one at a time. We will take turns presenting one idea each, and then we can collectively build upon or combine them to generate even more solutions.
2. Remember, there are no bad ideas!

Group Discussion and Idea Building

1. Micro-markets with self-service kiosks in convenient neighborhood locations.
2. E-grocery delivery services using bikes or electric vehicles for faster and more environmentally friendly options.
3. Subscription boxes with curated selections of seasonal fresh produce delivered directly to residents' doorsteps.
4. 'Click and Collect' options at grocery stores allowing pre-ordering of fresh produce online for pick-up at designated locations within the store.
5. Partnerships with public transportation systems offering discounted fares or dedicated routes with stops near grocery stores or farmers markets.

Design Visualization Question 4.3

Latent Need 3: Maintain independence and dignity when acquiring fresh produce. This could involve offering self-service options with clear signage and assistance readily available upon request, or exploring mobile market formats that cater specifically to senior citizen residences.

Carry out brainwriting and identify at least 5 ideas for the above latent need.

4.4.4 Reverse Brainstorming

A distinctive technique that can be employed during the ideation phase of the design thinking process is reverse brainstorming. This unconventional approach assists designers in contemplating their challenges from a novel perspective and crafting ingenious solutions. By inverting the traditional brainstorming methodology, reverse brainstorming stimulates individuals to transcend conventional thought patterns and cultivate trailblazing concepts.

Reverse brainstorming operates by meticulously scrutinizing problems/risks from diverse angles and subsequently formulating prospective resolutions. Rather than concentrating on what could or ought to be undertaken, reverse brainstorming urges participants to concentrate on what should be avoided or eradicated from an extant solution. This empowers designers to contemplate hitherto unexplored avenues, thereby yielding more innovative solutions to complex problems (Table 4.2).

For example, suppose a designer is working on creating an effective online learning platform. They may consider improving current platforms, such as reducing user navigation confusion or increasing engagement among learners through interactive activities such as games and quizzes. Reverse brainstorming could help them develop different strategies by asking themselves, 'what should we avoid when creating this online platform?' For example, they may want to avoid adding

Table 4.2 Brainstorming versus reverse brainstorming

S.No	Feature	Brainstorming	Reverse Brainstorming
1	Goal	Generate a large quantity of ideas to solve a problem	Identify the weaknesses, flaws, or potential problems of a solution or idea
2	Focus	Finding positive solutions and improvements	Identifying challenges, obstacles, and negative aspects
3	Mindset	Positive and solution-oriented	Critical and problem-focused
4	Evaluation	Ideas are typically not judged during the session	Ideas are evaluated and analyzed to understand potential issues
5	Structure	Can be less structured, relying on conversational flow	May follow a specific structure to encourage critical thinking
6	Quantity versus Quality	Focuses on generating a large number of ideas	Aims to identify the most significant potential problems
7	Output	List of potential solutions and ideas	List of potential weaknesses, flaws, and risks
8	Suitability	Effective for sparking creativity and exploring possibilities	Useful for refining ideas, mitigating risks, and ensuring solutions are well-rounded
9	Use Case	Early stage of problem-solving, idea generation	Later stage of problem-solving, idea refinement
10	Example	"How might we improve access to fresh produce?"	"What are the potential downsides of offering a grocery delivery service?"

too many choices for users to make (as this could add to confusion) and overloading pages with text (which would reduce engagement). Reverse brainstorming can also help identify weaknesses within existing products by forcing people to look at them from entirely different perspectives.

Reverse Brainstorming: Reducing Travel Time for Fresh Produce

Here are the reverse brainstorming pointers for reducing travel time and effort spent acquiring fresh produce:

- **Overly Inconvenient Locations:** Instead of focusing solely on convenience, what if grocery stores or farmers markets were located in hard-to-reach areas, creating unnecessary travel for everyone? This could highlight the need for a more distributed network of fresh produce options.
- **Bulk Purchases Only:** What if stores only offered produce in large quantities, requiring more frequent shopping trips and difficulty managing storage for smaller households? This highlights the need for various portion sizes and options for single individuals or smaller families.
- **Unreliable Public Transportation:** Imagine unreliable public transportation schedules or routes that bypass areas with high demand for fresh produce. This emphasizes the need for reliable public transportation options or partnerships to improve access in underserved communities.
- **Unfriendly Staff:** Imagine if grocery store staff were unhelpful or dismissive of customer inquiries about fresh produce. This underscores the importance of training staff to be knowledgeable and provide excellent customer service, especially for those seeking assistance navigating produce selections.

- **Limited Operating Hours:** Envision supermarkets operating within narrow timeframes, constraining shoppers to meticulously plan their visits, underscoring the significance of unhindered access to farm fresh produce throughout the day and week.
- **Confusing Store Layouts:** Visualize disorganized store layouts with ambiguous section labels, obstructing the swift procurement of nutritious fruits and veggies. This scenario accentuates the necessity for clear signage and intuitive store designs to facilitate seamless shopping experiences.
- **Slow Check-out Process:** Contemplate extended queues at check-out counters, substantially prolonging the shopping ordeal. This circumstance highlights the urgency for expedited and efficient payment options, such as self-service check-outs or mobile payment systems.
- **Limited Parking Availability:** Envision limited parking availability, compelling residents to expend precious time scouring for vacant spots or traversing considerable distances from remote parking areas. This scenario emphasizes the indispensability of ample and conveniently located parking facilities.
- **Lack of Delivery Options:** Deliberate the absence of delivery services for fresh produce, compelling all individuals, regardless of physical limitations or mobility constraints, to undertake in-person visits to procure essential groceries. This situation underscores the imperative for diverse delivery alternatives, encompassing bicycle couriers, dedicated grocery delivery services, or collaborative partnerships with ride sharing platforms. By reimagining these scenarios, we can enhance our collective understanding of the essential elements that foster a seamless and accessible grocery shopping experience for all members of our community.
- **Inaccessible Shopping Carts:** Envision a scenario where shopping carts pose challenges, are devoid of essential features like child seats or bottle holders, or their availability is limited. Such circumstances underscore the necessity for accessible, user-centric shopping carts that cater to diverse needs, ultimately elevating the overall shopping experience.

Design Visualization Question 4.4

Latent Need 2: How might we feel a sense of security and safety when obtaining fresh produce, especially for residents with mobility limitations. This could involve well-lit locations, accessible entrances and exits, or assistance programs for carrying groceries (volunteer grocery shoppers, designated bagging areas).

Perform reverse brainstorming with other design thinking experts and identify at least 5 ideas for the above latent need.

4.4.5 Mind Mapping

Conceptualizing and structuring ideas is an integral part of the ideation process known as mind mapping, which is capable of generating a diverse array of ideas. This approach starts with a central concept and branches out into associated ideas and sub-themes. The objective is to create a visual representation of all the concepts pertinent to the central theme.

Mind mapping is frequently employed to generate and organize ideas, identify relationships between concepts, and devise a coherent plan of action. We can initiate this by positioning the main concept or topic at the center of the page. Subsequently, we branch out with related ideas, connecting them with lines and keywords. Each idea can be further expanded upon with sub-ideas and details, culminating in an interconnected web of concepts. Mind mapping can be undertaken individually or in a group setting. It facilitates non-linear thinking and promotes the exploration of diverse possibilities and connections between ideas.

For instance, a marketing team might utilize mind mapping to conceptualize ideas for a new campaign. They could initiate a main theme such as 'summer' and subsequently branch out with associated ideas like 'outdoor pursuits' and 'travel'. Each of these ideas could then be further expounded upon with sub-ideas such as 'hiking' and 'beach vacations', thereby creating a comprehensive and interlinked map of potential campaign concepts (Fig. 4.4).

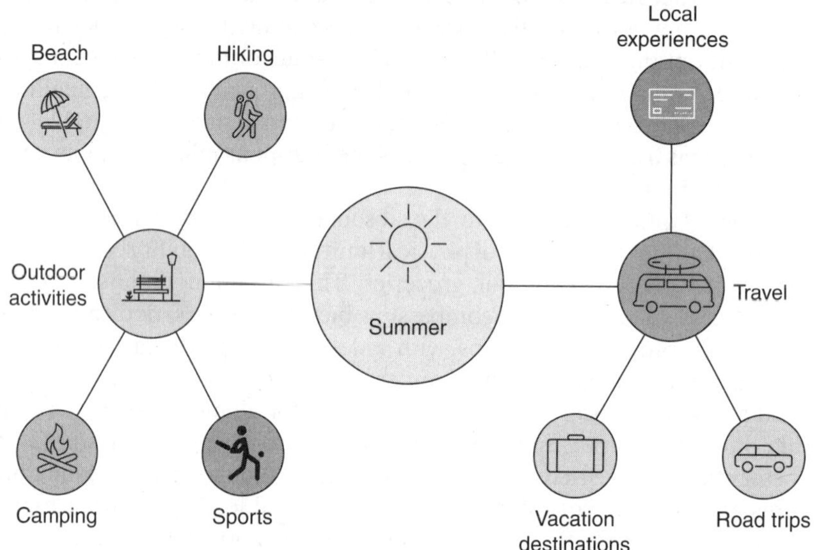

Figure 4.4 Mind mapping example

Design Visualization Question 4.5

Central Theme: Develop New Fitness Tracker

Branches:

1. Features
2. Target Audience
3. Design Considerations
4. Integration Opportunities

Expand the above branches into its sub-branches and draw a mind map for the same.

4.4.6 Rapid Prototyping

Rapid prototyping is an invaluable technique that enables designers to quickly create physical or digital representations of their ideas. This process facilitates iterative refinement through user testing and feedback. By swiftly producing tangible prototypes, innovators gain real-life insights, which inform further enhancements or pivots. Rapid prototyping streamlines the design journey, allowing for a deeper understanding of concepts before committing substantial time and resources.

Three-dimensional (3D) printing exemplifies rapid prototyping's applications during ideation. With a single click, designers can fabricate physical models directly from their digital designs.

Unlike traditional manufacturing methods, which require time-consuming mold creation, 3D printing empowers rapid iteration and experimentation. Designers can seamlessly develop diverse prototype versions, fine-tuning each iteration until the desired outcome is achieved.

Another example is virtual reality (VR), which uses computer-generated images to simulate real-life scenarios or environments, so designers can test various ideas within these settings before producing prototypes. For instance, furniture designers could test out how different layouts will work in a room by using VR instead of moving around pieces in a physical space every time something needs to be adjusted; this way, they can save both time and energy while being able to accurately visualize their design concept.

Finally, there is **low-fidelity prototyping** which involves mockups created using paper or other materials; this technique helps designers get an early understanding of how something might look without having to invest resources in its creation. For example, if someone wants to build new chairs for living rooms but has no idea what shape would work best, they could easily make multiple paper versions that look similar enough so they would know whether their initial plan was feasible.

All these examples show how rapid prototyping plays a vital role during the ideation phase by allowing creators to craft tangible models from abstract ideas so improvements can be made before investing too many resources into development.

4.4.7 Role Playing

Role playing allows individuals to unleash their creativity, exploring diverse concepts during the ideation stage of design thinking. Acting as someone else, such as a customer or entrepreneur, enables participants to re-enact potential scenarios and uncover novel insights. Moreover, role playing fosters different viewpoints, stimulating innovative solutions.

Consider an entrepreneur striving to craft a product or service that caters to customers' needs. To excel, they must comprehend customer mindsets and desires. Role playing empowers entrepreneurs to embody their clientele, gaining invaluable understanding of decision-making processes and potential areas for product enhancement. This methodology extends to app or website design; by simulating user interactions, designers can identify features requiring refinement or functionalities warranting expansion.

School Cafeteria Redesign: Role-playing Activity

Scene: We are in our college cafeteria at lunchtime. Let us see how things go!

Characters:

- **Cafeteria Staff (2–3 students):** Responsible for serving lunch, keeping things clean, and managing the flow of students.
- **Students (4–5 students):** Represent diverse needs:
  - **Latha:** Vegetarian
  - **Raj:** Peanut allergy
  - **Maria:** Gluten intolerance
  - **Abdul:** Wants a quick lunch due to extracurricular activities
  - **Kumar:** Looking for a healthy and balanced meal

The Role Play: (Imagine a designated space as the cafeteria or simply use your classroom)

- *Cafeteria Staff*: We're busy preparing for the lunch rush. We have hot dogs, pizza, a salad bar, and assorted fruits. We hope things run smoothly today!

(Students enter the cafeteria line)

- *Latha*: (Looking at the menu) Hmm, not much for vegetarians today. Maybe just some salad and fruit.
- *Raj*: (Scanning nervously) I hope they have something safe for me to eat. Peanuts are a big no-no!
- *Maria*: (Approaching the staff) Excuse me, do you have any gluten-free options besides the salad?
- *Cafeteria Staff* 1: (Checks the labels) Unfortunately, not today. We usually have gluten-free pasta on Wednesdays.
- *Maria*: (Sighs) Guess it's just salad then.
- *Abdul*: (Looks at his watch) Ugh, the line is moving so slowly! I only have 20 minutes before football practice.
- *Kumar*: (Picks at the pizza) This doesn't look very healthy. Are there any whole-wheat options like brown rice or whole-wheat pasta?
- *Cafeteria Staff 2*: (Shakes head) Sorry, not on the menu today.

(The scene continues with students facing various challenges)

Debriefing and Outcome: (After the role play, gather as a class)

- *Teacher*: Alright everyone, how was lunch today? What were your experiences?
(Students share their perspectives):
    - *Cafeteria Staff*: We felt overwhelmed with the long lines and students with specific dietary needs. It's hard to keep everyone happy!
    - *Latha*: It's frustrating to have limited vegetarian options. More variety would be great.
    - *Raj*: I felt anxious about finding safe food. Maybe a separate section for allergens would be helpful.
    - *Maria*: There weren't many gluten-free choices. Having more options would be a big improvement.
    - *Abdul*: The long line made me stressed about getting back to practice on time. Maybe a pre-ordering system?
    - *Kumar*: There wasn't much healthy food available. More balanced options would be nice.
- *Teacher*: We've identified some key pain points! How can we use this information to improve our school cafeteria?

Students Brainstorm Solutions

- Offer more vegetarian and gluten-free options.
- Clearly label allergen information.
- Consider a pre-ordering system for faster service.
- Introduce healthier and more balanced meals.
- Explore ways to streamline the serving process.

By reflecting on this role-playing activity, we can work towards a cafeteria that caters to everyone's needs and makes lunchtime a more enjoyable experience!

Design Visualization Question 4.6

Library Book Recommendation System

Scenario: Students role-play as librarians and patrons with different reading interests (science fiction, historical fiction, fantasy).

How to Conduct: Research popular book genres and reader preferences. Students role-play a library interaction where the 'librarian' recommends books using a hypothetical recommendation system. The 'patron' provides feedback based on their interests.

Outcome: Identify strengths and weaknesses of the recommendation system. This can spark ideas for incorporating user preferences, genre filters, or personalized recommendations to improve the book-finding experience in the library.

4.4.8 Storytelling

Crafting captivating narratives is an influential tool used in the ideation stage of the design thinking approach. This involves creating a story that brings an idea to life, making it more relatable and compelling. Through storytelling, designers can effectively communicate their ideas to stakeholders and generate enthusiasm and garner support.

Storytelling can be used at various stages of design thinking. For example, in the empathize and define stages, it helps designers comprehend the users' needs and challenges. By actively listening to users' stories, designers can gain insights into their experiences and identify areas where they can make a difference. In the ideation phase, storytelling can be used for generating and refining ideas. Designers can create stories around their conceptual ideas, testing their feasibility and evaluating their impact. For instance, a designer crafting a new product might create a story that depicts how the product would be used and how it would benefit the user, thereby identifying potential issues and refining the idea to meet the user's needs.

To harness the power of storytelling effectively in the ideate phase, designers should focus on creating engaging and memorable stories. They should employ vivid language and imagery to bring the story to life, making it more relatable and inspiring. Moreover, designers must also consider their audience when crafting stories.

Storytelling Approach: Educators and parents share stories about children's struggles with traditional learning methods and their hopes for a more engaging and interactive learning experience.

Impact: Listening to these stories inspires the creation of an app that incorporates gamification elements, personalized learning paths, and interactive activities to enhance children's learning and motivation.

The Struggles and Dreams of Learning

"My classroom walls are plastered with colorful charts, but some students just seem to switch off," Sarah, a dedicated elementary school teacher, lamented. "Lectures and worksheets feel outdated. I wish there was a way to ignite their curiosity and make learning truly engaging, something that sparks their imaginations and lets them explore at their own pace."

"My son, Abdul, spends hours glued to his tablet, but gets frustrated with traditional learning materials," Salim, a tech-savvy father, explained. "There's got to be a way to bridge the gap. An app that uses the same interactive elements Abdul loves in games, but focuses on educational content, could be a game-changer."

"My daughter, Asha, is a bright child, but struggles to focus in a large classroom setting," Priya, a concerned mother, confided. "An app that personalizes learning based on her strengths and weaknesses would be ideal. Something that caters to her individual learning style and keeps her motivated."

The Outcome

By listening to Sarah's desire to make learning interactive, Salim's call for engaging educational technology, and Priya's hope for personalized learning experiences, a clear picture emerges. Children today require a new approach to education, one that leverages technology and caters to their diverse learning styles.

Impact: Designing an App that Inspires

Inspired by these stories, the design team starts crafting an educational app that incorporates the following elements:

- **Gamification:** Points, badges, and leaderboards transform learning into an exciting adventure.
- **Personalized Learning Paths:** The app adapts to each child's strengths and weaknesses, offering targeted activities and challenges.
- **Interactive Activities:** Educational content is presented through engaging games, simulations, and puzzles.
- **Rich Multimedia:** Animations, sound effects, and captivating visuals make learning come alive.
- **Offline Accessibility:** The app allows for continued learning even without an internet connection.

This app becomes a valuable tool for educators, a fun and engaging resource for children, and a source of comfort and support for parents. It personalizes the learning journey, fostering curiosity, motivation, and a love for knowledge in every child.

Design Visualization Question 4.7

Redesigning Public Transportation for Senior Citizens

Storytelling Approach: Design teams interview and record stories from senior citizens about their challenges using public transportation (such as difficulty navigating stairs, limited seating, unclear signage).

Impact: These personal stories evoke empathy for the user group, leading to design solutions like prioritizing accessible entrances, installing grab bars and wider seats, and implementing clear visual and audio announcements.

Storytelling in design thinking provides a powerful tool to connect with users on an emotional level, fostering empathy and understanding of their needs. Use this approach to record the challenges and come out with ideas to solve the same.

4.4.9 Sketching

Rendering ideas through rough sketches is an effective technique employed in the ideation stage of design thinking to visualize and effectively convey concepts. This process involves crafting low-fidelity drawings that capture the essential components of a proposed design. Sketches can be produced using traditional tools like pencils and paper, digital mediums, or a harmonious blend of both. During the ideation stage, sketching serves as a swift and versatile means to explore and cultivate promising design concepts (Fig. 4.5).

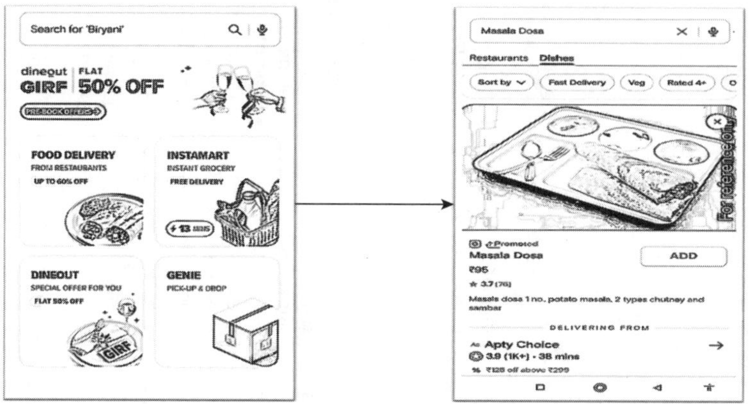

Figure 4.5 Sketching example

Visualizing thoughts and refining concepts are fundamental benefits of sketching for designers. This initial phase is crucial as it allows designers to iterate rapidly without getting stuck in complicated details. By sketching potential products or solutions, designers gain a better grasp of how their ideas might manifest and function in the real world.

Furthermore, sketching is an invaluable tool for fostering shared understanding within a design team. When team members illustrate their ideas through sketches, they not only explore new concepts but also share their thought processes. This collaborative effort builds a collective comprehension of the design challenge and potential resolutions. In essence, sketching is an indispensable tool during the ideation stage of the design thinking process.

4.4.10 SCAMPER

The acronym SCAMPER denotes a framework used for the systematic exploration of creative ideas. It involves applying distinct operations like Substitute, Combine, Adapt, Modify, Put to another use, Eliminate, and Reverse. This technique encourages generating novel concepts by introducing purposeful changes to an existing product or idea. The process leverages prompts representing each letter to methodically consider potential alterations or enhancements (Fig. 4.6).

Latent Need: Feel assured that the purchased produce is fresh, ripe, and free from contaminants.

SCAMPER in Action

Substitute

- **Material:** Replace plastic packaging with biodegradable or compostable alternatives.
- **Process:** Instead of relying solely on visual inspection, explore non-destructive testing methods to detect contaminants.

Combine

- **Information:** Integrate origin information with freshness indicators like color-changing stickers or QR codes with harvest dates and storage tips.
- **Technology:** Combine traditional labeling with smartphone apps that provide real-time information on proper handling and storage based on specific produce.

Adapt

- **Existing Systems:** Adapt current traceability systems to track produce journey from farm to shelf, offering consumers transparency.

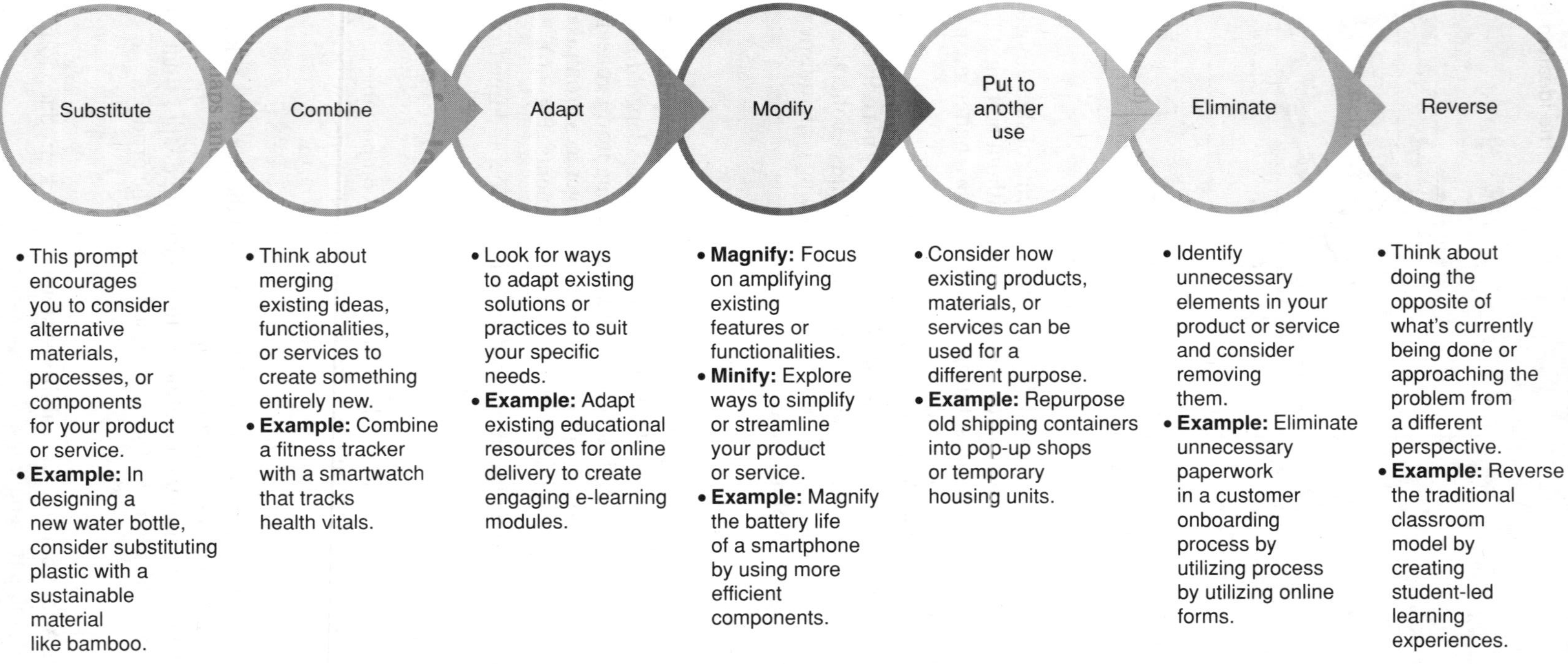

Figure 4.6 SCAMPER for ensuring fresh produce: Addressing Latent Need 1

- **Practices:** Adapt existing good agricultural practices (GAP) to include consumer education materials at the point of purchase.

Modify

- **Labeling:** Modify labels to include information on optimal storage conditions and shelf life for different types of produce.
- **Inspections:** Enhance visual inspections at distribution points by including trained personnel to assess ripeness and potential damage.

Put to Another Use

- **Packaging:** Utilize leftover produce scraps or byproducts to create new packaging materials.
- **Consumer Education:** Repurpose existing educational resources on food safety and adapt them for use in grocery stores or online platforms.

Eliminate

- **Unnecessary Packaging:** Eliminate excessive plastic wrapping on produce that has a natural protective skin.
- **Information Overload:** Streamline labels to focus on key information like origin and freshness indicators, avoiding overwhelming consumers.

Reverse

- **Consumer Perception:** Reverse the current system where responsibility solely lies with consumers. Implement a system where producers and distributors share the responsibility for ensuring fresh produce reaches consumers.
- **Supply Chain:** Reverse the traditional supply chain by sourcing local produce whenever possible, reducing transportation time and potential spoilage.

Design Visualization Question 4.8

Latent Need: Minimize food waste and get the most out of the purchased produce.
Substitute, Combine, Adapt, Modify, Put to another Use, Eliminate, and Reverse are all letters in the acronym SCAMPER. This ideation process entails using these prompts to produce new ideas based on tweaks or alterations to the basic concept of an existing idea or product.

Use SCAMPER to produce new ideas based on the above latent need.

4.4.11 Visualization

Visualization can be used throughout the ideation phase, but it is essential during the evaluation and refinement stages. Teams can create visual representations of their ideas and use them to evaluate the feasibility, impact, and usability of each idea. This process helps teams identify the most promising ideas and discard those that could be more practical or impactful.

The ideation process frequently employs storyboarding, a visualization technique. Storyboarding entails crafting a sequence of illustrations or sketches that narrates a narrative or reveals a procedure. This methodology finds widespread application in the entertainment realm, notably for the conceptualization of cinematic productions and animated features.

Kaveri, a sprightly woman with laughter lines etched around her eyes, settled into the chair. "Public transportation used to be my lifeline," she began, a touch of wistfulness in her voice. "Now, those high bus steps feel like mountains I have to conquer every time. The other day, the doors almost closed on me as I struggled up. It's a scary feeling." (Fig. 4.7).

Figure 4.7 Storyboarding example 1

Ramesh, a retired carpenter, recounted a different struggle. "The buses are always packed during rush hour," he said. "Even if I manage to get a seat, it's usually a small one. Holding on while the bus swerves is very difficult! My knees just can't handle it anymore." (Fig. 4.8)

Figure 4.8 Storyboarding example 2

Generating numerous ideas constitutes the pivotal ideation phase within the design thinking methodology, encompassing a comprehensive array of potential solutions to address a specific challenge. By approaching this phase with an open, curious mindset coupled with techniques like brainstorming, sketching, and exploring diverse avenues, designers can formulate groundbreaking ideas and insights, thereby propelling the innovation process forward.

4.4.12 Creative Matrix Technique

This is a tool for problem-solving that uses a matrix to organize and mix different ideas to create innovative solutions. It is a good technique for producing new ideas and dealing with complicated problems. We can list some characteristics or features that relate to each component, such as the design, layout, content, functionality, etc. We can then use a matrix to insert the components and the characteristics in rows and columns and fill the cells with potential ideas for improvement. The creative matrix technique helps us to try out different combinations of ideas and find new ways to improve the customer experience.

Suppose you want to design a new product for a coffee shop. You can use the creative matrix technique to generate some ideas, as shown in Table 4.3.

Table 4.3 Creative matrix to design a new product for a coffee shop

Product	Coffee	Tea	Juice	Smoothie
Cake	Coffee cake	Tea cake	Juice cake	Smoothie cake
Cookie	Coffee cookie	Tea cookie	Juice cookie	Smoothie cookie
Muffin	Coffee muffin	Tea muffin	Juice muffin	Smoothie muffin
Pie	Coffee pie	Tea pie	Juice pie	Smoothie pie

To begin, you establish categories along two axes, such as various ingredients or product features. Then, you generate ideas by pairing elements from each axis, like 'juice cake' or 'tea cookie'. This structured approach helps identify intriguing possibilities. In addition, you can further refine the matrix by creating subcategories or modifying the axes to explore more specific areas.

This versatile tool can be applied to diverse domains, from product development to marketing strategies, educational initiatives, or social problem-solving. In product design, one axis might represent desired product features, such as battery life, camera quality, screen size, and storage capacity. The other axis could encompass user needs like portability, durability, affordability, and ease of use (Table 4.4). By systematically considering how each feature might address a specific need, designers gain insights into developing well-rounded, innovative products tailored to user requirements.

For example, when designing a new smartphone, the matrix could lead to concepts like combining superior battery life with enhanced portability or pairing high-resolution cameras with durability for outdoor enthusiasts. This comprehensive approach ensures that various user needs are thoughtfully addressed, leading to products with broad appeal and practical functionality.

Table 4.4 Creative matrix to design a smart phone

Product	Portability	Durability	Affordability	Usability
Battery life				
Camera Quality				
Screen Size				
Storage Capacity				

The creative matrix methodology enables companies to find openings in the market by pinpointing consumer needs that existing products do not fully address. In addition, it aids in ranking product features based on their potential to enhance user satisfaction. This systematic approach guarantees all conceivable combinations receive consideration, ensuring no important aspect goes unnoticed – a critical factor in the competitive realm of product design.

4.4.13 Walls in Design Thinking

Design thinking necessitates walls as versatile tools throughout various stages. In the empathizing stage, walls enable designers to visualize users' perspectives and experiences. During problem definition, walls help organize insights and articulate challenges coherently. The ideation stage leverages walls' expansive canvas for free-flowing brainstorming and capturing diverse ideas. Walls also facilitate rapid prototyping by allowing teams to sketch, build, and iterate solution concepts collaboratively. Finally, during testing, walls support data visualization and analysis for refining prototypes based on user feedback.

Brainstorming on Walls: Brainstorming sessions thrive on walls' interactive nature, fostering creativity and collaboration. Individual or group brainstorming can benefit from walls' spatial advantages. Walls provide ample surface areas to capture thoughts visually, promoting focus and engagement. Techniques like mind mapping and word association flourish on walls. Mind mapping organizes ideas radiating from a central concept, showcasing relationships and connections. Word association involves rapidly listing words associated with the subject matter, triggering imaginative leaps and unexpected insights. On walls, these words can be grouped, rearranged, and linked, fueling more ideas and patterns.

Visualizing Ideas on Walls: Representing concepts visually is a crucial step in the design thinking methodology, fostering shared understanding, and aligning stakeholders towards a unified objective. Visual representation enables effective communication of ideas, assumption testing, and solution refinement. Various techniques exist, encompassing sketches, diagrams, charts, graphs, models, and prototypes. Walls provide an excellent canvas for creating and showcasing visual representations of ideas. They enable real-time collaboration and iteration by offering a large, visible space for sketching, drawing, or arranging materials. In addition, walls ensure visual representations remain accessible and visible, facilitating easy reference and comparison.

Collaborating on Walls: Collaboration lies at the core of design thinking, involving teamwork to comprehend challenges, generate concepts, and craft solutions. Synergy leverages diverse skills, perspectives, and expertise, fostering more innovative and effective outcomes. It cultivates trust, rapport, and commitment, enriching the design process. Walls facilitate collaboration by providing a communal space for idea exchange, discussion, and refinement. They serve as communication channels for sharing opinions, suggestions, and concerns, creating a sense of ownership and accountability. Moreover, walls enable group brainstorming sessions, where creativity thrives, alternative viewpoints emerge, and synergy blossoms. The six thinking hats technique, using colored hats to represent different thinking modes like creative, analytical, and critical, can be employed during these sessions. Design reviews also benefit from walls, where concepts, prototypes, and mockups are displayed, enhancing visualization, in depth exploration, and immediate feedback. These reviews are integral to design thinking, allowing evaluation and refinement based on constructive input.

Communicating on Walls: Successful design thinking demands effective communication. Sharing concepts, ideas, and solutions with team members, stakeholders, and users is crucial. Communication fosters a shared vision, aligns expectations, and garners support and buy-in. Importantly, it enables gathering feedback, learning from users, and enhancing solutions. Walls can boost communication by providing a visual focal point for teams. They offer a platform to visually represent ideas and concepts, conveying messages more powerfully and persuasively. In addition, walls create an engaging, interactive experience for audiences by allowing them to see, touch, and interact with concepts.

Useful tools include sticky notes for easy writing and rearranging, and whiteboards for erasable, modifiable notes. For presenting final designs to stakeholders and users, walls provide a large, visible canvas to showcase visual representations. They create an immersive, engaging experience by allowing audiences to view designs at scale and in context. Design walls that highlight concepts, prototypes, or mockups, and versatile, updatable digital displays are effective presentation methods.

4.5 Divergence and Convergence

The ideation phase of the design thinking process is characterized by divergent thinking, which encourages generating as many ideas as possible without constraints. However, at some point, the team needs to converge on a few promising ideas that can effectively solve the identified problem. To facilitate this process, the team uses divergence and convergence (Fig. 4.9).

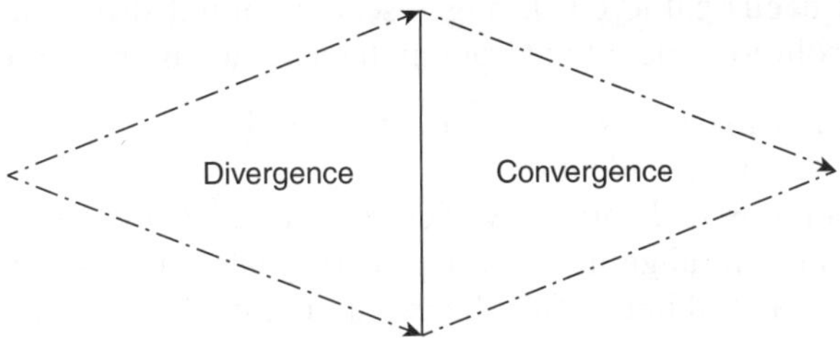

Figure 4.9 Divergence and convergence

Creative thinking necessitates producing numerous concepts without judging or filtering them immediately. Exploring multiple possibilities and discovering novel solutions to the issue at hand becomes feasible through this approach. Brainstorming, mind mapping, and SCAMPER are divergent thinking techniques crucial in the ideation phase of the design thinking process. These methods enable teams to generate a wide range of ideas, explore multiple avenues, and uncover innovative solutions to the problem they are tackling. Moreover, when dealing with intricate challenges, these techniques prove instrumental by providing a structured approach to ideation and breaking down the problem into smaller, more manageable components.

Convergence techniques play a vital role in the design thinking process, assisting the team in evaluating and refining the generated ideas. Several examples of convergence techniques exist. Voting is one such technique that involves team members selecting the most promising ideas based on predetermined evaluation criteria. Each team member receives a certain number of votes, which they can utilize to select the ideas they deem strongest. For instance, in a team developing a new product, each member might receive three votes and be asked to choose the three ideas they consider have the most potential.

4.6 Evaluation of Ideas

A crucial component of the ideation phase of the design thinking process is idea evaluation. It involves analyzing and refining the generated ideas to determine their feasibility, effectiveness, and potential for implementation. The goal is to identify the most promising ideas that have the potential to address the problem or challenge effectively. The evaluation process typically involves criteria such as feasibility, impact, novelty, user needs, and alignment with the project's goals and objectives. Each criterion is used to assess the ideas from a different perspective, providing a comprehensive analysis of the potential of each idea:

- **Feasibility** is one of the most critical criteria for evaluating the generated ideas. It assesses whether an idea is practically possible and can be implemented within constraints such as time, budget, and available resources. For example, an idea may be innovative and promising. However, it is only feasible if it can be executed due to these constraints.
- **Impact** is another criterion used to evaluate ideas. It assesses the potential impact of an idea on the target audience or the problem at hand. An idea with a high impact can significantly affect the end-users, making it more desirable and valuable.
- **Novelty** is also a crucial criterion that evaluates the uniqueness and originality of an idea. It assesses whether an idea is new or built upon existing ideas, making it more innovative and potentially disruptive.
- **Prioritizing user requirements** is vital when appraising concepts. This criterion examines if an idea addresses the target audience's needs and preferences. A solution tailored to user pain points and necessities is more likely to succeed.
- **User insights and needs** gathered during research should drive ideation. This user-centric approach ensures solutions meet the target audience's needs and preferences.

Effective ideation often involves sketching or visualizing ideas, facilitating better communication, quicker iteration, and collaborative ideation.

Unconventional solutions and innovative ideas require ideators to take risks and embrace potential failures. In addition, alignment with project goals and objectives is crucial, ensuring generated ideas are relevant and impactful. The evaluation process typically involves stakeholders like the design team, project sponsors, end-users, and others. They can utilize scoring systems, ranking, or voting to evaluate and prioritize the generated ideas. This process selects the most promising and feasible ideas for further development.

4.7 Tools for the Ideation Stage of Design Thinking

The ideation phase is crucial for creating original and creative solutions to challenging issues. Several tools and methods may be applied to help with this process. Among these, the ones most frequently used for ideation are shown in Fig. 4.10.

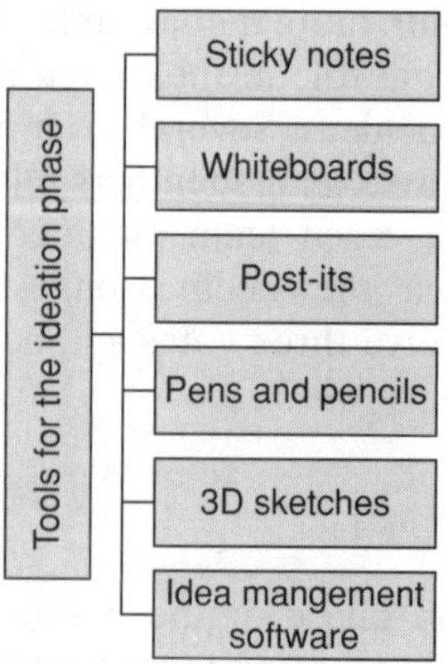

Figure 4.10 Tools for the ideation stage

Sticky Notes: This is a straightforward yet powerful tool for capturing and grouping concepts with flexibility. Teams often utilize sticky notes during ideation sessions for product development, generating ideas for enhancements or novel features. Color coding allows categorization into clusters like usability, functionality, and aesthetics. Arranging sticky notes based on grouping and vote tallies highlights the most compelling prospects to explore further, streamlining prioritization.

Whiteboards: Visually captivating canvases facilitate organized ideation and brainstorming. These versatile surfaces enable fluid collaboration from initial concept generation to refinement and planning phases. Particularly advantageous for group sessions, whiteboards ensure all participants can actively contribute and observe the creative process unfold.

Examples

- During product design sessions, to visualize and refine product concepts.
- During marketing brainstorming sessions, to generate and organize marketing ideas.
- During the process, improvement sessions map out current processes and identify areas for improvement.

Overall, whiteboards are a versatile and effective tool for ideation that can help to stimulate creativity and collaboration.

Post-its: These versatile sticky notes facilitate idea capture and organization. Available in diverse sizes and hues, they streamline grouping and prioritization of concepts. Post-its excel as an ideation tool, enabling users to physically record and arrange thoughts. Their compact, adhesive nature renders them highly portable and malleable, allowing for effortless rearrangement and categorization by color or theme. Suitable for collaborative brainstorming sessions or individual ideation, Post-its empower participants to visually map out their ideas on whiteboards or walls. This tangible representation promotes easy visualization and refinement of concepts. Although unsuitable for long-term idea storage due to adhesive degradation, Post-its thrive in dynamic, temporary settings, excelling in both in-person and remote team environments.

Pens and Pencils: Writing tools are indispensable for ideation, enabling swift and effortless recording of ideas and sketches. Pens and pencils can be employed throughout the entire ideation process, from initial concept generation to final refinement of plans. They empower users to visually transcribe ideas through sketches or textually through words and phrases that encapsulate the essence of a concept. However, there may be instances where specialized digital tools or software prove more suitable, particularly for projects with a significant digital component. In such cases, digital pens or styluses may better align with the ideation workflow.

3D Sketches: Visualizing and refining concepts during the design thinking process's ideation phase is facilitated by the powerful 3D sketching technique. It involves creating quick, rough sketches to represent ideas in three dimensions. This approach enables designers to explore spatial relationships among idea elements and consider how they integrate into the final design. A primary advantage is allowing rapid iteration and refinement by quickly creating 3D sketches to explore various design options and identify potential issues or areas for improvement. This streamlines the journey from concept to prototype, accelerating the design process while reducing development time and costs. In addition, 3D sketching effectively communicates complex ideas by conveying crucial information about shape, scale, and proportion, enhancing understanding and facilitating constructive feedback. Designers can sketch 3D models using various techniques like pen and paper, digital software, or even physical prototype materials. SketchUp is a widely used 3D sketching tool that enables designers to quickly and effortlessly create detailed 3D models.

Idea Management Software: Idea management software aids individuals and teams in ideation and idea organization. These tools enable brainstorming, structuring, evaluating, and implementing ideas. They offer remote access, promoting collaboration and idea sharing from any location. Such software proves beneficial for complex projects involving numerous ideas and input from multiple stakeholders. It also facilitates remote teamwork or projects necessitating a high degree of organization and tracking. However, idea management software may not be required for simple projects with minimal collaboration and input. Similarly, it may not suit individuals or teams preferring traditional ideation techniques like pen and paper or whiteboards.

Trello, Asana, IdeaScale, Miro, and MindMeister are some popular ideas management software. They offer varied features and pricing plans. Furthermore, these tools can be customized to cater to specific team and project requirements. Ideation tools should prioritize simplicity, adaptability, and user-friendliness. They should enable swift ideation and iteration cycles, while facilitating seamless idea sharing and organization.

4.8 Case Studies of the Ideation Stage

Example 1: Redesigning a Retail Store
A retail company was struggling with declining sales and needed more customer engagement in its stores. They used design thinking to redesign their stores and improve the customer experience. The team used brainstorming and mind mapping during the ideation phase to generate various ideas. They also researched customer needs, behavior, and trends in retail design. Using these insights, they generated multiple ideas, such as redesigning the store layout, creating interactive displays, and offering personalized customer service. After evaluating the ideas, the team used rapid prototyping to test different store layouts and displays. They also used Post-it notes and whiteboards to gather feedback from customers and team members. Through this iterative process, they created a new store design that increased customer engagement and sales.

Example 2: Developing a New Mobile App
A tech company wanted to develop a new mobile app to help people manage their finances. They used design thinking to create a user-centered app that would meet the needs of their target audience. The team used brainstorming and mind mapping during the ideation phase to generate various ideas. They also researched user needs, behavior, and trends in mobile app design. Using these insights, they generated multiple ideas, such as creating a simple and intuitive user interface, integrating budget tracking features, and offering personalized financial advice. After evaluating the ideas, the team used rapid prototyping to test user interfaces and features. They also used user testing to gather feedback from their target audience. Through this iterative process, they created a mobile app that met the needs of their users and received positive reviews.

Example 3: Improving a Healthcare System
A medical organization wanted to enhance its patient information management system. They employed design thinking principles to create an efficient and user-friendly solution. During the ideation phase, the team utilized brainstorming and mind mapping techniques to generate diverse ideas. In addition, they researched user needs, behaviors, and healthcare technology trends. Leveraging these insights, they proposed various concepts, such as developing a mobile app for patients to access their medical records, implementing an intuitive interface for healthcare providers to retrieve patient information, and utilizing data analytics to identify areas for improvement. After evaluating the ideas, the team employed rapid prototyping to test user interfaces and features. They also conducted user testing to gather feedback from healthcare providers and patients. Through this iterative process, they developed a more efficient and user-friendly system for managing patient information. This resulted in improved patient satisfaction and a streamlined healthcare system.

4.9 Ideation with SIT

Water bottles are an essential item in our daily lives, yet their design often lacks innovation. By applying systematic inventive thinking (SIT) methods, we can reimagine this ubiquitous product in eco-friendly and user-friendly ways.

Case Study: Ideating a New Water Bottle with SIT

Imagine that a company seeks to create a water bottle that is environmentally conscious, portable, and convenient. Applying SIT techniques can yield innovative solutions:

- **Addition:** Enhance the bottle by incorporating a detachable cup, enabling users to drink without unscrewing the cap. This addition simplifies the drinking experience while maintaining portability.
- **Subtraction:** Eliminate the cap entirely and replace it with a spill-proof spout. This subtraction eliminates the need to remove the cap each time, making hydration effortless.
- **Multiplication:** Duplicate the bottle's interior by creating two separate compartments. Users can now carry multiple beverages or separate hot and cold liquids within a single vessel.
- **Division:** Deconstruct the bottle into a modular design, allowing customization to suit individual preferences and needs. This division enables personalization and versatility.
- **Multifunctional Design:** This approach involves integrating new capabilities or tasks into existing product features. An idea could be creating a water bottle with a built-in filtration system, enabling users to purify water on the move.
- **Systematic Inventive Thinking:** This guides designers to generate diverse potential solutions that may not emerge through conventional brainstorming. Following its prescribed templates (addition, subtraction, multiplication, division, and task unification) helps designers transcend habitual thought patterns. They can then develop ingenious concepts tailored to user needs. However, ideation demands an iterative mindset. Designers must continually refine and polish ideas until converging on the optimal solution.

4.10 Three-Box Thinking

This is an innovative strategic approach devised to assist organizations in seamlessly integrating innovation while sustaining their core operations. Conceptualized by Vijay Govindarajan, a renowned business professor at Dartmouth College, this framework comprises three distinct boxes symbolizing the past, present, and future.

The first box, or Box 1, represents the present, where existing operations occur. This box optimizes current operations to improve efficiency, quality, and profitability. The second box, or Box 2, represents the past, where outdated practices and ideas reside. This box involves letting go of old practices that no longer serve the organization's needs and creating a sense of urgency for innovation. Finally, the third box, or Box 3, represents the future, where new ideas and opportunities exist. This box is concerned with exploring and developing new products, services, and business models that will ensure the organization's success in the future (Fig. 4.11).

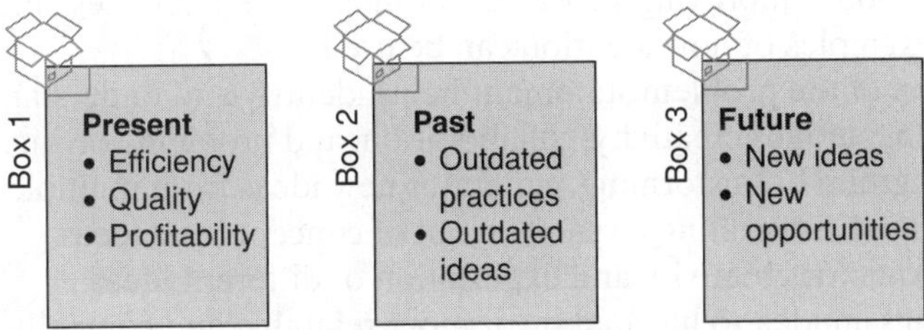

Figure 4.11 Three-box thinking

The three-box thinking framework serves as an invaluable tool for organizations to strategically navigate through times of disruption and change. This approach enables companies of all sizes and industries to strike a balance between fostering innovation while simultaneously maintaining and enhancing their existing operations, ultimately ensuring long-term competitiveness.

The framework's implementation involves allocating resources and attention across the three boxes based on the organization's current priorities. Box 1, which encompasses core operations, necessitates the majority of resources as it is pivotal to the company's present success. In contrast, Box 2 activities, which create a sense of urgency for innovation and identify outdated practices that require discontinuation, demand fewer resources. Lastly, Box 3 activities, aimed at developing new products, services, and business models crucial for future prosperity, require the least allocation of resources.

Organizations seeking to innovate while sustaining their existing operations find the three-box thinking framework immensely beneficial. It facilitates the prioritization of activities and effective allocation of resources, thereby ensuring long-term success. This framework is particularly useful when an organization aims to concentrate on innovation, whether to address current challenges or prepare for future opportunities.

Examples:

- Netflix exemplifies the successful implementation of the three-box thinking approach. In Box 1, the company manages and optimizes its current streaming service operations. Box 2 saw the company discontinue its DVD rental service, recognizing its obsolescence. Notably, in Box 3, Netflix created original content like *House of Cards*, which became a resounding success, driving future growth.
- Toyota exemplifies the utilization of three-box thinking for continuous enhancement. Box 1 involves managing and optimizing current production processes. The company constantly improves these processes in Box 2, eliminating waste and boosting efficiency. Box 3 entails exploring novel technologies and designing innovative vehicles like the popular Prius hybrid, driving future growth.

In summation, the three-box thinking framework is a potent tool for managing organizational innovation. It aids organizations in balancing innovation with the necessity of maintaining and improving existing operations. Box-3 ideation, specifically, is a valuable technique for generating fresh ideas and propelling future growth. By embracing this framework, organizations can become more agile, adaptable, and successful in today's rapidly evolving market.

Summary

- Ideation is a crucial step in the design thinking process, involving brainstorming and creative solutions to complex problems. It encourages divergent thinking, generating a wide range of ideas without judgment or criticism.
- Designing new goods, improving processes, designing new services, and creating marketing campaigns are examples of how ideation can be used.
- Clear articulation of the problem statement helps identify and understand users' needs.
- Brainstorming encourages creativity, collaboration, and problem-solving.
- Brainwriting, or group brainstorming, generates new ideas from multiple perspectives.
- Mind mapping involves creating a visual layout of concepts and ideas.
- Role-playing allows for creativity and exploration of different ideas.
- Storytelling brings an idea to life, making it more relatable and compelling.

- Sketching visualizes and communicates ideas.
- SCAMPER prompts are used to produce new ideas based on tweaks or alterations to an existing idea or product.
- Visual representations of ideas are used to evaluate the feasibility, impact, and usability of each idea.
- Divergent thinking involves generating a wide range of ideas without judging or filtering them.
- Convergence techniques include voting, clustering, and affinity diagramming.
- Idea evaluation involves analyzing and refining the generated ideas to determine their feasibility, effectiveness, and potential for implementation.
- Key tools for ideation are sticky notes, whiteboards, Post-its, pens and pencils, 3D sketches, and idea management software.
- Systematic inventive thinking (SIT) methods generate potential ideas and solutions. They help designers break away from conventional thinking and generate innovative solutions.
- Three-box thinking is a strategic framework for managing innovation while maintaining existing operations.

Solutions to Design Visualization Questions

Q 4.1

User Needs

1. **Affordability (Surface Need):** Affordable options for healthy food within budget.
   - **Latent Need 1:** Maximize the value for money spent on fresh produce. This could involve offering educational resources on budgeting and meal planning, extending shelf life of purchased produce (such as storage tips, recipe suggestions for using 'ugly' produce), or promoting recipes that minimize waste.
   - **Latent Need 2:** Feel empowered to make informed decisions about purchasing fresh produce. This could involve clear labeling with price per unit information, educational signage about seasonal produce availability and pricing, or workshops on identifying good quality at affordable prices.
   - **Latent Need 3:** Access financial assistance programs or discounts to stretch their budget further. This could involve integrating voucher programs into mobile app purchases, partnering with food banks for bulk discounts or 'rescue produce' boxes, or exploring loyalty programs at participating stores offering fresh produce.
2. **Variety and Choice (Surface Need):** Diverse range of fresh and culturally relevant healthy food options.
   - **Latent Need 1:** Feel a sense of connection to one's cultural background through available produce. This could involve offering culturally relevant fruits and vegetables, partnering with ethnic grocery stores for mobile market collaborations, or hosting cooking demonstrations featuring diverse cuisines.
   - **Latent Need 2:** Discover new and exciting ways to incorporate fresh produce into meals. This could involve providing recipe inspiration based on seasonal availability or dietary preferences, offering pre-cut vegetables for convenience, or hosting cooking classes focusing on healthy and delicious meal preparation.
   - **Latent Need 3:** Feel a sense of control and personalization over their dietary choices. This could involve offering a variety of portion sizes to cater to individual needs, promoting 'build-your-own' salad bars at mobile markets, or providing recipe customization suggestions.

3. **Quality and Safety (Surface Need):** Confidence in the quality and safety of available food options.
   - **Latent Need 1:** Feel assured that the purchased fresh produce is fresh, ripe, and free from contaminants. This could involve transparent labeling with origin information, visible inspections of produce at distribution points, or educational resources on safe handling and storage practices.
   - **Latent Need 2:** Minimize food waste and get the most out of purchased produce. This could involve offering tips on selecting ripe produce, providing storage recommendations based on specific items, or suggesting creative ways to use leftover produce.
   - **Latent Need 3:** Trust the source and freshness of the available produce. This could involve partnering with local farmers or reputable distributors, highlighting certifications or quality control measures, or offering opportunities to visit local farms or gardens (when feasible).
4. **Convenience (Surface Need):** Convenience of purchasing and preparing healthy food options.
   - **Latent Need 1:** Minimize the time and effort required to prepare meals with fresh produce. This could involve offering pre-washed and pre-cut vegetables, promoting quick and easy recipe options, or integrating meal prepping workshops into the solution.
   - **Latent Need 2:** Reduce the stress associated with grocery shopping and meal preparation. This could involve creating a user-friendly mobile app for ordering and managing fresh produce purchases, offering delivery or pick-up options, or providing resources for meal planning and grocery list creation.
   - **Latent Need 3:** Feel a sense of accomplishment and satisfaction from cooking with fresh produce. This could involve offering beginner-friendly cooking tutorials, highlighting the health benefits of incorporating fresh produce into meals, or creating a community forum for recipe sharing and meal planning inspiration.

Q 4.2

Brainstorming Session: Safe and Secure Fresh Produce Access

Challenge: Feel a sense of security and safety when obtaining fresh produce, especially for residents with mobility limitations.

Design Thinking Experts:

- You (Design Thinking Expert)
- Expert 2 (Accessibility Specialist)
- Expert 3 (Community Outreach Specialist)
- Expert 4 (Technology & Innovation Specialist)

Brainstorming Ideas:

- Grocery Assistance Program (Experts 3 and 4):
  - Develop a mobile app or phone hotline allowing residents with mobility limitations to place grocery orders, including fresh produce.
  - Partner with local volunteers or a designated shopping service to fulfill the orders and deliver them directly to users' homes.
  - Integrate features like live chat or video calls for order customization or special requests.
- Accessible Mobile Markets with Staff Support (Experts 2 and 3):
  - Design mobile market vehicles with wide aisles, lowered counters, and ramps to ensure accessibility for users with mobility aids.
  - Train mobile market staff to be patient, helpful, and offer assistance with selecting and carrying groceries.

  - Partner with community centers or senior living facilities to host pre-scheduled mobile market visits for residents with limited mobility.
- Designated 'Safe Zones' in Grocery Stores (Experts 2 and 4):
  - Partner with local grocery stores to establish designated 'Safe Zones' with wider aisles, grab bars, and lower shelves for easier navigation.
  - Equip 'Safe Zones' with call buttons or wearable panic alarms for immediate assistance in case of emergencies.
  - Utilize technology like digital signage or in-app notifications to inform users about available 'Safe Zones' within stores.
- Volunteer Grocery Shopping Network (Experts 3 and 4):
  - Establish a volunteer network through a mobile app or community center outreach.
  - Residents can request assistance from vetted volunteers for grocery shopping trips, prioritizing fresh produce options.
  - Integrate scheduling features and clear communication tools within the app for a seamless experience.
- Community Garden Network with Assisted Harvesting (Experts 1 and 3):
  - Support the development of accessible community gardens with raised beds, accessible pathways, and designated seating areas.
  - Organize volunteer programs or partner with local organizations to offer assisted harvesting services for residents with mobility limitations.
  - Promote a sense of community ownership and encourage social interaction while ensuring access to fresh, locally-grown produce.
- Safety Escort Services for Grocery Shopping (Experts 2 and 3):
  - Partner with volunteer organizations or security services to offer safety escort programs for residents with mobility limitations who prefer in-person shopping.
  - Trained escorts can accompany users to grocery stores, assist with navigating the store, and ensure a safe return home.

Q 4.3

Brainwriting: Independent and Dignified Fresh Produce Access

Instructions:

- Imagine yourself as a senior citizen who wants to maintain independence and dignity while acquiring fresh produce.
- Silently write down ideas on separate sheets of paper for 5 minutes, focusing on ways to maintain your independence and dignity when buying fresh produce.
- Don't judge or discuss your ideas yet.
  (Individual Brainstorming - 5 Minutes)
  (Timekeeper Note: Ring a bell or announce the end of the 5-minute period)
- Sharing and Building on Ideas: Now, let's share our ideas one at a time. We will take turns presenting one idea each, and then we can collectively build upon or combine them to generate even more solutions.
- Remember, there are no bad ideas!
  (Group Discussion and Idea Building)

Examples of Ideas:

1. Senior-friendly shopping carts with ergonomic handles, wider bases for stability, and built-in magnifying glasses for reading labels.

2. Self-service kiosks with large buttons, voice-activated interfaces, and magnified text options for placing produce orders and contactless payment.
3. 'Grab-and-Go' pre-packaged fresh produce bags with clear labeling and nutritional information, allowing for quick and convenient selection.
4. Mobile market with a lowered counter for easier access, staff trained in assisting seniors with selecting produce and carrying groceries.
5. Intergenerational grocery shopping program connecting volunteers with senior citizens for assistance with shopping or transportation to grocery stores.

Q 4.4

Reverse Brainstorming: Security and Safety for Fresh Produce Access

Challenge: How might we create situations that could make obtaining fresh produce feel unsafe or insecure for residents with mobility limitations?

Design Thinking Experts:

- You (Design Thinking Expert)
- Expert 2 (Security Specialist)
- Expert 3 (Accessibility Specialist)
- Expert 4 (Urban Planning Specialist)

Brainstorming Ideas (as Issues to Avoid):

- **Unreliable Staff Training:** Imagine if staff assisting residents with mobility limitations lacked proper training, potentially causing accidents or injuries while helping navigate the store or carry groceries.
- **Poor Signage and Communication:** Unclear signage or lack of communication about designated parking for disabled individuals, accessible entrances, or assistance programs could lead to confusion, frustration, and feelings of being unwelcome.
- **Unattended Personal Belongings:** Consider situations where limited mobility makes it difficult for residents to keep an eye on personal belongings while shopping, creating a risk of theft.
- **Impeding Slippery Surfaces:** What if grocery store floors were not properly maintained, with uneven surfaces, spills, or moisture creating a risk of slips and falls for residents with mobility limitations?
- **Poor Lighting in Parking Lots and Aisles:** Imagine poorly lit parking lots or dimly lit aisles within the store, creating visibility challenges and potentially increasing the risk of trip-and-fall accidents or even security concerns in dimly lit areas.

Q 4.5

Central Theme: Develop New Fitness Tracker

Branches:

1. Features: Heart rate monitoring, sleep tracking, GPS functionality, calorie tracking.
2. Target Audience: Athletes, casual fitness enthusiasts, health-conscious individuals.
3. Design Considerations: Durability, comfort, water resistance, battery life, style options.
4. Integration Opportunities: Compatibility with existing fitness apps, social media sharing features.

Sub-Branches:

1. Under 'Features,' expand on heart rate monitoring by exploring options like continuous monitoring, real-time alerts, and heart rate variability analysis.

Q 4.6

Library Book Recommendation System

1. **Scenario:** Students role-play as librarians and patrons with different reading interests (science fiction, historical fiction, fantasy).
2. **How to Conduct:** Research popular book genres and reader preferences. Students role-play a library interaction where the 'librarian' recommends books using a hypothetical recommendation system. The 'patron' provides feedback based on their interests.
3. **Outcome:** Identify strengths and weaknesses of the recommendation system. This can spark ideas for incorporating user preferences, genre filters, or personalized recommendations to improve the book-finding experience in the library.
4. **Library Book Recommendation System:** Role-playing activity

The Scene: We're at the local library! Let's see how the new book recommendation system works.

Characters:

- Librarian: (1 student) Uses the library's new book recommendation system to suggest books to patrons.
- Patrons: (3 students) Each with a different reading interest:
  - Anitha: Loves thrilling science fiction adventures.
  - Rakesh: Prefers historical fiction based on true events.
  - Fatima: Enjoys epic fantasy worlds with magical creatures.

The Role-play:

(Students approach the librarian's desk)

Anitha: Hi! I'm looking for a new book to read. I love science fiction, especially stories with space travel and alien encounters.

Librarian: (Types keywords into the recommendation system) Great! Our new system suggests "The Andromeda Strain" by Michael Crichton. It's a classic sci-fi thriller about a team investigating a deadly alien organism.

Anitha: Hmm, that sounds interesting, but I've already read it. Does the system recommend anything else based on my interest in space exploration?

Librarian: (Clicks a button) Let me see... How about "Project Hail Mary" by Andy Weir? It's a recent sci-fi novel about an amnesiac astronaut on a mission to save Earth.

Anitha: That sounds perfect! Thanks for the recommendation.

(Rakesh approaches the librarian)

Rakesh: Hi, I'm looking for some historical fiction that's based on real events. Maybe something about World War II or ancient civilizations.

Librarian: (Types keywords into the system) Absolutely! The system recommends "Unbroken" by Laura Hillenbrand. It's the true story of an American bombardier who survives a plane crash in the Pacific Ocean during World War II.

Rakesh: Sounds gripping! But I'm more interested in ancient history, particularly the Roman Empire. Does the system offer any recommendations in that area?

Librarian: (Refines the search) Let's see... Ah, "SPQR: A History of Ancient Rome" by Mary Beard might be a good fit. It's a comprehensive and engaging look at the rise and fall of the Roman Empire.

Rakesh: Excellent! That's exactly what I was looking for. Thanks for the help!

(Fatima approaches the librarian)

Fatima: Hi! I'm looking for a new fantasy book with a captivating storyline and well-developed characters. Dragons, magic, and epic quests would be ideal.

Librarian: (Types keywords into the system) No problem! The system recommends "A Song of Ice and Fire" by George R.R. Martin. It's a fantasy series known for its complex characters and intricate plotlines.

Fatima: That series is a bit long for me right now. I was hoping for something standalone with a complete story. Does the system allow you to filter based on book length?

Librarian: (Looks at the system interface) Unfortunately, that feature isn't available yet. However, I can search for shorter fantasy novels separately. How about "The Lies of Locke Lamora" by Scott Lynch? It's a fantasy heist novel with a witty protagonist and a fast-paced plot.

Fatima: That sounds intriguing! Thanks for taking the time to search for something that fits my preferences.

Debriefing and Outcome:

(After the roleplay, gather as a class)

Teacher: How did the new book recommendation system work for you?

(Students share their experiences):

Anitha: The system offered a good suggestion initially, but it didn't consider my specific preferences after I mentioned reading a book.

Rakesh: The recommendation based on real-world events was good, but the system lacked options for filtering by historical period.

Fatima: The system didn't allow me to filter for book length, which limited my options.

Teacher: We've identified some potential weaknesses in the recommendation system. Based on this feedback, what improvements can we suggest?

Students Brainstorm Solutions:

- Allow users to specify their reading preferences (genre, subgenre, themes).
- Incorporate filters for book length, publication date, and reading level.
- Offer personalized recommendations based on user reading history.
- Develop a system to learn from user feedback and improve suggestion accuracy over time.

By reflecting on this role-playing activity, we can help the library improve their recommendation system and ensure a better book-finding experience for all patrons!

Q 4.7

Redesigning Public Transportation for Senior Citizens

Storytelling Approach: Design teams interview and record stories from senior citizens about their challenges using public transportation (such as difficulty navigating stairs, limited seating, unclear signage).

Impact: These personal stories evoke empathy for the user group, leading to design solutions like prioritizing accessible entrances, installing grab bars and wider seats, and implementing clear visual and audio announcements.

Redesigning Public Transportation: Voices of Our Community

Kaveri: Public transportation used to be my lifeline, she said, a touch of wistfulness in her voice. Now, those high bus steps feel like mountains I have to conquer every time. The other day, the doors almost closed on me as I struggled up. It's a scary feeling.

Ramesh: The buses are always packed during rush hour, he said, his brow furrowed. Even if I manage to grab a seat, it's usually a tiny one. Holding on while the bus swerves is very difficult. My knees just can't handle it anymore.

The Outcome: By listening to stories like Kaveri's and Ramesh's, a common thread emerges. Senior citizens face a multitude of challenges using public transportation. These stories not only highlight physical limitations but also the emotional toll of feeling vulnerable and excluded.

Impact: Designing with Empathy

Armed with these real-life experiences, the design team approaches the project with a newfound empathy. Solutions begin to take shape, inspired by the voices of the community:

- Lower bus entrances with ramps or lifts, echoing Esther's need for easier boarding.
- Sturdy grab bars inside and outside, a response to Harold's concerns about stability.
- Wider, more comfortable seats, acknowledging the physical limitations expressed by both Harold and Esther.
- Larger, clear signage at bus stops, addressing Mildred's confusion about routes.
- Louder, well-articulated audio announcements, ensuring everyone hears their stop.

By incorporating these solutions, public transportation transforms from a source of anxiety to a tool for social connection and continued independence. The stories of senior citizens become the foundation for a more inclusive and user-friendly experience for everyone.

Q 4.8

Latent Need: Minimize food waste and get the most out of the purchased produce.

- **Substitute:**
  - **Materials:** Instead of plastic produce bags, offer reusable mesh bags for better air circulation and longer shelf life.
  - **Packaging:** Substitute bulky packaging with size-adjustable containers that adapt to the quantity of produce purchased.
- **Combine:**
  - **Information:** Combine shelf-life information on labels with QR codes that link to recipes using leftover ingredients.
  - **Technology:** Develop smart refrigerators with built-in inventory management systems and personalized recommendations for using up expiring produce.
- **Adapt:**
  - **Existing Apps:** Adapt existing recipe apps to include a 'use it up' feature that suggests recipes based on available ingredients.
  - **Educational Materials:** Adapt existing food preservation techniques like canning or pickling for use with commonly wasted produce.
- **Modify:**
  - **Storage Recommendations:** Provide more specific storage recommendations based on ripeness stage (for example, store unripe mangoes at room temperature, ripe ones in the fridge).
  - **Shopping Habits:** Encourage mindful shopping practices through loyalty programs that reward buying smaller quantities more frequently.

- **Put to Another Use:**
  - **Leftovers:** Utilize leftover vegetable scraps and trimmings to create flavorful broths or soups.
  - **Overripe Produce:** Repurpose overripe fruits for jams, smoothies, or frozen fruit mixes for later use.
- **Eliminate:**
  - **Confusing Labels:** Eliminate unclear or generic storage advice on labels. Replace them with simple and actionable icons for optimal storage.
  - **Impulse Purchases:** Develop in-store signage and educational campaigns to promote mindful grocery shopping and meal planning to reduce impulse purchases that contribute to waste.
- **Reverse:**
  - **Supply Chain:** Reverse the typical 'perfect produce' standards at grocery stores. Offer slightly imperfect fruits and vegetables at discounted prices to reduce waste.
  - **Consumer Perspective:** Shift the focus from individual responsibility to a collaborative effort. Partner with local food banks or composting programs to create solutions for handling excess produce.

By applying SCAMPER, we generate a multitude of ideas to tackle food waste and maximize produce usage. These ideas can be further refined and combined to create a holistic approach that benefits consumers, retailers, and the environment.

Exercises

Part A (Objective Questions)

1. A team is tasked with developing a new mobile app for a grocery delivery service. During the ideation phase, they decide to explore different user personas. Which of the following techniques would be most suitable for this purpose?
   (a) Reverse brainstorming (b) Mind mapping
   (c) Role-playing (d) Rapid prototyping
2. A design team is struggling to come up with innovative ideas for a new product. They decide to try a technique that involves reversing traditional brainstorming. Which technique are they using?
   (a) Mind mapping (b) Role-playing
   (c) Reverse brainstorming (d) Rapid prototyping
3. A design team wants to quickly visualize and organize their ideas for a new marketing campaign. Which technique would be most helpful for this purpose?
   (a) Role-playing (b) Mind mapping
   (c) Rapid prototyping (d) Reverse brainstorming
4. A design team wants to test their initial concept for a new product before investing significant resources. Which technique would be most suitable for this purpose?
   (a) Mind mapping (b) Role-playing
   (c) Rapid prototyping (d) Reverse brainstorming
5. A design team wants to create a compelling narrative that highlights the benefits of their new product. Which technique would be most helpful for this purpose?
   (a) Mind mapping (b) Role-playing
   (c) Rapid prototyping (d) Storytelling

6. A design team wants to explore different perspectives on a complex problem. Which technique would be most suitable for this purpose?
(a) Mind mapping (b) Role-playing
(c) Rapid prototyping (d) Reverse brainstorming

7. A design team wants to generate a large number of ideas quickly and efficiently. Which technique would be most suitable for this purpose?
(a) Mind mapping (b) Role-playing
(c) Rapid prototyping (d) Brainstorming

8. A design team wants to explore the potential risks and challenges associated with their new product. Which technique would be most suitable for this purpose?
(a) Mind mapping (b) Role-playing
(c) Rapid prototyping (d) Reverse brainstorming

9. In the three-box thinking framework, which box represents the need to let go of outdated practices?
(a) Box 1 (b) Box 2 (c) Box 3 (d) None of the above

10. What is the primary focus of Box 3 in the three-box thinking framework?
(a) Optimizing current operations (b) Identifying outdated practices
(c) Creating the future (d) Analyzing past performance

11. Which of the following is an example of a Box 2 activity?
(a) Implementing a new customer relationship management system
(b) Developing a new product line
(c) Analyzing past sales data
(d) Discontinuing a product that is no longer profitable

12. A design team is trying to come up with new ideas for a sustainable packaging solution. They decide to use a technique that involves combining, adapting, and modifying existing ideas. Which technique are they using?
(a) SCAMPER (b) Sketching
(c) Divergent thinking (d) Convergence techniques

13. A design team wants to visualize their initial ideas for a new mobile app. Which technique would be most suitable for this purpose?
(a) SCAMPER (b) Sketching
(c) Divergent thinking (d) Convergence techniques

14. A design team wants to evaluate and select the most promising ideas from a large pool of options. Which techniques would be most helpful for this purpose?
(a) SCAMPER (b) Sketching
(c) Divergent thinking (d) Convergence techniques

15. A design team wants to generate a wide range of ideas for a new product without judging or filtering them. Which technique would be most suitable for this purpose?
(a) SCAMPER (b) Sketching
(c) Divergent thinking (d) Convergence techniques

16. A design team wants to organize and categorize their ideas for a new marketing campaign. Question: Which tool would be most helpful for this purpose?
(a) Sticky notes (b) Whiteboards
(c) SCAMPER (d) Sketching

17. A design team wants to facilitate a group ideation session and encourage everyone to participate. Which tool would be most helpful for this purpose?
(a) Sticky notes (b) Whiteboards
(c) SCAMPER (d) Sketching

18. A design team wants to explore the potential benefits and drawbacks of different design options. Which technique would be most suitable for this purpose?
(a) SCAMPER (b) Sketching
(c) Divergent thinking (d) Convergence techniques
19. A design team wants to create a visual representation of their design concept to share with stakeholders. Which technique would be most suitable for this purpose?
(a) SCAMPER (b) Sketching
(c) Divergent thinking (d) Convergence techniques
20. A design team is brainstorming ideas for a new product. They want to capture and organize their thoughts in a visual and flexible way. Which tool would be most suitable for this purpose?
(a) Post-its (b) Whiteboards
(c) Sketching (d) Mind mapping
21. A design team wants to create a safe and inclusive environment for ideation. Which best practice should they prioritize?
(a) Using a diverse team (b) Setting clear objectives
(c) Creating a safe environment (d) Encouraging collaboration
22. A design team wants to generate innovative ideas for a new product by applying systematic techniques. Which method would be most suitable for this purpose?
(a) SIT (b) Post-its (c) Whiteboards (d) Mind mapping
23. A design team wants to generate a large number of ideas quickly and efficiently. Which technique would be most helpful for this purpose?
(a) SIT (b) Post-its (c) Whiteboards (d) Mind mapping
24. A design team wants to evaluate the feasibility and impact of their ideas. Which aspect of the design thinking process is most relevant to this task?
(a) Ideation (b) Prototyping
(c) Testing (d) Implementation
25. A design team wants to develop new products and services that meet the changing needs of their customers. Which aspect of design thinking is most relevant to this goal?
(a) Strategic innovation
(b) Systematic Inventive Thinking
(c) Post-its
(d) Whiteboards
26. A design team wants to break away from conventional thinking and generate innovative solutions. Which technique would be most helpful for this purpose?
(a) SIT (b) Post-its
(c) Whiteboards (d) Mind mapping
27. A design team wants to ensure that their ideas are user-centered and meet the needs of their target audience. Which best practice should they prioritize?
(a) Using a diverse team
(b) Setting clear objectives
(c) Creating a safe environment
(d) Encouraging collaboration

Part B (Short Answer Questions)

1. Write a short note on the ideation phase of the design thinking process.
2. How does brainstorming help in the ideation phase of design thinking?
3. What is brainwriting? Where is it used in design thinking?

4. What is reverse brainstorming? How is it used in the ideation phase?
5. What is mind mapping? How is it used in the ideation phase?
6. What is rapid prototyping?
7. What is role-playing? How is it used in the ideation phase?
8. What is storytelling? How is it used in the ideation phase?
9. What is sketching? How is it used in the ideation phase?
10. What is SCAMPER? How it is related to the ideation phase?
11. How does visualization help in the ideation phase?
12. What is divergent thinking?
13. What is convergence thinking?
14. What are the key characteristics of ideation?
15. How are sticky notes used in the ideation phase?
16. How are whiteboards used in the ideation phase?
17. How are Post-its used in the ideation phase?
18. What are the best practices of the ideation phase?
19. Define systematic inventive thinking.
20. What is three-box thinking?

Part C (Essay Questions)

1. How and where can ideation be used?
2. Write an essay on clear articulation of the problem statement focusing on latent needs.
3. Write an essay on various techniques for ideation.
4. Write an essay on brainwriting.
5. Explain reverse brainstorming in detail.
6. Explain creative ideation techniques in detail.
7. What are the key characteristics of effective ideation?
8. Explain various tools used in the ideation phase of design thinking.
9. Discuss various best practices of the ideation phase.
10. Write an essay on three-box thinking.

Answer Key

Part A

1. (c)	**2.** (c)	**3.** (b)	**4.** (c)	**5.** (d)	**6.** (b)	**7.** (d)	**8.** (d)	**9.** (b)	**10.** (c)
11. (d)	**12.** (a)	**13.** (b)	**14.** (d)	**15.** (c)	**16.** (a)	**17.** (b)	**18.** (d)	**19.** (b)	**20.** (a)
21. (c)	**22.** (a)	**23.** (b)	**24.** (a)	**25.** (a)	**26.** (a)	**27.** (a)			

CHAPTER 5

The Prototype Stage

Learning Objectives

At the end of this chapter, you will be able to:

- Explain the fundamental concepts of the prototype phase in design thinking, including its definition, purpose, and significance in the overall design process
- Describe how prototyping serves as a bridge between conceptualization and realization, enhancing the design thinking process by allowing for tangible experimentation
- List the techniques for developing various forms of mockups, models, and prototypes, and the importance of each in different stages of design validation
- Distinguish between different types of prototyping, such as paper prototypes, low-fidelity, mid-fidelity, and high-fidelity prototyping, and when to use each
- Explain the role of animatics, comps, and role-playing in simulating and testing design concepts and user interactions
- State the principles of user centricity in prototyping and its critical importance in ensuring the end product meets user needs and expectations
- Explain proof of concept in prototyping, and how it differs from full-scale prototyping in terms of scope and objectives
- Describe the lean startup methodology for prototype development, focusing on rapid iteration and feedback to refine the product efficiently
- Explain the creation and utilization of a virtual ecosystem for prototype development, which allows for testing in a controlled yet realistic digital environment
- List the essential skills for crafting effective prototypes and strategies for presenting them to stakeholders to communicate design intent and gather valuable feedback

5.1 Introduction

Several years ago, a design team had to create a mobile app for their employer. Even after extensive planning and brainstorming sessions over many months, consensus remained elusive. Ultimately, one designer proposed developing an initial prototype to solicit feedback from potential users. The team agreed on a low-tech prototype using basic materials like paper and pencils. When presented to a focus group, their valuable insights helped pinpoint areas requiring improvement in usability and functionality. Incorporating this feedback, the designers then built a more realistic digital prototype with specialized software tools.

After reviewing this enhanced version, another user group provided further constructive input. Through multiple cycles of revision and real-world testing, the team progressively refined their design until they reached a polished, high-fidelity prototype ready for full-scale development. This iterative prototyping process proved invaluable by facilitating early user input and allowing for adjustments before committing substantial resources. The final app was warmly received as user friendly and meeting its target audience's needs, resulting in a triumphant launch.

5.2 What and Why of Prototyping

Creating a prototype involves constructing a working model (Fig. 5.1). This process typically includes sketching ideas, drawing potential designs, crafting mock-ups from materials like cardboard or foam, 3D printing, or coding in software like JavaScript.

Figure 5.1 Example of prototyping

Prototyping aims to gain feedback throughout the design thinking process so that team members can make any necessary adjustments before finally committing resources to build the final product. A prototype allows designers and engineers to get a hands-on feel while making informed decisions based on feedback gained along the way, ultimately resulting in a successful launch. In addition, prototyping will help with proper planning and testing in product development.

By quickly developing a prototype, the ideas from the ideation stage can be tested, and functionalities can be verified, saving significant amounts of time and resources before the final product development process is initiated. We can quickly obtain a review of the user interface design and its positioning in the product from the potential user. This will ensure that the product we are developing matches the functionalities expected by the user in the early phase of product development.

To illustrate how this works, let us say you want the design team to create an app to help people plan trips more efficiently. As part of the prototype phase, the team may create some low-fidelity sketches on paper, showing what this app could look like when it is finished, perhaps displaying how users could enter details such as destination cities and hotels and compare prices. This would allow them to figure out what features are missing from their initial concept and also identify any usability issues before investing more development time into creating something which may not work in practice once released!

5.3 How Prototyping Enhances the Design Thinking Process

Prototyping plays a vital role in enhancing the design thinking process. It allows designers to evaluate and validate their ideas before investing considerable time and money in developing the final product. Figure 5.2 shows some ways whereby prototyping enhances the design thinking process.

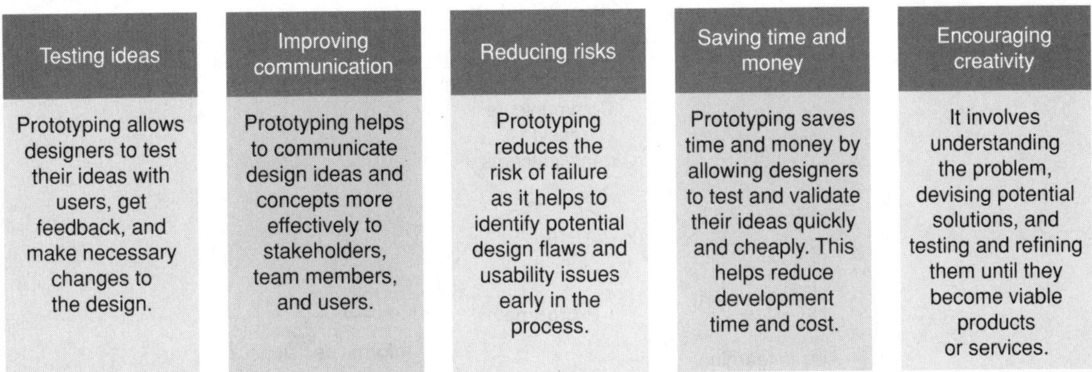

Figure 5.2 Prototypes enhance design thinking

Testing ideas: Prototyping enables designers to obtain user input and refine their concepts. A straightforward low-fidelity prototype with core functionality is first created. Potential users then assess this prototype, offering feedback on user experience, usability, and overall impression. The designers take this feedback into account, modifying the design as needed before creating an updated prototype (Fig. 5.3). This iterative cycle continues until the design fully meets user needs and expectations through repeated evaluation and refinement.

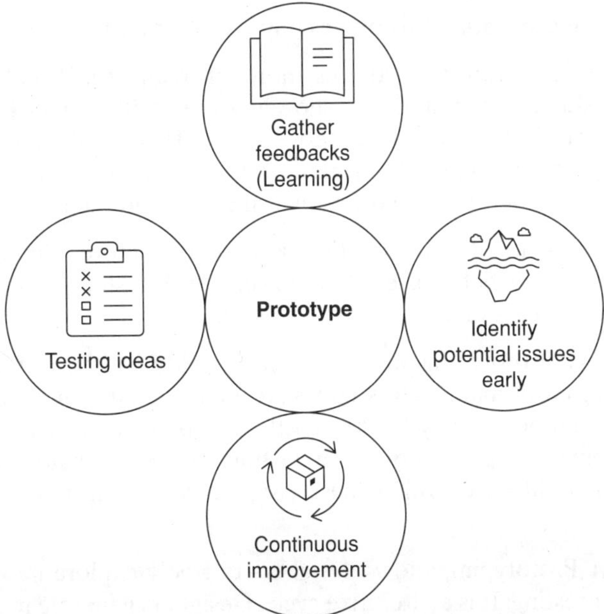

Figure 5.3 Prototyping helps to evaluate ideas

Improving communication: Prototyping aids in conveying design notions and concepts more clearly to stakeholders, colleagues, and users (Fig. 5.4). Visualizing and demonstrating the design ideas through prototypes ensures that everyone understands them. Prototyping effectively communicates design ideas and concepts because it allows people to experience the design interactively.

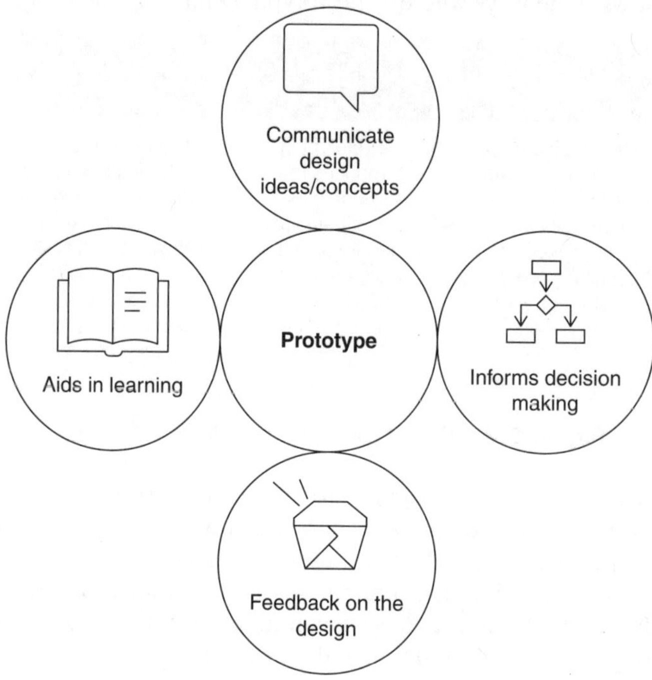

Figure 5.4 Prototypes improve communication

Designing new products and websites requires thorough planning. Prototyping helps make the process smoother. Teams create basic models to show how users will interact. Low-fidelity prototypes, like paper sketches, let stakeholders visualize website flows. This enables feedback on designs early on. For physical products, high-fidelity 3D-printed prototypes demonstrate functionality. Investors and customers can thus understand the features by using the prototypes.

Reducing risk: Prototyping identifies potential issues early before significant investment. This allows for updating designs for better user experience. A well-tested prototype leads to a refined final product with higher success rates.

Saving time and money: Prototyping validates ideas quickly and cost effectively. It streamlines development by enabling early changes. Resources are allocated efficiently based on user feedback. Without prototyping, assumptions may lead to costly mistakes. For instance, a software company spends heavily developing an app without user testing. However, major usability flaws make it unpopular. Prototyping could have caught these issues early, saving money while improving the product.

Encouraging creativity: Prototyping allows designers to freely explore new concepts by creating tangible models for user testing. It is an iterative cycle. Designers generate multiple mockups, refine them through feedback, and arrive at the best solution. This hands-on approach sparks innovative thinking and problem solving. Low-fidelity prototypes enable quick visualization of ideas. They reveal flaws and inspire fresh perspectives on addressing user needs. For instance, a mobile app team might prototype various interface layouts, evaluate usability, and creatively enhance the design.

5.4 Developing Mockups, Models, and Prototypes

Design thinking is a way of producing solutions to problems. It involves understanding the problem, devising potential solutions, and testing and refining them until they become viable products or services. Mockups, models, and prototypes are essential components in design thinking (Table 5.1).

Table 5.1 Mockups, models and prototypes

Feature	Mockup	Model	Prototype
Goal	Visualize the look and feel of a product	Represent a product in a physical or digital form	Simulate the functionality and user interaction of a product
Fidelity	High fidelity (realistic appearance)	Variable (low to high fidelity)	Variable (low to high fidelity)
Functionality	Static, non-functional	Can be static or functional	Functional, simulates user interaction
Materials	Digital design tools (for example, Figma, Photoshop)	Physical materials (cardboard, wood, clay) or digital tools (3D modeling software)	Physical materials (cardboard, foam) or digital tools (design and prototyping software)
Investment	Lower investment of time and resources	Variable investment based on complexity	Variable investment based on complexity and functionality
Output	Digital image or presentation showcasing the visual design	Physical or digital representation of the product's form and features	Functional model that allows users to interact with and experience the product
Iteration	Possible, but can be time-consuming	Possible, depends on model complexity	Iterative process with frequent refinements based on testing
Stakeholders	Designers, clients, and stakeholders for visual feedback	Designers, engineers, and stakeholders for overall product understanding	Designers, engineers, and users for testing functionality and user experience
Next Step	Prototyping or development based on approved mockup	Prototyping or further design refinement	User testing, further prototyping, or development based on prototype results

Mockups are service representations that can be used to evaluate ideas in the early stages of development. This helps ensure that design decisions align with business goals before proceeding down a more expensive path.

Models are higher fidelity simulations that allow users to interact with the product before it is sent to production. Models often contain detailed representations of how users will interact with the system by simulating interactive elements such as buttons, menus, etc., so they can test different workflows before coding begins. Models also enable designers to test functionality before launch by running 'what if' scenarios that simulate how users would interact with specific features in real-world settings. This helps identify potential flaws ahead of time while ensuring desired outcomes once the product is sent to the production phase.

Prototypes bridge the gap between models and actual implementation by incorporating code elements in their design structure, allowing for visual representation (mockup) and functional representation (model). Prototypes provide a realistic demonstration of what an end-user would experience when interacting with a product or service, which helps identify any issues related to user interface (UI) design as well as overall flow/usability before moving forward into the actual development phase.

For example, we want to develop a user-friendly mobile app for ordering fresh produce from local grocery stores or farmers markets.

Mockups: Exploring the Look and Feel

Goal: Define the basic layout and visual elements of the app.

Low-fidelity Mockup: Using pen and paper or a basic design tool, sketch out the main screens of the app. This might include a home screen with the featured produce, a product browsing screen with filtering options, a shopping cart screen, and a check-out process.

Focus on the Layout: At this stage, focus on the placement of elements like buttons, menus, and product information. Do not worry about detailed graphics or color schemes.

User Feedback: Present the mockups to potential users (shoppers and store owners) and gather feedback on the overall flow, clarity of information, and ease of use.

Models: Simulating User Interaction

Goal: Enhance the mockup by incorporating interactive elements to simulate the user experience.

Interactive Prototype: Use a prototyping tool to create a clickable model. This model should replicate core functionalities like browsing products, adding items to the cart, and navigating the check-out process.

Focus on Functionality: While the visuals may still be basic, the focus shifts to user interaction. Test how users navigate the app, complete tasks, and interact with features.

Usability Testing: Conduct usability testing with potential users and observe their interactions with the model. Identify any confusing elements or areas for improvement in the user flow.

Prototypes: Refining the Experience

Goal: Craft a highly detailed prototype that closely mirrors the intended final application.

High-fidelity Prototype: Employing an advanced prototyping tool, construct a prototype featuring realistic visuals and comprehensive functionalities. This prototype should exhibit an appearance and behavior reminiscent of the intended final application.

Focus on the User Interface (UI): Refine the visual design elements, including color schemes, typography selections, and product imagery, to enhance the overall user experience.

Realistic Testing: Conduct user testing sessions utilizing the high-fidelity prototype. This approach enables users to experience the application in a context more closely aligned with the intended final product, allowing them to provide insightful feedback regarding usability, information accessibility, and overall appeal.

5.5 Types of Prototyping

Prototyping is an important component of the design thinking process. There are different types of tests that you can use in thought making, and these are discussed in this section.

5.5.1 Paper Prototypes

These are usually basic mockups made from paper or cardboard (Fig. 5.5). You can use them to try ideas quickly, improve user flows, and check for ease of use. Paper testing means drawing the user pictures. This type of testing is cheap since you only need some paper and scissors. These tests are used to make websites, phone apps, comics, newspaper ads, and more. It lets designers check and improve their ideas quickly.

Figure 5.5 Example of paper prototype

For example, a designer is creating a new house and wants to assess the layouts. She can create a paper prototype using sketches and assess it with users to obtain feedback on the user experience. Paper prototyping can be used for two purposes:

- **To share ideas:** Paper models let us quickly show how the product will look, work, and move around. Everyone involved can give their thoughts early on.
- **To test the usability of the product:** Paper models enable us to test if the product works well for users. If users need changes, we can update the product's interface before building it.

Design Visualization Question 5.1

Paper prototyping is used in the design process to create quick, low-fidelity representations of an interface or product. It involves sketching ideas and concepts on paper, which can be easily modified and tested. At the same time, it may appear to be an old-fashioned method in the digital age, but paper prototyping has several advantages over other forms of prototyping.

List the various advantages of paper prototyping for a design thinking project.

Design Visualization Question 5.2

List the various disadvantages of paper prototyping with explanations.

5.5.1.1 When to Use Paper Prototypes

People can use easy prototypes when creating new objects or services that are very different from what is currently available. For instance, a team working on a new health device that tracks important signs may use easy prototypes to test various design ideas before building a real prototype. The team can make simple drawings of the device's interface and test the design with possible users, allowing them to improve the design and fix any usability problems before using expensive prototyping tools.

Sometimes, easy prototypes may not be needed if the design team is changing an existing solution without changing the user interface. For example, a team working on an online store may not need easy prototypes if all they need to do is add a new feature to it. However, easy prototypes can still be helpful if the team wants to explore different design options for the new feature. By creating simple drawings of the feature's user interface and testing it with possible users, the team can quickly try different design ideas and find the best solution.

5.5.2 Fidelity of Prototyping

Fidelity is about how detailed the prototype should be. It can be simple or complex.

Low-fidelity prototypes are quick rough versions used to test basic ideas for digital products like websites or apps. They help designers check if the flow and layout work well. Mid-fidelity prototypes are more detailed than low-fidelity ones but are still not fully polished. They include more accurate representations of the layout, design elements, and interactions. These prototypes often use grayscale or limited color schemes and provide a clearer idea of the user interface and experience. They help test specific functionalities and get feedback on the overall design without getting bogged down by visual details. On the other hand, high-fidelity prototypes are very close to the final product. They include detailed design elements, colors, typography, and interactions. These prototypes look and function almost like the actual product, allowing for thorough user experience and design testing. High-fidelity prototypes are often used for final user testing and presentations to stakeholders, as they provide a realistic view of the end product. Table 5.2 compares low-, mid- and high-fidelity prototypes.

Table 5.2 Comparison of low-, mid- and high-fidelity prototypes

Feature	Low-Fidelity Prototype	Mid-Fidelity Prototype	High-Fidelity Prototype
Looks	Like a very sketchy drawing	More detailed, like a drawing with some color	Looks almost like the real app, with graphics and icons
Materials	Paper, pen, sticky notes	Can be digital (on a computer) or physical (cardboard, markers)	Mostly digital (on a computer)

(Continued)

Feature	Low-Fidelity Prototype	Mid-Fidelity Prototype	High-Fidelity Prototype
Functionality	Limited interaction, mostly shows layout and basic ideas	Some clickable elements, hints at how the app might work	Most features are interactive, feels very close to the real app
Time and Effort	Fastest and easiest to make	Takes a bit more time and effort	Takes the most time and effort to create
Good for	Early brainstorming, getting basic ideas down	Testing specific features and user flows	Getting final user feedback, refining the design
Imagine it as.	A napkin sketch of your app	A more detailed storyboard for your app	A playable demo of your app

5.5.2.1 Low-Fidelity Prototyping

Several types of low-fidelity prototypes can be used in the design process. Here are some common examples (Fig. 5.6).

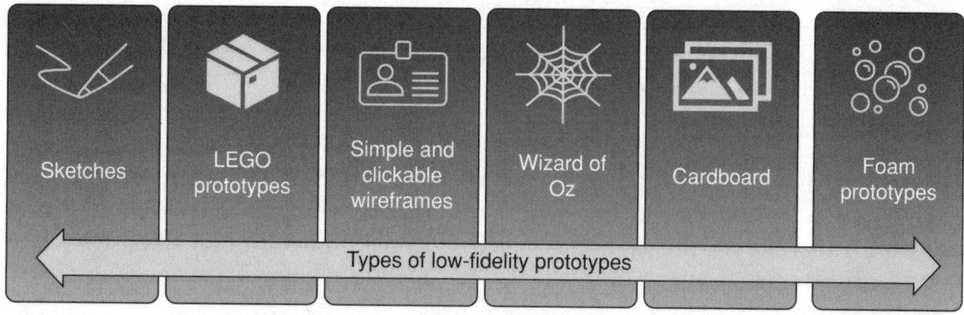

Figure 5.6 Types of low-fidelity prototypes

Sketches: This involves sketching the design on paper or using Post-it notes to represent different user interface elements and interactions. Sketches are drawn quickly with paper and pen or on a board with a chalk/marker (Fig. 5.7).

Figure 5.7 Sketches

In general, sketches are not technical but help make decisions. Sketches can be easy to draw and can be updated or discarded; in addition, it does not involve much time and cost. Moreover, to draw sketches, the person need not be artistic; hence it is the most preferred tool.

Sketches can be used in the initial stages of the design process. Your ideas can be sketched with symbols and text to evaluate their feasibility. For complex ideas, where many entities and their interactions are involved, we can use many diagrams such as sequence diagrams, flow diagrams, and behavior maps.

Design Visualization Question 5.3

Your Mission: Imagine you are tasked with designing a brand new mobile app that helps students stay organized and on top of their studies. Here's the catch: you can only use sketches to develop your ideas!

The Process:

1. **Brainstorming:** Get your creative mind working! Spend 10 minutes sketching out as many ideas as you can for features and functionalities in your student organizer app. Don't worry about perfect artistry; focus on getting your ideas down quickly and clearly.
2. **Refine and Focus:** Now, take a step back and review your sketches. Choose 3–5 ideas that you find most promising and interesting. Refine these sketches, adding details and labels to make them easier to understand.
3. **User Journey:** Let's think about how a student would use your app. Create a sketch storyboard that depicts the key steps a student would take to complete a specific task within your app. For example, how would a student add an assignment due date or create a study schedule?
4. **Collaboration and Feedback:** The beauty of design thinking is collaboration! Share your sketches with your classmates and get their feedback. What do they like? What could be improved? Be open to suggestions and use this feedback to further refine your ideas.

Bonus Challenge: Think about different types of students with different learning styles. How could your app cater to their needs? Sketch out some ideas for features that would be helpful for visual learners, auditory learners, or kinesthetic learners.

Remember: There are no wrong answers in brainstorming! The more ideas you generate, the better. Don't be afraid to experiment and have fun with this process.

What to Submit: At the end of this session, you should have a collection of sketches showcasing your ideas for the student organizer app. This could include:

- Initial brainstormed features
- Refined sketches of your top 3–5 ideas
- A storyboard depicting a user journey
- Any bonus sketches for catering to different learning styles

By the time you put pen to paper, you will be well on your way to designing a user-friendly student organizer app.

LEGO Prototypes: Plastic LEGO toys enable children to build diverse structures like buildings, robots, and vehicles (Fig. 5.8). The Danish LEGO Group manufactures these colored, interlocking bricks. The best feature is their easy disassembly, allowing reuse in other creations. LEGO prototyping forgoes words, using art to express product designs. Even complex concepts can be modelled with LEGO. These vibrant, eye catching bricks facilitate rapid prototyping of diverse designs.

Figure 5.8 LEGO prototype

Prototypes made with LEGO toys are easy to change. We can take apart, add, or remove bricks from the prototype. It is also fun to work with LEGO toys. LEGO prototypes can be the exact size of the physical product, so users can see how much space they would up. We can also check the weight of the product by adding materials with the same weight as the final product.

However, LEGO toys are not good for digital products because making them with LEGO is difficult. Also, it does not support the user interface in the prototype.

Design Visualization Question 5.4

The Challenge: Imagine you have been tasked with designing a brand new product for college students. The goal is to create something that will help them stay organized, manage their workload, and maybe even add a touch of fun to their daily routines!

The LEGO Twist: Here's the catch: you can only use LEGO bricks to develop your prototype. This might seem like a limitation, but it can actually spark your creativity and help you focus on the core functionality of your product.

The Process:

1. **Brainstorming:** Spend 15 minutes sketching out as many ideas as you can for your college student product. Don't worry about perfect artistry; focus on getting your ideas down quickly and clearly.
2. **Select your Bricks:** After your brainstorming session, choose the most promising idea you want to develop further. Think about the key features and functionalities of your product and start building a physical prototype using LEGO pieces.

3. **Functionality:** While building your prototype, keep the user experience in mind. How will college students interact with your product? Can they easily understand how it works? Use different colors and shapes to represent different functionalities.
4. **User Testing:** Gather some of your classmates and ask them to interact with your LEGO model. Observe their reactions, listen to their feedback, and see if they can understand the purpose and functionality of your product.
5. **Iteration is Key:** The beauty of LEGO prototyping is its ease of modification. Based on the user feedback, make changes and iterate on your design. Rebuild your prototype with your newfound insights and test it again.

Bonus Challenge: While LEGO bricks can help represent the size of your product, consider using other materials to add weight or simulate different textures. This can give users a more complete understanding of your idea.

Deliverables:

- A brief description of your chosen college student product and its intended functionalities.
- A picture of your final LEGO prototype.
- A summary of the user feedback you received during testing and how you iterated on your design based on that feedback.

Remember: There are no wrong ideas in brainstorming! The more creative you are, the better. So, have fun building, testing, and iterating.

Simple Wireframes: Wireframes are basic plans for screens of digital products (Fig. 5.9). They show the layout of each screen or page. People often make wireframes with tools like Sketch or Figma, but can draw them too. The goal is to plan the basic layout to look at the design and how people use it. Wireframes give you the outline shape of your product. This first plan will not look at the interface or how it looks. Wireframe first plans can change quickly based on what people need since they do not look at the interface or design. Unlike other first plans, wireframe first plans let you know how the different pages connect.

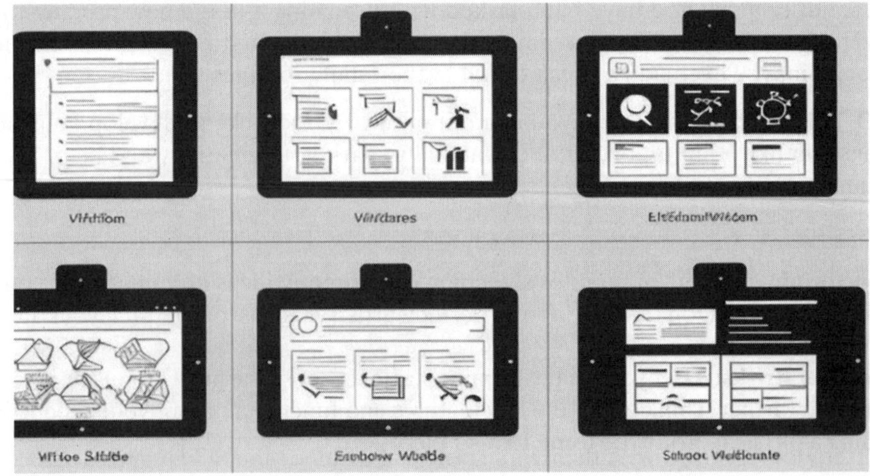

Figure 5.9 Simple wireframe

Wireframes help create user flows on different product pages. They show the layout of your product, not its appearance. Wireframes have templates that guide you in creating products. They do not use color. For consistency, use one font in the wireframe and different sizes for headings. Minimize placeholder text so your wireframes are fully usable. Use placeholders only when they will not affect usability.

Clickable wireframes are used when designers want to assess the flow and navigation of a product or website. They allow users to interact with the design and provide feedback on the user experience. Clickable wireframes can be easily created using tools like Sketch, Figma, or Adobe XD.

Clickable wireframes are best used when you need to see a simple layout and how parts connect for a digital product. However, they may not work well for testing complex elements like animations or moving content. In addition, they cannot be used for checking accessibility, since they may not include tools for people with disabilities.

Wizard of Oz Prototypes: These prototypes are used to make users believe that the prototype is fully functional, whereas in reality, only a part of it is. A specific complex part of the product can thus be assessed without building the entire product (Fig. 5.10).

Figure 5.10 Wizard of Oz prototype

This type of prototype helps us to validate the design before implementing it. However, a lot of time needs to be spent to build it as we need to make the user believe that the prototype is fully functional. This prototype should be used only in the last stage of the design process. We can train the Wizard for a predefined set of instructions. These instructions should be from standard or predictable scenarios so that the user may assess the reaction. The Wizard of OZ prototype cannot be used to test the reliability and accuracy of the product, as it needs to be fully functional.

Cardboard Prototypes: Cardboard prototypes are those created using cardboard material (Fig. 5.11). They are easy to create and can be quickly manipulated to test different design ideas. This can be used when the design is still in the ideation stage.

Figure 5.11 Cardboard prototype

Cardboard prototypes offer advantages such as swift creation, low cost, and straightforward modification. However, drawbacks exist: reduced realism and detail, restricted interaction testing abilities, potential unsuitability for intricate designs.

Design Visualization Question 5.5

Eco-Friendly Classroom: Challenge yourself to design a new and improved recycling system for your classroom. Use cardboard to create prototypes for different collection bins, sorting stations, or even a fun and educational display to promote recycling habits.

Foam Prototypes: These are optimal for evaluating physical form and interaction. Foam materials, easily shaped and cut, can be used to construct physical product models (Fig. 5.12). Lightweight and modifiable, they enable quick iterations. Suitable for initial design refinement stages, they test form and user physical interaction.

Figure 5.12 Foam prototype

However, they cannot be used to recreate electronic components, limiting their functionality. Also, they may lack durability for extended testing or referencing. The best practice is to use quality foam for longevity, test physical interaction by user handling, use with other prototypes for both physical and digital testing, and test different component setups and layouts to optimize the design.

5.5.2.2 Other Types of Low-Fidelity Prototypes

Rough Prototyping: This allows for rapid testing of ideas and assumptions, bringing concepts to life. This 'fail fast to succeed sooner' mindset is crucial in design thinking. First, user needs and goals are identified before creating any solution. Once understood, a rough working prototype is built to evaluate if the hypothesis about user needs is accurate. This iterative approach highlights what works and what does not, enabling informed decisions. Rough prototypes offer several advantages over traditional development cycles: they are typically more affordable and quicker to create; they simplify complex problems into manageable parts; they foster better user understanding through direct feedback; and they establish a shared language across teams with different expertise. For instance, if developing a grocery shopping assistance app, conversations with potential users about shopping challenges and efficiencies would precede wireframe sketches and clickable prototypes using tools like Sketch, Adobe XD, and InVision. User testing and feedback drive iterations until the minimum viable product is reached for public release, while insights gained continually enhance future versions.

Trying out new ideas carries risks. However, by building early versions, design thinking manages failures sensibly. This makes slip-ups seem less alarming than wasting huge efforts only to quit later. So, when facing major challenges, we should remember to embrace small failures, learn from mistakes, adapt swiftly, and persist with rough drafts until we attain success.

Walkthroughs: This is a straightforward technique for mapping out and evaluating new services or processes. It involves simulating the sequence of steps involved, permitting designers to assess the flow and user friendliness before full implementation. For instance, if creating a new online ordering system, a designer could construct a mock walkthrough guiding users about how to place an order from start to finish. This would entail simulated screens and prompts, enabling observation of the experience. The designer could then identify usability issues, unclear instructions, or procedural bottlenecks. This vital feedback informs refinements prior to launch, ensuring a smooth, optimized service or process. Walkthroughs are invaluable for preempting potential problems early in the design thinking process. They afford a controlled testing environment, empowering designers to iterate and perfect their vision before committing substantial resources. Whether for customer facing services or internal operations like onboarding, walkthroughs are an efficient, low-cost means of user experience validation. Their simplicity calls into question their immense utility in realizing intuitive, streamlined solutions.

Maquettes: These are simple 3D models that allow designers to test layout and usability before final production (Fig. 5.13). Imagine a designer crafting a retail display for a client. They build a maquette prototype, a basic representation of the intended design. This model enables user testing and feedback gathering to refine the display's layout and engagement. Maquettes serve as practical tools for recreating retail displays or packaging concepts prior to manufacturing the actual product. Their purpose is to facilitate design evaluation and adjustments, ensuring a compelling and user-friendly final result. For instance, when developing a new shelf arrangement for a retail store, a designer might construct a maquette to experiment with product placement and organization. This inexpensive, preliminary model allows for meaningful testing and optimization of the design concept.

Figure 5.13 Maquette prototype

Another example of maquettes in design thinking is in packaging design. A designer might create a maquette of a package design to test the packaging's size, shape, and functionality. They can also test different materials and textures to see how they impact the overall design and user experience. Overall, maquettes are a valuable tool in design thinking as they allow designers to test and refine their ideas before investing in the final product.

5.5.2.3 Mid-Fidelity Prototyping

Mid-fidelity prototypes are digital mockups that offer more realistic visuals and basic functionality. These are popular for showcasing designs with clickable elements while requiring minimal coding skills. The key distinctions between low-fidelity and mid-fidelity prototypes revolve around their level of detail and interactivity:

- **Details**: Low-fidelity prototypes are bare and basic, with little detail. Mid-fidelity ones have more realistic details. A low-fidelity website prototype might just have rough layout sketches, while a mid-fidelity one could show actual text, images, and color schemes.
- **Interaction**: Low-fidelity prototypes cannot be interacted with, but mid-fidelity ones sometimes let you click buttons or links. For instance, a low-fidelity app prototype could just be paper sketches, whereas a mid-fidelity one might let you click through different screens.
- **Materials**: Low-fidelity prototypes often use basic craft supplies like paper or cardboard. Mid-fidelity ones might use special tools like wireframing software or 3D printing. For example, a low-fidelity product prototype could be made from duct tape and cardboard, but a mid-fidelity version might 3D-print a more realistic model.
- **Cost and Time**: Creating low-fidelity models is fast and cheap. Making mid-fidelity models takes more time and money. For example, you can draw a basic website plan with paper and pen in just hours. However, to make a mid-fidelity model, you may need days or weeks using special software.
- **Feedback**: Low-fidelity models are good for getting overall comments on concepts and designs. Mid-fidelity models allow more specific feedback on features and functions. For instance, a simple product model may gather ideas on the general concept. A more detailed mid-fidelity model can get input on particular capabilities.

When developing applications, designers might employ mid-fidelity prototyping concepts. They could swiftly create a few introductory screens (with buttons/links) representing the core functions that must operate correctly. They could then add additional visual elements like graphics/textures once these core functions have been validated by tests with users or other stakeholders. This approach ensures that all critical requirements are met without wasting resources on aesthetic changes after functionality is completed. Figure 5.14 shows some examples of mid-fidelity prototypes with explanations.

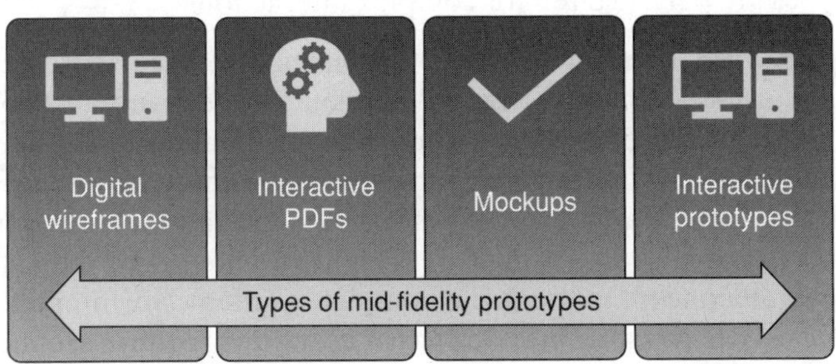

Figure 5.14 Types of mid-fidelity prototypes

Digital Wireframes: These are useful when designing products' usability and performance. They allow designers to test ideas during the development phase. Wireframes help gather feedback on concepts before advancing to high-fidelity prototypes. However, wireframes should not be used for evaluating complex features or visual elements. Their strength lies in assessing basic functionality and usability. Wireframes are easy to create, enabling rapid iterations. They facilitate sharing of designs for collaborative testing and feedback. However, wireframes provide incomplete representations, lacking the final products' full capabilities. In addition, they do not convey comprehensive user experiences, concentrating more on core usability.

Interactive PDFs: Interactive PDFs let designers simulate user interactions through clickable links, dropdown menus, and form fields. A mobile app designer could create an interactive PDF prototype with clickable buttons for navigation, input fields for user data, and dropdown menus for selections. Such prototypes are useful in the following situations:

- When designing more intricate, multi-page layouts or forms.
- When basic interactivity is required for testing and gathering feedback.
- When presenting the design to stakeholders for review and approval.

However, interactive PDFs are not suitable in these circumstances:

- When advanced interactivity beyond basic links and forms is necessary.
- When a more realistic and immersive user experience is essential.
- When the prototype needs testing on actual devices or platforms.

The advantages of using interactive PDFs as mid-fidelity prototypes include ease of creation and editing using tools like Adobe Acrobat, detailed visuals superior to low-fidelity wireframes, and basic interactivity for user testing. Conversely, the limitations are restricted interactivity beyond essential features, inability to provide a fully immersive experience, and potential compatibility issues with certain devices or platforms.

Mockups with Basic Functionality: Mockups that include some interactive elements like dropdown menus or clickable buttons are a step ahead of low-fidelity prototypes. They offer more detail and interactivity. However, they lack the full functionality of high-fidelity prototypes. These mockups have a refined visual design. Designers can use tools to create them with basic interactions. A designer creating an e-commerce mockup could include a dropdown for product categories and a cart button. This tests how users interact and identifies any navigation or check-out issues. But these mockups cannot accurately simulate advanced functionality like search bars or payment gateways. High-fidelity prototypes are better suited for complex interactions.

Interactive Prototypes with Limited Content: At times, it makes sense to create interactive prototypes containing just key content. These allow you to effectively test specific user flows or interactions. This approach is useful when building more detailed prototypes would be overly time consuming or unnecessary. Interactive prototypes with limited content enable designers to identify potential design issues early. This allows for quick iteration. However, it is important to remember that these prototypes do not fully represent the final product. Users may need help understanding the overall concept without the complete content. So, interactive prototypes with limited content work best when testing interactions or user flows requiring refinement. For instance, a designer might create a prototype solely focused on the check-out process for an e-commerce site. This would allow them to test and refine the purchase completion steps. However, using interactive prototypes with limited content is not recommended when trying to test the overall user experience. Nor should they be used when the final product will contain a significant amount of content. In such cases, more detailed prototypes are better to ensure users grasp the full scope of the product.

Scenario-based Prototyping: This is a way to design visuals. It combines user interface design with storyboarding and simulation. It involves creating multiple prototypes, getting closer to the desired result with each one. Scenario-based prototyping allows for creating experiences that users can interact with, using design thinking. The goal is to understand how the user would feel when using the designed product or service. Designers create scenarios describing how people might use their offering. They then turn these into sketches, wireframes, animations, or interactive prototypes. This shows how users will interact with specific functions or features. Designers can then quickly see what works and what does not, in terms of user experience, before creating the actual product or service.

For instance, consider an e-commerce website for an online store. Designers could create storyboards and wireframes illustrating how shoppers find products, go through check-out, payment options, shipping details, etc. They could also make interactive prototypes to test these scenarios before developing the actual e-commerce platform code. This enables them to identifying potential issues early in the development process, saving time and money by avoiding revisions after launch.

5.5.2.4 High-Fidelity Prototyping

Prototypes with a high level of detail and functionality are known as high-fidelity prototypes. Advanced tools or coding are used to create these highly interactive models. The look, feel, and functionality closely mirrors the final product. User testing, design validation, and stakeholder presentations often utilize high-fidelity prototypes. Designers can create realistic features and functions to test with users. This prototyping approach is part of design thinking, allowing idea testing before proceeding with development or production.

Some examples of high-fidelity prototyping include:

- Interactive prototypes with full functionality
- Virtual reality (VR) prototypes

- 3D-printed prototypes
- Video prototypes
- Fully functional physical prototypes
- HTML/CSS prototypes
- Mobile app prototypes
- Augmented reality (AR) prototypes

Design Visualization Question 5.6

High-fidelity prototyping is a form of rapid prototyping that emphasizes the details and accuracy of the design. List the various advantages of high-fidelity prototyping.

Design Visualization Question 5.7

List the various disadvantages of high-fidelity prototyping.

Once designers validate a basic prototype, they craft a high-fidelity version. This detailed prototype closely resembles the final product. For example, after testing a simple prototype, a designer creates an intricate version with designs and interactions to ensure user needs are met. Progressing from basic to advanced prototypes is crucial in the design process. Basic prototypes are affordable, easy-to-make models that allow designers to test and refine ideas quickly. They are typically created with simple tools like pens, paper, whiteboards, or basic software.

As the design evolves, prototypes become more realistic and product-like. High-fidelity prototypes enable testing of functionality, usability, and aesthetics. They utilize sophisticated tools like Adobe Photoshop or Sketch. Imagine a mobile app design team starting with paper wireframes and user flows to test layout and functions. Iterating on these basic prototypes, they move to digital wireframes using InVision or Figma. After refining the user interface and experience, they build a high-fidelity prototype with Adobe XD or Sketch. This realistic prototype closely resembles the final app, allowing comprehensive testing of functionality, usability, and appearance.

High-fidelity prototypes can broadly be divided into three main types: animatics, comps and role-playing.

Animatics: Animation companies use animatics to check if a story works smoothly before making a full animation. Animatics are basic and rough animations created with software like Adobe After Effects. They show the timing and flow of the animation. Companies make an animatic first instead of animating everything right away. This lets them test the pacing and camera angles. They can see if the story makes sense or needs changes. For example, a studio planning a new short film would test it with people first. They could get comments on the story timing and then update the animatic based on that feedback. Animatics also reveal animation issues early on. Some scenes might be too difficult to animate on time and within budget. By checking the animatic, the creators can simplify those parts before fully animating them. In short, animatics can save effort by letting studios refine animation pacing and spot complications beforehand. This tool is essential for smooth animation production.

Comps: For printed materials like brochures, advertisements, or packaging, high-fidelity prototypes are used. They are called comps or comprehensives (Fig. 5.15). Comps provide a realistic idea of the look-and-feel of the final design. Software like Adobe InDesign or Photoshop are used to create comps. Clients can review printed or digital comps and give feedback.

Comps help clients better understand how the final product will appear. This allows them to provide accurate feedback and make informed design decisions. Design teams also use comps internally. They test different concepts and layouts before presenting to clients. An advantage of comps is that they are easily adjustable without costly processes. For instance, a designer creates a brochure comp. The client requests color scheme or layout changes. The comp can be modified accordingly.

Figure 5.15 Comps

Comps are digital designs that closely resemble the final product's appearance. They allow designers to efficiently present and modify ideas before production. One key benefit is quickly updating comps based on client feedback, saving time and resources. In addition, comps enable designers to identify potential issues early, like misalignment with packaging die cut lines. This problem can be resolved in the digital file, preventing costly production errors.

However, comps have limitations too. They provide a realistic visual representation but lack the tactile experience of holding or using the actual product. This can be crucial for certain designs like packaging or physical products. Moreover, creating high-quality comps requires advanced software skills, which may not be feasible for all design teams or projects. Some clients might struggle to visualize the final product from a comp, leading to misunderstandings. Despite these drawbacks, comps remain an essential prototyping tool for printed materials, allowing designers to test and refine concepts before production. Their advantages, such as ease of modification and early issue detection, outweigh their limitations when used appropriately and with awareness of their constraints.

Role-playing: Acting out scenarios is a technique called role-playing. It is a realistic method used in design thinking. Role-playing helps designers comprehend how users will interact with a product or service. Designers recreate situations to identify difficulties and positive experiences. They might use props, sounds, and other elements to make scenarios seem real. This helps designers understand user interactions better.

For example, a design team creating a healthcare provider's mobile app might use role-playing. They could test how users interact with the app when scheduling appointments, accessing medical records, or receiving alerts. The team could act out different scenarios, playing user and app roles, to gain insights into usage in different situations. They might use props or simulations like a smartphone app mockup to make the environment realistic. Another example could involve a design team creating a retail store product. They could use role-playing to test how customers interact with the product and its place in the store's layout and experience.

Overall, role-playing helps designers gain insights into user behaviors and needs. By simulating real-life scenarios, designers identify pain points and positive user experiences, leading to human-centered design solutions.

5.6 User Centricity in Prototyping

Conceptualizing ideas is vital in the design process, allowing creators to explore and evaluate concepts before finalizing products. Regardless of the prototype type, the user's needs must remain central to ensure effective, efficient, and enjoyable solutions. User testing with low-fidelity prototypes exemplifies user-centric designs. Through real user feedback, designers gain valuable insights to enhance user experiences. Another approach utilizes high-fidelity prototypes, providing accurate previews of products' appearance and functionality.

A common prototyping strategy begins with low-fidelity wireframes, gradually increasing fidelity as designs refine. Teams may advance from basic sketches to mid-fidelity prototypes incorporating more detailed visuals and basic interactivity, culminating in high-fidelity, near-final versions with advanced interactions and polished aesthetics. This gradual progression allows for continuous user testing and refinement.

5.7 Proof of Concept and Prototyping

Proof of concept (POC) and prototyping are processes used in design thinking (Table 5.3). The primary purpose is to test an idea with users and stakeholders to see how it works in practice. The two concepts often need clarification; however, some crucial differences must be understood.

Table 5.3 Proof of concept versus prototyping

Feature	Proof of Concept (POC)	Prototyping
Goal	Validate feasibility of a core idea or technology	Refine and test design ideas
Fidelity	Low-fidelity (basic, often non-functional)	Variable fidelity (low-fidelity to high-fidelity)
Focus	Functionality	Functionality, usability, and user experience
Next Step	Decision on further development based on POC results	Further prototyping and user testing

(*Continued*)

Feature	Proof of Concept (POC)	Prototyping
Materials	Basic materials (paper, sketches, simulations)	Wider range of materials (cardboard, foam, 3D printing)
Investment	Low investment of time and resources	Variable investment based on fidelity
Output	Report, document, or basic model demonstrating core functionality	Functional or semi-functional model
Iteration	Limited iteration	Iterative process with frequent refinements based on testing
Stakeholders	Technical feasibility for internal teams or investors	Designers, engineers, and users
Next Step	Decision on further development based on POC results	Further prototyping and user testing

POC is a process in which a concept, idea, or service is tested through experimentation to prove its feasibility or ability to function as intended. This process involves breaking down a problem into more minor problems and testing each solution individually until you have found a suitable resolution. POCs can range from simple experiments involving computer code to complex multi-party interactions between people realizing an idea. An example could be trying out various website designs before officially launching them.

Prototyping allows the creation of physical replicas of products before actual development. This lets designers visualize the final product, gain user feedback, and make improvements before committing resources. It is an effective way to understand practical functionality and ensure the end product meets user expectations efficiently.

An example could be creating 3D-prints for furniture design prototypes so customers can see what their piece would look like without having to invest time or money into constructing the actual item first. POC verifies whether an idea is feasible, while prototyping tests the user experience by simulating the actual product experience

5.8 Lean Startup Method of Prototype Development

This approach aims to create products efficiently with customer input. It focuses on rapid testing, learning from feedback, and improving products step by step. This method speeds up development by making a basic version called a minimum viable product (MVP). The MVP tests the core idea at a low cost. Customers try the MVP and give feedback. Companies then use this input to refine the product before the next version.

Traditional methods often guessed at what people wanted without testing for it first. However, lean startup validates ideas early through the MVP, avoiding costly mistakes. It embraces an iterative cycle of building, testing, and enhancing based on actual user data. Lean startup complements design thinking, which puts people at the center of product creation. Moreover, lean startup and design thinking enable rapid prototyping. With continual input, companies quickly evolve ideas into better solutions. The methods work in parallel, allowing creativity without compromising quality standards.

A lean startup methodology helps businesses create better products faster while reducing development costs like materials and labor without compromising client quality standards. This results in happier customers because their expectations are met through consistent dialogue between them and project managers, especially in the early pre-prototype phase when requirements are discussed. Failure to follow this leads to unsatisfied outcomes and disappointed stakeholders, as well as financial losses if preventive measures are not taken earlier.

5.9 Virtual Ecosystem for Collaborative Prototyping

A virtual ecosystem for collaborative prototyping is a network of tools and platforms to create, test, and refine prototypes. It is an efficient way of working together that saves time and money while allowing teams to access the best ideas. This virtual space provides opportunities for creative solutions through collaboration and iteration. Designers can exchange feedback on their projects with each other to improve their designs quickly.

One example of a virtual ecosystem for collaborated prototyping is the Marvel app, which consists of three main components: a sketch studio, a prototype web studio, and an online cloud platform. The sketch studio helps designers bring their creative ideas in the form of sketches to life using vector drawing tools; the web studio allows you to quickly build web interfaces using HTML5/CSS3, while the cloud platform makes sure that your prototype models can easily be shared across multiple platforms like iOS/Android devices. In addition, these three components also allow users to collaborate on projects with other designers through version control and task management tools built into the system, making it easy for team members from anywhere around the globe to stay up to date with changes being made. The InVision app is a collaboration, and more details about it are available at www.invisionapp.com (Table 5.4).

Table 5.4 Marvel app versus InVision app

Feature	Marvel App	InVision App
Focus	Lightweight prototyping and design hand-off	Design-to-development workflow, rich interactive prototypes
Prototyping Fidelity	Low to medium fidelity	Low to high fidelity
Collaboration Features	Basic commenting and feedback	Advanced features like live collaboration (Liveshare), whiteboarding, and video conferencing
Design Hand-off	Simple developer specs with annotations	Detailed developer specs with code snippets and design assets
Integrations	Popular design tools (Sketch, Figma) and project management tools (Asana, Jira)	Wide range of design, development, and project management tools
Learning Curve	Easier to learn and use	Steeper learning curve with more features
Pricing	Freemium model with limitations, paid plans for advanced features	Freemium model with limitations, paid plans with more features and storage
Strengths	Fast and user-friendly for basic prototyping and feedback	Powerful for complex, interactive prototypes and robust collaboration features

By using virtual ecosystems such as Marvel or InVision, design thinkers can leverage powerful toolsets such as visual editing tools, task management software, user experience analytics, and testing data pipelines. This makes the design process more accessible and efficient. In addition, the collaborative nature of these apps enables rapid iteration cycles needed to reach improved versions of products faster than traditional methods.

5.10 Developing Skills for Making and Presenting Prototypes

Creating and showcasing sample versions of planned solutions individually and as a team demands unique abilities. Developing skills for crafting and presenting prototypes offers numerous advantages:

- **Enhanced user understanding:** Constructing prototypes allows designers to gain insights into user desires for products or services by observing interactions during testing sessions; this facilitates identifying areas needing improvement before investing resources into creations that may lack usability due to unfulfilled user expectations.
- **Swifter refinement cycles:** By generating models permitting quick modifications, designers experience shorter turnaround times when attempting fixes; this reduces overall project costs since work need not be repeated multiple times due to reworking issues that should have been addressed earlier.
- **Improved communication accessibility:** When all project members access visual representations of each other's concepts, it becomes simpler for everyone to comprehend others' objectives, thus promoting team collaboration.
- **Tangible deliverable:** Creating physical objects aids people in understanding a concept's appearance, enabling them to provide meaningful suggestions; this is crucial because without comprehending the concept, it is challenging to offer relevant feedback.

In conclusion, developing skills to make and present prototypes is an essential part of the design thinking process. These abilities enable faster iteration processes, better communication, and tangible output for testers to evaluate progress. Upon completion of these activities, the iterations continue until the desired results are achieved efficiently.

Summary

- Building a prototype helps test an idea before committing resources fully. A prototype serves as a smaller version of a product or concept. It allows evaluation prior to large-scale production. There are many types of prototypes.
- Low-fidelity prototyping focuses on the details of the prototype, used to test digital products like websites or apps. They include paper prototypes, sketches, LEGO prototypes, simple and clickable wireframes, foam prototypes and Wizard of OZ prototypes.
- Mid-fidelity prototyping involves a higher level of detail, interactivity, materials used, cost and time, and feedback. They include digital wireframes, interactive PDFs, mockups with basic functionality, and interactive prototypes with limited content.
- High-fidelity prototypes are more detailed and interactive than mid-fidelity prototypes. Examples include interactive prototypes, VR prototypes, 3D-printed prototypes, and video prototypes such as animatics and comps.

- Rough prototypes are early versions of a product or solution used to quickly test ideas and verify assumptions.
- Scenario-based prototyping is a method of designing visual media that combines elements of user interface design, storyboarding, and simulation techniques.
- Prototyping and the MVP (minimum viable product) are critical tools in the design thinking process.
- Proof of concept (POC) and prototyping are both processes used in the design thinking process.

Solutions to Design Visualization Questions

Q 5.1

Pros of Paper Prototyping

One of the primary benefits of paper prototyping is its low cost and ease of use. Unlike other prototyping techniques that require specialized software and tools, all that is needed for paper prototyping is a pencil and paper. In addition, paper prototyping requires only basic materials such as paper, scissors, and glue, making it a cost-effective and environmentally friendly option. For instance, an industrial design team may use paper prototypes to test different shapes and sizes of a new product before committing to more resource-intensive manufacturing processes. This means anyone can create a paper prototype regardless of technical skill level. In addition, this makes it an accessible and inclusive tool for teams to collaborate and iterate on ideas quickly. For instance, a mobile app development team may use paper prototypes to test different layouts and functionalities before investing in more expensive prototyping tools.

Another advantage of paper prototyping is that it allows designers to involve users in the early stages of the design process. By showing the paper prototype to users, designers can get immediate feedback and make modifications on the spot. This allows for quick and effective user testing, essential for ensuring that the final product meets user needs and expectations. Involvement of the user at an early stage: For example, a web design team may create a paper prototype of a new website, ask users to interact with it, and provide feedback on the layout and navigation.

In addition to user involvement, paper prototyping also encourages creativity. With the tool's simplicity, designers can explore multiple design concepts without being limited by technical constraints. This encourages designers to think outside the box and generate innovative ideas that may not have been possible with other prototyping techniques. For example, a graphic design team may create paper prototypes of different packaging designs for a new product line to explore different creative options.

While paper prototypes may not fully represent the look and feel of a final product, they can be used to test the concept of an idea. For example, a paper prototype of a website can be used to test the flow of information and the navigation structure, which are critical components of user experience. In addition, simple animations can be added to paper prototypes to provide a better understanding of how the interface works. Finally, changes can be easily made to paper prototypes on the fly, making it an efficient and adaptable process. For example, a UX designer can quickly change a paper prototype during a usability test based on user feedback.

Paper prototyping can be rapidly developed and tested. Unlike other prototyping methods, such as digital prototyping, paper prototyping does not require time-consuming coding or programming. This means that changes can be made quickly and tested in real time, which allows for a more efficient and effective design process. For example, a game development team may create paper prototypes of different game mechanics to test and refine the gameplay before investing in more expensive prototyping tools.

Q 5.2

Cons of Paper Prototyping

While paper prototyping has several advantages, it also has some limitations that designers should be aware of.

- **Limited visual fidelity:** One of the primary limitations of paper prototyping is its limited visual fidelity. Paper prototypes are hand-drawn, so they cannot accurately represent the look and feel of the final product. This may make it difficult for users to understand how the product looks and works. The visual fidelity of a product is its ability to represent the final product's visual design, aesthetics, and overall user experience. Visual fidelity is essential in ensuring users can relate to the product and understand how it works. When users interact with a product, they form an impression of it based on its visual design and aesthetics, among other factors. If a prototype lacks visual fidelity, users may not be able to visualize the final product, resulting in design flaws and usability issues.
- **Not suitable for testing complex interactions:** Another area for improvement of paper prototyping is that it may not be suitable for testing complex interactions or user flows. Since paper prototypes are static, they cannot accurately represent dynamic user interfaces or complex interactions. This means that designers may need help identifying navigation, usability, or interaction design issues. More sophisticated prototyping tools may be required to test complex user flows and interactions in such cases.
- **Remote collaboration is not possible:** Paper prototyping is a helpful technique for collaboration, especially when team members can work together in person. However, when team members work remotely, there may be better choices than paper prototyping. This is because remote collaboration requires tools that allow team members to work together in real-time, share feedback, and make changes to the design simultaneously. With paper prototyping, team members cannot easily collaborate remotely. If a team member changes the paper prototype, it may be difficult for others to see and provide feedback. This can lead to miscommunication, ultimately resulting in a less effective prototype.
- **Paper prototypes are static:** Paper prototypes are static and do not allow for interactions with the product. This means that designers must refrain from testing the product's functionality, such as user flow or navigation, with users.
- **Limited reusability:** Paper prototypes have limited reusability compared to digital prototypes because they are physical and cannot be easily modified or reused for different purposes. Once a paper prototype is created, it is typically used for a specific design iteration or product and cannot be easily adapted for future projects. For example, a designer creates a paper prototype for a mobile app they are working on. After conducting user testing, they realize they need to make significant changes to the app's user flow and layout. The designer may need to create a new paper prototype to reflect these changes, which can be time-consuming and may delay the design process. Furthermore, if the designer wants to use the paper prototype for a different platform, such as a tablet or desktop, they must create a new prototype to reflect the changes. This not only adds time and resources to the design process but also limits the flexibility and adaptability of the paper prototype.
- **Not accessible for users with disabilities:** One of the significant limitations of paper prototypes is that they may not be accessible to users with disabilities. Paper prototypes lack the

necessary features and technologies required to support users with visual, auditory, or motor impairments. For example, a paper prototype may not have the necessary contrast ratio or font size required for low-vision users. Similarly, it may not have alternative text or audio descriptions required for users with visual impairments. Moreover, paper prototypes may not be compatible with assistive technologies such as screen readers, which rely on digital content to provide information to users with visual impairments.

- **More physical space required:** Moreover, scaling paper prototypes may also require more physical space, storage, and transportation. Large-scale paper prototypes may require a dedicated workspace to store and manage them, which can add logistical challenges and costs. At the same time, paper prototyping has advantages but may not be the most scalable approach for larger projects or products. Other prototyping methods, such as digital or 3D printing, may be more effective in handling complex designs and interactions.
- **Collecting automatic user data is difficult:** One of the limitations of paper prototypes is that they may need to provide designers with accurate and comprehensive data on user behavior. Unlike digital prototypes, paper prototypes do not allow for collecting user data, such as analytics or user behavior metrics. This makes it difficult for designers to understand how users interact with the product, what elements work well, and what needs improvement.
- **Limited durability:** One of the limitations of paper prototypes is their limited durability. Paper prototypes are physical objects that are susceptible to wear and tear and can easily be damaged or lost. This can be particularly problematic when conducting long-term or repeated testing, as the paper prototype may become damaged or unusable over time. In addition, paper prototypes can be lost or misplaced, especially if passed around between different team members or stakeholders.

Guidelines for prototyping:

- **Start with a clear objective:** Before you begin prototyping, you must clearly understand what you want to achieve. Define your goals, target audience, and what you want to test.
- **Start with simple sketches:** When it comes to Prototyping, it's essential to start with simple sketches. Sketching is a quick and effective way to write your ideas down on paper and develop them further. In addition, sketches can be used to explore different design options and can be created with minimal resources.
- **Think big but start small:** Prototyping is an integral part of the design process and must be approached with the proper mindset. One of the most crucial principles of Prototyping is to think big but start small. This approach helps designers to break down complex projects into smaller, more manageable parts, allowing them to concentrate on one aspect at a time and measure progress more efficiently.
- **Don't be afraid to fail:** Designers can use prototyping to test and refine their ideas before investing large sums of money in the final product. However, it is critical to remember that only some prototypes will be successful. Failure is a natural part of the prototyping process, and designers should not be afraid to embrace it. Failure is inevitable in Prototyping because it allows designers to identify flaws and problems with their ideas early on. By testing and experimenting with different approaches, designers can quickly discover what works and what does not.
- **Use both low-fidelity and high-fidelity prototypes:** Using both low-fidelity and high-fidelity prototypes can be beneficial throughout the design process. Low-fidelity prototypes are quick and easy to create and helpful in testing early user ideas. They allow designers to explore different concepts and quickly iterate based on user feedback. For example, a team designing

a new mobile app may start with low-fidelity paper prototypes to test different layouts and user interactions. As the design progresses, high-fidelity prototypes can provide more accurate information about a product's appearance and performance. They can be created using digital tools and mimic the final product's functionality, making them useful for testing specific user interactions.

- **Test as much as possible:** Testing is a crucial part of prototyping. It allows designers to gather user feedback and make necessary changes to ensure the final product meets their needs. Therefore, testing should be done as much as possible throughout development, from early low-fidelity prototypes to more advanced high-fidelity ones. One way to test prototypes is through usability testing. Usability testing involves:
  - Observing users interact with the prototype.
  - Asking them to perform tasks.
  - Recording their feedback.
- **Focus on user experience:** Remember your target audience when creating your prototype. Make sure that the user experience is at the center of the design. When creating a prototype, it's essential to remember the target audience for whom the product is intended. The design should be centered around the user experience, making it easy and intuitive for users to navigate and interact with the product. This can be achieved by understanding the target audience's needs, preferences, and pain points through research and user testing.
- **Use the right tools:** Many different prototyping tools are available, each with strengths and weaknesses. Choose the tool that is best suited to your needs and skill level. When it comes to Prototyping, there are a plethora of tools available that can be used for various purposes. These tools vary from low-fidelity to high-fidelity prototypes, depending on the complexity of the design being tested. Paper and pencil, prototyping software, and 3D modeling software are some of the most commonly used tools for Prototyping. Choosing the right tool for your needs is essential based on your skill level and the detail required for your prototype.
- **Test and iterate:** Prototyping is an iterative process. Test your prototype with real users, gather feedback, and improve based on that feedback. Testing and iteration are crucial parts of the prototyping process because they help identify potential issues and refine the design to improve the user experience.
- **Be open to feedback:** Feedback is essential for improving your prototype. Be open to feedback from your team and users and use it to improve your prototype. Being open to feedback means listening to different perspectives and opinions. When creating a prototype, it's essential to understand that it's not a finished product and that feedback will help to improve it. This requires having an open mind and being receptive to criticism and suggestions. When receiving feedback, it's important to listen actively and ask questions to clarify the feedback. Try to understand the reasoning behind the feedback and consider whether it aligns with your goals and target audience. Be open to making changes based on the feedback, but also use your judgment to determine if it's appropriate to make specific changes. Creating a culture of open communication and constructive criticism within your team is essential. Encourage team members to share their ideas and thoughts and create a safe environment where everyone feels comfortable giving and receiving feedback. Remember that feedback is an opportunity to improve your work, not a personal attack. Accept it as a learning opportunity and use it to improve your prototype.
- **Please keep it simple:** Do not try to include too many features in your prototype. Please keep it simple and focused on the core functionality. Keeping your prototype simple means focusing

on the essential features and functionality necessary to achieve your goals. Adding too many features can make the prototype clearer and more manageable for users, which can lead to poor feedback and results.

- **Use real data:** Whenever possible, use real data in your prototype to make it more realistic and accurate. Using real data in a prototype can be highly beneficial for making informed decisions and ensuring accuracy.
- **Be creative:** Be bold when creating your prototype. Try new things and explore different design ideas. Being creative is an essential aspect of Prototyping, as it allows you to explore new ideas and push the boundaries of what's possible. Here are some ways you can be creative when prototyping:
  - **Use brainstorming:** Start by brainstorming a variety of ideas and solutions. Feel free to suggest wild or unconventional ideas.
  - **Experimenting:** Try out new tools and techniques to create your prototype. For example, you could use virtual reality to create an immersive experience or unconventional materials to build a physical prototype.
  - **Collaboration:** Work with other designers or experts from different fields to get fresh perspectives and new ideas.
  - Storytelling: Use storytelling techniques to create scenarios and narratives to help users better understand how the product or service works.
  - **Visual design:** Use color, typography, and other design elements to create a visually appealing prototype that captures users' attention. For example, a team prototyping a new fitness app might use virtual reality to create a 3D environment where users can interact with the app's features. They could also collaborate with fitness experts to ensure the app includes features that meet users' needs. Finally, they could use storytelling techniques to create scenarios illustrating how users could use the app in their daily lives.
  - **Use storytelling:** Use storytelling to help users understand the problem you are solving and how your solution addresses that problem. Storytelling is a powerful tool in design thinking that can create empathy and understanding among users. When developing a prototype, it can be helpful to use storytelling techniques to help users understand the problem to solve and how your solution addresses it. This can be done through narratives, scenarios, or even personas. For example, if you are designing a new app that helps people find local restaurants, you could create a persona of a busy working mom who struggles to find time to cook dinner for her family. You could then create a scenario where she is running late and needs to find a restaurant quickly. By using storytelling techniques, you can help users understand how your app can quickly and easily solve the problem of finding a restaurant quickly and easily.

Using these tips and strategies, you can create practical prototypes that help you test and validate your ideas and ultimately create better products and services for your users.

Q 5.3

Sample Brainstorming Outcomes

Core features

- **Calendar:** Visualize assignments, exams, and deadlines.
- **Task Manager:** Break down large projects into smaller tasks.
- **Note-taking:** Capture class notes, research, and study materials.
- **Time Management:** Set study timers and track time spent on different subjects.

- **Resource library:** Store important documents, links, and study guides.
- **Community forum:** Connect with peers for study groups and discussions.

Additional features

- **Personalized study plans:** Create custom study schedules based on individual needs.
- **Smart notifications:** Receive timely reminders and alerts.
- **Integration with learning management systems (LMS):** Sync assignments and deadlines directly from college portals.
- **Gamification:** Earn rewards and badges for completing tasks and achieving milestones.
- **Mindfulness tools:** Incorporate meditation and relaxation techniques to reduce stress.

Refining and Focusing: Based on the brainstorming session, we can prioritize the following features:

- **Calendar:** A visually appealing and intuitive calendar to help students stay organized.
- **Task manager:** A flexible task management system to break down large projects into smaller, manageable tasks.
- **Note-taking:** A robust note-taking tool that allows students to capture information in various formats (text, images, audio).
- **Time management:** A time management feature to help students allocate time effectively and avoid procrastination.

User Journey

Adding an assignment:

- Student opens the app and taps the "Add Assignment" button.
- Student enters the assignment details (title, description, due date, course).
- Student selects the appropriate course and saves the assignment.
- The assignment is added to the calendar and task manager.

Creating a study schedule:

- Student opens the "Study Planner" feature.
- Student selects the subjects they need to study.
- Student allocates specific time slots for each subject.
- The app generates a personalized study schedule based on the student's preferences and priorities.

Catering to Different Learning Styles

Visual Learners:

- Mind mapping tools
- Colorful themes and icons
- Infographic creation

Auditory Learners:

- Audio recording features
- Voice-to-text functionality
- Podcasts and audiobooks

Kinesthetic Learners:

- Interactive quizzes and games
- Physical activity trackers
- Hands-on project ideas

By combining these elements, we can create a powerful and user-friendly student organizer app that empowers students to succeed.

Q 5.4

Product Idea: The LEGO Productivity Planner

Concept: A physical planner made of LEGO bricks that allows users to visually organize their schedules, tasks, and goals.

Core Functionalities

- Modular design: Users can customize the planner's layout and size to fit their specific needs.
- Color-coded system: Different colored LEGO bricks can represent different subjects, priorities, or moods.
- Task tracking: Users can build LEGO towers to represent tasks and break them down into smaller steps.
- Goal setting: Larger LEGO structures can symbolize long-term goals, while smaller ones can represent daily or weekly objectives.
- Mind mapping: Users can create visual mind maps using LEGO bricks to brainstorm ideas and connect concepts.

User Testing Feedback

Positive feedback:

- Users appreciated the visual and tactile nature of the planner.
- They found it easy to understand and use.
- The modular design allowed for customization and personalization.

Areas for improvement:

- Some users suggested adding component, such as a smartphone app, to sync tasks and reminders.
- Others suggested incorporating a storage solution for loose LEGO pieces.

Iterations: Based on the feedback, we can consider the following improvements:

- Digital integration: Develop a companion app to sync tasks and reminders between the LEGO planner and a digital device.
- Storage solution: Design a LEGO storage container that can be attached to the planner.
- Additional features:
  - Incorporate a LEGO timer to help users manage their time effectively.
  - Develop a set of LEGO stamps for labeling tasks and events.

By combining the tangible nature of LEGO bricks with digital technology, the LEGO Productivity Planner can provide a unique and engaging way for college students to stay organized and motivated.

Q 5.6

Pros of high-fidelity prototyping

- High-fidelity prototypes are typically the **most advanced** type of prototype, closely resembling the final product in terms of design and functionality. They can include detailed visual designs, advanced interactions, and even real content, giving users a more realistic experience of the final product. High-fidelity prototypes are useful for testing specific details of the product and gathering feedback on the overall user experience. For example, imagine a team is designing a mobile app for a banking service. A high-fidelity prototype of the app would include realistic images and content, as well as advanced interactions such as swiping between screens and tapping on buttons to simulate banking transactions. Users could test the app on their own devices, providing feedback on the user interface and overall usability. High-fidelity prototypes can also be useful for presenting the product to stakeholders and investors, as they provide a more polished and professional-looking representation of the final product. This can help secure funding and support for the project.

- High-fidelity prototypes are useful in **identifying design flaws** and issues that may not have been apparent in low or mid-fidelity prototypes. By providing a more accurate representation of the final product, high-fidelity prototypes allow designers to better assess the product's usability and functionality, and test how users interact with it in a more realistic setting. This can help to identify problems and challenges that may not have been apparent in lower fidelity prototypes, and to refine the design before investing significant resources into development. For example, a software company creating a new mobile app may start with low-fidelity sketches or wireframes to test out different design concepts and user flows. Once they have identified a promising design, they may create a mid-fidelity prototype using a prototyping tool such as Sketch or Figma to test out more detailed interactions and user flows. Finally, they may create a high-fidelity prototype using a tool like InVision or Adobe XD, incorporating more realistic design elements and interactions such as animations and micro-interactions.
- High-fidelity prototypes provide designers with the ability to **experiment with different concepts** and refine them to achieve the best possible design. By providing a more realistic representation of the final product, high-fidelity prototypes allow designers to explore different aesthetics, user interfaces, and interactions in a more nuanced way. This can lead to more effective decision-making and ultimately save time and resources later in the design process. For example, a designer working on a new mobile app can create a high-fidelity prototype to test different color schemes, font styles, and layouts. By testing these various visual design elements in a realistic context, the designer can quickly identify which concepts are most effective and refine them accordingly. This can save time and resources later in the development process, as the designer will have a more solid foundation upon which to build the final product.

Q 5.7

Cons of high-fidelity prototyping

High-fidelity prototyping, while highly detailed and accurate, does come with several disadvantages: Creating high-fidelity prototypes takes significantly longer compared to low-fidelity versions. The detailed design and functionality require more effort and time to develop. The increased effort and resources needed to create high-fidelity prototypes often translate to higher costs. This includes the use of professional prototyping tools and potentially more skilled personnel. High-fidelity prototypes are less flexible. Once created, making changes can be time-consuming and complex. This rigidity can hinder the iterative process of design. Stakeholders and designers may become attached to the polished appearance of a high-fidelity prototype, making them resistant to changes even if necessary. Users may mistake the prototype for the final product and form biases based on its appearance and functionality. This can lead to unrealistic expectations and feedback. When changes are needed, a series of pages or elements in a high-fidelity prototype also need to be modified, which can be cumbersome and time-consuming. These disadvantages highlight the importance of balancing the level of fidelity in prototypes with the needs and constraints of the project.

Exercises

Part A (Objective Questions)

1. Which of the following is NOT a benefit of prototyping in product development?
   (a) Gathering feedback from users
   (b) Saving time and resources
   (c) Identifying design and functionality issues early on
   (d) Producing a final, fully functional product
2. During the prototyping stage, what is the purpose of testing prototypes with real users who represent the target market?
   (a) To identify design and functionality issues early on
   (b) To gather feedback on the user interface
   (c) To ensure the product meets the user's demands
   (d) All of the above
3. Which of the following is NOT a typical method of creating a prototype in product development?
   (a) Developing a 3D printed version
   (b) Coding on computer software such as JavaScript
   (c) Building a final, fully functional product
   (d) Sketching ideas and drawing possible designs
4. What is the main benefit of prototyping in the design thinking process?
   (a) Reducing the cost of developing a final product
   (b) Allowing designers to test and validate their ideas
   (c) Enhancing communication between stakeholders and team members
   (d) Reducing the time required to complete the design thinking process
5. How can prototyping be used to improve communication in a design project?
   (a) By visualizing and demonstrating design ideas through prototypes
   (b) By reducing the cost and time required to complete a design project
   (c) By allowing designers to quickly develop a final product
   (d) By automating the design thinking process
6. How does prototyping save time and resources in the design thinking process?
   (a) By allowing designers to skip the testing and validation phase
   (b) By automating the design thinking process
   (c) By enabling designers to identify potential issues and make necessary changes early in the design process
   (d) By allowing designers to quickly develop a final product
7. What is the benefit of using prototyping in project management?
   (a) It increases the chances of project success
   (b) It creates a final product without any design flaws
   (c) It saves time and money by skipping the testing phase
   (d) It encourages project managers to work in isolation
8. How does prototyping help project managers save time and money?
   (a) By allowing them to test and validate ideas quickly and cheaply
   (b) By skipping the testing phase and investing more resources into the final product
   (c) By relying on guesswork and assumptions, leading to costly mistakes
   (d) By creating the final product without any design flaws

9. How does prototyping encourage creativity in project management?
   (a) By limiting the number of design concepts
   (b) By discouraging experimentation
   (c) By allowing designers to experiment with various design ideas
   (d) By relying on guesswork and assumptions
10. Which of the following is NOT an advantage of using prototypes in the design thinking process?
   (a) Identifying UI design issues before implementation
   (b) Testing functionality before launch
   (c) Saving time and money during the production phase
   (d) Providing low-fidelity product representations
11. What is the main benefit of using mockups in the design thinking process?
   (a) Identifying UI design issues before implementation
   (b) Testing functionality before launch
   (c) Providing a realistic experience for end-users
   (d) Incorporating code elements into design structure
12. Which of the following best describes the purpose of models in the design thinking process?
   (a) To provide a low-fidelity product representation
   (b) To test functionality before launch
   (c) To simulate how users will interact with the system
   (d) To bridge the gap between conceptualization and implementation
13. What is the primary purpose of using paper prototypes in the early stages of a design project?
   (a) To create a high-fidelity representation of the final product
   (b) To test the usability of the product
   (c) To save time and money on development costs
   (d) To share ideas and gather feedback
14. What is the advantage of using paper prototypes in usability testing?
   (a) They are high-fidelity representations of the final product.
   (b) They are quick and easy to create.
   (c) They can be used to test the market appeal of the product.
   (d) They are only useful in the early stages of a project.
15. What is the main difference between paper prototypes and other types of prototypes?
   (a) Paper prototypes are only used in the early stages of a project.
   (b) Paper prototypes are high-fidelity representations of the final product.
   (c) Paper prototypes are low-fidelity representations of the final product.
   (d) Paper prototypes are more expensive to create than other types of prototypes.
16. What is one advantage of paper prototyping in the design process?
   (a) It is a high-fidelity representation of the final product
   (b) It requires specialized software and tools
   (c) It encourages creativity and exploration of multiple design concepts
   (d) It is time-consuming and requires extensive programming
17. How can paper prototyping benefit the user testing process in the design process?
   (a) It allows designers to test the final product with users
   (b) It provides a low-cost alternative to user testing
   (c) It allows designers to involve users in the early stages of the design process
   (d) It is not effective in providing user feedback
18. What is a key advantage of paper prototyping in comparison to other prototyping methods?
   (a) It provides a high-fidelity representation of the final product
   (b) It requires specialized software and tools

(c) It is a cost-effective and environmentally friendly option
(d) It is more efficient than other prototyping methods

19. What is one of the primary limitations of paper prototyping?
(a) Limited functionality
(b) Limited visual fidelity
(c) Limited collaboration options
(d) Limited usability testing

20. When may paper prototyping not be suitable for testing user flows?
(a) When the user flows are simple
(b) When the team is working remotely
(c) When the interactions are complex
(d) When the prototype requires greater visual fidelity

21. Why may digital prototyping tools be more suitable for remote collaboration?
(a) They provide greater visual fidelity
(b) They are easier to use
(c) They allow for paper prototypes to be digitized
(d) They are less expensive than paper prototypes

22. What is one limitation of paper prototyping when it comes to testing user interactions?
(a) It cannot simulate interactions
(b) It cannot gather data on user behavior
(c) It cannot optimize usability
(d) It cannot accurately represent visual design

23. In which scenario might paper prototyping not be necessary?
(a) When designing a new healthcare device
(b) When modifying an existing solution without changing the user interface
(c) When creating an e-commerce website
(d) When exploring different design options for a new feature

24. What is the advantage of using paper prototyping for a new healthcare device?
(a) It allows the team to test various design concepts before building a physical prototype
(b) It ensures that the user interface accurately represents the final product
(c) It provides greater visual fidelity than other prototyping tools
(d) It allows the team to gather valuable data on user interactions

25. Why is paper prototyping a valuable tool for teams looking to create innovative solutions?
(a) It is a flexible and accessible tool that can be used in various design thinking scenarios
(b) It allows teams to simulate dynamic user interfaces and complex interactions
(c) It provides greater visual fidelity than other prototyping tools
(d) It allows teams to gather valuable data on how users complete specific tasks or workflows

26. What is the primary advantage of low-fidelity prototyping?
(a) It is relatively inexpensive.
(b) It allows designers to create highly detailed designs.
(c) It is faster to produce than high-fidelity prototypes.
(d) It is better suited for testing usability issues.

27. What is an example of a low-fidelity prototyping method?
(a) Card sorting exercises
(b) A fully functional website
(c) A high-fidelity wireframe
(d) A detailed 3D model

28. What is the main purpose of low-fidelity prototyping?
(a) To create highly detailed designs
(b) To test usability issues
(c) To refine existing designs
(d) To explore ideas and concepts quickly

29. What is the benefit of using sketches in the design process?
    (a) Sketches are artistic representations that are easily understood by all team members.
    (b) Sketches are a quick and cheap tool to portray ideas and evolve designs.
    (c) Sketches are the only way to convey interactions between components in the application.
    (d) Sketches are the best prototype for selecting the final design.
30. What types of diagrams can be used to illustrate complex ideas in sketches?
    (a) Sequence diagrams, flow diagrams, and behavior maps
    (b) Wireframes, paper prototypes, and storyboards
    (c) Post-it notes, symbols, and text
    (d) Stakeholder meetings, customer interviews, and card sorting exercises
31. What is the main advantage of using LEGO prototypes in product design?
    (a) LEGO prototypes are cheap and easy to acquire.
    (b) LEGO prototypes can be quickly dismantled, modified, and reworked.
    (c) LEGO prototypes allow for easy creation of user interfaces.
    (d) LEGO prototypes are suitable for creating digital products.
32. In which scenario would a LEGO prototype be the most appropriate choice for product design?
    (a) Designing a digital product with a complex user interface.
    (b) Designing a physical product with fixed dimensions and weight.
    (c) Designing a product that requires detailed technical specifications.
    (d) Designing a product with a simple design that will not require significant changes.
33. What skill can be improved by working with LEGO prototypes?
    (a) Programming (b) Writing
    (c) Drawing, art, and craft (d) Public speaking
34. What is the primary goal of wireframes in design thinking?
    (a) To test the overall layout and navigation of each screen
    (b) To design the complete visual appearance of the product
    (c) To address the user interface aspects of the product
    (d) To finalize the product design
35. What is the difference between low-fidelity wireframes and wireframe prototypes?
    (a) Low-fidelity wireframes focus on the content structure, while wireframe prototypes focus on the visual appearance
    (b) Low-fidelity wireframes are drawn by hand, while wireframe prototypes are created using software tools
    (c) Low-fidelity wireframes deal with the user interface and design, while wireframe prototypes do not
    (d) Low-fidelity wireframes can be modified quickly, while wireframe prototypes cannot
36. When is it appropriate to use wireframes in the product design process?
    (a) In the initial design phase of the product
    (b) After finalizing the product design
    (c) When creating user flows on various pages of the product
    (d) When you want to focus on the aesthetic sense of the product
37. What is the primary benefit of using a Wizard of Oz prototype?
    (a) To make users believe that the prototype is fully functional
    (b) To save time and effort in building a fully functional prototype
    (c) To test the reliability and accuracy of the product
    (d) To use in the early stages of the design process
38. When should a Wizard of Oz prototype be used in the design process?
    (a) In the early stages of the design process
    (b) In the middle stages of the design process

(c) In the last stages of the design process
(d) At any stage of the design process

39. What are some best practices to follow while using a Wizard of Oz prototype?
(a) Train the Wizard for unpredictable scenarios
(b) Use the Wizard to test the reliability and accuracy of the product
(c) Discover what questions you need answers to through the Wizard before building it
(d) Use the Wizard in the early stages of the design process

40. What is the main advantage of using cardboard prototypes?
(a) They are easy and quick to create.
(b) They are highly realistic and detailed.
(c) They can test complex interactions and features.
(d) They are suitable for testing the final product experience.

41. When should clickable wireframes be used?
(a) To test complex animations or transitions.
(b) To test a product's basic layout and navigation.
(c) To test the final product experience.
(d) To test a product's visual design.

42. What is a disadvantage of cardboard prototypes?
(a) They lack realism and detail.
(b) They are difficult and time-consuming to create.
(c) They are suitable for testing highly detailed designs.
(d) They are expensive and require high-fidelity design resources.

43. What is a disadvantage of clickable wireframes?
(a) They are highly realistic and detailed.
(b) They can test complex interactions and features.
(c) They require minimal design and development resources.
(d) They may not accurately replicate the final product experience.

44. When should cardboard prototypes not be used?
(a) When the design is still in the ideation stage.
(b) When the team wants to quickly test out different design concepts.
(c) When working on a highly complex product.
(d) When the design has already been finalized.

45. What is the main advantage of using foam prototypes?
(a) They are lightweight and easy to handle
(b) They can replicate the electronic components of a digital product
(c) They are suitable for testing the functionality of a product
(d) They are made of inexpensive materials

46. When is it best to use foam prototypes in product development?
(a) When testing the functionality of the product
(b) When the product design is finalized
(c) When testing the physical form and interaction of the product
(d) When testing the flow and navigation of a website

47. What are some best practices for using foam prototypes in product development?
(a) Use low-quality foam materials to save costs
(b) Use foam prototypes to test the digital components of the product
(c) Test the physical interaction of the product by having users interact with the prototype
(d) Use foam prototypes as the sole prototype for the product

48. What is the main advantage of using mid-fidelity prototypes over low-fidelity prototypes in the design process?

(a) Cost efficiency (b) Aesthetics
(c) Feedback gathering (d) General design concepts

49. What is the main difference between low-fidelity and mid-fidelity prototypes in terms of level of detail?
(a) Mid-fidelity prototypes have more detailed wireframes with specific text, images, and color schemes.
(b) Low-fidelity prototypes use specialized tools and materials, such as wireframing software and 3D printing.
(c) Mid-fidelity prototypes are generally non-interactive.
(d) Low-fidelity prototypes are more detailed and realistic.

50. What is the main benefit of using mid-fidelity prototypes in design thinking?
(a) Speed and cost efficiency (b) Aesthetics and branding
(c) Collaboration and usability testing (d) Technical details and features

51. When is it appropriate to use digital wireframes in the design process?
(a) When testing basic usability and functionality
(b) When testing complex functionality that cannot be easily simulated with wireframes
(c) When testing visual design elements of the product
(d) When gathering feedback on the overall concept design

52. What are some pros of using digital wireframes in the design process?
(a) They allow for rapid iteration and feedback
(b) They accurately represent the final product
(c) They focus on complex functionality
(d) They provide a complete picture of the user experience

53. When is it appropriate to use digital wireframes in the design process?
(a) When testing basic usability and functionality of the product
(b) When testing complex functionality that cannot be easily simulated with wireframes
(c) When testing visual design elements of the product
(d) None of the above

54. Which of the following is a suitable scenario for using interactive PDFs as a mid-fidelity prototype?
(a) When advanced interactivity is required beyond essential clickable links and form fields.
(b) When the design requires a fully immersive user experience.
(c) When creating complex designs with multiple pages or forms.
(d) When testing the prototype on actual devices or platforms.

55. Which of the following is not a pro of using interactive PDFs as a mid-fidelity prototype?
(a) Easy to create and edit using software like Adobe Acrobat.
(b) Can include more detailed visual designs than low-fidelity prototypes.
(c) Advanced interactivity allows testing and feedback on user interactions.
(d) Basic interactivity allows testing and feedback on user interactions.

56. What is the main limitation of using interactive PDFs as a mid-fidelity prototype?
(a) They cannot provide a fully immersive user experience.
(b) They are difficult to create and edit using software like Adobe Acrobat.
(c) They are incompatible with most devices and platforms.
(d) They require advanced coding skills to create.

57. What is the benefit of using interactive prototypes with limited content?
(a) They are quick to create and easy to modify, helping identify potential design issues early on.
(b) They fully represent the final product, giving users a complete understanding of the concept.

(c) They allow for advanced functionality and realistic user experiences.
(d) They are best used for testing overall user experience.

58. When is it best to use interactive prototypes with limited content?
(a) When trying to test the overall user experience.
(b) When the final product will have a significant amount of content.
(c) When testing specific interactions or user flows that need to be refined.
(d) When the prototype needs to be tested on actual devices or platforms.

59. What is the disadvantage of using interactive prototypes with limited content?
(a) They are quick to create and easy to modify, helping identify potential design issues early on.
(b) They may not fully represent the final product, and users may need help understanding the overall concept without the full content.
(c) They allow for advanced functionality and realistic user experiences.
(d) They are best used for testing overall user experience.

60. What is the primary difference between mid-fidelity and high-fidelity prototypes?
(a) High-fidelity prototypes offer more detail and functionality
(b) Mid-fidelity prototypes are quicker and easier to create
(c) Mid-fidelity prototypes are highly interactive and resemble the final product
(d) High-fidelity prototypes are used for specific user flows and interactions only

61. Which type of prototyping is used in design thinking to test ideas before moving forward with development or production?
(a) Low-fidelity prototyping
(b) Mid-fidelity prototyping
(c) High-fidelity prototyping
(d) Rapid prototyping

62. What are some examples of high-fidelity prototyping?
(a) 2D drawings and sketches
(b) Wireframes and mockups
(c) Interactive prototypes with full functionality
(d) Low-fidelity physical prototypes

63. What is the main advantage of high-fidelity prototypes?
(a) They provide a more realistic experience of the final product to users
(b) They are less time-consuming and resource-intensive than low-fidelity prototypes
(c) They can be used for testing basic design concepts and user flows
(d) They are best used for securing funding and support for the project

64. Which stage of prototyping is best suited for testing specific details of the product and gathering feedback on the overall user experience?
(a) Low-fidelity prototypes
(b) Mid-fidelity prototypes
(c) High-fidelity prototypes
(d) None of the above

65. When should high-fidelity prototypes be used in the product design process?
(a) At the beginning of the design process
(b) Once the design has been thoroughly tested and validated through earlier stages of prototyping and user testing
(c) Only after the product has been developed
(d) Throughout the entire design process

66. Which of the following is a benefit of using high-fidelity prototypes in design?
(a) They allow designers to test different concepts and refine them more effectively.
(b) They save time and resources by skipping the lower fidelity prototyping stages.
(c) They provide a less realistic representation of the final product, making it easier to identify flaws.
(d) They are only useful for presenting the product to stakeholders and investors.

67. What is the primary advantage of using high-fidelity prototypes in the design process?
    (a) They allow designers to experiment with different concepts and refine them to achieve the best possible design.
    (b) They provide a more realistic representation of the final product, allowing for more effective decision-making.
    (c) They help identify design flaws and issues that may not have been apparent in lower fidelity prototypes.
    (d) They can be used to present the product to stakeholders and investors, securing funding and support for the project.
68. What is the main disadvantage of creating high-fidelity prototypes?
    (a) They can be time-consuming and resource-intensive.
    (b) They may not accurately represent the final product's functionality.
    (c) They may not accurately represent the final product's aesthetic design.
    (d) They may not be suitable for testing with users.
69. What is the typical process for creating high-fidelity prototypes?
    (a) Start with low-fidelity prototypes made from cardboard or foam, then create mid-fidelity prototypes using more advanced materials such as 3D printed parts or CNC-machined components, and finally create high-fidelity prototypes using materials and finishes that closely match the final product.
    (b) Start with high-fidelity prototypes and refine the design through user testing before beginning development.
    (c) Start with mid-fidelity prototypes made using prototyping tools such as Sketch or Figma, then create high-fidelity prototypes using a tool like IN Vision or Adobe XD.
    (d) Start with low-fidelity sketches or wireframes to test different design concepts and user flows, then create mid-fidelity prototypes using a prototyping tool such as Sketch or Figma, and finally create high-fidelity prototypes incorporating more realistic design elements and interactions such as animations and micro-interactions.
70. In which phase of the project management process is role-playing most commonly used?
    (a) Planning (b) Execution
    (c) Monitoring and Controlling (d) Closing
71. How can role-playing be used to improve the design of a new product for a retail store?
    (a) By testing how customers interact with the product and how it fits into the store's layout
    (b) By testing the durability of the product in different environmental conditions
    (c) By determining the production cost of the product
    (d) By testing the product's packaging and labeling.
72. How can role-playing help a design team develop a new mobile app for a healthcare provider?
    (a) By testing how the app looks on different devices
    (b) By identifying pain points and positive aspects of the user experience
    (c) By determining the app's programming language
    (d) By testing the app's compatibility with different operating systems
73. In design thinking, which technique is used to gain insights into user behaviors and needs by simulating real-life scenarios?
    (a) Brainstorming (b) Prototyping
    (c) Role-playing (d) Mind mapping
74. How can a design team use role-playing to test a new product for a retail store?
    (a) By creating a mockup of the product on a smartphone
    (b) By setting up a mock display of the product in the store
    (c) By conducting a survey with customers
    (d) By testing the product in a laboratory setting

75. Which of the following is a benefit of using role-playing in design thinking?
(a) Identifying pain points and positive aspects of the user experience
(b) Creating a detailed project plan
(c) Reducing the overall project cost
(d) Increasing the project timeline

76. What is the purpose of a walkthrough in the design thinking process?
(a) To fully develop new services or processes
(b) To test the flow and usability of new services or processes
(c) To gather feedback on completed services or processes
(d) To simulate user behavior after the service or process has launched.

77. How can walkthroughs help identify areas for improvement in a new online customer ordering system?
(a) By providing simulated screens or pages for users to interact with
(b) By observing the user's experience and gathering feedback
(c) By streamlining the ordering process
(d) By launching the system and gathering user feedback.

78. What type of processes can walkthroughs be used to test?
(a) Employee onboarding (b) Customer service protocols
(c) Both A and B (d) Neither A nor B.

79. What are maquettes used for in design thinking?
(a) Recreating point-of-purchase designs (b) Creating digital designs
(c) Conducting market research (d) Testing software programs

80. How do maquettes help designers in the design process?
(a) By allowing them to test and refine their ideas before investing in the final product
(b) By automatically creating the final product
(c) By reducing the amount of time needed to create the final product
(d) By eliminating the need for user testing

81. What is an example of how maquettes are used in retail design?
(a) Testing different software programs
(b) Conducting market research
(c) Creating a maquette of a shelf display to test the placement and arrangement of the product
(d) Creating digital designs

82. What is the primary purpose of using animatics in film and video production?
(a) To test the effectiveness of animations or motion graphics in telling a story.
(b) To create a fully animated version of the film or video.
(c) To identify potential technical issues in the final animation.
(d) To save time and resources in the long run.

83. How can animatics be helpful in identifying potential technical issues before creating the final animation?
(a) By testing the pacing and storytelling of animation.
(b) By adjusting the animation's timing to convey the intended message.
(c) By revealing that certain scenes or transitions are too complex to animate within the given timeline or budget.
(d) By refining the story and testing different camera angles and transitions.

84. What is an example of how animatics can be used in animation production?
(a) To create a fully animated version of a short film.
(b) To identify potential technical issues in a storyboard.

(c) To test the story and pacing before committing to the final animation.
(d) To refine the animation's timing and transitions.

85. What is the primary purpose of creating comps?
(a) To test the final look and feel of printed materials designs before production.
(b) To provide clients with a tactile experience of the final product.
(c) To save time and resources during the production process.
(d) To test the pacing and storytelling of animation before investing resources into creating a fully animated version.

86. What is an advantage of using comps in the design process?
(a) They provide a tactile experience of the final product.
(b) They help identify potential production issues early on.
(c) They require advanced design skills and software.
(d) They are cost-effective to produce.

87. What is a limitation of using comps in the design process?
(a) They provide a realistic representation of the final design.
(b) They require advanced design skills and software.
(c) They can be easily adjusted and modified as needed.
(d) They provide a tactile experience of the final product.

88. What is the primary benefit of using rough prototypes in design thinking?
(a) They are usually much cheaper and faster to make.
(b) They are more visually appealing to potential users.
(c) They provide a common language for teams to understand each other's jargon.
(d) They guarantee success in product development cycles.

89. What is the first step in the design thinking process?
(a) Creating a rough working model.
(b) Identifying the user's needs and understanding their goals.
(c) Brainstorming potential solutions.
(d) Conducting market research.

90. What is the primary purpose of using software like the InVision app in the prototyping process?
(a) To demystify complex problems by simplifying them into smaller pieces.
(b) To help teams understand each other's jargon.
(c) To receive direct feedback from potential users on the prototype.
(d) To guarantee success in product development cycles.

91. What is the primary goal of scenario-based prototyping in design thinking?
(a) To gain insight into how the user would feel when using the product or service is designed.
(b) To create wireframes and animations for products or services.
(c) To develop multiple versions of the same product or service.
(d) To finalize the product or service before testing with users.

92. How does scenario-based prototyping save time and resources in the development process?
(a) By allowing designers to create wireframes and animations quickly.
(b) By identifying potential issues early in the development process.
(c) By finalizing the product or service before testing with users.
(d) By creating multiple versions of the same product or service.

93. In what ways can scenario-based prototyping be used in e-commerce website development?
(a) To create wireframes and animations for the website.
(b) To test out scenarios for finding products and going through the checkout process.
(c) To develop multiple versions of the same e-commerce platform.
(d) To finalize the e-commerce platform before testing with users.

94. What is the primary goal of an MVP in the design thinking process?
(a) To release a fully functional product or service to the market
(b) To test the market and gather feedback from users
(c) To build a prototype with all of the features and functionality
(d) To skip the testing phase and launch the product or service directly

95. What is the main advantage of using prototypes in the design thinking process?
(a) To quickly release a product or service to the market
(b) To save time and money on development efforts
(c) To gather feedback from users before investing too much time and resources
(d) To skip the testing phase and launch the product or service directly

96. What is the iterative process in the design thinking process?
(a) A process of understanding people's needs and developing innovative solutions to problems
(b) A process of researching, experimenting, testing, refining, and ultimately delivering the best possible product or service
(c) A process of releasing the product or service directly to the market
(d) A process of building the product or service with all of the features and functionality at once

97. What is the primary purpose of a proof of concept (POC)?
(a) To test an idea with users and stakeholders
(b) To create physical models of products
(c) To simulate the actual product experience
(d) To build out a finished product

98. How do prototypes differ from POCs in the design thinking process?
(a) Prototypes simulate the actual product experience, while POCs test an idea's feasibility
(b) Prototypes test an idea's feasibility, while POCs simulate the actual product experience
(c) Prototypes and POCs have the same purpose
(d) Prototypes and POCs are completely different processes

99. What is an example of using POCs or prototypes in design thinking?
(a) Creating a finished product for testing with users
(b) Building a physical model of a product before testing it with users
(c) Trying out various website designs before officially launching them
(d) Designing a product without any testing

100. What is the main benefit of using lean startup methodology in product development?
(a) Faster product development time
(b) Lower costs associated with development cycles
(c) Increased customer satisfaction
(d) All of the above

101. What is a minimum viable product (MVP) in the context of lean startup methodology?
(a) A fully developed product that is ready for market launch
(b) A prototype that is tested extensively before being launched
(c) A product with only essential features that is used to validate an idea or concept
(d) None of the above

102. How does design thinking complement lean startup methodologies in product design?
(a) Design Thinking allows for more creative freedom in product design
(b) Design Thinking focuses on understanding how users think and behave
(c) Design Thinking helps reduce costs associated with development cycles
(d) Design Thinking replaces the need for MVP testing

103. Which of the following is a crucial aspect to consider before beginning the prototyping process?

(a) Defining your goals, target audience, and what you want to test
(b) Creating a high-fidelity prototype
(c) Skipping the sketching process
(d) Testing the prototype with a small group of users

104. What is the importance of starting with simple sketches in the prototyping process?
(a) It allows you to create a high-fidelity prototype quickly.
(b) It is a cost-effective method.
(c) It helps to explore different design options.
(d) None of the above.

105. What is the significance of understanding your target audience in the prototyping process?
(a) It helps to create a prototype tailored to your audience and effectively addresses their needs.
(b) It reduces the need for user testing.
(c) It helps to create a prototype with high-fidelity.
(d) It helps to speed up the prototyping process.

106. Which of the following is a benefit of using both low-fidelity and high-fidelity prototypes in the design process?
(a) Low-fidelity prototypes are more accurate in representing the final product's appearance.
(b) High-fidelity prototypes are more efficient in testing early user ideas.
(c) Using both types of prototypes can save time and money by catching problems early in the design process.
(d) Using only low-fidelity prototypes is sufficient for gathering user feedback.

107. What is usability testing?
(a) A way to gather user feedback by observing users interact with the prototype and asking them to perform tasks.
(b) A way to gather data on user behavior using analytics tools.
(c) A way to create two prototype versions and test them with different groups of users to see which version performs better.
(d) A way to choose the appropriate prototype for each stage of the design process.

108. Which of the following is a way to test prototypes using analytics tools?
(a) Observing users interact with the prototype and asking them to perform tasks.
(b) Creating two prototype versions and testing them with different groups of users to see which version performs better.
(c) Gathering data on user behavior, such as how long they spend on a specific page, using analytics tools.
(d) Choosing the appropriate prototype for each stage of the design process.

109. What is the importance of being open to feedback when creating a prototype?
(a) It helps to improve the prototype
(b) It delays the completion of the prototype
(c) It makes the prototype more complex
(d) It is not necessary for creating a prototype

110. Why is it essential to keep your prototype simple and focused on core functionality?
(a) It makes the prototype more manageable for users
(b) It ensures that all possible features are included
(c) It makes the prototype more complex
(d) It doesn't affect the feedback from users

111. What should be prioritized when prototyping a mobile app for ordering food?
(a) Adding all possible features
(b) Focusing on the core functionality

(c) Making the prototype complex
(d) Avoiding feedback from users

112. Which of the following is an example of using storytelling in prototyping?
(a) Conducting user testing
(b) Collaborating with team members
(c) Creating a scenario of a busy working mom struggling to find time to cook dinner
(d) Conducting design reviews

113. What is an effective way to involve stakeholders in the prototyping process?
(a) Conduct user testing
(b) Collaborate with team members
(c) Conduct design reviews
(d) Involve stakeholders in the prototyping process to ensure the prototype aligns with their goals and expectations

114. Which of the following is an effective way to collaborate in prototyping?
(a) Using collaboration tools
(b) Creating personas
(c) Conducting design reviews
(d) All of the above

115. What is the main advantage of developing skills for making and presenting prototypes during a design project?
(a) Improved understanding of user needs
(b) Increased project costs
(c) Reduced collaboration among team members
(d) Longer turnaround times

116. How can creating physical objects help in the design process?
(a) By slowing down the project timeline
(b) By making it more difficult to understand concepts
(c) By allowing team members to provide meaningful suggestions
(d) By decreasing collaboration among team members

117. Which tool can designers use to arrive at the best possible outcome faster during the prototyping phase?
(a) Sketches and paper
(b) "None of the above"
(c) 3D printing
(d) All of the above

Part B (Short Answer Questions)

1. What is the purpose of prototyping in product development and how does it benefit the project team?
2. Why is it important to test prototypes with real users during the prototyping phase?
3. How does prototyping help product designers and developers ensure that the product meets the user's demands in terms of design and functionality?
4. How can prototyping enhance the design thinking process?
5. What is the importance of prototyping in improving communication between stakeholders and designers?
6. How can creating prototypes help promote collaboration among team members?
7. How can prototyping help reduce the risk of failure in a project?
8. What are the benefits of prototyping in terms of saving time and money?
9. How does prototyping encourage creativity in the design thinking process?

10. What is the purpose of using mockups in design thinking?
11. How do prototypes help in delivering better quality products?
12. How can models be used to identify potential flaws before coding begins?
13. What is the advantage of using low-fidelity prototypes in product development?
14. In what scenarios is low-fidelity prototyping most effective?
15. How does low-fidelity prototyping benefit design thinking processes?
16. What is the primary advantage of low-fidelity prototyping?
17. What are some common examples of low-fidelity prototypes?
18. What are the potential drawbacks of using low-fidelity prototypes in the design process?
19. What is the advantage of using LEGO prototypes in design thinking?
20. Can sketches be used to convey the interactions between components in the application?
21. When should we prefer Lego prototypes over other types of prototypes in design thinking?
22. What is the purpose of wireframes in the design thinking process?
23. Can wireframes be modified easily according to user needs? Why or why not?
24. When should wireframes be shown to outside team members? Why is this important?
25. What is the main advantage of using Wizard of Oz prototypes?
26. When should you use Wizard of Oz prototypes in the design process?
27. What are some best practices to follow while using Wizard of Oz prototypes?
28. What are cardboard prototypes and when should they be used?
29. What are the advantages of using clickable wireframes?
30. When might clickable wireframes not be appropriate for testing a product?
31. In which stage of product development are foam prototypes most suitable?
32. What are some of the advantages of using foam prototypes?
33. What are the advantages of using mid-fidelity prototypes over low-fidelity prototypes in product development?
34. In what stage of product development would low-fidelity prototypes be most useful?
35. What are some examples of materials that can be used to create low-fidelity prototypes?
36. What is the main benefit of using mid-fidelity prototyping in design thinking?
37. What are the potential drawbacks of using mid-fidelity prototypes in design thinking?
38. How can mid-fidelity prototypes help bridge conversations between different perspectives within organizations?
39. When is it appropriate to use digital wireframes in the design process?
40. What are the advantages and disadvantages of using digital wireframes?
41. What are some examples of basic interactivity that can be included in an interactive PDF prototype?
42. What are the limitations of using interactive PDFs as a mid-fidelity prototype?
43. What is the primary difference between mid-fidelity and high-fidelity prototypes?
44. What are some examples of high-fidelity prototyping?
45. How can high-fidelity prototypes be used in the development of a physical product?
46. When is the best time to create a high-fidelity prototype in the design process?
47. What is the main advantage of high-fidelity prototypes over low or mid-fidelity prototypes?
48. What are some challenges that may arise when creating high-fidelity prototypes?
49. How can high-fidelity prototypes be used to improve decision-making and ultimately save time and resources in the design process?
50. What is the purpose of using role-playing in design thinking?
51. How can role-playing be used in designing a new mobile app for a healthcare provider?
52. How can role-playing be used in designing a new product for a retail store, and what are some examples of props or simulations that can be used?

53. What is the purpose of using walkthroughs in the design thinking process?
54. How can a company use walkthroughs to test the usability of a new online ordering system?
55. What are some benefits of using walkthroughs in the design thinking process?
56. What are maquettes used for in design thinking?
57. How can maquettes help designers improve the customer experience?
58. Can maquettes be used for non-physical designs, such as digital products?
59. What is the primary purpose of using animatics in film and video production?
60. How can animatics help creators identify potential technical issues in animation production?
61. Why are animatics considered an essential tool in animation production?
62. What is the purpose of creating comps in the design process?
63. What are the advantages of using comps in the design process?
64. What are some limitations of using comps in the design process, and how can they be addressed?
65. What is the benefit of creating rough prototypes in design thinking?
66. How can rough prototypes help teams with different expertise work better together?
67. What are the key steps in the design thinking process, and how does the use of rough prototypes fit into those steps?
68. What is the goal of scenario-based prototyping?
69. How can scenario-based prototyping help in the development of an e-commerce website?
70. How can scenario-based prototyping help designers form more robust designs?
71. Why is it important to keep the user's needs in mind during the prototyping process?
72. How can prototyping with low-fidelity prototypes help designers improve the user experience?
73. How can prototyping help reduce the chance of costly redesigns down the line? Provide an example.
74. What is the purpose of an MVP in the design thinking process?
75. What is the benefit of testing low-fidelity prototypes with real users early on in the design process?
76. Why are prototyping and MVPs essential tools for any successful design thinking project?
77. What is the primary goal of a proof of concept (POC), and what are some examples of its use in design thinking?
78. How does prototyping differ from proof of concept (POC)?
79. Why are proof of concept and prototyping important in design thinking?
80. What is the importance of defining goals before starting the prototyping process?
81. How can starting with simple sketches benefit the prototyping process, and what are its limitations?
82. What is the principle of 'thinking big but starting small' and how can it benefit the prototyping process?
83. What is one advantage of creating prototypes during the design thinking process?

Part C (Essay Questions)

1. Why are prototypes used in design thinking projects?
2. How does prototyping enhance the design thinking process?
3. Differentiate between mockup, model, and prototype.
4. Write an essay on paper prototypes along with its pros and cons.
5. What are the best practices for paper prototypes?
6. Write an essay on low-fidelity prototyping.
7. What are the types of low-fidelity prototypes?
8. What are the main differences between low-fidelity and mid-fidelity prototypes?

9. Write an essay on digital wireframes.
10. Write an essay on interactive PDFs.
11. Write an essay on mock-ups with basic functionality.
12. Write an essay on interactive prototypes with limited content.
13. Write an essay on high-fidelity prototyping.
14. Explain some of the pros of high-fidelity prototyping.
15. Explain some of the cons of high-fidelity prototyping.
16. How can we move from low fidelity to high fidelity prototypes?
17. Write an essay on role-playing of design thinking.
18. Write an essay on walkthroughs.
19. Write an essay on maquettes.
20. Write an essay on animatics.
21. Write an essay on comps.
22. Write an essay on rough prototyping.
23. Write an essay on scenario-based prototyping.
24. Write an essay on user centricity in prototyping.
25. Compare and contrast MVP and prototyping.
26. Compare and contrast proof of concept and prototyping.
27. Write an essay on the lean start-up method of prototype development.
28. List some of the guidelines for prototyping.
29. What are the ways you can be creative when prototyping?

Answer Key

Part A

1. (d)	**2.** (d)	**3.** (c)	**4.** (b)	**5.** (a)	**6.** (c)	**7.** (a)	**8.** (a)	**9.** (c)	**10.** (d)
11. (a)	**12.** (c)	**13.** (d)	**14.** (b)	**15.** (c)	**16.** (c)	**17.** (c)	**18.** (c)	**19.** (b)	**20.** (c)
21. (a)	**22.** (a)	**23.** (b)	**24.** (a)	**25.** (a)	**26.** (a)	**27.** (a)	**28.** (d)	**29.** (b)	**30.** (a)
31. (b)	**32.** (b)	**33.** (c)	**34.** (a)	**35.** (c)	**36.** (c)	**37.** (a)	**38.** (c)	**39.** (c)	**40.** (a)
41. (b)	**42.** (a)	**43.** (d)	**44.** (d)	**45.** (a)	**46.** (c)	**47.** (c)	**48.** (a)	**49.** (a)	**50.** (c)
51. (a)	**52.** (a)	**53.** (a)	**54.** (c)	**55.** (c)	**56.** (a)	**57.** (a)	**58.** (c)	**59.** (b)	**60.** (a)
61. (c)	**62.** (c)	**63.** (a)	**64.** (c)	**65.** (b)	**66.** (a)	**67.** (b)	**68.** (a)	**69.** (d)	**70.** (a)
71. (a)	**72.** (b)	**73.** (c)	**74.** (b)	**75.** (a)	**76.** (b)	**77.** (b)	**78.** (c)	**79.** (a)	**80.** (a)
81. (c)	**82.** (a)	**83.** (c)	**84.** (c)	**85.** (a)	**86.** (b)	**87.** (d)	**88.** (a)	**89.** (b)	**90.** (c)
91. (a)	**92.** (b)	**93.** (b)	**94.** (b)	**95.** (c)	**96.** (b)	**97.** (a)	**98.** (a)	**99.** (c)	**100.** (d)
101. (c)	**102.** (b)	**103.** (a)	**104.** (c)	**105.** (a)	**106.** (c)	**107.** (a)	**108.** (c)	**109.** (a)	**110.** (a)
111. (b)	**112.** (c)	**113.** (d)	**114.** (a)	**115.** (a)	**116.** (c)	**117.** (d)			

CHAPTER 6

Testing and Implementation

Learning Objectives

At the end of this chapter, you will be able to:

- Explain the significance of testing and implementation within the design thinking framework and how it influences the final outcome
- Define clear objectives for the testing and implementation phases to ensure alignment with project goals
- Explain the importance of identifying and engaging key stakeholders during the testing phase to gather diverse insights and enhance the solution's effectiveness
- List the common challenges faced during testing and implementation and strategies to navigate these obstacles effectively
- Describe the piloting process, including its role in the design thinking methodology and tips for conducting successful pilot tests
- List the techniques for analyzing test results to extract meaningful insights and make informed decisions moving forward
- Explain the methods for tracking and measuring the success of a solution post-implementation to validate its impact and performance
- Utilize feedback and data to refine and improve testing procedures and implementation strategies continuously
- Explain the strategies for scaling testing processes in design thinking to accommodate larger user groups or more complex systems
- Explain the concept of continuous improvement in testing and how it contributes to the iterative nature of design thinking
- Provide tips for avoiding common pitfalls that can occur during the testing phase and how to preemptively address them
- Give an overview of the Kano model and its application in desirability testing to prioritize features based on user satisfaction
- State the principles of usability and ergonomic testing to ensure the solution's ease of use and user comfort
- Explain the role of agility in the testing phase, allowing for flexible adaptation to new information and changes in the project scope
- Explain the process of revisiting user needs and aspirations to ensure the solution remains user-centered throughout the testing and implementation stages

6.1 Introduction

Imagine that you and classmates want to create an app to help students stay organized and learn better. You and your friends brainstormed about innovative ideas and made drawings of the app. Now it is time for the last two steps: testing and implementation (Fig. 6.1).

Think of testing like giving your app a final exam. Here's how we make sure it passes with flying colors:

- **Does it solve the problem?** Just like your math homework solves a problem, your app needs to solve the issue it was designed for. During testing, you will check if students can use the app to stay organized, access learning materials, or collaborate on projects.
- **Is it feasible and easy to use?** Imagine a very complex math equation – it may work, but it is not very practical. We need to test if your app works smoothly and efficiently. Is it fast enough? Can students with different tech skills use it easily? This is where usability testing comes in. You will observe students interacting with the app, identify any confusing parts, and check if it meets their expectations.

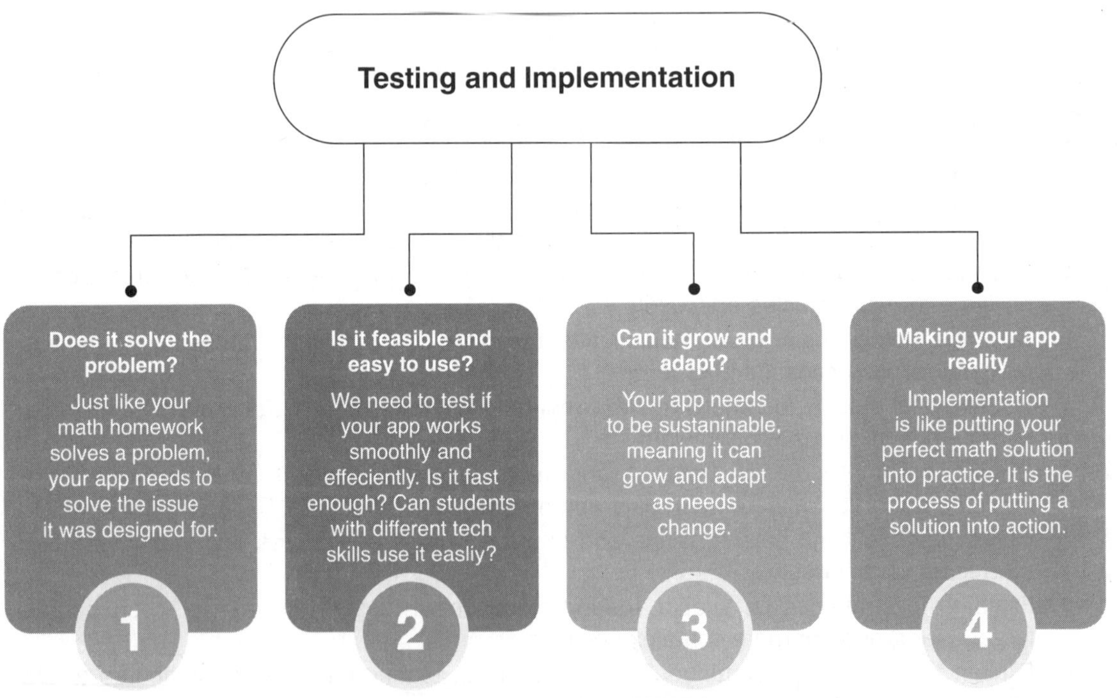

Figure 6.1 Testing and implementation

Let us say your app has a complex calendar view. During usability testing, you may find that students struggle to add due dates and color-code their assignments. This would be a sign that the calendar needs to be simplified.

- **Can it grow and adapt?** Imagine learning new things in different subjects throughout your school years. Your app needs to be sustainable, meaning it must grow and adapt as needs change. During testing, consider if the app's design allows for future updates and new features. Sustainability testing assesses how well the solution can be upheld and enhanced over time. This may entail evaluating the solution's capacity for growth, adaptability to shifting demands, and future development.

Once your app passes the test, it is time to bring it to life! Implementation is like putting your perfect math solution into practice. The process of putting a solution in action and making it accessible to users is called implementation. Here are the steps involved:

1. **Creating a Plan:** Just like you would not solve a math problem without a strategy, you need to create a plan to implement your app. This could involve deciding how the app will be distributed, training teachers on how to use it, and creating support resources for students.
2. **Teaching and supporting:** Imagine explaining your math solution to your classmates. You may need to teach students and teachers how to use your app effectively. This could involve creating tutorials, workshops, and online guides.

6.1.1 Types of Testing

There are different types of tests, just like there are different sections in your final exam:

- **User testing**: This is similar to having classmates use your app and give feedback. User testing entails observing users engage with the solution to find any problems or difficulties. Testing the solution with users with varying degrees of experience or skill may also be necessary.
- **Functionality testing**: This is similar to checking if all the features of your app, like adding notes or creating quizzes, work properly. Functionality testing entails examining all of the solution's features and functions.
- **Performance testing**: This is similar to making sure your app does not crash or take too long to load, just like you would not want your calculator to freeze during a math test. Performance testing checks the solution's speed and responsiveness.

6.2 Defining Testing and Implementation Goals

Have you ever read a detective story? They never accuse people right away. A good detective learns about the situation, finds clues, and tests their ideas before making an accusation. This is a human-centered approach to problem-solving.

Let us say you and your friends need to design the college cafeteria. Here's how design thinking helps solve this problem:

Step 1: The Cafeteria Case

Understanding the problem: First, we act like detectives and figure out the problem. Is the cafeteria food boring? Are the lines too long? We can interview students, teachers, and cafeteria workers to find clues.

Step 2: Brainstorming

Coming up with solutions: Now that we know the problem, we brainstorm possible solutions. This is like the detective thinking of theories about who stole the cafeteria cookies. Maybe we could offer healthier options, create a faster ordering system, or have themed food days.

Step 3: Mock Cafeterias – Building Prototypes

Prototyping: Detectives build mini crime scenes to test theories. In design thinking, we create prototypes, which are like tiny versions of our solutions. This could be a sketch of a new menu, a cardboard self-serve station, or even acting out different ordering ways.

Step 4: Testing Our Theories

Testing: Just like the detective checks their ideas by asking questions, we need to test our plans with real students. This helps us to find out if our ideas fix the problem. Perhaps the new menu is difficult to understand or the self-serve station does not work as well as we think it does. Testing helps us find any substandard areas in our detective work (design answers).

Step 5: Putting the Best Solution in Action

Implementation: Once we have tested all the plans and found the best answer, it is time to put it to work. This could mean working with the cafeteria workers to use a new menu, building the self-serve station, or training students on how to use a new ordering system.

Why are Testing and Implementation Goals Important?

Imagine a situation where the detective solves the case by accusing the wrong person. Setting clear goals for testing and implementation helps us avoid mistakes.

Testing Goals

- Are students happy with the food options?
- Can students order their lunch quickly and easily?
- Is the new system easy to understand for everyone?

6.2.1 Implementation Goals

- Can the new system be implemented within budget?
- Do we have the staff and resources needed to make it work?
- How will we measure the success of the new cafeteria system?

By setting clear goals, we can make sure our design thinking process is on track and that the final solution truly solves the problem and meets the needs of students, teachers, and staff.

Determining testing and implementation goals is a crucial step in the design thinking process. Designers must ensure that they are working towards a defined goal and assess the solution's performance in relation to those goals by establishing explicit goals for testing and execution. Goal setting also helps ensure that the final product meets the demands and preferences of people.

Design Visualization Question 6.1

Imagine you have been tasked with improving the user experience of a popular bike-sharing app in your city. Cyclists have expressed frustration with the current app, ridership is declining.

The Challenge: Your design thinking team will develop a plan to test and refine the bike-sharingapp, ensuring it meets the needs of cyclists and encourages ridership.

Think User-Centric: Who are the users? Consider demographics, cycling habits, and pain of typical bike-share app users. What are their needs and frustrations? Conduct user research through interviews and surveys to understand their challenges with the current app.

Define Success: What does successful outcome look like? This could be increased ridership, improved user satisfaction ratings, of a reduction in app-related complaints.

Testing Goals: Our testing phase will identify areas for improvement. Here's what we want to achieve: Identify usability issues, Evaluate app functionality, Gather user feedback

Deliverables:

- A user profile outlining the target audience for the bike-sharing app, including their needs and frustrations.
- A set of clearly defined success metrics that will measure the effectiveness of the improved app.
- Specific testing goals that outline how you will identify usability issues, evaluate functionality, and gather user feedback.

6.3 Identifying Key Stakeholders of the Testing Stage

In the design thinking process, spotting key people who will try out the solution during the testing stage is very important (Fig. 6.2).

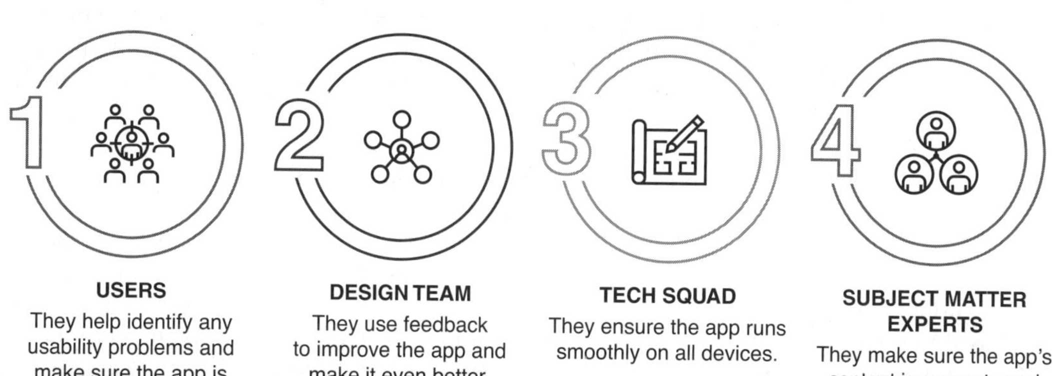

Figure 6.2 Identifying key stakeholders

6.3.1 Users

These are the people who will use the finished product. So it is vital to have them in the testing stage to make sure the product is easy to use and meets their needs. Also, users can give designers helpful comments during testing that can be used to improve the solution and ensure its success. There are many reasons why it is crucial to involve users in the testing process.

First, it enables designers to pinpoint any usability problems or user pain points. Second, designers can spot opportunities for development and hone the solution to better suit users' demands by watching people interact with it. Third, users who participate in the testing procedure can give designers illuminating feedback and comments that can be used to improve the solution. Fourth, users may offer ideas for new features or upgrades to current functions that designers may have yet to consider. Finally, design professionals may provide more user-friendly solutions and better satisfy consumers' demands by incorporating user feedback into the design process. Including consumers in the testing process helps boost customer satisfaction and user adoption rates. Users are more inclined to use and refer the good or service to others when they believe that their feedback has been considered. In the end, companies may see higher sales and revenue due to this.

6.3.2 Design Team

The design team is in charge of watching users engage with the product during testing and identifying any potential usability problems or pain points. To further hone the solution, they might also be in charge of gathering customer feedback and implementing it into the design process. The design team can learn a lot about the usability and efficacy of the solution by participating in the testing process. To ensure that the solution satisfies the user's wants and expectations, they can check for areas that could be used better and make the necessary changes. The team that plans designs is in charge of planning to put the solution into action. They tell people how to use it. They also give continuous help and keep it is working well. Being part of the testing stage helps them understand how people use the solution. They can spot any issues or problems before the solution is put into action. Their participation in the testing stage can also aid them in developing a better understanding of how to properly install the solution and offer continuous support and maintenance to guarantee its long-term success.

6.3.3 Technical or IT Support Team

It is crucial to identify any technical or IT support teams that may be required to deploy the solution during the testing phase of the design thinking process. They are frequently in charge of managing databases, setting up hardware and software, and ensuring the system is secure and reliable. The technical viability and scalability of the solution may be tested during the testing phase by the technical or IT support teams. They might also be in charge of spotting any potential implementation-related technical problems or difficulties and developing a strategy to deal with them. These teams may offer end-user training and support in addition to their technical skills when the solution is implemented. To guarantee that users can use the system correctly and efficiently, they can be in charge of developing user manuals, holding training sessions, and offering continuing technical support. Assuring a smooth and successful system rollout, their presence can also help detect any potential technical issues or challenges that may develop during implementation. Their technical knowledge and resources are essential for assuring the success of the solution and for its efficient implementation.

6.3.4 Subject Matter Experts

Subject matter experts should be considered the fourth key stakeholder to identify throughout the testing process. These specialists can offer helpful insights and input during the testing process since they have particular knowledge and skill in the area that the solution is meant to solve. Experts might come from various fields, including academia, business, or government. In addition, they might be knowledgeable in engineering, medicine, education, or law. They can aid designers in identifying potential problems or difficulties relating to the solution's design and ensuring that the solution satisfies the end-users' needs. Subject matter experts can offer input on the solution's technical viability, usability, and efficacy throughout the testing process. Also, they might help discover any parts that need enhancing or reworking by participating in user testing. Their opinions can ensure that the solution is produced to address the issue or opportunity it was intended to address and is effective. The development of the solution's content or curriculum may involve subject matter experts and their feedback during the testing phase. For instance, while developing lesson plans and curricula for an educational solution, subject matter experts may also offer advice on instructional design. Designers may ensure that the solution adheres to industry best practices and that any legal or compliance needs are satisfied by including subject matter experts in the testing process.

Design Visualization Question 6.2

Design Thinking Challenge: Building a StudyBuddy App

Your design thinking team has developed a revolutionary study app prototype called StudyBuddy, designed to help students learn collaboratively and conquer their courses. Now it is time to refine your creation and ensure it is user-friendly and effective.

The Challenge: This assignment focuses on the crucial testing phase of the design thinking process. You will identify essential stakeholders who will participate in testing StudyBuddy and develop a plan to gather their valuable feedback.

Deliverables:

- A detailed stakeholder recruitment plan outlining how you will identify and recruit participants from each stakeholder group.
- A comprehensive testing plan that defines specific testing methods for each stakeholder group (users, design team, tech squad, subject matter experts).
- A clear plan for collecting, analyzing, and synthesizing feedback from all stakeholders.

6.4 Key Challenges in Testing and Implementation

The main challenges designers might face during testing and launching are shown in Fig. 6.3.

Key challenges in testing and implementations

1 **Not enough resources**
Testing and launching an app takes resources, just like building a treehouse which needs wood, nails, and friends.

4 **Technical glitches**
Sometimes, things just do not work the way they are supposed to.

Change is difficult
This can make it difficult to get everyone on board with a new solution.

Communication problems
Testing and launching the app requires clear communication between everyone involved.

The app will not work for everyone
This is a scalability issue – the app needs to work for everyone, not just a select few.

Launching without a plan
Just like you would not build a treehouse without a blueprint, you need a plan.

Figure 6.3 Key challenges in testing and implementation

6.4.1 Challenge 1: Not Enough Time, Money, or Resources

Testing and launching an app requires resources. It is like building a treehouse, which requires wood, nails, and help from friends. Sometimes, there might not be enough time, money, or people to test everything. This can happen in small startups with small budgets. For example, you only have a week to test your app before presenting it to your college principal. This might not be enough time to get feedback from everyone and make all the necessary changes.

How to Fix It: Focus on getting feedback from a small group of students with different learning styles and tech skills. You can also use online surveys or forums to gather more comprehensive input.

6.4.2 Challenge 2: Change is Difficult

People must test the product thoroughly. Some teachers (or even students) may not want to use a new app, mainly if they are happy with the current system. This can make it difficult for you to ensure that they test the new peoduct. For example, some teachers may be worried that the app will take too much time to learn or that it will disrupt their lessons.

How to Fix It: Get teachers and students involved early in the design process. This way, they will feel invested in improving and using the app. Communicate to the stakeholders how the app will make learning fun and easy for all.

6.4.3 Challenge 3: The App Will Not Work for Everyone

The app may work well on mobile phones but may crash on older school tablets. This is a scalability issue. The app must work for everyone, not just a select few. For example, the app may require a lot of memory, making it run slow on older devices.

How to Fix It: Test the app on different devices during the testing phase. This will help identify any compatibility issues. You might also need to adjust the app to ensure it runs smoothly on all devices.

6.4.4 Challenge 4: Technical Glitches

Sometimes, the product will not work the way it is supposed to. There may be some technical bugs in the app's code, or the server might overload if too many users try to access it simultaneously. For example, the app may lose your assignments if the internet connection goes down.

How to Fix It: Test the app thoroughly before launching it. Also, have a back-up plan in case something goes wrong. This might involve having a tech-savvy student on standby or creating offline versions of essential features.

6.4.5 Challenge 5: Communication Problems

Testing and launching the app requires clear communication between everyone involved. If there are misunderstandings or people are not kept in the loop, it can cause delays and frustration. For example, if the teachers were not informed about the new app's training session and were therefore not prepared to answer student questions.

How to Fix It: Establish clear communication channels from the beginning. Hold regular meetings to discuss progress and address any concerns. Also, ensure everyone involved has access to the latest information about the app.

6.4.6 Challenge 6: Launching Without a Plan

Just like you would not put up a tree house without a plan, you need to make a plan for the app launch. This involves assigning jobs to people, timetables for jobs, and listing the issues that could be encountered. For example, if there is no plan for troubleshooting technical issues that students might encounter while using the app, it could result in unhappy users.

How to Fix It: Develop a detailed implementation plan that outlines roles, responsibilities, and potential challenges. This will help ensure a smooth launch and address any problems that come up along the way.

Design Visualization Question 6.3

Potential obstacles for testing and implementation:

- **Limited Resources:** Time, budget, and expertise may be restricted.
- **Stakeholder Resistance:** Gaining buy-in from key stakeholders can be challenging.
- **Shifting User Needs:** User needs and preferences may evolve, requiring ongoing adaptation.
- **Scalability Challenges:** Ensuring your solution can accommodate future growth and user base expansion can be difficult.

Deliverables:

- A detailed implementation plan outlining resource allocation, stakeholder engagement, and scalability strategies.
- A brief description of potential obstacles you anticipate facing and how you will overcome them using your chosen strategies.

6.5 Overview of Piloting and Launching in Design Thinking

Let us suppose that you and your friends have come up with a new method for studying history using virtual reality (VR) equipment. You have built a model, but before rolling it out to the whole college, you must first try it out with a smaller group. This is called a pilot test.

A pilot test lets you check if your idea works well. You first obtain input from a few people. This way, you can fix any issues before the actual launch. For example, some students may feel dizzy using the VR headset (Fig. 6.4). Or the history lessons may need more visuals. Getting feedback early helps improve your design.

Figure 6.4 A new method for studying history using VR equipment

6.5.1 Steps in the Pilot Test

1. **Setting Test Goals:** What do you want to learn from the pilot test? Is it to see if the VR experience is fun and engaging? Or maybe to check if students actually learn more history this way. Having a clear goal helps you focus your test and get the information you need.
2. **Selecting Test Participants:** You need to find a small group of students who are interested in history and comfortable using VR technology. This way, their feedback will be most helpful.
3. **Prototyping:** Your pilot test should not use the final VR experience. Instead, you can create a simpler version with the key features you want to test. This way, you can make changes easily based on feedback.

4. **Inviting Participants:** When your VR experience is ready for a trial, call your test participants. Give them clear information on what to do and how to give feedback. Let them know what goals you want them to achieve. Ask what worked well and what did not.
5. **Gathering Feedback:** After the pilot test, it is time to listen closely to what your test group has to say. Ask them questions about their experience. Did they find the VR experience fun and engaging? Did they learn anything new about history? Their feedback will help you improve your VR experience before launching it to the whole college.

By following these steps, you can conduct a successful pilot test and ensure your VR history project is useful to everyone.

It is important to remember that design thinking is all about learning from mistakes and adapting your ideas based on user feedback. So do not be afraid to test and iterate (make improvements) before launching your project.

6.5.2 Conducting a Successful Pilot Test

Defining the test's goal is the first step in executing a successful pilot test. The goal must be precise, measurable, and do-able in the allotted time. As a result, designers will be better able to concentrate their efforts and resources on reaching the desired result. In addition, the pilot test's goal should align with the project's overall objectives. Finally, it should contribute to validating the developed solution.

The second phase is the choice of a representative sample of the intended audience for the pilot test (Fig. 6.5). Those who are likely to utilize the solution and can offer insightful input on its usability, effectiveness, and relevance should be included. Again, the sample should be varied enough to include a variety of viewpoints and experiences without being too big to handle.

Making a testable prototype of the solution is the third phase. The final product should resemble this prototype as closely as feasible and have all the essential features and capabilities required to provide the intended results. To ensure the prototype is workable and practical, it should be tested in a real-world environment.

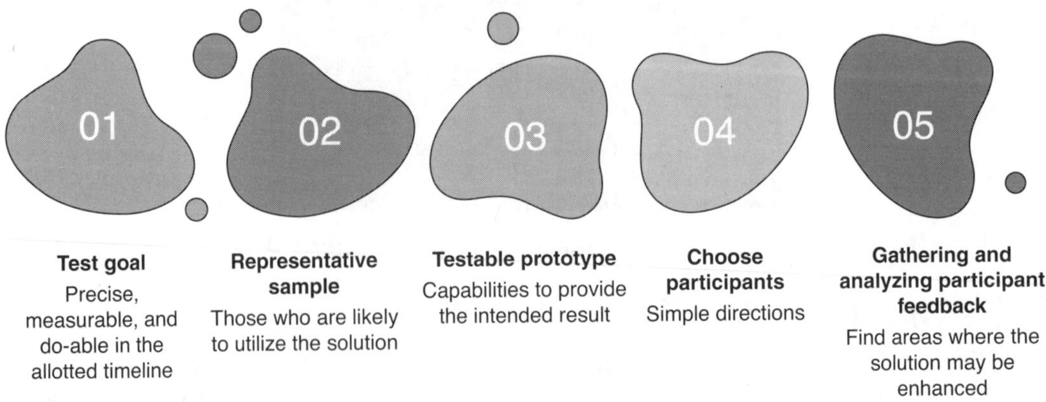

Figure 6.5 Conducting a successful pilot test

Choosing participants for the pilot test and giving them detailed instructions on using the solution are the final two steps. The directions should be simple to understand and created to aid participants in achieving the desired result. Participants should be given enough time to try the solution and express their opinions.

Gathering and analyzing participant feedback is the fifth phase. Surveys, interviews, and observation can all be used to get feedback. The feedback should be reviewed to find areas where the solution may be enhanced and to confirm its efficacy and usability. Finally, the solution should be improved and the design should be polished using the input.

Thus, careful planning, execution, and assessment are necessary for a successful design thinking pilot test. Among the crucial steps are determining the test's objective, choosing a representative sample of the intended audience, developing a solution prototype, enlisting participants, and gathering and analyzing participant feedback. By following these procedures, designers can ensure that their solutions are usable, practical, and functional and satisfy their consumers' needs.

Design Visualization Question 6.4

Pilot testing involves running a small-scale version of your solution with a representative user group to gather valuable feedback before full-scale implementation.

The Challenge: Imagine you have developed a revolutionary fitness app designed to motivate users and help them achieve their fitness goals.

Your Task:

1. **Define Your Test Goal:** Craft a clear, measurable, and achievable goal for your pilot test. For example, 'Increase user engagement with the app by 20% within two weeks.'
2. **Recruit Your Testers:** Describe the ideal user profile for your fitness app. How will you select a representative sample of 10–15 users for your pilot test?
3. **Prototype:** Briefly describe the key features of your app prototype. How will you ensure your prototype functions smoothly during the pilot test?
4. **Instructions and Feedback:** Develop clear and concise instructions for your pilot test participants. How will you gather feedback on the app's usability, effectiveness, and user experience?

6.6 Analyzing the Test Results

After the pilot test, it is time to analyze the feedback from the test group (Fig. 6.6) to make changes and improve the performance of your product.

1. **Gather Your Data:** This can be accomplished by conducting interviews, surveys, or even by observing the test group's interactions with the product. There are two main types of data:
   - **Quantitative:** This involves numbers. For example, how long did it take students to complete the VR experience on average?
   - **Qualitative:** This is more about feelings and experiences. For example, what did students like or dislike about the VR experience? Did they find it confusing or easy to use?
2. **Data Analysis:** It is now necessary to analyze and derive meaning from the data that has been gathered. Observe trends and patterns. Did numerous students become fixated on a particular segment of the VR experience? Did everyone appreciate the same portions?
3. **Prioritizing Fixes:** Focus on the issues that will make the biggest difference in the user experience. For example, if many students found a part of the VR experience confusing, that might be a higher priority to fix than something only a few students mentioned.
4. **Relaunch and Refine:** Once you have made changes based on the feedback, it is time to test your VR experience again with a small group. Observe if the changes you made actually improved the experience. This process of testing, getting feedback, and making improvements is called iteration. By iterating, you can keep improving your VR experience.

Figure 6.6 Analyzing the test results

By carefully analyzing the test results and user feedback, you can make sure your VR history project is an engaging and educational experience for everyone.

6.7 Tracking Results and Measuring Success

1. **Goals and Metrics:** Your VR history endeavor must have distinct objectives. What were the desired outcomes for students through its utilization? Did you intend to impart knowledge regarding a particular era in history? Alternatively, perhaps your objective was to enhance the level of engagement in history courses. After establishing your objectives, you must determine how to quantify them. The term for these is metrics. If improving history test scores was your objective, for instance, you could compare the mean score before and after utilizing the VR experience.
2. **Gathering Feedback:** You need to gather feedback from students about their experience with the VR history project. This can be done through surveys, interviews, or even informal chats.
3. **Analyzing the Data:** Once you have all your data (test scores, feedback, etc.), it is time to analyze it and check if you achieved your goals. Did students learn more history? Did they enjoy using the VR experience?
4. **Making Improvements:** Using the feedback you gathered, you can make improvements to your product. For example, if students found a certain part of the VR experience confusing, you can modify it to make it clearer.

Monitoring outcomes and gauging the effectiveness of tests is crucial to the design thinking process' testing and implementation phase. It aids in ensuring that the solution satisfies user wants and corporate goals. Businesses can develop successful solutions that add value for users and stakeholders by setting clear goals, getting feedback, and analyzing data.

Design Visualization Question 6.5

Design Thinking Challenge: Tracking Metrics

The Challenge: Imagine you have launched a new community garden initiative to promote healthy eating and environmental awareness:

- **Define Success:** Outline 3–5 key metrics you would use to measure the success of your community garden initiative. Consider both quantitative (measurable) and qualitative (descriptive) metrics.
- **Data Collection Tools:** Describe specific tools and methods you would use to collect data for each of your chosen metrics.
- **Evaluation Timeline:** Develop a realistic timeline for data collection and evaluation. How often will you assess your metrics, and how will you analyze the data?
- **Adapt and Improve:** Explain how you would utilize the gathered data to adapt and improve your community garden initiative. For example, how might changes in user behavior or feedback influence future planning?

Deliverables:

- A table outlining your chosen success metrics, data collection tools, and analysis frequency.
- A brief explanation of how you would use the data to inform future iterations and improvements of your community garden initiative.

6.8 Leveraging Feedback and Data to Improve Testing and Implementation

Imagine that you hear from students that a part of the VR experience is confusing. This feedback indicates that there is a problem that needs fixing. Feedback can come from different sources:

- **Students (Users):** They can tell you what they liked and disliked about the VR experience.
- **Teachers (Stakeholders):** They might have ideas on how to integrate the VR experience into their lessons.
- **Your Teammates:** They might notice things you missed during development.

We can gather feedback through surveys, interviews, or even just talking to students after they use the VR experience. Your VR experience may also track data, like how long students spend in different parts. We can collect data through different methods:

- **Analytics tools:** These can track metrics such as how many students use the VR experience and for how long.
- **User testing:** We can observe students using the VR experience and see where they get stuck.
- **Surveys:** We can ask students questions about their experience, like how easy it was to use.

Utilizing data and feedback is essential for the design thinking process to be successful. Feedback and data give designers insightful information about user wants and preferences, which can improve design decisions. Therefore, the design thinking process can be improved by including user feedback and data to help designers produce more user-centered and efficient solutions. In addition, designers may guarantee that the solution is extensively tested and executed in the most advantageous way to the consumers by leveraging feedback and data to inform testing and implementation.

6.9 Scaling the Testing in Design Thinking

Imagine that you have launched your VR history project in your college and it has become very popular. Now, more colleges from all around the country want to use it. But before you roll it out to everyone, you need to make sure it can handle a bigger crowd. This is called scaling the testing process (Fig. 6.7).

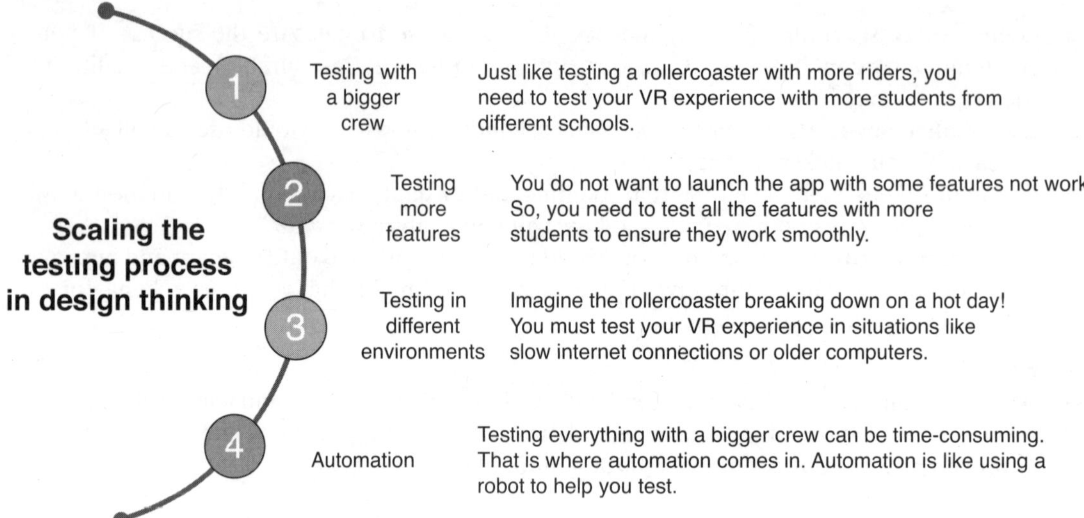

Figure 6.7 Scaling the testing process

Testing with more significant user populations may be necessary to scale the testing process and provide complete information about how users interact with the solution. In addition, this enables the designers to spot other patterns and trends that may have gone unnoticed during testing on a smaller scale. By testing more features, the testing process may also be scaled up. Designers can learn which features people value most and which may benefit from refinement by testing a more comprehensive selection of features. Furthermore, testing in more complex setups might assist designers in understanding how users interact with the solution in more difficult circumstances. This may be especially crucial for solutions intended for various settings or circumstances.

It is crucial to remember that scaling the testing procedure may also result in additional difficulties, like higher prices, extended testing durations, and specialized equipment requirements. Therefore, meticulous planning and resource allocation is required to guarantee that the testing process is successful and efficient. To ensure that the solution satisfies the needs of a broad user population, scaling the testing process is a crucial step in the design thinking process.

But, again, automation is helpful in this situation. Automation involves automating time-consuming, repetitive processes using tools and software. For example, automation can speed up the testing process and reduce the time and resources needed to perform tests in the context of design thinking testing. In addition, an application's functionality can be assessed using automated testing methods to ensure it functions as intended on all supported platforms and devices.

One advantage of automation is its capacity to carry out routine tasks efficiently and precisely. As a result, testers may feel less pressure and have more time to focus on harder-to-test cases that require manual testing. Automating repeated tasks allows testing to be done more efficiently while saving time and resources. Yet it is crucial to remember that automation does not entirely replace manual testing. Automation can speed up testing, but it is still vital to review the outcomes of automated tests and perform manual testing when required. Moreover, carefully prepared and planned test cases are a requirement for effective automation. Automation can result in false positives or negatives, leading to incorrect test results if test cases are not correctly written. As a result, it is essential to combine manual and automated testing and ensure test cases are correctly written.

Making use of a test management system is another strategy for scaling testing. A test management system offers an organized location to coordinate testing efforts and monitor test results. This ensures that testing is carried out consistently and that the entire team has easy access to the test data. A test management system can also assist in identifying testing process flaws so that improvements can be made continuously.

User testing is an important way to get feedback on how well a product works. It helps find areas that need improvement. There are many methods for user testing. Some are usability testing, surveys, and interviews. Including users in testing makes sure the product is easy to use. It also ensures the product meets user needs.

Scaling testing is essential for the effectiveness of the design thinking methodology. Testing activities must be scaled as a project grows to account for the broadened scope. Scaling testing efforts can be accomplished through automation, test management software, and user testing. Scaling testing allows designers to validate that a solution works and satisfies user needs, resulting in a more successful project conclusion.

6.10 Continuous Improvement in Testing

Reviewing and analyzing test findings frequently is one method of testing's continual development. Finding places where the solution can be enhanced entails reviewing the data gathered during testing. For instance, if a user is having trouble finishing a task, this may be a clue that the user interface needs to be improved. Likewise, design professionals can find areas for development and make the necessary adjustments to the solution by routinely reviewing test results.

Using user feedback in testing is another method of continual improvement. User input can help discover development areas and offer insightful information about how the solution is being utilized. User opinions can show if a tool is hard to use. Say people cannot find a feature. That means it may need to be easier to find. You can look at what users say while testing the tool. This way you know it works well for people. Regular usability testing is the third method for testing ongoing improvement. Usability testing entails watching consumers engage with the solution to see any problems or locations where they are having trouble. Regular usability testing can assist designers in identifying problem areas and making the necessary adjustments to the solution. Testing for usability can also guarantee that the solution is simple to understand and utilize. Another method of continual improvement is to automate the testing procedure. Testing is an important step to make sure software works well. Doing tests manually can take a lot of time. Tools can test software faster than humans. These tools check if an app works well on different phones and computers. With tools, testers have more time to look at tricky issues. Tools can run simple tests so people do not have to.

6.11 Avoiding Common Pitfalls in the Testing Stage

Here are some common testing mistakes and how to fix them:

- **Testing with an unsuitable audience:** Imagine if you showed your VR experience to teachers instead of students. Their feedback would not be constructive. This is why testing your solution with the appropriate audience is essential. In this case, you would want to test it with students, the actual users of your VR experience. Consider age, interests, and technical skills when choosing your test group. The more your test group matches your target audience, the better the feedback you will receive.
- **Unclear objectives:** Imagine testing your VR experience without knowing what you are looking for. Are you checking if it is easy to use? Is the history information accurate? Having

clear testing goals helps you focus your test and get the feedback you need. For example, a goal might be to see if students can learn about a specific historical event using the VR experience. By setting clear goals, you can get more relevant feedback that helps you improve your project.

- **Leading the test:** Imagine you are testing a VR game you made. You want the students testing it to pick the visuals as the best part of the experience. However, if you hint at that, it could spoil the results as it would be unfair. The correct way is to let the students explore the game freely. Ask open questions like "What did you enjoy?" or "What was unclear?" That way, you get their honest thoughts without guiding them.
- **Ignoring the test results:** Imagine testing your VR experience and then ignoring the feedback. That would be a big mistake. Test results show you what is working well and what needs improvement. For example, if many students say a part of the VR experience is confusing, you know you need to modify it. By carefully analyzing test results and user feedback, you can improve your VR experience.
- **Limited testing:** Let's say you create a VR game and test it with a few friends. They think it is good. But when more people play it, they find major problems. This is why testing with more people is key during the design process. The more you test, the more likely it is that you will find and fix issues before launch.

6.12 The Kano Model

Imagine that you are designing a pizza delivery app for students. You want it to be the best app possible, but how do you know what features students really want? This is where the Kano model comes into play.

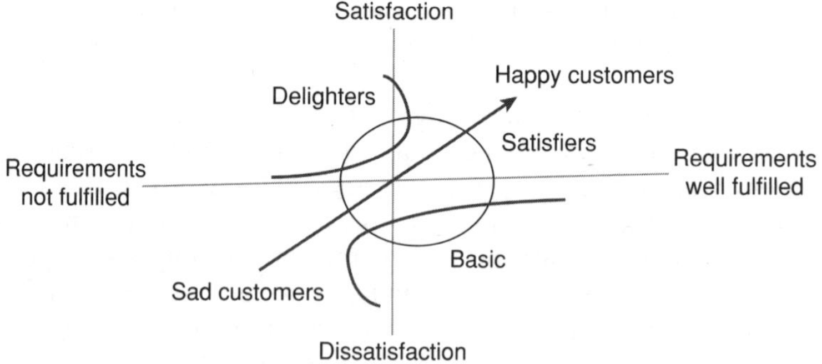

Figure 6.8 The Kano model

The main features of this model are as follows (Fig. 6.8):

- **Fundamental Features (Essential):** Users require these features in order for the application to function. For example, the essential components of a pizza would be the dough, cheese, and sauce. A pizza would be impossible without these ingredients. The essential features of your application may include real-time order tracking, a menu with prices, and streamlined order placement. In the absence of these functionalities, students will become dissatisfied and discontinue their usage of your application.
- **Performance Features (Satisfiers):** While not crucial to the app's functionality, these elements enhance the user experience. Imagine providing different toppings for your pizza, such as

chicken, mushrooms, or capsicum. Although these toppings are actually not required, they enhance the flavour of your pizza. Implementing performance features in your application may involve:

- Providing users with the ability to select their preferred delivery driver
- Offering coupons and discounts
- Incorporating a tip calculator

The more performance-oriented functionalities an application possesses, the more satisfied the users will be.

- **Delight Features (Delighters):** These are the features that students might not expect, but will be very happy to use. For example, getting a free dessert with your pizza order. Delight features for your app could be letting users track their pizza's progress from the oven to their doorstep, offering exclusive student deals, or integrating with games or social media. These features will set your app apart from the competition and excite students to use it.

Design thinkers use the Kano model to decide which elements to include in a product first. To prevent customer dissatisfaction, the product must have essential features. In contrast, performance features can be gradually introduced to raise customer satisfaction. In addition, using appealing features can set a product apart from its rivals. Customer feedback is gathered through interviews or surveys to implement the Kano model. First, customers are questioned about their expectations and reactions to whether a particular trait is present. Then, features are divided into the three categories above based on user input.

6.12.1 Steps in Using the Kano Model

- **User Feedback:** Just like you would not add pineapple on your pizza without asking your friends if they like them, you should never guess what features users want. Talk to students, interview them, or give them surveys to find out what features they expect (essential), would appreciate (performance), and would love to see (delight).
- **Sort the Features:** Once you have the feedback, categorize the features. This will help you know which features are essential, which will improve the experience, and which will really wow the users.
- **Prioritize and Create:** Start by building the essential features. Then, you can add performance features to make it more user-friendly. Finally, if you have resources left, consider adding some delightful features to make your app stand out.

The Kano model thus helps you focus on the features that users care about and create a product that will be a hit with everyone.

The Kano model has several advantages, one of which is that it facilitates resource allocation. Basic features are required, and performance features can be introduced depending on the available resources. In addition, delight features can be introduced if there is a chance to distinguish the product and raise customer satisfaction. The Kano model also has the advantage of assisting in predicting customer requirements. For example, while delight features are based on exceeding customer expectations, basic and performance features are based on what customers anticipate. As a result, a competitive advantage for the product can be created by anticipating customer requirements.

The Kano model is a helpful tool for the design thinking process testing step. It helps to allocate resources effectively by classifying features based on consumer expectations and satisfaction. In addition, anticipating customer requirements can help the product gain a competitive edge.

Design Visualization Question 6.6

Design Thinking Challenge: Kano Model

The Challenge: You are developing an online shopping platform that caters to environmentally conscious consumers.

Your Task:

- **Essential Functionality:** What core features are essential for users to navigate your platform and make eco-friendly purchases easily? List 5–7 essential features, like clear product sustainability labels, detailed carbon footprint information for each item, and secure payment processing.
- **Performance Perks:** How can you enhance the user experience and encourage repeat visits? Brainstorm 5–7 performance features that offer additional value, such as personalized product recommendations based on a user's sustainability preferences, educational content about eco-friendly brands and practices, or a loyalty program with rewards for choosing sustainable products.
- **Beyond Expectations:** What unexpected features would truly wow users and strengthen their connection to your platform? Develop 3–5 delightful features that might include curated 'sustainable swaps' for commonly purchased items, a carbon offset program integrated with purchases, or partnerships with environmental NGOs to donate a portion of sales.

6.13 Desirability Testing

Consider a scenario in which you have created an exceptionally stylish phone case that incorporates a fidget spinner, but it fails to appeal to any of your acquaintances. That certainly would not be desirable, would it? When this occurs, desirability testing is utilized. Here, understanding how users feel about your creation and incorporating their feedback into its development is the objective. Desirability testing involves the following:

- **Gaining insight into your target market**: It is imperative to ascertain the intended audience of your project prior to presenting it to others. Consider designing a phone case for educators in which each individual design is adorned with glitter and emoticons. It may not be the most suitable match. Similar to fictitious characters, personas symbolize the ideal user. Through audience research, it is possible to develop personas that encapsulate their desires, requirements, and preferences. This assists you in creating an item that will appeal to them.
- **User-specific testing**: Consider a phone case that is aesthetically pleasing but unfeasible to install on your device. Clearly, that is not preferable. Usability testing consists of observing user interactions with a given application. This may involve anything from experimenting with a new app to testing a phone case. Through observation of its usage, one can ascertain whether or not it is intuitive and straightforward to navigate. If they are becoming perplexed or frustrated, you know that adjustments must be made.
- **Obtaining feedback**: Obtaining feedback from actual users is the most vital component of desirability testing. This may be accomplished through surveys, interviews, or focus groups. Communicate with them, "What do you like about this?" or alternatively "What would make this better?". The candid feedback of others will assist you in pinpointing areas that require enhancement. Perhaps you have a cool-looking phone case, but the fidget spinner renders it cumbersome. This feedback enables you to make necessary adjustments to your project in order to align it more closely with what people truly desire.

Desirability testing is important for the following reasons:

- **Satisfying user requirements**: One can guarantee that the endeavor is beneficial and attractive to the intended audience by soliciting feedback from actual individuals. Similar to ensuring that your pizza is topped with every topping that your peers enjoy.
- **Greater success with fewer setbacks**: No one wants to devote their entire day to something that no one desires. Desirability testing enables the early detection of issues, allowing for their resolution prior to the project's launch. This enhances the likelihood that your endeavor will achieve success.

Testing for desirability is an integral component of the design thinking methodology. Designers can increase the desirability and marketability of a product or service by seeking and implementing user feedback. Furthermore, desirability testing can guarantee that the product satisfies the needs and demands of the target market and reduce the probability of market failure.

6.14 Usability and Ergonomic Testing

Usability and ergonomics testing are the final checks you need to perform before launching your project. They help you identify areas for improvement and ensure your creation is user-friendly and enjoyable.

Usability testing checks how simple it is for a user to complete tasks. In contrast, ergonomic testing looks at the form and design of a product or service to see how pleasant and user-friendly it is. Usability testing involves watching how customers use a product or service and getting their feedback. This feedback can help designers identify areas that need improvement and make changes. There are various methods for usability testing, including in-person testing, remote testing, and moderated testing. Choosing the best method for the product or service being tested and the intended audience is essential.

Ergonomic testing checks if a product or service is easy to use. It looks at the design and layout. This includes the size and shape of the product, where the buttons are, and how useful it is. Ergonomic testing may also look at how the product works in different places. It is essential to know who will use the product before testing. The test instructions must be clear. Testing should take place in a controlled space. The test team needs to understand how to get user feedback and watch how they use the product.

Testing for ease of use and ergonomics is key to a product's success. It helps designers find ways to improve the user experience and make users happier. By testing during the design process, teams can make sure their products meet user needs and are simple to use.

Design Visualization Question 6.7

Design Thinking Challenge: Usability and Ergonomic Testing

The Challenge: Your team has designed a revolutionary smart kitchen gadget that chops, dices, and slices vegetables with a single touch.

Your Task:

1. **Usability Testing Plan:** Develop a usability testing plan for your smart kitchen gadget. This plan should include:
   - **Target Users:** Describe your ideal user group for this product (age, cooking experience level, etc.).

- **Testing Tasks:** Outline 3–5 specific tasks you want users to complete with the gadget, such as chopping an onion or slicing carrots.
- **Testing Methodology:** Choose a suitable testing method (such as in-person testing with observation, remote testing with screen recordings).
- **Data Collection:** Describe the methods you will use to gather user feedback (such as post-test questionnaires, observation notes).

2. **Ergonomic Considerations:** Identify 3–5 key ergonomic considerations for your smart kitchen gadget. This might include:
   - **Size and Weight:** Is the gadget comfortable to hold and maneuver for users of different hand sizes?
   - **Button Placement:** Are the buttons easily accessible and intuitive to use?
   - **Stability and Grip:** Does the gadget offer a secure grip during operation to prevent accidents?

6.15 Agility in the Testing Phase of Design Thinking

Agility means demonstrating flexibility and adjusting the project in accordance with insights gained from testing. An advantage of integrating agility in design thinking testing is the ability to promptly adapt to changes that may arise; this eliminates the need to expend time and effort on obsolete solutions. Better ideas can be generated through the practice of receptiveness to feedback and willingness to embrace change.
The main features of agility in the testing phase of design thinking are as follows:

- **Small-Step Testing (Iterative Testing):** Iterative testing entails modifying and evaluating a project in small increments. In this manner, you can obtain feedback while testing a rudimentary version of your app with simple principles. Before exerting significant effort, you can modify the entire concept, add new features, or modify the regulations in response to the feedback of your peers. It is analogous to constructing an app piecemeal and verifying the functionality of each component prior to proceeding.
- **Rapid Prototyping:** This entails the construction of basic, quick models of a project in order to test concepts in advance. This could take the form of a rudimentary diagram of a game board, handwritten instructions on cardboard pieces, or even a group of friends acting out the game. The purpose is to convey the fundamental concept and determine whether or not it is enjoyable. You can then improve your game and refine your concepts based on their feedback prior to devoting a substantial amount of time and energy to a complex final product.
- **Constantly Learning and Adapting:** Suppose you disregard the feedback of your peers on your game on the grounds that you believe your concept to be flawless. That would hardly constitute an open mentality. It is essential to be adaptable to change in agile testing. You must be open to receiving feedback from your peers, even if it is critical. Perhaps they find the game to be overly complicated or uninteresting. Incorporate their recommendations to enhance the design and increase the overall enjoyment of the game for all participants. Keep in mind that the objective is to produce something that individuals will appreciate, so be receptive to learning from and incorporating their suggestions.
- **Engaging in Open Communication:** Consider a scenario where your acquaintances offer unintelligible feedback regarding a particular game. Open communication is therefore essential. It is essential that all members of your design team (in this instance, your friends and

you) possess the ability to exchange ideas and comprehend one another's criticism. Discuss openly what is functioning and what is not. Keeping everyone on the same page will ensure that their contributions are instrumental in developing the highest quality game conceivable.

- **Develop an Appealing Project**: Through iterative testing and refinement, one can guarantee that the ultimate product is an undertaking that will be embraced by all.

Summary

- The testing and implementation phase is crucial in determining the viability, usability, and sustainability of a design solution.
- Techniques used include user testing, performance testing, and functionality testing.
- Testing objectives confirm assumptions made during the ideation phase and ensure the solution meets user requirements.
- Implementation objectives include ensuring the final solution is efficient and long-lasting, creating a strategy for implementation, identifying training or support requirements, and setting metrics for tracking the solution's progress.
- The primary stakeholders in the testing process include users, design teams, technical or IT support teams, and subject matter experts.
- Challenges include lack of resources, resistance to change, communication issues, and the need for a clear implementation strategy.
- The design thinking pilot test process includes defining the test's goal, selecting a representative sample, creating a testable prototype, selecting participants, analyzing test results, identifying frustrating components, scaling the testing, and continuously improving.
- Best practices include early stakeholder involvement, extensive testing, examination of test results and comments, improvement and iteration, and clear communication.
- Key tools include the Kano model, desirability testing, usability and ergonomic testing, and agile testing.

Solutions to Design Visualization Questions

Q 6.1

Building a Better Bike-Sharing App

Part 1: Defining Goals

User Profile

- **Demographics:** Target users likely include college students, young professionals, and urban residents who value eco-friendly transportation and convenience. Age range could be 18–45, with a tech-savvy population.
- **Cycling Habits:** Usage patterns may vary, with some users relying on the app for daily commutes, while others use it for occasional leisure rides.
- **Pain Points:** Common frustrations might include difficulty finding available bikes, confusing user interface, unreliable unlocking mechanisms, lack of clear trip information, and limited reporting options for app malfunctions.

Success Metrics

- **Increased Ridership:** Track the number of app-initiated bike rentals compared to previous periods. Aim for a measurable increase (such as 15%) in ridership within a set timeframe (such as 3 months).

- **Improved User Satisfaction Rating:** Implement an in-app survey system or utilize app store reviews to gauge user satisfaction. Target a specific improvement in user rating (such as a 0.5 star increase on a 5-star scale).
- **Reduction in App-Related Complaints:** Monitor the number of support tickets submitted through the app or customer service channels. Aim for a decrease in complaints related to usability or functionality issues (such as a 20% reduction).

Part 2: Testing Goals

Usability Testing: Recruit a diverse group of cyclists with varying levels of experience using the app. Conduct usability tests where participants are observed completing typical tasks like locating bikes, unlocking them, and reporting a malfunction.

Observe for:

- Difficulty navigating the app interface.
- Confusion with specific features or functionalities.
- Time taken to complete tasks.

Conduct A/B testing on different app interface designs to see which layouts users find most intuitive and user-friendly.

Functionality Testing: Develop a comprehensive test plan that covers all app features, including:

- Bike availability display accuracy.
- Seamless unlocking and locking mechanisms.
- Accurate trip duration and distance tracking.
- Functionality of payment integration and account management features.
- System stability and performance across different devices and network conditions.

Gathering User Feedback: Conduct post-testing interviews with participants to gather qualitative feedback on their experience. Questions could focus on:

- Ease of use and intuitiveness of the app.
- Clarity of information displayed.
- Suggestions for improvement of specific features.

Implement in-app surveys to collect user feedback on a broader scale. Surveys could ask users to rate features, report any issues, and suggest improvements.

Part 3: Implementation Goals

App Distribution Strategy: Utilize a smooth app store update process to ensure users receive the latest version automatically.

- Partner with the bike-sharing company to promote the updated app through their social media channels, website, and on-site signage.

User Training and Support: Develop a series of short video tutorials showcasing the new app features and functionalities.

- Create a comprehensive FAQ section within the app to address common user questions.
- Offer in-app chat support with customer service representatives for real-time assistance.

Communication Plan

- Issue a press release announcing the launch of the improved app, highlighting the new features and benefits for users.

- Develop targeted social media posts engaging with potential users and promoting the app's improvements.
- Partner with local cycling advocacy groups to spread awareness about the updated app through their networks.

Conclusion: By following these steps, the design thinking team can ensure a successful testing and implementation process for the bike-sharing app. The focus on user needs, clear goals, and a well-defined plan will ultimately lead to an improved app experience that encourages ridership and empowers cyclists to navigate their city efficiently and conveniently.

Q 6.2

StudyBuddy App: Stakeholder Testing Plan

Introduction: This document outlines the stakeholder testing plan for StudyBuddy, a revolutionary collaborative learning app designed to support student success. The plan ensures comprehensive app evaluation through participation from key stakeholder groups.

Stakeholder Recruitment

- **Users (Students)**
- **Recruitment Strategy:** Partner with student organizations and academic departments to reach a diverse group of students. Utilize social media platforms and campus flyers to promote participation in user testing sessions. Offer incentives like coffee coupons or small gift cards for participation.
- **Selection Criteria:** Consider students from various academic years and majors to obtain a well-rounded perspective. Recruit students with a range of technical experience levels to ensure the app caters to diverse user needs.

Design Team

- **Recruitment:** No external recruitment necessary. The design team will actively participate in all testing phases.

Tech Squad

- **Recruitment:** No external recruitment necessary. The tech squad will be responsible for technical testing.
- Subject Matter Experts (Professors/Teachers):

Recruitment Strategy

- Collaborate with faculty advisors or department heads to identify professors familiar with relevant course content.
- Offer professors early access to the app and the opportunity to shape its educational value.

Testing Methods

User Testing

- Conduct individual user testing sessions with students to observe their interaction with the app's features.
- Facilitate group testing sessions to encourage student interaction and gather diverse perspectives on collaboration functionalities.
- Utilize screen recording software to capture user behavior and identify potential usability issues.
- Administer post-testing surveys to gather qualitative feedback on user experience, satisfaction, and suggestions for improvement.

Design Review: The design team will conduct internal reviews of user testing data (screen recordings, surveys) to identify recurring usability issues and areas for improvement.

- Design team members will participate in user testing sessions to observe user behavior firsthand and gain deeper insights.
- The tech squad will conduct performance testing to assess app loading times, response speed, and resource utilization.
- Compatibility testing will ensure the app functions smoothly across a variety of devices and operating systems.
- The tech squad will utilize automated testing tools and manual testing to identify and resolve bugs and technical glitches.
- Subject matter experts will review the learning materials integrated within the app for accuracy, comprehensiveness, and alignment with relevant course objectives.
- Experts can provide feedback on the quality and relevance of resources, including study guides, practice quizzes, and educational content.
- Professors may suggest additional learning materials or suggest modifications to improve the app's educational value.

Feedback Analysis

- All feedback will be documented using a centralized system like a project management tool or a dedicated feedback form.
- User testing data (surveys, screen recordings) will be analyzed to identify trends and common pain points.
- Bug tracking software will be used to log and prioritize technical issues identified by the tech squad.
- Content review feedback from subject matter experts will be compiled and categorized based on specific learning materials and areas of improvement.
- A dedicated team member will be responsible for synthesizing all feedback and presenting key findings to the design team for further action.

Conclusion: This comprehensive stakeholder testing plan ensures that StudyBuddy receives valuable feedback from students, the design team, the tech squad, and subject matter experts. By analyzing the collective insights, the design team can refine the app's usability, functionality, technical performance, and educational content. This iterative approach will lead to a StudyBuddy app that empowers students to collaborate effectively, optimize learning, and achieve academic success.

Q 6.3

Design Thinking Challenge: Prototyping

This assignment focuses on the crucial stages of testing and implementation within the design thinking process. You will explore potential roadblocks and develop strategies to overcome them, ensuring your solution not only meets user needs but also achieves sustainable success.

Understanding the Importance

- **Testing:** Validates your solution's effectiveness and identifies areas for improvement before full-scale implementation. User testing ensures your solution truly addresses the problem and caters to a positive user experience.
- **Implementation:** Transforms your tested solution into a real-world application. This phase involves planning, resource allocation, and stakeholder engagement to bring your idea to life.

Potential Obstacles

- **Limited Resources:** Time, budget, and expertise may be restricted.
- **Stakeholder Resistance:** Gaining buy-in from key stakeholders can be challenging.
- **Shifting User Needs:** User needs and preferences may evolve, requiring ongoing adaptation.
- **Scalability Challenges:** Ensuring your solution can accommodate future growth and user base expansion can be difficult.

Overcoming the Obstacles

- **Resource Prioritization:** Develop a clear plan outlining which resources are most essential for successful testing and implementation.
- **Stakeholder Integration:** Actively involve key stakeholders throughout the process. Address their concerns, and leverage their expertise for a more effective solution.
- **User-Centered Design Culture:** Maintain a user-centric approach. Gather continuous user feedback throughout testing and implementation, iterating on your solution as needed.
- **Scalability Considerations:** Design your solution with future growth in mind. Consider a modular architecture that can be easily adapted to accommodate an expanding user base.

Your Task

- **Problem and Solution:** Briefly describe the problem your design thinking team is addressing and your proposed solution.
- **Testing Plan:** Outline a plan for testing your solution, including:
    - **Target user group:** Who will be involved in user testing?
    - **Testing methods:** How will you gather user feedback (surveys, interviews, usability testing)?
    - **Evaluation criteria:** How will you determine whether your solution is effective and user-friendly?
- **Implementation Plan:** Develop a plan for implementing your solution, including:
    - **Resource allocation:** How will you allocate resources (time, budget, people) for implementation?
    - **Stakeholder engagement strategy:** How will you keep stakeholders informed and involved during implementation?
    - **Scalability strategy:** How will your solution adapt to accommodate future growth?
    - **Addressing Obstacles:** Identify potential obstacles you might face during testing and implementation. Describe how you will overcome each obstacle using the strategies discussed above.

Deliverables

- A one-page summary outlining your problem, solution, and a high-level overview of your testing and implementation plans.
- A detailed testing plan outlining the target user group, testing methods, and evaluation criteria.
- A detailed implementation plan outlining resource allocation, stakeholder engagement, and scalability strategies.
- A brief description of potential obstacles you anticipate facing and how you will overcome them using your chosen strategies.

Remember

- Testing and implementation are not linear processes. Be prepared to iterate and adapt your plans based on feedback and ongoing evaluation.
- Communication is key, Keep stakeholders informed throughout the process and address their concerns proactively.
- Embrace challenges. Obstacles are opportunities for learning and refining your solution.

By following these steps and embracing a user-centered approach, your design thinking team can successfully bridge the gap between a brilliant idea and a tangible solution that delivers lasting impact. Go forth and innovate!

Q 6.4

Design Thinking Challenge Solutions: Pilot Testing

Challenge: Fitness App

- **Define Your Test Goal:** Our pilot test aims to increase user engagement with the fitness app by 20% within two weeks. We will measure engagement by tracking daily active users, time spent using the app, and completion rates of workout routines.
- **Recruit Your Testers:** We will target individuals aged 22–45 who are interested in improving their fitness but may struggle with consistency. We will recruit participants through social media ads targeting fitness communities and local gyms. Our goal is to select a diverse group of 10–15 users with varying fitness levels and technological experience.
- **Prototype:** Our app prototype will include features like personalized work-out plans, progress tracking, motivational challenges with friends, and integration with wearable fitness trackers. We will ensure a smooth testing experience by conducting the pilot test on a user-friendly platform that allows easy app download and functionality testing.
- **Instructions and Feedback:** We will provide clear instructions on downloading and using the app prototype. After two weeks, participants will complete a survey on their experience, including ease of use, enjoyment, and impact on motivation. We will also conduct follow-up interviews with a subset of users to gain deeper insights.

Q 6.5

Design Thinking Challenge: Tracking Metrics

- **Your Task:** Imagine you have launched a new community garden initiative to promote healthy eating and environmental awareness.
- **Define Success:** Outline 3–5 key metrics you would use to measure the success of your community garden initiative. Consider both quantitative (measurable) and qualitative (descriptive) metrics.
- **Data Collection Tools:** Describe specific tools and methods you would use to collect data for each of your chosen metrics.
- **Evaluation Timeline:** Develop a realistic timeline for data collection and evaluation. How often will you assess your metrics, and how will you analyze the data?
- **Adapting and Improving:** Explain how you would utilize the gathered data to adapt and improve your community garden initiative. For example, how might changes in user behavior or feedback influence future planning?

Deliverables

- A table outlining your chosen success metrics, data collection tools, and analysis frequency.
- A brief explanation of how you would use the data to inform future iterations and improvements of your community garden initiative.

Data Collection Tools

- **Sign-up Sheets and Attendance Logs:** Track initial garden participant numbers and active involvement in maintenance and harvest.
- **Weight Measurements and Harvest Logs:** Quantify the overall produce yield from the garden.
- **Event Attendance Records and Volunteer Sign-up Sheets:** Measure community engagement through participation in events and volunteering.

- **Surveys and Post-Event Feedback Forms:** Gather qualitative user feedback on overall experience, enjoyment, and perceived benefits.

Evaluation Timeline

- **Bi-weekly:** Track produce yield and analyze harvest logs to monitor garden productivity.
- **Monthly:** Review participant sign-up sheets and attendance logs to assess garden participation trends.
- **Bi-monthly:** Distribute surveys to gauge user satisfaction and collect feedback on the overall experience.
- **Quarterly:** Analyze data on community engagement through event attendance and volunteer participation.
- **Quarterly:** Review surveys on reported consumption of homegrown produce to assess impact on healthy eating habits.

Adapting and Improving

- **Low Participation:** If participation is low, analyze survey data and user feedback to understand potential barriers. Consider offering workshops, educational events, or schedule adjustments to attract more involvement.
- **Poor Produce Yield:** Analyze data on weather patterns, utilized planting methods, and harvest logs. Consult with experienced gardeners or agricultural experts to adapt planting strategies or address pest control issues.
- **Limited Community Engagement:** If community events are not attracting a large audience, consider diversifying event types or offering educational workshops related to gardening and healthy eating.
- **User Feedback:** Utilize user feedback from surveys to identify areas for improvement. This could involve modifying garden layout, offering additional resources, or providing signage with educational information on produce varieties and healthy recipes.
- **Healthy Eating Habits:** Track changes in reported homegrown produce consumption over time. If results are stagnant, conduct focus groups or in-depth interviews to understand user challenges and identify ways to encourage increased consumption.

By continuously monitoring these metrics and adapting the initiative based on the data and user feedback, the design thinking team can ensure the community garden thrives, fosters a sense of community, and promotes healthy eating habits.

Q 6.6

Design Thinking Challenge Solutions: Kano Model

Essential Functionality (Must-Haves)

- **Product Search and Filtering:** Allow users to easily search for products based on keywords, categories, and sustainability criteria.
- **Clear Sustainability Labels:** Provide clear and consistent labeling on each product page that communicates its environmental impact and sustainability certifications.
- **Carbon Footprint Information:** Display detailed information about a product's carbon footprint across its lifecycle, from production to transportation.
- **Secure Payment Processing:** Offer a secure and reliable payment gateway for completing online purchases.
- **Order Tracking and Delivery Management:** Enable users to track their orders and manage delivery options with transparent communication about eco-friendly packaging and shipping methods.

- **Account Management:** Allow users to create accounts and store preferences for a more personalized shopping experience.
- **Reviews and Ratings:** Facilitate a platform for users to read and leave reviews on products and their sustainability claims.

Performance Perks (Nice-to-Haves)

- **Personalized Recommendations:** Based on a user's past purchases and sustainability preferences, recommend eco-friendly alternatives for commonly purchased items.
- **Educational Content Hub:** Offer informative articles, blog posts, and videos that educate users about sustainable brands, practices, and the environmental impact of different products.
- **Loyalty Program with Rewards:** Implement a loyalty program that rewards users for choosing sustainable products, encouraging repeat purchases and customer loyalty.
- **Sustainability Brand Spotlight:** Feature interviews with eco-conscious brands and their efforts towards creating environmentally friendly products and packaging.
- **Partnership with NGOs:** Offer users the option to donate a portion of their purchase to environmental NGOs directly through the platform.

Delightful Surprises (Wow Factors)

- **Curated 'Sustainable Swaps':** Based on a user's shopping cart, suggest sustainable alternatives for specific products with a similar function but a lower environmental impact.
- **Carbon Offset Program:** Offer a carbon offset program where users can choose to offset the carbon footprint of their purchases with a simple click and contribution.
- **Partnership with Environmental NGOs:** Partner with environmental NGOs to allow users to directly support specific sustainability initiatives or conservation projects through the platform. This could involve offering limited edition products where a portion of the proceeds go towards a particular cause.

Q 6.7

Design Thinking Challenge Solutions: Usability and Ergonomic Testing

Usability Testing Plan

- **Target Users:** Our target users are busy professionals (aged 25–45) who value convenience and healthy cooking habits. They may have limited cooking experience but appreciate user-friendly kitchen tools.

Testing Tasks

- **Task 1:** Chopping an onion into medium dice.
- **Task 2:** Slicing a carrot into thin julienne strips.
- **Task 3:** Dicing a tomato for a salad.
- **Task 4:** Cleaning and storing the smart kitchen gadget.
- **Task 5:** (Optional) Setting custom settings for chop size or slice thickness (if applicable).

Testing Methodology: We will conduct in-person testing sessions with 5–7 participants in a kitchen environment. A moderator will observe user interactions and ask follow-up questions to understand their thought processes. The session will be recorded with screen capture software to document user actions on the gadget's interface (if applicable).

Data Collection

- **Post-Test Questionnaire:** We will administer a questionnaire to gather user feedback on task completion ease, intuitiveness of controls, overall efficiency, and satisfaction with the gadget's performance.

- **Observation Notes:** The moderator will document user behavior during the tasks, noting any difficulties encountered, areas of confusion, and overall comfort level using the gadget.

Ergonomic Considerations

- **Size and Weight:** The gadget should be lightweight and compact enough for comfortable one-handed operation by users with varying hand sizes. Consider offering interchangeable grip attachments for added customization.
- **Button Placement:** Large, clearly labeled buttons positioned on the side opposite the chopping/slicing blade for easy access and to prevent accidental activation.
- **Stability and Grip:** The base of the gadget should be slip-resistant and incorporate a textured grip to ensure stability during operation and minimize the risk of slipping.
- **Noise Level:** Consider noise levels during operation and implement noise reduction mechanisms to create a more pleasant user experience.
- **Safety Features:** Include clear safety instructions and incorporate safety features like a blade guard or automatic shut-off mechanism to prevent injuries.

Exercises

Part A (Objective Questions)

1. Which phase of the design thinking process determines the viability, usability, and sustainability of the solution?
   (a) Ideation phase (b) Testing and implementation phase
   (c) Empathizing phase (d) Defining the problem phase
2. What are some techniques that can be used in testing the design solution?
   (a) User testing (b) Performance testing
   (c) Functionality testing (d) All of the above
3. Which stage of the design thinking process is critical in determining the solution's viability, usability, and sustainability?
   (a) Ideation stage (b) Prototyping stage
   (c) Testing and implementation stage (d) Empathizing stage
4. What are the objectives of the testing phase in design thinking?
   (a) To come up with prospective solutions (b) To evaluate usability and functionality
   (c) To gather user input (d) All of the above
5. Which phase of design thinking involves prototyping possible solutions?
   (a) Ideation phase (b) Testing phase
   (c) Empathizing phase (d) Defining the problem phase
6. What is the ultimate goal of design thinking?
   (a) To find user pain points (b) To create innovative solutions
   (c) To understand user needs (d) To evaluate usability and functionality
7. What are some objectives of the implementation phase in design thinking?
   (a) To identify user pain points
   (b) To create a strategy for implementing the solution
   (c) To test the solution's viability
   (d) All of the above
8. What is the ultimate goal of the implementation phase in design thinking?
   (a) To create innovative solutions
   (b) To evaluate usability and functionality

(c) To guarantee the final solution is efficient and long-lasting
(d) To understand user needs

9. Which phase of design thinking involves identifying any training or support requirements for the final solution?
(a) Ideation phase
(b) Testing phase
(c) Implementation phase
(d) Empathizing phase

10. Why is it important to include users in the testing process of a design thinking project?
(a) To ensure that the solution is efficient
(b) To guarantee the solution's success
(c) To identify user pain points
(d) To save time and money

11. How can user feedback during the testing process improve a design solution?
(a) By identifying training or support requirements
(b) By establishing metrics for tracking progress
(c) By providing insightful comments that can be used to enhance the solution
(d) By creating a strategy for implementing the solution

12. Who is responsible for identifying any potential usability problems or pain points during the testing phase of the design thinking process?
(a) Users
(b) Design team
(c) Technical support team
(d) Stakeholders

13. Who is responsible for managing databases, setting up hardware and software, and ensuring the system is secure and reliable during the testing phase of the design thinking process?
(a) Users
(b) Design team
(c) Technical support team
(d) Stakeholders

14. What is one of the primary challenges associated with testing and implementation?
(a) Lack of resources
(b) Inadequate stakeholder involvement
(c) Insufficient user feedback
(d) Poor design thinking process

15. What is one of the primary reasons why communication can be an issue during the testing and deployment phase?
(a) Poor team management
(b) Inadequate testing tools
(c) Resistance to change
(d) Misunderstandings among team members or stakeholders

16. What is one of the key challenges that may arise during the implementation phase?
(a) Lack of resources
(b) Poor communication
(c) Resistance to change
(d) Inadequate design thinking

17. What is the first step in conducting a successful pilot test?
(a) Choosing participants for the pilot test
(b) Making a testable prototype of the solution
(c) Defining the test's goal
(d) Giving participants detailed instructions on using the solution

18. Which step in conducting a successful pilot test involves selecting a representative sample of the intended audience for the test?
(a) Defining the test's goal
(b) Making a testable prototype of the solution
(c) Choosing participants for the pilot test
(d) Giving participants detailed instructions on using the solution

19. What is the final step in conducting a successful pilot test?
    (a) Defining the test's goal
    (b) Choosing participants for the pilot test
    (c) Making a testable prototype of the solution
    (d) Giving participants detailed instructions on using the solution
20. What is one strategy for scaling the testing process in design thinking?
    (a) Including users in the testing process
    (b) Reducing the number of features being tested
    (c) Decreasing the user population being tested
    (d) Testing only essential features
21. What is one benefit of using a test management system in scaling the testing process?
    (a) Reduced need for user participation
    (b) More efficient use of resources
    (c) Faster deployment of solutions
    (d) Increased flexibility in solution design
22. Why might it be necessary to test with a larger user population when scaling the testing process in design thinking?
    (a) To reduce the number of features being tested
    (b) To decrease the time required for testing
    (c) To provide more complete information about user interactions with the solution
    (d) To limit the need for technical or IT support teams
23. Which category of features in the Kano model exceeds customer expectations?
    (a) Essential features (b) Performance features
    (c) Delight features (d) None of the above
24. What is the primary purpose of the Kano model in the design thinking process?
    (a) To gauge customer satisfaction with a product's features
    (b) To decide which elements to include in a product first
    (c) To test a product's essential, performance, and delight features
    (d) None of the above
25. Which type of features in the Kano model can result in customer dissatisfaction if they are missing?
    (a) Essential features (b) Performance features
    (c) Delight features (d) None of the above
26. What is the goal of desirability testing in design thinking?
    (a) To understand how users engage with and feel about a product.
    (b) To create a prototype of the solution.
    (c) To select a representative sample of the intended audience.
    (d) To choose participants for the pilot test.
27. Which technique is used in desirability testing?
    (a) Market analysis (b) User research
    (c) Competitive analysis (d) Prototype testing
28. What is the benefit of desirability testing?
    (a) It increases sales.
    (b) It reduces costs.
    (c) It improves customer satisfaction.
    (d) It eliminates the need for user research.

29. What is the purpose of usability testing in design thinking?
    (a) To determine how user-friendly a product or service is.
    (b) To assess the form and design of a product or service.
    (c) To gauge how pleasant and user-friendly a product or service is.
    (d) To determine how well a product or service performs.
30. What is the focus of ergonomic testing in design thinking?
    (a) To determine how user-friendly a product or service is.
    (b) To assess the form and design of a product or service.
    (c) To gauge how pleasant and user-friendly a product or service is.
    (d) To determine how well a product or service performs.
31. What does usability testing gauge in design thinking?
    (a) How simple it is for a user to carry out tasks.
    (b) The form and design of a product or service.
    (c) How pleasant and user-friendly a product or service is.
    (d) How well a product or service performs.
32. What is the main benefit of an iterative testing process?
    (a) It allows for large changes to be made quickly.
    (b) It avoids the need for user feedback.
    (c) It enables the team to make modest changes and pivot as necessary.
    (d) It only tests the solution once.
33. Why is open communication essential in the testing phase?
    (a) It ensures that everyone speaks the same language.
    (b) It eliminates the need for user feedback.
    (c) It avoids the need for an iterative testing process.
    (d) It enables the team to make large changes quickly.

Part B (Short Answer Questions)

1. Write short notes on the testing and implementation phase of design thinking.
2. What is the objective of the testing phase?
3. What is the objective of the implementation phase?
4. Explain the importance of users and the design team in the testing phase.
5. Explain the importance of the IT support team in the testing phase.
6. Explain the importance of SME in the testing phase.
7. What are the key challenges in the testing and implementation phase of design thinking?
8. Explain the pilot test in detail.
9. How can we scale testing in design thinking?
10. What are the best practices of the testing and implementation phase?
11. What are the common pitfalls in the testing phase?
12. Write short notes on the Kano model.
13. What is desirability testing?
14. What is usability and ergonomic testing?
15. Write notes on agility in the testing phase.

Part C (Essay Questions)

1. Explain the role of testing and implementation in the design thinking process.
2. Who are the key stakeholders of the testing phase? Why?

3. What are the key challenges in testing and implementation? Explain in detail.
4. Write an essay on identifying the appropriate solution to test and other factors related to it.
5. Write an essay on piloting and launching in design thinking.
6. How can we scale testing in design thinking?
7. What are the best practices for the testing and implementation phase?
8. What are the best practices for interviews and surveys while testing?
9. Explain how the Kano model is used the testing phase of the design thinking process.
10. Write an essay on desirability testing.

Answer Key

Part A

1. (b)	**2.** (d)	**3.** (c)	**4.** (b)	**5.** (a)	**6.** (b)	**7.** (b)	**8.** (c)	**9.** (c)	**10.** (b)
11. (c)	**12.** (b)	**13.** (c)	**14.** (a)	**15.** (d)	**16.** (c)	**17.** (c)	**18.** (c)	**19.** (d)	**20.** (a)
21. (b)	**22.** (c)	**23.** (c)	**24.** (b)	**25.** (a)	**26.** (a)	**27.** (b)	**28.** (c)	**29.** (a)	**30.** (b)
31. (a)	**32.** (c)	**33.** (a)							

CHAPTER 7

Sustainable Design Approaches

Learning Objectives

At the end of this chapter, you will be able to:

- Define and state the importance of sustainable design, explaining its necessity in the modern context for environmental conservation and resource management
- State the objectives of sustainable design approaches, which aim to minimize negative environmental impact, while maximizing product functionality and efficiency
- Apply the life cycle assessment approach to evaluate the environmental impacts associated with all the stages of a product's life, from cradle to grave
- State the principles of circular economy modeling, which focuses on designing out waste and pollution, keeping products and materials in use, and regenerating natural systems
- Explain the role of green chemistry in sustainable design, which involves designing products and processes that reduce or eliminate the use and generation of hazardous substances
- Elaborate on the concept of biomimicry, which is the design and production of materials, structures, and systems that are modeled on biological entities and processes
- Describe the cradle-to-grave production methodology, which assesses a product's environmental impact from the raw material extraction phase to its ultimate disposal

7.1 Introduction

Design thinking creates not just a product but a solution that addresses core-to-life human needs. However, focusing on users alone is insufficient, because we should also think about the Earth. For this reason, sustainable design has come into play. We are talking about environmentally friendly products; for instance, clothes that last long without wearing out quickly, implying less garbage generation. Through a sustainable design approach, these requirements can be turned into user-centered solutions that are also friendly to our surroundings. Think of a sleek laptop – beautifully designed, easy to fix, and lasting for years. No more e-waste pile-up – just satisfied users, with a trusty companion.

Sustainable design attempts to reduce a product's environmental negative impact by prioritizing resource efficiency and using materials responsibly. This perfectly aligns with design thinking's core principle: creating solutions that benefit both the user and society. It is a win–win situation – users get products that meet their needs, and the planet gets an environmentally friendly product.

Examples in Action

- **Reusable shopping bags:** Single-use plastic bags harm the environment. Design thinking solves this problem by proposing reusable shopping bags that are stylish, convenient for consumers, and which promote responsible consumption.
- **Shared mobility services:** Design thinking recognizes the primary need for transport options and concerns about the vehicle's environmental impact. Sustainable development incorporates its principles in creating car-sharing programs or bike-sharing to provide users with convenience while reducing dependence on private cars.
- **Energy-efficient appliances:** User research shows that people want appliances that can save electricity and work well. To achieve this goal, designers create high-performance systems with lower power consumption rates, among other functions.

7.2 What and Why of Sustainable Design

Sustainable design is not an afterthought – it is woven into the entire design thinking process (Fig. 7.1). We do not consider only a product's functionality; we also think about its impact throughout its lifecycle – from creation to disposal – on society and the environment. This includes financial (economic) considerations, social effects, and cultural implications, alongside environmental impact. Sustainable design aims to create compelling, efficient, and eco-friendly products that are easily distributed.

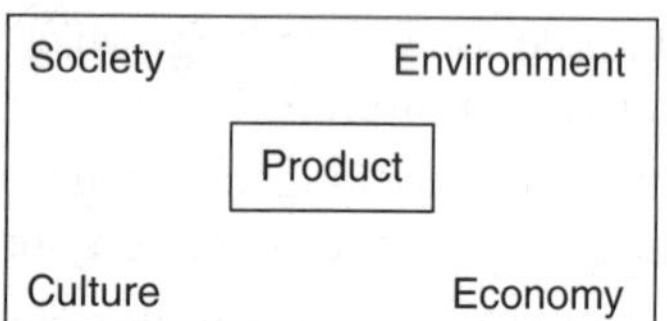

Figure 7.1 A product in the environment

Consider a car seat constructed from recycled materials (Fig. 7.2). This eliminates waste when a product's life cycle ends – the user can recycle the entire item, rather than take it apart into smaller pieces. This not only reduces waste, but new seats also require fewer resources since traditional car seats, usually made using non-recycled materials, need more resources to produce. A company that incorporates sustainable design principles into its operations reduces its adverse environmental impact and produces goods that satisfy customer needs, besides cutting down considerably on production waste levels.

Sustainable design meets the user requirements; at the same time it minimizes the ecological footprint across all stages of a product's existence, including manufacturing, utilization, and disposal. In addition, it enables products to adjust to evolving consumer requirements, hence minimizing the necessity for repeated replacements. This results in reduced energy consumption during the manufacturing process and decreased waste generated from discarded models. Sustainable design thinking necessitates examining the complete life cycle of a product, from its inception to its retirement, to guarantee a thriving planet for future generations while simultaneously providing outstanding user experiences in the present.

Figure 7.2 Car seat made from recycled materials

As an example of sustainable design in practice, we have Apple's 2020 MacBook Pro, which, when recycled, reduces aluminum usage besides cutting down on its carbon footprint each time a new model is manufactured by using 100 post-consumer plastic bottles as packaging materials.
Think of a product's life as a journey:

- **Birth (Making the Product):** Sustainable design uses recycled materials like plastic bottles or old car parts to make new things. Factories use less energy, or perhaps even harness solar or wind power, to be kind to the planet.
- **Life (Using the Product):** Sustainable products are made to last longer, so we do not throw them away quickly. Your phone case is very strong and protects the phone from falling, lasting for years.
- **Afterlife (What Happens When We Are Done):** Sustainable products can be recycled easily or can be safely disposed of without polluting the environment. Your old phone case, if made from recycled materials, can be turned into something new.

Why is this Important?

We utilize fewer resources and produce less waste, which maintains our planet's integrity. An environmentally safe world would mean cleaner air and water and brighter prospects for everyone involved. From the extraction of raw materials through to production, packaging, transportation, use, and disposal, examine the complete trajectory of a product. Carefully select materials with preference given to those that can be reused or recycled into other products; design items that will last long periods without losing their utility value because they have become outmoded.

Design Visualization Question 7.1

Assignment: Sustainable Redesign Challenge (Group)

The Challenge: Redesign an existing product using sustainable design principles.

Steps:

1. **Choose a Product:** Select a common household product like a water bottle, phone case, or food packaging.
2. **Research:** Investigate the product's life cycle, materials used, and current environmental impact.

3. **Reimagine:** Redesign the product with sustainability in mind. Consider aspects like material selection, reusability, recyclability, and energy efficiency during production.
4. **Presentation:** Develop a visual presentation showcasing your original product, its environmental impact, and your proposed sustainable redesign. Explain the benefits of your design for both users and the environment.

Deliverables:

- A visually engaging presentation (10–15 slides) explaining the original product, its environmental impact, and your sustainable redesign.
- Include details about the chosen materials, production processes, and potential user benefits.

7.3 Objectives of Sustainable Design Approaches

There are a variety of approaches that businesses can take to create sustainable designs, all of which share the same objectives in general (Fig. 7.3).

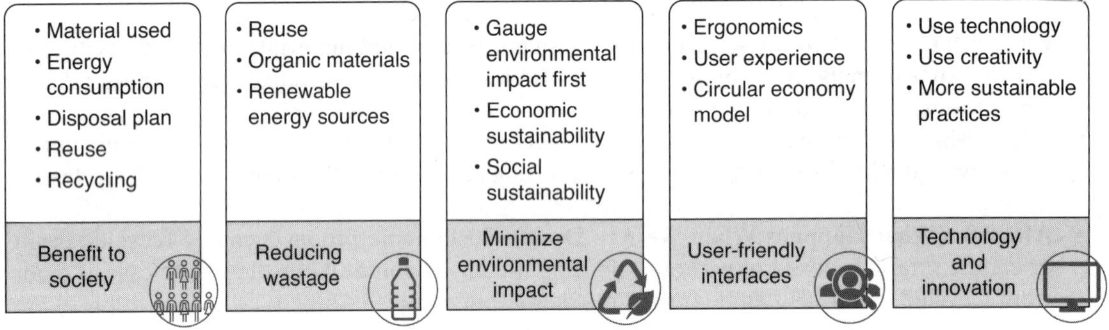

Figure 7.3 Objectives of sustainable design approaches

- Creating systems and products that benefit society while having the least possible adverse effects on the environment.
- Reducing waste by making the most of already available resources.
- Minimizing environmental impacts through thoughtful material selection (design for the environment or DFE).
- Improving customer experiences by emphasizing user-friendly interfaces and consistent performance levels.
- Pushing existing boundaries even further through technology and innovation.

7.3.1 Benefit to Society and Less Adverse Effects on the Environment

Imagine that you are designing a new phone. Sustainable design means thinking about everything – the materials used, the energy it takes to make it, and even how it will be recycled at the end of its life (Fig. 7.4). The goal is to create products that last a long time, use resources wisely, and do not pollute our environment.

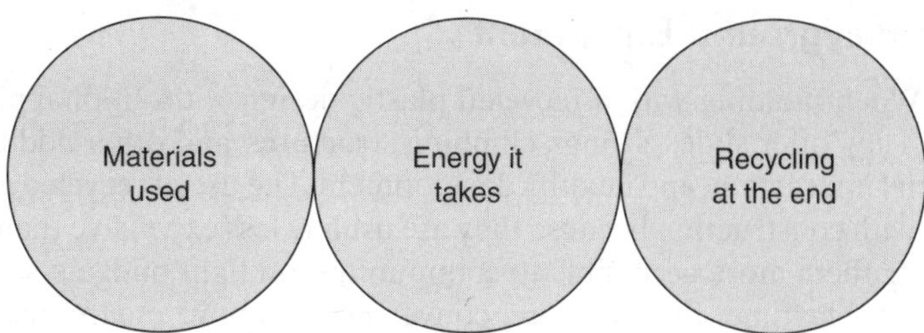

Figure 7.4 Top three characteristics of sustainable design

Reusing and recycling are the superstars in sustainable design. Instead of always creating something new, we can find ways to use things again and again. For example, using recycled plastic in construction projects instead of virgin plastic. This saves money and keeps waste out of landfills. Reusing materials also lowers emissions when identical materials are created from scratch.

In sustainable design thinking, how energy is used can make a big difference. This means that designers may want to set up their production processes so that they do not waste resources while creating things and can use them repeatedly. This could involve developing new ways to use less power when making things or using better equipment. They should also think about how someone will take care of (maintenance) what they do in the future.

Sustainable design has two main objectives (Fig. 7.5). Firstly, it would like to cause as little harm as possible through a product's life cycle by reducing carbon emissions due to manufacturing processes and using recycled materials whenever available. Secondly, the products are intended to be kept operational for the longest time, having been created strong and durable or easily modifiable; tools like recyclers should thus contribute at the design stage. Besides, they must think about how users will use their designs to fit in with all needs and expectations while creating no room for wastage during any of the usage periods.

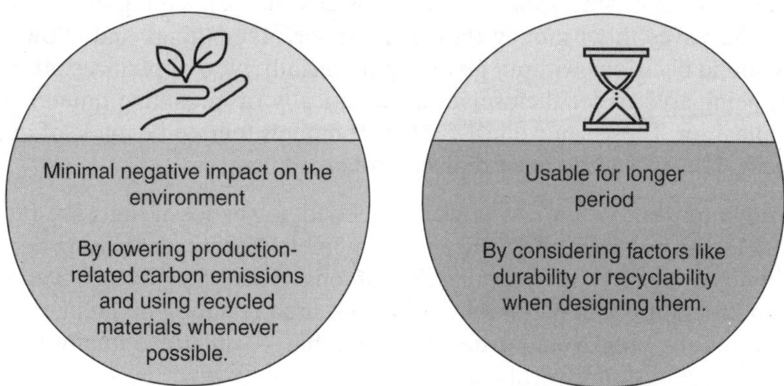

Figure 7.5 Two main objectives of sustainable design

Organizations that adopt sustainable design methodologies may obtain a variety of advantages. It can make them stand out from rivals by demonstrating dedication to safeguarding the planet's resources despite the short-term expenses. This will bring us all closer to establishing all-encompassing and long-lasting solutions for people and the environment. The higher efficiency levels connected with green operations can help organizations cut operational expenses in areas like waste management or energy usage, eventually leading to corporate growth through increased revenue streams. But equally crucially, implementing sustainability in business procedures helps recruit skilled workers who want to work for a firm that prioritizes environmental protection by creating a desirable work environment.

Recycled Plastic Playground Equipment

Societal Benefits: When building with a recycled plastic design, a traditional playground can still be fun for children. They offer slides, swings, climbing structures, and other additions that promote physical activity, social interaction, and healthy development. The use of recycled materials can lower the costs associated with construction because they are usually less expensive than new ones while at the same time making them more accessible to communities on tight budgets, so no child is left out from enjoying healthy playtime. Furthermore, conversations about environmental responsibility and resourcefulness are started by using trash to create something new; this is especially important since it may help change people's attitudes towards littering or illustrate ways in which we can reduce what ends up being thrown into the garbage. Another way we can do this would be by involving community members in designing or building these structures, thereby creating a sense of ownership amongst them over such communal assets.

Environmental Advantages: Plastic playgrounds incorporating recycled material divert waste from landfills. These structures prevent the plastic materials from being buried in a landfill where they will sit for hundreds of years before finally breaking down into small pieces that can then be consumed by animals or infiltrate water supplies with harmful chemicals. When we use recycled plastics instead of producing new ones, it cuts down on the amount of energy consumed during extraction processes and protects natural habitats like rainforests which might otherwise have been destroyed had their resources been exploited continuously without respite. Here again, education comes into play by creating awareness among children about various environmental concerns, including but not limited to, pollution control measures such as proper disposal methods and waste recycling strategies aimed at conserving resources for future generations.

Energy-Efficient Appliances

Societal Benefits: Energy-saving appliances use less electricity, meaning they cost less to run for people at home. This saves them money they can use for other things and allows them to make environmentally sound decisions without giving up financially. New appliances often have different features, such as being able to set themselves automatically or becoming quieter. This makes life easier and more pleasant. These same energy-efficient models tend to be made of quality parts that last longer, reducing how often one must replace broken appliances.

Environmental Advantages: When less power is needed, fewer fossil fuels are burned, releasing harmful gases into the atmosphere and warming our planet; likewise, decreasing demand upon said non-renewable reserves ensures their availability among future generations while limiting heat-trapping pollution. In addition, new standards spur research resulting in 'greener' products across this sector, so continuous improvement becomes possible – which eventually leads us closer to utterly renewable energy systems worldwide.

Modular Furniture

Societal Benefits: Modular furniture enables users to personalize items to fit individual needs and desires, thus leading to more comfort and satisfaction in living spaces. It also allows for rearrangement or expansion whenever necessary due to the ever changing needs, providing flexibility and adaptability. This is especially helpful for people living in small spaces or those with dynamic lifestyles.

Environmental Advantages: Modular furniture enhances the life of individual pieces by allowing repairs and upgrades, which reduces the need for frequent replacement and the accompanying waste from discarded items. Modular designs often use less material than traditional ones and are more sustainable. In addition, the use of recycled materials during manufacture further lowers their environmental impact. Emphasis on repair and reuse fosters responsible consumption patterns that encourage consumers to buy long-lasting and versatile products.

Design Visualization Question 7.2

Creating systems and products that benefit society while having the least possible adverse effects on the environment is the basis of sustainable design, which is a crucial component of design thinking.
List 5 products that benefit society and have fewer adverse effects on the environment.

7.3.2 Reducing Waste by Optimizing the Use of Already Available Resources

Reusing or recycling previously used items rather than tossing them away is one way to reduce waste. Resources are not being used up when they can still be used for other things, which helps to conserve them. As you do not have to buy new materials each time you need something, reusing products also help you save money; for instance, by upcycling old clothing for quilting projects or turning old jars into planters.

Recycling and composting things whenever possible instead of tossing them in landfills or releasing toxins into the environment through other methods is another crucial component of minimizing waste through sustainable design thinking.

Recycling commodities like paper, plastic, glass, electronics components, and metal allows these materials to be broken down and turned into new products and lessens pollution from factories that generate these materials from scratch each time they are required. Organic materials like food scraps that have been composted into soil enhance it with nutrients while preventing the unneeded release of greenhouse gases like methane, which can harm our ecosystem if not properly handled. Finally, choosing renewable energy sources like solar energy whenever possible lessens our reliance on non-renewable energy sources like coal or oil, which cause more environmental damage over their lifetimes than renewable sources do when it comes to producing the electricity or heat needed by both homes and businesses.

Where possible, choose renewable energy sources to avoid using polluting ones that, over time, harm our planet without offering anything in return outside the electricity they produce. Decreasing waste by making the most of already available resources involves careful planning. However, if put into practice, it offers several benefits, like improved soil quality, cleaner air, and cost savings.

Examples

Repurposing Clothes: You could attempt to get creative with your old wardrobe items, instead of throwing them away. This may mean changing ripped jeans into stylish shorts or using long-forgotten shirts as rags as cleaning cloth. When you do this, remember it is not only about saving money on new clothes, it is also important because our planet needs us. We should never underestimate the significance of reducing waste through everyday practices.

Reusable Shopping Bags: To begin with, clear out flimsy plastic bags in your home and instead use only reusable bags. Keep some cloth or canvas bags in your purse or bag to ensure you are always ready. Besides being highly durable compared to the former, which may fall apart after a single use, they also significantly affect plastic pollution.

Composting Food Scraps: Composting is a fantastic way to transform your food scraps into nutrient-rich compost, which is gold for your garden (Fig. 7.6). Not only does this keep food waste out of landfills (where it creates harmful methane gas), but it also helps your plants thrive.

Figure 7.6 Composting food scraps (*Courtesy*: Lane composters, CDD India, July 2023; https://commons.wikimedia.org/wiki/File:Community_level_composting,_Devanahalli,_Bengaluru.jpg; CC-BY-SA-4.0)

These practices can significantly reduce waste, conserve resources, and create a more sustainable future. Even small changes in individual behavior can have a collective positive impact on the environment.

7.3.3 Minimizing Environmental Impact Through Thoughtful Material Selection (Design for Environment: DFE)

In general, materials matter a lot. The resources we use, the energy required to process them, and the waste they generate add up. DFE or design for environment encourages designers to think beyond aesthetics and consider a material's entire life cycle. Imagine a phone case made from recycled plastic bottles instead of non-reusable plastic materials. We are giving new life to plastic waste while reducing the need to extract fresh resources. But DFE is not only about just recycling. It is also about choosing materials that are kind to the environment from the beginning. Think bamboo bikes or furniture made from sustainably harvested wood. These materials are renewable and often require less processing than traditional options.

DFE is not just about saving trees and reducing landfills, although that is important. It is also about energy efficiency. Imagine a building designed with unique heat-reflecting panels, reducing the need for air conditioning (Fig. 7.7).

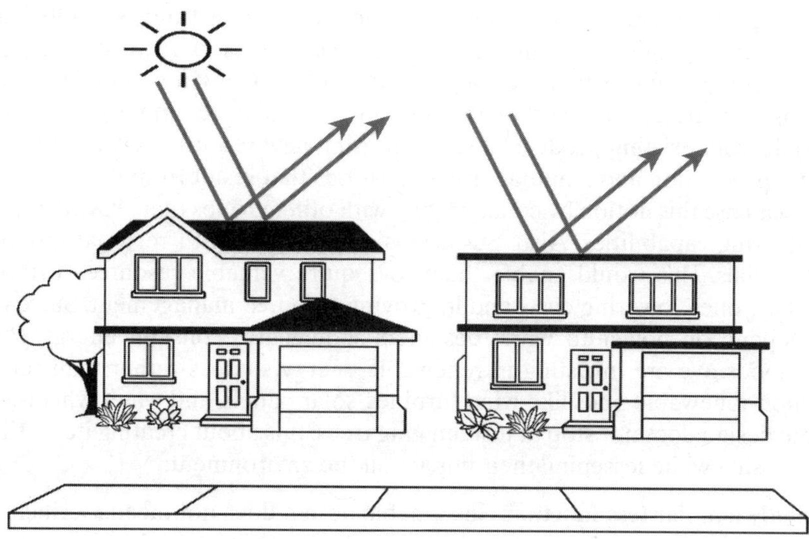

Figure 7.7 Heat reflecting panels

DFE is also about making good products for people. Nobody wants a phone case that cracks once dropped or furniture that falls apart after one year. Surprisingly, sustainable materials can often be very robust. In addition, there is also the possibility of coming up with new and exciting designs that are attractive and useful.

So next time you shop for a new device or even renovate your house, try thinking about the importance of the choice of materials. Seek out those items made explicitly according to DFE standards, too. All these little decisions will help make our combined efforts much more impactful towards an overall better tomorrow for everyone concerned. It is worth remembering that every bit helps – from each recycled bottle right down to any sustainably sourced wood board used in construction work carried out anywhere around us presently or in years to let alone future generations.

Economic sustainability looks at the future cost of things. How much will it cost to produce these new designs if we use certain materials or technologies? We need to think about whether rare materials are worth using because their value keeps increasing due to them becoming scarcer day by day; in addition, some setups might be expensive but cheapen prices for consumers who buy products created with them later on, so there are many factors involved.

Social sustainability considers quality-of-life issues, including access to clean water, safe housing, adequate healthcare, educational opportunities, and environmental implications. By considering all these factors, designers can ensure that their designs are environmentally friendly while being economically efficient, socially beneficial from a quality-of-life perspective, and culturally sensitive towards various groups affected by new designs. Ultimately, sustainable design thinking methods result in healthier societies that are advantageous to everyone—including the designers themselves.

7.3.4 User-friendly Interfaces and Consistent Performance Standards

Consumer experiences are enhanced through sustainable design that minimizes negative environmental impact. To achieve this, they must consider the physical and psychological interactions between users regarding ergonomics and user experience. Besides, knowing what clients want helps companies make goods that satisfy those wants, leaving minimal environmental footprint. Another increasingly popular strategy for sustainable design is circular economy models, which involve reusing materials from existing products instead of using new resources every time. This approach reduces the overproduction and manufacturing emissions that result from it.

Businesses can use this notion by collaborating with other groups that provide recycling services and remanufacturing capabilities. Also, businesses can connect with regional groups with access to recycled materials. This would enable them to acquire valuable resources without constantly having to buy new ones, lowering costs and improving resource management. Since many modern technologies depend on power to work, designers should also consider energy efficiency while building their goods. We are investing in renewable energy sources rather than relying solely on fossil fuels or non-renewable ones like wind turbines, solar panels, and water wheels.

Sustainable design does not stop at just hugging trees. It is about creating items that individuals can enjoy using using while lessening their impact on the environment:

- **User-friendly and flawless function:** Sustainable design does not mean sacrificing a great user experience. Imagine a product that is easy to use, feels good in your hands, and works perfectly every time. Designers who think sustainably consider both physical comfort (think ergonomics) and how users interact with the product on an emotional level.
- **Meeting needs with a smaller footprint:** By understanding what people truly need and want, companies can design products that fulfil those needs without leaving a significant environmental footprint. It is about creating things that last and do not end up in landfills after a few uses.
- **The circular economy:** Imagine a world where old products get new life instead of constantly using fresh resources. That is the circular economy in action. Sustainable designers love this approach because it reduces waste and reduces emissions from making new products all the time. Companies can partner with recycling and remanufacturing businesses to keep materials in circulation.

By incorporating these ideas, sustainable design makes user-friendly, high-performing products that are kind to the Earth.

7.3.5 Pushing Existing Boundaries Further Through Technology and Innovation

Making a sustainable product does not necessarily mean ignoring excellent user experience. A device that is not hard to utilize is comfortable to handle, does its job beautifully every time, and has a positive emotional customer experience. This is an example of such an efficient product. Designers who are ecologically friendly should consider people's physical comfort and emotional attachment to the item. This idea of modern sustainable design thinking is vital today as it employs technology and creativity to deliver energy or environmentally conscious goods, services, and processes. Sustainable design thinking goes beyond this to reduce human impact on the environment while building a sustainable future for all. Such goals can only be achieved by applying cutting-edge technologies like renewable sources of energy, eco-friendly building materials, and production methods.

Greener Buildings, Brighter Future: Design for sustainability focuses on creating structures that are good for the environment and our wallets. A building that cools in the summer and heats in the winter should do so with ease. This is where green construction materials come into play. These materials reduce the power a structure needs, thus cutting electricity costs. On another note, solar panels have been hailed as heroes regarding renewable energy sources. Sunlight hits them and gets converted into electricity, which can then be used for lighting or even turning on your washing machine. This is not limited to buildings themselves because using recycled materials where possible is also part and parcel of sustainable design by lowering waste production levels, like forest conservation.

Recycling Creativity, Reducing Waste: Sustainable design is about using creativity to make products that are good for the planet. It lets you reuse objects instead of throwing them away, saving resources, and keeping our planet happy. For example, a furniture company could use leftover bits of wood from other projects to create unique new pieces. Doing so saves money on materials and keeps waste from getting into landfills.

Trash to Treasure: When it comes to sustainable designs, it is not only saying no to new things but also creatively using what is already there. Imagine turning empty plastic bottles into fleece jackets or more substantial beams to make chairs and tables out of them. Such is the might of eco-design. Instead of throwing things away, we can find new uses for them. Companies are turning old plastic bottles into clothes and even lumber for furniture. This keeps junk out of landfills, where it can leak chemicals into the ground.

Saving Energy, Saving Money: Imagine making products with less energy, like using solar power instead of relying on fossil fuels. In general, factories use up a lot of energy. Sustainable design helps us find ways to make them run more efficiently. In addition, businesses are less affected by rising energy prices because they would rely less on fossil fuels.

Overall, the goal of sustainable design thinking is ambitious yet achievable: it seeks to push existing boundaries even further through technology and innovation so that we may have a greener future filled with more sustainable practices which protect our planet's fragile ecosystems against further harm. By embracing these principles now, businesses, large and small, can help create healthier communities worldwide, ensuring long-term economic survival too.

Design Visualization Question 7.3

Assignment: Sustainable Service Design Challenge (Individual)

The Challenge: Design a sustainable service that benefits society and minimizes environmental impact. (mobile app for food rescue)

Steps:

1. **Empathize:** Research a specific societal need that could be addressed through a service. Consider issues like social justice, education, or community development.

2. **Define:** Clearly define the societal need and how it relates to sustainability. For example, the need might be 'affordable access to fresh produce' and the sustainable aspect could be 'reducing food waste.'
3. **Ideate:** Brainstorm service ideas that tackle the identified need while minimizing environmental impact. Think about ways to reuse resources, promote local businesses, and minimize energy use,
4. **Prototype:** Develop a low-fidelity prototype of your service concept. This could be a service blueprint, a user journey map, or even a role-playing scenario.
5. **Test:** Present your service prototype to potential users and stakeholders. Gather feedback on feasibility, impact, and sustainability benefits.

Deliverables:

- A short report (3–5 pages) outlining your societal need, design process, service prototype, and potential impact analysis (environmental and social).
- Include visuals like diagrams of your service blueprint or user journey map.

7.4 Methods for Incorporating Sustainable Design

Understanding eco-design concepts (Fig. 7.8), which emphasize choosing materials with the least possible environmental impact, optimizing the manufacturing process, and using renewable energy sources, is the first step in sustainable design.

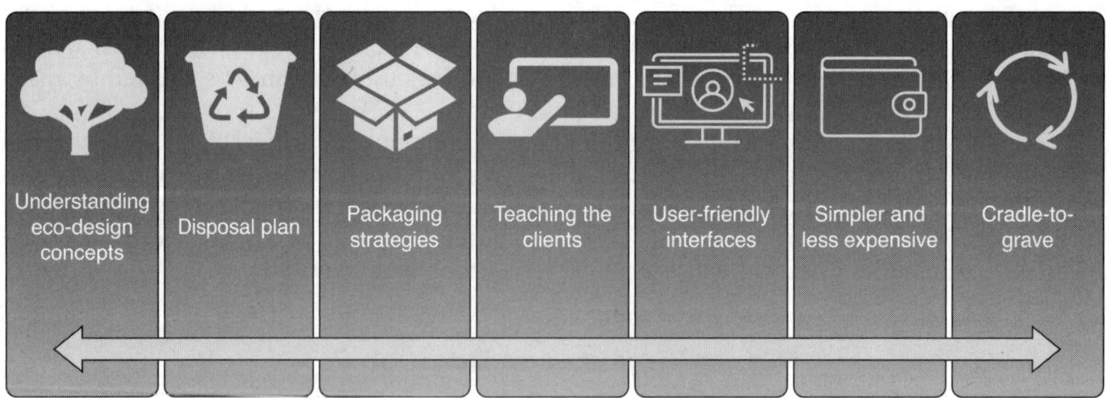

Figure 7.8 Different methods for incorporating sustainable design

Understand eco-design concepts: This entails picking products made of low-toxic components that can be used for the intended purpose. Designers also consider using those components throughout the production as efficiently as possible by employing recycled materials or minimizing waste. They might think about using renewable energy sources such as solar power or wind turbines to fuel their manufacturing processes instead of non-renewable sources like coal, oil, and natural gases. These produce a lot of carbon dioxide and are responsible for most global warming, leading to climate change.

Disposal plan: When a product has reached the end of its useful life, the designer must consider how well it works during disposal to avoid harming the environment. For this reason, they are also advised to develop designs that can be easily recycled or reused. This will reduce the amount of waste generated. This entails designing for disassembly so that parts can be separated for recycling right away instead of sending them all to the landfill, where they will not decompose properly.

Packaging strategies: Designers must consider how to adapt their packaging strategies to minimize the number of layers of wrapping. If possible, they may even consider 'zero waste' solutions. Consumers only purchase the items they need, with no additional packaging, making everything infinitely recyclable without adding to environmental damage further down the line.

Teaching their clients: Businesses need to make sure they are teaching their clients about responsible post-purchase disposal procedures, as well as staff about sustainable design principles while adhering to industry regulations about toxins and hazardous materials. We should start to see beneficial changes take hold throughout creative industry sectors globally as we become more mindful of our planet's finite resources and restricted capacity for natural habitats.

User-friendly interfaces: Prioritizing energy efficiency in products through user-friendly interfaces or simple maintenance procedures is one sustainable design method. For instance, smart home appliances like automatic thermostats enable customers to remotely regulate heating settings with little to no effort while gradually lowering energy consumption. In addition to being more energy-efficient than conventional incandescent bulbs at comparable brightness levels, LED lighting solutions produce fewer emissions due to lower overall energy demand from electrical grids in areas where these technologies are widely used. As a result, end-users can save money using LED lighting solutions.

Simpler and less expensive: Making goods simpler and less expensive to repair so that their lifespan can be increased without compromising functionality is another way sustainable design encourages more effective resource use. With this strategy, designers could use modular designs or replaceable parts to reduce waste and labor costs associated with maintenance tasks. In addition, users could easily replace faulty components themselves rather than having manufacturers do it for them every time something breaks, allowing them to save money and reduce e-waste.

Cradle to grave: Considering potential ecological implications when developing new products or services by considering how they might affect nearby habitats or ecosystems before they are even put into practice, helping to avoid irreversible damages caused by careless developments, is another crucial aspect of sustainable design. When all of those tactics are combined, they point us in the direction of genuinely effective sustainability-driven design methods that simultaneously address the present requirements while protecting the environment for future generations. Sustainable methods are becoming more and more significant in design thinking. Designers must consider using resources sensibly and morally while simultaneously producing goods that offer customers real value. Thinking about a product's whole lifecycle or that of a service is essential in sustainable design. This is called 'cradle-to-grave' thinking and examines the totality of the process from extraction through production to disposal for any given item or idea.

Design Visualization Question 7.4

Assignment: Eco-Audit and Sustainable Redesign Challenge (Individual)

The Challenge: Analyze an existing product and redesign it using sustainable design principles.

Steps:

1. **Product Selection:** Choose a commonly used household product like a coffee maker, lamp, or clothing item.
2. **Eco-Audit:** Conduct an eco-audit of the product, considering the materials used, manufacturing process, packaging, and end-of-life options. Identify areas for improvement in terms of environmental impact.
3. **Sustainable Redesign:** Redesign the product with a focus on eco-design concepts.

Consider aspects like:

- **Material selection:** Use recycled or low-impact materials.
- **Manufacturing optimization:** Minimize waste and energy use during production.
- **Disassembly for easy recycling:** Design for parts separation and easy reuse.
- **Sustainable packaging:** Minimize packaging materials or incorporate recycled content.
- **Presentation:** Develop a presentation showcasing your chosen product, its eco-audit findings, and your proposed sustainable redesign. Explain how your design addresses each eco-design concept.

Deliverables:

- A visually engaging presentation (10–15 slides) outlining the original product, its environmental impact, and your sustainable redesign. Include details about your eco-audit findings and how your redesign incorporates different eco-design strategies.
- Include visuals like diagrams of your service blueprint or user journey map.

7.4.1 Life Cycle Assessment Approach

When creating something sustainable, you need to consider it from the very beginning to the very end. This means considering where all the materials come from and what happens to your product after you throw it away. Life cycle assessment (LCA) is a way of doing just that: examining every stage of a product's existence to determine its environmental impact (Fig. 7.9).

For instance, imagine trying to figure out how much energy an item uses, starting with mining the raw materials and ending when it is put into a landfill. All these different steps offer opportunities for designers to reduce harm to our world, for example, through lower energy use during manufacture or using materials that can be replaced by those that are renewed.

If we were making phones, for instance, LCA might suggest that the highest energy consumption happens during the production phase, so developers could brainstorm some activities aimed at making this process more efficient, such as using renewable sources of power. In addition, it also enables us to choose safe materials originating from non-exhaustible sources, such as bamboo instead of plastics.

The production stage is not the only one involved in LCA. It also considers the transportation of these goods as well as their disposal afterward. To illustrate, think about packaging made out of recycled materials, which can decompose quickly, unlike plastics that take centuries to biodegrade. Viewing products within whole life cycles enables making them beneficial to both humans and the environment.

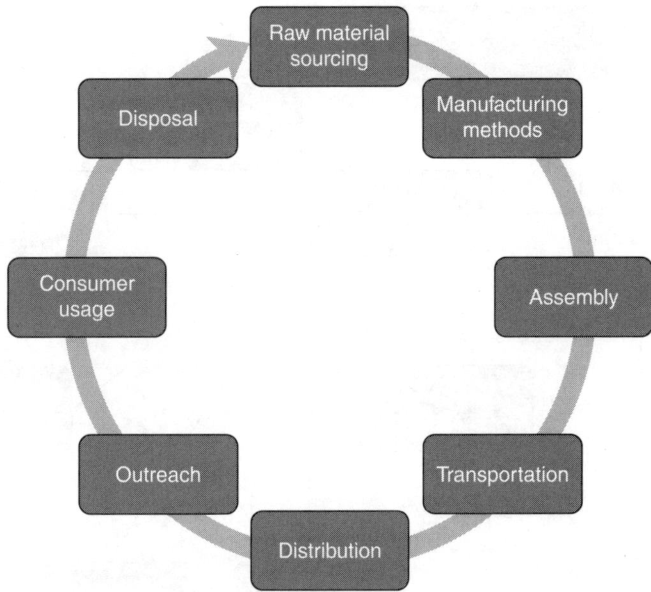

Figure 7.9 Life cycle assessment approach

LCA is thus a powerful tool because it provides a comprehensive vision of the design. When everything from the birth of a product to its end, whether it is discarded, is taken into consideration, a designer can come up with products that can be maintained, are user-friendly, and which benefit the environment. The next time you see a label on a product with the words 'eco-friendly' or 'green', know it has probably gone through a very thorough LCA.

7.4.2 Circular Economy Modeling

Designers have developed a circular economy modeling method to lessen the environmental impact and support resource conservation (Fig. 7.10). This approach encourages designers to consider reuse potential over many years rather than just the short lifecycle of each product. Instead of simply replacing their products with something completely different every time, designers can significantly extend the usable lifespans of their products by finding ways for customers to pass along their goods after they no longer require them, such as directly donating them or reselling them online. This concept employs resources sensibly and effectively to build an environmentally friendly cycle.

It examines every step in a product's life cycle so that nothing is wasted or thrown away before being fully used. This, in turn, means there will be less pollution going into our air and water from manufacturers. In addition, it helps ensure that items come from restorative resources like reused materials rather than finite ones such as oil or gas. As a result, less energy is needed to produce designs that employ renewable resources, which results in fewer carbon emissions and helps safeguard our planet from global warming.

As an illustration, fashion designer Stella McCartney introduced a 'Buy Back' program for selecting items from online. Consumers who participate in this program can return things from their collection in exchange for savings or shop credit that can be used to buy other goods. McCartney decreases waste associated with producing new clothing by encouraging consumers to contribute goods they no longer want rather than discarding them. This also encourages reusing and repurposing existing items that might otherwise go unused.

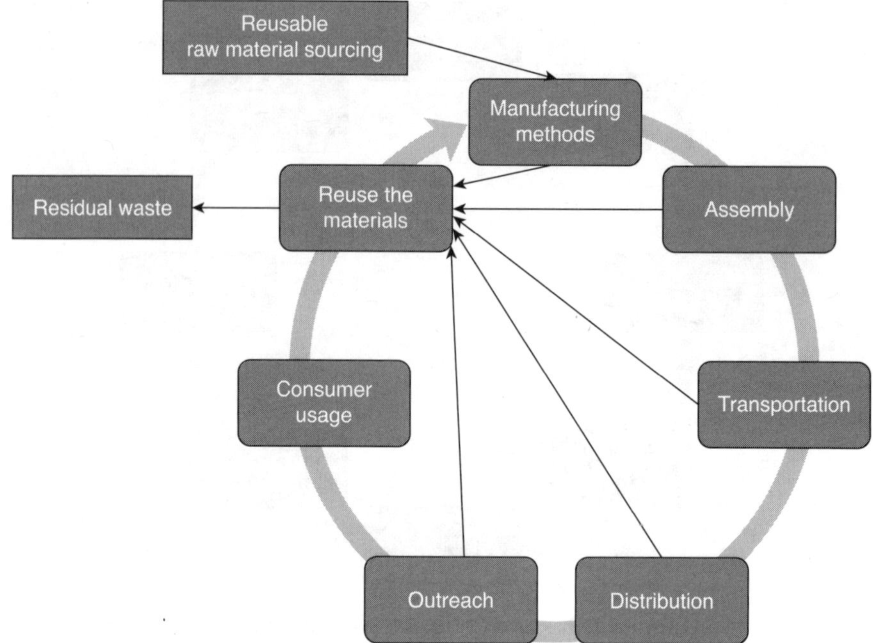

Figure 7.10 Circular economy model

As an alternative to replacing older models with newer ones every few years, some businesses employ technology like blockchain databases to track ownership throughout the entire product lifecycle. This includes clothes recycling programs. For instance, the automaker Volvo developed a cutting-edge system using physical and digital components to track vehicles throughout their lifetimes using blockchain technology. This system enables Volvo technicians throughout Europe to quickly diagnose mechanical problems without the need for additional tools or service centers, which not only streamlines the repair process but also helps reduce waste associated with manufacturing.

7.4.3 Green Chemistry

Green chemistry refers to a methodology requiring companies to look out for cleaner alternatives among chemicals used in manufacturing processes, hence reducing toxicity levels within the environment (Fig. 7.11). Also, materials should not be solely synthetic ones created within laboratories but instead include those occurring naturally, if possible, even plant-based substitutes. Designers employ principles related to green chemistry, creating unique, valuable, sustainable pieces, and caring for the environment.

When creating new packaging for food products, businesses should ensure that the materials do not contain hazardous substances, such as lead derivatives; instead, they should choose environmentally friendly options, like biodegradable plastics derived from plant sources, such as corn or sugarcane. Similarly, businesses should consider using recycled water whenever possible instead of fresh supplies when reducing water usage during manufacturing processes.

They should also consider using rainwater harvesting techniques to store collected rainwater during rainy seasons so it can be used again during dry spells. Designers should choose paints and varnishes for industrial applications that contain minimal to no volatile organic compounds (VOCs). By limiting the usage of VOCs, which are proven hazards that contribute to air pollution and respiratory ailments, manufacturers may safeguard their workers and reduce environmental pollution from industrial activity.

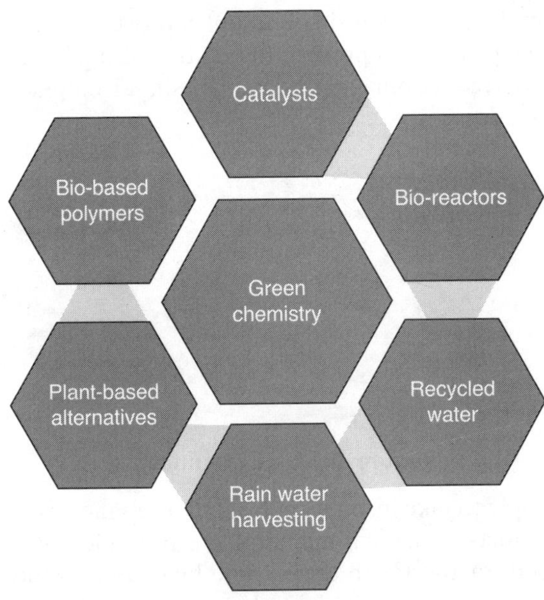

Figure 7.11 Green chemistry ecosystem

Businesses can ensure that their products comply with safety regulations while being kinder to the environment by implementing green chemistry strategies that reduce waste generation and emissions from manufacturing processes used in production cycles and end-of-life stages where product disposal occurs after it has passed its expiration date. In addition, by incorporating green chemistry strategies into design thinking frameworks, organizations have a better chance of producing goods with improved sustainability standards while still enjoying the performance standards expected of these goods without compromising on any health hazard-related outcomes. We can drastically lessen our environmental impact while creating high-quality goods with fewer resources by developing more effective ways to make things like paper and textiles without producing vast amounts of hazardous waste.

Green chemistry has several advantages for sustainable design methods. First, it enables us to create practical solutions that lessen environmental impact without sacrificing performance requirements or the output of high-quality products. Furthermore, by lowering hazardous emissions from industrial processes and providing dependable products manufactured with eco-friendly production techniques, designers who adhere to this ideology help us take better care of our planet's finite resources.

7.4.4 Biomimicry

By copying nature, a science called biomimicry is being used to envision and build a better and more sustainable world. Scientists may study how fish move through water with little effort and use those same principles to design more efficient boats or submarines. Engineers may look at how a plant's leaves collect sunlight for energy and use that principle for rooftop solar panels (Fig. 7.12). Architects may take inspiration from bird nests or beehives when designing homes that withstand extreme weather conditions while still energy efficient.

The potential lifespan of biomimicry above conventional engineering or manufacturing techniques is a significant advantage. We may access answers that have been tried and tested for millions of years by imitating nature's patterns. Also, these designs are frequently significantly more durable than those built by humans, requiring less upkeep over time, which lowers maintenance costs and emissions from the production process. In addition, using fewer fossil fuels in production processes, biomimicry helps us reduce our carbon footprint since it emphasizes resource conservation rather than resource exploitation.

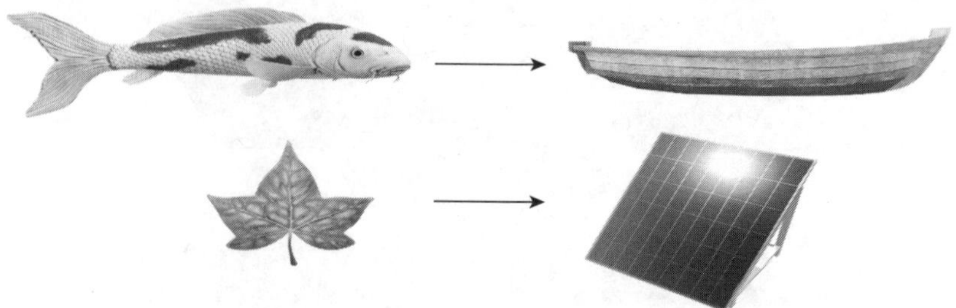

Figure 7.12 Biomimicry

Biomimicry is a way for people to take inspiration from nature's most successful methods while still generating high-quality products in an environmentally responsible way. We can create long-lasting improvements that are good for the Earth and people by carefully studying natural systems and applying them to our actions, such as developing solar panels or structures.

For example, solar vehicles with nearly identical wings, like birds, help reduce wind drag significantly because air flows around car bodies much more smoothly, significantly improving fuel efficiency.

7.4.5 Cradle-to-Grave Production Methodology

C2G, or cradle-to-grave, is tasked with designing items that can be recycled or reused after they have finished their first job. This approach reduces the amount of waste disposed in landfills and burned to produce electricity, contributing to air pollution. Sustainable materials should be chosen whenever possible according to the C2G method. For example, the C2G strategy lowers carbon footprints while eliminating potential overharvesting issues using bamboo instead of plastics. During production, more resources are required to make plastic than bamboo; hence, people should stop using them. When we choose renewable sources like bamboo instead of non-renewable ones such as metal or plastic, we can still produce durable quality items over very long periods, even reducing our dependence on finite natural resources.

To ensure that there is a lower negative impact on the environment from businesses for generations to come, they should use resources that can be replenished, like solar power. This type of renewable energy is becoming increasingly popular among companies today because, apart from not emitting greenhouse gases or pollutants into the atmosphere, very little maintenance work needs to be done. Therefore, instead of using fossil fuels to run their operations, thereby causing harm to our surroundings, firms should switch to solar energy, not only cutting down on their environmental footprint but also ensuring a consistent power supply for their products.

Companies can prevent contributing to landfill problems and unnecessary pollution just by thinking about what will happen to any waste material they produce after using it. For example, several firms now have facilities that allow employees to separate recyclables from other garbage, which would otherwise have found its way into them. If this stage of waste management is maintained throughout the entire production process rather than waiting until everything has already been made before trying to start recycling, then not only will natural resources be saved, but pollution levels at landfills too can be kept low.

Companies are driven by the cradle-to-grave technique to assess how their new goods could serve the community rather than just themselves during manufacture. A business, for example, would rather use materials that can be broken down organically rather than plastics, thus reducing carbon footprints while offering environmentally friendlier options for clients needing them.

Another option is for a company to donate a percentage of its revenues to charitable causes, such as the construction of schools or the distribution of food to areas hit by natural disasters. These decisions show that businesses care about bringing about constructive social change in addition to their financial line.

Summary

- Design thinking is a creative problem-solving approach focusing on understanding user needs and creating human-centered designs.
- Sustainable design is crucial for meeting user needs and environmental requirements.
- The objectives of sustainable design approaches are to create systems and products benefiting society while minimizing the environmental impact.
- Sustainable design considerations in the product life cycle encompass the development phase, utilization phase, end-of-life phase, and recycling/reuse.

Solutions to Design Visualization Questions

Q 7.1

Assignment: Sustainable Redesign Challenge

Product Redesign Ideas

- **Water Bottle:** Redesign a single-use plastic water bottle into a reusable, insulated bottle made from recycled stainless steel.
- **Phone Case:** Replace a traditional plastic phone case with a biodegradable case made from plant-based materials like bamboo or recycled paper.
- **Food Packaging:** Redesign a cardboard takeout container with a wax lining to be fully compostable and eliminate the need for plastic liners.

Tips for Redesigning Products

- Research the environmental impact of the current product's materials and production process.
- Explore alternative materials that are sustainable, durable, and readily available.
- Consider the product's functionality and how it can be redesigned to be more user-friendly while minimizing waste.

Additional Tips for Assignments

- Encourage students to think creatively and explore innovative solutions.
- Emphasize the importance of user testing and feedback throughout the design process.
- Connect the assignments to real-world examples of sustainable design for inspiration.

By following these prompts and completing these assignments, students will gain valuable experience in user research, sustainable design principles, and creative problem-solving – all core skills for design thinking in today's world.

Q 7.2

These are just a few examples:

- Reusable grocery bags
- Compostable packaging
- Solar-powered phone chargers
- Water-saving showerheads
- Passive house design
- Refill stations for cleaning products
- Upcycled clothing

Q 7.3

Assignment: Sustainable Service Design Challenge

Example: Mobile App for Food Rescue

- **Societal Need:** Reducing food waste and increasing access to fresh produce for low-income communities.
- **Sustainable Aspect:** Connecting grocery stores with expiring food to charities and individuals who need it, minimizing food waste and promoting healthy eating.
- **Service Prototype:** Develop a mobile app that allows grocery stores to post information about soon-to-expire produce. Charities and individuals can browse available food and reserve items for pickup, reducing waste and creating a win-win situation for both businesses and communities.

Additional Tips for Students

- Conduct thorough research to support their chosen ideas.
- Explore existing examples of sustainable businesses and services for inspiration.
- Consider the feasibility and scalability of their solutions.
- Focus on clear communication and user-centered design principles.
- Be creative and think outside the box!

By following these guidelines and delving deeper into their chosen topics, students can develop well-rounded solutions that showcase their understanding of sustainable design thinking principles. Remember, the goal is to encourage critical thinking, creativity, and a commitment to building a more sustainable future.

Q 7.4

Assignment: Eco-Audit and Sustainable Redesign Challenge

Example: Sustainable Coffee Maker

Original Product: Traditional plastic coffee maker with disposable paper filters.

Eco-Audit Findings: Plastic parts, energy consumption during brewing, and landfill waste from paper filters.

Sustainable Redesign

- **Materials:** Use stainless steel or recycled plastic for the machine body.
- **Manufacturing:** Optimize production processes to minimize waste.
- **Disassembly:** Design for easy disassembly and component replacement.
- **Packaging:** Use minimal recycled cardboard packaging and offer reusable filters.

Exercises

Part A (Objective Questions)

1. What is the aim of sustainable design in the design thinking process?
   (a) To create compelling and efficient goods
   (b) To consider financial costs only
   (c) To ignore cultural implications
   (d) To create products that harm the environment
2. What is considered during the sustainable design process in the design thinking process?
   (a) Only the environment
   (b) Only the financial costs
   (c) Only the social ramifications
   (d) Environment, financial costs, social ramifications, and cultural implications
3. What are the objectives of sustainable design approaches?
   (a) Creating products with maximum environmental impact
   (b) Minimizing resource usage and waste
   (c) Improving customer experiences through inconsistent performance levels
   (d) Prioritizing profitability over environmental considerations
4. Which of the following is not an objective of sustainable design?
   (a) Pushing existing boundaries through technology and innovation
   (b) Emphasizing user-friendly interfaces and consistent performance levels
   (c) Maximizing environmental impact through material selections
   (d) Reducing waste by making the most of already-available resources
5. What is the goal of sustainable design?
   (a) To create systems and products that benefit society while having no impact on the environment
   (b) To push existing boundaries through technology and innovation
   (c) To maximize profits through cost-cutting measures
   (d) To create products that benefit society while having the least possible adverse effects on the environment
6. Which approach is focused on designing products with minimal waste and a closed-loop system for materials?
   (a) Circular Economy Modeling
   (b) Green Chemistry
   (c) Biomimicry
   (d) Cradle-to-Grave production methodology
7. Which approach involves looking to nature for inspiration in design solutions?
   (a) Life Cycle Assessment Approach (b) Circular Economy Modeling
   (c) Green Chemistry (d) Biomimicry
8. Which approach involves evaluating the environmental impacts of a product throughout its entire lifecycle, from creation to disposal?
   (a) Life Cycle Assessment Approach (b) Circular Economy Modeling
   (c) Green Chemistry (d) Biomimicry
9. Which phase of the product life cycle should sustainable design principles be considered?
   (a) Development phase (b) Manufacturing phase
   (c) Use phase (d) Recycling phase

10. What is the foundation of sustainable design during the development phase of the product life cycle?
    (a) Material usage
    (b) Energy use
    (c) Reduced waste
    (d) Recycling
11. At which stage of the product life cycle is the product retired?
    (a) Development phase
    (b) Manufacturing phase
    (c) Use phase
    (d) Recycling phase
12. What should be the focus during the utilization phase of a product's life cycle?
    (a) Minimizing environmental impact
    (b) Maximizing profits
    (c) Increasing advertising
    (d) Reducing manufacturing costs
13. What is the purpose of making a product durable during the utilization phase?
    (a) To increase manufacturing costs
    (b) To increase advertising
    (c) To minimize the need for replacement
    (d) To maximize profits
14. What is one way to increase a product's longevity during the utilization phase?
    (a) Making it difficult to repair
    (b) Making it energy-efficient
    (c) Using non-recyclable materials
    (d) Making it disposable
15. What should be considered during the end-of-life phase of a product?
    (a) Durability and energy efficiency
    (b) Material usage reduction
    (c) Recycling and reuse of components
    (d) User-friendly interfaces
16. Why is it important for products to be made with recyclable materials?
    (a) To reduce waste
    (b) To improve customer experiences
    (c) To increase the product's longevity
    (d) To push existing boundaries even further through technology and innovation
17. What is the purpose of making a product easily disassembled?
    (a) To increase the product's longevity
    (b) To reduce energy use
    (c) To improve customer experiences
    (d) To facilitate recycling or reuse of components
18. What is the purpose of considering sustainable design principles during the end-of-life phase of a product's life cycle?
    (a) To ensure the product components are made of recyclable materials.
    (b) To increase the product's longevity.
    (c) To minimize energy use during the utilization phase.
    (d) To reduce the adverse environmental effects of the manufacturing process.
19. Why should sustainable design principles be considered during the development phase of a product's life cycle?
    (a) To reduce energy use during the utilization phase.
    (b) To minimize waste, energy use, and material usage.
    (c) To ensure the product is durable and energy-efficient.
    (d) To simplify the disassembly and repair of the product.
20. What is the advantage of considering sustainable design principles during the utilization phase of a product's life cycle?
    (a) To minimize the need for replacement.
    (b) To increase the product's longevity.
    (c) To ensure the product components are made of recyclable materials.
    (d) To simplify the disassembly and repair of the product.

Part B (Short Answer Questions)

1. How does sustainable design help design thinking?
2. What are the objectives of sustainable design approaches?
3. What are the different methods for incorporating sustainable design?
4. What is a product life cycle?
5. How does the development phase of the product consider sustainability?
6. How does the utilization phase of the product consider sustainability?
7. How does the end-of-life phase of the product consider sustainability?

Part C (Essay Questions)

1. What is sustainable design? Why is it important?
2. What are the objectives of sustainable design approaches? Explain in detail.
3. Explain the different methods for incorporating sustainable design.
4. Explain the life cycle assessment approach.
5. Explain circular economy modeling with an example.
6. Explain green chemistry in detail.
7. Explain biomimicry in detail.
8. Explain the cradle-to-grave production methodology in detail.

Answer Key

Part A

1. (a) **2.** (d) **3.** (b) **4.** (c) **5.** (d) **6.** (d) **7.** (d) **8.** (a) **9.** (a) **10.** (c)
11. (d) **12.** (a) **13.** (c) **14.** (b) **15.** (c) **16.** (a) **17.** (d) **18.** (a) **19.** (b) **20.** (a)

CHAPTER 8

Analyzing User Experience

Learning Objectives

At the end of this chapter, you will be able to:

- State the principles of design thinking and how it informs user experience (UX) to create products that not only function well but also provide a seamless and satisfying user experience
- Explain the concept of killer UX design, which goes beyond aesthetics to ensure that every aspect of the product is optimized for the best user experience
- Construct a work activity affinity diagram (WAAD) to visually organize user data and insights, facilitating a deeper understanding of user behaviors and needs
- Explain the development and application of user models, usage models, and work environment models to anticipate user requirements and design for maximum efficiency and satisfaction
- Describe the fundamentals of user experience analysis, including effective methods for prioritizing usability problems and generating innovative solutions
- List the user research methods and how to address common objections to UX research, ensuring that user feedback is effectively integrated into the design process
- Explain the creation and use of personas and customer journey maps to empathize with users and chart their interactions with the product, identifying pain points and opportunities for enhancement
- Give the steps to create a user journey map, which traces the user's path through the product, highlighting areas for improvement
- Describe the design and implementation of a user experience dashboard that aggregates key user metrics and provides a comprehensive overview of the user experience
- Define the key metrics for user experience analysis, which help in measuring the effectiveness of the UX and guiding iterative design improvements
- Explore future trends in UX analysis, preparing you to adapt to emerging technologies and user expectations
- Give some real-life case studies in UX analysis, offering insights into successful strategies and common pitfalls in UX design and evaluation

8.1 Introduction

User experience (UX) analysis is a crucial aspect of design that is frequently disregarded. It involves assessing a user's interactions with a product or service and identifying methods to enhance that experience. By performing a comprehensive user experience analysis, designers can develop products that possess both aesthetic appeal and user-friendliness.

Apple is well known for its efforts in analyzing user experience. They are very good at it, and they have some of the most elegant products on the market, with very intuitive interfaces. This is because they spend a lot of time and energy trying to understand how people use their product. By doing so, Apple builds products that work well while also looking attractive because all of the features that do not add value get weeded out through constant user feedback reviews.

Another example is the design of Netflix. The streaming service's success hinges mainly upon an interface so straightforward that now it seems like common sense. However, through deeply diving into user research and tests, Netflix has managed not only to create content recommendation engines but also to completely customize pages based on individual interests.

Virtually anything can benefit from looking at how people interact with that product, from websites or mobile apps to physical objects. If we know why users do what they do, then crafting interfaces becomes easier while simultaneously being more effective.

8.1.1 Design Thinking and User Experience

Thinking from a user's view is key in design thinking. Looking at what people need and finding the appropriate solutions is the key to UX. Design thinking meshes well with UX. When both come together, the result is products and services that people find helpful and enjoyable (Fig. 8.1).

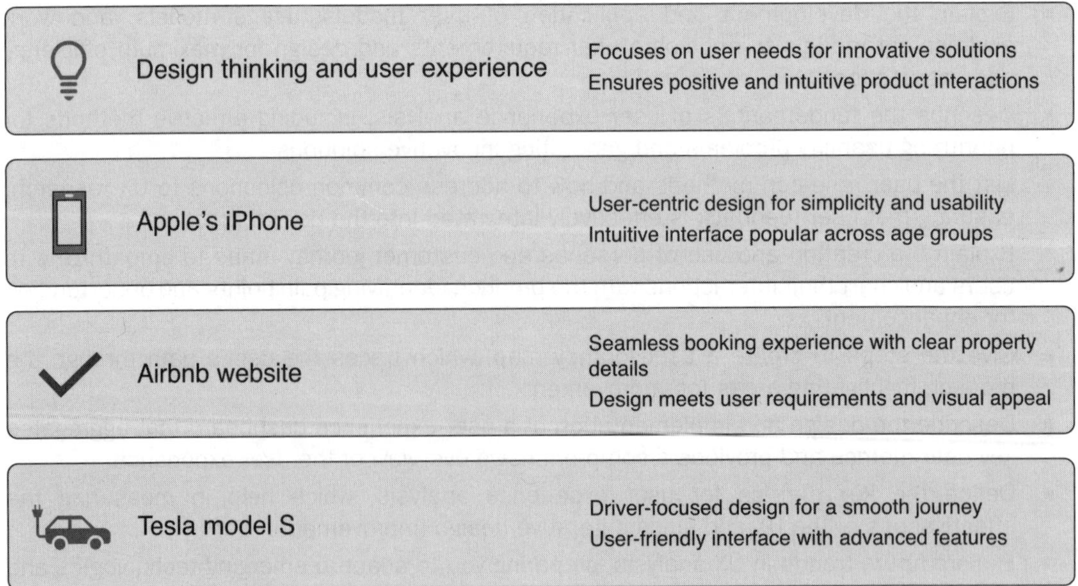

Figure 8.1 Sample products developed using design thinking

Apple's iPhone, as mentioned earlier, is a prime example of design thinking and user experience. It was created keeping users in mind; this means creating an easy, straightforward device anyone could work with without fuss. Users of every age love its simplicity. The designers also used design thinking ideas to create a functional and aesthetically pleasing product.

Another great use of design thinking and user experience is Airbnb's website. The site was designed to make booking vacation rentals a smooth, pleasant process. Everything is easy to follow, with clear details on each listing. The designers aimed to satisfy users' needs while also making the site visually appealing.

Tesla's Model S shows off design thinking and user-friendly technology. The car was crafted to give drivers a seamless, comfortable experience behind the wheel. The controls, like the huge touchscreen, regulate the vehicle's settings easily. Tesla's designers prioritized the driver's needs and an aesthetically pleasing style.

8.1.2 Killer UX Design

A killer UX design offers users a positive experience. It entails understanding what your audience needs and wants in order to come up with a straightforward, intuitive way of meeting those requirements through the design of the product (Fig. 8.2).

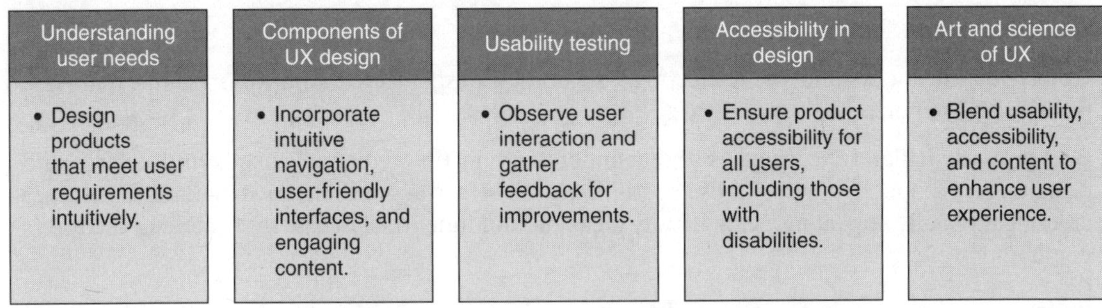

Figure 8.2 Characteristics of killer UX design

Both the art and science that goes into creating digital products, which can offer exceptional experiences for those who use them, have been dubbed killer UX design. The users should feel that they are having a pleasant experience whenever they interact with these products. To ensure this happens, we should take into consideration the surrounding environment (context), behavior patterns exhibited while operating such systems, and personal tastes plus preferences, if any exist. A killer UX design has different parts such as navigation that is easy to use, interfaces designed with the user in mind, and content that is engaging for your audience.

An excellent killer UX design must first look attractive visually and also function well at the same time. In addition, it should be aesthetically pleasing. Furthermore, the layout needs to consider people's needs and desires so they can find things quickly – whether it is information or products/services – and complete tasks rapidly such as signing up for an account or making a purchase.

In short, usability testing comes in handy during the development stages, since it helps identify bugs before the final release. In addition, testing the design with actual users is necessary to ensure that it fulfills their requirements and preferences.

It is important to keep in mind that everybody matters, and this is especially true when it comes to creating a top-notch UX design. We need to make sure that a product can be used by anyone who wants or needs it – including those with disabilities. This means they have to design interfaces using assistive technology.

Here are some examples:

- **Slack:** It is a communication tool used by teams worldwide. Its designs mainly focus on enabling collaboration between different people during communication processes. The interface is straightforward and to the point, and chat rooms are categorized based on topics discussed at that time. Also, a powerful search feature makes it easy for users to find specific conversations or files.
- **Dropbox:** It has designed its UX around simplicity when it comes to file storage and sharing. Uploads can also be done quickly since the interface design has an uncomplicated drag-and-drop functionality and no clutter. In addition, intuitive sharing options such as sending through email/link/social media make everything about this service straightforward.
- **Google:** This is the king of UX design. All of Google's products, including the search engine and productivity tools, aim to fulfil the needs of the user. Consequently, the interfaces are neat and simple, with strong search features that help users find everything they are looking for easily.

Design Visualization Question 8.1

Student Project: Killer UX Design

Objective: To understand the concept of killer UX design and its importance in creating a positive and seamless user experience.

Background: Killer UX design is about understanding the audience's needs and desires and designing a product that meets those needs in a straightforward and intuitive manner. It involves creating a visually appealing, aesthetically pleasing, and functional design that caters to the user's needs and preferences.

Steps:

- Research the concept of killer UX design and its components, including intuitive navigation, user-friendly interfaces, and engaging content.
- Choose a product or service and analyze its current UX design.
- Identify areas for improvement and create a new killer UX design for the chosen product or service.
- Present your new design to the class and explain how it improves the user experience.

8.1.3 Constructing a Work Activity Affinity Diagram

A work activity affinity diagram (WAAD) is a valuable method for organizing and understanding the various duties and activities involved in a given work process (Fig. 8.3).

The design team should include people from different departments or fields of knowledge who can provide various views on how the work should be performed. After putting the team together, the next thing is to identify all the main activities involved in carrying out this task. Brainstorming might help, or making an activity list containing each process. When these activities have been recognized, they should be grouped by similarity or interdependency.

One way to group is by using Post-it notes or index cards, where each activity must be written down and physically arranged on a whiteboard. The groupings should be discussed among the team members until they are logical and meaningful enough for all activities therein to appear organized, after which they are refined.

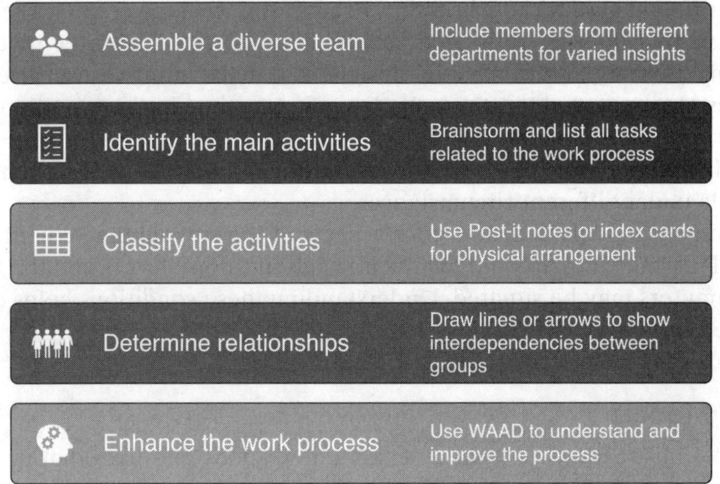

Figure 8.3 Work activity affinity diagram, drawing steps

After the groups are made, it becomes important to establish connections between different categories. What we can do here is draw lines or even arrows joining various groups to show how they depend on one another or relate to each other in any way possible. This process may also help identify other activities missing from the WAAD that might be required to complete it fully.

Developing WAADs could greatly assist people in understanding and improving their working processes. When teams arrange process activities and determine their relations, they become more knowledgeable about their functioning points and areas that need enhancements.

8.1.4 Models Used in UX

Understanding the user is crucial when designing software applications. User models, usage models, and work environment models are vital in ensuring that the software developed meets the user's needs (Fig. 8.4).

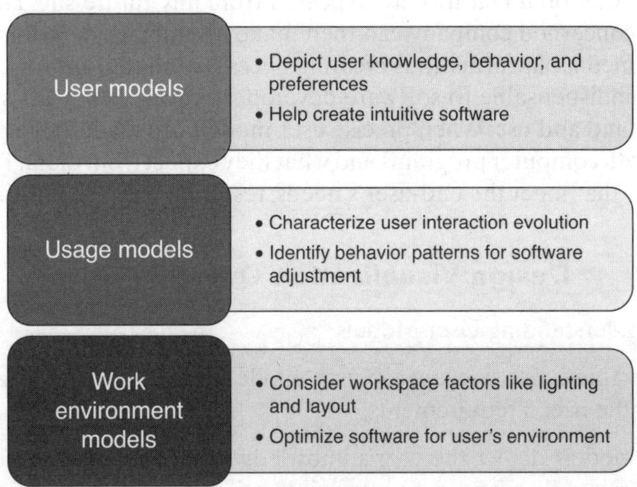

Figure 8.4 Vital characteristics of user needs

User models describe what users know, how they behave, and what they prefer. They help developers understand how people interact with programs and the kinds of features that are likely to be necessary. Creating user models also enables designers to make intuitive, user-friendly systems.

Usage models are employed to represent changes over time in the ways people use programs or systems. They assist developers to identify patterns of user behavior and modify software correspondingly. In addition, they can help forecast future interactions with a given piece of software by different people under different circumstances.

Work environment models depict various aspects of the surrounding conditions under which software is used. They take into account factors like lighting, noise levels, and the layout of physical spaces where computers may be situated. Understanding these conditions helps developers create systems best suited for particular working environments.

We will now discuss each of thes models in detail.

8.1.4.1 User Models

Models of users are abstractions of what a person knows, does, and likes that make it possible for developers to build easy and enjoyable software. It is necessary to have broad knowledge about these ideas because they help in creating programs that will be needed or anticipated by the final user.

Different methods can be used in creating user models, such as surveys and interviews with users, among others, like observation during use. Good models showing what users want can be constructed by gathering information on their behavior patterns and what they prefer. For instance, suppose there is a company that wants to create an app for delivering food using mobile phones. It may send out questionnaires to its clients to obtain knowledge about the types of foods people like the most, the time expected for delivery, and methods through which payments should be made, among other things. When this data is analysed, such an organization can develop an accurate model showing each client's preference or behavior, enabling them to design a user interface that meets all these requirements.

Another scenario could be the development of a new social media platform where companies wish to reach more people through internet-based communication systems. They may conduct interviews among different individuals, asking how they usually carry out activities on existing social sites and what additional features are expected from any future site. Having performed this kind of research, the concerned company can then make a summary describing what people know and like about social media platforms, thus creating necessary conditions for user engagement.

User models are indispensable to software developers because they assist in making software that is easy to understand and use. When precise user models are made, developers can understand how people interact with computer programs and what they expect from them. This information helps in designing programs that meet the end-user's needs, resulting in more satisfactory experiences.

Design Visualization Question 8.2

Student Project: Understanding User Models

Objective: To understand the concept of user models and their importance in developing software that meets the user's requirements.

Background: User models depict the user's knowledge, behavior, and preferences. They assist developers in comprehending how consumers interact with software and what features they anticipate. By developing user models, developers can design intuitive and user- friendly software,

Steps:
- Research the concept of user models and their components, including user knowledge, behavior, and preferences.
- Choose a software product and analyze its current user model.
- Identify areas for improvement and create a new user model for the chosen software product.
- Present your new user model to the class and explain how it improves the user experience.

8.1.4.2 Usage Models

It is essential to comprehend user behavior when developing software. This is where usage models become relevant (Fig. 8.5).

Figure 8.5 Steps in drawing usage models

These models characterize the evolution of user interactions with software, enabling developers to recognize patterns and modify their products accordingly. For example, they may discover that clients interact with some features more often than others. With such details, the developers can adjust their applications to better suit the users' needs.

Usage models are also helpful in predicting future user interactions and optimizing existing software. By analyzing usage patterns over time, developers can obtain insight into the likely evolution of user behavior. This enables them to anticipate user requirements and create software that better meets them. Creating effective usage models requires meticulous data analysis and interpretation. Developers must recognize significant data patterns and make informed decisions about how to modify their software. With the proper tools and knowledge, usage models can enhance the user experience and help us develop software that genuinely meets user needs.

Design Visualization Question 8.3

Student Project: Understanding Usage Models

Objective: To understand the concept of usage models and their importance in developing software that meets the user's requirements.

Background: Usage models are used to characterize the evolution of user interactions with software. They assist developers in identifying user behavior patterns and adjusting software accordingly. Usage models can also assist developers in predicting future user interactions with software.

Steps:

- Research the concept of usage models and their components, including user behavior patterns and future user interactions.
- Choose a software product and analyze its current usage model.
- Identify areas for improvement and create a new usage model for the chosen software product.
- Present your new usage model to the class and explain how it improves the user experience.

8.1.4.3 Work Environment Models

In our contemporary world, as software increasingly controls our everyday activities, it becomes vital for designers to understand its use context. One way to understand the working environment is through models related to work environments; these consider lighting and air quality, among other things, in the workspace (Fig. 8.6).

The software created should be able to meet the users' needs under these conditions by considering some factors. For example, if someone is operating from a place with poor visibility, they may need brighter colors or larger fonts so that reading becomes easier. Where noise levels are high, instead of hearing information delivered through sound effects on their computers' screens, they may display it graphically.

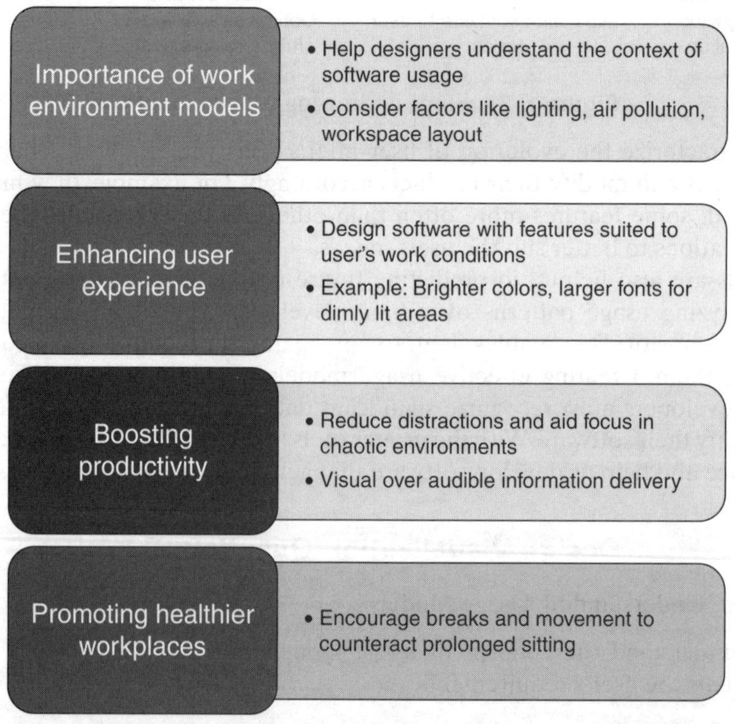

Figure 8.6 Characteristics of work environment models

Work environment models improve not only the user experience but also productivity. This can be achieved by designing optimized applications within specific work environments, hence minimizing distractions and enabling individuals to focus more on what needs to be done. However, this benefit is not limited to just enhancing employee satisfaction and output alone. It extends further into creating healthier spaces, too. Designers should, therefore, consider physical arrangement when developing such systems because, through them, people will have short breaks, thus reducing the effects brought about by prolonged sitting.

8.2 Fundamentals of User Experience Analysis

Suppose you are creating a new food delivery app. UX analysis helps predict how people will interact with it. It consists of a series of steps that reveal user needs, frustrations, and expectations, ultimately leading to a design that is easy to use and enjoyable for the customer (Fig. 8.7).

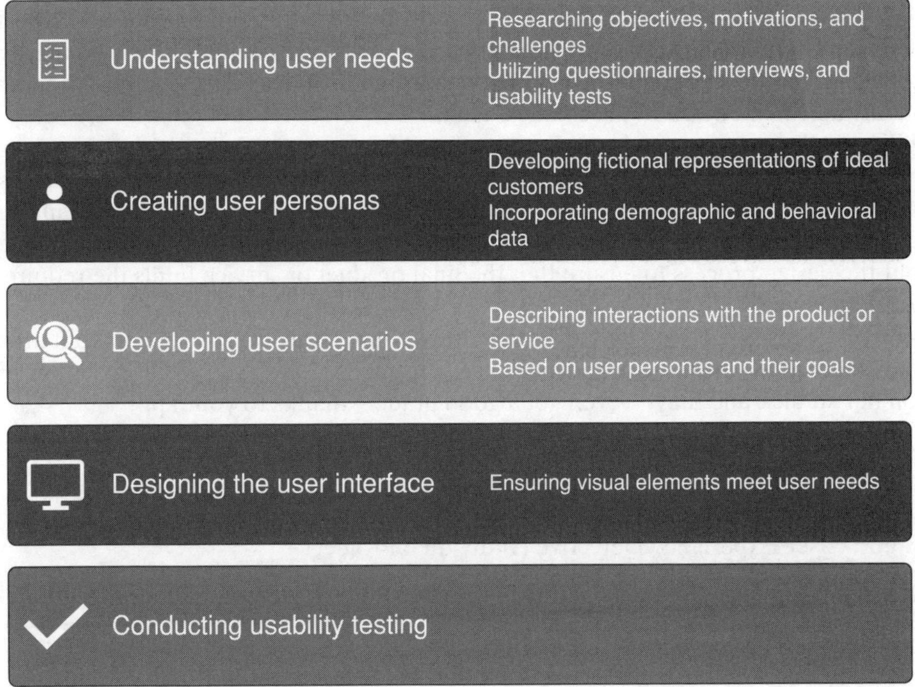

Figure 8.7 User experience analysis steps

Think of yourself as Sherlock Holmes, but instead of solving crimes, you are solving user issues! The aim during UX anaylsis includes the identification of such things as the objectives of your customers (what they hope to achieve), their motivations (why they want to buy from me), and pain points or problems they encounter along their way while using a service or product. This can be achieved through various means, such as:

- **Questionnaires:** Online surveys designed to gather general information about users' preferences, also known as personality tests.
- **Interviews:** Deep conversations with genuine individuals who have used the system before. Ask them different questions concerning how often they order food online, what type they prefer most among others, etc.
- **Usability testing:** This is the stage where we come up with a prototype for users to interact with. It involves watching them struggle and seeing where exactly that happens to make necessary changes accordingly. The point here is not just understanding but digging deep into these needs, thus informing what should be designed.

After understanding the user's needs, the next step is to create user personas. A user persona refers to a fictional character that you make up based on your research. It embodies the characteristics of actual people you interviewed during questionnaire sessions or observed while conducting usability tests together with other relevant sources such as social media profiles to paint an accurate picture of this individual., For instance, Sarah is a 22-year-old college student staying in a dormitory.

In the next stage, user scenarios are developed. Think about a scenario for Sarah using your app. Scenario: Sarah is cramming for an exam and suddenly wants pizza. She opens the app, selects 'late-night delivery' under filters, quickly picks out her favourite pizza place, and places an order in minutes. User scenarios could be a narrative description of how users will interact with a product or service. They should originate from personas and reflect their goals, what drives them, or even where it hurts the most. These stories help test products but also reveal areas that need more work.

The next stage is user interface design. Think of the visual design of your app. The interface refers to any part of products/services that people can see or touch. It must meet requirements from various types, such as described in the user persona which includes color scheme, typography style, and layout arrangement, down to the smallest detail.

Usability testing represents the fifth stage. Just like a car needs test drives, your app needs usability testing. Real users interact with the app prototype, providing feedback on its ease of use. This helps you identify and fix any issues before launch. Imagine Sarah testing the app and suggesting a 'reorder favourites' feature for those late-night cravings. Usability testing should be performed throughout the design process to ensure that the final product or service fulfils the requirements of the intended audience.

By following these steps, you end up with a user-centered design. It is an app built around your users' needs, leading to a positive user experience. This means Sarah can easily order her pizza, stay focused on her studies, and maybe even get a good grade – thanks to your app!

Design Visualization Question 8.4

Assignment: User Experience Detective (Individual Project)

Objective: Develop a user persona and user scenario for a chosen product or service.

The Case: You are a UX Designer tasked with improving a specific product or service. Choose something you use regularly, like a campus library website, a food delivery app, or a gym membership system.

Your Tools:

- **Research:** Conduct online surveys or interviews with fellow students to gather user needs and pain points related to your chosen product/service.
- **Analysis:** Organize your findings to identify common themes and user frustrations.

Deliverables:

1. **User Persona:** Create a detailed profile of your ideal user for the chosen product/service. Include demographics, goals, motivations, and pain points. (Think of this as a 'character sketch' for your user).
2. **User Scenario:** Develop a narrative describing how your user persona interacts with the product/service. Include their goals, the steps they take within the product/service, and any challenges they encounter.

8.2.1 How to Prioritize Usability Problems

The design of products or services must always consider usability. It should ensure that users can navigate and interact with the product successfully. With so many potential issues, it might take time to figure out where to start (Fig. 8.8).

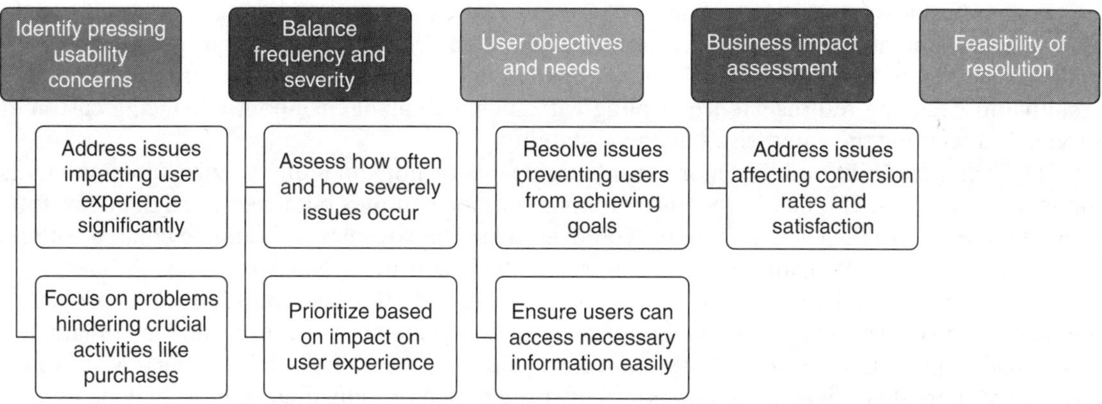

Figure 8.8 Steps in prioritizing usability problems

First, identify the most significant usability problems. These will impact the user experience the most and may lead to frustration or abandonment of the product. For example, if buyers need assistance to complete an important task such as making a purchase or submitting a form, this should be your first concern.

Next, consider how often each problem occurs and how severe it is when it does occur. Some problems could occur all the time but hardly affect anybody, while others could be encountered rarely but completely ruin the experience for those rare few who do. By weighing up these factors, you can work out what needs fixing right away and what can wait until later.

Another way of deciding what needs attention is to think about what the users are trying to accomplish. If something stops them from doing this, it has to be fixed immediately; for instance, if people cannot find information that would help them make informed decisions, this should be given top priority.

Furthermore, consider how each problem might affect your business or organization if left unresolved. If something significantly reduces sales conversions or customer satisfaction, we must deal with it immediately. On the other hand, if its impact is minimal within either context, we can leave this particular issue for later.

To make usability problem resolution more practical, consider each problem's difficulty. Some may take longer to fix than others. The most easily addressed should be dealt with first. Many factors must be considered when arranging usability problems in order of importance for design thinking. Critical problems should be identified to solve user interface issues best; one should also evaluate how often they occur and their severity, consider what the user wants or needs to be done, and determine how this will affect business or organization interests before deciding on feasibility.

For example, a booking system is essential in a dining establishment. It is the first place where a customer interacts with the restaurant. The problem starts when it shows that only a few time slots are available. This can significantly affect the user's journey. This not only limits people's ability to choose but can also create a feeling that the place is not accessible or the services are not good. Although this issue does not occur frequently, it significantly impacts the client's experience.

If these problems occur, customers may end up feeling annoyed or let down if they cannot get their desired reservation slot. Failure to secure a booking time of choice is regarded as quite serious since most guests look forward to it while planning events or trying to fit into other people's schedules. Not being able to do this might make the hotel less attractive, thus driving clients away who would find another place to feel more catered for.

From a business point of view, failure of the reservation system to adapt to users' wants could lead to losing potential earnings. For example, suppose someone finds it hard to get a table. They may decide to go to a competing establishment. When one person steps out, others may follow suit, resulting in declining returns. Hence, dealing with such a challenge is about enhancing customer service and securing the enterprise's financial stability.

Regarding feasibility, adding more visible time slots or implementing waitlist functionality is moderately complex. This means that the solution is not too complex but needs to be done carefully to fit seamlessly into the current system. Moreover, these improvements should be created with an eye for scalability to anticipate future growth and shifts in consumer behavior.

The restaurant is advised to deal with other more urgent issues first, considering this problem's medium priority level. However, the importance of this issue should not be underestimated. A well-rounded plan that considers both immediate and long-term tactics is necessary. Meanwhile, temporary alternatives like manual bookings over the phone or individual support may be used to lessen its impact on user experience.

In summary, even though it may occur infrequently, failing to address such matters can significantly affect customer satisfaction and business performance. Hence, by prioritizing what the users want and looking at possible options, the eatery can improve its reservation system, thus making clients happy while solidifying its position in the market.

8.2.2 Generating Solutions to Usability Problems

Issues with practicality may arise at any point in a project, so we must think of ways to solve them (Fig. 8.9).

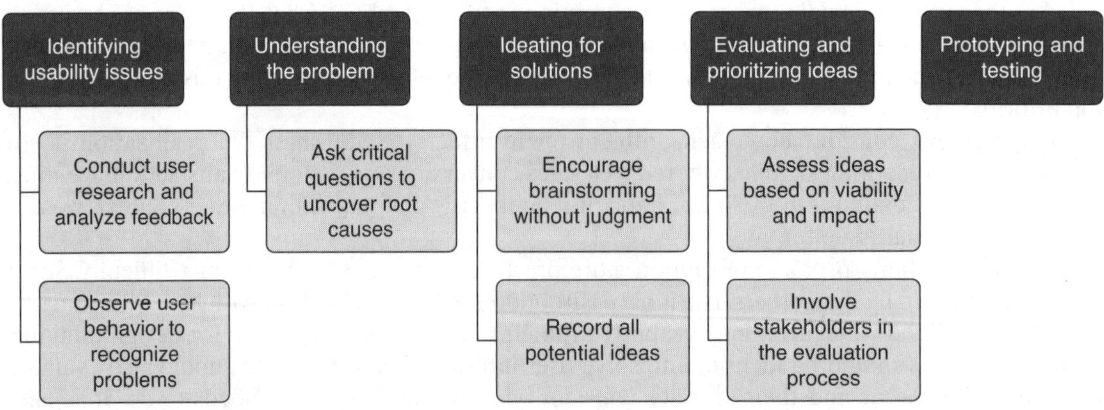

Figure 8.9 Generating solutions to usability problems

The first step is to recognize the issue by conducting user research, analyzing user feedback, and observing user behavior. Once the problem has been identified, the next step is to determine its underlying cause. This can be achieved by asking "Why is this happening?" and "What factors are contributing to the issue?"

At the next stage, we need to come up with some possible solutions. The more diverse these ideas, the better. Write down every thought that occurs because each could contain a kernel of truth. Following the generation of ideas, the next stage is to evaluate and rank them. This can be accomplished by considering viability, impact, and implementation simplicity. Again, involving stakeholders ensures that the proposed solutions correlate with the organization's objectives and core values.

After prioritizing the solutions, it is necessary to prototype and test them. This can be easily achieved by creating low-fidelity prototypes, which includes wireframes, and testing them with end-users. Finally, it is vital to iterate on solutions based on user feedback and to continue testing until the underlying issue is resolved.

Thus, design thinking calls for designers to identify the problem, find what is causing it, brainstorm possible solutions, and test them. This means that the steps of design thinking are understanding, observation, point of view, defining (reframing), ideating (brainstorming), prototyping, and testing. This ensures that products designed are user-friendly and meet user needs and requirements.

Returning to our restaurant reservation problem, in response to the critical problem of limited time slots in the online reservation system, different actions can be taken by the restaurant authorities. Firstly, current reservation data analysis can be constructive in understanding busy hours and what customers like most when it comes to eating. This will give them a better plan for giving out the remaining slots. It may also be good for them to adjust their back-end system architecture so that availability would shift dynamically according to real-time demand.

Secondly, they should consider introducing a waitlist feature that can act as a backup for clients who fail to get their preferred slot times due to the restaurant being fully booked. It provides an alternative and aids in proper cancellation control measures put in place by management.

Equally important is rewarding people for making reservations during off-peak periods to even out the number of clients at any given hour while not necessarily reducing business during peak hours. Another aspect is keeping customers engaged through automating notifications about available slots or immediate table seating whenever they come up. Furthermore, integrating with various platforms like social media sites and dining apps would be beneficial since it will make the service more accessible to different people.

From a technical perspective, making the reservation system user-friendly and compatible with mobile devices can attract more online bookings. In addition, updating it regularly to meet new usability standards and interface design best practices contributes significantly towards enhancing the overall user experience.

For the system to work effectively, staff should be trained to handle bookings both online and offline. By giving employees, the tools and authority they need to decide on reservations, it is possible to provide more individualized service and better address special requests from clients. Finally, gathering continuous feedback from users about their reservation experience will help make future improvements. If customers can easily give their suggestions through a feedback loop, this not only improves the system but also shows how much a restaurant cares about satisfying its clients.

8.2.3 User Research Methods

Before any product or service is designed, techniques must be fully understood to comprehend the users' wants, needs, and challenges. The design thinking process requires various methods of user research and feedback gathering (Fig. 8.10).

User interviews

Direct conversations to understand objectives, motivations, and challenges

Importance of open-ended questions for detailed insights

Observation

Studying user–product interactions to identify pain points

Reveals actual usage and areas for improvement

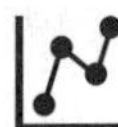

Surveys and questionnaires

Gathering quantitative data through structured queries

Effective for feedback from a larger audience

User testing

Evaluating prototypes to find usability issues

Crucial for refining design iterations

Figure 8.10 Various user research methods

Interviewing people has a high success rate and can be done through one-on-one conversations/face-to-face/over the phone. Designers must talk to individuals about their main goals and why those goals are critical to them, and what could stop them from achieving them. The use of open-ended questions allows users to give more detailed and comprehensive solutions.

Another method is observation, which could involve observing how people interact with products/services during use (usability testing). This method shows where pain points exist within the system and areas that could be improved.

Surveys and questionnaires can also provide valuable feedback from many individuals who may not have time for an interview. A set number of questions is sent to these people, which helps collect data quantitatively.

User testing is another way of gathering feedback from users. This entails testing prototypes with representatives of the intended audience to identify potential issues related to ease of use or opportunities for improvement.

Design thinking depends on user research methodologies because they enable designers to understand users so that they can create products and services that align with their needs while solving their problems. Furthermore, through frequent early collection of user feedback, iteration becomes possible in design, thus enabling the creation of products tailored to meet actual user requirements.

8.2.4 Dealing with Common Objections to UX Research

When it comes to UX research, numerous objections may be raised. However, it is necessary to establish successful user experience to address these objections (Fig. 8.11).

Cost and time investment in UX research	Designer bias versus user insights	Navigating UX research complexity	Importance of exhaustive UX research
• Identifies and resolves issues early • Essential for product success despite costs	• Risks in assuming user needs without research • Research provides valuable user perspective	• Availability of resources and methods • Surveys, interviews, usability tests, A/B testing	• Leads to user-friendly designs • Addresses specific user concerns effectively

Figure 8.11 Dealing with common objections in UX research

People often consider UX research costly and time-consuming. While this is true, it is also important to consider the intension in making the product successful. Potential problems can be fixed before they become significant issues through research.

Another argument against user experience research is that it is not necessary because designers already know what people want. However, this assumption is dangerous since designers usually have biases that may cloud judgment. Conducting a study provides insights into consumer needs and wants, thus leading to better satisfaction among them.

Someone might also say that carrying out extensive UX research is quite complicated. This should not deter you, as many resources are available for such inquiries. Several techniques can also be applied in different situations, such as surveys, interviews, usability tests, or A/B tests. Even though some may object to the idea of UX research, it is still necessary to provide good user experiences. Therefore, we must address these concerns and conduct a comprehensive inquiry.

For example, let us assume you are creating a new e-commerce site. Through research, you could learn from users that they need assistance in finding specific items or a simplified check-out process. Such changes would help create a website that meets their needs quickly.

8.2.5 Personas and Customer Journey Mapping

Understanding the user is essential for creating a successful product or service. To this end, personas and customer journey mapping serve as two major aids that can help designers better understand users by ensuring that the experiences are tailored according to their needs. Personas are imaginary depictions of several groups of users that have been designed based on research and data. They help to create an image of users by identifying such things as demographics, behaviors, goals, and pain points, among others. Therefore, through this, businesses can develop products and services specifically intended for their target audience (Fig. 8.12).

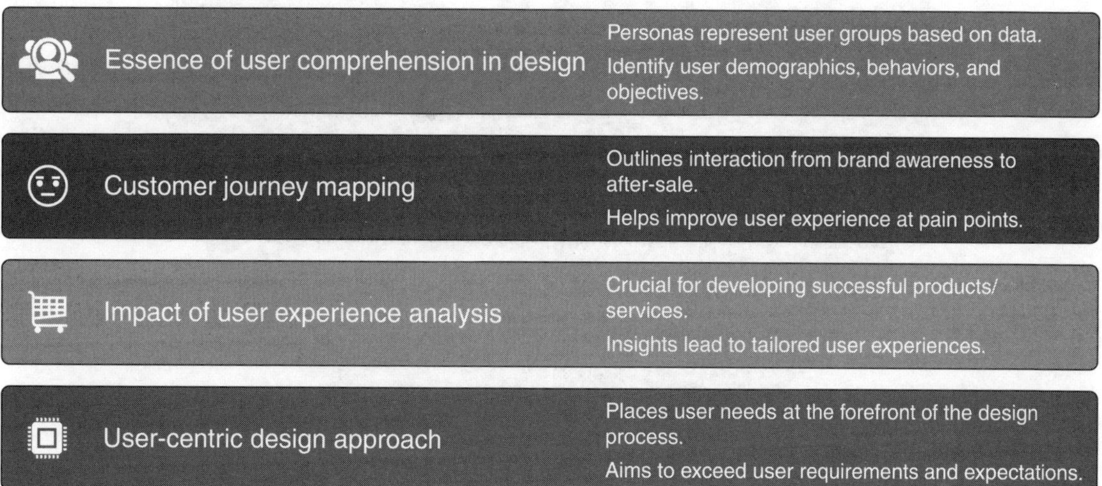

Figure 8.12 Personas and customer journey mapping

On the other hand, customer journey mapping traces the entire interaction between a consumer and the product or service. This includes all points of contact, from when they first become aware of the brand until after they have made a purchase, and post-sale as well. By mapping out this process, organizations can find out where users may be getting frustrated or confused and fix those parts of their site so people have better experiences.

Understanding what drives users when coming up with new ideas is also crucial. Businesses must, therefore, know what their customers want so that they can provide them with something unique and exciting. Tools like personas and customer journey mapping will help understand who the users are by giving insights into their needs. In light of this information, businesses can design experiences tailored to meet those requirements. Putting users at the heart of the design process means creating products/solutions beyond what is expected or desired, which exceeds customer expectations accordingly.

8.2.6 How to Create a User Journey Map

To create a successful user experience, you must have a user journey map. It is a design tool that shows how an individual interacts with a product or service. This process should identify pain points, opportunities for improvement, and the emotions and motivations of the users at different stages (Fig. 8.13).

Figure 8.13 Steps in creating a user journey map

The journey begins with the user's awareness of the product or service and ends after the purchase has been completed. Hence, all points of interaction should be included, such as website visits, social media interactions, and emails.

For example, if you have created an app that delivers food, the journey may start when someone sees an advertisement on social media platforms like Facebook or X, and downloads and and installs the application in their device(s). A user creates an account and then browses the available restaurants before choosing what to order for a meal. The next step is placing an order, after which tracking delivery status follows suit until finally, the food arrives at the destination so that they can enjoy their delicious food and later leave feedback.

Opportunities for improvement may be experienced throughout the user journey. For example, a person may require assistance with app navigation or the delivery time could take longer than expected. By identifying such pain points, you will be able to enhance customer satisfaction levels and improve their overall experience.

To create a user journey map, you must include it in a prospective user's experience. It allows us to find where we need to make changes, improve their experience, and increase customer satisfaction by identifying different touchpoints with our products or services.

For example, imagine that Kiran, a busy professional, loves trying new restaurants. Her user journey map for the food delivery app she uses might look like this:

- **Awareness stage:** Kiran sees a photo of a delicious dish on the app's Instagram page. (**Touchpoint:** Social media advertisement) (**Emotion:** Curious, hungry)
- **Consideration stage:** Kiran downloads the app and browses the restaurant options. (**Touchpoint:** Mobile app) (**Emotion:** Intrigued, overwhelmed by choices)
- **Decision stage:** Kiran filters restaurants by cuisine and finds a new Italian place. She reads positive reviews and creates an account. (**Touchpoint:** Mobile app) (**Emotion:** Hopeful, engaged)
- **Action stage:** Kiran selects her meal, customizes it with extra cheese, and places the order. (**Touchpoint:** Mobile app) (**Emotion:** Excited)
- **Post-purchase stage:** Kiran tracks the delivery status on the app and receives a notification when the food arrives. She enjoys her delicious meal and writes a glowing review. (**Touchpoint:** Mobile app) (**Emotion:** Satisfied, gratified)

During the journey, we may encounter 'friction points' or areas for improvement. For example, Kiran might struggle to navigate the app's complex filtering system (Pain Point: Confusing interface). The delivery might take longer than expected, leaving Kiran frustrated. (Pain Point: Long wait time).

By determining these pain points, we can improve usability by simplifying the app's interface and enhance user satisfaction by offering order tracking updates. To increase customer retention, we could ensure that we provide an experience that is smooth and enjoyable.

8.2.7 Creating a User Experience Dashboard

Creating a dashboard for user experience is essential for your product to work well (Fig. 8.14).

The dashboard gives an insight into the user experience, such as page load time, bounce rate, and conversion rate. With this information, you can recognize areas of concern in your product and make changes for a better user experience.

To create such a dashboard, you must first figure out what data points need tracking. For example, standard metrics are as follows: How long do pages take before fully loading? What makes people leave without clicking anything else after landing on one page? Why isn't anyone buying products despite them adding to the cart more frequently than before?

There are many instruments that can be used for collecting data, such as Google Analytics, Mixpanel and Kissmetrics. Using these tools, we can examine user behavior, among other things, thus providing awareness on how users interact with the site/application. After all the required information has been gathered, it should undergo analysis to identify weaknesses in the system.

One of the most important parts of setting up a UX-focused dashboard is presenting the findings in an understandable manner; consider representing them as charts or graphs. This makes it easier to locate areas that need improvement.

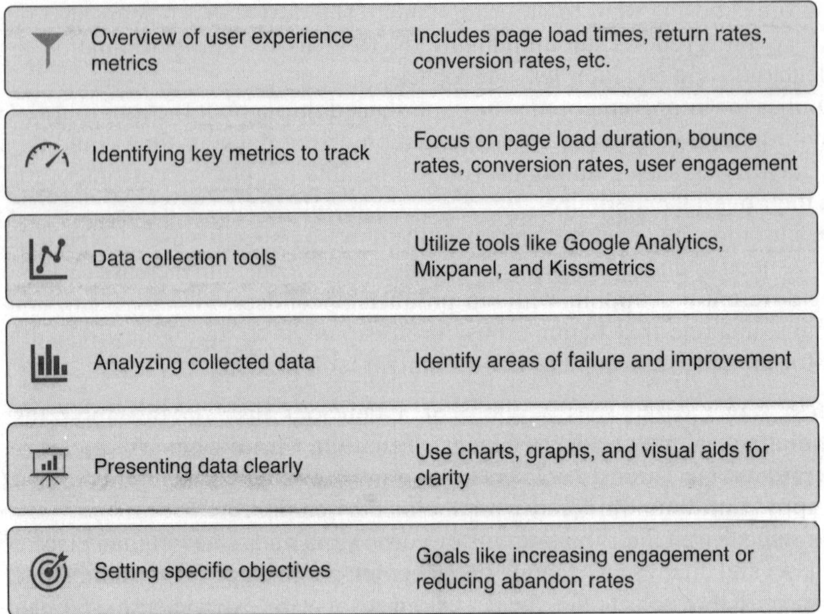

Figure 8.14 Creating user experience dashboards

Setting goals plays another crucial role in creating such dashboards; for example, increasing customer engagement might further reduce bounce rates while keeping track of progress towards these goals, which helps determine whether more changes are required based on specific cases.

Establishing a user experience dashboard is essential for your website or application to satisfy its customers. This dashboard will help you know where to improve the satisfaction of people using your website or app by monitoring main indexes, interpreting data, and setting goals.

8.3 Key Metrics for User Experience Analysis

In this digital age, what matters most when it comes to the success of any product or service is the nature of the user experience. Therefore, it is crucial for anyone looking forward to making his/her clients happy through their platforms, be it websites or any other application. To achieve this goal, one needs to measure and evaluate key metrics used to assess user engagement, satisfaction, and behavior. Here are some of the most important analytical metrics for UX studies (Fig. 8.15):

- **User engagement:** Companies should measure user interaction on their sites or products because it helps them know if people find the content exciting and easy to navigate. For example, measuring how many pages a person opened while on your site can tell you more about its engagement levels than saying that they stayed for a long time. However, the time spent per session may also give insights into what type of information is being sought by visitors. On the flip side, a high bounce rate would mean little or no engagement, where a visitor leaves after opening only one page. This shows a lack of interest. Lastly, click-through rate (CTR) shows the frequency with which individuals click links or call for action, portraying the effectiveness with which these items direct users into taking specific website actions. Therefore, businesses must keep track of such metrics to improve overall user experiences.
- **Conversion rate**: This refers to the rate at which visitors to a website are converted into paying customers. This means persuading people through these platforms to buy a product or service.

This number has revenue and ROI implications. Conversion rate optimization means improving systems or processes or designs so that more people become paying customers. It is done by identifying areas that need fixing and making informed decisions through numbers.

- **Customer satisfaction:** Businesses must succeed in fulfilling the product or service requirements and expectations of their consumers, which is an essential element of business success. Enterprises can measure their customers' satisfaction using surveys and client feedback. For instance, surveys enable firms to collect firsthand buyers' feelings about specific products or services. Reviews can provide customer feedback and evaluations on different products.
- **Usability:** Usability also refers to the ease of use of a product. It could be a website's ease of use or efficiency in web systems such as computer software programs. Specifically for webpages and digital products, easy navigation speeds up the consumers' ability to access required information. Withdrawal may occur if an individual encounters unnecessary menus or excessively extended loading time while navigating through pages. A practical design of products will make labeling obvious and always maintain/specify the exact location for every component throughout different interfaces. A simple but rich experience ensures visitor retention, where people stay longer, and explore much more than they originally intended, so this increases the chances of converting them into buyers.
- **Retention rate:** This is the percentage of users who return to a product or website after initially using it. A high retention rate indicates that the product or website is valued and satisfies the users, which can result in more earnings through increased user loyalty. On the other hand, a low retention rate may show problems with the product or website, such as poor user experience or lack of attractive features. In addition, retention rates enlighten businesses about the effectiveness of their marketing campaigns in retaining clients and motivate them to create retention strategies that will improve the overall user experience. Therefore, understanding this data is crucial for any company that wants to keep and grow its customer base over time.
- **Task completion rate:** This is an essential measure for every website or product that meets users' needs and provides a good user experience. It shows the percentage of users who have completed a specific task or goal on a website or product. When people find it difficult to accomplish their goals through your site, you would be considered having failed them since

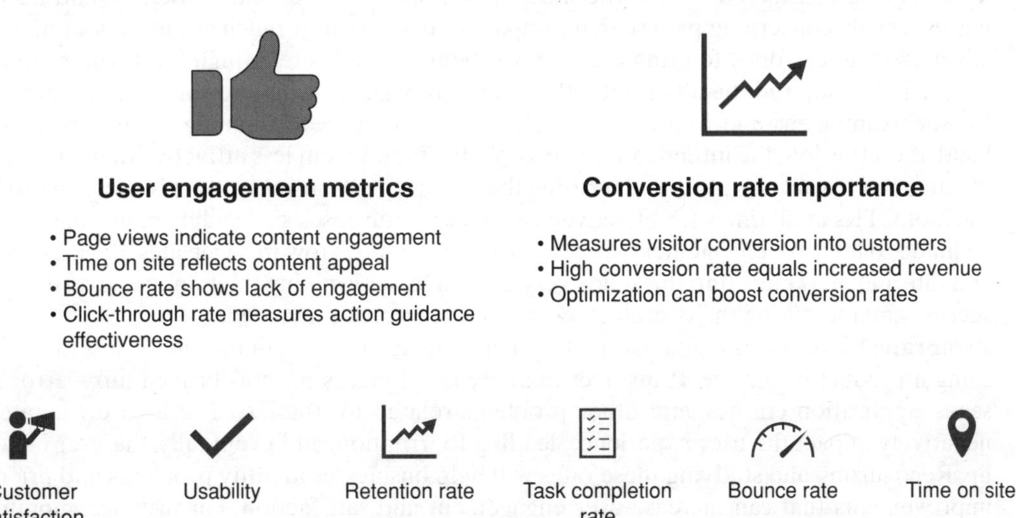

Figure 8.15 Key metrics of UX analysis

they take too long trying to figure out certain parts with no success at all. A high task completion rate means that individuals can easily navigate your webpage and achieve their objectives without any hiccups. Conversely, if this number is low, some assistance might be needed regarding user interface design. Also, possible barriers encountered while trying to reach desired outcomes should be highlighted, so that developers can know where improvements should be made to ensure the satisfaction of those using such platforms. After all these steps have been addressed, a high task completion rate will lead to more user engagement, increased consumer brand loyalty, and positive word-of-mouth referrals.

- **Bounce rate:** This is a vital measurement that might help webpage owners know how effective their site is. The high rate indicates that individuals must be more into the content or the website's design before leaving after looking at just one page. This could be because of poor navigation, slow loading times, insufficient exciting material, or a generally unpleasant user experience. Having many people leaving through only one page indicates that there is something wrong with your source of traffic, whereas a low exit rate shows that guests are participating more on a page and going through several pages. Sometimes, it might mean that, this specific link is performing well since users may spend a lot of time without taking action. So, as a result, among other performance metrics, website owners need to measure bounce alongside other performance indicators to come up with an overall effectiveness measure for their website.
- **Time on site:** This measures the average duration a visitor spends during one internet browsing session. Site owners should use it as it guides them when finding out how long people stay at their sites and whether they are interested in what is in them. If someone spends a lot of time reading through this content, they will find much value, engagement, and relevance in such information, thus improving their rankings on their engines because there will be more daily visits. On the other hand, if someone takes a short time while on your website, it could mean they did not find what they were looking for, affecting the return rate (RR), conversion rate (CR), and income generation. Therefore, time on site is a very important parameter that website owners must keep track of because when increased, it gradually leads to higher user engagement levels and, consequently, expansion in business operations.
- **Click-through rate (CTR):** This refers to the number of users who click on a specific link or icon. CTR is considered one of the most critical metrics in digital marketing and advertising, especially concerning paid search campaigns. It shows how much attention a campaign or advertisement can draw to bring prospective clients to one's site. A high CTR will mean many people have followed the ad or link to land on this page, showing they are relevant audiences for such campaigns and indicating excellent interactivity levels among them. On the other hand, if CTR is low, the intended viewers probably found them less attractive than expected or did not match what was promised by using these concepts. Consequently, it is necessary to keep track of CTRs at all times for effectiveness checking purposes since adjustments may need to be made to improve engagement, increasing traffic volumes towards websites. Business people and internet marketers find this index very helpful in determining their online advertisements' success and measuring the overall efficiency of the websites involved.
- **Error rate:** Error rate is a vital metric for measuring the number of mistakes users make while using a product or service. It involves many types of errors, such as broken links, error messages, application crashes, and other problems related to usability. The high error rate can negatively impact the user experience, leading to irritation, and eventually, the user may give up. Recognizing and studying these rates will help businesses identify problems and prioritize improvements that can increase user engagement and satisfaction. For instance, monitoring error rates in A/B tests enables one to find the most effective user interface designs, thereby optimizing them. Similarly, after making changes to your website or app, you need to keep an

eye on its error rate so as not only to get an insight into what users feel about such modifications but also to give room for future updates based on their responses. Products should be frequently checked by organizations, offering them the opportunity to slash these figures, integrate feedback from clients, and make sure that they prioritize the user's experience, which will lead to more loyalty, among other things. This will make them easy to use, decrease mistakes, and increase customer interaction and affection.

8.4 Future Trends in UX Analysis

Technological advancements are constantly changing how we interact with different products and services. As a result, UX analysis must be able to adjust to fit into the changed environment.

8.4.1 Voice-driven UX Analysis

It is one way to find out what people think of voice-driven applications. We can achieve this by looking at how users interact with the app – for example, what parts of it they talk to, if any, and whether their commands are clear enough. That way, you can see which part should be improved or developed further, and also learn more about general interactions. For example, the voice UX analysis could show that a person had trouble understanding an instruction or moving from one place to another in the interface.

Another area where voice UX analysis has potential is in enhancing the overall usability of these types of apps. For instance, it could reveal places where the interface needs some work, like making things easier/more transparent for users and increasing functionality in different areas. Alternatively, it might also highlight opportunities to create more engaging experiences through personalized feedback systems.

Besides, examining voice-driven applications' user experience through a comprehensive approach will ultimately lead to enhancements across various fronts. The analysis might not only point out ways to improve our UI design – making it more user-friendly by simplifying processes or integrating additional tools – but also suggest certain features that have not been included yet.

8.4.2 Contextual UX Analysis

Contextual UX analysis looks at the environment in which a user interacts with a product or service to understand their experience. This form of analysis involves studying the customer's surroundings, their goals, and those of this system itself. For example, one cannot reply to messages or emails without knowing who sent them originally; therefore, a personal name should be used each time somebody communicates so that their identity can be verified easily, showing touchpoints between different things within the user experience.

Moreover, contextual UX analysis can help determine a person's goals and motivations when using a particular website or application. For instance, when a customer is looking for information about where to buy coffee makers, he/she probably wants to find out which one best suit his/her needs. Knowing this will enable us to select the products that meet his expectations, thus improving customer satisfaction levels through our online platforms.

It may also be used to investigate the user's environment around them. To improve their mobile UX, designers must consider people's conditions while in transit during peak hours. By doing so, these experts can build interfaces that work across different devices, which will give rise to high-quality performance and excellent user experiences under harsh environmental conditions.

8.4.3 Augmented Reality-driven UX Analysis

Augmented reality (AR) has gained popularity in recent years as it can transform how we interact with our surroundings. AR-driven UX analysis refers to using AR to analyze user experience to improve a product or service's usability.

By utilizing AR, businesses can observe how users interact with a product or service in real time and understand user behavior better. Thus organizations can gain insight into what happens during customer interaction with their products/services, thereby enabling them to know the areas in which they need to improve. In addition, this helps them develop related changes to enhance clients' satisfaction levels.

This method can also offer enterprises valuable information that may be used in future development of goods and services.

The retail sector is one where this analysis would be most beneficial. By implementing AR, retailers can observe how their customers interact with products while still at the store, thus giving them an opportunity to understand consumer behavior towards those items. This will help them identify areas requiring improvement and make necessary adjustments for a better customer experience.

Using AR, medical professionals can see how patients interact with their services and understand how they use them. This enables them to identify certain areas for improvement where they can make changes to enhance the patient's experience. For example, a healthcare provider could use AR to visualize patient interactions with a given service and highlight areas of improvement, such as patient flow and waiting times, among others.

8.4.4 Wearable UX Evaluation

Wearable UX analysis appraises the value and user experience of a wearable device. It is fundamental to developing products that meet users' needs correctly.

The initial step in wearable UX analysis is to identify the user's needs and objectives, including understanding users' lifestyles, the environment they live or work in, and their activities. Also required is knowledge of what features potential customers prefer and the desired expectations for such devices. Various methods can be used to acquire this information, including interviews with people using similar products and surveys.

After identifying the user's needs and objectives, the gadget's usability is assessed. This involves examining how well the design, features, and user interface function. At the same time, this process ascertains other areas where effectiveness could be realized, that is, battery life and connectivity responsiveness, depending on the requirements set by different user groups.

8.4.5 Mobile-first UX Research

Mobile devices are becoming increasingly essential to consumers and businesses in the digital age. Therefore, companies must design their websites and applications with a mobile-first mentality. This means the user experience should be optimized for mobile devices before anything else. Thus, mobile-first UX analysis examines a website or application to ensure it is mobile-optimized.

The first step is evaluating the user interface (UI). This entails looking at icons' sizes and positions, menu locations, and other components; all these should be easily accessible without many struggles from the user side since they need to navigate through them. In addition, UIs should have responsive layouts to adjust to different screen sizes.

The next step involves evaluating the UX. In this case, we check how easy or difficult users find in accomplishing tasks on our site. We also consider the sensitive factor of interfaces during applications' working period, loading times for websites or apps, because if more time is taken, then people might get bored waiting for too long, hence ultimately leaving before seeing anything useful.

Third comes content evaluation, which includes checking the quality standards, such as readability level such as accessibility details. In mobile device optimization, where plain and short materials work best, images and videos also should not be left behind since they must suit these gadgets, too.

Lastly, there is a performance review, whereby loading times and overall performance (speed) of sites or apps are analysed thoroughly.

8.4.6 Cross-platform UX Research

When several platforms are available, it is important to ensure that users have the best experience with a product or service. This is called cross-platform UX analysis. The process involves testing how well products or services work on different devices, operating systems, and browsers. For businesses that want their goods to be used everywhere, this is a must.

To perform practical cross-platform UX analyses, one should take into account elements such as:

- **User interface:** Evaluation should include layout navigation systems, among other things. Usability is about how easily users can perform different tasks using your products or services on different platforms. Consideration should be given to the fact that people experience the same product differently when they use other devices with various operating systems and browsers.
- **Performance:** This involves checking loading time across devices with varied screen sizes. It also entails evaluating product or service responsiveness and general effectiveness on different platforms.
- **Accessibility:** For example, if someone has a disability, they may need special software or hardware devices that must be compatible with specific applications. This means such apps must be designed to enable all users to access them irrespective of their abilities or disabilities.
- **Safety**: Look at the safety of the users on different systems. This means seeing what precautions are taken to protect users' details and stop harmful programs from causing harm.

8.4.7 Forecasting UX Analysis

UX design utilizes data and analytics to predict user needs and behaviors. By understanding or empathizing with user behavior and preferences, designers can create more intuitive and compelling user experiences. This analysis is used to determine user requirements, preferences, and behaviors to improve the user experience.

The first step of predictive UX analysis is the acquisition of data. This information can originate from various sources, including user surveys, interviews, and analytics. This information is then analyzed to determine user requirements, preferences, and conduct.

Utilizing machine learning algorithms to predict user behavior is one example of predictive UX analysis. One can analyze user data and identify behavioral patterns. By grasping these patterns, designers can create user experiences that are more intuitive and effective. For instance, a machine learning algorithm can predict which features a user is likely to utilize and which they are likely to disregard.

Utilizing sentiment analysis is another example of predictive UX analysis. Sentiment analysis is a form of natural language processing (NLP) that analyses user comments and feedback through algorithms. By comprehending user sentiment, designers can create more compelling and intuitive user experiences. For instance, a sentiment analysis algorithm can determine how a user feels about a specific feature or product.

Lastly, predictive UX analysis can be utilized to determine user preferences. Designers can create more intuitive and compelling user experiences by understanding user preferences. For instance, a predictive UX analysis algorithm can be used to determine which features users prefer and which they are likely to disregard.

Overall, predictive UX analysis is an effective method for designing more intuitive and efficient user experiences.

8.4.8 Gamification-driven User Experience Analysis

This is essential for comprehending the user experience and enhancing user engagement. Gamification-driven UX analysis seeks to identify and address user pain points, create a more pleasant user experience, and boost user engagement.

It is essential to first comprehend the concept of gamification. Gamification is using game elements, such as points, rewards, and leaderboards, to encourage user participation in a product or service. Incorporating game elements into a product or service increases the likelihood that users will be engaged and complete tasks or objectives.

Once the concept of gamification is understood, UX analysts can begin analyzing user behavior and product interactions. This analysis can be conducted using questionnaires, interviews, and data analysis. Interviews can provide valuable insights into user behavior, while data analysis can assist in identifying opportunities for improvement.

Once the analysis is complete, UX analysts can use the insights to create a more engaging experience. For example, adding game elements, such as points and rewards, can help increase user engagement. In addition, UX analysts can use these insights to enhance the user experience by addressing user pain points and making the product or service more straightforward.

Lastly, UX analysts can use gamification-driven UX analysis to evaluate the success of their modifications. UX analysts can determine whether their modifications have improved the user experience by monitoring user engagement.

8.5 Real-life Case Studies in UX Analysis

Real-world case studies shed light on how UX analysis can enhance user satisfaction and, ultimately, business success.

One such case study is redesigning the National Health Service (NHS) website in the United Kingdom. The NHS is an extensive organization with a difficult-to-use website that can intimidate users. The redesign aimed to simplify the site's navigation and make it easier for users to locate the desired information. The result was a more user-friendly website that received positive feedback from patients and healthcare professionals.

The redesign of the Lyft mobile application is another illustration. Lyft wanted to enhance the user experience for drivers, who frequently expressed frustration with the app's navigation. Through UX analysis, the team identified the primary pain points and refined the application interface. This resulted in enhanced driver satisfaction and retention rates.

The redesign of apparel retailer ASOS's e-commerce website constitutes the third case study. The company wanted to increase revenues by enhancing the website's user experience. The team determined through UX analysis that users needed help locating and purchasing their desired products. The redesign aimed to simplify the purchasing experience and make it less complicated for users to complete transactions. This led to a substantial rise in the company's sales.

These case studies illustrate the effectiveness of UX analysis in enhancing user satisfaction and, by extension, business success. By understanding how users interact with a product or service, businesses can identify areas for enhancement and implement modifications to increase customer satisfaction and loyalty. As the world becomes increasingly digital, UX analysis will become crucial for businesses seeking to remain competitive.

Summary

- User experience analysis evaluates user interactions with a product or service, identifying enhancement opportunities.
- A killer UX design is the art and science of creating digital products with an exceptional user experience. Itincludes intuitive navigation, user-friendly interfaces, and engaging content.
- Usability testing is a crucial component of effective UX design, observing user interactions and gathering feedback.
- Accessibility is a crucial component of a winning UX design, including designing interfaces that can be accessed with assistive technology and providing alternative text for images and videos.
- Work activity affinity diagram (WAAD) is a valuable tool for organizing and understanding various tasks and activities in a given work process.
- Usage models and work environment models are essential tools for developing software that meets the user's needs.
- User research methods involve gathering user insights and feedback is crucial to the design thinking process.
- A user journey map depicts a user's interactions with a product or service, identifying pain points, improvement opportunities, and the user's emotions and motivations at each stage.
- A user experience dashboard provides an overview of the user experience, including page load times, return rates, and conversion rates.
- User engagement, conversion rate, customer satisfaction, usability, retention rate, task completion rate, bounce rate, time on site, click-through rate (CTR), error rate are critical UX analysis metrics.
- UX analysis facilitates teamwork and collaboration, reducing development risks.
- User-centered design involves accumulating user insights and feedback to understand user preferences and needs.
- AI tools can identify patterns and trends from large amounts of data, save costs on data collection and analysis, and enhance user experience. Personalization and speech recognition capabilities are enhancing user experience.
- Accurately capturing user behavior and attitudes is a significant challenge in UX research and analysis. External factors such as environment, device type, and context can affect user behavior and attitudes. The volume of data collected can be overwhelming, making it difficult to quantify and analyze.
- Future trends include voice-driven UX analysis, contextual UX analysis, augmented reality-driven UX analysis, wearable UX evaluation, mobile-first UX research, cross-platform UX research, and gamification-driven UX analysis.

Solutions to Design Visualization Questions

Q 8.1

Student Project: Killer UX Design

Solution:

- The student will research the concept of killer UX design and its components, including intuitive navigation, user-friendly interfaces, and engaging content.
- The student will choose a product or service and analyze its current UX design, identifying areas for improvement.
- The student will create a new killer UX design for the chosen product or service, incorporating the components of killer UX design to improve the user experience.
- The student will present their new design to the class, explaining how it improves the user experience by making it more visually appealing, aesthetically pleasing, and functional.

Q 8.2

Student Project: Understanding User Models

Solution:

- The student will research the concept of user models and their components, including user knowledge, behavior, and preferences.
- The student will choose a software product and analyze its current user model, identifying areas for improvement.
- The student will create a new user model for the chosen software product, incorporating the components of user models to improve the user experience.
- The student will present their new user model to the class, explaining how it improves the user experience by making it more intuitive and user-friendly.

Q 8.3

Student Project: Understanding Usage Models

Solution:

- The student will research the concept of usage models and their components, including user behavior patterns and future user interactions.
- The student will choose a software product and analyze its current usage model, identifying areas for improvement.
- The student will create a new usage model for the chosen software product, incorporating the components of usage models to improve the user experience.
- The student will present their new usage model to the class, explaining how it improves the user experience by making it more intuitive and user-friendly.

Q 8.4

Assignment: User Experience Detective

Research

- **Surveys:** Design a short online survey with questions about user habits, preferences, and frustrations related to the chosen product/service.

- **Interviews:** Conduct brief interviews with 5–7 users, asking open-ended questions to delve deeper into their experiences.

Analysis

- Organize survey responses and interview notes. Identify recurring themes and categorize them as user needs, goals, pain points, and frustrations.
- Look for patterns and commonalities in user feedback.

User Persona

- Based on your research, create a user persona with a name, age, occupation, and a brief bio.
- Include their goals, motivations, and tech-savviness when using the product/service.
- Highlight their biggest pain points and frustrations.

User Scenario

- Craft a story that describes your user persona interacting with the product/service.
- Include details like the context (lunchtime at the library), the user's specific goals (finding a research paper), and the steps they take within the product/service.
- Describe any challenges they encounter and how they feel during the interaction.

Bonus: Wireframe

- Sketch a basic wireframe of the product/service interface.
- Focus on the key elements users interact with to achieve their goals.
- Use this wireframe to illustrate potential improvements based on user research, like clearer navigation or more prominent search bars.

Exercises

Part A (Objective Questions)

1. What is the main objective of a killer UX design?
   (a) To provide users with a frustrating experience.
   (b) To design a product that meets users' needs straightforwardly and intuitively.
   (c) To create a product that is difficult to navigate.
   (d) To make a product that is aesthetically displeasing.
2. What is the importance of considering the user's context, behavior, and preferences in UX design?
   (a) It's not important to consider the user's context, behavior, and preferences in UX design.
   (b) It ensures the product meets the user's requirements and expectations.
   (c) It makes the product more difficult to use.
   (d) It provides an inferior user experience.
3. What are some components of a killer UX design?
   (a) Confusing navigation and interfaces.
   (b) Visually displeasing design.
   (c) Intuitive navigation, user-friendly interfaces, and engaging design.
   (d) None of the above.
4. Why is it important for a killer UX design to be visually appealing and aesthetically pleasing?
   (a) It is not important for a killer UX design to be visually appealing and aesthetically pleasing.
   (b) It helps the user navigate the product more easily.
   (c) It provides a superior user experience.
   (d) It makes the product more difficult to use.

5. What is the overall goal of a killer UX design?
   (a) To make a product that is difficult to use.
   (b) To create a visually unappealing product.
   (c) To provide users with a positive and seamless experience.
   (d) To create a product that does not meet users' needs.
6. What is usability testing in UX design?
   (a) Testing the functionality of a product
   (b) Observing users' interactions with a digital product
   (c) Checking the aesthetics of a design
   (d) Evaluating the marketing strategy of a product
7. Why is usability testing important in UX design?
   (a) To check the product's aesthetics
   (b) To evaluate the marketing strategy
   (c) To identify areas for enhancement
   (d) To test the functionality of the product
8. Who should be involved in usability testing?
   (a) Only the UX designer (b) Only the developer
   (c) The UX designer and the developer (d) Users of the digital product
9. What is the purpose of gathering user feedback in usability testing?
   (a) To identify areas for enhancement
   (b) To check the product's aesthetics
   (c) To evaluate the marketing strategy
   (d) To test the functionality of the product
10. How can usability testing improve UX design?
   (a) By testing the functionality of the product
   (b) By observing users' interactions with the product
   (c) By evaluating the marketing strategy
   (d) By testing the aesthetics of the design
11. What is the purpose of designing interfaces that can be navigated easily with assistive technology?
   (a) To improve website traffic
   (b) To make the website more visually appealing
   (c) To ensure the website is accessible to users with disabilities
   (d) None of the above
12. Why is it necessary to provide alternative text for images and videos?
   (a) To make the website more visually appealing
   (b) To improve website traffic
   (c) To ensure the website is accessible to users with disabilities
   (d) None of the above
13. Who benefits from designing interfaces that can be navigated easily with assistive technology?
   (a) Only users with disabilities (b) Only users without disabilities
   (c) Both users with and without disabilities (d) None of the above
14. What is the consequence of not making a digital product accessible to users with disabilities?
   (a) No consequence (b) Legal repercussions
   (c) Decreased website traffic (d) None of the above
15. What is the main purpose of designing a product that is accessible to all users?
   (a) To improve website traffic (b) To increase revenue
   (c) To provide equal access to digital products (d) None of the above
16. What is the primary purpose of creating a work activity affinity diagram (WAAD)?
   (a) To identify potential customers

(b) To organize and comprehend various duties and activities involved in a given work process
(c) To create a prototype
(d) To conduct usability testing

17. Who should be included in the team for creating a WAAD?
    (a) Only members from the same department
    (b) Members from various departments or fields of expertise
    (c) Only members from upper management
    (d) Only members who are already familiar with the work process
18. What is the first step in creating a WAAD?
    (a) Designing the final product
    (b) Assembling a team of individuals conversing with the in-question work process
    (c) Conducting market research
    (d) Creating a user persona
19. What is the benefit of having a team with diverse perspectives for creating a WAAD?
    (a) It allows for a quicker completion of the process
    (b) It eliminates the need for usability testing
    (c) It ensures that all team members have the same background knowledge
    (d) It offers different viewpoints and insights into the work process
20. Which of the following is NOT a benefit of creating a WAAD?
    (a) Organizing and comprehending various duties and activities involved in a given work process
    (b) Identifying potential customers
    (c) Finding opportunities for improvement in the work process
    (d) Providing a visual representation of the work process
21. What are usage models used for?
    (a) Identifying user behavior patterns and adjusting software
    (b) Characterizing the software usage context
    (c) Creating software optimized for the user's needs
    (d) All of the above
22. What do work environment models consider?
    (a) User behavior and preferences
    (b) Factors such as lighting and pollution
    (c) Software context of use
    (d) All of the above
23. What are user models used for?
    (a) Identifying user behavior patterns and adjusting software
    (b) Characterizing the software usage context
    (c) Creating software optimized for the user's needs
    (d) All of the above
24. Why are usage models important in software development?
    (a) They help developers predict future user interactions with software
    (b) They help developers identify user behavior patterns and adjust software accordingly
    (c) They help developers consider the user's knowledge, behavior, and preferences
    (d) None of the above
25. What do work environment models assist software designers in doing?
    (a) Creating software that is optimized for the user's needs
    (b) Identifying user behavior patterns and adjusting software
    (c) Predicting future user interactions with software
    (d) None of the above

26. What is the purpose of user experience analysis?
    (a) To identify the user's requirements, obstacles, and expectations.
    (b) To create a product that meets the business's requirements.
    (c) To market the product to potential users.
    (d) To assess the product's financial success.
27. What are the stages involved in user experience analysis?
    (a) Ideation, Prototype, Testing
    (b) Research, Analysis, Design, Testing
    (c) Conceptualization, Implementation, Launch
    (d) None of the above.
28. What is the benefit of conducting user experience analysis?
    (a) To create a product that satisfies the business's requirements.
    (b) To gain insight into how users interact with the product.
    (c) To reduce costs associated with product development.
    (d) To improve the product's search engine optimization.
29. Why is user experience analysis important for businesses?
    (a) To gain insight into user behavior.
    (b) To increase sales and revenue.
    (c) To reduce costs associated with product development.
    (d) To create a product that meets the business's requirements.
30. What is the ultimate goal of user experience analysis?
    (a) To create a product that is aesthetically pleasing.
    (b) To create a product that is easy to use.
    (c) To create a product that satisfies the user's requirements and expectations.
    (d) To create a product that is profitable.
31. What is a common objection to UX research?
    (a) It is too simple.
    (b) It is unnecessary.
    (c) It is too complex.
    (d) None of the above.
32. What is a typical objection to UX research?
    (a) It is cost-effective. (b) It is time-consuming.
    (c) It is simple. (d) None of the above.
33. What is one of the arguments against UX research?
    (a) It is too complex. (b) It is too simple.
    (c) Designers already know what consumers want. (d) None of the above.
34. What is a common misconception about UX research?
    (a) It is too complex to conduct. (b) It is cost-effective.
    (c) It is unnecessary. (d) None of the above.
35. What is a typical criticism of UX research?
    (a) It is too easy. (b) It is too complicated.
    (c) It is too expensive. (d) None of the above.
36. What is the purpose of creating a user journey map?
    (a) To identify the user's emotions and motivations.
    (b) To define the user persona.
    (c) To depict the user's interactions with a product or service.
    (d) To map out the post-purchase experience.

37. What is the first step in creating a user journey map?
(a) Identifying touchpoints.
(b) Mapping out the post-purchase experience.
(c) Defining the user persona.
(d) Identifying pain points.

38. What touchpoints should be included in a user journey map?
(a) Website visits.
(b) Social media interactions.
(c) Email communications.
(d) All of the above.

39. What is the purpose of identifying pain points in a user journey map?
(a) To define the user persona.
(b) To identify the user's emotions and motivations.
(c) To map out the post-purchase experience.
(d) To identify improvement opportunities.

40. What is the final stage of a user journey map?
(a) Identifying touchpoints.
(b) Mapping out the post-purchase experience.
(c) Defining the user persona.
(d) Depicting the user's emotions and motivations.

41. Which metric measures the percentage of website visitors who leave after visiting only one page?
(a) Bounce rate
(b) Conversion rate
(c) Usability
(d) Time on site

42. Which metric measures the percentage of users who complete a specific task on your website or application?
(a) Retention rate
(b) Task completion rate
(c) Error rate
(d) Click-through rate

43. Which metric measures how long users stay on your website or application?
(a) Bounce rate
(b) Conversion rate
(c) Time on site
(d) Click-through rate

44. Which metric measures the number of users who return to your website or application over a given period?
(a) Retention rate
(b) Task completion rate
(c) Error rate
(d) Click-through rate

45. Which metric measures how many times users click on a specific link or call to action?
(a) Bounce rate
(b) Conversion rate
(c) Click-through rate
(d) Time on site

46. Which metric measures the percentage of users who remain on a website or app after initially arriving?
(a) Bounce rate
(b) Time on site
(c) Task completion rate
(d) Conversion rate

47. Which metric measures the percentage of users who successfully complete a task or goal on a website or app?
(a) Usability
(b) Conversion rate
(c) Customer satisfaction
(d) Click-through rate

48. What is the primary goal of user-centered design?
(a) To create products that solve actual problems for users.
(b) To create products that are visually appealing.
(c) To create products that are cheap to produce.
(d) To create products that are trendy and fashionable.

49. Which approach emphasizes the establishment of a continuous feedback loop between consumers and developers?
(a) User-centered design
(b) Agile software development
(c) Both A and B
(d) None of the above
50. What is the main benefit of using AI-powered tools in user experience analysis?
(a) They can identify patterns and trends from large amounts of data
(b) They can replace human researchers entirely
(c) They can only collect data, not analyze it
(d) They are not useful for improving the user experience
51. What is a potential benefit of using AI-powered tools in user research?
(a) They can only collect data, not analyze it
(b) They can replace human researchers entirely
(c) They can analyze vast amounts of data more efficiently
(d) They are not useful for improving the user experience
52. What is a powerful application of AI in enhancing the user experience?
(a) Automating the data collection process
(b) Using speech recognition to interact with devices
(c) Replacing human researchers with AI-powered tools
(d) Collecting and analyzing large amounts of data
53. How can AI-powered tools help businesses save costs on data collection and analysis?
(a) By making data collection and analysis more time-consuming
(b) By replacing human researchers with AI-powered tools
(c) By automating the data collection and analysis process
(d) By requiring more resources than manual data collection and analysis
54. What is another way in which AI is being used to enhance the user experience?
(a) By replacing user researchers with AI-powered tools
(b) By analyzing data more efficiently than human researchers
(c) By allowing users to interact with systems through gestures or pointing
(d) By automating the data collection process
55. What is one of the significant challenges in UX research and analysis?
(a) Finding enough participants for the study
(b) Collecting quantitative data
(c) Capturing user behavior and attitudes accurately
(d) Conducting research in a controlled environment
56. What is one factor that can affect user behavior and attitudes in UX research?
(a) The researcher's qualifications
(b) The type of device used
(c) The number of participants in the study
(d) The length of the study
57. What type of data is frequently collected during UX research?
(a) Quantitative data
(b) Qualitative data
(c) Demographic data
(d) Observational data
58. What is one challenge in evaluating efficacy with non-native speakers of a language in UX research?
(a) Finding participants for the study
(b) Collecting quantitative data
(c) Communicating with the participants
(d) Conducting the study in a controlled environment

59. What is one challenge in making sense of the data collected during UX research?
    (a) Collecting enough data
    (b) Finding patterns in the data
    (c) Quantifying the data
    (d) Conducting the research in a controlled environment
60. What is a best practice for UX research?
    (a) Clearly defining research objectives and goals
    (b) Using closed-ended questions during research sessions
    (c) Limiting research participants to a single demographic
    (d) Rushing the research process to save time
61. What is an example of a future trend in UX analysis?
    (a) Focus groups
    (b) Mobile-first UX research
    (c) Paper surveys
    (d) Telephone interviews
62. What is an industry best practice for recruiting research participants?
    (a) Recruiting only individuals with high incomes
    (b) Recruiting only individuals with a certain level of education
    (c) Recruiting representative and diverse research participants
    (d) Recruiting only individuals who are familiar with the product or service
63. What is an example of a challenge in UX research and analysis?
    (a) Clearly defining research objectives and goals
    (b) Validating research findings through triangulation
    (c) Quantifying qualitative data
    (d) Recruiting representative and diverse research participants
64. What is an example of a future trend in UX analysis?
    (a) Telephone interviews
    (b) Wearable UX evaluation
    (c) Paper surveys
    (d) Focus groups
65. What is an industry best practice for obtaining consent from research participants?
    (a) Providing incomplete information about the research study
    (b) Obtaining consent after the research session has already begun
    (c) Obtaining informed consent from research participants
    (d) Skipping the consent process altogether
66. What is an example of a challenge in UX research and analysis?
    (a) Using open-ended and neutral questions during research sessions
    (b) Conducting research in a comfortable and non-threatening environment
    (c) Limiting researcher bias through a rigorous and systematic data analysis process
    (d) Assuring that the collected data effectively reflect user behavior and attitudes
67. What is an industry best practice for selecting appropriate research methodologies?
    (a) Choosing the methodology that is quickest and easiest to implement
    (b) Choosing the methodology that is most popular among other companies
    (c) Choosing the methodology that addresses the research objectives
    (d) Choosing the methodology that is most affordable
68. What is an example of a future trend in UX analysis?
    (a) Paper surveys
    (b) Voice-driven UX analysis
    (c) Telephone interviews
    (d) Focus groups
69. What is an industry best practice for conducting research sessions?
    (a) Using closed-ended questions during research sessions
    (b) Conducting research in a threatening environment
    (c) Using open-ended and neutral questions during research sessions
    (d) Conducting research without proper planning or preparation

70. What is the primary goal of using open-ended and neutral questions during research sessions?
    (a) To validate research findings through triangulation
    (b) To limit researcher bias
    (c) To obtain informed consent from research participants
    (d) To allow research participants to share their opinions and thoughts freely
71. What is the best way to limit researcher bias during UX research?
    (a) Conducting research in a comfortable and non-threatening environment
    (b) Using open-ended and neutral questions during research sessions
    (c) Validating research findings through triangulation
    (d) Following a rigorous and systematic data analysis process
72. What is the importance of recruiting representative and diverse research participants in UX research?
    (a) To limit researcher bias
    (b) To obtain informed consent from research participants
    (c) To ensure the research findings are applicable to the target audience
    (d) To conduct research in a comfortable and non-threatening environment
73. Which of the following is an example of a future trend in UX analysis?
    (a) Using open-ended and neutral questions during research sessions
    (b) Conducting research in a comfortable and non-threatening environment
    (c) Augmented Reality-driven User Experience Analysis
    (d) Validating research findings through triangulation
74. What is the primary goal of conducting UX research in a comfortable and non-threatening environment?
    (a) To limit researcher bias
    (b) To obtain informed consent from research participants
    (c) To validate research findings through triangulation
    (d) To ensure research participants feel at ease and are more likely to share their thoughts and opinions freely

Part B (Short Answer Questions)

1. What is user experience analysis?
2. What is design thinking?
3. What is the importance of combining design thinking and user experience?
4. What is a killer UX design?
5. What are the components of killer UX design?
6. Why is usability testing important in UX design?
7. Why is accessibility an important component of UX design?
8. What is a work activity affinity diagram (WAAD)?
9. What are usage models used for?
10. What are work environment models used for?
11. Why are user models, usage models, and work environment models essential for developing software?
12. Why is user research crucial in the design thinking process?
13. What are some common objections to UX research?
14. What is a user journey map?
15. What is a user persona?
16. What should a user journey map include?

17. Why is creating a dashboard for the user experience important?
18. What are some key metrics for user experience analysis?
19. Why is creating aesthetically pleasing and straightforward products important?
20. What is a user journey map and why is it important in creating a successful user experience?
21. What is a work activity affinity diagram (WAAD) and how is it useful in designing a work process?
22. What are some common objections to UX research and how can they be addressed?
23. Why is accessibility a crucial component of a winning UX design?
24. What are key metrics for user experience analysis and why are they important in optimizing user engagement and satisfaction?

Part C (Essay Questions)

1. Write an essay on killer UX design.
2. Write an essay on user models, usage models and work environment models.
3. How can we prioritize usability problems?
4. How can we deal with common objections to UX research?
5. What are the key metrics for user experience analysis?
6. Write an essay on the impact of artificial intelligence on user experience analysis.
7. What are the challenges in UX research and analysis?
8. Write an essay on contextual UX analysis.
9. Write an essay on augmented reality-driven user experience analysis.
10. Explain mobile-first UX research in detail.
11. Explain gamification-driven user experience analysis in detail.
12. List various industry best practices for UX research.

Answer Key

Part A

1. (b)	**2.** (b)	**3.** (c)	**4.** (c)	**5.** (c)	**6.** (b)	**7.** (c)	**8.** (d)	**9.** (a)	**10.** (b)
11. (c)	**12.** (c)	**13.** (c)	**14.** (b)	**15.** (c)	**16.** (b)	**17.** (b)	**18.** (b)	**19.** (d)	**20.** (b)
21. (a)	**22.** (b)	**23.** (c)	**24.** (b)	**25.** (a)	**26.** (a)	**27.** (b)	**28.** (b)	**29.** (a)	**30.** (c)
31. (b)	**32.** (b)	**33.** (c)	**34.** (c)	**35.** (c)	**36.** (c)	**37.** (c)	**38.** (d)	**39.** (d)	**40.** (b)
41. (a)	**42.** (b)	**43.** (c)	**44.** (a)	**45.** (c)	**46.** (a)	**47.** (b)	**48.** (a)	**49.** (c)	**50.** (a)
51. (c)	**52.** (b)	**53.** (c)	**54.** (c)	**55.** (c)	**56.** (b)	**57.** (b)	**58.** (c)	**59.** (b)	**60.** (a)
61. (b)	**62.** (c)	**63.** (c)	**64.** (b)	**65.** (c)	**66.** (d)	**67.** (c)	**68.** (b)	**69.** (c)	**70.** (d)
71. (d)	**72.** (c)	**73.** (c)	**74.** (d)						

CHAPTER 9

Integrating Design Thinking With Other Disciplines

Learning Objectives

At the end of this chapter, you will be able to:

- Explain how design thinking can be leveraged to develop innovative business models and strategies
- Describe the impact of design thinking on business performance and operations
- List the ways in which design thinking and technology intersect to foster innovation
- Describe the methods for integrating design thinking into educational curricula
- List the strategies for utilizing design thinking to address and solve educational challenges
- Explain the applications of design thinking principles in the healthcare industry
- Explain the role of design thinking in creating significant social impact
- List the techniques for applying design thinking to social innovation
- Explain the approaches for implementing design thinking in non-profit and social impact organizations
- Describe the use of design thinking in the process of constructing buildings and in architectural design

9.1 Introduction

Design thinking is a method of problem-solving focused on people's needs. It is an approach that employs imagination and empathy to resolve challenging issues. Design thinking has gained popularity in recent times because businesses use it to innovate and spur growth. However, cross-disciplinary cooperation is crucial for design thinking to be successful (Fig. 9.1).

Collaboration leads to diverse perspectives: Design thinking values cross-disciplinary collaboration because it fosters a diversity of viewpoints. When professionals from many fields collaborate, they each contribute their unique talents and experiences. A product designer, for instance, might view a problem from a different angle than a social scientist or a biologist. Combining these viewpoints can result in more original and creative solutions.

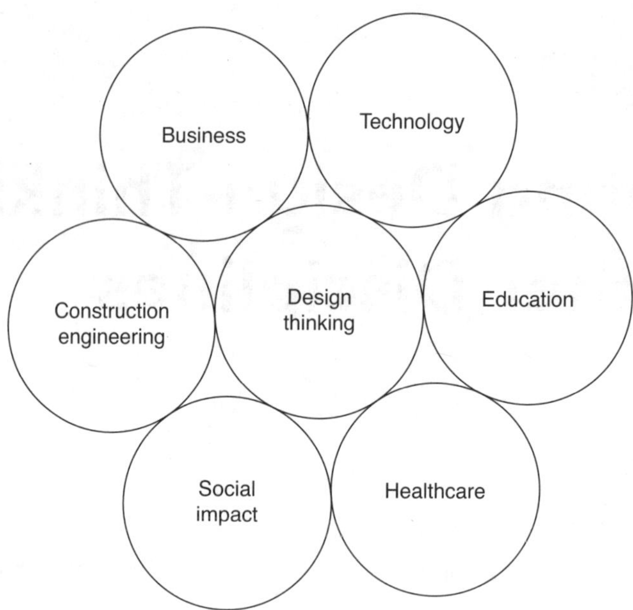

Figure 9.1 Design thinking interaction with other disciplines

The creation of the Nike Flyknit sneaker is an instance of cross-disciplinary cooperation. Nike gathered scientists, engineers, and designers to produce an innovative and sustainable sneaker. The outcome was a shoe that was more robust and utilized less material, making it economical and environmentally beneficial.

Collaboration leads to a deeper understanding of user needs: Collaboration across disciplines is crucial to design thinking because it helps us understand consumer demands better. Moreover, cross-disciplinary cooperation may ensure that the user's demands are thoroughly understood and met because design thinking is user-centered. For instance, a team of designers, engineers, and healthcare specialists can work together to make sure a medical device not only functions well but is also user-friendly and fits patient demands.

The creation of the Embrace newborn warmer is an instance of this. The team worked together to develop a device to keep preterm babies warm and lower infant death rates in underdeveloped nations. The team included designers, engineers, and healthcare specialists. The result was a tool that was not only reliable but also inexpensive and simple to use.

Collaboration leads to more effective problem-solving: When experts from several fields work together, they combine various techniques and tools to address an issue. For instance, a group of designers, engineers, and business experts can work together to identify a problem, develop solutions, and then market those answers.

The creation of the Tesla Model S is an illustration of this. The Tesla team, made up of designers, engineers, and business experts, worked together to produce a car that was not only electric but also powerful. The team employed cutting-edge engineering methods to produce a vehicle that could travel large distances on a single charge. In addition, the designers used their imagination to produce an eye-catching vehicle. The result was a car that became popular and altered how people perceive electric cars.

9.2 Design Thinking and Business

As businesses strive to differentiate themselves and foster innovation within competitive markets, the design thinking approach has gained traction as a key strategy. It is increasingly being adopted by organizations seeking to develop solutions that resonate with their target audience and deliver meaningful value. This user-centric philosophy is instrumental in driving the creation of products and services that not only meet but exceed customer expectations (Fig. 9.2).

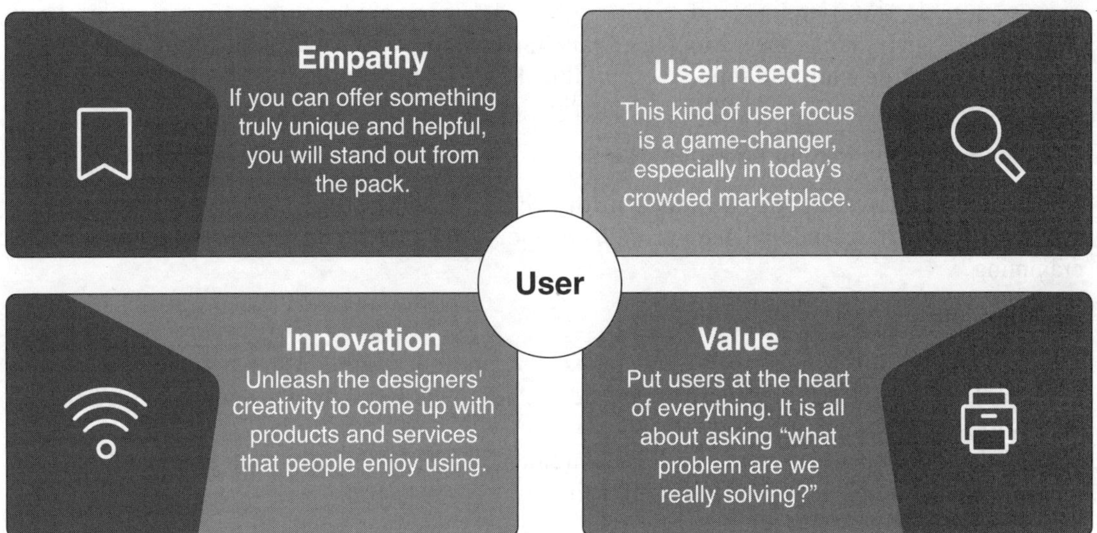

Figure 9.2 Design thinking and business

Design thinking encourages innovation: Design thinking enables businesses to unleash their creativity and come up with products and services that people will find attractive. For example, Airbnb used design thinking to first understand what travellers were looking for: a comfortable place to stay, a local experience, and a way to connect with new people. So, they built a platform that catered to those needs, offering an alternative to traditional hotels. This focus on the user experience made Airbnb a billion-dollar success story.

Design thinking leads to better customer experiences: By understanding the customer's needs and frustrations, businesses can design products and services that fit seamlessly into their lives.

Flipkart, India's e-commerce giant, started on a captivating journey to remodel its website and mobile app interfaces, giving users a shopping experience that is not only user-friendly but also inspiring. They have made the navigation easier, redesigned the check-out to be more intuitive, and developed a more responsive design that can adjust to various screen sizes and devices. This single-minded concentration on user experience has not only enabled Flipkart to maintain a large portion of the market in the highly competed Indian e-commerce industry, but it has also become a standard for others to imitate.

Design thinking can improve problem-solving: Finally, design thinking can enhance organization problem-solving. Companies can create solutions that address real-world issues in novel and creative ways by concentrating on the demands of users. This may result in higher productivity, cost savings, and income.

9.2.1 Understanding Design Thinking's Impact on Business

Design thinking has become very popular recently, especially in the business world. The impact of design thinking on business is varied.

Design Visualization Question 9.1

Remember the struggle of sharing large files a few years ago. Dropbox completely changed the game with their user-friendly cloud storage service. Their initial idea was not a perfect hit. They then used design thinking, specifically the Lean Startup approach (which is all about rapid testing and iteration), to develop and refine their product based on user feedback. The result is a billion-dollar business that has disrupted the file-sharing industry.

The Challenge: Building Better Study Habits

Effective studying often gets sacrificed in the chaos of college life. How might we design a system or tool to help students manage their workload, prioritize learning, and avoid last-minute cramming?

Your Mission:

1. **Empathize:** Investigate the study habits of your fellow students. What are the biggest challenges they face in staying organized and focused? (time management, competing priorities, lack of motivation)
2. **Define:** Formulate a clear problem statement. What specific barrier are you trying to overcome to improve student study habits?
3. **Ideate:** Come up with innovative solutions. Could there be a scheduling app that integrates with course syllabi and to-do lists? A personalized study planner with built-in reminders and accountability systems?
4. **Prototype:** Develop a basic prototype of your solution. This could be a wireframe for a mobile app, a sample scheduling template, or a flowchart of your proposed system.
5. **Test:** Share your prototype with other students and gather feedback. Does it address the core problem? Is it feasible and user-friendly?

Design thinking helps to create customer-centric solutions: Design thinking can be a game-changer for creating solutions that people truly desire. By focusing on what customers really want and the struggles they face, businesses can design solutions that fit perfectly into their lives.

While designing the iPhone, for example, Apple used design thinking to understand what people wanted in a phone: something intuitive, user-friendly, and aesthetically pleasing. So, they left out the complicated buttons and clunky interfaces, and created a sleek, touchscreen experience. This customer focus made the iPhone a runaway success, propelling Apple to the top of the smartphone market.

Design thinking promotes collaboration and creativity: The potential of design thinking to foster creativity and collaboration has an additional effect on business. Companies can develop fresh, original ideas that could result in game-changing advancements by bringing together people with various backgrounds and specialties. In addition, this collaborative approach can aid in dismantling organizational silos and fostering an innovative culture.

The international design firm IDEO is an excellent example of design thinking that encourages cooperation and creativity. Cross-functional teams of designers, engineers, and business experts collaborate to create solutions that address the demands of their clients as part of the company's problem-solving strategy.

Design thinking encourages experimentation and iteration: Another benefit of design thinking is that it promotes experimentation and iteration, both of which have a significant influence on business. Companies can quickly determine what works and what does not by testing and refining ideas through prototyping and user feedback and then adjusting their strategy appropriately. This strategy can assist businesses in remaining flexible and adjusting to changes in their market and sector.

Experimentation and Iteration

Working backwards
Envisioning the final product from the customer's perspective and then moving backwards to the initial product conception.

FAQ document
FAQ document and a user manual for the new product, which forces the team to confront potential problems and questions ahead of time.

Amazon Kindle
A series of iterations that responded to how customers consume books and media.

Amazon Prime
What began as a premium shipping service has grown to include streaming video, music, and more.

Figure 9.3 Amazon's approach to product development

Amazon's approach to product development, characterized by its 'working backward' methodology, is a ideal example of design thinking in action (Fig. 9.3). This customer-centric strategy begins with clearly focusing on the end-user's needs and experiences. The process involves envisioning the final product from the customer's perspective and then moving backward to the initial product conception and development stages. By doing so, Amazon ensures that the product fulfills and anticipates customer needs, leading to innovative solutions that resonate with users. The iterative nature of this process means that products are not created in a vacuum but are constantly refined through cycles of experimentation, feedback, and improvement. This allows Amazon to adapt quickly to changing market demands and technological advancements.

The development of the Kindle, for instance, was not a one-time event but a series of iterations that responded to how customers consume books and media. Each version of the Kindle is an improvement on the last, with enhancements that make reading more accessible and enjoyable for users. Similarly, Amazon Prime's evolution reflects continuous refinement and expansion of services. What began as a premium shipping service has grown to include streaming video, music, and more, all because Amazon kept iterating based on customer usage and feedback. This willingness to experiment and iterate is not without risks, but Amazon's strategy accepts failure as a necessary step in innovation. The company's culture encourages bold bets and accepts that not all will pay off, but those that do can be transformative.

The 'working backward' methodology also involves writing a press release for the not-yet-existent product, which outlines the product's features, benefits, and customer experience. This hypothetical press release is shared internally to align the development team's vision and serves as a litmus test for the product's market viability. If the press release excites internal teams, it is a good indicator that it will excite customers, too. Moreover, Amazon's approach includes creating a frequently asked questions (FAQ) document and a user manual for the new product, which forces the team to confront potential problems and questions ahead of time. This proactive problem-solving ensures that when the product hits the market, it is innovative, user-friendly, and well-supported.

In conclusion, Amazon's product development strategy exemplifies how a relentless focus on the customer and a willingness to experiment and embrace failure can lead to groundbreaking products and services.

9.3 Design Thinking and Technology

With the aid of technology, designers can acquire information and insights to guide their design thinking process. Technology enables designers to perform user research, gather and analyze data, and develop prototypes swiftly and effectively. For instance, designers can use digital tools like questionnaires, interviews, and user testing to acquire customer feedback and guide the design process. With the aid of technology, designers can acquire information and insights to guide their design thinking process (Fig. 9.4).

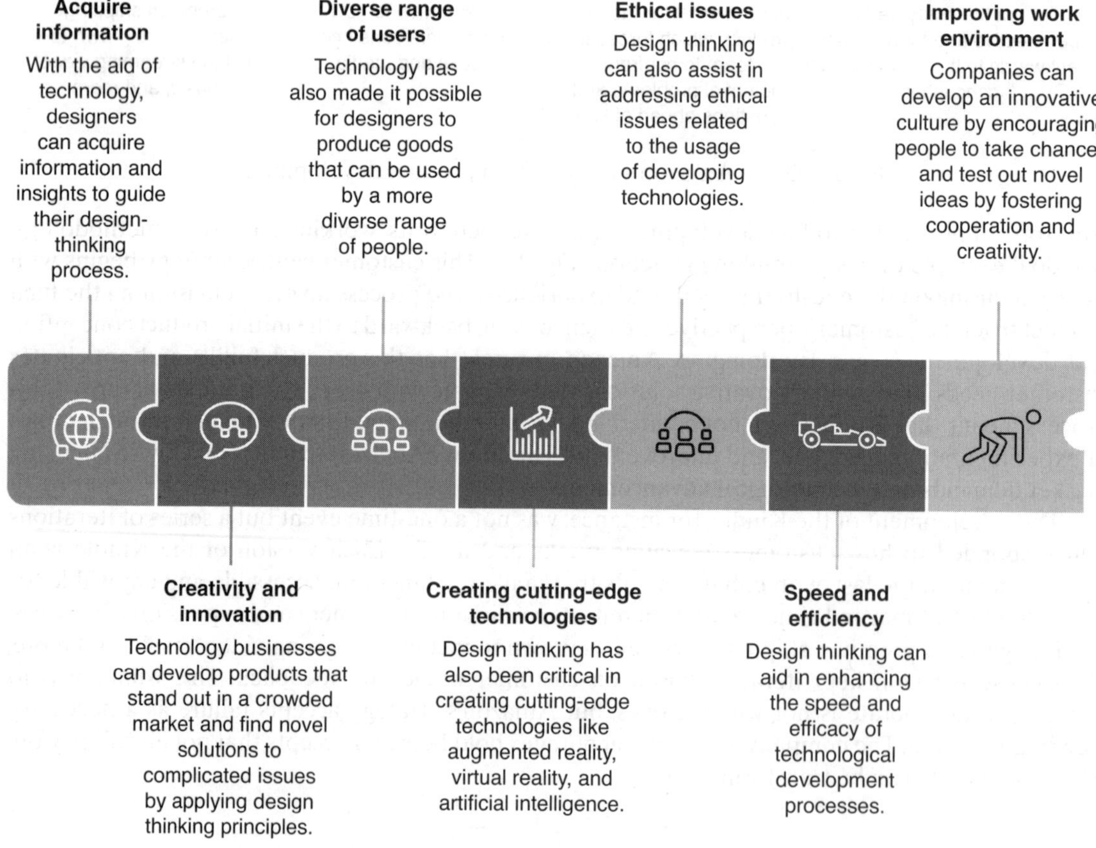

Figure 9.4 Design thinking and technology

Technology has also made it possible for designers to produce goods that can be used by a more diverse range of people. For instance, assistive technologies like text-to-speech software and screen readers have enabled people with impairments to access digital information. Creating smart houses is another instance of technology and design ideas working together. Designers are using technology to build safer, more secure, and more user-friendly homes. Automated lighting, climate control, and security systems are a few features that can be found in smart homes, all of which are created with the user's needs in mind.

Design thinking has also had an impact on the advancement of technology. In the past, human experience was rarely considered when designing technology, which was frequently more concerned with functionality and technical requirements. On the other hand, design thinking has questioned this methodology and given users' wants and experiences more weight. This user-centered approach has led to the creation of more user-friendly, intuitive, and pleasurable technology. Smartphones and other devices, for instance, now offer more user-friendly features and intuitive interfaces that make it simple for users to carry out tasks and obtain information. In addition, technology design now places a greater emphasis on the requirements of people to develop products that better consumers' lives.

Design thinking has promoted creativity and innovation in the technology sector. Technology businesses can develop products that stand out in a crowded market and find novel solutions to complicated issues by applying design thinking principles. For instance, companies like Apple and Google have applied design thinking to develop products that have altered how users engage with technology.

Design thinking has also been critical in creating cutting-edge technologies like augmented reality, virtual reality, and artificial intelligence (AI). However, although these technologies can potentially transform the way we work and live entirely, they also bring brand-new usability and accessibility issues. Companies may develop better user-friendly and accessible interfaces for these technologies, enabling more people to use their potential by applying design thinking principles. For instance, design thinking has contributed to the development of more immersive and exciting virtual reality experiences and more user-friendly augmented reality applications.

Design thinking can also assist in addressing ethical issues related to the usage of developing technologies. For instance, AI can potentially transform sectors like healthcare and banking, but it also raises ethical questions about algorithmic prejudice and data privacy. As a result, businesses may develop AI systems that are more open, accountable, and reliable by addressing these issues with design thinking.

One of the main advantages of design thinking in technology is that it aids in developing goods and services that better satisfy consumer wants. By emphasizing empathy, businesses can better understand their customers and develop more logical, simple, and practical products. This can boost client happiness and loyalty while promoting corporate success. Technology design thinking also has the potential to encourage innovation. Companies can find new possibilities and create innovative solutions that meet unmet requirements by adopting a user-centered approach to problem-solving. As a result, new goods, services, and business models that benefit the company, and its consumers may result.

Design thinking can aid in enhancing the speed and efficacy of technological development processes. Companies may produce more effective, efficient, and economical products by incorporating user feedback and iteration into the development process. This can speed up development and eliminate waste, which can be particularly crucial in highly competitive businesses.

Design thinking can also contribute to improving the working environment for technology professionals. For example, companies can develop an innovative culture by encouraging people to take chances and test out novel ideas by fostering cooperation and creativity. This may be essential for attracting and keeping top personnel in fields that depend heavily on skilled labor.

User interface and user experience (UI/UX) design is another area of technology where design thinking is having an impact. In the past, technology companies paid little attention to the user experience and instead concentrated mainly on the functionality of their products. Design thinking has helped to change this perspective, and more businesses now understand how critical it is to make valuable and entertaining products. Examples of businesses incorporating design thinking principles into their UI/UX design processes include Google and Facebook. These businesses can design user interfaces that are clear, interesting, and simple to use by utilizing techniques like empathy mapping, prototyping, and user testing. Users are hence more likely to continue using these goods more regularly.

The creation of AI and machine learning (ML) systems is another field in which design thinking is impacting. These technologies are growing increasingly common in our lives, but they are frequently opaque and challenging to comprehend. Companies may guarantee that these systems are moral, open, and simple to use by including design thinking ideas throughout development.

Design thinking can also be used to solve complicated challenges in fields like cybersecurity, where more conventional methods have frequently failed. Teams can create creative solutions that tackle complicated problems in novel and unexpected ways by assembling specialists from many disciplines and using design thinking methodologies to foster collaboration and innovation.

To further illustrate the impact of design thinking in technology, let us look at some real-world examples:

- Apple is a company that uses design thinking ideas prominently in its product design process. The business prioritizes comprehending consumer wants and behaviors, which has aided it in developing some of the most recognizable and user-friendly technology products available. The user-friendly iPhone interface and the svelte MacBook design are just two examples of how well Apple understands its customers' demands and is dedicated to making beautiful and valuable products.
- Another illustration is Tony Fadell, the former head of Apple's iPod division, who created the Nest thermostat. Instead of using conventional thermostats, Fadell developed one that was more user-friendly, intuitive, and energy efficient. In addition, Fadell developed a more user-friendly device that was better for the environment by including features like learning algorithms and remote control.
- IBM's design thinking methodology has created ground-breaking AI-related technologies. For example, the human-centered design was emphasized during the development of the company's Watson AI system, which has contributed to creating more understandable and user-friendly solutions. For instance, Watson Health, a platform for medical professionals, uses natural language processing to assist physicians and nurses in reliably and swiftly diagnosing patients.

9.4 Design Thinking and Education

In education, design thinking is crucial. We can encourage children to think critically, be more creative, and solve problems by incorporating design thinking into the classroom. Understanding the requirements and viewpoints of students, instructors, parents, and other stakeholders is necessary in the field of education. We can build solutions that meet their demands and are more likely to be effective if we know their needs and viewpoints (Fig. 9.5).

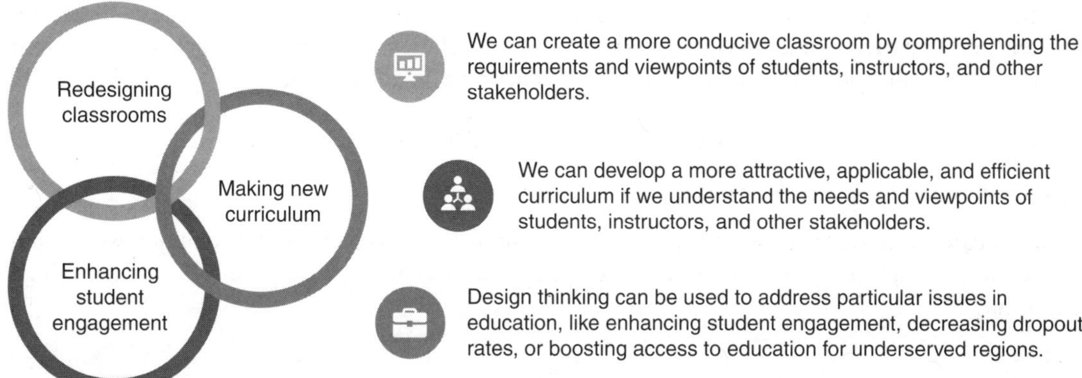

Figure 9.5 Design thinking and education

Redesigning a classroom illustrates the use of design thinking in education. We can create a more conducive classroom by comprehending the requirements and viewpoints of students, instructors, and other stakeholders. For example, to address the demands of various learners, we could design a classroom with flexible seating options, natural light, and a range of learning spaces.

Making a new curriculum is another illustration. We can develop a more attractive, applicable, and efficient curriculum if we understand the needs and viewpoints of students, instructors, and other stakeholders. For instance, we may construct a curriculum that includes more hands-on, project-based learning to aid students in acquiring critical thinking and problem-solving skills.

In addition, design thinking can be used to address particular issues in education, like **enhancing student engagement**, decreasing dropout rates, or boosting access to education for underserved regions. We can create creative solutions that tackle the underlying causes of the issue and are more likely to be sustainable by applying design thinking to these problems.

9.4.1 Integrating Design Thinking into the Curriculum

As students prepare to navigate the twenty-first century's demands successfully, a practical approach is to incorporate design thinking into the curriculum. This problem-solving approach emphasizes experimentation, creativity, and empathy and can assist students in acquiring the skills necessary for success. By integrating design thinking into the curriculum, we can encourage children to think critically and creatively and prepare them for success in the ever-changing landscape of the future. Integrating design thinking into the curriculum can take many different forms. Here are some examples:

- **Design thinking assignments:** Teachers can give students design thinking assignments that call for them to recognize a problem, feel for those affected by it, come up with solutions, create a prototype, and test their concepts. For instance, students might devise a plan to lessen the trash in the school cafeteria or develop a service to address an issue in their neighborhood.
- **Design thinking tasks:** Teachers can make design thinking tasks that call on students to apply design thinking to a particular issue. Students might be asked, for instance, to create a product that benefits those with impairments or a plan to enhance city transport.
- **Workshops on design thinking:** Teachers can lead workshops on design thinking that instruct students on the method and offer them a chance to put their knowledge to use. Students might participate in a workshop on prototyping and testing or one on designing for empathy, for instance.

- **Integrated design thinking:** Math, physics, and social studies are just a few examples of areas teachers can incorporate design thinking into. For instance, students could apply design thinking to a social studies project or to real-world arithmetic difficulties.

Design Visualization Question 9.2

The Challenge: Combating Cafeteria Chaos

College cafeterias often generate a significant amount of food waste. How might we design a system or program to reduce food waste and promote sustainable practices in the college cafeteria?

Your Mission:

1. **Empathize:** Observe the cafeteria during lunch periods. How much food waste is being generated? What factors contribute to it? (portion sizes, limited choices, lack of awareness about food waste)
2. **Define:** Formulate a clear problem statement. What specific aspect of food waste are you trying to tackle? (uneaten main course options, excessive fruit and vegetable scraps)
3. **Ideate:** Brainstorm creative solutions. Think beyond just composting. Could there be a system for pre-ordering lunch to reduce overproduction? A student-led campaign to raise awareness about food waste reduction?
4. **Prototype:** Develop a basic prototype of your solution. This could be a poster campaign mockup, a flowchart of a pre-ordering system, or a script for a student-led presentation.
5. **Test:** Present your prototype to other students and cafeteria staff. Does it address the core problem? Is it feasible and easy to implement?

Integrating design thinking into the curriculum has many benefits for students. Here are some examples:

- **Develops critical thinking abilities**: Design thinking requires students to improve their problem-solving abilities and increase their critical thinking abilities.
- **Fosters creativity**: Encourages students to think creatively and come up with original ideas through design thinking. Including design thinking in the curriculum helps pupils develop their originality and creativity.
- **Encourages collaboration**: Collaboration and teamwork are critical components of design thinking. Students learn how to communicate with others and work effectively in teams by incorporating design thinking into the curriculum.
- **Increases engagement**: Design thinking is a practical, experiential method of education—students' interest and engagement in their learning increase when design thinking is incorporated into the curriculum.

9.4.2 Using Design Thinking to Solve Educational Challenges

Using design thinking to address problems in education is effective. Here are some examples of using design thinking to solve educational challenges:

- **Improving student engagement:** Maintaining students' interest in their studies is a typical educational difficulty. We can develop solutions that are more engaging and pertinent to their interests by using design thinking to understand students' requirements and perspectives better. For instance, a design thinking team might develop a mobile application that enables students to monitor their development and receive incentives for meeting their learning objectives.

- **Reducing dropout rates:** Dropout prevention is another issue in education. Using design thinking, we can pinpoint the causes of student dropouts and create ways to deal with them. For instance, a design thinking team could develop a mentoring program that links at-risk students with accomplished alums to offer support and direction.
- **Increasing access to education:** Increasing access to education, especially for impoverished people, is another educational challenge. We can recognize the obstacles to education and create solutions to overcome them by applying design thinking. For instance, a design thinking team could develop a program that offers free laptops and an internet connection to students who do not have access to these tools at home.
- **Enhancing teacher professional development:** For their professional growth and to stay updated with best practices, teachers need continual professional development. We can create more efficient and exciting professional development programs by utilizing design thinking. For example, to make learning more engaging and interactive, a design thinking team might produce online seminars incorporating gamification.

9.5 Design Thinking and Healthcare

With its empathetic and user-centered approach, design thinking can revolutionize healthcare by tailoring solutions to the specific needs of patients and healthcare professionals. For instance, consider a patient's journey from diagnosis to treatment. Design thinking can be applied to streamline this process, making it more intuitive and less stressful (Fig. 9.6).

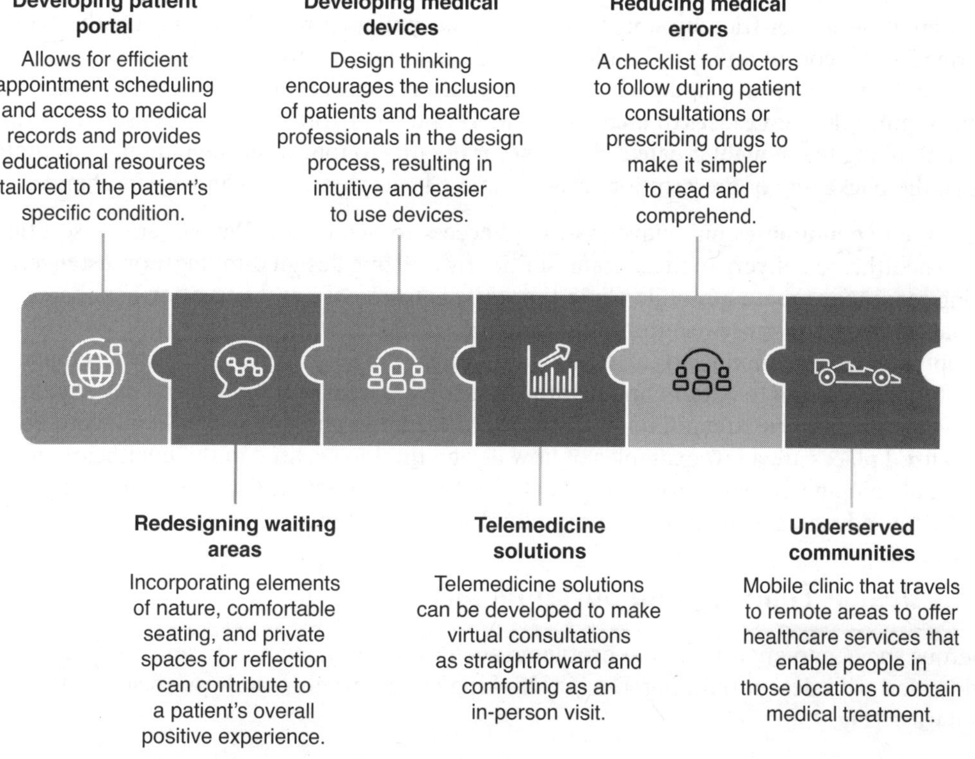

Figure 9.6 Design thinking and healthcare

A design thinking team might observe the patient's journey, identify pain points, and create a more seamless experience. This could involve **developing a patient portal** that allows for efficient appointment scheduling and access to medical records and provides educational resources tailored to the patient's specific condition, empowering them with knowledge and control over their health journey.

Moreover, design thinking can address the **physical environment of healthcare facilities**. Often, hospitals and clinics are designed for functionality, overlooking the impact of the environment on a patient's well-being. By applying design thinking, spaces can be transformed to promote healing and comfort. For example, redesigning waiting areas to be more welcoming and less clinical can reduce anxiety. Incorporating elements of nature, comfortable seating, and private spaces for reflection can contribute to a patient's overall positive experience.

Another area where design thinking can significantly impact is the **development of medical devices.** Traditionally, the focus has been on technical functionality, sometimes at the expense of user-friendliness. Design thinking encourages the inclusion of patients and healthcare professionals in the design process, resulting in devices that are not only cutting-edge in terms of technology but also intuitive and easier to use. For example, redesigning a blood glucose monitor to be less intimidating and more engaging could encourage consistent use and better management of diabetes.

Furthermore, design thinking can enhance the way healthcare is delivered. **Telemedicine**, for example, has become increasingly important, and design thinking can optimize its delivery. By understanding the barriers patients face in accessing telemedicine, solutions can be developed to make virtual consultations as straightforward and comforting as an in-person visit. This might involve creating a user-friendly app that guides the patient through setting up the technology, preparing for the consultation, and understanding the follow-up procedures.

Patients who experience medical blunders may suffer severe repercussions. Using design thinking, we can **pinpoint the root causes of medical blunders** and create preventative measures. For instance, a design thinking team might create a checklist for doctors to follow during patient consultations or redesign the packaging of prescription drugs to make it simpler to read and comprehend.

Underserved communities may have restricted access to healthcare. We can create solutions that enhance healthcare delivery in these communities by utilizing design thinking. For instance, a design thinking team may create a mobile clinic that travels to remote areas to offer healthcare services that enables people in those locations to obtain medical treatment.

Applying design thinking to the healthcare industry is an effective strategy to create cutting-edge solutions catering to patient and healthcare provider demands. Improving patient experience, lowering medical errors, streamlining healthcare procedures, and enhancing healthcare delivery in marginalized places are a few examples of how design thinking is used in the healthcare industry. In addition, developing empathy, fostering creativity, fostering cooperation, and enhancing outcomes are just a few advantages of applying design thinking to healthcare.

9.6 Design Thinking and Social Impact

Numerous social and environmental problems, such as poverty, inequality, and climate change, can be addressed with design thinking. Design thinking can be used to address social impact issues in several ways (Fig. 9.7).

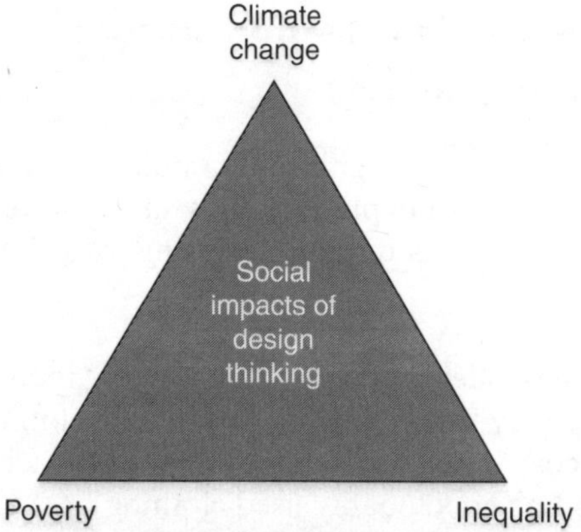

Figure 9.7 Design thinking and social impact

- **Understand the needs of marginalized communities**: Using design thinking, we may better comprehend the needs and experiences of marginalized communities, such as those of low-income and disabled individuals. Understanding their requirements will enable us to create solutions that address their particular problems and enhance their quality of life.

Design Visualization Question 9.3

The Challenge: Bridging the Digital Divide

Many marginalized communities lack access to technology, the internet, and digital literacy skills. This 'digital divide' can limit their access to education, employment opportunities, and essential services. How might we design a program or service to bridge the digital divide and empower marginalized communities?

Your Mission:

1. **Empathize:** Research or interview members of a marginalized community. What are the biggest challenges they face in accessing technology and the internet? What skills and resources do they need? (affordability of devices and internet plans, lack of digital literacy training, limited access to public Wi-Fi hotspots)
2. **Define:** Craft a clear problem statement. What specific aspect of the digital divide are you focusing on? (lack of affordable laptops for students, limited access to internet safety training for seniors)
3. **Ideate:** Brainstorm creative solutions! Think beyond just providing free computers. Could there be a mobile device lending program with digital literacy workshops? A community center offering free Wi-Fi access and tech support programs?
4. **Prototype:** Develop a basic prototype of your solution. This could be a flyer promoting a digital literacy workshop, a flowchart for a mobile device lending program, or a sample lesson plan for internet safety training.
5. **Test:** Present your prototype to community members and organizations. Does it address the core problem? Is it culturally sensitive, accessible, and sustainable?

- **Create sustainable solutions:** Design thinking can assist us in developing environmentally friendly solutions that foster long-term social and economic growth. For instance, a design thinking team might create a sustainable farming system that uses less water and encourages regional economic development.

Design Visualization Question 9.4

The Challenge: Combating Fashion Waste

The fast-fashion industry generates a significant amount of textile waste, contributing to environmental pollution and resource depletion. How might we design a system or service to promote sustainable fashion practices and reduce clothing waste?

Your Mission:

1. **Empathize:** Talk to college students or young adults about their clothing consumption habits. What are the challenges they face in buying sustainable clothing? What motivates them to discard clothing? (high cost of sustainable clothing brands, lack of awareness about clothing lifecycle, difficulty in finding good quality used clothing)|
2. **Define:** Formulate a clear problem statement. What specific aspect of clothing waste are you trying to tackle? (encouraging students to buy fewer new clothes, promoting the reuse of existing clothing)|
3. **Ideate:** Come up with innovative solutions. Think beyond just clothing donation drives. Could there be a student-run clothing swap event? A mobile app for buying and selling pre-owned clothing with a focus on ethical brands?
4. **Prototype:** Develop a basic prototype of your solution. This could be a flyer promoting a clothing swap event, a wireframe for a clothing resale app, or a social media campaign promoting sustainable fashion choices.
5. **Test:** Share your prototype with fellow students and fashion retailers. Does it address the core problem? Is it user-friendly, accessible, and promotes a positive change in consumer behavior?

- **Foster collaboration and community engagement:** People with various backgrounds and viewpoints can work together on challenges with societal significance using design thinking. We can design more efficient and sustainable solutions by involving communities and stakeholders.
- **Address systemic issues:** Systemic concerns that contribute to social and environmental problems can be addressed via design thinking. For instance, a design thinking team could create a plan to deal with poverty's underlying issues, like access to healthcare and education.

Examples of design thinking on social impact:

- **IDEO.org**: This non-profit organization works to combat inequality and poverty worldwide. They have created several cutting-edge solutions, including smartphone software that aids Kenyan farmers in managing their crops and a reasonably priced prosthetic knee joint for amputees in underdeveloped nations.
- **OpenIDEO**: This is an online platform. They work with a global network of designers, activists, and businesspeople to develop solutions, such as a program to cut food waste in cities and a website that connects refugees with employment opportunities.
- **Embrace Innovations**: This is a social venture that creates healthcare options for at-risk groups by applying design thinking. For example, they have created an inexpensive newborn warmer that has helped thousands of preterm infants in impoverished nations survive.
- **The Unreasonable Institute**: This is a company that supports social entrepreneurs in creating creative answers to problems with a social impact. They offer mentorship, money, and training to help these entrepreneurs scale their ideas and have a more significant effect.

9.6.1 The Role of Design Thinking in Addressing Social Issues

Design thinking can be critical in addressing social issues in several ways. For example, it can help:

- **Identify and understand social issues:** Designers can better grasp the problem and the individuals affected by it by conducting research and talking to those affected by these concerns.

Design Visualization Question 9.5

The Challenge: Combating Social Isolation in Seniors

Social isolation is a growing problem among seniors, leading to loneliness, depression, and health issues. How might we design a program or service to address social isolation and promote community connection for older adults?

Your Mission:

1. **Empathize:** Research senior living facilities or interview older adults in your community. What are the biggest challenges they face in staying connected with others? (limited mobility, lack of access to transportation, difficulty using technology to stay in touch)
2. **Define:** Formulate a clear problem statement. What specific aspect of social isolation in seniors are you focusing on? (difficulty for homebound seniors to connect with others, lack of engaging activities for seniors in assisted living facilities)
3. **Ideate:** Brainstorm creative solutions. Think beyond just senior centers. Could there be an intergenerational pen pal program connecting seniors with students? A volunteer program that trains technology-savvy teenagers to teach basic digital skills to seniors?
4. **Prototype:** Develop a basic prototype of your solution. This could be a flyer promoting an intergenerational pen pal program, a flowchart for a volunteer training program, or a sample lesson plan for teaching basic online communication tools to seniors.
5. **Test:** Present your prototype to senior centers, community organizations, and potential volunteers. Does it address the core problem? Is it culturally sensitive, inclusive, and promotes intergenerational connections?

- **Engage communities:** Communities and stakeholders can be involved in the design process by using design thinking. Designers may ensure that the solutions they create are pertinent, efficient, and sustainable by involving the individuals affected by the social issue.
- **Create positive change:** By addressing the underlying causes of societal challenges, design thinking can bring about constructive change. Designers can bring about long-lasting change that enhances people's lives by creating solutions that address the fundamental causes of societal challenges.

Design Visualization Question 9.6

The Challenge: Rethinking Mental Health Support in Schools

Mental health issues among adolescents are on the rise. Traditional school support systems often lack the resources or capacity to address the diverse needs of students struggling with mental well-being. How might we design a system or program to promote mental health awareness, early intervention, and accessible support services within schools?

Your Mission:

1. **Empathize:** Research mental health resources in schools. Talk to students, teachers, and school counselors. What are the biggest barriers students face in accessing mental health support? (stigma surrounding mental health, limited access to counselors, lack of awareness about available resources)
2. **Define:** Craft a clear problem statement. What specific aspect of mental health support in schools are you focusing on? (reducing stigma around seeking help, increasing access to peer support networks)
3. **Ideate:** Brainstorm creative solutions. Think beyond just hiring more counselors. Could there be an anonymous online forum for students to share struggles and connect with peers? A peer-to-peer training program educating students on mental health resources and how to support their classmates?
4. **Prototype:** Develop a basic prototype of your solution. This could be a mock-up of a school website with a dedicated mental health resources section, a sample lesson plan for a peer-to-peer mental health awareness training session, or a flyer promoting an anonymous online student support forum.
5. **Test:** Present your prototype to students, educators, and mental health professionals. Does it address the core problem? Is it culturally sensitive, promotes inclusivity, and creates a safe space for students to seek help?

Examples where design thinking solutions have been used to address social issues:

- **Design for America:** This is a student-run organization that uses design thinking to address social challenges. They have created a wide range of solutions, such as a tool that helps Parkinson's patients write more clearly and a program that facilitates access to wholesome food for low-income families.
- **The Nike Foundation:** This empowers young women in impoverished nations using design thinking. They have created several cutting-edge solutions, such as a program that gives girls access to economic, healthcare, and education opportunities.
- **The Ellen MacArthur Foundation:** This foundation uses design thinking to advance a circular economy and lessen waste. They have created several solutions, including a program to encourage the use of reusable packaging and a platform that links businesses with recycled materials.
- **The Humanitarian Innovation Fund:** This fund uses design thinking to create solutions to humanitarian situations. They have created many solutions, including a tool that makes clean water more accessible to individuals with disabilities and a program that aids refugees in getting access to education and training.

9.6.2 Design Thinking and Social Innovation

The process of coming up with fresh approaches to societal issues to improve society is known as social innovation. Because it centers problem-solving around the needs and experiences of people, the design thinking process is especially well suited to social innovation.

First, it is necessary to identify the problem to be resolved to employ design thinking for social innovation. This might be anything from environmental sustainability or healthcare access to poverty and inequality. Understanding the requirements and experiences of those impacted by the issue comes next after the problem has been recognized. This can entail holding focus groups, surveys, or interviews with individuals directly experiencing the issue.

The next stage is to come up with concepts for potential fixes. This is where design thinking's inventiveness and teamwork skills are used. Workshops, brainstorming sessions, and other group activities can all be used to produce ideas. Without criticizing or rejecting any of the ideas at this point, the emphasis should be on coming up with various concepts.

The next phase is to evaluate and improve the ideas after a variety of them have been developed. This could entail making mockups or prototypes of potential solutions and testing them on those who the issue would impact. Feedback can be used to improve the solutions and ensure that they address the demands of the target population.

After a solution has been created and improved, it can be put into practice, and its results can be assessed. This may entail assessing the solution's efficacy in resolving the social problem and its effects on the people they impact.

There are numerous instances when design thinking has been applied to social innovation. One illustration is the national network of college students involved in the Design for America program, who utilize design thinking to create solutions to social issues in their areas. The IDEO.org program is another illustration of how design thinking is used to solve various social challenges, such as poverty, healthcare, and education.

9.7 Design Thinking in Constructing Buildings

Design thinking may be used in various industries, including architecture and construction. It is not applicable only to digital or product design. Design thinking is becoming increasingly popular among architects and builders to produce structures that are aesthetically pleasing but also practical and sustainable.

Empathy, or comprehending the needs and desires of the end-users, is one of the fundamental tenets of design thinking. This refers to the practice of considering the intended users' wants and preferences when designing a structure. The demands of patients, medical personnel, and visitors must all be considered while constructing a hospital, for instance. The architect may design a cozy and helpful structure for everyone by being aware of their requirements and desires.

The iterative process of prototyping and testing is a crucial component of design thinking in architecture. Using design thinking, architects can develop prototypes and test them to see if they satisfy the needs of the end-users before a building is ever built. This can guarantee that the building achieves the project's objectives and help prevent expensive mistakes throughout the construction period.

Seattle's The Bullitt Centre is a building that used design thinking in its construction. The architects employed design thinking to construct a structure that was both environmentally friendly and comfortable for the people working there. This structure has these qualities: solar panels, natural ventilation, rainwater collection, and comfortable workplaces and communal areas.

Another illustration is the luxury resort Alila Villas in Bali, created using design thinking ideas. The resort is located in a natural setting, and the architects employed empathy to comprehend not just the demands of the visitors but also those of the nearby neighborhood and environment. The outcome was a stunning and environmentally friendly resort that blends in with its surroundings and offers visitors a relaxing and unforgettable experience.

Summary

- Cross-disciplinary cooperation is crucial for successful implementation of design thinking. Examples include the Nike Flyknit sneaker and the Embrace newborn warmer.
- Businesses like IDEO have used design thinking to create innovative solutions in healthcare.

- Technology allows designers to gather and analyze data, develop prototypes quickly, and create products that can be used by a wider range of people.
- Design thinking has shifted the focus from functionality to user experience, leading to more user-friendly, intuitive, and pleasurable technology.
- Examples of businesses incorporating design thinking principles into their UI/UX design processes include Google and Facebook.
- Design thinking is influencing the creation of AI and ML systems. Companies can ensure these systems are moral, open, and easy to use by including design thinking ideas in development.
- Design thinking encourages critical thinking, creativity, and empathy in education. Examples include redesigning classrooms, creating new curricula, and addressing specific issues in education.
- Examples of the use of design thinking in healthcare include improving patient experience, streamlining healthcare processes, and improving healthcare delivery in underserved communities.
- Design thinking can address social and environmental problems like poverty, inequality, and climate change. Examples include understanding the needs of marginalized communities, creating sustainable solutions, fostering collaboration and community engagement, and addressing systemic issues.

Solutions to Design Visualization Questions

Q 9.1

The Challenge: Building Better Study Habits

Solution 1: The 'Smart Scheduler' App

- **Function:** A mobile app that integrates with course syllabi, calendars, and to-do lists to create a personalized study schedule.
- **Benefits:** Improved time management, reduced stress, better organization, ability to prioritize tasks and deadlines.
- **Features:** Automatic schedule generation based on course syllabi, built-in Pomodoro timer for focused study sessions, progress tracking and gamification elements to boost motivation.

Solution 2: The Study Buddy Platform

- **Function:** An online platform that connects students based on their courses and learning styles to form study groups or find accountability partners.
- **Benefits:** Improved understanding of course material through collaboration, increased motivation through social learning, peer support, and feedback.
- **Features:** Matching algorithms based on learning styles and study goals, built-in video chat and document sharing tools, collaborative study resources and note-taking features.

Q 9.2

The Challenge: Cafeteria Crusaders

Solution 1: The Waste Warrior Program

- **Function:** A student-led initiative that promotes awareness and action to reduce food waste in the cafeteria.

- **Benefits:** Reduces landfill waste, saves money on food costs, promotes environmental responsibility.
- **Activities:**
  - Educational campaigns about the impact of food waste.
  - 'Waste audits' to track the types and amount of food being thrown away.
  - Collaboration with cafeteria staff to adjust portion sizes and offer more sustainable options.
  - Student-led composting program (if feasible).

Solution 2: The Cafeteria Choice App

- **Function:** A mobile app that allows students to pre-order their lunch selections.
- **Benefits:** Reduces overproduction of food, caters to student preferences, minimizes leftover meals.
- **Features:**
  - Daily menu display with photos and descriptions.
  - Pre-ordering option for specific menu items within a designated timeframe.
  - Ability to customize portions or request dietary substitutions.

Q 9.3

The Challenge: Bridging the Digital Divide - Empowering Solutions

Solution 1: The Tech Connect Mobile Hub

- **Function:** A converted van or trailer equipped with laptops, tablets, and a mobile Wi-Fi hotspot that travels to underserved neighborhoods.
- **Benefits:** Provides free and accessible technology resources for community members.
- **Features:**
  - Trained facilitators offering basic digital literacy workshops on internet navigation, email, and essential online skills.
  - Lending library of laptops and tablets pre-loaded with educational resources and productivity tools.
  - Assistance with setting up affordable internet plans and discounted device purchases for qualified residents.

Solution 2: The Community Tech Corps Training Program

- **Function:** A program that trains unemployed or underemployed individuals from marginalized communities to become digital literacy instructors.
- **Benefits:** Empowers community members, promotes digital inclusion, and creates local employment opportunities.
- **Activities:**
  - Recruitment and training of program participants on essential digital skills and adult education techniques.
  - Collaboration with local community centers and libraries to offer ongoing digital literacy workshops.
  - Mentorship and career development support for program graduates who wish to pursue careers in the tech sector.

Q 9.4

The Challenge: Sustainable Fashion Solutions

Solution 1: The Remix Revolution Clothing Swap App

- **Function:** A mobile app specifically designed for college students to organize and participate in clothing swap events.
- **Benefits:** Promotes clothing reuse, reduces textile waste, and fosters a sense of community among students.
- **Features:**
  - User-friendly interface to list unwanted clothing items with photos and descriptions.
  - Geolocation feature to connect students organizing or attending clothing swap events in their area.
  - 'Wish list' function allowing users to browse available items and request swaps with other participants.

Solution 2: The Thriftify & Tailor Collaborative Platform

- **Function:** An online platform that connects students with local tailors and second-hand clothing stores, promoting clothing repair, alterations, and upcycling.
- **Benefits:** Extends the life of existing clothing, reduces the need to buy new clothes, and supports local businesses within the fashion ecosystem.
- **Features:**
  - Directory of local tailors and second-hand stores with user reviews and pricing information.
  - Online tutorial library showcasing simple clothing repair and upcycling techniques.
  - Booking system for appointments with tailors for alterations or custom design projects using pre-loved clothing.

Q 9.5

The Challenge: Combating Social Isolation in Seniors

Solution 1: The GrandPals Intergenerational Pen Pal Program

- **Function:** Connects senior citizens with students through a pen pal program, fostering meaningful connections and combating loneliness.
- **Benefits:** Reduces social isolation for seniors, promotes intergenerational understanding, and provides companionship for both generations.
- **Activities:**
  - Matching program based on interests and hobbies to create a sense of connection.
  - Facilitation of regular letter exchange with prompts and conversation starters.
  - Optional virtual or in-person meet-ups (with safety precautions) to strengthen bonds.

Solution 2: The Tech Savvy Seniors Volunteer Program

- **Function:** Trains tech-savvy teenagers as volunteers to provide digital literacy workshops and one-on-one support to seniors, helping them connect with others online.
- **Benefits:** Empowers seniors to utilize technology for communication and social connection, reduces digital divide for older adults, and creates valuable learning experiences for teenagers.
- **Activities:**
  - Recruitment and training of volunteers on patience, communication, and basic digital skills.
  - Interactive workshops for seniors covering online communication tools, video chat platforms, and social media basics (with a focus on safety).
  - Individualized support sessions to help seniors connect with family and friends online.

These solutions address different aspects of social isolation in seniors. The GrandPals program focuses on building emotional connections through intergenerational friendships, while Tech Savvy Seniors empowers older adults to utilize technology for social interaction.

Q 9.6

The Challenge: Rethinking Mental Health Support in Schools

Solution 1: The Mindful Moments Peer Support Network

- **Function:** A student-led peer support network that provides a safe space for students to share experiences, connect with others, and access mental health resources.
- **Benefits:** Reduces stigma around mental health, fosters supportive peer relationships, and empowers students to advocate for their well-being.
- **Activities:**
  - Training workshops for student volunteers on active listening, empathy, and mental health awareness.
  - Weekly peer support groups led by trained student facilitators, offering a confidential space for students to share their struggles.
  - Creation of online resources (for example, an anonymous forum) where students can connect with peers and access mental health information.

Solution 2: The Wellness Warriors App

- **Function:** A mobile app providing students with self-care tools, mental health resources, and access to professional support services.
- **Benefits:** Offers students a readily available resource for managing mental health, promotes self-awareness and coping skills, and provides a discreet way to connect with professionals.
- **Features:**
  - Interactive exercises and guided meditations to promote relaxation and stress management.
  - Mood tracking tools to help students monitor their well-being.
  - Directory of on-campus and local mental health professionals with easy appointment booking options.
  - Anonymous mental health quizzes and self-assessments with tailored recommendations for further resources.

These solutions address different aspects of improving mental health support in schools. Mindful Moments focuses on building a supportive peer community, while Wellness Warriors provides a digital platform for self-care and access to professional help. The key is to create a multi-faceted approach that empowers students to seek help, reduces stigma, and promotes overall well-being within the school environment.

Exercises

Part A (Objective Questions)

1. What is the main benefit of design thinking in the business world?
   (a) Encourages innovation and differentiation
   (b) Reduces costs and saves time
   (c) Increases profits and revenue
   (d) None of the above
2. Why has design thinking become popular in business?
   (a) It is a low-cost method of innovation
   (b) It emphasizes user sensitivity and understanding
   (c) It is a highly technical process
   (d) None of the above

3. How can design thinking help organizations set themselves apart in a crowded market?
   (a) By reducing costs and saving time
   (b) By emphasizing user sensitivity and understanding
   (c) By increasing profits and revenue
   (d) All of the above
4. What is the main reason why design thinking has become popular in business?
   (a) It is a highly technical process
   (b) It is a low-risk, low-cost method of innovation
   (c) It encourages collaboration and creativity
   (d) None of the above
5. What is the focus of design thinking in terms of solutions?
   (a) Design thinking focuses on profit over people.
   (b) Design thinking focuses on finding a quick solution.
   (c) Design thinking focuses on creating customer-centric solutions.
   (d) Design thinking focuses on creating solutions without customer input.
6. What is the role of collaboration in design thinking?
   (a) Collaboration is discouraged in design thinking.
   (b) Collaboration is not important in design thinking.
   (c) Collaboration is critical to design thinking.
   (d) Collaboration is only important in the ideation stage.
7. How has technology influenced design thinking?
   (a) It has allowed for more efficient user research and prototyping.
   (b) It has decreased the importance of user experience in design.
   (c) It has made it more difficult to produce goods that are usable by a wide range of people.
   (d) None of the above.
8. What was the focus of technology design before the advent of design thinking?
   (a) Human experience
   (b) Technical requirements
   (c) User wants and needs
   (d) None of the above
9. What impact has design thinking had on technology design?
   (a) It has made technology more functional.
   (b) It has decreased the importance of user wants and experiences.
   (c) It has given user wants and experiences more weight.
   (d) None of the above.
10. How has technology enabled designers to create products that are more usable by a wider range of people?
    (a) By making user research and prototyping more efficient.
    (b) By focusing on technical requirements rather than human experience.
    (c) By decreasing the importance of user wants and needs.
    (d) None of the above.
11. What role does technology play in the design-thinking process?
    (a) It replaces the need for human creativity.
    (b) It allows for more efficient data analysis.
    (c) It makes the design-thinking process unnecessary.
    (d) None of the above.
12. What is the impact of design thinking on technology?
    (a) It has made technology more user-friendly.
    (b) It has made technology more complex.
    (c) It has made technology less accessible.
    (d) It has made technology less innovative.

13. How has design thinking impacted UI/UX design?
    (a) It has made companies focus solely on functionality.
    (b) It has made companies prioritize the user experience.
    (c) It has made companies prioritize the technical requirements.
    (d) It has made companies prioritize the aesthetics.
14. How can design thinking principles be applied in the development of AI and ML systems?
    (a) By ensuring these systems are opaque and difficult to understand
    (b) By including design thinking ideas throughout development
    (c) By only focusing on technical requirements
    (d) By neglecting user experiences.
15. What is the role of design thinking in making AI and ML systems more user-friendly?
    (a) It doesn't play a role
    (b) It ensures these systems are opaque
    (c) It incorporates transparency and user-friendliness into development
    (d) It only focuses on technical requirements
16. What is the benefit of assembling specialists from different disciplines in design thinking?
    (a) It helps in promoting collaboration and innovation.
    (b) It increases the cost of the project.
    (c) It leads to conflicts and disagreements.
    (d) It slows down the project development process.
17. What is the benefit of using design thinking methodologies in collaborative projects?
    (a) It encourages experimentation and iteration.
    (b) It leads to conflicts and disagreements.
    (c) It increases project cost.
    (d) It decreases the speed of the project development process.
18. What is design thinking in education?
    (a) A problem-solving method that includes experimentation, creativity, and empathy
    (b) A method of teaching that focuses only on technical skills
    (c) A method of teaching that emphasizes memorization and rote learning
    (d) A method of teaching that encourages competition among students
19. How can design thinking benefit students in education?
    (a) Encourages critical thinking, creativity, and problem-solving
    (b) Encourages rote memorization of information
    (c) Encourages competition among students
    (d) Encourages conformity among students
20. What skills can children learn through design thinking in education?
    (a) Collaboration and communication skills (b) Memorization skills
    (c) Competitive skills (d) Conformity skills
21. What is the goal of incorporating design thinking into the classroom?
    (a) To encourage critical thinking, creativity, and problem-solving skills
    (b) To promote conformity among students
    (c) To encourage memorization skills
    (d) To promote competition among students
22. What societal issues can design thinking be used to address?
    (a) Inequality, poverty, and environmental deterioration.
    (b) Animal rights, climate change, and economic growth.
    (c) Immigration, political corruption, and education.
    (d) Cybersecurity, technological advancements, and healthcare.

Part B (Short Answer Questions)

1. How do technology and design thinking work together?
2. How do a user-centered approach and design thinking work together?
3. How do AI/ML and design thinking work together?
4. How do design thinking and education work together?
5. How does design thinking help to solve educational challenges?
6. How does design thinking make an impact on society?

Part C (Essay Questions)

1. Why is cross-disciplinary cooperation crucial for design thinking to be successful?
2. How can design thinking help businesses?
3. Write an essay on the intersection of design thinking and technology.
4. Write an essay on integrating design thinking into the curriculum.
5. How can we use design thinking to solve educational challenges?
6. How can design thinking be used in healthcare?
7. Write an essay on the role of design thinking in addressing social issues.
8. How can we apply design thinking to non-profit and social impact organizations?

Answer Key

Part A

1. (a) **2.** (b) **3.** (b) **4.** (c) **5.** (c) **6.** (c) **7.** (a) **8.** (b) **9.** (c) **10.** (a)
11. (b) **12.** (a) **13.** (b) **14.** (b) **15.** (c) **16.** (a) **17.** (a) **18.** (a) **19.** (a) **20.** (a)
21. (a) **22.** (a)

CHAPTER 10

Measuring the Impact of Design Thinking

Learning Objectives

At the end of this chapter, you will be able to:

- Explain the methodologies for assessing the effectiveness of design thinking in various contexts
- List the common obstacles encountered while attempting to measure the impact of design thinking
- Describe the innovation funnel framework and how it applies to design thinking
- Give insights into the design scorecard framework and its relevance to evaluating design initiatives
- Explain the types of metrics that can be employed to gauge the success of design thinking processes
- Explain how design thinking influences user experience and the ways to measure this impact
- Elaborate on the significance of design thinking in shaping organizational culture and the metrics for its assessment
- Describe the broader societal implications of design thinking and the approaches to measure its extensive influence
- List the key lessons learned from analyzing the outcomes of design thinking applications

10.1 Introduction

The results of using design thinking methodology and guiding principles in various situations are referred to as its impact. These impacts can be observed in how the user experience has improved, team collaboration has increased, creativity and invention have increased, and corporate culture has improved. Understanding how the design thinking process influences these outcomes and identifying areas for development are the two main objectives of measuring the impact of design thinking.

For instance, a business that uses design thinking to enhance its products may tangibly affect customer satisfaction and loyalty. Design thinking may help the business to pinpoint and resolve customer journey pain points, leading to more satisfying encounters and, eventually, more sales.

Another illustration would be a non-profit group developing solutions for social issues through design thinking. The organization can develop more successful and long-lasting initiatives that benefit society by interacting with the community and empathetically understanding their needs.

In both situations, the effects of design thinking are evident in observable results like **increased consumer satisfaction or positive social change.** However, the influence can also be seen in less obvious ways, like **enhanced teamwork and more creative company culture.** Therefore, organizations can better understand how the process affects their objectives and make wise decisions about how to apply design thinking to produce positive results by measuring the influence of the process in these numerous aspects.

10.2 How to Measure the Impact of Design Thinking

The impact of design thinking can be measured in various ways:

- **Observing changes in user experience (UX):** When you implement design thinking solutions, you aim to make products easier and more enjoyable for users to use. Observing their experience after implementing your design is an excellent measure of impact. For example, let us imagine that you redesigned the college library website. Previously, it was confusing and complicated to find information. After applying design thinking, the website became clear and user-friendly. You can observe changes in UX by:
  - **Watching students interact with the website:** Do they seem frustrated or confused? Can they find what they need quickly?
  - **Asking for feedback:** Conduct surveys or hold focus groups to get students' opinions on the new website.
  - **Tracking website analytics:** Tools like Google Analytics show how many people visit the website, which pages they view, and how long they stay. This data tells you if the redesign makes the website more user-friendly.
- **Analyzing customer feedback:** People are the heart of design thinking. Their feedback is invaluable in understanding if your solution is actually addressing their needs. Imagine you designed a new cafeteria menu system based on student preferences. Analyze customer feedback by:
  - **Collecting surveys:** Ask students if they find the new menu options more appealing and more accessible to choose from.
  - **Setting up suggestion boxes:** Encourage students to leave anonymous feedback on what they like or dislike about the new system.
  - **Holding open forums:** Organize discussions where students can voice their opinions and suggestions for improvement.
- **Tracking data from prototyping processes:** A prototype is a basic, early version of your design solution. It is like a test run before building the final product. By tracking prototype data, you can see if users respond positively and identify any potential problems early on. Let us say you created a prototype of a new recycling program with different colored bins for other materials. Track data by:
  - **Observing how students use the prototypes:** Do they understand which bin to use for each material? Are there any initial confusions?
  - **Recording user interactions:** Track how many students use each bin and if there are any mistakes in sorting waste.
  - **Analyzing feedback on prototypes:** Ask students for their initial impressions on the clarity and effectiveness of the new system based on the prototype.

By using these three methods, you can measure the impact of design thinking and check if your solutions are making a positive difference. Remember, design thinking is an iterative process. The data you collect will help you refine your solutions and ensure they truly meet the needs of the users.

Here's an analogy to remember: imagine throwing a pebble into a pond. The ripples extend outwards, affecting the entire surface. In design thinking, your solution is the pebble, and your impact – a more user-friendly website, a tastier cafeteria menu, or a more sustainable recycling program – is the ripple effect.

By carefully observing user experience, analyzing feedback, and tracking data, you can ensure your design thinking solutions create positive and lasting ripples in the lives of the people you are trying to help.

10.3 Challenges of Measuring Design Thinking

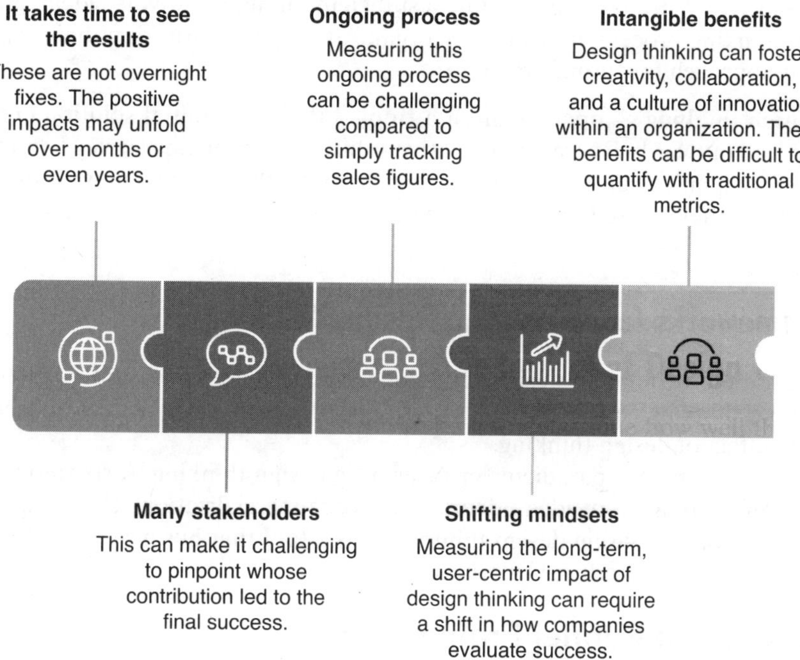

Figure 10.1 Challenges of measuring design thinking

Design thinking has become a popular approach for companies seeking innovation. It is a creative problem-solving process that emphasizes understanding user needs. However, measuring the impact of design thinking can be tricky, for the following reasons (Fig.10.1):

- Design thinking tackles **complex challenges**. Imagine improving healthcare delivery or redesigning public transportation systems – these are not overnight fixes. The positive impacts may unfold over months or even years.
- Design thinking is a **collaborative effort**. Project managers, designers, and, most importantly, the end-users are all involved. This can make it challenging to pinpoint whose contribution led to the final success.
- Design thinking is an **iterative process**. There is a lot of brainstorming, prototyping (building basic test versions), and refining of ideas before a final solution is reached. Measuring this ongoing process can be challenging compared to simply tracking sales figures.

- Traditional business metrics often focus on short-term gains. Measuring the long-term, user-centric impact of design thinking can require a **shift in how companies evaluate success**.
- Design thinking can foster creativity, collaboration, and a culture of innovation within an organization. These **benefits can be difficult to quantify** with traditional metrics.

However, there are ways to navigate these challenges and assess the effectiveness of design thinking:

- **Track the number of innovative solutions** generated during the design thinking process. Did the team develop many fresh ideas for new products, services, or ways to improve existing ones? This can be a good indicator of design thinking's ability to spark creativity.
- **Poll project stakeholders**, including end-users, to gather feedback on their experience with the design thinking process and the final solution. Did it effectively address their needs? This feedback helps gauge the impact and identify areas for improvement.
- **Post-project reviews** are valuable tools. Ask questions like: "Did we truly understand the user's perspective?" or "Did we generate a sufficient number of diverse ideas?" By dissecting the design thinking process after the fact, organizations can learn from their experiences and refine their approach for future projects.

Remember, design thinking's impact is often a ripple effect. The initial solution creates positive changes that spread outwards. By tracking creative solutions, conducting surveys, and holding post-project reviews, companies can gain valuable insights into the effectiveness of design thinking. This, in turn, allows them to refine their strategies and unlock even more significant innovation potential.

10.4 Frameworks for Measuring Design Thinking

To fully appreciate the benefits of design thinking, a business must measure its effects. However, quantifying design thinking can be difficult. There are numerous frameworks that businesses can use to gauge the effect of design thinking.

The innovation funnel is a paradigm for measuring design thinking. A six-step method, it aids enterprises in transitioning from idea generation to commercialization. The design scorecard is another framework for evaluating design thinking. It is a tool that businesses use to evaluate how well their design thinking procedure is working.

10.4.1 Innovation Funnel Framework

With this framework, businesses can view the innovation process as a funnel that gathers a vast number of ideas before selecting the finest ones to put into practice (Fig. 10.2).

In the first stage – the **idea generation** stage – businesses use brainstorming, ideation sessions, and other creative methods to produce many ideas. As it enables businesses to investigate a wide range of alternatives and opportunities, this stage is essential to the design thinking process.

The **screening or harvesting** stage is the second stage of the innovation funnel. Organizations assess the ideas produced in the idea generation stage to decide which ones need further investigation. At this step, the ideas are systematically assessed in light of specified standards like viability, desirability, and practicality.

Idea development is the third stage, where businesses develop the chosen concepts from the screening stage into more intricate ones. This phase involves prototyping, testing, and iterating to hone the concepts further. The goal is to comprehend the wants and problems of the user in its entirety.

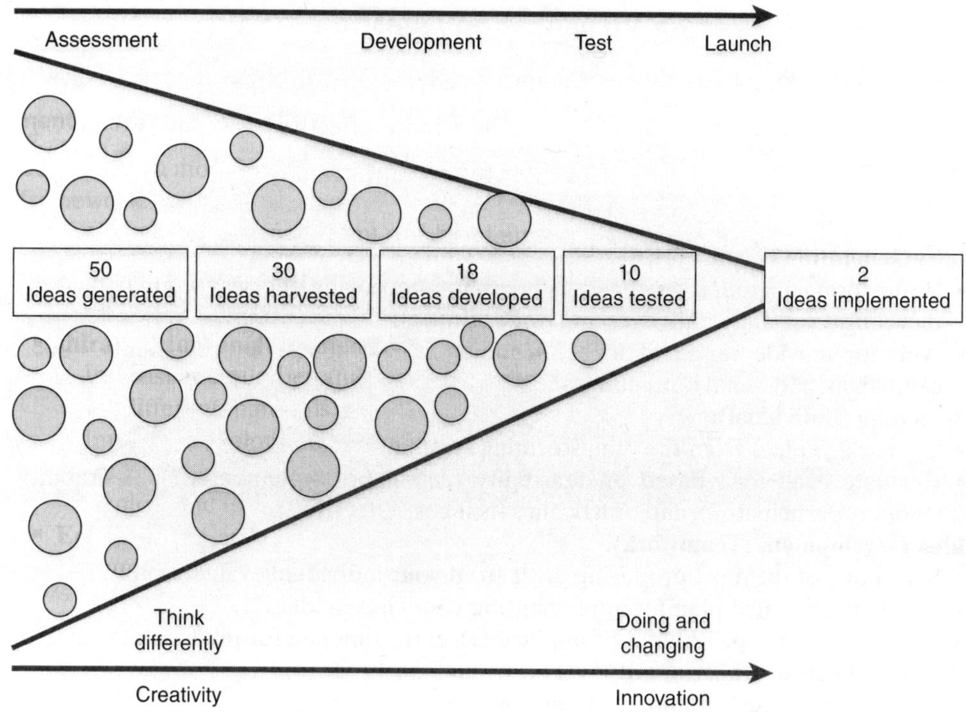

Figure 10.2 Innovation funnel framework

The **business analysis or testing** stage is the fourth level in the innovation funnel. Organizations assess the financial viability and potential market impact of the concepts created in the concept development stage. To assess the viability of the concepts, this stage entails market research, financial analysis, and other business-related activities.

The **implementation** stage is the last stage of the innovation funnel. In this phase, businesses advertise the concepts created during the concept development and business analysis stages. This stage encompasses product development, launch, and continuous review to ensure the product satisfies user demands and business goals.

The innovation funnel framework lets businesses see the innovation process as a funnel and gauge how well their design-thinking methodology works at each level. Businesses can use this framework to stimulate creativity and develop products that cater to their target market.
We can measure effectiveness through the funnel as follows:

- **Idea generation:** Track the number of ideas generated during brainstorming sessions.
- **Screening:** Analyze the criteria used for selecting ideas and the number of ideas that move forward.
- **Idea development:** Measure the success of prototypes through user testing and feedback.
- **Business analysis:** Assess the financial viability and potential market impact (improved student health) of the chosen solution.

By evaluating each stage of the innovation funnel, we can gain valuable insights into the effectiveness of the design thinking process.

Design Visualization Question 10.1

Assignment: Rethinking Recycling on Campus

Objective: Use the innovation funnel to design a more effective recycling program on your college campus.

Instructions:

1. **Idea Generation (Teamwork):**
   - Brainstorm in groups to generate ideas for improving the way your college handles recycling. Consider challenges and opportunities.
   - Aim for a wide range of ideas, including infrastructure improvements, educational campaigns, and behavioral nudges.
2. **Screening (Individual):**
   - Choose 2–3 ideas from the brainstorming session.
   - Evaluate each idea based on feasibility (can it be implemented?), desirability (will students participate?), and practicality (is it cost-effective?).
3. **Idea Development (Teamwork):**
   - Select one of the most promising ideas from your individual evaluations.
   - Develop a detailed plan for implementing your chosen idea.
   - Include sketches, prototypes (if applicable), and a timeline for pilot testing.
4. **Business Analysis (Individual):**
   - Analyze the potential impact of your proposed solution.
   - Consider environmental benefits, cost savings for the college, and potential changes in student behavior.
5. **Present Your Innovation (Teamwork):**
   - Prepare a presentation showcasing your team's project.
   - Explain your design thinking process, the chosen solution, and its potential effectiveness.

10.4.2 Design Scorecard Framework

An effective technique for assessing the effectiveness of design thinking is the design scorecard framework. This framework offers a method for assessing design projects using established standards.

A design project's success is measured using several criteria that comprise the design scorecard framework. The user experience, functionality, aesthetics, and technological performance are frequently included in these criteria. The design scorecard aims to offer a methodical method for assessing design work based on quantifiable standards.

One of its main advantages is that this framework offers a straightforward and impartial method of assessing design projects. When several stakeholders are involved in the design process, this might be very crucial. Stakeholders can evaluate design projects based on a shared set of criteria by utilizing the design scorecard, which can help ensure everyone is on the same page.

The design scorecard also aids in pinpointing areas where the design process might be strengthened. The design team may need to spend more time investigating and comprehending the demands of the target audience if a project obtains a poor score for user experience, for instance. In addition, the design scorecard can encourage ongoing development in the design process by highlighting areas that need to be improved.

Organizations often begin by setting the standards by which design projects will be judged before applying the design scorecard structure. These standards should be based on the target market's needs and the business's aims and objectives. Design projects can be assessed depending on how well they adhere to the criteria once they have been established.

Consider a scenario in which a business is creating a new mobile application. Criteria like usability, utility, aesthetics, and technical performance could be on the design scorecard. The business might then assess the app according to how effectively it satisfies each requirement. For example, suppose the app earns good marks for usability and aesthetics but low marks for usability and functionality. In that case, the design team may need more time to perfect the app's visual layout.

The design scorecard framework is a valuable tool for assessing the effectiveness of design thinking. It helps guarantee that design initiatives satisfy the demands of the target audience and the organization's objectives by offering a methodical approach to evaluating design projects. In addition, the framework can aid in pinpointing areas where the design process needs attention, which can spur innovation and continual development.

Design Visualization Question 10.2

Assignment: Evaluating a Redesigned Product (Individual)

Objective: Apply the design scorecard to evaluate a recently redesigned product you have encountered.

Instructions:

1. **Choose a Product:** Select a consumer product that has undergone a recent redesign (packaging, website, mobile app).
2. **Define the Evaluation Criteria:** Identify 4–5 key criteria relevant to the chosen product and its target audience. Consider factors like:
   - **User experience (UX):** Is the product intuitive and easy to use?
   - **Functionality:** Does the product effectively perform its intended purpose?
   - **Aesthetics:** Is the design visually appealing and appropriate for the target audience?
   - **Technological performance (if applicable):** Does the product function smoothly and reliably (for apps or websites)?
3. **Develop a Scoring System:** Establish a scoring system for each criterion. This could be a simple point system (1–5 points) or a descriptive scale (excellent, good, fair, poor).|
4. **Evaluate the Product:** Analyze the redesigned product based on your defined criteria and scoring system:
   - Conduct research to understand the target audience and intended use of the product.|
   - Consider your own experience or user reviews to assess user experience and functionality.
   - Evaluate the visual design and its alignment with the target audience.
   - If applicable, assess technical performance through testing or user feedback.
5. **Present Your Evaluation:** Create a presentation or report summarizing your findings:
   - Briefly describe the redesigned product and the target audience.
   - Explain your chosen evaluation criteria and scoring system.
   - Present your evaluation results for each criterion and discuss your reasoning.
   - Conclude with an overall assessment of the product redesign's success based on the design scorecard evaluation.

10.5 Types of Metrics for Measuring Design Thinking

To measure the impact of design thinking, it is essential to use appropriate metrics (Fig. 10.3). Metrics that emphasize subjective observations, such as user feedback or subjective evidence, are called qualitative metrics. On the other hand, quantitative metrics involve numerical data that may be examined to produce quantifiable results. The use of either qualitative or quantitative metrics depends on the goals and objectives of the measurement because both have strengths and disadvantages. Hybrid metrics integrate quantitative and qualitative data to provide a more thorough knowledge of the effects of design thinking.

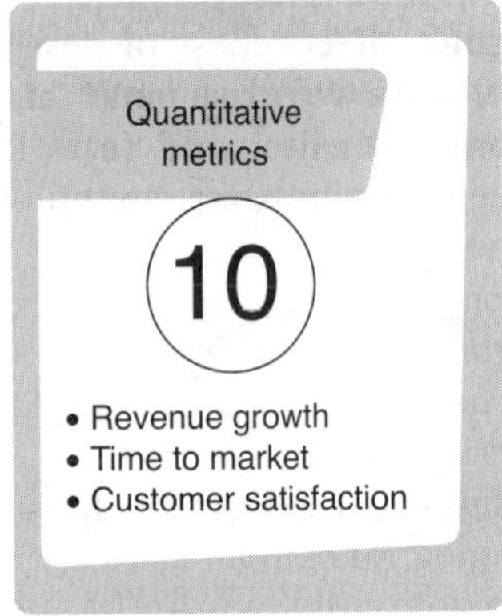

Figure 10.3 Quantitative, qualitative and hybird metrics

10.5.1 Quantitative Metrics

Quantitative metrics are objective and measurable, such as the number of new product launches or the percentage increase in sales. Some examples of quantitative metrics for measuring design thinking are:

- **Revenue growth:** This metric tracks the financial impact of design thinking by comparing the revenue generated before and after implementing design thinking methodologies. It provides a precise, objective measure of the financial success of design thinking initiatives. Increased revenue suggests that design thinking helped create products or services that resonate with customers and drive sales. Revenue growth can be influenced by factors beyond design thinking, such as market trends, competitor activity, and pricing strategies. Attributing revenue growth solely to design thinking requires careful consideration of other influencing factors. It is helpful to track revenue growth over an extended period to capture the long-term impact of design thinking. Analyse revenue growth alongside metrics like customer satisfaction or product adoption to build a more comprehensive picture.

  For businesses to defend their investment in design thinking, it is essential to measure its financial benefit. Making defensible choices about the application of design thinking in upcoming initiatives requires understanding the return on investment (ROI) of design thinking. The financial impact of design thinking can be evaluated in various ways. A typical strategy is calculating the cost savings or revenue gained by a project that uses design thinking. For instance, a business might employ design thinking to develop a new product that is less expensive and more user-friendly. Alternatively, a business might utilize design thinking to enhance the customer experience, raising client happiness and loyalty and, consequently, boosting sales.

Calculating the value of intellectual property produced through the design thinking process is another method for assessing the financial impact of design thinking. For instance, a business might utilize design thinking to create a new patentable product, which could result in more income from sales or licensing fees. Also, businesses can utilize design thinking to locate fresh markets and sources of income. For instance, design thinking can be employed to find unmet customer demands and create new products or services that address those needs. Again, this will create new markets and revenue streams. Calculating the financial benefits of design thinking can be challenging, and the data may only be sometimes accurate. Therefore, it is crucial to set precise criteria for gauging financial effects and ensure they align with the organization's overarching business objectives. To apply design thinking effectively and make wise decisions regarding future investments in this strategy, businesses must be able to quantify its financial impact. Therefore, organizations measure the value of design thinking and utilize it to promote innovation and growth by identifying cost reductions, income generation, intellectual property creation, and new business prospects.

- **Time-to-market:** This metric focuses on speed. It compares the time it takes to launch a product before and after using design thinking. Design thinking can streamline development by encouraging user-centered design, early prototyping, and iterative testing. Reduced time-to-market can lead to a competitive advantage by getting products to market faster. Not all products require a rapid launch. Complexity or regulatory requirements necessitate a longer development cycle. Focusing solely on speed might compromise quality or overlook crucial user needs. It is important to balance speed with quality. Track time-to-market alongside metrics like customer satisfaction or product defect rates to ensure a faster launch does not sacrifice user experience.
- **Customer satisfaction:** This metric assesses customers' satisfaction level with a product or service designed or redesigned through design thinking. Customer satisfaction surveys, ratings, and net promoter scores (NPS) are standard tools for measuring this. Customer satisfaction is crucial to a product or service's success. Design thinking should lead to solutions that address user needs and provide a positive user experience. Increased customer satisfaction can translate to higher customer loyalty, repeat business, and positive word-of-mouth marketing. Customer satisfaction can be subjective and influenced by factors beyond the product, such as customer service interactions. Track customer satisfaction throughout the product life cycle to understand how it evolves. Analyse customer feedback alongside design thinking activities to identify specific design choices that positively impact customer experience.

These quantitative metrics offer valuable insights into the effectiveness of design thinking. Remember, the most powerful approach combines these metrics with qualitative data (such as user interviews, focus groups) to paint a complete picture. By understanding the 'what' (quantitative results) and the 'why' (qualitative feedback), you can truly assess the impact of design thinking and continuously refine your approach to create solutions that not only meet business goals but also resonate with users.

10.5.2 Qualitative Metrics

Qualitative metrics, such as customer feedback or employee engagement, are subjective and more complex to measure. Examples of qualitative metrics for measuring design thinking include:

- **User experience:** This metric focuses on how users interact with a product or service. It encompasses ease of use, accessibility, intuitiveness, and overall enjoyment. Design thinking emphasizes user-centered design, so successful implementation should lead to a positive UX. User testing sessions, usability studies, A/B testing of design elements, and collecting user feedback through surveys, interviews, and reviews are all valuable tools for measuring UX. A positive UX translates to user satisfaction, increased product adoption, and loyalty. Measuring UX helps ensure that design thinking leads to solutions that address user needs and provide a seamless experience.

- **Brand perception:** This metric delves into how customers perceive a brand. Design thinking promotes user empathy and understanding, which can translate into design choices that resonate with target audiences and strengthen brand identity. Brand tracking studies, social media sentiment analysis, customer surveys about brand image, and focus groups exploring brand association are helpful tools. Positive brand perception leads to customer trust, loyalty, and advocacy. You can gauge how design thinking influences brand image and user experience by measuring brand perception.
- **Employee engagement:** This metric assesses employee satisfaction and motivation. Design thinking workshops and training can empower employees to be more creative, innovative, and problem-solving, potentially leading to increased engagement. Employee satisfaction surveys, focus groups on design thinking workshops, and tracking participation in design challenges or innovation initiatives can provide insights. Highly engaged employees are more productive, satisfied, and likely to stay with the company. Measuring employee engagement helps organizations understand how design thinking fosters a culture of innovation and collaboration.

10.5.3 Hybrid Metrics

Hybrid metrics integrate quantitative and qualitative data to provide a more thorough knowledge of the effects of design thinking. Examples of hybrid metrics for measuring design thinking include:

- **Net promoter score (NPS):** This metric combines a quantitative measure (customer loyalty score) with qualitative feedback on the reasons behind that score. Customers are asked on a scale of 0–10 how likely they are to recommend the product/service to others. Detractors (scores 0–6) are unhappy and may spread negative word-of-mouth. Passives (scores 7–8) are satisfied but not enthusiastic. Promoters (scores 9–10) are loyal and likely to recommend the product/service. NPS is calculated by subtracting the percentage of detractors from the percentage of promoters. Design thinking emphasizes understanding user needs and creating solutions that address them. By fostering empathy and user-centered design, NPS can be used to assess how effectively design thinking leads to customer satisfaction and loyalty. Qualitative feedback from the NPS survey can reveal specific areas where design thinking has improved the product or service, or identify areas needing further design thinking efforts.
- **Innovation index:** This metric offers a holistic view of an organization's innovation process. It combines quantitative and qualitative data points to assess the overall innovation capability. Quantitative measures could include revenue growth from new products or services, number of patents filed and time-to-market for new products. Qualitative measures could include employee surveys on design thinking implementation and creativity, customer feedback on the innovativeness of products or services, and the number of ideas generated through design thinking workshops. By measuring the innovation index, you can assess how design thinking contributes to generating a higher volume of innovative ideas, bringing innovative products or services to market faster, and achieving financial success through those innovations.

10.5.4 Leading and Lagging Indicators

Leading and trailing indicators can be used to assess the effects of design thinking. Lagging indicators quantify the effects of previous acts, whereas leading indicators forecast or signal future success (Fig. 10.4).

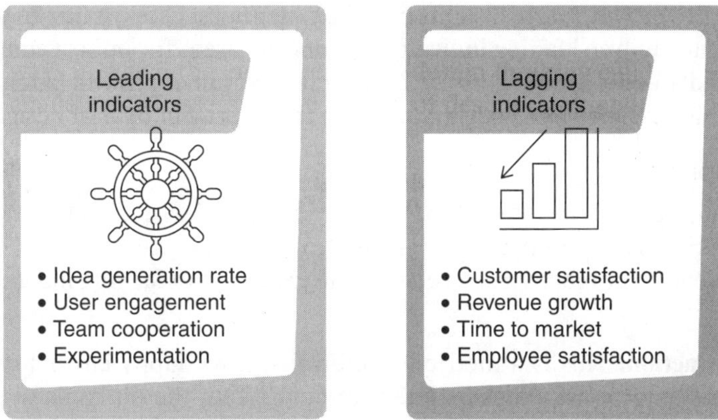

Figure 10.4 Leading and lagging indicators of design thinking

Leading Indicators

Using leading indicators to gauge design thinking can help teams assess their progress and determine whether they are on track to meet their objectives. Here are some examples of the mainleading indicators for measuring design thinking:

- **Idea generation rate:** This metric tracks the number of ideas generated during a design thinking workshop or brainstorming session. A high idea generation rate suggests a creative and engaged team. It indicates the team is actively exploring various solutions and not settling for the first idea. Not all ideas are created equal. Focus on the quality and diversity of ideas alongside quantity.
- **User engagement:** This metric assesses how satisfied users are with a proposed solution developed through design thinking. User testing, surveys, and interviews can be used to gather user feedback. Early user engagement ensures solutions address user needs and expectations.
- **Team cooperation:** This metric assesses how effectively team members collaborate during the design thinking process. Observing team dynamics, conducting team surveys, or using project management tools to track communication and collaboration patterns can provide insights. Strong team cooperation fosters a culture of open communication, shared ownership of ideas, and the ability to build upon each other's strengths. This leads to more innovative and well-rounded solutions.
- **Experimentation:** This indicator assesses how frequently teams test out fresh concepts when engaging in design thinking. A willingness to experiment demonstrates openness to new ideas and a growth mindset. Testing early and often allows for rapid iteration and ensures solutions are feasible and effective.

Additional Leading Indicators

- **Problem definition clarity:** A clear and concise understanding of the problem being addressed is crucial for developing effective solutions.
- **Empathy with users:** The design thinking process emphasizes user empathy. Teams that actively seek to understand user needs are more likely to design solutions that resonate.
- **Prototyping speed:** The ability to quickly create prototypes allows for early testing and feedback, accelerating the design process and reducing the risk of developing solutions that do not meet user needs.

Leading indicators thus provide early insights into the potential success of design thinking initiatives. Regularly monitor and analyze leading indicators to identify areas for improvement and adjustment of approach if needed. Leading indicators are best used in conjunction with lagging indicators (such as customer satisfaction, revenue growth) to measure the overall impact of design thinking.

Lagging Indicators

Teams can better comprehend the effects of their activities and decisions by using lagging indicators to gauge design thinking. These metrics give information about whether the design thinking process has successfully achieved its objectives. Here are some examples of lagging indicators for measuring design thinking:

- **Customer satisfaction:** This is a metric to determine how happy customers are with a given good or service. It can assist teams in determining whether the outcome of their design thinking process is a solution that satisfies user requirements and expectations.
- **Revenue growth:** This indicator assesses an organization's financial impact of a design thinking approach. It can assist teams in determining whether their use of design thinking has resulted in the development of new revenue sources or an increase in overall revenue.
- **Time to market:** This measures the time it takes for a good or service to reach the market. It can assist teams in determining whether their use of design thinking has resulted in the development of easily implementable solutions.
- **Employee satisfaction:** This is a metric used to gauge employees' happiness with their jobs and contributions to the design thinking process. It can assist teams in determining whether their use of design thinking supports a productive workplace and innovation.

It is critical to include both leading and lagging indications when assessing the effectiveness of design thinking. While trailing indicators offer information into the overall effectiveness of the design thinking process, leading indicators can assist teams to stay on course and modify their approach as needed. Organizations may ensure they are accomplishing their objectives and promoting innovation through design thinking by combining both metrics.

10.6 The Impact of Design Thinking on User Experience

Design thinking has gained importance in enhancing user experience by centering the design process around the user. The strategy emphasizes developing solutions that cater to user wants and expectations, leading to a more fulfilling and exciting experience. The impact of design thinking on user experience is as follows:

- **Simplifying complex interfaces:** Many goods and services were created with technological capabilities in mind, with user experience receiving minimal consideration. This method has been altered by design thinking, which has simplified and improved interfaces. For example, to enhance user experience, Google, a business renowned for its minimalist design, has implemented design thinking ideas in its search engine. The result is a user-friendly design that is clear and simple to use.
- **Personalization:** Another strategy to enhance the user experience is personalization. By gathering consumer input and insights, design thinking enables the creation of more customized products and services. Personalization enhances the user experience, user engagement, and company brand loyalty. For a more exciting experience and increased user retention, Netflix, for instance, has successfully applied this method. The streaming service employs data analytics to make subscriber-specific content recommendations. Design thinking has enhanced user experience through innovation. By focusing on users' needs and difficulties, designers can

create unique solutions that solve their requests and problems. An example is the Nest thermostat, which was developed with straightforward controls and energy-saving features, leading to a user-friendly product. It also enhances the overall user experience.

- **Emotive Design:** User experience has also been altered by design thinking through emotive design. Designing goods and services to arouse emotions and establish a stronger connection with customers is known as emotional design. By establishing an emotional connection, design professionals may improve user engagement and brand loyalty. With its sleek, simple, and aesthetically pleasing designs that serve a purpose, Apple is a corporation that has perfected inspirational design.

By putting the user at the center of the design process, design thinking has drastically improved user experience. Designers may produce more engaging, user-friendly, and rewarding solutions by streamlining interfaces, customizing goods and services, encouraging innovation, and embracing emotional design. Businesses that have used design thinking ideas have enhanced user experience while boosting revenue, brand recognition, and customer loyalty.

10.6.1 Metrics for Measuring User Experience

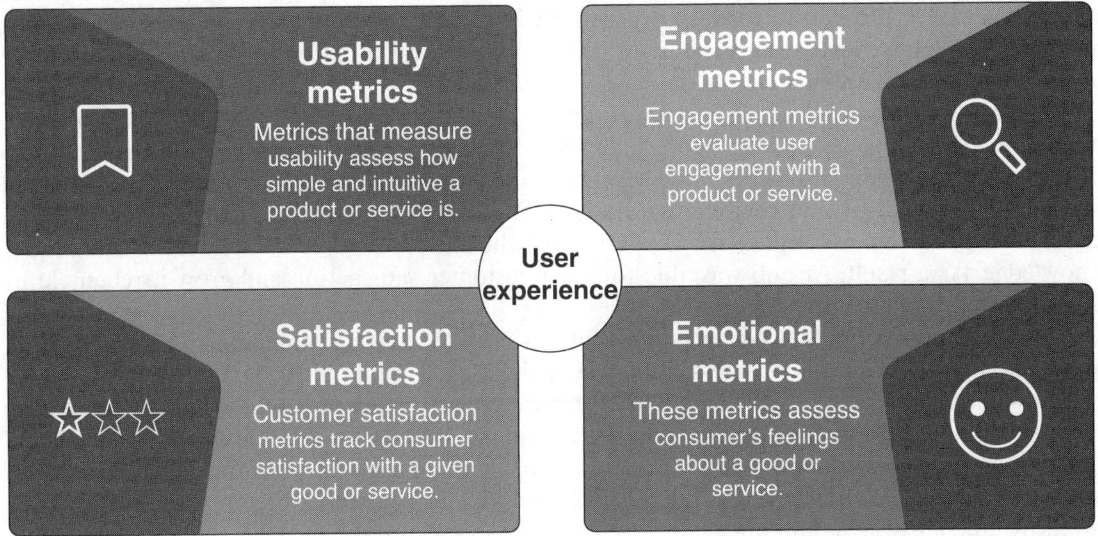

Figure 10.5 Metrics for measuring user experience

With a user-centric strategy, design thinking strives to develop solutions that satisfy users' demands and improve their experience. Therefore, the impact on user experience must be evaluated to determine the effectiveness of design thinking. Following are a few metrics used in the design thinking process to gauge user experience (Fig. 10.5):

- **Usability:** Metrics that measure usability assess how simple and intuitive a product or service is. Task completion time, mistake rate, and ease of use are all examples of usability metrics. Users, questionnaires, or expert evaluations can all be used to measure these parameters.
- **Engagement:** Engagement metrics are metrics that evaluate user engagement with a product or service. For example, time spent using a product, interactions, and frequency of use are all engagement indicators. These metrics can be determined using analytics software, polls, or user reviews.

- **Customer satisfaction:** Customer satisfaction metrics track consumer satisfaction with a given good or service. For example, customer effort score (CES), net promoter score (NPS), and customer satisfaction score are all measures of customer satisfaction (CSAT). In addition, surveys or consumer reviews can also be used to measure these parameters.
- **Emotional:** These metrics assess consumers' feelings about a good or service. Among the emotional measures are contentment, elation, and annoyance. Surveys, interviews, and user feedback are all effective ways to measure these variables. These analytics track how user experience affects financial results like sales and client retention. Analytics software, questionnaires, or company data can all be used to measure business indicators.

10.6.2 The Relationship between Design Thinking and Customer Satisfaction

Empathy with end-users is a critical component of the design thinking methodology, underpinned by a thorough knowledge of their needs, wants, and preferences. As a result, companies can produce goods and services that genuinely resonate with their customers and increase satisfaction levels by applying the concepts of design thinking. Design thinking promotes in-depth customer insight, which can increase empathy and improve understanding of their demands. Understanding consumer demands enables businesses to design goods and services tailored to those needs, increasing customer happiness. Several businesses use this strategy to raise customer satisfaction and forge closer connections with their clients.

Airbnb is a business that has employed design thinking to raise customer satisfaction levels. Airbnb recognized a demand for more individualized and genuine travel experiences thanks to design thinking. Under its Experiences program, the firm reinvented how people traveled and started to provide distinctive regional experiences. Through this program, tourists can reserve local excursions and activities conducted by expert hosts who can provide recommendations and insider knowledge. As a result, Airbnb was able to boost customer satisfaction and grow its clientele by adopting a customer-centric strategy.

Warby Parker is another organization that has employed design thinking to raise consumer satisfaction. The eyeglasses business uses design thinking to pinpoint a demand for reasonably priced, stylish spectacles that are simple to purchase online. The company's virtual try-on feature lets customers upload a photo and try on glasses digitally. Because of this feature, customers could now try on glasses without leaving the comfort of their homes, removing the inconvenience of visiting a real store. Warby Parker developed a seamless client experience that increased satisfaction levels by utilizing design thinking.

10.7 Measuring the Impact of Design Thinking on Organizational Culture

In addition to being a method for solving problems, design thinking also acts as a catalyst for cultural change inside an organization. It emphasizes empathy, collaboration, and iteration, which causes a change in both individual and team mindsets. Understanding the effectiveness of this methodology in fostering an environment of innovation, experimentation, and creativity requires measuring the effect of design thinking on corporate culture.

Many companies, like Apple, Google, and IBM, have effectively embraced design thinking, which has had a substantial impact on the organizational cultures of those companies. For instance, design thinking has changed the corporate culture at IBM by motivating staff members to think creatively and collaborate. As a result, cutting-edge goods and services, including Watson, a platform for cognitive computing, have been created. A comprehensive strategy that considers both qualitative and quantitative indicators is needed to assess the effect of design thinking on corporate culture. Employee feedback, team dynamics, and cultural values are examples of qualitative measures. In contrast, quantitative metrics include employee engagement, retention rates, and innovation metrics.

Organizations can use several frameworks to assess the influence of design thinking on organizational culture. The **design value index**, created by the Design Management Institute, for instance, tracks the stock performance of businesses that make investments in design and can gauge how design thinking affects corporate culture. The **cultural transformation framework** is another framework that evaluates an organization's intended and current culture and offers a path for cultural change.

As a result of encouraging cooperation, innovation, and creativity, design thinking can change company culture. To fully appreciate design thinking's worth and keep bringing about change inside an organization, measuring its effects on organizational culture is crucial. Organizations may effectively assess and advance their cultural change journeys by combining qualitative and quantitative measurements and frameworks.

10.7.1 Metrics for Measuring Organizational Culture

The collective ideals, attitudes, and practices that influence how individuals interact and make decisions within an organization are called organizational culture. A healthy company culture may boost productivity, encourage employee involvement, and enhance overall business performance. A valuable tool for influencing and enhancing company culture is design thinking. Several measures can be employed to assess the effect of design thinking on company culture:

- **Employee satisfaction and engagement:** Employee engagement and satisfaction are crucial measures for assessing organizational culture. Employees who are actively involved in their work are more dedicated, motivated, and productive. Surveys, focus groups, and feedback sessions can all be used to gauge employee happiness. In addition, design thinking can assist in identifying employee pain spots, creating solutions to solve them, and putting into practice methods to increase employee engagement and happiness.
- **Diversity and inclusion:** A positive organizational culture must value diversity and inclusiveness. An inclusive and varied workplace can promote innovation, creativity, and improved decision-making. Some measures used to gauge diversity and inclusion are the number of minority employees, retention rates, and promotion rates. By detecting prejudices and developing solutions, design thinking can assist organizations in building a more inclusive workplace.
- **Collaboration and communication:** A healthy organizational culture depends on effective collaboration and communication. To gauge cooperation and communication, metrics, including meeting productivity, response times, and feedback quality, can be used. By identifying communication gaps, creating ways to close them, and implementing these solutions, design thinking can assist in increasing collaboration and communication.
- **Innovation and creativity:** Innovation and creativity are crucial for accelerating growth and maintaining an edge over the competition. Innovation and creativity can be measured using metrics like the number of original ideas developed, the success rates of their implementation, and the money produced by new goods and services. In addition, organizations can benefit from using design thinking to develop novel ideas, test and improve them, and implement effective solutions.

- **Learning and development:** For staff growth and retention, learning and development are essential. Learning and development can be measured using metrics like training attendance rates, skill growth, and employee satisfaction with training. In addition, organizations can use design thinking to identify skill gaps, create training programs, and implement measures to support learning and development.

Organizations must thus evaluate the effect of design thinking on organizational culture to determine the success of their design thinking projects.

10.7.2 The Role of Leadership in Promoting a Design Thinking Culture

Design thinking has grown in popularity in recent years as an approach to problem-solving and creativity in businesses. However, strong leadership is necessary for a design thinking culture to flourish within a company. For a company to be really good at design thinking, it needs leaders who believe in these steps and show everyone else how it is done. These leaders are like the captains of a sports team, setting thc tone and leading by example. They do not just tell others to be empathetic and cooperative; they do it themselves. They are the first to suggest trying new things and are not afraid to learn from mistakes.

For example, a famous company that makes computers started by understanding that people wanted easy-to-use and beautiful products. The leaders worked closely with designers and engineers, tried many prototypes, and kept improving their products. This company is known for its innovation and has a strong design thinking culture because its leaders live by these principles. In another case, a large shoe manufacturer spent a lot of time understanding athletes' needs. They collaborated with sportspeople to design shoes, tested them rigorously, and kept updating the designs. This company's leaders were involved in every step, ensuring that the shoes not only looked good but also performed well.

By offering resources and support for design thinking efforts, leaders may encourage design thinking. This can involve allocating funds for design thinking initiatives, scheduling specific times and places for design thinking activities, and supporting training and development programs. Also, leaders are essential in fostering a culture of innovation and risk-taking. It can be difficult for businesses to use design thinking since it calls for experimentation and iteration. At the same time, efficiency and predictability are valued more highly. Therefore, leaders must be prepared to accept failure and inspire their staff to try new things and make mistakes.

Building cross-functional teams and promoting departmental cooperation are additional ways leaders can support a design thinking culture. Design thinking requires collaboration since it combines many viewpoints and skill sets. Leaders may promote collaboration by allowing workers to collaborate on design thinking initiatives and projects.

Finally, executives must constantly emphasize the value of design thinking and how it affects the organization's achievement. Regular communication and feedback, praising and rewarding team members and individuals who apply design thinking principles, and implementing design thinking in the company's values and goals are all effective ways to do this.

Several businesses with strong leadership support have effectively introduced a design thinking culture. IBM is one organization that has incorporated design thinking into its procedures and culture. In addition, the business has created cross-functional teams focusing on design thinking projects and developed a Design Thinking Academy to train and support staff.

Another illustration is Airbnb, which promotes collaboration, experimentation, and iteration within a design-centric culture. The company's management established a framework for establishing and upholding design consistency across the firm as part of a Design Language System.

Leadership is essential for establishing and maintaining an organization's design thinking culture. Leaders must be familiar with the ideas and tenets of design thinking, support initiatives that use them with resources and assistance, promote experimentation and collaboration, and constantly emphasize their significance in attaining the objectives of the business. By doing this, leaders can develop a culture that encourages success, innovation, and creativity.

10.8 Measuring the Impact of Design Thinking on Society

The social influence of design thinking is enormous. This process allows businesses and people to provide novel answers to pressing social issues. Healthcare, education, transportation, and sustainability are just a few industries that have benefited from design thinking.

The quantity of social issues that have been resolved utilizing design thinking is one of the critical measures for gauging its influence on society. For instance, in India, the issue of rural electrification has been addressed using the design thinking methodology. Thanks to a government initiative, every village in the nation can have access to power. Design thinking was employed to find the program's implementation potential and problems. With this strategy, the government created a strategy that addressed the issues and took advantage of the chance to bring power to more than 18,000 villages.

The number of individuals who have profited from design thinking is another indicator for assessing its influence on society. For instance, design thinking has been applied to the healthcare industry to create technologies and medical products to enhance patient outcomes. For example, Embrace Warmer is a low-cost incubator explicitly made for premature infants in underdeveloped nations. The Embrace Warmer controls the baby's body temperature, lowering the likelihood of hypothermia. In nations like India and Nepal, this technology has been instrumental in saving thousands of lives.

The degree of accessibility design thinking provides can also be used to gauge its influence on society. For instance, the design thinking process has provided affordable housing solutions for low-income families. As a result, the government of Singapore has put in place a policy to give its people access to inexpensive homes. The program employs a design thinking methodology to provide cutting-edge, environmentally friendly housing options available to all inhabitants.

The sustainability of design thinking can be evaluated to determine the extent of its social influence. For instance, eco-friendly transportation choices that reduce carbon emissions have been developed using design thinking. One example of this is the Copenhagen Wheel. This electronic bicycle wheel generates power as the cyclist pedals and stores it when the bike brakes. With the help of this device, carbon emissions can be reduced, and environmentally friendly transportation can be promoted.

Design thinking has a significant impact on society, to sum it up. It can be gauged by looking at how many social issues have been resolved, how many people have benefited, how accessible it is, and how much sustainability is encouraged. In addition, design thinking has been utilized to create novel solutions that help society in several industries, including healthcare, education, transportation, and sustainability. The influence of design thinking on society will increase as more businesses and people adopt this strategy.

10.8.1 Metrics for Measuring Social Impact

Design thinking aims to improve society by doing more than just finding solutions to problems. Hence, it is crucial to gauge how design thinking affects society. Therefore, metrics for quantifying social impact should concentrate on how design thinking solutions advance social progress and have long-term effects on society.

The social impact of design thinking can be measured using a variety of social metrics, including the number of people who have benefited from a design solution, the number of jobs created, and the extent to which the target population's quality of life has improved. For instance, the number of individuals who now have access to clean water could be used as a measure of the social impact of a design solution that aims to increase access to clean water in a rural community.

Assessing the degree of community engagement and participation in the design thinking process is another criterion for gauging social effects. This statistic is essential for verifying that design solutions satisfy the requirements of the community they are intended to serve. Design thinking that involves community involvement and cooperation can produce solutions more in line with the values and ambitions of the community.

In addition, the outcomes of design thinking should be long-lasting and beneficial to society. Hence, metrics for measuring social effects should consider the design solution's level of sustainability and its capacity to impact the community in the long term. For instance, the number of plastic bags prevented from ending up in landfills or the oceans might be used to gauge the success of a design solution that tries to decrease plastic waste in a city.

Last but not least, social impact indicators should gauge the extent to which design thinking solutions improve society. It should concentrate on how much the solution has advanced social fairness and inclusion, the economic growth and development rate, and the quality of life in the community. For example, to measure the success of a design strategy intended to lessen social inequality in a community, one could look at factors such as income redistribution or the number of persons lifted out of poverty.

10.8.2 Ethical Considerations of Measuring the Impact of Design Thinking on Society

Design thinking is being more frequently applied as a problem-solving method to develop original solutions that advance society. Yet, ethical issues must be considered when assessing the influence of design thinking on society. The possibility of unforeseen effects is one ethical factor to take into account. There is always a chance that implementing design thinking solutions will have unexpected repercussions that hurt society. For instance, a design thinking solution to provide clean water in a rural location may unintentionally degrade regional ecosystems or affect regional livelihoods. Therefore, design thinkers must conduct a thorough study and include stakeholders to predict and reduce unexpected outcomes to address this ethical challenge.

The possibility of prejudice in the design thinking procedure is another ethical problem. Empathy and user comprehension are necessary for design thinking, but individual prejudices and experiences can influence them. This can result in decisions that are not fair or inclusive. For instance, a design thinking proposal to increase access to healthcare might include something other than the needs of disadvantaged groups. To solve this ethical challenge, design thinkers must be conscious of their prejudices and participate in continuing training and education to promote diversity, equity, and inclusion.

The possibility of exploiting weaker people is a third ethical factor to consider. Be sure that disadvantaged people are not taken advantage of for the benefit of others when developing social impact solutions. For instance, a design thinking solution that depends on unpaid labor or unscrupulous business methods could hurt the people it intends to serve. Design thinkers need to put each stakeholder's autonomy and dignity first to handle this ethical issue and prevent any exploitation or unfair treatment.

Many indicators can be used to gauge the societal impact of design thinking. A few of these are as follows:

- **Accessibility**: How widely is the solution available, and how simple is it?
- **Affordability**: How affordable is the solution, and how easily accessible is it to those with few financial resources?
- **Sustainability**: How environmentally friendly is the proposed solution, and how does it affect nearby ecosystems?
- **Integrity**: To what extent does the solution consider the demands of underprivileged groups?
- **Equity**: How does the solution promote justice and alleviate ingrained inequalities?

Engaging in open, inclusive assessment processes that include all stakeholders is crucial to address the ethical issues involved in assessing the social impact of design thinking. This can involve regular monitoring and assessment, participatory research techniques, and community input meetings. Design thinkers must also be conscious of power relationships and take care to collaborate with communities rather than imposing their solutions on them.

Assessing the influence of design thinking on society necessitates carefully weighing ethical issues and using the proper measures. In addition, design thinkers can ensure that their solutions are long-lasting, just, and advantageous for everyone by emphasizing transparency, inclusion, and community involvement.

10.9 Key Takeaways from Measuring the Impact of Design Thinking

Companies must measure the impact of design thinking to determine how well the process works in reaching desired results. There are several ways to gauge the results of design thinking, including the effect on user experience, the degree of teamwork, the level of risk-taking within a company, and the level of consumer participation and feedback.

First, assessing a product or service's happiness and usability can be used to gauge the impact of design thinking on the user experience. For instance, Airbnb used design thinking to give its users a simple and personalized booking experience. Airbnb determined the effectiveness of its design thinking methodology in enhancing user experience by tracking user engagement and feedback.

Second, assessing the degree of cooperation and communication among team members can be used to gauge the level of collaboration within teams. Collaboration is crucial to the success of design thinking, and businesses can gauge its efficiency by gauging how well teams collaborate. For instance, IBM has reshaped its corporate culture and promoted employee collaboration using design thinking. As a result, IBM determined how well design thinking promoted teamwork and innovation by assessing the level of collaboration within teams.

Thirdly, the degree of experimentation and innovation in product development can be used to gauge the level of risk-taking inside a firm. The effectiveness of design thinking can be determined by evaluating the degree of risk-taking inside a business. Design thinking encourages organizations to take chances and experiment with new ideas. For instance, Procter & Gamble (P&G) increased revenue and market share using design thinking to develop new products. The effect of design thinking on the organization's innovation and growth might be assessed by assessing the level of risk-taking within P&G.

The degree of consumer interaction and feedback can also be used to determine the amount of customer engagement. Organizations can gauge the success of design thinking by looking at the level of consumer interaction and feedback because it emphasizes understanding and empathizing with the customer. Apple is a company that has applied design thinking to its product development process. Apple could comprehend the influence of design thinking on its performance in developing consumer-centric products by monitoring customer happiness and feedback.

Organizations must measure the impact of design thinking to know how well the process works in reaching their desired results. Organizations may learn a lot about the effectiveness of design thinking by assessing the influence on user experience, amount of team cooperation, level of risk-taking within a company, and level of consumer engagement and feedback. With this knowledge, businesses may continue to apply design thinking more effectively while fostering innovation and expansion.

Some key takeaways from measuring the impact of design thinking include profitability, market share, and revenue growth. While developing goods and services that fulfill consumer demands and expectations, measuring the influence of design thinking on user experience is essential. Building a solid company culture that encourages creativity, teamwork, and continual development can help with design thinking. By using social impact indicators, organizations can evaluate the consequences of design thinking on society, including problems with diversity, equity, and inclusion.

Summary

- The impact of design thinking is likened to throwing a pebble into a pond, with the solution being the pebble and the impact being the ripple effect.
- By observing user experience, analyzing feedback, and tracking data, design-thinking solutions can create positive and lasting ripples in the lives of the people they aim to help.
- The innovation funnel is a six-step method that aids businesses in transitioning from idea generation to commercialization.
- The design scorecard is a tool to evaluate how well the design thinking procedure is working.
- Qualitative metrics emphasize subjective observations, such as user feedback or subjective evidence.
- Quantitative metrics involve numerical data that can be examined to produce quantifiable results.
- The use of either qualitative or quantitative metrics depends on the goals and objectives of the measurement.
- Usability metrics measure how simple and intuitive a product or service is. Task completion time, mistake rate, and ease of use are examples of usability metrics.
- Engagement metrics evaluate user engagement with a product or service. Time spent using a product, interactions, and frequency of use are engagement indicators.
- Customer satisfaction metrics track consumer satisfaction with a given good or service.
- Emotional metrics assess consumers' feelings about a good or service. Surveys, interviews, and user feedback are effective ways to measure these variables.
- Design thinkers must be aware of their prejudices and participate in ongoing training and education to promote diversity, equity, and inclusion.

Solutions to Design Visualization Questions

Q 10.1

Assignment 1: Rethinking Recycling on Campus - Sample Solution using the Innovation Funnel

Objective: Design a more effective recycling program on your college campus using the innovation funnel framework.
Here's a sample solution you can adapt and build upon:

1. **Idea Generation**
   - **Brainstorming Ideas:** Here are some potential ideas to get you started:
     - **Infrastructure Improvements:**
       - Increase the number and visibility of recycling bins around campus, with clear signage for different materials.
       - Implement color-coded bins for easy identification (blue for paper, green for glass, etc.).
       - Explore the feasibility of installing specialized bins for compostable materials.
     - **Educational Campaigns:**
       - Launch awareness campaigns about the importance of recycling on campus.
       - Use posters, social media, and flyers to educate students about what can and cannot be recycled.
       - Organize workshops on proper sorting techniques and the environmental impact of recycling.
   - **Behavioral Nudges**
     - Implement a reward system for students who consistently use recycling bins correctly.
     - Partner with student organizations to host 'recycling challenges' with incentives for participation.
     - Utilize design elements on bins or in common areas that encourage proper recycling habits (playful messages or visual cues).

2. **Screening**
   - **Feasibility:** Consider the budget, resources, and manpower available to implement each idea.
   - **Desirability:** Gauge student interest in participating in educational campaigns or reward systems.
   - **Practicality:** Evaluate the ease of implementation and ongoing maintenance for infrastructure improvements.

   Here's an example of applying the screening criteria:
   - **Idea:** Implement a reward system for consistent recycling.
   - **Feasibility:** Moderate. Requires setting up a tracking system (swipe cards or tokens) and managing rewards.
   - **Desirability:** High. Students are likely to be motivated by the potential for rewards.
   - **Practicality:** Moderate. Requires initial setup and ongoing monitoring, but can be streamlined with digital solutions.

3. **Idea Development:** Select the most promising idea(s) based on your screening process. Let's develop the 'reward system for consistent recycling' idea further:
   - **Reward Options:** Consider offering small rewards like discounts at the campus store, free coffee coupons, or entries into a raffle for larger prizes

- **Tracking System:** Explore options like swipe cards for designated recycling bins, a mobile app for logging recycling activity, or a point system based on bin usage
- **Pilot Testing:** Implement the reward system in a test area like a single dorm building or a specific department to assess its effectiveness and gather student feedback.

4. **Business Analysis:** Analyze the potential impact of your proposed solution. Consider these factors:
   - **Environmental Benefits:** Increased recycling rates lead to less waste going to landfills and a reduced environmental footprint for the college.
   - **Cost Savings:** Recycling can save money on waste disposal fees.
   - **Student Engagement:** A well-designed reward system can increase student participation and awareness of recycling importance.
5. **Present Your Innovation:** Prepare a presentation for your classmates or college administration. Showcase your design thinking process:
   - Briefly explain the challenges of the current recycling program.
   - Present your brainstormed ideas and the chosen solution for development.
   - Detail the reward system plan, including tracking methods and pilot testing strategy.
   - Highlight the potential benefits of your Solution: improved recycling rates, cost savings, and increased student engagement in sustainability efforts.

Remember: This is just a sample solution. Feel free to adapt and modify it based on the specific challenges and opportunities present on your college campus.

Q 10.2

Assignment: Evaluating a Redesigned Product (Individual) - Sample Solution

Product: Let's evaluate the recent redesign of a popular brand's cereal packaging.

Evaluation Criteria

- User Experience (UX): Is the packaging easy to open, pour from, and reclose?
- Functionality: Does the packaging effectively protect the cereal and keep it fresh?
- Aesthetics: Is the design visually appealing and appropriate for the target audience (children, families)?
- Sustainability (Bonus Criterion): Is the packaging made from recycled materials or is it easily recyclable?
- Scoring System: We will use a simple 1–5 point scale (1 = poor, 5 = excellent).

Evaluation

- User Experience: The packaging has a resealable pouch, scoring well for convenience (4 points). However, the opening requires some effort, especially for children (3 points).
- Functionality: The cereal appears to stay fresh and protected within the packaging (4 points).
- Aesthetics: The design features vibrant colors and playful characters, likely appealing to children (5 points).
- Sustainability: The packaging information indicates it is made from partially recycled materials (3 points).

Presentation

- Briefly describe the redesigned cereal packaging and its target audience (families with children).
- Explain the chosen evaluation criteria and scoring system.

- Present the evaluation results for each criterion:
  - User Experience (4 points): Packaging is convenient but opening requires some effort.
  - Functionality (4 points): Cereal stays fresh and protected.
  - Aesthetics (5 points): Design is visually appealing and likely resonates with children.
  - Sustainability (3 points): Packaging is partially made from recycled materials.

Conclude by suggesting that while the redesign excels in aesthetics and functionality, improving the opening mechanism would enhance user experience. Additionally, using fully recyclable materials would strengthen the sustainability aspect.

EXERCISES

Part A (Objective Questions)

1. What is one of the biggest challenges in assessing the impact of design thinking?
   (a) Lack of collaboration
   (b) Short-term focus
   (c) Difficulty in measuring effectiveness
   (d) Limited stakeholder perspectives
2. Why is it difficult to gauge the effect of design thinking on a project?
   (a) Each stakeholder has a different perspective on the process.
   (b) It is a short-term process.
   (c) The impact is always negative.
   (d) The design thinking process is not effective.
3. How long can it take to solve complex challenges through design thinking?
   (a) Hours (b) Days
   (c) Months or even years (d) Weeks
4. Why can measuring the impact of design thinking be challenging?
   (a) Design thinking is always successful
   (b) There is no standardized method for measuring impact
   (c) The process is too short
   (d) The process is not collaborative
5. What is the innovation funnel?
   (a) A four-step process for concept generation and refinement
   (b) A six-step process for transitioning from idea generation to commercialization
   (c) A five-step process for measuring the effectiveness of design thinking
   (d) None of the above
6. Which of the following is NOT one of the steps in the innovation funnel?
   (a) Ideation (b) Concept Development
   (c) Implementation (d) Testing
7. The innovation funnel is a paradigm for measuring what?
   (a) Customer satisfaction (b) Revenue growth
   (c) Design thinking (d) Employee engagement
8. How many steps are in the innovation funnel?
   (a) Four (b) Five
   (c) Six (d) Seven

9. What is the design scorecard?
   (a) A tool for measuring the effectiveness of design thinking
   (b) A design thinking framework
   (c) A method for generating new ideas
   (d) A tool for prototyping
10. What are some elements the design scorecard uses to gauge the effectiveness of design thinking?
   (a) Ideation, validation, and commercialization
   (b) Empathy, inventiveness, and experimentation
   (c) Discover, define, develop, and deliver
   (d) Ideation, concept development, validation, prototype development, testing, and commercialization
11. What can a low score for user experience on the design scorecard indicate?
   (a) The design team needs to spend more time investigating and understanding the needs of the target audience
   (b) The project needs more time for ideation and concept development
   (c) The design team needs to spend more time on prototype development and testing
   (d) The project is ready for commercialization
12. What is the innovation funnel?
   (a) A tool for measuring the effectiveness of design thinking
   (b) A design thinking framework
   (c) A method for generating new ideas
   (d) A tool for prototyping
13. What is the difference between lagging and leading indicators?
   (a) Lagging indicators predict future success
   (b) Leading indicators quantify the effects of previous acts
   (c) Both lagging and leading indicators quantify the effects of previous acts
   (d) Both lagging and leading indicators forecast future success
14. What do lagging indicators do?
   (a) Provide information about future success
   (b) Give information about past success
   (c) Determine the effectiveness of design thinking
   (d) None of the above
15. Which of the following is an example of a lagging indicator for measuring design thinking?
   (a) Number of prototypes developed
   (b) Amount of time spent on ideation
   (c) Revenue growth
   (d) Number of team members involved in the process
16. Why arc lagging indicators important for measuring design thinking?
   (a) They forecast future success
   (b) They determine the effectiveness of design thinking
   (c) They provide information about past success
   (d) None of the above
17. What is an example of a lagging indicator that measures the success of design thinking in terms of customer satisfaction?
   (a) Number of prototypes developed
   (b) Amount of time spent on ideation
   (c) Revenue growth
   (d) Customer feedback rating

18. How can lagging indicators be used to improve the design thinking process?
    (a) By forecasting future success
    (b) By determining the effectiveness of design thinking
    (c) By providing information about past success
    (d) None of the above
19. What are some of the business outcomes that can result from incorporating design thinking into operations?
    (a) Greater employee dissatisfaction
    (b) Higher consumer happiness
    (c) Decreased operational effectiveness
    (d) Lower income
20. How can design thinking help businesses set themselves apart from their competitors?
    (a) By focusing solely on operational effectiveness
    (b) By producing inferior goods and services
    (c) By increasing employee dissatisfaction
    (d) By creating superior goods and services
21. What is one of the essential business results of design thinking?
    (a) Increased employee turnover
    (b) Decreased consumer satisfaction
    (c) Higher operational inefficiency
    (d) Greater employee engagement
22. How can design thinking help businesses achieve their objectives?
    (a) By producing inferior goods and services
    (b) By increasing employee dissatisfaction
    (c) By integrating design thinking into operations
    (d) By decreasing consumer happiness
23. What are some of the potential benefits of using design thinking in business?
    (a) Greater employee dissatisfaction and decreased revenue
    (b) Lower consumer happiness and employee turnover
    (c) Increased employee engagement and higher consumer satisfaction
    (d) Higher operational inefficiency and lower income
24. What are some financial outcomes that businesses can achieve by integrating design thinking into their operations?
    (a) Cost reductions (b) Intellectual property creation
    (c) Income generation (d) All of the above
25. How can businesses make wise decisions about future investments in design thinking?
    (a) By measuring its financial impact
    (b) By increasing employee satisfaction
    (c) By improving customer experience
    (d) None of the above
26. What are some business outcomes that can be achieved by integrating design thinking into operations?
    (a) Higher consumer happiness
    (b) Greater operational effectiveness
    (c) Higher employee engagement
    (d) All of the above

27. What are lagging indicators used for measuring design thinking?
    (a) Forecasting future success
    (b) Quantifying the effects of previous acts
    (c) Identifying cost reductions
    (d) None of the above
28. How can design thinking help businesses set themselves apart from their rivals?
    (a) By increasing customer satisfaction
    (b) By improving employee satisfaction
    (c) By generating intellectual property
    (d) All of the above
29. Which of the following is an example of a usability metric for measuring user experience?
    (a) Customer satisfaction (b) Net Promoter Score (NPS)
    (c) Task completion time (d) Market share
30. Which metric measures how easy it is for customers to use a product or service?
    (a) Customer satisfaction score (b) Net promoter score
    (c) Customer effort score (d) Usability score
31. Which metric tracks consumer satisfaction with a given good or service?
    (a) Usability score (b) Customer effort score
    (c) Net promoter score (d) Task completion time
32. Which parameter can be used to measure customer satisfaction?
    (a) Expert evaluations (b) Task completion time
    (c) Surveys (d) Mistake rate
33. Which metric measures how likely customers are to recommend a product or service to others?
    (a) Customer satisfaction score (b) Net promoter score
    (c) Usability score (d) Mistake rate
34. Which metric measures the overall satisfaction of customers with a product or service?
    (a) Usability score (b) Customer effort score
    (c) Customer satisfaction score (d) Task completion time
35. What are the metrics used to measure emotional response to a product or service?
    (a) Task completion time, mistake rate, and ease of use
    (b) Customer effort score, net promoter score, and customer satisfaction score
    (c) Contentment, elation, and annoyance
    (d) Sales and client retention
36. How can business metrics be measured?
    (a) Through user surveys
    (b) By analyzing company data
    (c) Using emotional response measures
    (d) Through expert evaluations
37. What are the metrics used to measure customer satisfaction?
    (a) Task completion time, mistake rate, and ease of use
    (b) Contentment, elation, and annoyance
    (c) Customer effort score, net promoter score, and customer satisfaction score
    (d) Sales and client retention
38. What are the metrics used to measure usability?
    (a) Sales and client retention
    (b) Customer satisfaction score
    (c) Contentment, elation, and annoyance
    (d) Task completion time, mistake rate, and ease of use

Part B (Short Answer Questions)

1. What are the ways in which the effectiveness of design thinking can be measured?
2. What are the challenges of assessing the impact of design thinking?
3. Explain the innovation funnel.
4. What is a design scorecard?
5. Give examples for quantitative metrics of design thinking.
6. Give examples for qualitative metrics of design thinking.
7. How are hybrid metrics helpful in design thinking?
8. Give examples for lagging indicators of design thinking.
9. How will you measure the impact of design thinking on user experience?
10. How can we measure customer satisfaction?
11. How will you measure the impact of design thinking on organizational culture?
12. How will you measure the impact of design thinking on society?
13. What are the metrics for measuring the social impact of design thinking?

Part C (Essay Questions)

1. How can we measure the impact of design thinking?
2. Discuss various frameworks for measuring design thinking.
3. Explain the innovation funnel framework in detail.
4. Explain the design scorecard framework in detail.
5. Explain the leading and lagging indicators of design thinking.
6. What is the impact of design thinking on user experience?
7. What is the relationship between design thinking and customer satisfaction?
8. How can we measure the impact of design thinking on organizational culture?
9. What is the role of leadership in promoting a design thinking culture?
10. Write an essay on measuring the impact of design thinking on society.

Answer Key

Part A

1. (c)	**2.** (a)	**3.** (c)	**4.** (b)	**5.** (b)	**6.** (c)	**7.** (c)	**8.** (c)	**9.** (a)	**10.** (b)
11. (a)	**12.** (b)	**13.** (b)	**14.** (b)	**15.** (c)	**16.** (c)	**17.** (d)	**18.** (c)	**19.** (b)	**20.** (d)
21. (d)	**22.** (c)	**23.** (c)	**24.** (d)	**25.** (a)	**26.** (d)	**27.** (b)	**28.** (d)	**29.** (c)	**30.** (c)
31. (c)	**32.** (c)	**33.** (b)	**34.** (c)	**35.** (c)	**36.** (b)	**37.** (c)	**38.** (d)		

CHAPTER 11

Ethical Considerations in Design Thinking

Learning Objectives

At the end of this chapter, you will be able to:

- Explain the significance of integrating ethical considerations into design thinking processes
- Define the methods by which design thinking can effectively address and incorporate ethical concerns
- Explain the role of diversity and inclusion in enhancing the design thinking approach
- List the strategies for ensuring design thinking initiatives consider and benefit underserved populations
- Describe the importance of privacy in design thinking, encompassing aspects such as security measures, encryption techniques, and authentication protocols
- List the best practices for processing and storing user data to uphold privacy standards
- Explain the influence of user interface design on user privacy and how to optimize it for ethical considerations
- List the critical elements of privacy policies and how they should be structured within the design thinking framework
- Explain the approaches to user education about privacy and security to foster informed and responsible use of design products
- Describe the additional ethical considerations that are paramount in the realm of design thinking

11.1 Introduction

Ethical considerations are very important when it comes to design thinking. Design thinking is about coming up with creative solutions to problems, but these solutions must consider the ethical issues involved. Ethical considerations ensure that solutions are not only innovative and effective, but also responsible and sustainable.

11.2 Importance of Ethical Considerations in Design Thinking

Design thinking should incorporate ethical concerns to ensure that the solutions produced do not hurt people or communities. The potential effects of the designs must be considered, and designers must ensure that they are consistent with moral standards and ideals. Design thinking solutions must consider the potential effects on all parties, including end-users, suppliers, and the larger community (Fig. 11.1). For instance, a design solution that lowers manufacturing costs can be attractive to a company's bottom line. However, it might also lead to job losses or environmental harm.

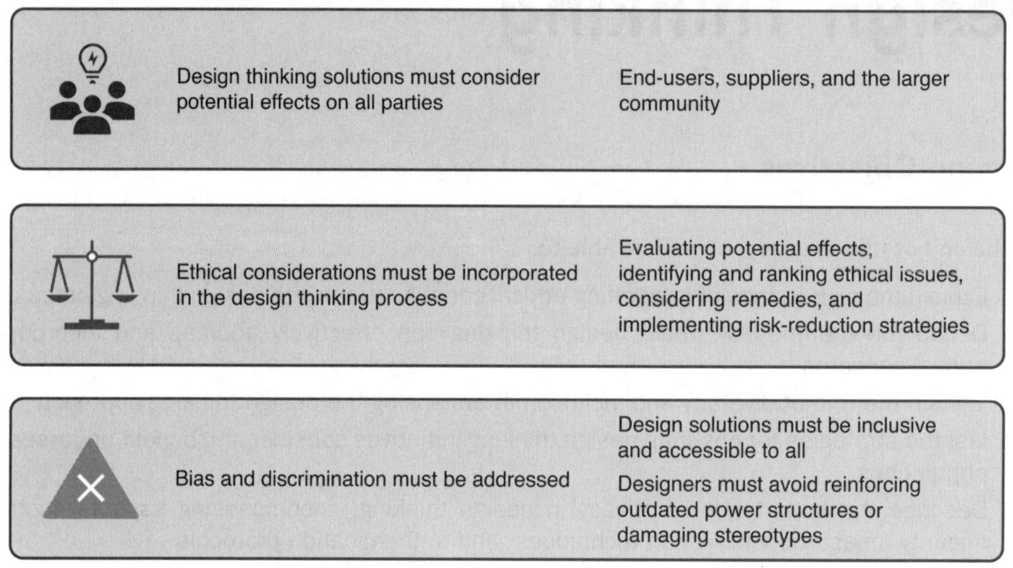

Figure 11.1 Importance of ethical considerations in design thinking

The design thinking process entails incorporating ethical considerations by evaluating the potential effects of solutions on diverse stakeholders. Identifying and ranking ethical issues may be necessary, considering potential remedies, and putting risk-reduction strategies into action during this process. Designers might consider how their solutions affect the environment, the possible harm to end users, and the effects on the larger community.

Addressing bias and discrimination issues is another aspect of ethical considerations. Design solutions must be inclusive and accessible to all. Designers must also watch out for reinforcing outdated power structures or damaging stereotypes.

Design thinking requires ethical considerations. Designers must consider how their ideas could affect diverse stakeholders and ensure they adhere to moral standards and ideals.

11.3 How Design Thinking Incorporates Ethical Concerns

Design thinking can incorporate ethical considerations by emphasizing user-centeredness and empathy. Design professionals may develop solutions that are not only inventive but also responsible and sustainable by comprehending the demands and viewpoints of stakeholders. Designers might also use ethical frameworks and guidelines to ensure that their solutions adhere to ethical principles and values (Fig. 11.2).

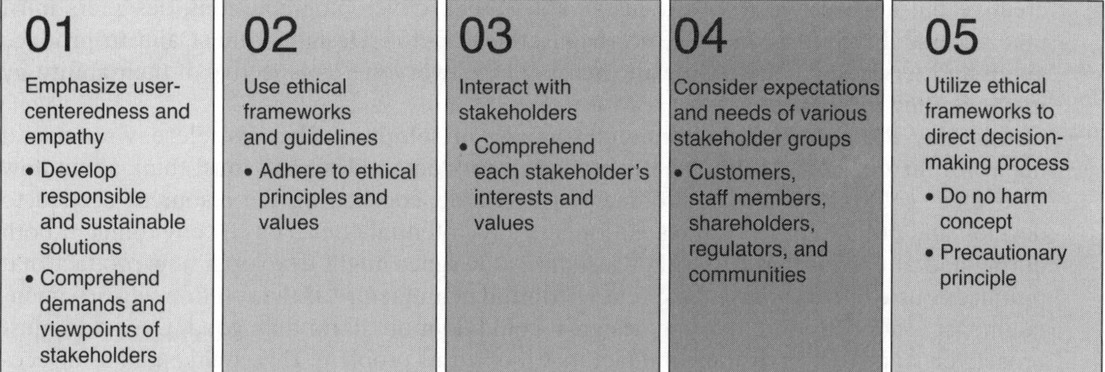

Figure 11.2 Design thinking and ethical concerns

Designers must provide original solutions that not only consider stakeholders' demands and viewpoints but also **advance moral values and principles.** Design professionals may develop solutions that are not only inventive but also responsible and sustainable by comprehending the demands and viewpoints of stakeholders. So, to comprehend each stakeholder's particular demands, interests, and values, designers must interact with them.

Customers, staff members, shareholders, regulators, and communities are just a few examples of the various people and organizations that comprise stakeholders. Therefore, designers must consider the different expectations and needs of various stakeholder groups while developing solutions. For instance, a designer creating a new product must consider not just the wants and desires of the end consumers but also **how the product will affect society and the environment.**

Designers might also **use ethical frameworks and guidelines** to ensure that their solutions adhere to ethical principles and values. Designers can utilize a variety of ethical frameworks to direct their decision-making process. For instance, the **'do no harm' concept** mandates that designers abstain from developing solutions that might hurt people or communities. In addition, some conceptual frameworks, such as the **'precautionary principle,'** exhort designers to exercise caution and consider any potential long-term effects of their designs.

Further considerations in design thinking include the following:

- **Ensuring that solutions are accessible to all individuals:** By using design thinking, problems can be solved in novel ways. Although the primary goal of is to come up with original solutions, designers must also consider ethical considerations when coming up with these answers. Accessibility is one of the most critical ethical issues in design thinking. Accessibility is the term used to describe how easy it is for anyone, regardless of ability, to utilize a product or service. This means that when developing solutions, designers must consider people with impairments. For instance, while designing a website or mobile application, the designer must ensure that the final product can be used by those with visual, auditory, or movement impairments. Designers can use a range of strategies, such as universal design principles, which call for creating solutions that can be accessed by the broadest audience possible to ensure accessibility. For instance, to make their ideas more accessible, designers can use legible typefaces, vivid colors, and audible or visual clues. In addition, designers must ensure that their ideas are usable and accessible. This entails creating simple products to understand and use, regardless of a user's level of technical proficiency or experience with the technology. Ethical considerations are crucial in design thinking to ensure that solutions are not only creative but also responsible and sustainable. When developing solutions, designers must take accessibility into account as a crucial ethical factor. Designers must aim to produce goods and services that are usable and accessible to everyone, irrespective of their ability, by implementing these ideas.

- **Considering the potential environmental impact of solutions:** The possible environmental impact of the developed solutions is a crucial ethical factor. Designers must think about how their ideas could affect the environment. This entails considering the resources needed to develop and put into practice the solution and any potential effects on the environment both during and after those processes. For instance, a designer might develop a new product that produces waste or consumes a lot of energy during manufacture. If the solution's environmental impact is not considered during design, it could do more harm than good. Designers must proactively approach environmental factors to solve this problem. This could entail using eco-friendly resources and manufacturing techniques or developing energy-efficient solutions. For instance, a designer might develop a new product that uses recycled materials or consumes less energy during production. Designers can produce solutions that are not only practical but also eco-friendly by following these guidelines. The disposal of the solution after usage is another important factor. Many goods and solutions are disposed of at landfills or other waste facilities, which may harm the environment. Designers must think about developing products that can be readily recycled or that may be used in another way as a strategy to solve this problem. For instance, a designer might develop a brand-new item built of biodegradable components that can be disassembled and used once more.
- **Avoiding unintended consequences:** Design thinking encourages the development of innovative and practical solutions to issues or demands. Therefore, it is crucial to consider any potential unintended consequences that may result from putting the solutions into practice when creating them. An ethical aspect that is essential to design thinking is the consideration of unintended consequences. When designers fail to consider the long-term repercussions of their solutions or their designs' broader social, economic, and environmental impacts, unintended consequences may result. The usage of single-use plastics in packaging is one illustration of unintended effects in design thinking. The use of plastics has long been widespread, but it has had unforeseen consequences, including the planet's environmental impact. Polymers can have catastrophic effects on ecosystems, especially marine life, and can take hundreds of years to disintegrate. Designers need to approach design thinking holistically to prevent unintended outcomes. They should consider the long-term repercussions and prospective impacts on diverse stakeholders in addition to the short-term advantages of their solutions. In addition, designers should consult with stakeholders to detect potential dangers and ensure that their solutions adhere to moral and ethical standards. Design thinking must incorporate ethical issues to ensure that solutions are responsible and sustainable.

11.4 Diversity and Inclusion in Design Thinking

In design thinking, diversity and inclusion are crucial ethical factors. Design thinking is fundamentally about developing goods, services, and experiences that cater to the requirements of everyone. When coming up with solutions, designers must consider a wide range of viewpoints and areas of expertise to ensure they satisfy as many needs as feasible (Fig. 11.3).

Diversity and inclusion are crucial ethical factors in design thinking

- Designers must consider various cultures, beliefs, and values
- Design thinking is about developing goods, services, and experiences for everyone

The design process must include people from various backgrounds and viewpoints

- Offers access to innovative ideas and creative thinking
- Ensures all potential demands are considered
- Reduces prejudice and stereotyping in the design process

Microsoft's Xbox Adapted Controller for those with disabilities

- Created by engaging with organizations advocating for individuals with disabilities
- Resulted in a controller that suits the demands of its users

Figure 11.3 Diversity and inclusion in design thinking

Those involved in the design process must come from **various backgrounds and viewpoints** for design thinking to be inclusive and diverse. This could include various sexual orientations, genders, ethnicities, ages, socioeconomic statuses, faiths, physical prowess, life experiences, and more. In addition, each process participant should feel listened to, appreciated, and validated.

There are several advantages to including various people in the design process. First, it offers designers the chance to access innovative ideas from a range of people who need to be more typically taken into account during conventional design procedures. This leads to more creative thinking, resulting in improved services and goods for all. Second, having a range of viewpoints can ensure that all potential demands are considered when developing a good or service.

Third, as a result, it is simpler to create products and services that appeal to a broad demographic. Last but not least, including diverse designers might assist in lessening prejudice and stereotyping in the design process. By ensuring that every voice is heard and considered during the design process, the chance that someone's viewpoint will be disregarded or not taken into account due to their ethnicity, gender, religion, or other background characteristics is reduced.

It is crucial to remember that everyone participating must be committed if true diversity and inclusion in design thinking is to be achieved. Ensure that you aggressively seek out a wide range of opinions from diverse backgrounds, perspectives, and designers. Businesses must deliberately promote an inclusive culture where all employees feel appreciated and valued regardless of their backgrounds or identities. Also, customers must be informed that diversity and inclusion are crucial ethical factors to consider when designing goods and services and must demand that businesses adhere to these ethical standards.

Let us look at how Microsoft made its Xbox Adapted Controller, created especially for those with disabilities, by including diversity and inclusiveness. To ensure they addressed their users' demands, Microsoft engaged with several organizations that advocate for individuals with disabilities when building the controller. The outcome was a controller that completely suits the demands of its users, thanks to its capacity to alter buttons and switches based on their unique preferences or impairment. This illustration demonstrates how crucial it is to integrate a variety of viewpoints in the design process to produce goods that satisfy the demands of all users.

11.5 Addressing the Needs of the People

Designers should think about how their ideas would benefit individuals who are disadvantaged or in need (Fig. 11.4).

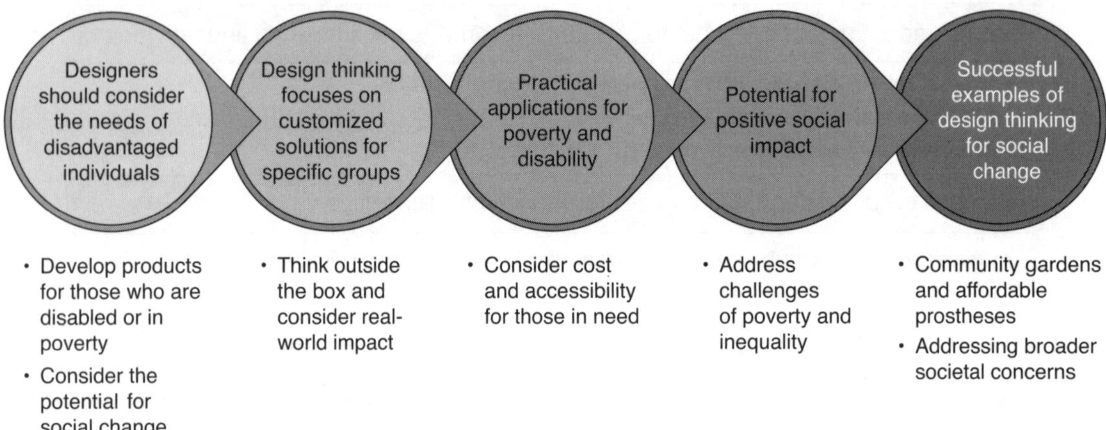

Figure 11.4 Addressing the needs of the people

Designers should work to develop products that address the needs of those who are disabled or live in poverty while also considering how their products could affect social change.

Design thinking is fundamentally concerned with developing solutions customized to the demands of certain groups or communities. This calls for designers to look outside the box and consider how their creations will impact the lives of real-world users. Those who are struggling with poverty, impairments, and other obstacles are included in this. By doing this, designers can produce valuable solutions that advance social change while assisting those in need.

Design thinking can be applied practically to provide better solutions for people who are **economically challenged or have impairments**. For instance, a business could utilize design thinking to pinpoint its target market and how the product would meet its needs if it intended to create a new aid for people with physical limitations. From there, they can create solutions by thinking about how the product could be made cheaper or more easily accessible for those with lower disposable income or how the product could be built in a way that would make it easier for users with disabilities to use comfortably.

Designers can apply design thinking to their consideration of the potential social impact of their products. Designers can produce goods that not only help those in need but also affect positive social change by considering how their designs might solve challenges of poverty or inequality. For instance, a corporation could utilize design thinking to find methods to make food more accessible while lowering prices or boosting efficiency if they created a new product to help fight hunger in underdeveloped areas.

Many businesses and organizations have used design thinking successfully in recent years to develop valuable solutions that simultaneously address user needs and contribute to constructive societal change. This includes setting up new community gardens to improve low-income communities' access to nutritious food and designing reasonably priced prostheses for persons with impairments. In addition, designers can use design thinking to develop solutions that address more general societal concerns and directly aid those struggling with poverty and other disadvantages.

11.6 Privacy in Design Thinking

Designers may ensure that their solutions adhere to ethical principles and values by considering ethical concerns early on and averting potential problems in the future. Reviewing and assessing them periodically is crucial to ensure that ethical issues are adequately addressed throughout the design thinking process. The values and standards of ethics serve as a guide for appropriate conduct and decision-making. Ethics are crucial in design thinking because they ensure everyone will benefit from the solutions developed, not just a select few.

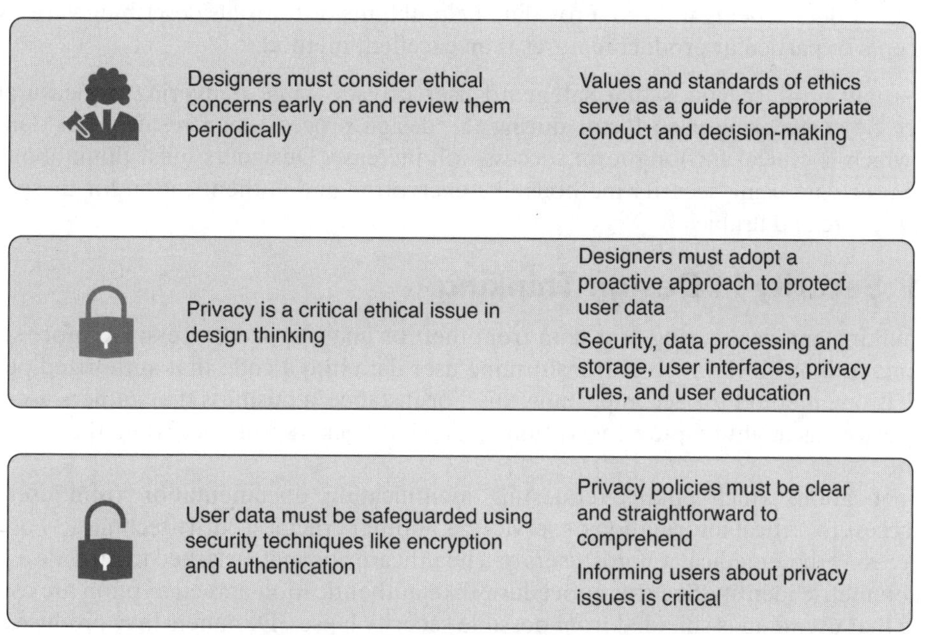

Figure 11.5 Privacy in design thinking

Privacy is one of the critical ethical issues in design thinking (Fig. 11.5). Designers must be conscious of any potential privacy concerns as they develop solutions. For instance, a corporation must make sure that the information about employees that is gathered is kept private and that only authorized individuals have access to it when building a recruit onboarding system. The importance of privacy in the modern world makes it crucial to consider it while developing new products or revamping old ones. Designers must adopt a proactive approach when considering privacy in design thinking. This includes looking for ways to protect user data, ensuring that data is treated responsibly, and giving consumers clear choices about how their data is used. Security, data processing and storage, user interfaces, privacy rules, and user education are the primary areas to concentrate on when integrating privacy into design thinking.

- **User data:** This must be safeguarded using security techniques like encryption and authentication. Encryption can prevent damage if data is stolen or intercepted while in transit. By forcing users to demonstrate their identity, authentication helps prevent illegal access to user data.
- **Processing and storing user data:** Considering how and where it is processed and stored is critical. Additional security measures, such as multi-factor authentication, should be implemented if the data is kept on a server owned by a third party.

- **User interfaces:** Designers should employ user interfaces that are simple to comprehend and provide people control over how their data is used. Taking into account how consumers interact with the UI is also crucial. Can they grasp their options? Can they terminate their account or alter their preferences with ease?
- **Privacy policies:** Privacy rules must be clear and straightforward to comprehend. It is critical to provide detailed information about the data the business gathers, how it is used, who has access to it, and how long it is retained.
- **Education of users:** Finally, informing users about privacy issues is critical. Hence, they know how their data is being utilized. Providing helpful hints or tutorials describing various privacy concepts or particular product features is an excellent method.

Designers may produce goods that safeguard user privacy while delivering a pleasurable user experience by considering each factor during the design process. As a result, users' faith in the product, which is crucial for long-term success, will increase. Designers must think about how to safeguard user data using security methods like encryption and authentication for these solutions to be both secure and usable.

11.6.1 Security in Design Thinking

Design thinking entails securing user data from theft or unauthorized access; therefore security is crucial. Encryption, which involves transforming user data into a code that authorized people can only read, is one method for accomplishing this. For instance, a business that gathers user data for online transactions might employ encryption to prevent hackers from accessing the financial data of its users.

Authentication, which entails requesting identification documentation from users before granting access to critical information or services, is another crucial security technique. For instance, before accessing their medical records, users of a healthcare app may be asked to provide a password or give a biometric identity. Security procedures like authentication and encryption are essential to guarantee that user data is shielded from possible security lapses. Designers may produce solutions that put the security and privacy of their consumers first by including these precautions in the design-thinking process.

Encryption

Encryption is a form of security technique used to guard against data theft or transmission interception (Fig. 11.6).

Data is encrypted into an unintelligible format that a person with the proper key or code can only decode. Even if someone were to intercept the data, they would not be able to read it without this key or code. Encryption is a crucial security precaution designers can employ in design thinking to safeguard user data.

Assume, for instance, that a business is creating a mobile application that holds user data such as passwords, private information, and financial information. Designers should ensure that data is encrypted before being sent to the app's server through the internet. In addition, to prevent data from being read or comprehended, it should be in an unreadable format even if hackers intercept it. Encryption can thus be used to safeguard private communication routes between the app and the server.

For instance, designers can secure the communication channel between the app and the server using SSL/TLS encryption, making it more difficult for attackers to eavesdrop on the communication. Moreover, user data kept on the server can be secured using encryption. With a symmetric key only known to the server in this situation, the designer can encrypt the user data. Because the user data is encrypted, even if an attacker manages to access the server, they cannot read it.

Encryption: A security technique

- Used to guard against data theft or transmission interception
- Data is encrypted into an unintelligible format
- Only a person with the proper key or code can decode the data

Encryption in design thinking

- Crucial for safeguarding user data
- Designers should ensure data is encrypted before being sent to the app's server
- Encryption can also secure communication channels between the app and the server
- User data stored on the server can also be secured using encryption

Overall importance of encryption

- Protects user data from unauthorized access and theft

Figure 11.6 Encryption in design thinking

Overall, encryption is a critical security measure in design thinking that protects user data from unauthorized access and theft.

Authentication

Authentication is a crucial security mechanism in design thinking that aids in preventing unwanted access to sensitive user data (Fig. 11.7). Before allowing users access to specific features or data, designers must verify that they are who they say they are. Using usernames and passwords is one popular technique. Before accessing their account or other secure services, users must enter a unique username and password that only they know. However, designers must understand that password and username authentication may only sometimes be safe enough.

Authentication is a crucial security mechanism in design thinking

- It aids in preventing unwanted access to sensitive user data

Designers must verify the user's identity before allowing access to specific features or data

- Various authentication techniques can be employed
- Username and password is one popular technique
- Two-factor authentication (2FA) adds an extra layer of security

Designers must consider authentication to safeguard sensitive user data from unauthorized access

- Only authenticated users should be able to access specific data or functionalities

Figure 11.7 Authentication in design thinking

For instance, a hacker might be able to determine a user's password or access it using a phishing scam. Designers can solve this with two-factor authentication (2FA), which asks users to input a second authentication factor besides their username and password. Using a mobile phone to get a code that is then entered as a second authentication factor illustrates 2FA in design thinking. By doing this, you may be sure that anyone who accesses your account is using the correct password and having access to your phone.

To safeguard sensitive user data from unauthorized access, designers must consider authentication while using design thinking. For example, designers can assist in maintaining the safety and security of user data by making sure that only authenticated users can access specific data or functionalities.

11.6.2 Processing and Storing User Data

It is critical to consider user data processing and storage when building a product or service (Fig. 11.8). Considerations such as where the data will be kept, how it will be accessible, and who will have access to it are all part of this process. For instance, a business creating a mobile app that gathers user information must maintain the information securely. First, they must protect the data; this may entail deploying encryption or other security measures. Suppose the data is kept on a server owned by a third party. In that case, the business must ensure that the third party is reliable and that the necessary security measures are in place.

Figure 11.8 Processing and storing user data

Designers must take into account potential dangers associated with data processing in addition to security. Companies must guarantee that user data is being gathered and processed in a morally and legally correct way. This entails being open and honest about the information gathered and its intended purpose. It also entails granting consumers access to tools for editing or deleting their data.

Also, designers should consider employing multi-factor authentication, which requests numerous information from users before granting access to their data. For instance, a user may be required to input a password and a verification number sent to their phone to get into an app. Even if a password is hacked, this prevents unwanted access to user data. Design thinkers may create secure products and services that respect user privacy by carefully examining data processing and storage.

11.6.3 User Interfaces

Designers should use user interfaces (UIs) that are simple to comprehend and provide people control over how their data is used. Taking into account how consumers interact with the UI is also crucial. Can they grasp their options? Can they terminate their account or alter their preferences with ease? While using design thinking, it is essential to consider user privacy when designing the user interface.

For consumers to make intelligent judgments about their data, designers must create interfaces that are simple to use and comprehend. To choose who can view their posts or personal information, users can change the privacy settings on a social networking platform. Users should be able to find and alter these options quickly, provided the interface is created and uncomplicated. The use of clear and straightforward language to describe how data is being used in user interfaces is another factor to consider.

Designers must be open and honest about data gathering and processing to earn users' trust. For instance, an app that gathers user data for advertising purposes should make this evident in its UI so that consumers can choose whether or not to continue using the app. User interfaces should enable users to erase their accounts and the data they have connected with them. Because it enables users to delete their personal information from the site if they decide they no longer wish to use it, this feature is crucial for safeguarding user privacy.

11.6.4 Privacy Policies

Privacy rules must be clear and straightforward to comprehend. It is critical to provide detailed information about the data the business gathers, how it is used, who has access to it, and how long it is stored. Privacy rules should be created using design thinking to give people clear and understandable information.

For example, what information is being gathered, how it will be used, who will have access to it, and how long it will be retained should all be crystal clear in a privacy policy. Avoiding too much technical terminology that can be difficult for people to grasp is crucial when applying design thinking. For instance, if a business is creating a mobile app that gathers user data, its privacy policy should be straightforward to understand and available on the app's settings. In addition, what information is being gathered, such as user location or device information, and how it will be used, such as to enhance the app's functioning, should be made clear in the policy.

The privacy policy should also clarify who has access to the data, such as employees or outside service providers, and how long the data will be stored. The policy might specify, for instance, that user information will be removed when an account is requested to be deleted or after a predetermined amount of time. By creating a transparent and open privacy policy, design thinkers may help users feel more comfortable sharing their data. This will also help designers establish trust with their audience.

11.6.5 User Education

It is important to inform consumers about privacy issues so they know how their data is used. Giving helpful hints or tutorials that describe various privacy concepts or particular product features is an excellent method. Teaching consumers about privacy issues in design thinking is essential for fostering transparency and confidence. A social media site may, for instance, offer instructions on how to modify privacy settings and restrict the availability of personal data. This tutorial might also explain why these settings are essential and what might happen if the user does nothing. Also, businesses can offer tools that customers can utilize to contact them with any queries or concerns, including a frequently asked questions (FAQ) section or a privacy hotline. Companies can give customers the power to take control of their data and make educated decisions about how it is used by teaching them design thinking about privacy.

11.7 Other Considerations

Designers must also consider other situations where user privacy needs to be protected, such as when collecting personal data. In addition, they must consider the types of user consent required and ensure that all data is stored securely using the necessary safeguards, such as encryption and secure databases with stringent access control protocols. By using design thinking, creators must consider user privacy when collecting personal data from them. Before collecting users' personal information, this involves getting the required consent from them. In addition, designers should explicitly inform users of why and how their personal information is required.

As an illustration, a social media site that gathers user information for targeted advertising should inform consumers of how their information will be used and allow them to decline this service. Designers must also ensure that any personally identifiable data is stored safely and according to industry standards.

As part of this, secure databases with stringent access control mechanisms are used to prevent unauthorized access, as well as encryption to protect data while it is in transit. For instance, a medical app that gathers sensitive patient data must be encrypted and kept in a secure database with access limited to licensed medical personnel.

Designers may preserve user privacy and increase the likelihood that customers will continue to trust and use their goods or services by considering these aspects when applying design thinking.

Summary

- Design thinking emphasizes user-centeredness and empathy and uses ethical frameworks and guidelines to ensure solutions adhere to ethical principles and values.
- The main considerations in design thinking are ensuring solutions are accessible to all individuals, consideration of the potential environmental impact of solutions and avoiding of unintended consequences.
- Diversity and inclusion in design thinking considers various cultures, beliefs, and values and aims to cater to the needs of everyone.
- Sustainability in design thinking ensures solutions do not harm the environment or society. It also addresses the needs of the people.
- Privacy in design thinking protects user data using security techniques like encryption and authentication.

Exercises

Part A (Objective Questions)

1. How can design thinking incorporate ethical considerations?
   (a) By focusing on user-centeredness and empathy
   (b) By ignoring the viewpoints of stakeholders
   (c) By prioritizing speed over responsibility
   (d) By disregarding ethical frameworks and guidelines
2. What are some ethical principles that designers can follow in design thinking?
   (a) Honesty, fairness, and respect
   (b) Deception, discrimination, and bias
   (c) Exploitation, plagiarism, and insensitivity
   (d) None of the above
3. What is the importance of considering ethical issues in design thinking?
   (a) To come up with more inventive solutions
   (b) To avoid legal issues
   (c) To develop responsible and sustainable solutions
   (d) All of the above

4. What are some ways in which designers can understand the viewpoints of stakeholders?
   (a) Through surveys and interviews
   (b) By ignoring their perspectives
   (c) By imposing their own opinions
   (d) By disregarding their feedback
5. How can designers ensure that their solutions adhere to ethical principles?
   (a) By following ethical frameworks and guidelines
   (b) By ignoring ethical considerations altogether
   (c) By prioritizing financial gain over ethical concerns
   (d) By disregarding the viewpoints of stakeholders
6. What is the importance of diversity and inclusion in design thinking?
   (a) It is not necessary to consider diverse perspectives in design thinking.
   (b) Design thinking only caters to a specific group of people.
   (c) Designers must consider different cultures, beliefs, and values when creating solutions.
   (d) Design thinking does not have anything to do with ethical considerations.
7. What is the role of empathy in design thinking?
   (a) It is not important to consider the feelings of the user in design thinking.
   (b) Design thinking does not require designers to put themselves in the user's shoes.
   (c) Designers must empathize with the user to develop responsible and sustainable solutions.
   (d) Designers should not worry about the user's needs in design thinking.
8. What is the significance of ethical considerations in design thinking?
   (a) Ethical considerations are not relevant in design thinking.
   (b) Designers do not need to consider ethical issues when developing solutions.
   (c) Designers must consider ethical issues when developing solutions.
   (d) Ethical considerations are only important in certain fields of design.
9. Why is user-centeredness important in design thinking?
   (a) Design thinking does not require designers to focus on the user.
   (b) Designers must focus on the user to create solutions that are responsible and sustainable.
   (c) User-centeredness is not relevant in design thinking.
   (d) Designers should not worry about the user's needs in design thinking.
10. How can designers ensure their solutions adhere to ethical principles and values?
    (a) By not considering ethical issues when developing solutions.
    (b) By developing solutions that only cater to a specific group of people.
    (c) By using ethical frameworks and guidelines.
    (d) By ignoring the viewpoints of stakeholders.
11. What is one of the primary areas to concentrate on when integrating privacy into design thinking?
    (a) User satisfaction
    (b) Product cost
    (c) Data processing and storage
    (d) Advertising techniques
12. What should designers ensure while developing new products or revamping old ones according to the given content?
    (a) Ignore the privacy concerns
    (b) Ensure that data is treated responsibly
    (c) Maximize profits
    (d) Develop products without considering user experience

13. What security technique can prevent damage if user data is stolen or intercepted while in transit?
    (a) Authentication (b) Multi-factor authentication
    (c) Encryption (d) User education
14. What technique can help prevent illegal access to user data?
    (a) Encryption (b) User education
    (c) Authentication (d) Multi-factor authentication
15. When processing and storing user data on a server owned by a third party, what additional security measure should be implemented?
    (a) User education (b) Encryption
    (c) Multi-factor authentication (d) Authentication
16. What is the primary area to concentrate on when integrating privacy into design thinking?
    (a) User interfaces (b) Privacy rules
    (c) Security (d) User education
17. How can designers protect user data?
    (a) By giving consumers clear choices about how their data is used
    (b) By authenticating users
    (c) By encrypting user data
    (d) All of the above
18. What is encryption?
    (a) A form of security technique used to guard against data theft or transmission interception.
    (b) A technique to increase data processing speed.
    (c) A technique to make data more visible to unauthorized parties.
    (d) A technique to delete data permanently.
19. How does encryption protect data?
    (a) By making it impossible to access.
    (b) By encoding it into an unintelligible format that requires a key or code to decode.
    (c) By deleting it permanently.
    (d) By increasing the speed of data processing.
20. What is the purpose of encryption?
    (a) To increase data processing speed.
    (b) To make data more visible to unauthorized parties.
    (c) To protect data from theft or interception during transmission.
    (d) To permanently delete data.
21. Who can decode encrypted data?
    (a) Anyone who intercepts the data during transmission.
    (b) Only those who have the proper key or code.
    (c) Those who have access to the server where the data is stored.
    (d) No one can decode encrypted data.
22. What happens if someone intercepts encrypted data?
    (a) They can decode it easily.
    (b) They cannot decode it.
    (c) They can decode it if they have the proper key or code.
    (d) They can decode it if they have access to the server where the data is stored.
23. What is the purpose of privacy policies in design thinking?
    (a) To confuse consumers about how their data is used
    (b) To provide detailed information about data collection, usage, and storage
    (c) To make it easy for businesses to misuse user data
    (d) To prevent users from accessing their own data

24. What is user education in design thinking?
 (a) Teaching users about design thinking
 (b) Teaching users about privacy issues
 (c) Teaching users how to misuse data
 (d) Teaching users how to hack into servers

25. What is the purpose of encryption in design thinking?
 (a) To create unintelligible data
 (b) To create easy-to-read data
 (c) To prevent data theft or transmission interception
 (d) To make data easily accessible to everyone

Part B (Short Answer Questions)

1. Diversity and inclusion are ethical factors in design thinking. How?
2. How can we ensure privacy in design thinking?
3. How does user data need to be safeguarded?
4. What is encryption?
5. What is authentication?

Part C (Essay Questions)

1. How does design thinking incorporate ethical concerns?
2. Write about diversity and inclusion in design thinking.
3. How is privacy taken care of in design thinking?

Answer Key

Part A

1. (a)	**2.** (a)	**3.** (c)	**4.** (a)	**5.** (a)	**6.** (c)	**7.** (c)	**8.** (c)	**9.** (b)	**10.** (c)
11. (c)	**12.** (b)	**13.** (c)	**14.** (c)	**15.** (c)	**16.** (c)	**17.** (d)	**18.** (a)	**19.** (b)	**20.** (c)
21. (b)	**22.** (c)	**23.** (b)	**24.** (b)	**25.** (c)					

CHAPTER 12

Design Thinking Case Studies

12.1 Introduction

In this chapter, we will discuss six different case studies, as listed below (Table 12.1):

- **Airbnb:** Using design thinking to create a personalized and seamless experience for travelers with their mobile app.
- **Delta Airlines:** Using design thinking to improve the airport experience with innovations such as mobile check-in and redesigned boarding processes.
- **Kaiser Permanente:** Using design thinking to improve the patient experience with solutions such as a mobile app for tracking health information and redesigned clinics.
- **IDEO:** Using design thinking to create innovative solutions for clients, such as a redesigned check-in process for a major hotel chain and a more personalized patient experience for a healthcare organization.
- **Ford:** Using design thinking to create a more human-centered approach to car design, such as incorporating technology to improve safety and the user experience.
- **Indian Railways:** Using design thinking to improve and enhance the passenger experience, infrastructure, safety aspects, and digital services.

Table 12.1 Summary of case studies

Company	Industry	User Focus	Design Thinking Applications	Impact
Airbnb	Travel	Travelers and Hosts	• Personalized accommodation search • Direct host–guest communication • User reviews and recommendations • Unique experiences offered by locals	Personalized travel experiences, built trust and community, industry leader
Delta Airlines	Airline	Passengers	• Mobile check-in • Redesigned boarding process • Streamlined airport experience	Improved passenger experience, reduced travel stress, increased efficiency
Kaiser Permanente	Healthcare	Patients	• Mobile app for health information • Redesigned clinics	Enhanced patient experience, improved access to health information, potentially better health outcomes

(Continued)

Table 12.1 *(Continued)*

Company	Industry	User Focus	Design Thinking Applications	Impact
IDEO (Design Consultancy)	Various	Client-specific (Hotel check-in, Patient experience)	• User research and empathy building • Brainstorming innovative solutions • Prototyping and testing • Iterative design based on user feedback	Wide range of innovative solutions across industries, focus on human-centered design
Ford	Automotive	Drivers and Passengers	• Technology for improved safety • User-centered car design • Enhanced in-car experience	Safer and more user-friendly vehicles, potentially increased customer satisfaction and brand loyalty
Indian Railways	Travel	Passengers	• Enhancing customer experience • Infrastructure and safety improvements • Digital transformation • Collaborative innovation	Improved passenger experience, better infrastructure and safety measures, and comprehensive digital services

12.2 Airbnb

Airbnb is a popular online marketplace that allows people to rent out their homes or apartments to travelers. The company has used design thinking to create a seamless and personalized experience for its users. By understanding the needs and pain points of its customers, Airbnb has been able to design an app that provides a hassle-free booking experience.

12.2.1 Personalized Experience

One of the key features of the Airbnb app is the ability for hosts and guests to communicate directly and easily. This has created a strong sense of community and trust among its users.

Through messaging, users can ask hosts questions, share details about their arrival time, and other key communications. The company has also made it easy for hosts to manage their listings, including setting availability, pricing, and house rules.

The app offers a personalized experience by recommending listings based on a user's search history and previous bookings. This makes it easier for users to find the appropriate accommodation that suits their needs. For example, if a user searches for a specific type of accommodation or location, the app will suggest similar options based on their preferences. This feature has helped users to save time and find the perfect place to stay.

In addition, the app has a simple and intuitive user interface, making it easy to navigate and book accommodation. Users can filter their search results by various criteria such as price, location, and amenities, and can easily view photos and read reviews of each listing. The app also provides useful information about the surrounding neighborhood, including popular attractions and local restaurants.

Airbnb has also used design thinking to create a sense of community and belonging among its users. The app offers various experiences and activities hosted by local residents, which allows users to explore new destinations and meet new people. By facilitating connections and interactions between hosts and guests, Airbnb has been able to create a unique travel experience that goes beyond just booking accommodation.

12.2.2 Safe and Secure Platform

Airbnb has utilized design thinking to create a safe and secure platform for both hosts and guests. This is a crucial aspect of their business model as trust and safety are key factors in the success of a peer-to-peer platform. One of the key safety measures implemented by Airbnb is a rating system for both hosts and guests (Fig. 12.1). After each stay, both the host and guest can rate and review each other. This helps to build trust and accountability within the community and encourages users to maintain high standards.

Airbnb has also implemented safety measures such as background checks for hosts and secure payments. Hosts are required to verify their identity and provide information about themselves and their listing before they can list their property on the platform.

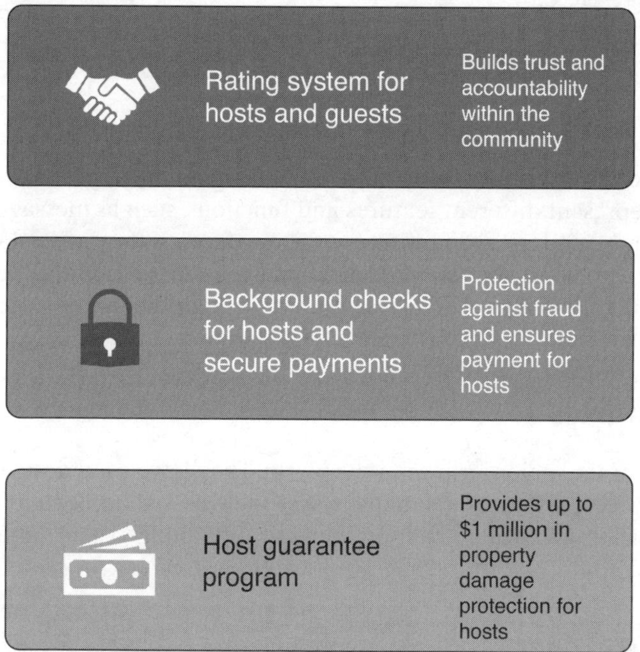

Figure 12.1 Safe and secure platform characteristics of Airbnb

Guests are also required to verify their identity before booking a stay. In addition, all payments are processed through Airbnb's secure payment system, which provides protection against fraud and ensures that hosts are paid for their services.

Another example of Airbnb's use of design thinking for safety is their Host Guarantee program. This program provides up to $1 million in property damage protection for hosts in case of damage caused by guests during their stay. This provides peace of mind for hosts and encourages them to list their properties on the platform.

12.2.3 User-friendly Interface

Airbnb has utilized design thinking to create a visually appealing and user-friendly interface.

The app is designed to be intuitive, with clear and simple navigation (Fig. 12.2). This has made it easy for users to search and book accommodations, which has contributed to the company's success. One way that Airbnb has achieved this is by using a minimalist design approach. The app is uncluttered, with a clean and simple layout that emphasizes the most important information. This makes it easy for users to quickly find what they are looking for, without feeling overwhelmed or confused.

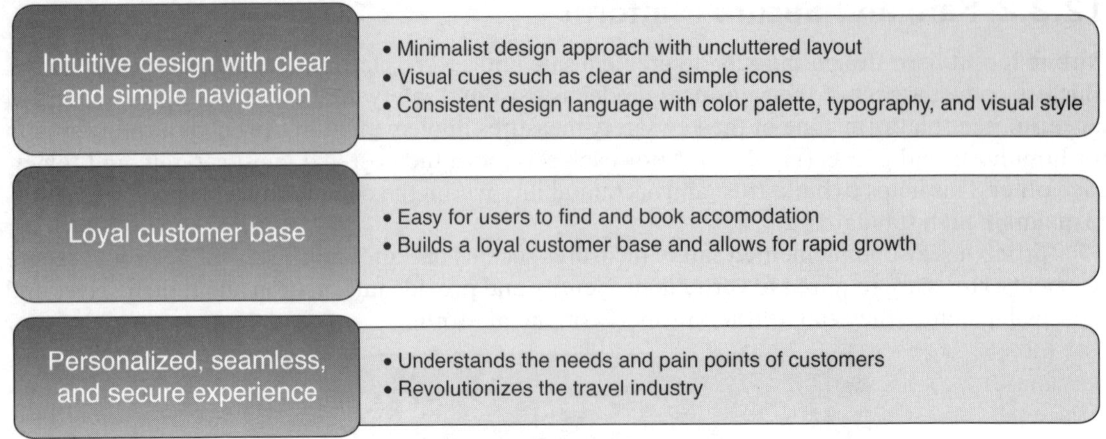

Figure 12.2 User-friendly interface characteristics of Airbnb

Airbnb has also made use of visual cues to help users navigate the app. For example, they use clear and simple icons to represent different features and functions, such as messaging and booking. This makes it easy for users to understand how to use the app, even if they are unfamiliar with it.

Furthermore, the app has a consistent design language that is used throughout, which helps to create a sense of familiarity and trust. This is achieved through the use of a consistent color palette, typography, and visual style.

12.3 Delta Airlines

Delta Airlines is one of the major airlines in the world. They have used design thinking to improve the user experience for customers in many ways, such as by implementing mobile check-in, redesigning the boarding process as well as their airport lounges, and improving their in-flight experience (Fig.12.3).

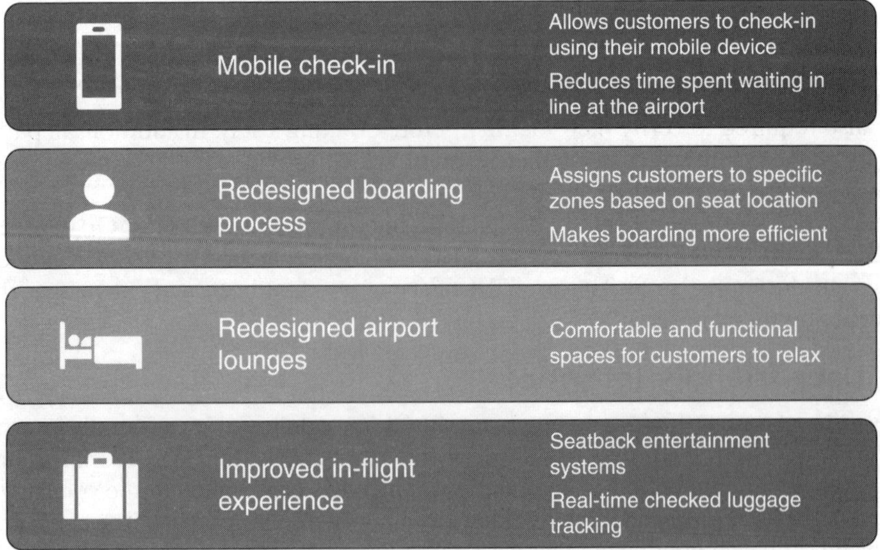

Figure 12.3 Design thinking approach in Delta Airlines

12.3.1 Mobile Check-in

One of the key innovations that Delta has introduced is mobile check-in, which allows customers to check in for their flight using their mobile device. This has not only made the check-in process more convenient for customers, but it has also reduced the time that they spend waiting in line at the airport.

12.3.2 Redesigning the Boarding Process

Delta's new boarding process involves a four-color system that identifies the order in which passengers should board the plane (Fig. 12.4). Passengers in first class and premium cabins board first, followed by those in the main cabin seated in the window seats, then those seated in the middle, and finally, those in the aisle seats. By dividing the boarding process into smaller groups, it helps reduce the amount of time that customers spend waiting in line to board the plane, and also helps to minimize the crowding that can occur in the boarding area.

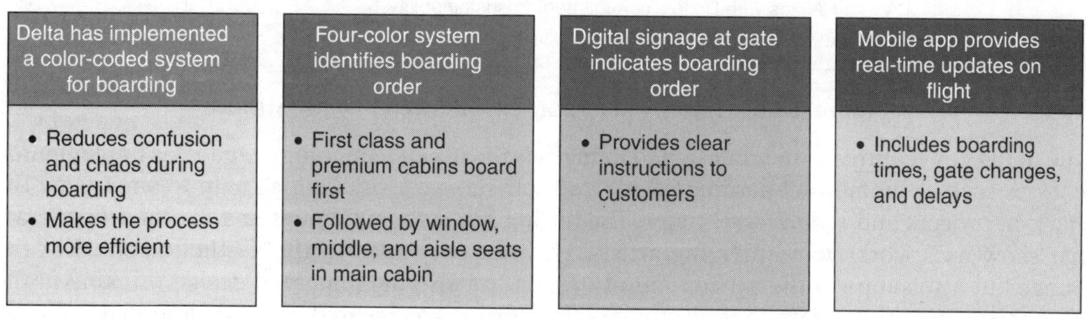

Figure 12.4 Redesigning the boarding pass in Delta Airlines

Delta has also implemented digital signage at the gate to indicate when boarding will begin and the boarding order. This provides clear instructions to customers and helps to ensure that everyone understands the new boarding process. Delta has also used design thinking to create a mobile app that provides customers with real-time updates on their flight, including boarding times, gate changes, and delays.

These improvements have reduced wait times and confusion, making air travel a more enjoyable and efficient experience for customers.

12.3.3 Improved Airport Experience

Delta has also used design thinking to improve the airport experience by redesigning their airport lounges (Fig. 12.5).

The redesigned Delta Sky Club lounges are intended to make the airport experience more comfortable and enjoyable. The lounges have been furnished with comfortable seating, modern decor, and plenty of natural light. This creates an environment that is more relaxing and less stressful than the hustle and bustle of the airport terminal. In addition, the lounges are designed to be more functional and convenient, with amenities such as charging stations, Wi-Fi, and printers.

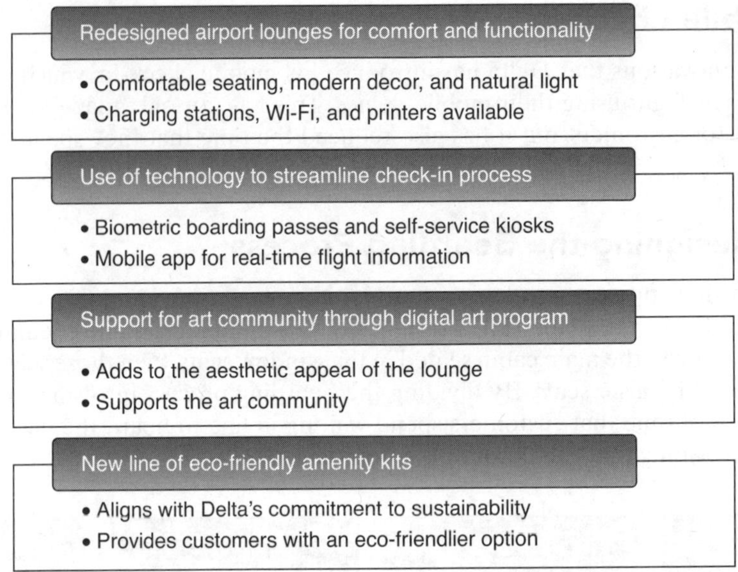

Figure 12.5 Improved airport experience in Delta Airlines

One of the key features of the redesigned lounges is the use of technology. Delta has implemented features such as biometric boarding passes and self-service kiosks, which help to streamline the check-in process and reduce wait times. The airline has also implemented a digital art program that showcases work from emerging artists. This not only adds to the aesthetic appeal of the lounge but also supports the art community. Delta has also implemented design thinking in the way they communicate with their customers. The airline has created a mobile app that provides customers with real-time flight information, gate changes, and weather updates. This helps to reduce stress and anxiety for travelers by providing them with all the information they need in one place.

Furthermore, Delta has introduced a new line of amenity kits that include environmentally friendly products. This move aligns with Delta's commitment to sustainability and provides customers with an eco-friendlier option.

12.3.4 Improved In-flight Experience

In addition to these initiatives, Delta has also used design thinking to improve their in-flight experience (Fig. 12.6).

Delta collaborated with design firm IDEO to create seats that provide more legroom and recline further back. The new seats have also been designed with a slim profile to create more space in the cabin.

Delta worked with Panasonic Avionics to develop a new entertainment system that provides passengers with a wide range of content, including movies, TV shows, and games. The system is also equipped with a feature that allows customers to create personalized playlists and save their favorite content for future flights.

Delta has also introduced new food and beverage options that cater to different dietary preferences and tastes. They have worked with celebrity chefs to create new menus that offer a variety of options, including vegetarian, gluten-free, and kosher meals. In addition, Delta has started serving craft beer and premium wines to enhance the in-flight dining experience.

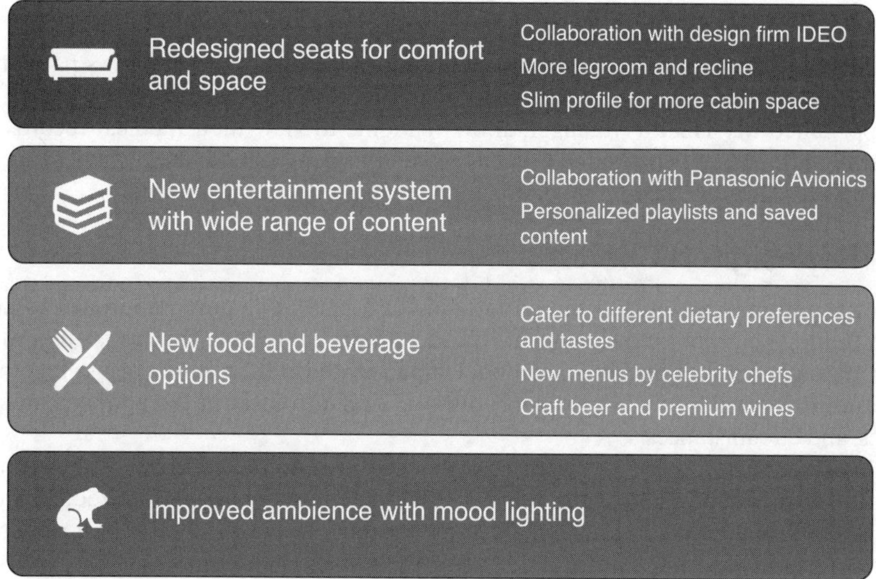

Figure 12.6 Improved in-flight experience in Delta Airlines

Furthermore, Delta has introduced mood lighting, which creates a more relaxed and calming environment for passengers. The lighting changes throughout the flight to reflect the time of day and the stage of the flight, which helps passengers to adjust to different time zones and feel more refreshed upon arrival.

12.4 Kaiser Permanente

Kaiser Permanente, a healthcare organization in the United States, has utilized design thinking to improve the patient experience (Fig. 12.7).

Mobile app 'My health manager' for tracking health information and communication

- View medical records, schedule appointments, receive test results

Clinics redesigned with design thinking principles

- Natural lighting, calming colors, comfortable furniture
- Electronic check-in and self-service kiosks
- Team-based care approach

'Thrive' campaign to promote healthy lifestyles

- Classes, workshops, and online resources on nutrition, stress management, and physical acitivity

'Total health' program to improve medication management

- Medication synchronization and therapy management

Figure 12.7 Design thinking characteristics in Kaiser Permanente

12.4.1 Improving the Patient Experience

One way they have done this is through the creation of a mobile app that allows patients to track their health information and communicate with their healthcare providers.

The app, called My Health Manager, allows patients to view their medical records, schedule appointments, and receive test results. This has made it easier for patients to stay engaged in their healthcare and has improved communication between patients and providers.

12.4.2 Redesigned Clinics

Kaiser Permanente has recognized the importance of a patient-centered approach to healthcare, and design thinking has played a significant role in achieving this goal. The redesign of their clinics is a perfect example of this. The care team model implemented at their clinics brings together a team of healthcare professionals to work collaboratively, taking into account the patient's unique needs, preferences, and circumstances.

The clinics' design is also a critical aspect of the patient-centered approach. The natural lighting and comfortable furniture create a calm and inviting environment, helping to reduce anxiety and stress levels. The artwork and other elements also contribute to the welcoming atmosphere, making patients feel more relaxed and comfortable during their visits.

Kaiser Permanente has also used design thinking to improve the accessibility of healthcare services for their patients. For instance, they have introduced telemedicine options, allowing patients to receive medical care from the comfort of their homes. This innovation has made healthcare more convenient and accessible for patients, especially those living in remote areas or with mobility issues.

Moreover, Kaiser Permanente has also used design thinking to enhance patient education. They have developed online resources, including articles, videos, and interactive tools, to help patients understand their health conditions and treatments better. This has empowered patients to take an active role in their healthcare, leading to better outcomes.

12.4.3 Improving Online Presence

Kaiser Permanente has also used design thinking to improve their online presence (Fig. 12.8).

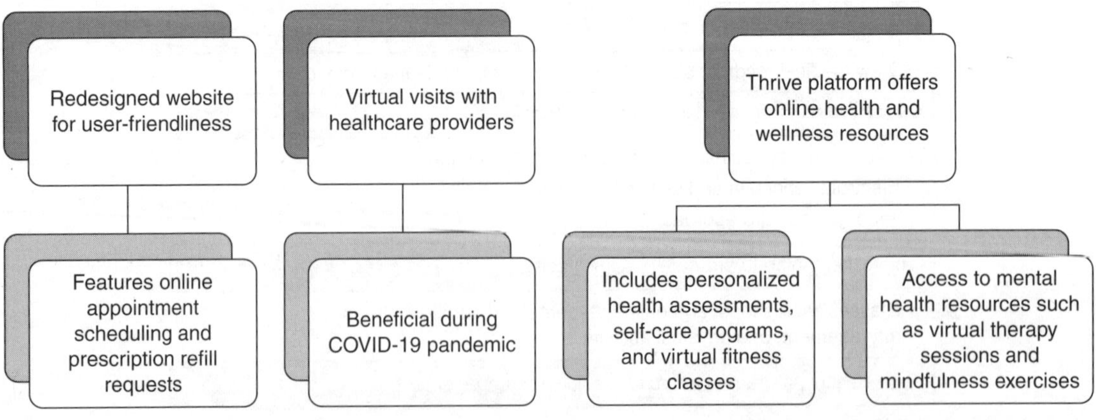

Figure 12.8 Improving online presence in Kaiser Permanente

They have redesigned their website to be more user-friendly and have added features such as online appointment scheduling and virtual visits with healthcare providers. This has made it easier for patients to access care and has improved their overall experience with the organization. Kaiser Permanente's implementation of design thinking to improve the patient experience also includes improving their online presence. They have redesigned their website to be more user-friendly, allowing patients to easily access information about their health and medical care. The website features clear navigation, simple language, and easy-to-use tools such as online appointment scheduling and prescription refill requests. This has made it more convenient for patients to manage their health and communicate with their healthcare providers.

In addition, Kaiser Permanente has introduced virtual visits with healthcare providers, allowing patients to receive care from the comfort of their own homes. This was especially beneficial during the COVID-19 pandemic when many people were hesitant to visit a medical facility in person. Through the use of video conferencing technology, patients can receive care from their healthcare providers without having to leave their homes, saving them time and reducing the risk of exposure to the virus.

Another example of Kaiser Permanente's use of design thinking to improve their online presence is the implementation of their Thrive platform. This platform offers a variety of online health and wellness resources, including personalized health assessments, self-care programs, and virtual fitness classes. The platform also includes access to mental health resources, including virtual therapy sessions and mindfulness exercises. This has made it easier for patients to take a proactive approach to their health and wellbeing, with the convenience of accessing resources from their own devices.

Kaiser Permanente's implementation of design thinking to improve their online presence has made it easier for patients to access care and manage their health. The combination of a user-friendly website, virtual visits, and the Thrive platform has created a comprehensive and convenient approach to healthcare that puts the patient at the center.

12.4.4 Improving Clinical Processes

In addition to these initiatives, Kaiser Permanente has used design thinking to improve their clinical processes (Fig. 12.9).

Kaiser Permanente has also focused on improving their clinical processes using design thinking principles. One of the most significant changes they have implemented is the 'pre-visit planning' process. In this process, healthcare providers review a patient's medical history and prepare for their visit ahead of time. This includes identifying any necessary tests or procedures and ensuring that the

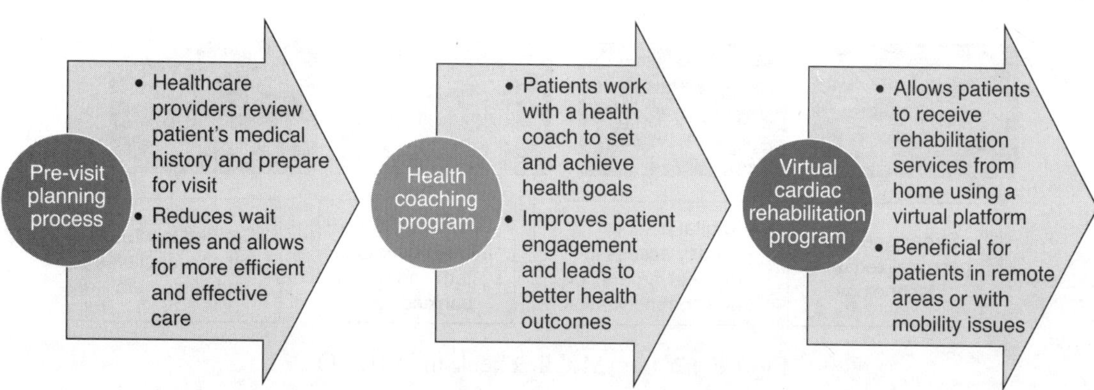

Figure 12.9 Improving the clinical process in Kaiser Permanente

patient is up to date on any necessary vaccinations or medications. By doing so, the healthcare team can optimize the patient's visit, reduce wait times, and ensure that the patient receives the care they need in a timely and efficient manner.

Another way that Kaiser Permanente has used design thinking to improve their clinical processes is through their 'health coaching' program. In this program, patients work with a health coach to set and achieve health goals. The health coach provides guidance and support to the patient, helping them make positive lifestyle changes that can improve their overall health and wellbeing. By using a design thinking approach, Kaiser Permanente has been able to create a program that is tailored to the needs and preferences of each individual patient. This has led to high levels of patient engagement and has resulted in better health outcomes.

Kaiser Permanente has also used design thinking to develop innovative solutions for patients with chronic conditions. For example, they have created a 'virtual cardiac rehabilitation' program for patients who have experienced a cardiac event. This program allows patients to receive rehabilitation services from the comfort of their own home, using a virtual platform. By doing so, patients can receive the care they need without having to leave their home, which can be particularly beneficial for patients who live in remote areas or who have mobility issues.

Kaiser Permanente has also used design thinking to improve the medication management process. They have implemented a program called 'Total Health' which aims to improve medication adherence and reduce medication errors. This program includes features such as medication synchronization, where patients can have all their prescriptions filled at the same time, and medication therapy management, where patients receive personalized support and guidance from pharmacists. This has improved patient outcomes and has reduced healthcare costs associated with medication-related complications.

12.5 IDEO

IDEO is a design and innovation consulting firm that has been at the forefront of design thinking. They have worked with a wide range of clients across industries to create innovative solutions that solve complex problems.

12.5.1 Innovative Solutions

One example of their work is the redesign of the check-in process for a major hotel chain (Fig. 12.10).

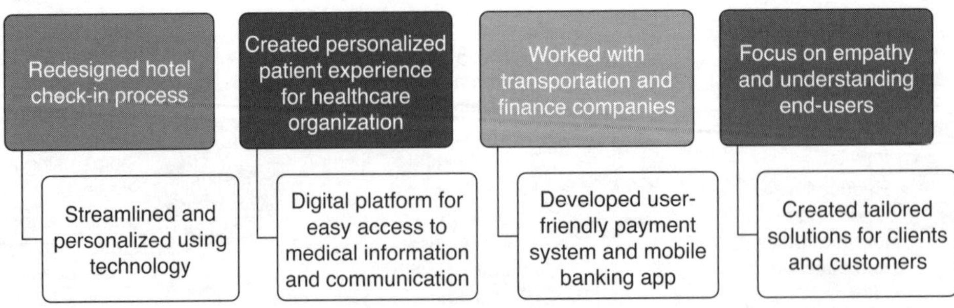

Figure 12.10 Mobile check-in in IDEO

IDEO used design thinking to identify pain points in the existing check-in process, such as long wait times and a lack of personalization. They then developed a solution that involved using technology to streamline the check-in process and make it more personalized. The new process involved using mobile devices to check-in and select room preferences, as well as providing personalized recommendations for local attractions and restaurants based on the guest's interests.

IDEO has also worked with companies in various industries, such as transportation and finance, to create innovative solutions using design thinking. For example, they worked with a transportation company to develop a new payment system that is more user-friendly and convenient for riders. They also worked with a financial institution to redesign their mobile banking app to make it more user-friendly and personalized.

One of the key strengths of IDEO's approach to design thinking is their focus on empathy and understanding the needs and experiences of the end-users. This allows them to create solutions that are truly tailored to the needs of their clients and their customers. IDEO's work has not only resulted in innovative solutions but has also helped to shape the way that organizations approach problem-solving and design.

12.5.2 Improved Healthcare Solutions

Another example of IDEO's work is their collaboration with a healthcare organization to create a more personalized patient experience (Fig. 12.11).

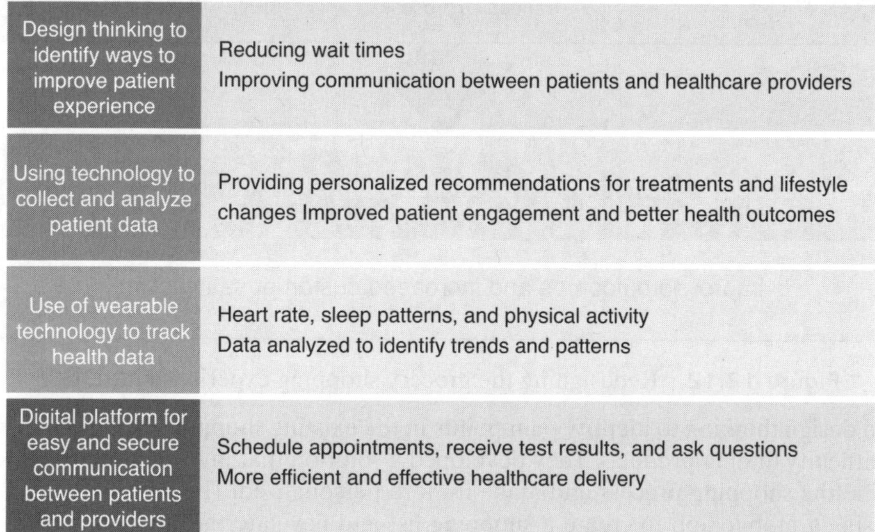

Figure 12.11 Improved healthcare solutions in IDEO

In their collaboration with a healthcare organization, IDEO utilized design thinking to improve the patient experience. The design thinking process allowed them to identify key pain points and opportunities for improvement and develop innovative solutions that addressed these issues. One such solution was the use of technology to collect and analyze patient data, which allowed for a more personalized approach to healthcare. With wearable technology, patients could track their health data such as their heart rate, sleep patterns, and physical activity. This data was then analyzed to identify trends and patterns that could be used to provide personalized recommendations for treatments and lifestyle changes. For example, if a patient's data showed that they were not getting enough physical activity, they could be recommended exercises that are tailored to their fitness level and interests.

IDEO also addressed the issue of communication between patients and healthcare providers. They developed a solution that involved the use of a digital platform that allowed for easy and secure communication between patients and providers. Patients could schedule appointments, receive test results, and ask questions, while providers could review patient data and respond to inquiries in a timely manner. This improved communication has led to more efficient and effective healthcare delivery, as well as increased patient satisfaction.

12.5.3 Redesigning the Grocery Shopping Experience

Another example of IDEO's work is their redesign of the grocery shopping experience for a major chain (Fig. 12.12).

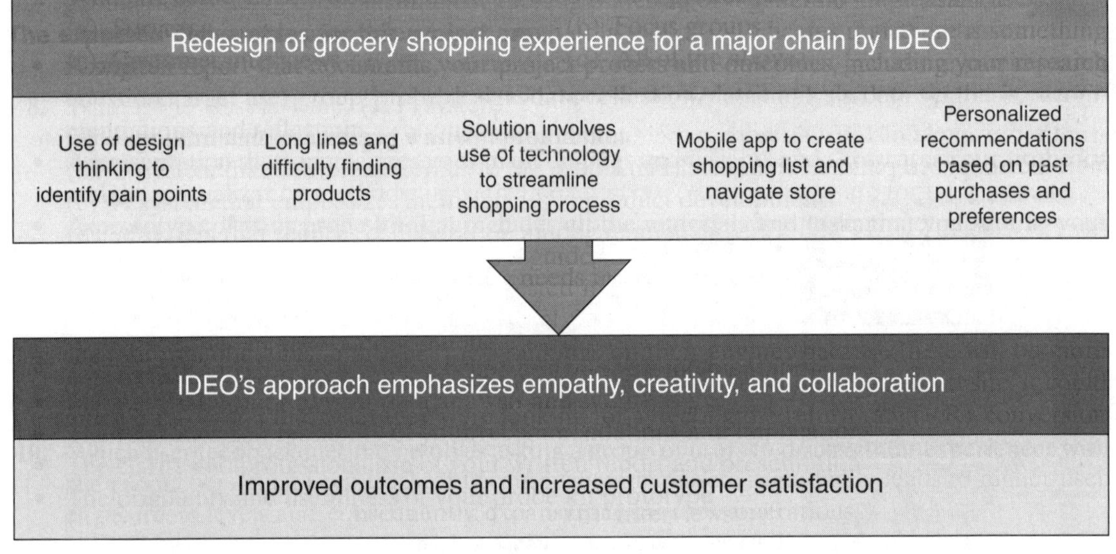

Figure 12.12 Redesigning the grocery shopping experience in IDEO

IDEO used design thinking to identify pain points in the existing shopping experience, such as long lines and difficulty finding products. They developed a solution that involved the use of technology to streamline the shopping process and make it more personalized. The new shopping experience involved using a mobile app to create a shopping list and navigate the store, as well as providing personalized recommendations based on the customer's past purchases and preferences.

12.5.4 Designing a Self-Driving Car and Home Blood-testing Kit

IDEO has also worked with clients to develop innovative products, such as a self-driving car for a major automaker and a home blood-testing kit for a healthcare company (Fig. 12.13).

IDEO used design thinking to identify user needs and pain points, such as safety concerns and the need for a seamless driving experience. They developed a solution that involved using advanced technology, such as sensors and machine learning algorithms, to create a car that could safely and efficiently navigate roads without human input. The design also emphasized user experience, with features such as a comfortable interior and intuitive controls.

In another project, IDEO worked with a healthcare company to develop a home blood-testing kit. They used design thinking to identify user needs, such as the need for accurate and easy-to-use testing equipment.

IDEO's collaboration with major automaker

Developed a self-driving car using design thinking

Identified user needs and pain points

Used advanced technology for safe and efficient navigation

Emphasized user experience with comfortable interior and intuitive controls

IDEO's collaboration with a healthcare company

Developed a home blood-testing kit using design thinking

Identified user needs for accurate and easy-to-use testing equipment

Resulting product was compact and user-friendly

Design thinking's versatility and impact on diverse industries

Improves experiences of individuals in healthcare, transportation, and more

Figure 12.13 IDEO innovation projects

The resulting product was a compact and user-friendly kit that could be easily used at home to monitor health metrics such as cholesterol levels and blood sugar. These examples demonstrate the versatility of design thinking and the impact it can have on a variety of industries. By prioritizing user needs and collaborating with clients to develop innovative solutions, IDEO has helped to improve the experiences of individuals in diverse contexts, from healthcare to transportation.

12.6 Ford

Ford, one of the largest automobile companies in the world, has been using design thinking to create a more human-centered approach to their car design. By incorporating technology to improve safety and user experience, Ford has been able to stay ahead of the curve in the competitive automotive industry.

12.6.1 Safety Features

Ford has developed a system called Co-Pilot360, which includes features such as automatic emergency braking, blind spot monitoring, and lane keeping assistance. These features not only make driving safer for the driver and passengers but also for pedestrians and cyclists on the road.

12.6.2 Improving User Experience

Another way Ford has used design thinking is by improving the user experience of their vehicles. They have integrated technology such as voice-activated controls, touchscreen displays, and smartphone connectivity to make the driving experience more convenient and enjoyable. For instance, Ford's SYNC 3 system enables drivers to control various functions such as music, navigation, and climate control using voice commands or the touchscreen display.

12.6.3 Eco-friendly and Sustainable Vehicles

Ford has used design thinking to improve the manufacturing process of their vehicles. They have adopted an approach called 'lean manufacturing', which focuses on eliminating waste and improving efficiency. This has resulted in a more streamlined manufacturing process and has enabled Ford to produce vehicles at a lower cost.

Ford has also used design thinking to develop electric and hybrid vehicles that are more sustainable and eco-friendly. The Ford Mustang Mach-E, for example, is an all-electric SUV that has been designed to offer the performance and style of a traditional Mustang while also being environmentally friendlyThe Mach-E is equipped with a long-range battery that can travel up to 300 miles on a single charge, making it a practical choice for everyday use. It also comes with advanced features such as hands-free driving and over-the-air software updates.

Ford has developed hybrid vehicles that combine a gasoline engine with an electric motor to achieve better fuel efficiency. The Ford Escape Hybrid, for example, has a range of up to 582 miles on a single tank of gas and can achieve an estimated 41 miles per gallon in the city. This makes it a practical choice for families who want a fuel-efficient SUV that can handle both city and highway driving.

Another example of Ford's commitment to sustainability is the Ford F-150 Lightning, an all-electric version of the popular F-150 pickup truck. The F-150 Lightning is designed to be both rugged and eco-friendly, with a towing capacity of up to 10,000 pounds and a range of up to 300 miles on a single charge. It also comes with features such as Pro Power Onboard, which allows the truck to act as a portable generator, and a large front trunk for extra storage.

12.6.4 Human-centered Approach

Ford has used design thinking is by incorporating a human-centered approach in their car design (Fig. 12.14).

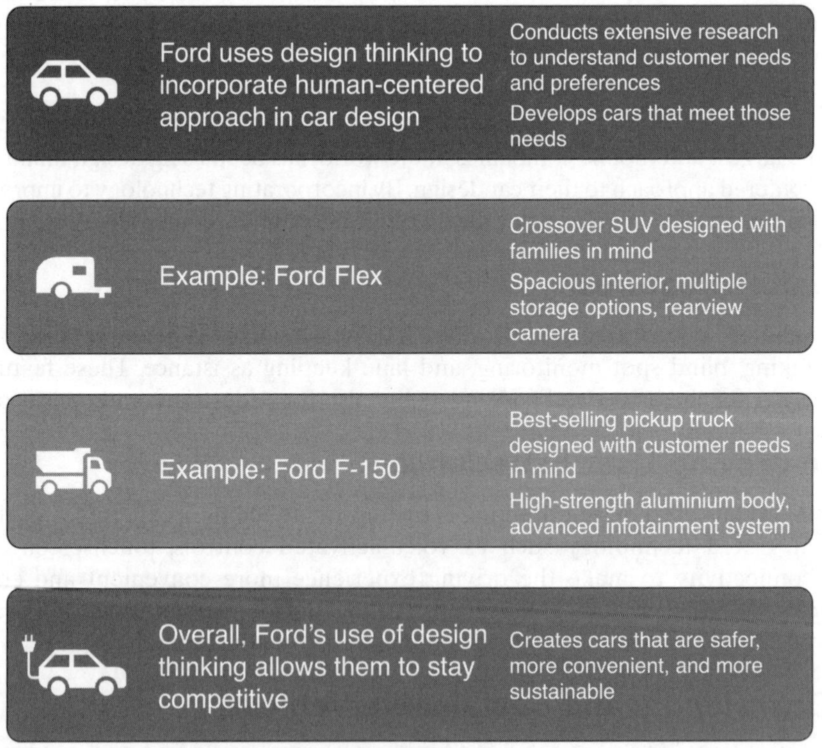

Figure 12.14 Ford innovation projects

In addition to safety features, Ford has incorporated technology such as touchscreens, voice recognition, and smartphone integration to make driving more convenient and enjoyable. For example, many Ford models now come equipped with SYNC, a system that allows drivers to use voice commands to control features such as music, navigation, and climate control.

Ford has also used design thinking to create more comfortable and versatile interior spaces in their vehicles. They have implemented features such as adjustable seats and storage compartments to make the driving experience more personalized and convenient for the user. For example, the Ford Escape offers a sliding second row of seats, allowing passengers to adjust their seating position for maximum comfort. The Ford F-150 pickup truck also features a versatile storage system called the BoxLink system, which includes various hooks and brackets for securing cargo.

Another example of this human-centered design approach is the Ford Flex, a crossover SUV that was designed with families in mind. The Flex has a spacious interior that can accommodate up to seven passengers and multiple storage options, including under-seat storage and a rear cargo management system. The vehicle also has a rearview camera that makes it easier for parents to load and unload their children and their belongings. In addition, the Flex has a large panoramic sunroof that provides natural light and an open, airy feel for passengers.

The F-150 pickup truck has been one of the best-selling vehicles in the US for over 40 years and has been designed with the needs of its customers in mind. Ford has conducted extensive research to understand the needs of pickup truck buyers, and has used this information to develop a vehicle that is both functional and stylish. The F-150 has features such as a high-strength aluminum body, which makes it lighter and more fuel-efficient than other trucks in its class, as well as an advanced infotainment system that provides a variety of entertainment and connectivity options.

Ford has been using design thinking to create a more human-centered approach in their car design. By incorporating features such as advanced safety systems, innovative technology, and sustainable materials, Ford has been able to create vehicles that meet the needs and preferences of their customers. This approach has helped Ford to develop cars that are not only functional and practical but also aesthetically pleasing and enjoyable to drive.

12.7 Indian Railways

Indian Railways, one of the world's largest and most complex railway networks, has increasingly adopted design thinking to tackle various challenges and improve the overall passenger experience. Design thinking, a user-centric approach to problem-solving, has enabled Indian Railways to innovate and enhance its services in several significant ways:

- Enhancing customer experience
- Infrastructure and safety improvements
- Digital transformation
- Collaborative innovation

This approach has allowed Indian Railways to better meet the needs of its passengers and enhance the overall travel experience.

12.7.1 Enhancing the Customer Experience

Indian Railways has effectively employed design thinking to tackle various challenges and enhance the customer experience, especially within the Mumbai Local network, one of the busiest and oldest railway systems in the country. This initiative, facilitated by TinkerLabs, included a comprehensive ethnographic study aimed at understanding the daily experiences and pain points of commuters.

The project commenced with an ethnographic study. Multidisciplinary teams, comprising railway officials and professionals from various sectors, conducted field visits and immersive workshops. These teams engaged with daily commuters to gather valuable insights into their experiences and challenges.

Overcrowding

During rush hour, the Mumbai Local trains and platforms become extremely crowded, making it difficult for commuters to move freely. This overcrowding not only causes discomfort but also poses safety risks, as the high density of passengers can lead to accidents and injuries. The lack of space makes it challenging for passengers to efficiently board and alight from the trains, further worsening the congestion. For instance, many passengers often push into already-packed trains during peak hours, creating a stressful and unsafe environment.

To address this issue, Indian Railways has implemented several design thinking solutions:

- **Heat Maps for Commuter Distribution:** Technology was utilized to create heat maps that illustrate the distribution of commuters across trains and coaches. These heat maps assist in managing passenger flow, ensuring a more even distribution and reducing overcrowding in specific areas. This improvement enhances comfort and promotes safety by preventing accidents caused by excessive crowding.
  Sensors and data analytics tools were installed to monitor real-time passenger movement and density. These tools collected data on the number of passengers boarding and alighting at each station, as well as their distribution across different coaches. The gathered data was processed to produce heat maps that visually depicted passenger density in various parts of the train and on the platform. Color coding was used to indicate areas of high and low passenger concentration. By analyzing these heat maps, railway officials could identify overcrowded areas and implement measures to distribute passengers more evenly. For example, announcements and signage could guide passengers toward less crowded coaches, balancing the load across the train.
  With a more balanced distribution of passengers, overall comfort levels increased. Passengers enjoyed more space to move around and were less likely to experience discomfort and stress associated with overcrowding. Overcrowding can lead to accidents, such as passengers being pushed or falling while boarding or alighting. Reducing crowd density in specific areas helped minimize the risk of such incidents. In emergencies, a more evenly distributed passenger load facilitated easier evacuations and assistance, further enhancing safety.
  Insights from the heat maps also allowed railway officials to allocate resources more effectively. For instance, additional staff could be deployed to manage passenger flow in high-density areas during peak hours. Understanding passenger distribution patterns helped optimize train schedules and frequencies, ensuring that trains were available when and where they were needed most.
- **Additional Services During Peak Hours:** Increasing the frequency of trains during peak hours to accommodate the higher number of passengers. This reduces the number of passengers per train, alleviating congestion and making it easier for commuters to board and alight safely.
  Indian Railways adjusted train schedules to increase the frequency of services during peak hours. This involved adding more trains to the timetable and reducing the intervals between trains. Additional resources, such as train crews and maintenance staff, were allocated to support the increased frequency of services. This ensured the additional trains could operate smoothly without compromising safety or reliability. Increasing the number of trains reduced the number of passengers per train. This alleviated congestion, making it easier for commuters to find space and move comfortably within the trains. With fewer passengers per train, boarding, and alighting became more orderly and efficient. Passengers no longer had to rush or push onto crowded trains, reducing the risk of accidents and delays.
  The increased frequency of trains provided a more comfortable and convenient travel experience. Passengers had more options for travel times, reducing the need to wait for long periods

and allowing for a more flexible commute. The reduction in overcrowding and the availability of more trains helped to reduce the stress and anxiety associated with peak-hour travel. Commuters could travel with greater peace of mind, knowing they would have a better chance of finding a seat or standing space. The increased frequency of trains allowed for better utilization of the railway infrastructure. Trains were used more efficiently, and the network's overall capacity was maximized. With a more even distribution of passengers and reduced congestion, trains could adhere more closely to their schedules. This improved the overall punctuality of the service, enhancing the reliability of the railway system.

- **Platform Management:** Deploying staff to manage the flow of passengers on platforms, especially during peak hours. Additional staff members, often called platform marshals or attendants, are deployed on platforms during peak hours. Their primary role is to manage the flow of passengers, assist with boarding and alighting, and ensure safety protocols are followed. These staff members are trained in crowd management techniques, emergency response, and customer service. They are equipped to handle large crowds and assist passengers, especially during busy times. The presence of platform staff helps in organizing the boarding and alighting process. They guide passengers to designated boarding areas, ensure that passengers wait for alighting passengers to exit first, and manage the flow of people to prevent bottlenecks. By managing the flow of passengers, platform staff reduce the chaos and confusion that often occurs during peak hours. This leads to a smoother and more orderly boarding process, minimizing delays and improving overall efficiency. Platform staff play a crucial role in preventing accidents. They monitor the platform for any safety hazards, assist passengers needing help, and ensure passengers do not crowd too close to the platform's edge. Platform staff are trained to respond quickly and effectively in emergencies. They can provide first aid, manage evacuations, and coordinate with emergency services to ensure passenger safety. Platform staff provide valuable assistance to passengers, answering questions, giving directions, and helping with luggage. This enhances the overall passenger experience, making travel more pleasant and stress-free. With platform staff managing the flow of passengers, trains can adhere more closely to their schedules. This improves the punctuality and reliability of the service, benefiting all passengers.
- **Awareness Campaigns:** This comprises running campaigns to educate passengers about the best practices for boarding and alighting and the importance of using all available doors and coaches. Creating and distributing educational materials such as posters, pamphlets, and digital content helps explain the best practices for boarding and alighting. These materials are placed in high-visibility areas such as platforms, ticket counters, and inside trains. Public announcement systems regularly remind passengers about the importance of following boarding and alighting guidelines. These announcements are made in multiple languages to ensure they reach a broad audience. Social media platforms are leveraged to spread awareness about safe and efficient boarding practices. Engaging content, including videos and infographics, is shared to educate passengers and encourage them to follow the guidelines. Workshops and live demonstrations are organized at major stations to show passengers how to board and alight from trains. These sessions are interactive and provide hands-on learning experiences. These campaigns help spread awareness about the best practices for boarding and alighting. Passengers become more informed about the importance of using all available doors and coaches, which helps distribute the passenger load more evenly. By educating passengers, these campaigns encourage them to follow the guidelines, which can significantly reduce congestion and improve safety. Passengers are more likely to adhere to the rules when they understand the benefits. With more passengers using all available doors and coaches, the boarding and alighting process becomes more efficient. This reduces congestion on platforms and inside trains, making the travel experience more comfortable.

Difficulty in Boarding

The chaotic process of boarding and deboarding trains is a significant issue. Passengers often struggle to get on and off the trains due to the rush and lack of organized entry and exit points. This disorganized boarding process leads to delays, as trains have to wait longer at each station to accommodate the flow of passengers. The risk of accidents increases, as passengers may fall or get injured in the scramble to board or alight. For instance, the absence of clear markers or designated areas for boarding and alighting can confuse people and cause crowds at train doors.

To address this issue, Indian Railways has implemented several design thinking solutions:

- **Entry and Exit Markers:** Clear markers were introduced at train doors and platforms to guide passengers during boarding and deboarding. These markers included arrows, lines, and signs indicating where passengers should stand while waiting to board and where they should move to exit the train. Different colors were used to distinguish between entry and exit points, making it easier for passengers to identify the correct areas quickly. Additional signage was installed to provide instructions on how to use the markers effectively. This included diagrams and text explaining the boarding and deboarding process. The clear markers helped organize the boarding and deboarding process, reducing the chaos typically seen during peak hours. Passengers clearly understood where to stand and move, facilitating a smoother flow of people. By guiding passengers to specific entry and exit points, the markers helped distribute the crowd more evenly across the platform and train doors. This reduced congestion and made it easier for passengers to board and alight without pushing or shoving. The organized flow of passengers minimized the risk of accidents, such as tripping or falling, common in crowded and chaotic boarding situations. Passengers could board and alight more safely, knowing exactly where to go.
  With a more orderly boarding process, trains could adhere more closely to their schedules. Reduced delays at stations meant that trains could depart on time, improving the overall efficiency of the railway system.
- **Dedicated Boarding Zones:** Specific zones on the platform were marked and designated for boarding and alighting. These zones were indicated with signs and floor markings to guide passengers. Different colors and signs were used to distinguish between boarding and alighting zones. This visual differentiation helped passengers quickly identify where they should stand while waiting to board and where they should move to exit the train. Regular announcements were made to inform passengers about the designated boarding and alighting zones, ensuring everyone was aware of the new system. The system reduced confusion and crowding at train doors by clearly designating specific areas for boarding and alighting. The organized flow of passengers ensured a smoother and faster boarding process. With a more orderly boarding and alighting process, trains could adhere more closely to their schedules. This reduced delays and improved the overall punctuality and reliability of the railway service.
- **Platform Assistants:** Deploying staff to assist passengers during peak hours, guiding them to the correct boarding zones, and helping with the boarding process. Additional staff members, often referred to as platform assistants or marshals, are deployed on platforms during peak hours. Their primary role is to manage the flow of passengers, assist with boarding and alighting, and ensure safety protocols are followed. These staff members receive training in crowd management, customer service, and emergency response. They are equipped to handle large crowds and assist passengers, especially during busy times. Platform assistants are easily identifiable by their uniforms or vests, making it simple for passengers to seek help when needed. The presence of platform assistants helps to organize the boarding and alighting process, reducing the chaos typically seen during peak hours.

- **Public Announcements and Signage:** Public announcement systems and clear signage should be used to inform passengers about boarding procedures and train schedules. Installing and utilizing public announcement systems at stations to provide real-time information about train schedules, boarding procedures, and any changes or delays. Announcements are made in multiple languages to cater to a diverse passenger base. Clear and visible signs should be placed throughout the station and on platforms to guide passengers. This includes signs indicating boarding zones, exit points, platform numbers, and directions to various facilities such as ticket counters and restrooms. Using digital displays and electronic boards to show real-time updates on train arrivals, departures, and platform changes. These displays are strategically placed to ensure they are easily visible to passengers. Public announcements and clear signage keep passengers well-informed about train schedules and boarding procedures. This reduces the likelihood of confusion and helps passengers plan their movements more effectively. Providing timely and accurate information enhances the overall passenger experience. Passengers feel more confident and less stressed when they have access to clear and reliable information about their journey.
- **Boarding Time Management:** Indian Railways adjusted train schedules to allocate additional time for boarding and alighting during peak hours. This involved analyzing passenger flow data to identify the busiest times and stations and then modifying the timetable accordingly. Introducing flexible timetables that can be adjusted dynamically based on real-time passenger data. This allows more responsive scheduling to adapt to varying daily demands. Ensuring train crews and platform staff are informed about the adjusted schedules and prepared to efficiently manage the extended boarding times. By allowing more time for boarding and alighting, passengers are not forced to rush, which decreases the likelihood of accidents and injuries. This creates a safer and more relaxed environment for commuters.

Under-utilization of ATVMs

Automatic ticket vending machines (ATVMs) are not being used effectively, resulting in long queues at ticket counters. Many passengers either do not know how to use the ATVMs or find them too complicated, leading to under-utilization. This inefficiency causes delays and frustration among commuters who have to wait in line to purchase tickets, adding to the overall congestion and reducing the efficiency of the ticketing process. For example, despite the availability of ATVMs, many passengers prefer to queue at ticket counters due to unfamiliarity with the machines or perceived complexity.

To address this issue, Indian Railways has implemented several design thinking solutions:

- **Simplified ATVM Interfaces:** The ATVM user interface was redesigned to be more intuitive and user-friendly. This involved simplifying the steps required to purchase a ticket and providing clear, easy-to-follow instructions. The redesign process focused on understanding the needs and behaviors of passengers. User feedback was gathered through surveys and usability testing to identify pain points and areas for improvement. The number of steps required to purchase a ticket was reduced. Clear, concise instructions were provided at each step, using simple language and visual cues to guide users through the process. The touchscreens were made more responsive and easier to navigate. Larger buttons and icons accommodated users of all ages and abilities. The interface was made available in multiple languages to cater to the diverse passenger base, ensuring that language barriers did not hinder the use of ATVMs. The redesigned interface made ATVMs much easier to use, leading to a significant increase in their utilization. More passengers opted to use the machines instead of waiting in line at ticket counters.

The improvements made the ATVMs more accessible to a wider range of passengers, including those with disabilities or limited technical skills. This inclusivity ensured that all passengers could benefit from the convenience of the machines.

- **User Education and Awareness Campaigns:** Conducting educational campaigns to teach passengers how to use ATVMs. This included station demonstrations, instructional videos, and posters with step-by-step guides. Organizing live demonstrations at major railway stations where staff members showed passengers how to use ATVMs. These demonstrations were scheduled during peak hours to reach maximum commuters. Creating and displaying instructional videos on screens at stations and on social media platforms. These videos provided a step-by-step guide on using ATVMs, making it easy for passengers to follow along. Designing posters and pamphlets with clear, illustrated instructions on how to use ATVMs. These materials were distributed at station ticket counters, waiting areas, and other high-traffic locations. Setting up interactive kiosks where passengers could practice using a simulated ATVM interface. This hands-on experience helped build confidence and familiarity with the machines. The increased use of ATVMs allowed station staff to focus on assisting passengers with more complex needs, improving overall service quality and operational efficiency.
- **On-site Assistance:** Deploying staff to assist passengers with using ATVMs, especially during peak hours. These staff members provided hands-on help and answered passengers' questions about the machines. Additional staff members were stationed near ATVMs during peak hours to assist passengers. These staff members were trained to provide hands-on help and answer any questions passengers might have about using the machines. The assisting staff wore uniforms or badges that made them easily identifiable to passengers seeking help. This ensured that passengers could quickly find assistance when needed. Staff members proactively approached passengers who appeared to be struggling with the ATVMs, offering guidance and support without waiting to be asked. The immediate assistance provided by the on-site staff helped passengers overcome any initial hesitation or confusion about using ATVMs. This support was particularly beneficial for first-time users or those unfamiliar with the technology. The hands-on help offered a more personalized experience, making passengers feel more comfortable and confident using the machines.
- **Feedback Mechanisms:** Installing feedback systems on ATVMs to gather user input on their experience and any difficulties encountered. A simple and intuitive feedback interface was added to the ATVMs, allowing users to rate their experience and provide comments immediately after completing their transaction. This could include options like rating the ease of use, reporting any issues, and suggesting improvements. In addition to on-machine feedback, QR codes were displayed on the ATVMs, directing users to an online feedback form. This provided an alternative way for passengers to share their experiences and suggestions. A dedicated team monitored the feedback collected in real time. This allowed for quick identification and resolution of recurring issues or common complaints. The feedback gathered from passengers provided valuable insights into their experiences and highlighted areas for improvement.
- **Incentives for Using ATVMs:** Offering incentives such as discounts or loyalty points for passengers who use ATVMs to purchase tickets. Providing a small discount on ticket prices for passengers who purchase tickets through ATVMs. This financial incentive encourages passengers to choose the self-service option over traditional ticket counters. Introducing a loyalty program where passengers earn points for each ticket purchased via ATVMs. These points can be redeemed for future travel discounts, upgrades, or other rewards. Running promotional campaigns to inform passengers about the incentives available for using ATVMs. This includes station advertisements, social media, and other communication channels. The financial and

reward-based incentives encouraged more passengers to use ATVMs, significantly increasing their utilization. Passengers were motivated by the immediate savings and the potential for future rewards. With more passengers opting to use ATVMs, the queues at ticket counters were reduced. This made the ticket-purchasing process more efficient and less time-consuming for everyone.

12.7.2 Infrastructure and Safety Improvements

Indian Railways has effectively employed design thinking to modernize its infrastructure and enhance safety measures. This user-centric approach has led to significant advancements, ensuring a safer and more efficient railway system.

The Vande Bharat Express

Also known as Train 18, this is a prime example of how design thinking has been applied to create a faster and more comfortable travel experience. These trains incorporate several user-centric features:

- **Advanced Safety Systems:** Vande Bharat trains are equipped with modern safety technologies such as the Train Collision Avoidance System (TCAS). This system helps prevent accidents by automatically controlling the train's speed and ensuring safe distances between trains. For instance, if the TCAS detects another train on the same track, it can automatically slow down or stop the train to avoid a collision. This significantly enhances passenger safety and reduces the risk of accidents. TCAS continuously monitors the train's speed and the distance to other trains on the same track. If it detects that the train is approaching another train too quickly, it can automatically reduce the speed or bring the train to a complete stop. This automatic control helps prevent rear-end collisions, a significant safety concern in railway operations. By maintaining safe distances between trains, TCAS ensures smoother and safer journeys for passengers. The system uses real-time data from various sensors and GPS to track the position and speed of the train. This data is constantly analyzed to detect potential hazards and take corrective actions. Real-time monitoring allows for immediate response to potential safety threats, significantly reducing the risk of accidents. Passengers can travel with greater peace of mind, knowing that advanced technology is working to keep them safe. TCAS is integrated with other safety systems on the train, such as automatic braking and signaling systems. This integration ensures a coordinated response to any detected threats. The seamless integration of multiple safety systems enhances the overall safety of the train.
- **Ergonomic Seating:** The trains feature comfortable, ergonomic seats designed to provide better support and comfort for passengers during long journeys. These seats are designed with adjustable headrests, ample legroom, and reclining features to ensure a comfortable travel experience. This design consideration reflects a deep understanding of passenger needs and comfort, making long-distance travel more pleasant and less tiring. The seats have adjustable headrests that passengers can modify to suit their height and preferred position. This feature provides better neck and head support, reducing strain during long journeys. The seat design includes generous legroom, allowing passengers to stretch their legs comfortably. This is particularly important for long-distance travel, where cramped seating can lead to discomfort and stiffness. The seats have reclining features that allow passengers to adjust the angle of the seat back. This enables passengers to find a comfortable seating position, whether sitting upright or reclining slightly. Reclining the seat adds to passenger comfort, especially during long journeys. It allows passengers to relax and rest more effectively, reducing fatigue and making the

journey more pleasant. The ergonomic design of the seats includes lumbar support and cushioning that conforms to the body's natural curves. This design helps maintain proper posture and provides consistent support throughout the journey. The supportive design reduces the risk of back pain and discomfort, common issues during long-distance travel.

- **Improved Amenities:** Vande Bharat trains offer a range of amenities that enhance the overall travel experience. Passengers can stay connected and productive during their journey with onboard Wi-Fi. High-speed Wi-Fi is available throughout the train, allowing passengers to access the internet for work, entertainment, or communication. This amenity ensures that passengers remain connected, making the journey more enjoyable and productive. It is particularly beneficial for business travelers who need to stay in touch with their work. Real-time updates on train location, upcoming stations, and expected arrival times are displayed on screens throughout the train, keeping passengers well-informed. Digital screens are installed in each coach, displaying real-time information about the train's progress, next stops, and expected arrival times. This system keeps passengers informed and reduces anxiety about their journey. Knowing the exact location and timing helps passengers plan their activities better, enhancing their overall travel experience. These toilets are designed to be more hygienic and environmentally friendly, reducing water usage and ensuring a cleaner travel environment. Bio-vacuum toilets use minimal water and have a vacuum system that ensures waste is efficiently managed and disposed of. These toilets provide a cleaner and more hygienic environment for passengers. They also contribute to environmental sustainability by reducing water usage and managing waste more effectively. The trains feature automatic doors and modern interiors with LED lighting, providing a more comfortable and aesthetically pleasing environment.

Upgrading Tracks and Signaling Systems

Indian Railways has embarked on a comprehensive modernization journey, upgrading its tracks and signaling systems to support higher speeds and enhance safety.

- **High-Strength Rails (R-350 Grade):** One of the significant advancements in Indian Railways' infrastructure is the adoption of high-strength rails, specifically the R-350 Grade. These rails are designed to withstand higher speeds and greater stress, making them ideal for modern, high-speed train operations. The R-350 grade rails are more durable than traditional rails, reducing the risk of track-related accidents and ensuring smoother train operations. Introducing these high-strength rails is part of a broader strategy to upgrade the railway network. For instance, the Steel Authority of India Ltd (SAIL) has been tasked with producing these rails domestically, ensuring that the Indian Railways can maintain a steady supply for its extensive network. The use of R-350 rails is expected to facilitate the operation of next-generation trains like the Vande Bharat Express, which are designed to run at speeds up to 220 km per hour.
- **Modern Signaling Technology: European Train Control System (ETCS):** In addition to upgrading the physical tracks, Indian Railways is investing in modern signaling technologies to enhance safety and efficiency. One of the key technologies being implemented is the European Train Control System (ETCS). This system provides real-time information to train drivers and control centers, enabling better decision-making and reducing the likelihood of human errors. ETCS operates at multiple levels, with Level 2 being particularly significant for Indian Railways. This level involves continuous communication between the train and trackside equipment, ensuring that trains can operate safely even at high speeds. The system includes Automatic Train Protection (ATP), which prevents collisions by automatically controlling the

train's speed and braking. Additionally, integrating Automatic Train Operation (ATO) and Automatic Train Supervision (ATS) further enhances operational efficiency and safety.

The upgrades to tracks and signaling systems have profound implications for the safety and efficiency of train operations in India. High-strength rails reduce the risk of derailments and other track-related accidents, while modern signaling systems like ETCS minimize the chances of human error, which is a significant factor in many railway accidents.

Moreover, these advancements are crucial for developing high-speed rail corridors in India. The ability to run trains at higher speeds without compromising safety is essential for reducing travel times and improving the overall passenger experience. For example, the Delhi–Mumbai and Delhi–Howrah corridors are being upgraded to allow trains to run up to 160 km/h, significantly reducing travel times between these major cities.

Infrastructure Modernization Projects

Indian Railways has embarked on several large-scale infrastructure modernization projects to enhance safety, efficiency, and passenger experience. Two of the most significant initiatives under this modernization drive are the construction of Dedicated Freight Corridors (DFCs) and the comprehensive redevelopment of railway stations across the country.

- **Dedicated Freight Corridors (DFCs):** DFCs are a transformative initiative designed to separate freight and passenger traffic, reducing congestion and the risk of accidents. The primary objective of the DFCs is to create a network of high-capacity. These high-speed freight lines can handle heavier and longer trains, significantly improving the efficiency of goods transportation in India. The DFC project involves the construction of two main corridors: the Eastern Dedicated Freight Corridor (EDFC) and the Western Dedicated Freight Corridor (WDFC). The EDFC stretches from Ludhiana in Punjab to Dankuni in West Bengal, covering a distance of approximately 1,856 kilometers. The WDFC runs from Jawaharlal Nehru Port in Mumbai to Dadri in Uttar Pradesh, spanning about 1,504 kilometers. These corridors are designed to accommodate double-stack container trains and are equipped with advanced signaling and communication systems. The tracks are built to handle higher axle loads, allowing for the transportation of heavier goods. Using electric traction further enhances the efficiency and sustainability of freight operations. As of 2024, significant portions of the EDFC and WDFC are operational, with the remaining sections nearing completion. The operationalization of these corridors has already begun to transform freight logistics in India. The separation of freight and passenger traffic has reduced delays and improved the punctuality of passenger trains. Additionally, the increased capacity and speed of freight trains have lowered transportation costs and enhanced the competitiveness of Indian goods in the global market. The DFCs are also expected to have a positive environmental impact by reducing the reliance on road transport, which is more polluting and less efficient. By shifting a significant portion of freight traffic to rail, the DFCs reduce greenhouse gas emissions and promote sustainable transportation practices.
- **Station Redevelopment:** In parallel with the construction of DFCs, Indian Railways has launched an ambitious redevelopment program to modernize railway stations nationwide. This initiative seeks to enhance passenger amenities, improve safety, and create world-class facilities that cater to the needs of modern travelers. The station redevelopment program focuses on upgrading the infrastructure and facilities at major railway stations. The redevelopment's key features include better lighting, CCTV surveillance, and improved accessibility features such as ramps and elevators for differently-abled passengers. The program also aims to enhance the passenger experience by providing modern amenities such as clean and spacious waiting areas, food courts, and retail outlets. One of the flagship initiatives under this program is the

Amrit Bharat Station Scheme, which aims to redevelop 1,275 stations nationwide. This scheme is designed to integrate the redevelopment of stations with other key government initiatives, such as the BharatNet project for high-speed internet connectivity and the One Station One Product scheme to promote local products. The station redevelopment program is progressing rapidly, with several stations already transformed into modern, passenger-friendly hubs. For instance, the redevelopment of stations like Habibganj in Bhopal and Gandhinagar in Gujarat has set new benchmarks in terms of design and amenities. These stations now feature state-of-the-art facilities, including energy-efficient buildings, green spaces, and advanced security systems. The impact of station redevelopment extends beyond passenger convenience. By creating commercial spaces within station premises, the program generates additional revenue for Indian Railways, which can be reinvested in further infrastructure improvements. Moreover, the enhanced station environments contribute to the overall urban development of the surrounding areas, boosting local economies and improving the quality of life for residents.

12.7.3 Digital Transformation

Indian Railways has embraced digital transformation by integrating digital tools and platforms, focusing on user experience and operational efficiency. This approach has significantly improved the accessibility, convenience, and reliability of railway services.

Ticket Booking App

The IRCTC (Indian Railway Catering and Tourism Corporation) mobile app has revolutionized the ticket booking process for Indian Railways, making it more convenient and efficient for passengers. This essay explores the features and benefits of the IRCTC mobile app, highlighting how it has transformed how people book train tickets in India. The IRCTC mobile app offers many features to simplify ticket booking and enhance user experience. Passengers can book tickets with just a few taps on their smartphones. The app allows users to search for trains, select their preferred class and seats, and complete the booking process quickly and efficiently. The app provides real-time information on seat availability, helping passengers make informed decisions. It also offers real-time updates on ticket status, train schedules, and platform numbers, ensuring that passengers are always well-informed. The IRCTC app supports various payment methods, including credit and debit cards, net banking, UPI, and e-wallets. This flexibility makes it easier for passengers to complete their transactions securely and conveniently. The app features an intuitive and user-friendly interface, making it accessible to all ages. It includes advanced security features such as biometric login and self-assigned PINs to ensure the safety of user data.

Beyond ticket booking, the app offers additional services such as booking meals, checking PNR status, and accessing travel insurance. It also supports special quotas for ladies, senior citizens, and differently-abled passengers. The app eliminates the need for passengers to visit physical ticket counters and wait in long queues.

The app's user-friendly design and comprehensive features enhance the overall passenger experience. Real-time updates and multiple payment options ensure a smooth and hassle-free booking process. For Indian Railways, the app improves operational efficiency by reducing the burden on physical ticket counters and minimizing manual errors. The digital platform also allows for better data management and analysis, helping Indian Railways optimize its services. The app's support for special quotas and accessibility features ensures that all passengers, including those with special needs, can easily book tickets and access railway services. The IRCTC mobile app has significantly transformed the ticket booking process for Indian Railways, making it more convenient, efficient, and user-friendly.

Real-time Train Tracking

The "Where is my Train" app provides:

- Real-time tracking of trains
- Current location
- Expected arrival times
- Platform numbers

This feature helps passengers plan their journeys better, avoid delays, and reduce anxiety about train schedules. Providing timely information also improves the overall travel experience.

The "Where is My Train" app has become an essential tool for passengers, offering real-time train tracking and providing crucial information that enhances the overall travel experience. This essay explores the features and benefits of the app, highlighting how it helps passengers plan their journeys more effectively and reduces the stress associated with train travel. The "Where is My Train" app is designed to provide passengers with accurate and timely information about their train journeys. Key features of the app include:

The app uses GPS technology to track trains' exact locations in real-time. Passengers can view their train's current position on a map, which helps them stay informed about its progress and any potential delays.

The app provides estimated arrival times for trains at various stations along the route. This information is continuously updated based on the train's current speed and location, allowing passengers to plan their arrival at the station accordingly. Knowing the platform number in advance can save passengers time and hassle, especially at busy stations. The app provides real-time updates on platform numbers, ensuring that passengers are ready to board their train as soon as it arrives. One of the app's standout features is its ability to function offline. Passengers can access train schedules and other essential information without an internet connection, which is particularly useful during long journeys with limited network connectivity. The app sends notifications about any changes in train schedules, delays, or platform numbers. These alerts help passengers stay informed and make necessary adjustments to their travel plans.

By providing real-time updates on train locations and expected arrival times, the app helps passengers plan their journeys more effectively. This feature is especially useful during peak travel times or in case of unexpected disruptions. The app enhances the travel experience by providing timely and accurate information. Passengers can enjoy a smoother journey with fewer surprises and better preparation.

Customer Feedback

The RailMadad app enables passengers to lodge complaints, provide feedback, and track the status of their grievances. This platform enhances customer service by ensuring that passenger issues are addressed promptly. It also helps Indian Railways gather valuable feedback to improve services.

Indian Railways uses IoT sensors and advanced analytics to monitor the condition of tracks, trains, and other infrastructure. By analyzing sensor data, Indian Railways can predict potential failures and schedule maintenance. This reduces downtime, prevents accidents, and ensures smoother operations. Data analytics tools analyze passenger flow, train occupancy, and travel patterns. This information helps optimize train schedules, ensuring that trains run on time and resources are used efficiently. It also helps manage peak travel times and reduce congestion. IoT devices monitor and manage energy consumption across railway stations and trains. This leads to more efficient energy use, reducing operational costs and the environmental footprint of Indian Railways. It also supports sustainability initiatives.

12.7.4 Collaborative Innovation

A key aspect of Indian Railways' design thinking approach is collaboration. By engaging with various stakeholders, including passengers, employees, and external experts, Indian Railways has been able to co-create innovative and practical solutions. This collaborative approach ensures that the solutions developed are well-aligned with the needs and expectations of all stakeholders.

Mumbai Local Project with TinkerLabs

One of the most notable examples of this collaborative approach is the Mumbai Local project facilitated by TinkerLabs. This initiative aimed to enhance the commuter experience on one of the country's busiest and oldest railway systems.

Here's how the collaboration unfolded:

Multidisciplinary teams, including railway officials and professionals from various sectors, conducted field visits and immersive workshops to understand commuters' daily experiences and pain points. This study revealed key issues such as overcrowding, difficulty in boarding during rush hours, and under-utilization of ATVMs. The teams participated in workshops where they brainstormed and prototyped solutions based on the insights gathered. These workshops encouraged participants to think creatively and explore a wide range of ideas without immediate concern for feasibility. Technology was used to create heat maps that displayed the distribution of commuters across trains and coaches, helping to manage passenger flow more effectively. Clear markers were introduced at train doors and platforms to streamline the boarding and deboarding process, reducing congestion and improving safety. The user interface of ATVMs was redesigned to be more intuitive and user-friendly, increasing their utilization. The solutions were prototyped and tested with real users to ensure their practicality and effectiveness. Feedback from commuters was used to refine the solutions. The successful implementation of these solutions improved the commuter experience and demonstrated the value of user-centric design.

Other Collaborative Efforts

Indian Railways has engaged in other collaborative efforts to enhance its services:

- **Partnership with the National Institute of Design (NID):** To improve various aspects of railway design, including station areas, coach layouts, and passenger amenities. This collaboration has led to the development of better-designed stations and coaches, improving the overall travel experience for passengers.
- **Engagement with Technology Experts:** To integrate advanced technologies such as IoT and data analytics into railway operations. These collaborations have enabled Indian Railways to implement predictive maintenance, optimize train schedules, and enhance operational efficiency.

By leveraging design thinking and fostering collaboration, Indian Railways has developed innovative solutions that address the specific needs and challenges of its stakeholders. These efforts have improved the commuter experience and established a culture of continuous innovation within the organization. As Indian Railways continues to embrace design thinking, it is well-positioned to meet the evolving needs of its passengers and maintain its status as a vital part of India's transportation infrastructure.

CHAPTER 13

Capstone Projects

13.1 Introduction

A capstone project is a final, integrative assignment that allows students to demonstrate their mastery of a specific topic, skill, or discipline. Capstone projects can take various forms, such as research papers, case studies, portfolios, prototypes, or presentations. They can be used in the design thinking process as a way to apply the stages of empathy, ideation, prototyping, and testing to a real-world problem or opportunity. Capstone projects can also foster creativity, collaboration, communication, and critical thinking among students and also enhance students' skills in innovation, teamwork, presentation, and reflection.

13.2 Capstone Project 1: Designing a Cultural Probe for Empathetic Leadership

In this project, you will design and implement a cultural probe to explore how empathetic leadership can be fostered in different contexts. You will use the tools and methods of human-centered design to understand the needs, challenges, and opportunities of potential users of your probe. You will also analyze and synthesize the data collected from your probe to generate insights and recommendations for empathetic leadership development.

Your project will consist of the following steps:

1. Identify a specific context or domain where empathetic leadership is relevant and important. For example, you could choose education, healthcare, social work, or any other field where leaders interact with diverse groups of people.
2. Define your target user group and research question. Who are the potential users of your probe and what do you want to learn from them? For example, you could focus on teachers, nurses, social workers, or managers and ask how they practice or experience empathetic leadership in their work environment.
3. Design your probe kit. A probe kit is a collection of materials and tasks that you send to your users to elicit their thoughts, feelings, and behaviors related to your research question. Your probe kit should include at least three different types of activities, such as surveys, photo diaries, storyboards, collages, drawings, etc. You should also provide clear instructions and guidelines for your users on how to complete and return the probe kit.

4. Implement your probe. You will need to recruit at least 10 participants from your target user group and send them your probe kit. You should also follow up with them regularly to ensure that they complete and return the probe kit within a specified time frame.
5. Analyze and synthesize your data. You will need to collect and organize the data from your probe kits and look for patterns, themes, and insights that answer your research question. You can use various methods such as affinity diagrams, personas, journey maps, etc. to help you structure and visualize your data.
6. Generate recommendations and implications. Based on your analysis and synthesis, you will need to propose some recommendations and implications for empathetic leadership development in your chosen context or domain. You should also reflect on the strengths and limitations of your probe design and implementation and suggest some improvements for future iterations.

The expected deliverables for this project are:

- A written report that documents your project process and outcomes, including your research question, target user group, probe design, data collection, data analysis, data synthesis, recommendations, and reflections.
- A presentation that summarizes your main findings and insights and showcases your probe kit and data visualization methods.
- A prototype of your probe kit that includes all the materials and tasks that you sent to your users.

The evaluation criteria for this project are:

- The quality and creativity of your probe design and implementation
- The depth and rigor of your data analysis and synthesis
- The relevance and feasibility of your recommendations and implications
- The clarity and professionalism of your written report and presentation
- The originality and usefulness of your probe kit prototype

13.3 Capstone Project 2: Designing a Community-based Healthy Food Access Solution

This project involves using the define phase of the design thinking process to design a solution that addresses the problem of limited access to healthy food options in a specific community.

Students will work in teams to:

1. Analyze and synthesize data collected during the empathize phase, using techniques such as affinity diagramming and coding to identify patterns and themes.
2. Define the core problem by formulating a clear and concise problem statement that summarizes the issue from a user-centric perspective.
3. Identify user needs and opportunities by prioritizing the most critical needs and exploring potential solutions from various angles.
4. Develop a point of view (POV) statement that expresses the team's perspective on addressing the problem and fulfilling user needs.
5. Create five 'how might we' questions to guide the ideation phase, focusing on potential solutions to the POV and user needs.

13.4 Capstone Project 3: Improving the User Experience of a Healthcare App

This project involves using the define phase of the design thinking process to improve the user experience of an existing healthcare app.

Students will work in teams to:

1. Analyze user data, such as feedback surveys and app usage metrics, to identify patterns and insights.
2. Define the core problem by formulating a clear and concise problem statement that summarizes the issue from a user-centric perspective.
3. Identify user needs and opportunities by prioritizing the most critical needs and exploring potential solutions from various angles.
4. Develop a point of view (POV) statement that expresses the team's perspective on addressing the problem and fulfilling user needs.
5. Create 'how might we' questions to guide the ideation phase, focusing on potential solutions to the POV and user needs.

13.5 Capstone Project 4: Designing a New Product

In this project, students will use the ideation phase of design thinking to design a new product. They will start by identifying a problem or need that their product will address. Then, they will use techniques such as brainstorming, mind mapping, and SCAMPER to generate a wide range of ideas for their product. Students will then evaluate their ideas based on criteria such as feasibility, impact, and user needs, and select the most promising ideas to move forward with. They will then use rapid prototyping to test and refine their ideas, and create a final design for their product.

Your project will consist of the following steps:

1. Start by identifying a problem or need that your product will address.
2. Use techniques such as brainstorming, mind mapping, and SCAMPER to generate a wide range of ideas.
3. Evaluate your ideas based on criteria such as feasibility, impact, and user needs.
4. Select the most promising ideas and use rapid prototyping to test and refine them.
5. Create a final design for your product.

13.6 Capstone Project 5: Improving a Service

In this project, students will use the ideation phase of design thinking to improve an existing service. They will start by identifying the pain points and challenges that users face when using the service. Then, they will use techniques such as brainstorming, mind mapping, and SCAMPER to generate a wide range of ideas for improving the service. Students will then evaluate their ideas based on criteria such as feasibility, impact, and user needs, and select the most promising ideas to move forward with. They will then create a plan for implementing their ideas and improving the service.

Your project will consist of the following steps:

1. Start by identifying the pain points and challenges that users face when using the service.
2. Use techniques such as brainstorming, mind mapping, and SCAMPER to generate a wide range of ideas for improving the service.
3. Evaluate your ideas based on criteria such as feasibility, impact, and user needs.
4. Select the most promising ideas and create a plan for implementing them and improving the service.

13.7 Capstone Project 6: Designing a User-friendly Mobile App for Ordering Fresh Produce

To develop a user-friendly mobile app for ordering fresh produce from local grocery stores or farmers markets.

Your project will consist of the following steps:

1. Use the design thinking process to understand the problem and devise potential solutions.
2. Create low-fidelity mockups to explore the look and feel of the app.
3. Enhance the mockup by incorporating interactive elements to simulate user experience.
4. Create a high-fidelity prototype that closely resembles the final app.
5. Conduct user testing with the high-fidelity prototype to gather feedback on usability, information accessibility, and overall appeal.

13.8 Capstone Project 7: Developing a New Healthcare Device

To develop a new healthcare device that tracks vital signs.

Your project will consist of the following steps:

1. Use the design thinking process to understand the problem and devise potential solutions.
2. Create paper prototypes to test various design concepts before building a physical prototype.
3. Use the feedback from the paper prototypes to refine the design and address any usability issues.
4. Create a high-fidelity prototype using 3D printing or other advanced tools.
5. Demonstrate the functionality and features of the product to potential investors or customers and gather valuable feedback on the design.

13.9 Capstone Project 8: Creating a New Online Customer Ordering System

To create a new online customer ordering system for a company.

Your project will consist of the following steps:

1. Use the design thinking process to understand the problem and devise potential solutions.
2. Create a walkthrough that simulates the experience of placing an order from start to finish.
3. Observe the user's experience and gather feedback on the system's ease of use, clarity of instructions, and overall effectiveness.

4. Use the feedback to adjust the storyboard and animation before creating the final animation.
5. Test the final product with users to ensure it is user-friendly and meets their needs.

13.10 Capstone Project 9: Design Thinking for a School App

To design and implement a school app that helps students stay organized and learn more effectively.

Your project will consist of the following steps:

1. Define the problem and gather information from students, teachers, and staff.
2. Brainstorm possible solutions and create prototypes.
3. Conduct usability and ergonomic testing to ensure the app is user-friendly.
4. Implement the app and gather feedback from users.
5. Continuously improve the app based on user feedback.

13.11 Capstone Project 10: Design Thinking for a School Cafeteria

To redesign the school cafeteria to improve the dining experience for students.

Your project will consist of the following steps:

1. Define the problem and gather information from students, teachers, and cafeteria staff.
2. Brainstorm possible solutions and create prototypes.
3. Conduct desirability testing to ensure the new design meets the needs and wants of the users.
4. Implement the new design and gather feedback from users.
5. Continuously improve the design based on user feedback.

13.12 Capstone Project 11: Design Thinking for a Classroom Experience:

To improve the classroom experience for students.

Your project will consist of the following steps:

1. Define the problem and gather information from students and teachers.
2. Brainstorm possible solutions and create prototypes.
3. Conduct Kano model analysis to determine which features are essential, performance, and delight.
4. Implement the new design and gather feedback from users.
5. Continuously improve the design based on user feedback.

13.13 Capstone Project 12: Designing a Sustainable Product

To design a sustainable product that meets user needs while minimizing environmental impact across its life cycle.

Guidance: Students should use sustainable design principles such as life cycle assessment approach, circular economy modeling, green chemistry, biomimicry, and cradle-to-grave production methodology to design a product that is environmentally friendly, user-friendly, and economically viable. Students should consider the product's entire life cycle, from raw material sourcing to end-of-life management, to minimize waste and environmental harm.

Expected Deliverables: A detailed report on the product design process, including research, sketches, prototypes, and final design. The report should include an analysis of the product's environmental impact and a comparison with similar non-sustainable products.

Your project will consist of the following steps:

1. Research and identify a need for a sustainable product.
2. Use sustainable design principles to brainstorm and sketch potential product designs.
3. Create prototypes and test them with potential users.
4. Refine the design based on user feedback and environmental impact analysis.
5. Create a final design and present it in a detailed report.

13.14 Capstone Project 13: Sustainable Design in the Fashion Industry

To research and propose sustainable design solutions for the fashion industry.

Guidance: Students should research the environmental impact of the fashion industry and identify areas where sustainable design principles can be applied to reduce waste and pollution. Students should consider the entire life cycle of fashion products, from raw material sourcing to end-of-life management, and propose solutions that are environmentally friendly, user-friendly, and economically viable.

Expected Deliverables: A detailed report on the environmental impact of the fashion industry and proposed sustainable design solutions. The report should include an analysis of the potential environmental and economic benefits of the proposed solutions.

Your project will consist of the following steps:

1. Research the environmental impact of the fashion industry.
2. Identify areas where sustainable design principles can be applied to reduce waste and pollution.
3. Propose sustainable design solutions for the fashion industry.
4. Analyze the potential environmental and economic benefits of the proposed solutions.
5. Present the findings and proposed solutions in a detailed report.

13.15 Capstone Project 14: Sustainable Design in the Built Environment

To research and propose sustainable design solutions for the built environment.

Guidance: Students should research the environmental impact of the built environment and identify areas where sustainable design principles can be applied to reduce waste and pollution.

Students should consider the entire lifecycle of buildings, from raw material sourcing to end-of-life management, and propose solutions that are environmentally friendly, user-friendly, and economically viable.

Expected Deliverables: A detailed report on the environmental impact of the built environment and proposed sustainable design solutions. The report should include an analysis of the potential environmental and economic benefits of the proposed solutions.

Your project will consist of the following steps:

1. Research the environmental impact of the built environment.
2. Identify areas where sustainable design principles can be applied to reduce waste and pollution.
3. Propose sustainable design solutions for the built environment.
4. Analyze the potential environmental and economic benefits of the proposed solutions.
5. Present the findings and proposed solutions in a detailed report.

13.16 Capstone Project 15: Developing an Innovative Business Model using Design Thinking

To develop an innovative business model for a startup company using design thinking principles.

Expected Deliverables: A detailed business plan that includes market research, customer analysis, value proposition, revenue model, and marketing strategy.

Your project will consist of the following steps:

1. Identify a problem or need in the market that the startup company aims to solve.
2. Conduct market research and gather data on customer needs and preferences.
3. Use design thinking principles to develop an innovative business model that addresses the identified problem or need.
4. Test and iterate the business model based on customer feedback.
5. Develop a detailed business plan that includes market research, customer analysis, value proposition, revenue model, and marketing strategy.

13.17 Capstone Project 16: Developing a User-centered Mobile Application using Design Thinking

To develop a user-centered mobile application that solves a specific problem using design thinking principles.

Expected Deliverables: A functional mobile application that has been tested and iterated based on user feedback.

Your project will consist of the following steps:

1. Identify a specific problem that the mobile application aims to solve.
2. Conduct user research to gather data on user needs and preferences.
3. Use design thinking principles to develop a user-centered mobile application that addresses the identified problem.

4. Test and iterate the mobile application based on user feedback.
5. Launch the final version of the mobile application.

13.18 Capstone Project 17: Developing a Social Innovation Project using Design Thinking

To develop a social innovation project that addresses a specific social issue using design thinking principles.

Expected Deliverables: A detailed project plan that includes research on the social issue, proposed solutions, and an implementation plan.

Your project will consist of the following steps:

1. Identify a specific social issue that the project aims to address.
2. Conduct research on the social issue to gather data and insights.
3. Use design thinking principles to develop innovative solutions that address the identified social issue.
4. Test and iterate the proposed solutions based on feedback from the target community.
5. Develop a detailed project plan that includes research on the social issue, proposed solutions, and an implementation plan.

13.19 Capstone Project 18: Measuring the Impact of Design Thinking on User Experience

To measure the impact of design thinking on user experience by analyzing changes in user experience, customer feedback, and data from prototyping processes.

Guidance: Students can choose a product or service that has been developed or improved using design thinking methodology. They can then collect data on user experience, customer feedback, and prototyping processes to measure the impact of design thinking on user experience.

Expected Deliverables: A report detailing the methodology used to collect data, the data collected, and the analysis of the data to measure the impact of design thinking on user experience.

Your project will consist of the following steps:

1. Choose a product or service that has been developed or improved using design thinking methodology.
2. Collect data on user experience, customer feedback, and prototyping processes.
3. Analyze the data to measure the impact of design thinking on user experience.
4. Write a report detailing the methodology used to collect data, the data collected, and the analysis of the data.

13.20 Capstone Project 19 Measuring the Impact of Design Thinking on Organizational Culture

To measure the impact of design thinking on organizational culture by analyzing employee satisfaction, collaboration, and innovation.

Guidance: Students can choose an organization that has implemented design thinking methodology. They can then collect data on employee satisfaction, collaboration, and innovation to measure the impact of design thinking on organizational culture.

Expected Deliverables: A report detailing the methodology used to collect data, the data collected, and the analysis of the data to measure the impact of design thinking on organizational culture.

Your project will consist of the following steps:

1. Choose an organization that has implemented design thinking methodology.
2. Collect data on employee satisfaction, collaboration, and innovation.
3. Analyze the data to measure the impact of design thinking on organizational culture.
4. Write a report detailing the methodology used to collect data, the data collected, and the analysis of the data.

13.21 Capstone Project 20: Measuring the Impact of Design Thinking on Society

To measure the impact of design thinking on society by analyzing the number of social issues resolved, the number of people benefited, and the level of sustainability.

Guidance: Students can choose a social issue that has been addressed using design thinking methodology. They can then collect data on the number of social issues resolved, the number of people benefited, and the level of sustainability to measure the impact of design thinking on society.

Expected Deliverables: A report detailing the methodology used to collect data, the data collected, and the analysis of the data to measure the impact of design thinking on society.

Your project will consist of the following steps:

1. Choose a social issue that has been addressed using design thinking methodology.
2. Collect data on the number of social issues resolved, the number of people benefited, and the level of sustainability.
3. Analyze the data to measure the impact of design thinking on society.
4. Write a report detailing the methodology used to collect data, the data collected, and the analysis of the data.

APPENDIX A

Model Course Structure

OPTION 1

Credits: 4 **Contact Hours per Week: 4**

MODULE-I

Design Thinking

Introduction: Why Design?, Four Questions, Ten Tools - Definition of Design Thinking, Need for Design Thinking, Objectives of Design Thinking, History and Evolution of Design Thinking, Principles of Design Thinking, Design Thinking Concepts and Brainstorming, Stages of the Design Thinking Process (explain with examples) - Empathize, Define, Ideate, Prototype, Test, How to Plan a Design Thinking Project, Benefits of Using Design Thinking, When to Use Design Thinking and When Not to, Alternatives to Design Thinking, How Design Thinking Differs from Traditional Problem-solving Approaches.

MODULE-II

The Empathize Phase

The Importance of Empathy in Design Thinking (See Things, from the End-user Perspective, Personalized Product Recommendations, Empathy-based Approach, Assertive Technologies, Mobile Banking, Voice Assistants, Fitness Apps, Vision Impairments Products), Develop a User-centered Approach, Analysing User Needs and Pain Points, Techniques for Conducting User Research and Gathering Information (User Interviews, User Interview Process, Focus Groups, Surveys, Observational Studies, Shadowing, Immersion, I Like I Wish Game, Empathy Maps, User Persona Development, Journey Maps, Cultural Probes, User Diaries), Empathetic Dimension to Leadership.

MODULE-III

The Ideate Phase

Creative Process and Creative Principles. Divergence and Convergence: Creative Ideation Techniques, Sketching, 3D Sketching, Visualization, Storytelling, Evaluation of Ideas.

The Prototype Phase

Lean Startup Method for Prototype Development, Visualization and Presentation Techniques, Developing Mockups, Models, and Prototypes, Quick and Dirty Prototyping, Role of Soft and Hard Materials.

MODULE-IV

Testing and Implementation

Test Phase - Tips for Interviews, Tips for Surveys, Kano Model, Desirability Testing, How to Conduct Workshops, Requirements for the Space, Material Requirements, Agility for Design Thinking, Checking Back with Users' Needs and Aspirations, Presenting and Communicating Design, Testing Prototypes, Obtaining Feedback to Refine Product Usability and Ergonomic Testing.

Sustainable Design Approaches

Concern for Environment and Sustainability in Design, Case Studies to Understand Good Design for Environment (DFE) Decisions, Design Considerations in the Five Stages of the Product Life Cycle.

MODULE-V

Ethical Considerations in Design Thinking

Importance of Ethical Considerations in Design Thinking, How Design Thinking Incorporates Ethical Concerns, Diversity and Inclusion in Design Thinking, Addressing the Needs of People, Privacy in Design Thinking (Security, Encryption, Authentication, Processing and Storing User Data, User Interfaces, Privacy Policies, User Education).

Measuring The Impact of Design Thinking

Outcomes of the Process, User Experience, Level of Collaboration within Teams, Level of Risk-taking within an Organization, Level of Customer Engagement and Feedback, Ethical Considerations in Design Thinking, Case Studies and Examples of Design Thinking in Action.

OPTION 2

Credits: 4 **Contact Hours per Week: 4**

MODULE-I

Design Thinking

Introduction: Why Design?, Four Questions, Ten Tools - Definition of Design Thinking, Objectives, History and Evolution, Principles of Design Thinking, Concepts and Brainstorming of Design Thinking, Stages of the Design Thinking Process with Examples - Empathize, Define, Ideate, Prototype, Test, How to Plan a Design Thinking Project, Benefits of Using Design Thinking, When to Use Design Thinking and When Not to, Alternatives to Design Thinking, How Design Thinking Differs from Traditional Problem-solving Approaches.

MODULE-II

The Empathize Phase

The Importance of Empathy in Design Thinking (See Things from the End-user Perspective, Personalized Product Recommendations, Empathy-based Approach, Assertive Technologies, Mobile Banking, Voice Assistants, Fitness Apps, Vision Impairments Products), Develop a User-centered Approach, Analysing User Needs and Pain Points, Techniques for Conducting User Research and Gathering Information (User Interviews, User Interview Process, Focus Groups, Surveys, Observational Studies, Shadowing, Immersion, I Like I Wish Game, Empathy Maps, User Persona Development, Journey Maps, Cultural Probes, User Diaries), Empathetic Dimension to Leadership.

MODULE-III

Ideation

Ideate Phase - Creative Process and Creative Principles.

Divergence and Convergence

Creative Ideation Techniques, Sketching, 3D Sketching, Visualization, Storytelling, Evaluation of Ideas.

Clear Articulation of Problem Statement with Focus on Latent Needs

Brainstorming Potential Solutions, Ideation Methods with Case Study-based Approach to Using Systematic Inventive Thinking (SIT) Methods: Addition, Subtraction, Multiplication, Division and Task Unification.

MODULE-IV

Prototype Phase

Lean Startup Method for Prototype Development, Visualization and Presentation Techniques, Developing Mockups, Models, and Prototypes, Quick and Dirty Prototyping, Role of Soft and Hard Materials.

Testing and Implementation

Test Phase - Tips for Interviews, Tips for Surveys, Kano Model, Desirability Testing, How to Conduct Workshops, Requirements for the Space, Material Requirements, Agility for Design Thinking, Checking Back with Users' Needs and Aspirations, Presenting and Communicating Design, Testing Prototypes, Obtaining Feedback to Refine Product Usability and Ergonomic Testing.

MODULE-V

Analysing User Experience (UX)

Design Thinking and User Experience, Killer UX Design, Constructing Work Activity Affinity Diagram (WAAD), User Models, Usage Models and Work Environment Models, Fundamentals of User Experience Analysis - How to Prioritize Usability Problems, Generating Solutions to Usability Problems, User Research Methods, Dealing with Common Objections, Personas and Customer Journey Mapping, Key Metrics for User Experience Analysis, Future Trends in UX Analysis (Voice-driven UX Analysis, Contextual UX Analysis, Augmented Reality-driven User Experience Analysis, Wearable UX Evaluation, Mobile First UX Research, Cross-platform UX Research, Forecasting UX Analysis, Gamification-driven UX Analysis, User-centered Design, Real-life Case Studies in UX Analysis.

Measuring the Impact of Design Thinking

Outcomes of the Process, User Experience, Level of Collaboration within Teams, Level of Risk-taking within an Organization, Level of Customer Engagement and Feedback, Ethical Considerations in Design Thinking, Case Studies and Examples of Design Thinking in Action.

OPTION 3

Credits : 4 **Contact Hours per Week : 4**

MODULE-I

Design Thinking

Introduction: Why Design?, Four Questions, Ten Tools - Definition of Design Thinking, Need for Design Thinking, Objectives of Design Thinking, History and Evolution of Design Thinking, Principles of Design Thinking, Concepts and Brainstorming, Stages of the Design Thinking Process (explain with examples) - Empathize, Define, Ideate, Prototype, Test, How to Plan a Design Thinking Project, Benefits of Using Design Thinking, When to Use Design Thinking and When Not to, Alternatives to Design Thinking, How Design Thinking Differs from Traditional Problem-solving Approaches.

MODULE-II

The Empathize Phase

The Importance of Empathy in Design Thinking (See Things from the End-user Perspective, Personalized Product Recommendations, Empathy-based Approach, Assertive Technologies, Mobile Banking, Voice Assistants, Fitness Apps, Vision Impairments Products), Develop a User-centered Approach, Analysing User Needs and Pain Points, Techniques for Conducting User Research and Gathering Information (User Interviews, User Interview Process, Focus Groups, Surveys, Observational Studies, Shadowing, Immersion, I Like I Wish Game, Empathy Maps, User Persona Development, Journey Maps, Cultural Probes, User Diaries), Empathetic Dimension to Leadership.

The Ideate Phase

Creative Process and Creative Principles.

Divergence and Convergence

Creative Ideation Techniques, Sketching, 3D Sketching, Visualization, Storytelling, Evaluation of Ideas.

Clear Articulation of Problem Statement with Focus on Latent Needs

Brainstorming Potential Solutions, Ideation Methods with Case Study-based Approach to Using Systematic Inventive Thinking (SIT) Methods: Addition, Subtraction, Multiplication, Division and Task Unification.

Strategic Innovation for Competition in Future

Linear Innovation vs. Non-linear Innovation, Understanding and Identifying Weak Signals, Three-box Thinking, Three-box Framework and Three-box Ideation.

The Prototype Phase

Lean Startup Method for Prototype Development, Visualization and Presentation Techniques, Developing Mockups, Models, and Prototypes, Quick and Dirty Prototyping, Role of Soft and Hard Materials.

Testing and Implementation

Test Phase - Tips for Interviews, Tips for Surveys, Kano Model, Desirability Testing, How to Conduct Workshops, Requirements for the Space, Material Requirements, Agility for Design Thinking, Checking Back with Users' Needs and Aspirations, Presenting and Communicating Design, Testing Prototypes, Obtaining Feedback to Refine Product Usability and Ergonomic Testing.

MODULE-III

Analysing User Experience (UX)

Design Thinking and User Experience, Killer UX Design, Constructing Work Activity Affinity Diagram (WAAD), User Models, Usage Models and Work Environment Models, Fundamentals of User Experience Analysis - How to Prioritize Usability Problems, Generating Solutions to Usability Problems, User Research Methods, Dealing with Common Objections, Personas and Customer Journey Mapping, Key Metrics for User Experience Analysis, Future Trends in UX Analysis (Voice-driven UX Analysis, Contextual UX Analysis, Augmented Reality-driven User Experience Analysis, Wearable UX Evaluation, Mobile First UX Research, Cross-platform UX Research, Forecasting UX Analysis, Gamification-driven UX Analysis, User-centered Design, Real-life Case Studies in UX Analysis.

MODULE-IV

Integrating Design Thinking with Other Disciplines

Design Thinking and Business, Design Thinking and Technology, Design Thinking and Education, Design Thinking and Healthcare, Design Thinking and Social Impact, Design Thinking in Constructing Buildings.

MODULE-V

Measuring the Impact of Design Thinking

Outcomes of the Process, User Experience, Level of Collaboration within Teams, Level of Risk-taking within an Organization, Level of Customer Engagement and Feedback, Ethical Considerations in Design Thinking, Case Studies and Examples of Design Thinking in Action.

Case Studies

- Airbnb (Personalized experience, safe and secure platform, user-friendly interfaces)
- Delta Airlines (Mobile check-in, redesigning the boarding process, improved airport experience, improved in-flight experience)
- Kaiser Permanente (Improving the patient experience, redesigned clinics, improving online presence, improving the clinical process)
- IDEO (Innovative hotel check-in, improved healthcare solutions, redesigning the grocery shopping experience, designing self-driving car)
- Ford (Safety features, improving the user experience, eco-friendly and sustainable vehicles, human-centered approach)

APPENDIX B

Model Test Paper 1

NAME OF THE COLLEGE
End Semester – (XXXX)

Programme: XXXXX **Course Code: XXXXX**
Course Title: DESIGN THINKING
Duration : 3 Hrs **Max Marks: 75**

Part-A (10 × 1 = 10)
Answer ALL the Questions

1. What is an example of a brand-new concept that is a result of innovation?
   (a) A smartphone that can fold into a tablet
   (b) A vaccine that can prevent a disease
   (c) A car that can run on electricity
   (d) A website that can sell products online
2. You are a design thinking consultant hired by a school that wants to have more space for students. What is the first step you would take to help them solve this problem?
   (a) Brainstorm ideas for adding another floor to the building or finding a way to store books in less space.
   (b) Build a prototype of a new classroom layout and test it with students and teachers.
   (c) Research the needs and preferences of the students, teachers, and staff using interviews and observations.
   (d) Define the problem statement and the criteria for success.
3. You are a designer working on a project to create a website for a local library. You have conducted some empathic research and learned about the needs and desires of the library users. How can you use empathy to define the problem you are trying to solve?
   (a) By creating a problem statement that reflects the users' point of view
   (b) By creating a list of features and functions that the website should have
   (c) By creating a map of the user journey and touchpoints
   (d) By creating a prototype of the website and testing it with users
4. How does prototyping encourage creativity in project management?
   (a) By limiting the number of design concepts
   (b) By discouraging experimentation
   (c) By allowing designers to experiment with various design ideas
   (d) By relying on guesswork and assumptions

5. What is the aim of sustainable design in the design thinking process?
(a) To create compelling and efficient goods
(b) To consider financial costs only
(c) To ignore cultural implications
(d) To create products that harm the environment

6. What are some components of a killer UX design?
(a) Confusing navigation and interfaces.
(b) Visually displeasing design.
(c) Intuitive navigation, user-friendly interfaces, and engaging design.
(d) None of the above.

7. What are some market research methods used in new product development?
(a) Surveys (b) Focus groups
(c) Customer interviews (d) All of the above

8. What is the "Just in Time" (JIT) system?
(a) A system that encourages waste in production
(b) A system that delivers materials to the production line only when they are required
(c) A system that emphasizes inefficiencies in product development
(d) A system that reduces collaboration among team members

9. What is the ultimate goal of deciphering needs in design thinking?
(a) To create a product that is easier to use
(b) To identify areas for development
(c) To find the true causes of issues or areas for development
(d) None of the above

10. Which user feedback method involves asking a group of users to discuss their experiences with the product?
(a) Surveys (b) Interviews
(c) Focus groups (d) Usability testing

Part-B (5 × 2 = 10)
Answer ALL the Questions

11. Define innovation imperatives and give examples.

12. What is empathy? Why is it important?

13. What are the objectives of sustainable design approaches?

14. How can the design of aircraft and spacecraft be integrative engineering?

15. Define deciphering needs.

Part-C (5 × 5 = 25)
Answer Any FIVE Questions

16. Explain the four questions of design thinking.

17. Explain the importance of the IT support team and subject matter expert (SME) during the testing phase.

18. What are the objectives of sustainable design approaches? Explain in detail.

19. Carrying out market research is an essential step in the new product development process. Explain this.

20. Explain sustainable building design as an example of integrative design solutions.

21. How are surveys used to get user feedback in design thinking?

22. Explain value proposition in detail.

Part-D (3 × 10 = 30)
Answer Any THREE Questions

23. Write an essay on the 10 tools of design thinking.

24. Why should a prototype be used in design thinking projects?

25. How can we deal with common objections to UX research? Discuss the key metrics of user experience analysis.

26. Write an essay on accessible metrics.

27. Write an essay on usability testing and A/B testing in detail.

Model Test Paper 2

NAME OF THE COLLEGE
End Semester – (XXXX)

Programme: XXXXX **Course Code: XXXXX**
Course Title: DESIGN THINKING
Duration : 3 Hrs **Max Marks: 75**

Part-A (10 × 1 = 10)
Answer ALL the Questions

1. A company wants to create a new product that meets the needs of its customers. Which of the following innovation imperatives should they focus on first?
   (a) Accept the Change
   (b) Focus on Customer Needs
   (c) Embrace Digital Transformation
   (d) Leverage Design Thinking and Agile Methodologies
2. Which stage of the design thinking process involves creating a rough draft or model of the solution?
   (a) Empathize (b) Define
   (c) Ideate (d) Prototype
3. Which of the following is NOT an advantage of using prototypes in the design thinking process?
   (a) Identifying UI design issues before implementation
   (b) Testing functionality before launch
   (c) Saving time and money during the production phase
   (d) Providing low-fidelity product representations
4. Which phase of the design thinking process determines the viability, usability, and sustainability of the solution?
   (a) Ideation phase (b) Testing and implementation phase
   (c) Empathizing phase (d) Defining the problem phase
5. Why is usability testing important in UX design?
   (a) To check the product's aesthetics
   (b) To evaluate the marketing strategy
   (c) To identify areas for enhancement
   (d) To test the functionality of the product
6. What is the benefit of using design thinking in understanding customers?
   (a) Improved customer loyalty (b) Reduced manufacturing costs
   (c) Increased market competition (d) Better employee training
7. What is the primary goal of integrated engineering design solutions?
   (a) To design products that look visually appealing
   (b) To integrate diverse subsystems and components into an efficient product

(c) To create systems that are easy to manufacture
(d) To reduce the cost of engineering projects

8. What techniques are involved in understanding the client thoroughly through design thinking?
(a) Active listening, observation, and empathy
(b) Cost reduction and profit maximization
(c) Technology integration and sustainability
(d) None of the above

9. How can design thinking help organizations set themselves apart in a crowded market?
(a) By reducing costs and saving time
(b) By emphasizing user sensitivity and understanding
(c) By increasing profits and revenue
(d) All of the above

10. What do work environment models consider?
(a) User behavior and preferences
(b) Factors such as lighting and pollution
(c) Software context of use
(d) All of the above

Part-B (5 × 2 = 10)
Answer ALL the Questions

11. What is digital disruption?

12. What is brainwriting? Where is it used in design thinking?

13. What is a killer UX design?

14. Define ergonomics and give an example.

15. How does design thinking make an impact on society?

Part-C (5 × 5 = 25)
Answer Any FIVE Questions

16. What are innovation imperatives? Explain any 5 innovation imperatives.

17. Explain the importance of analysing user needs and pain points with examples.

18. How can we prioritize usability problems?

19. Explain the design of aircraft/spacecraft and medical devices as examples of integrative design solutions.

20. Explain lean manufacturing in detail.

21. Write an essay on the intersection of design thinking and technology

22. How can we measure the impact of design thinking?

Part-D (3 × 10 = 30)
Answer Any THREE Questions

23. Explain the following misconceptions:
    (a) You need complex technology tools to implement design thinking
    (b) Design thinking ignores traditional methods of problem-solving
24. Who are the key stakeholders of the testing phase? Why?
25. Explain the life cycle assessment approach and circular economy modeling with examples.
26. What are the problems associated with diverse teamwork? How do we resolve the same?
27. How can we use design thinking to solve educational and healthcare challenges?

Model Test Paper 3

NAME OF THE COLLEGE
End Semester – (XXXX)

Programme: XXXXX **Course Code: XXXXX**
Course Title: DESIGN THINKING
Duration : 3 Hrs **Max Marks: 75**

Part-A (10 × 1 = 10)
Answer ALL the Questions

1. What is the main difference between product innovation and service innovation?
   (a) Product innovation focuses on creating new products, while service innovation focuses on improving how customers interact with products and services
   (b) Product innovation focuses on improving existing products, while service innovation focuses on creating new services
   (c) Product innovation focuses on meeting customer needs in different ways than before, while service innovation focuses on meeting customer needs in the same way as before
   (d) Product innovation focuses on making products more innovative and efficient, while service innovation focuses on making products more convenient and easy to use
2. What are some methods that can help you gain empathy towards your users?
   (a) Talking to people, observing them in their environment, or doing surveys or interviews
   (b) Consulting experts, conducting observations, or immersing yourself in your users' physical environment
   (c) Both (a) and (b)
   (d) Neither (a) and (b)
3. What is the ultimate goal of the implementation phase in design thinking?
   (a) To create innovative solutions
   (b) To evaluate usability and functionality
   (c) To guarantee the final solution is efficient and long-lasting
   (d) To understand user needs
4. Who is responsible for managing databases, setting up hardware and software, and ensuring the system is secure and reliable during the testing phase of the design thinking process?
   (a) Users
   (b) Design team
   (c) Technical support team
   (d) Stakeholders
5. How can design thinking foster creativity and innovation in businesses?
   (a) By limiting the scope of the project to a predetermined set of features.
   (b) By ignoring customer feedback.
   (c) By emphasizing user experience and fostering creativity and innovation.
   (d) By copying competitors' products.

6. What should be the focus during the utilization phase of a product's life cycle?
   (a) Minimizing environmental impact
   (b) Maximizing profits
   (c) Increasing advertising
   (d) Reducing manufacturing costs

7. What is the benefit of determining user needs in new product development?
   (a) It helps to increase the price of the product
   (b) It helps to develop a product that satisfies the target market's demands
   (c) It helps to reduce the cost of the product
   (d) It helps to increase the speed of product development

8. What is the importance of strategic foresight in design thinking?
   (a) It enables companies to anticipate future changes and prepare for them.
   (b) It helps companies focus only on the present moment.
   (c) It makes companies reactive to changes rather than proactive.
   (d) It hinders companies' ability to create long-term strategies.

9. What are some ways in which designers can understand the viewpoints of stakeholders?
   (a) Through surveys and interviews
   (b) By ignoring their perspectives
   (c) By imposing their own opinions
   (d) By disregarding their feedback

10. What is value chain analysis?
   (a) A strategic management tool for evaluating customer satisfaction
   (b) A method for identifying and evaluating steps in the production process
   (c) A process for segmenting a target market
   (d) A tool for analyzing employee productivity

Part-B (5 × 2 = 10)
Answer ALL the Questions

11. What is POV in design thinking?
12. What are the limitations of paper prototyping for testing complex interactions or user flows?
13. How does design thinking encourage creativity and innovation?
14. How can we integrate design thinking in a culture?
15. Explain the innovation funnel.

Part-C (5 × 5 = 25)
Answer Any FIVE Questions

16. What is the need for design thinking?
17. How and where can ideation be used?

18. Why is design thinking important for customer experience?
19. How does intellectual property help in product design?
20. How can we use storytelling to communicate innovation strategy?
21. How does design thinking incorporate ethical concerns?
22. Write an essay on the intersection of design thinking and technology

Part-D (3 × 10 = 30)
Answer Any THREE Questions

23. When do we use design thinking and when should we not? How does design thinking differ from traditional problem-solving approaches?
24. How can we deal with common objections to UX research? Discuss the key metrics of user experience analysis.
25. How does design thinking encourage creativity? How does design thinking help companies to be more agile?
26. How can we measure the impact of design thinking on organizational culture?
27. Explain the design scorecard framework and leading and lagging indicators of design thinking in detail.

Index

E

F

G

H

I

O

P

Q

R

S

T

U

W